CRITICAL SURVEY
OF
DRAMA

CRITICAL SURVEY
OF
DRAMA

REVISED EDITION

Essays

7

Edited by
FRANK N. MAGILL

SALEM PRESS

Pasadena, California   Englewood Cliffs, New Jersey

∞ The paper used in these volumes conforms to
the American National Standard for Permanence of
Paper for Printed Library Materials, Z39.48-1984.

**Library of Congress Cataloging-in-Publication
Data**
    Critical survey of drama. English language series/
edited by Frank N. Magill.—Rev. ed.
        p.   cm.
    Includes bibliographical references and index.
    1. English drama—Dictionaries. 2. American
drama—Dictionaries. 3. English drama—Bio-
bibliography. 4. American drama—Bio-bibliography.
5. Commonwealth drama (English)—Dictionaries.
6. Dramatists, English—Biography—Dictionaries.
7. Dramatists, American—Biography—Dictionaries. 8. Commonwealth drama (English)—Bio-
bibliography.
I. Magill, Frank Northen, 1907-   .
PR623.C75   1994
822.009'03—dc20   93-41618
ISBN 0-89356-851-1 (set)   CIP
ISBN 0-89356-858-9 (volume 7)

PRINTED IN THE UNITED STATES OF AMERICA

LIST OF ESSAYS

CRITICAL SURVEY
OF
DRAMA

DRAMATIC GENRES

The classification of Western dramatic works into genera owes less to playwrights than to critics and theorists. Every age has tried to redefine preexisting genres in terms of its own preoccupations or has tried to invent new genres in order to categorize novel phenomena that do not fit the terminology available. Occasionally playwrights themselves concur in using these labels and even, as in the Renaissance and neoclassical periods, meekly follow the guidelines set down for them by academicians. For the most part, however, whenever drama has thrived, the dramatist's creation has preceded or preempted the critical definition. Consequently, the study of dramatic genres is not so much that of taxonomy as an inquiry into theatrical and literary fashion, as reflections of a society's values and concerns.

The ubiquity of the laughing and frowning masks as a symbol of drama is a constant reminder that the two major genres, tragedy and comedy, took on definitive shape in Attica in the fifth century B.C. Speculating on the origins of Greek tragedy has been a favorite pastime of scholars for more than two hundred years, and there are more points of contention than there are extant Greek tragedies. Aristotle's speculation, which has been supported or endorsed by most classical scholars, is that tragedy originated in the wild Thracian rites of Dionysus or, more specifically, out of the later lyric dithyramb, a cantilena performed in the god's honor. Dionysus is a complex deity who combines the contradictions of life giving and death dealing, therapeutic bliss and wanton cruelty, dynamic possession of his worshipers and passive destruction by them. In accordance with his manifold nature, the choral plaint expressed both exuberant joy and profound grief, though with joy predominating.

Aristotle asserted that the word "tragedy" derived from *tragōn oidē*, a song of goats, usually taken to mean a hymn sung by a chorus, clad in goatskins to resemble Satyrs, as they danced around the altar of Dionysus. Gerald F. Else, in *The Origin and Early Form of Greek Tragedy* (1965), has pointed out that this is a linguistically impossible compound; a more likely etymology is a formation from *tragoidos*, "goat singer or goat bard," from the prize that he received in competition.

Whatever the case, tradition has assigned specific developments to specific individuals. Arion of Lesbos (seventh century B.C.) is said to have been the first to spurn improvisation and write a dithyramb in advance, and also the first to compose a dithyramb not about Dionysus but about a heroic subject. This narrative poem, sung to music, was a rudimentary drama, not unlike an operatic oratorio. Thespis of Athens, which was a chief seat of the Dionysian cult, is credited with composing the first tragedy in 534 B.C., a work consisting of a prologue, a series of choral songs, and a dramatic set speech, or *rhesis*, which had a strict tripartite structure, so that the thought enunciated at the start was restated at the end. Thespis eliminated the Satyrs and gave the choral leader, in this case himself, the part of *hypokritēs*, or "expositor," performing these recitations as monologues and advancing the action by brief dialogues with the chorus. By wearing a series of masks, he could assume different characters. In opposition to the lyric recitations of the chorus, these narrative passages were logical exhortations or straightforward descriptions which in turn elicited the choral response.

According to Else's suppositions, Thespis based his tragedy not on divine myths but on the Homeric legends, more native to Athens and very much in the tradition of the rhapsodist's recitations from Homer. With Thespis' innovations, the epic hero, the idea of impersonation, and iambic verse combined to give Greek tragedy its special character.

Thespis' innovations were so well approved that they became a leading feature in the Athenian festival of Dionysus, where further development was to be concentrated. Later improvements were made by Phrynichus, who introduced an actor who was distinct from the chorus leader, known as the *protagonistēs;* added female roles both in the chorus and for the *rhesis*; and modified the preponderance of the choral contribution, which at that time dominated the play. Aeschylus further subordinated the chorus, reducing its role by adding a second actor, the *deuteragonistēs;* finally, a third actor was introduced by Sophocles, completing what became the standard cast size: Any poet who entered the public competition would be subsidized only for up to three actors and a chorus of twelve (later expanded to fifteen by Sophocles). It should be made clear, however, that, by changing masks and costumes, the actors could portray many more than three characters; nonspeaking figurants were also employed.

At the dramatic competitions held during the City Dionysia of Athens, each poet staged a tetralogy, consisting of three tragedies followed by a Satyr play. The tragic trilogy is believed to have originated as an expanded form of the prologue-*rhesis*-*rhesis* sequence, designed to accommodate the second actor. In Aeschylus' time, the three tragedies were internally connected by plot, as in his *Oresteia* (pr. 458 B.C.), an association that Sophocles is said to have discarded. The Satyr play may have been a concession to public protests that the new tragic form had ousted the fun-loving roistering of the Dionysia. It was reputed to be an invention of Pratinas of Phlius (c. 500 B.C.), who adapted the dithyramb to a tragic format but retained the choric dances performed exclusively by Satyrs, as was customary in his birthplace. The Satyr play provided comic contrast to the tragedies that preceded it and, by featuring Silenus and his goatish entourage, emphasized the link with Dionysus. The plot of a Satyr play was not necessarily comic; indeed—deriving, like tragic plots, from epic or legend—it might be somber in tone. The merriment came from the intervention of the drunken, lecherous, impudent Satyrs capering about. Aeschylus was considered a master of the form, but the only extant Satyr play is Euripides' *The Cyclops* (pr. c. 450 B.C.).

Any discussion of Greek tragedy must be qualified by an admission of the paucity of extant texts. Some fourteen hundred tragedies may have been composed and performed in Athens alone, yet of these, only thirty-two by three authors, all of Athens, survive intact, along with a number of fragments and allusions. In general, however, tragedy is concerned less with gods than with people and especially with the hero's "pathos," or moment of emotional crisis. In tragedy, death is seen very much as the inevitable end of mortals; transfiguration or transcendence is seldom a possibility.

Before Aeschylus, the fit subjects for tragedy were the Homeric heroes and their progeny; Aeschylus enlarged the subject matter to include the struggles between gods and Titans, as in *Prometheus Bound* (pr. fifth century), and relatively current history, as in *The Phoenician Women* (pr. c. 411-409 B.C.) and *The Persians* (pr. 472 B.C.). He also intensified the conflict, or agon, between individuals and between the protagonist and the chorus, in order to lead up to the protagonist's pathos. For the most part, tragic poets recycled the same heroic stories but were free to formulate new motivations and variants. Agathon, a contemporary of Euripides, is said to be the first to have invented a purely original plot, in *Antheus*, or *The Flower* (pr. c. 425 B.C.), which is no longer extant.

Structurally, Greek tragedy generally comprises the "prologos," a scene that precedes the first entrance of the chorus; the "parodos," the first important choral sequence; the "epeisodion," a scene of dialogue or monologue that divides the choral songs; the "stasimon," the choral song following each episode; and finally, the "exodos," or withdrawal, following the last chorus. (On an open-air stage, chorus and actors would have to make their exits in full view of the audience.) There are, however, numerous variations on this pattern, and over time the chorus' role was reduced until Agathon turned it into a mere intermezzo, whose songs were unrelated to the plot. The prologue, which had been a relevant part of the action, was often used by Euripides as a set speech informing the audience of antecedent action (for which he was ridiculed by Aristophanes). In later days, when actors became virtuosos who toured the Greek world with their repertories, solos were introduced as star turns.

Reflecting the rhetorical nature of Attic civilization, almost all tragic action is unfolded in speech. Because the story begins close to its culmination, a large amount of exposition is required, and heralds, messengers, and similar ancillary figures report offstage occurrences at length. The chorus functioned as a moral regulator by which the spectator might gauge his reaction to events, a signpost to significant elements that might otherwise be overlooked, and a significant part of the spectacle. Most important, its songs abstracted the situation by drawing historical parallels and thus allowed time for reflection on past actions and on those to come.

Comedy shares with tragedy and Satyr drama a common origin in Dionysian revels; its name is related to the song of the *kōmos*, or mirth-making procession of Dionysus, that followed a ritual banquet. The Dorians of Megara claimed to have been the first to elaborate into full-fledged farce this impromptu horseplay, with its flaunting of totemic phalluses and its vigorous raillery. The genre gained a literary patina in Sicily from Epicharmus (c. 540-450 B.C.), who probably added a formal chorus to what had become a blend of philosophical debate, rhetoric, and monkeyshines; he also varied the mythological plots with stories taken from real life. These products were known as *motoriae*, because of their loose structure and violent action.

The chief seat of the worship of Dionysus in Attica was Icaria, where a more polished form of the Megarian comedy was introduced, possibly by one Susarion, about 580 B.C. Comedy remained a minor genre, however, until the Athenians, around the time of the Persian Wars, fused its phallophoric choruses to a structure based on that of tragedy. The State granted to the genre a subvention and status in an annual festival, possibly because of complaints that Satyr plays were not sufficient to represent riotous license at the Dionysian holidays.

This form of comedy, known as Old Comedy, flourished during the heyday of Athenian democracy and its immediate aftermath. Indeed, only in such a liberal society could Old Comedy have developed, with its sharp political satire and unbridled humor. The actors sported leather phalluses and wallowed in scatology and sexual innuendo, in both word and gesture. As in some of the village festivals that still survive in Greece, personal abuse and invective played a major role. Old Comedy bristled with in-jokes and scurrilous assaults, even on members of the audience, to such a degree that the Athenians prudently banned both foreigners and slaves from attendance. The raw material of real life was present in Old Comedy, heightened to a pitch of grotesquerie and lyric fantasy.

Originally, comedy had probably opened with a choral dance and ended with the *kōmos*. Its mature structure followed the pattern of tragedy, with a prologue, episodes, choruses, and an exodus, but it also featured a "parabasis," a production number that usually occurred in about the middle of the play and in which the enlarged chorus (twenty-four as opposed to tragedy's fifteen members) made a direct appeal to the audience. The author might use the parabasis to request the prize, or the chorus might harangue the public on a topical issue or offer advice on current events. In theory, it consisted of seven separate parts, but they were seldom all present. (As a rule, Greek comedy was a much more flexible and adaptable genre than tragedy.)

Unlike tragedy, which drew its stories from myth and legend, Old Comedy seldom began *in medias res*. The opening of the comedy would set forth the basic premise of the plot: Usually, a malcontent character sets out to remedy an abuse by an extreme measure. This convention is evident in the works of Aristophanes, the only comic dramatist of the period whose plays (eleven of them) have survived in complete form: In *Lysistrata* (pr. 411 B.C.), the title character resorts to a sex strike to bring about peace; in *The Birds* (pr. 414 B.C.), two dissatisfied Athenians leave their hometown to found a new community with the aid of the feathered kingdom; in *The Clouds* (pr. 423 B.C.), a father sends his dissolute son to be enrolled in Socrates' school, only to find that the boy grows even more dishonest under this Sophistic tutelage. Once the plot point is established, the play's structure is open enough to accommodate all sorts of tangents and digressions. Aristophanes, and most likely his competitors at the comic contests, sought first and foremost to amuse the audience; careful plot making and artistic refinements were not prime considerations. Whole episodes and stretches of dialogue were fabricated to raise laughs, built as a joke is built, with the necessary repetitions, key words, odd dialects, and retards to evoke the maximal mirth. As Peter Arnott has remarked in his essay "Aristophanes and Popular Comedy" (1977), "Scenes and groups of scenes have traditionally been explained in terms of reference to some external factor, when a more reasonable explanation may be found in the innate principles of comic writing, the mechanical laws which every draftsman must obey if he wishes his plays to work."

In Aristophanes' *The Women at the Festival* (pr. 411 B.C.), for example, the plot ostensibly concerns the revenge that the women of Athens plan to wreak on Euripides for his defamation of their sex in his tragedies. An Old Man is disguised as a woman and smuggled into the women's festival, the Thesmophoria, to spy on them, but he is discovered and trussed up to await further punishment. So far, the story line is followed reasonably closely, though not without pauses for literary satire, an elaborate slapstick shaving scene, and the parabasis. At this point, however, approximately halfway into the play, the women of the title disappear, and Aristophanes devotes himself to an extended and hilarious parody of Euripides' tragic innovations as well as a number of sexual sight gags. Even the finale—which, in Old Comedy, usually effects a reconciliation among warring parties and an invitation to a feast, as in *The Birds* and *Lysistrata*—is here performed in hugger-mugger, the conclusion curt and curtailed.

Less subject to religious decorum than tragedy, comedy also displayed more violence and action onstage and thus reduced messengers and expository speeches to a minimum (except when used to poke fun at tragic conventions). On the other hand, the reconciliatory banquet was seldom brought to view, perhaps because it was too closely connected to the religious rites from which comedy sprang. If, as some scholars contend, this was the case, it runs counter to the blasphemous mockery of the gods and their service that characterized Old Comedy. More plausibly, it might be argued that the final banquet was kept offstage as an event to which the audience might be invited, at least figuratively; in this way, comedy brought together a whole community which it had previously shown to be divided.

Both tragedy and comedy were spectacles, considerably embellished with stylized speech, music and dance, and a quantum of scenic effect; these elements were crucial to the planning and financing of the festivals. In his *Poetics* (334-323 B.C.), Aristotle, who had little taste for "opsis," the physical aspect of theater, belittled its significance, treating it as a side issue, and in this he has been closely followed by literary critics for centuries. For the original audience, however, much of the chorus displayed to best advantage in the parabasis; similarly, the thrill of Aeschylus' *The Furies* (pr. 458 B.C.) lay partly in the horrific masks and gestures of the title characters. If Euripides was mocked for his overreliance on machinery and costuming, the criticism came from conservative connoisseurs and not the popular audience.

The mention of Aristotle brings this discussion to the first formal definitions of tragedy and comedy, based on the types of drama that had evolved by 340 B.C. In his esoteric and fragmentary *Poetics*, Aristotle proposed a taxonomy of literary forms that he believed to be solidly grounded on the organic nature of the phenomena under discussion. As a natural scientist, he took a biological approach to literature and, by inductive reasoning, hoped to synthesize his analyses of representative specimens into a conclusive scheme of differentiation. Aristotle examined the available works and decided that the tragedy of Aeschylus, Sophocles, Euripides, and their colleagues represented a fully evolved form of poetry, which had been achieved only after passing through such stages as the epic and the ode. The nature of tragedy, therefore, lay in its entelechy; its constituent parts existed in order to perform tragedy's primary function, which was philosophical. Almost as if demonstrating how the physical attributes of a fish conduce to its behavioral survival, Aristotle anatomized tragedy to show how its features were part of a rational, well-functioning whole, productive of pleasure and reflection.

Aristotle's definition of tragedy, found in the *Poetics* (and given here in the familiar 1902 translation of Samuel Butcher), is the *locus classicus* of Western discussions of tragedy. For Aristotle, tragedy is

> an imitation of an action that is serious, complete, and of a certain magnitude; in language embellished with each kind of artistic ornament, the several kinds being found in separate parts of the play, in the form of action, not of narrative; through pity and fear effecting the proper purgation of these emotions.

Through the centuries, every item in this definition has been subjected to intense scrutiny and interpretation, but in essence, Aristotle's formulation has been accepted as the standard by which to distinguish tragedy from lesser genres of drama. The preeminence of tragedy is vital. Aristotle was the first to proclaim it the ultimate and superior dramatic form. In that, as in his sharp distinction between tragedy and comedy, most thinkers have followed him unquestioningly.

The instinct for imitation, or mimesis, was a basic principle of Greek art, the artist striving not "to express himself" but to perceive and body forth whatever was essential in nature. The imitation, a harmonized and purified version of the original, would thus complete nature by distilling its ideal qualities. In this way, it would transmit the abiding and universal Ideas or Forms to the observer and aid in what Plato called "sound opinion," the basis for wisdom. Plato himself had scorned art, seeing it as a reflection of the truth, but Aristotle exalted poetry as superior to "history, in that it deals with the universal." Tragedy chose only such actions to imitate as would best illustrate the persisting and permanent truths of human nature.

The "serious, complete action of a certain magnitude" is in turn imitated in action, through the actor's performance and byplay, as well as by the playwright's creation. This is less simplistic than it sounds, because, for Aristotle, action was the product of character and thought, the outward manifestation of inner motivation. Thought can only be represented onstage as speech, and in a culture as verbal as the Greek, this meant subtle argumentation and suasion rather than the cogitative soliloquies of a Hamlet. Indeed, in Greek tragedy there is nothing that can properly be called a soliloquy. A character explains his motives, intentions, or feelings to the chorus or to another character, to gain acceptance of his point of view. This rhetorical expertise confirms the tragic hero's intellectual prowess.

It has been argued that Aristotle's definition of tragedy is too narrow, that it fails to conceive of a "tragic vision" of the world or a dramatic work as a paradigm for existence. In fact, his proposal of purgation (catharsis) as the proper effect of tragedy is a fruitful place to look for a broader meaning. It is also the most debatable item in his definition, but all the other facets of tragedy are relevant only insofar as they discharge pity and fear. Among the Greeks, catharsis had manifold connotations. In medical theory, it was the flushing out of excessive and disproportionate humors in the body; in religion, it was a cleansing of the soul by expelling harmful psychic elements; in music, as Aristotle noted in his *Politics* (330 B.C.), it soothed and healed by purging overdone feelings such as religious zeal. In his *Rhetoric* (c. 330 B.C.), pity and fear are seen as dangerous and painful emotions: Fear is defined as an apprehension of disaster, proximate and inescapable, while pity is this fear applied to others who have not merited the disaster. Fear alone is a passive and deleterious state, and pity alone is a helpless and disaffected feeling. If one experiences merely the former, the result is the same gooseflesh with which one responds to a thriller. If one experiences merely the latter, the result is a warm bath of superficial emotion, the kind prompted by a melodrama or a soap opera. The combination, however, triggers and then expels emotions of identification, as one apprehends the common lot of humanity. It is unclear from Aristotle's comments whether these processes take place during or after the performance, or how the double action operates. What is clear is that the pleasure in watching tragic suffering comes partly from the delight in observing a well-conducted imitation and the aesthetic harmony of the tragedy, and partly from the purgation, which leaves one's mind unclouded and open to contemplation. As Stephan Dedalus put it in James Joyce's *A Portrait of the Artist as a Young Man* (1916), in true catharsis, "the mind is arrested and raised above desire and loathing."

There are optimal circumstances in which these effects can be achieved. Certain stories, personages, and events, according to Aristotle, are more conducive to catharsis than others, and the skill of the dramatic poet is to be judged by his choice and handling of material to this end. "The plot is soul and first principle," which the poet arranges into a sequence productive of tragic effect. The best plots are those already known to the audience, such as the history of a great house, which require less time in the exposition of antecedent information. Novelty and surprise come from the editing and rationalization of the familiar myth. Impossible probabilities (such as a convincing portrayal of a supernatural being) are preferred to improbable possibilities (such as a true but extraordinary coincidence) in securing the universality of the action.

Central characters must be of such sufficient stature that, when they undergo a change of fortune for the worse, their plight has resonance, but they must not be of such exalted status as to be remote from the audience. To exact fear, they should be like the members of the audience; yet, to exact pity, they must be undeserving of their great downfall in some degree. This downfall is the result not of a crime (for then it would be a retributive punishment) or merely of an accident or misadventure. Rather, it springs from the protagonist's "hamartia," a term which has been rendered as "tragic flaw" but which actually derives from the technical vocabulary of archery and means "a near miss of the mark." The tragic protagonist has somehow mistaken his aim, his identity, his choice of values; his moral responsibility becomes a complex issue. A character such as Sophocles' Oedipus in *Oedipus the King* (pr. 430-426 B.C.) is indeed foredoomed to incest and patricide (and in Aeschylus' lost tragedy on the subject, the curse entailed by a blasphemy was well to the fore). In Sophocles, however, the crimes have been committed before the play begins, and the action of the drama reveals Oedipus coming to self-knowledge of his hamartia, in his case having taken the form of headstrong self-assurance and heedlessness. As George Saintsbury pointed out, Aristotle's doctrine of hamartia was a stroke of genius in defining tragedy: The great tragic dramatists share "the sense that there is infinite excuse, but no positive justification, for the acts which bring their heroes and heroines to misfortune."

For Oedipus, the moment when he recognizes his lifelong misapprehension is also the moment of his true downfall; for this reason, Aristotle considered *Oedipus the King* to be a nearly perfect tragedy. The necessary "peripeteia," or reversal of fortune, the ironic boomerang of an intended purpose, coincides and coalesces with the "anagnorisis," the protagonist's realization of how badly he has gone wrong. In Greek tragedy, this realization is usually limited, on the protagonists' part, to an awareness of their own mistakes; it is left to the chorus to draw general principles from their plight. William Shakespeare and Jean Racine, on the other hand, allow their tragic heroes insight into their place in the universal scheme of things, thus ennobling or improving them. Later ages allowed tragic heroes to transcend the mundane reversals that caused their fall. The audience is left with a sense of reconciliation and, if not of justice, at least of balance in life. A genuine tragedy, predicated on those terms, would be neither depressing nor revolting but would inspire the audience with a heightened awareness of human beings' ability to overcome their fate. Greek tragedy seldom permits this consolation and recognizes no rewards beyond the mortal sphere: Sophocles' *Oedipus at Colonus* (pr. 401 B.C.) is the rare exception. Once Greek tragedy moved beyond Aeschylus' pious obeisance to the powers-that-be, it remained steadfastly anthropocentric.

Of Aristotle's other recommendations, the twenty-four-hour rule was regularly debated in later ages. He had desired a tragedy to be only as long as memory could embrace, and to preserve unity of action, by which he meant a unity of motive binding the characters together (as the crisis in *Oedipus the King* ensnares each character). The best means to accomplish this unity is to limit the length of the plot's action to a hypothetical day. Else postulated that Aristotle meant that the length of performance should not go beyond a day, but since the usual presentation of three tragedies and a Satyr play had of necessity to end by nightfall, this seems unlikely.

In sum, Aristotle saw tragedy as a way of bringing people to thoughtful contemplation, through their observation of action and passion. As the protagonist passes through pathos, that moment of extreme and unreasoning emotion, to reach a higher plane of understanding, the audience's feelings are heightened, discharged, leaving the mind clear to ponder the meaning of these events. Pleasure was a means, not an end, in this process.

Aristotle is more dismissive of comedy, and in this he followed Plato, who thought it suited only for slaves and aliens. In his *Philebus* (c. 400 B.C.), Plato argued that "those who are weak and unable to revenge themselves, when they are laughed at, may be truly called ridiculous. . . . Ignorance in the powerful is hateful and horrible, because hurtful to others both in reality and fiction; but powerless ignorance may be reckoned and, in truth, is ridiculous." In other words, one may safely laugh at the innocuous and impotent. Aristotle was more willing to grant that innocent amusement creates a relaxation that is a legitimate accompaniment of the pursuit of virtue. Even if laughter is a politically dangerous emotion, it may be safely purged through comedy. Lane Cooper, in *An Aristotelian Theory of Comedy* (1922), has glossed the comic catharsis as a purgation of anger (resentment of the comic victim's foolishness) and envy (longing to enjoy his happy ending). Comedy, Aristotle explained,

> is an imitation of characters of a lower type—not, however, in the full sense of the word bad, the ludicrous being merely a subdivision of the ugly. It consists of some defect or ugliness which is not painful and not destructive. To take an obvious example, the comic mask is ugly and distorted, but does not imply pain.

The emphasis on lower types of characters directed comedy toward a more realistic depiction of society—especially since, as Aristotle noted, comic poets did not borrow from mythology but invented their plots, building them along lines of probability. By Aristotle's time, Aristophanic comedy had long been extinct (Aristotle does not allow the mockery of individuals that was commonplace in Aristophanes), and Aristotle could have known only Middle Comedy (see below). Comic types, with a fixed vice that could be portrayed typically by a mask, had become the usual stage fare.

Attempts have been made to show that Aristotle did not intend to divide comedy and tragedy into mutually exclusive genres, since they presented different facets of the same elements. The hamartia in tragedy provokes pity and fear because the punishment is so vastly disproportionate to the error, whereas in comedy the hamartia is grossly exaggerated, but the punishment is trifling. Tragedy reveals the contradiction between the hero's view of himself and the universe around him; comedy reveals the contradiction between the hero's view of himself and the society around him. Tragedy effects a reconciliation in the audience's mind; comedy effects a reconciliation onstage. In an essay of 1948, entitled "The Argument of Comedy," Northrop Frye went so far as to suggest that tragedy is comedy that has not fulfilled its entelechy:

> The tragic catharsis passes beyond moral judgment, and while it is quite possible to construct a moral tragedy, what tragedy gains in morality it loses in cathartic power. The same is true of the comic catharsis, which raises sympathy and ridicule on a moral basis, but passes beyond both. . . . The audience gains a vision of that resurrection whether the conclusion is joyful or ironic, just as in tragedy it gains a vision of a heroic death whether the hero is morally innocent or guilty . . . tragedy is really implicit or uncompleted comedy; . . . comedy contains a potential tragedy within itself.

Any sharp distinction between tragedy and comedy had already begun to blur by the time of Euripides, who has been censured from Aristotle to Friedrich Nietzsche for not preserving the tragic "spirit" of his precursors. Many of his plays have happy endings (*Alcestis*, pr. 438 B.C.) or lack a downward peripeteia for the protagonist (*Helen*, pr. 412 B.C.), or edulcorate an otherwise tragic ending with a "euthanasia," or blessed death (*Hippolytus*, 428 B.C.), effected by a *deus ex machina*. In this respect, Euripides foreshadows the tragicomedies of a later day while maintaining the outward form of tragedy; certain of his characters come perilously close to the comic.

It is clear from Aristotle's definition that his view of comedy is a normative one; to deviate too radically from the established social norm is to render oneself comic. The character-types he listed in his ethics as examples of the vicious or deviant are suitable for ridicule, and two of them, the *eiron* and the *alazon,* are patterns for Western comic types. The *eiron* is the mock-modest man of cunning, an expert at sophistic argumentation, subtle, covert, and, as the term implies, ironic in attitude. Socrates, with his homely exterior and ironic humility concealing a razor-sharp mind, was Aristotle's prime example; the type recurs in the clever slaves of the New Comedy tradition, their servility masking their ingenuity. The *alazon* is the *eiron*'s dialectical opposite: the bullying braggart who claims to be more than he can validate, the boastful coward or would-be lady's man whose pretensions are exposed by the play's end. Aristotle lists variations ranging from the boorish loudmouth to the urbane wit, and in a complex comic figure such as Shakespeare's Falstaff, the *eiron* and the *alazon* are merged.

Aristophanic comedy had approached the normative only in the sense that Aristophanes himself, a conservative with strongly pronounced tastes for peace and the old-fashioned way, contrasted these ideals with the abuses and newfangled practices he saw around him. He did not necessarily speak for his society or set it up as an admirable model; his comic heroes, in fact, tend to be down-to-earth, plainspoken characters, comic only in terms of the physical situations into which they are thrust. A number of modifications to Old Comedy brought it inevitably closer to Aristotle's paradigm. The spectacular parabasis was omitted, in part as a result of financial considerations, in part as a result of a law instigated in 396 B.C. by the dithyrambic poet Cinesias, who had been personally attacked in a comedy. Gradually, the law took a firmer hand in moderating comedy's satiric excesses: In 414 B.C., a statute of Syracosius forbade poets from referring to current events in comedy, and in 404 B.C., a similar law prohibited the insertion of a personal name into comedy. By the time of Aristophanes' last play, *Plutus* (pr. 388 B.C.), with its diminished chorus and absent parabasis, the transition to Middle Comedy was well under way.

No entire plays of Middle Comedy are extant, but its distinguishing features can be reconstructed from surviving fragments and traces of its influence on its successors. It has been called a comedy of manners, although the manners shown are not very specific, since types govern the action. Certain recurring figures still connected with the festal origins of comedy—revelers, courtesans, cooks—as well as soldiers and parasites, are standard, and they speak a colloquial prose that never reaches heights of poetry or depths of scurrility but maintains an easy mean. For the most part, supernatural machinery is absent, although one style of Middle Comedy, invented by the Thasian Hegemon, specialized in parodies of tragic myths. Athenians were laughing at his *Gigantomaknia* (pr. late fifth century B.C.; war of the giants) when news of the Sicilian debacle reached them.

Essentially, the differences between tragedy and comedy were effaced less by Euripides' innovations than by the sentimental accretions of so-called New Comedy. This style, practiced by Menander (whose *Dyskolos*, pr. 317 B.C., is the only complete sample in existence), introduced a few new characters, such as the clever slave and the captain of mercenaries. Its plots, however, became stereotypical and unvaried. The central novelty of Menander and his colleagues was to place the emphasis on a love interest revolving around a sympathetic young man and young girl and to festoon the action with moral and sentimental reflections in the Euripidean fashion. In Aristophanes, there had been plenty of sex but no love; even in Middle Comedy, romantic involvement remained peripheral. In contrast, the pivot of the action in New Comedy was the young man's love, thwarted by the will or business dealings of an old crank; by the play's end, matters had been worked out, often through the machinations of a cunning slave, to bring the lovers together. As in tragedy, there was a late point of attack, close to the climax, and the hamartia, or mistaking of one's identity, in New Comedy became an external and mechanical use of disguises and concealed identities, until matters were cleared up by anagnorisis, or recognition of the truth. The *kōmos* feast at the finale became a wedding banquet, and the sententious commentary replaced the chorus, which had, by this time, atrophied into irrelevancy, as a group of nondancing singers whose contribution smacked of variety entertainment.

There were other, minor genres practiced during the heyday of New Comedy. The "mime," the only Greek dramatic form in which women performed, was basically a comic sketch spiced with the music of the cymbal, flute, and tambourine. In Doric regions, the mime was absorbed by local comedy, which tended either toward mythological fantasies treated bawdily (the *phlyakes*) or toward a tepid sort of realism. Rhinthon of Tarentum, around 300 B.C., wrote *phlyakographies*, more sophisticated recensions of the *phlyakes* farces, full of repartee and slapstick, while the almost apocryphal Sotades produced pornographic travesties. Yet these were side issues. The form in which Menander cast comedy was to become the basic mode for that genre (and later for straight drama) for two millennia.

Greek tragedy and New Comedy were transmitted by the Romans, who were not themselves adept at drama but were content to borrow what their neighbors had developed. In this habit they were not unlike the Victorian English, who regarded their French allies as immoral and frivolous but who pillaged, reworked, and prettified French dramatic works for decades. One of the reasons the Romans did not develop an indigenous and viable drama of their own was the lack of religious sanction. Early Roman religious rites were accompanied by revels and masquerades, part dance, part song, part backchat, mostly improvised; like the phallic Fescennine verses, later sung only at weddings, these quasi-dramatic rites never evolved into true drama. The *Saturae* (or goatish medleys) acted out comic stories to the sound of a flute, but they were not incorporated into a dramatic spectacle until, typically, non-Roman influence took hold. Etruscan dancers and mimes came to Rome in 364 B.C. and introduced the *ludi scenici*, or stage games, originally as part of the annual propitiatory rites. Later, the *Saturae*, reminiscent in this of the Satyr plays, were tacked on as *exodia*, or farcical interludes. The mime enjoyed a revival of popularity during the Empire, although even then, the principal feature of the form was gesticulation, not dialogue. The same holds true for the *fabulae attelanae*, or Atellan fables, simpleminded comedies of country life, with a gallery of stock characters. These included Pappus, the tyrannical father or husband; Maccus, the hunchbacked glutton; Bucco, the greedy and mendacious loudmouth; and Dossennus, the village pedant. To these occasionally were added other stock figures: dim-witted or tricky servants; Manducus, a jaw-snapping bogeyman; and the witch Lamia. Here, too, speech was improvised, the plots slender but full of complications (*tricae*, from which "intrigue" derives), and the actors' byplay the main ingredient for success. No wonder that under the Empire, such stock figures were readily absorbed into the popular pantomimes. The rustic characters, under other names and guises, would reappear in much folk comedy and take on fully fleshed forms in the Renaissance *commedia dell'arte* (see below).

Drama, then, was for the Romans neither a meaningful outgrowth from their religious beliefs nor an expression of communal solidarity, but purely and simply a rude recreation. According to tradition, Livius Andronicus, a Tarentine freedman of Greek ancestry, was the first to adapt tragedies and comedies from Greek originals, around 240 B.C.; unlike Aristotle, he was not very exact in drawing distinctions. An attempt was made to naturalize tragedy by means of the *fabula praetextata* (literally, the purple-hemmed-robe fable, a reference to the garb of superior court judges), which dramatized patriotic historical subjects and was meant to be performed as a eulogy at the funeral rites of the heroes whose victories it celebrated. It seems to have failed to catch on because the playwrights were permitted no latitude in dealing with the venerated Roman past and were not free to turn respected ancestors into human characters. The Romans did, however, invent the five-act structure, conventionalizing the episodes of Greek tragedy, with a standard prologue and epilogue. The chorus was retained but seldom took much part in the action, and the responsibilities of the performers became specialized. Dialogue was recited, often by a single actor, with intervals in which a boy, accompanied by a flute player, would sing while the actor mimed what was sung. This division of labor alienated performer from character and audience from action; dynamic interchanges between characters were sacrificed to rhetorical monologues, and the pity and fear discharged by a well-conducted plot were replaced by maudlin tear-jerking and sensational thrills.

Nevertheless, the tragedies of Lucius Annaeus Seneca have value beyond their intrinsic merit, for their influence on Renaissance and Elizabethan drama. It is still debated whether Seneca's tragedies, founded on Greek myths, were meant to be performed onstage or recited before a patrician audience. The latter opinion was long prevalent, but revivals of Seneca in the contemporary theater have proved that the tragedies have many stage-worthy and appealing features. What seems especially modern is Seneca's taste for the gruesome and the horrendous, in which he takes an almost sadistic delight; also noteworthy in this context is the speed in the development of the story, which may argue a lack of interest in characterization but which conduces to excitement and urgency. What is least modern about Seneca is his *sententiae*, the ponderous and artificial moralizing that clogs the movement of the drama and, rather than evolving organically from the characters, seems patently applied by the author.

Comedy became better acclimated to the Roman stage in two varieties: the *fabula palliata* (Greek-cloak fable), based on Greek originals and set in Greece, and the *fabula togata* (toga fable), which drew on the lives of the Roman proletariat. All that is known of the latter genre is based on titles and scholastic commentary, from which it can be inferred that the form was mildly satiric and topical, simple in cast and structure, and sexually unbridled.

Gnaeus Naevius, who is credited with inventing the *fabula praetextata*, also introduced the *contaminatio*, the conflation of two Greek plots into a single Latin one, thereby establishing the Italian comic formula of a rapid and complicated intrigue. Greek comedy was truly naturalized by the quasi-legendary plebeian Plautus, who translated the plays of Menander and his fellows into Latin, with their frustrated lovers, angry cooks, wily slaves, and meretricious courtesans adapted wholesale. The chorus was replaced by a prologue in which leading comic actors would ingratiate themselves with the audience and fill in the background. The setting was standardized: a street with two (occasionally three) house frontages, one entrance leading to the harbor and another to the forum. Plautus' genius lay in the complications he introduced into the plots, the elaborate weaving and unraveling of the intrigue. He also had a flair for comic dialogue, not as fanciful as Aristophanes' but still breezy and exuberant, with plentiful asides, and arrangements that have been characterized as the prototypes of the arias, duets, trios, and ensembles of comic opera. His Machiavellian slaves were clearly discriminated from one another, and he could heighten a conventional type such as the braggart soldier into a vital and recognizable human being (as in the play of that title, *Miles Gloriosus*, pr. 205 B.C.; *The Braggart Soldier*, 1825).

Moreover, even though Plautus' stories allegedly took place in Greece, it was obviously Roman morals and values that were being flouted, with masters befooled, slaves in charge, and mendacity, adultery, and the pleasure principle the order of the day. To license these affronts to Latin *industrias* and *honestas*, Plautus emphasized what can be called the "one mad day" aspect of comedy: Just as during the Saturnalia and similar religious festivals or holidays, the norm is perverted or challenged only to be ultimately restored and affirmed at the holiday's close, so, during the time of a comedy, antisocial activity is permitted, for the regular order will be reconfirmed at the finale. Henpecked husbands can feather lovenests; impertinent underlings can rule the roost; men can dress as women, and whores as virgins. By the final curtain, the irregularities have been resolved, the deviant characters either expelled from or reintegrated into society, and the unifying bond of community sealed anew. This pattern would remain a constant in traditional comedy from Thomas Dekker to Thornton Wilder.

Plautus' successor Terence was less rambunctious and more pallid, and his characters had not the vivacity or the variety of the earlier writer's; as with Menander, the love interest stands foremost. Terence even managed, in his *Andria* (pr. 166 B.C.?; *The Girl from Andros*, 1912) to introduce a situation in which the young man is smitten, not with a slave girl, but with a young lady of his own class. Terence's dialogue was so polished and elegant that he was preserved as a model for Latinists during the Middle Ages, and his influence on Renaissance comedy was as profound as Seneca's on Renaissance tragedy: He became an arsenal of plots and personae to be rifled and refurbished at will.

Terence's refinements on Plautus bespoke the increasing sophistication of the *palliatae,* but in the process they lost their broad comedy and also their appeal to the masses, and were performed for private audiences. The *togatae*, which flourished between 170 and 80 B.C., also enjoyed only a limited vogue. Roman audiences, coarsened by the sanguinary spectacles of the arena, found the theater tame, and the bellicose and austere national character never regarded drama as more than a frivolity. Horace's famous dicta on the drama in his *The Art of Poetry* (c. 17 B.C.), his insistence on clarity, common sense, fastidiousness, and decorum, were meant to groom a crude form of entertainment into one that was fit for the salon, since a discriminating patron of the arts should disdain vulgar amusements. Drama that conformed to Horace's urbanity would suit the taste of an elite class, but drama is by nature a public art, and the Roman public required stronger fare.

Consequently, in the early Empire, tragedy and comedy both gave way to ballets (*fabulae salticae*), which related the amorous expoits of the gods and heroes in a manner that was explicitly obscene, tricked out with spectacular effects like a Las Vegas nightclub show. Attempts were made to introduce crowd-pleasing features into tragedy: real executions and a slave tossed from a real tower. Comedy came to rely more heavily on slapstick and buffoonery. The pantomime, a lyric tragedy recited to a mimed solo with chorus and instruments, regained popularity; the mimes, who had a reputation for effeminacy, changed masks to represent different characters and excelled in the portrayal of voluptuous passion. Literary drama could not keep pace with the allurements of sex, spectacle, and female performers, and the pantomime remained the preeminent Roman dramatic form until the sixth century, at the time that it was banned by the Empress Theodora—who, in her salad days, had performed in sex shows at the circus.

From the foregoing survey of Greek and Roman dramatic forms, it should be apparent that, at their inception, tragedy and comedy were not distinct in nature. They arose from similar primitive impulses, and only gradually, and at the hands of individual creators, did their concerns and outward aspects grow far enough apart for them to be classified as mutually exclusive genres. Aristotle tried to demonstrate that these differences were intrinsic and organic, but the inability of the genres themselves to remain stable or meaningful outside post-Periclean society reveals their contingency. The classical genres of tragedy and comedy were not needed by a Christian world, and the Middle Ages had no interest in reviving them.

To begin with, there was the early Christian association of the theater with paganism and persecution; the only shows to be seen during the late Empire were so debased and sensual, the playhouses themselves ornamented with idols of the gods whose loves were played out onstage, that no self-respecting Christian would go near them. Furthermore, as Saint Augustine more subtly realized, if the spectator were to be moved to tears by a tragedy, he would waste the compassion that should be expended on actual objects. From such a perspective, plays leach off the fine emotions that human beings should reserve for real-life situations.

Greek drama, as noted, was anthropocentric, its interest focused on humans in their world. Christian thinking was metaphysical and theocratic and saw the function of art as a means of turning one's mind to God. The early fathers of the Church were vigorously outspoken in their contempt of the body and the world as snares and delusions, the instruments of Original Sin, the hindrances that bar souls from Heaven. When Saint Bernard of Clairvaux, in his *Meditationes Piissimae*, described humans as "nothing else than fetid sperm, a sack of dung, the food of worms," he was lending graphic images to a not uncommon attitude. It is ironic that Tertullian, who considered his belief heretical, in that the soul's activity is manifested and conditioned by the flesh, should be the Church father most explicit in his denunciation of the theater: He condemned it as a temple of Satan and maintained that, since all Christians at their baptism renounce Satan, to step inside a playhouse is automatically an act of apostasy.

Finally, the Middle Ages knew the literature of the ancients only piecemeal, and, despite attempts to adapt certain forms to Christian orthodoxy, the discrepancy between form and content was too great for success. The Byzantine *Khristōs paskhon* (c. 9th century; Christ's Passion) turned episodes from the Old and New Testaments into tragedy for educational purposes; in it, the Virgin Mary makes her first appearance onstage, lamenting her son's death with Agave's plaint from *The Bacchae* (pr. c. 405 B.C.) of Euripides. Within the isolation of her cloister, the nun Hroswitha of Gandesheim composed plays to glorify martyrdom and chastity in the style of Terence's comedies, faithful even to the bawdiness. These, however, were idiosyncratic cases, which had no effect on the world at large.

Classical tragedy could not be easily adapted, because its worldview ran counter to Christian tenets: In a universe where Christ has saved everyone and where His mercy is available on application by the sinner, no tragic fate is possible for the protagonist. Only if protagonists persist in their obstinacy and reject redemption can they be doomed; in that case, they are criminals and infidels who deserve damnation. Hamartia is simply not recognized. With Christ Himself as the central figure in tragedy, a happy ending cannot be avoided, despite the torments of the Passion; besides, as a divinity, Christ (not unlike Dionysus in *The Bacchae*) is incapable of hamartia, because He knows full well the import of His actions.

Consequently, all that the Middle Ages retained of the classical concept of tragedy was the notion of a fall from prosperity; the malevolent figure of Fortune spinning her wheel became a commonplace emblem. As Geoffrey Chaucer defined the genre in his poem *Troilus and Criseyde* (1372-1386), "Tragedye is to seyn, a dite of a prosperite for a tyme that endith in wrecchydnesse." The fall from high degree to misery was itself thought tragic, regardless of whether the protagonist was morally responsible. Tragedy had also lost its dramatic connotation, and the Monk in *The Canterbury Tales* (1387-1400) regarded his potted verse biographies of fallen greatness to be exemplary tragedies.

Similarly, comedy came to mean any dramatic presentation, with the Spanish *comedia*, the French *comédie*, and the Italian *commedia* frequently signifying the same broad range that the English word "play" does. Medieval plays were mixed in form, combining the sublime with the ridiculous and the grotesque. Dante entitled his great poem a *Commedia* (*Divina* was added only after his death) not because it is humorous but because its vision comprehends both the violent emotions of the damned and the incandescent spirituality of paradise and divine love, presented in an extravagant and fantastical mode yet couched in the realistic eloquence of the vulgar tongue.

Medieval drama, then, when it did begin to take shape, developed irregularly and with a teleological character. It was meant to instruct and focus the mind on God. The celebration of the Mass was itself a kind of performance, with the priest acting as both stage manager and star performer, and the communicants as both chorus and audience. As early as the sixth century, Pope Gregory the Great had fixed the antiphonal chant, which alternated the voices of soloists and choir, and this form was popularized by the Benedictines. Tutelon, a monk of Saint Gall, is credited with inventing Scriptural paraphrases called tropes (from *tropos*, a turn), some time in the tenth century. These tropes were inserted—"smuggled in," in Léon Gautier's phrase—before or after the sung portions of the breviary office to serve as Introits. The most renowned of these is the tenth century *Quem quaeritis,* sung on Easter Sunday. Half of the choir intoned to the three Marys come to the tomb, "*Quem quaertitis in sepulchro, o christicolae?*" (What seek you in the tomb, O Christians?), to which the other half replied, "*Iesum Nazarenum crucifixum, o caelicolae*" (Jesus of Nazareth who was crucified, O heavenly beings). The angelic half of the choir then announced, "*Non est hic, surrexit, sicut praedixerat/ Ite, nuntiate quia surrexit de sepulchro*" (He is not here. He has arisen as he foretold./ Go forth and proclaim that he has risen from the tomb).

The impetus for these tropes may have come from wandering clerics, the Goliards, who had introduced well-sung embellishments to the monasteries. When the *Regularis Concordia* (c. 970) of Ethelwold, Bishop of Winchester, recommended such devices "to fortify unlearned people in their faith," there was a sudden flowering of "dramatic" chanting and gesture (such as drawing the veil before the altar), as if the clergy had been suppressing for centuries an instinct for drama. Visual celebrations of the chief dates of the Church calendar became the rule. The earliest Latin liturgical play extant is based on the tale of the Magi and Herod, but by the eleventh century, plays were being produced in France on biblical subjects that had no connection with Church festivals: the Wise and Foolish Virgins, Adam and the Fall of Lucifer, Daniel, and Lazarus. Such plays, known as "mystery plays" or "mysteries," were written in the vernacular; their predecessors, the liturgical mysteries, had been written in Latin verse with some prose passages.

The earliest example of the vernacular mystery play is the Norman *Jeu d'Adam* (c. 1150). Indeed, it was in France that the terminology used to identify such plays originated. Technically, the term "mystery" (French *mystère*, a conflation of the Latin *ministerium*, meaning office or ceremony, with *mysterium*) covered plays depicting incidents from the life of Christ, while plays that dramatized the lives of saints were referred to as "miracle plays" or "miracles." This distinction, however, was not hard and fast even in France and did not exist at all in England, where the term "mystery" was not applied to these plays until the eighteenth century (by which time they were fodder for antiquarians). In any case, Christ's life was interpreted broadly to entail those episodes in the Old Testament that foretold his advent or symbolically prefigured his deeds. The Fall of Man, the Flood, and the sacrifice of Isaac were taken to be important prophecies of the redemption of the world, fulfilled by the Nativity, the Passion, and the Resurrection.

As these plays grew more elaborate, they were thrust out of the churches —sometimes for reasons of space, sometimes at the behest of an irate clergy—and into the churchyard or the public square. This shift, along with the adoption of the vernacular as the linguistic medium, enabled the plays to become less reverent and more profane, with heavy admixtures of comedy. As Benjamin Hunningher suggests in *The Origin of the Theater: An Essay* (1955), "When definite dramatic forms have been established, a church, no matter how opposed it might have been to theatre, may see some desirability in employing that theatre and even in participating directly in its further development." Thus, the Church sanctified the plays by associating them with the Corpus Christi festival in 1264 and with the solemn procession in which the symbol of the mystery of the Incarnation was borne (hence the term *processus* in ecclesiastic use to describe the plays). Occasionally, a council or a bishop would disown these spectacles and prohibit them, on the grounds that they had lost their religious character and were distracting the populace from true worship. (Robert Mannyng of Brunne, in his poem *Handlyng Synne*, 1288-1338, revived the legend of dancers in a churchyard who were cursed by the priest and condemned to dance for twelve months, in order to advertise the desecration of holy ground by such performances.) Plays performed by the clergy as didactic aids to religion were gradually supplanted by plays performed by laymen as expressions of secular concerns. In the process, Latin ceased to be a viable theatrical tongue (although it persisted in the *commedia erudita* and even enjoyed a revival in the Jesuit school dramas of the seventeenth century). Chanted speech was replaced by spoken dialogue, and the familiar figures of the Bible were ousted by original and more contemporary types.

In France, the drama was soon coopted by the laity; Jean Bodel, who wrote a relatively realistic *Le Jeu de St. Nicholas* (pr. c. 1200), was not a priest but a poet. (Saints' lives were particularly popular, since they could be given a local coloration and brought closer to the audience.) The Faust theme makes its first showing in Rutebeuf's *Théophilus* (pr. c. 1260; *Le Miracle de Théophile*, 1971), a miracle play of Our Lady that was still in the tradition of explicitly liturgical drama. As early as the thirteenth century, the vernal *Jeu de la feuillée* (pr. c. 1275; *The Greenwood Play*, 1971) of Adam de la Halle introduced pastoral elements; it was soon followed by his *Jeu de Robin et Marion* (pr. c. 1283; *The Play of Robin and Marion*, 1928), which announced a secular drama, more sophisticated in its structure than even so polished a Passion mystery as Greban's of the same period. By the end of the fourteenth century, the *Estoire de Griselidis* (pr. 1395; the tale of patient Griselda) by Philippe de Mézières appeared, a serious secular drama whose style was that of miracle plays of the Virgin but with a new Petrarchan Humanism conspicuous. Half a century later, Joan of Arc appeared for the first time on any stage in the tedious and overlong *Mystère du siège d'Orléans* (pr. c. 1450; mystery of the siege of Orleans, possibly by Jacques Milet), an embryonic chronicle play in its attempt to dramatize recent history. This relatively rapid secularization was assisted by the mime tradition—the old comic interludes and farcical scenes that had been preserved and spread by wandering minstrels and mountebanks from earliest times.

In England, the miracle plays did not begin to flourish until they came under the sponsorship of the trade guilds, which vied with one another in sumptuous staging and promotion. Many of the plays were translated from the French, but English authors also created their own reworkings of the Bible, the Apocrypha, and the lives of the saints. A characteristic of the English miracle plays was their grouping into series called cycles, which were performed in the course of one day, unfolding the totality of Scriptural history from Creation to the Day of Judgment. Some scholars believe that this synoptic approach was influenced by the Anglo-Saxon epics. It was certainly facilitated by the *pagonds*, or pageant wagons, which could trundle an episode from one end of a market town to another. The earliest English dramatic work, from the latter half of the thirteenth century, *The Harrowing of Hell*, comes from the East Midlands and exhibits a peculiarly English penchant for the gloomy. Indeed, each cycle bears the stamp of the locality in which it arose: The Towneley, or Wakefield, Cycle is exuberant and packed with humor and jocular invention and is not overly reverent in its treatment of religious figures; the York Cycle is more somber and dignified; and the Coventry Cycle is more wrought in a literary sense, more dramatically powerful, and shows a new sophistication in its use of abstract characters.

This growing abstraction came to fruition in the form known as the "morality play." Morality plays, like mystery and miracle plays, reflect not only the liturgical origins of medieval drama but also its increasing secularization; the distinctive feature of the form is the use of allegorical characters representing virtues, vices, warring spiritual principles, and so on. The genre is said to have been invented by Norman *trouvères* sometime before the thirteenth century, in an attempt to wrest dramatic control away from the ecclesiastical authorities, but morality plays did not appear onstage until the next century. In France, moralities were the first secular plays to be presented by university students (in 1426 and 1431).

A morality is constructed to depict a conflict among the personified qualities of the human soul, with the protagonist as a metaphor for all humankind. The French quickly adapted this scheme to nonreligious matters, such as political and social debates, and, with the clear-cut division between good and evil, injected a foretaste of melodrama. There is even a prototypal problem play: Nicolas de la Chesnaye's morality of hygienic abstinence, published in 1507, in which "Banquet" conspires with "Apoplexy," "Epilepsy," and similar diseases to endanger human health.

Genre diversification occurred in French drama because of increasing specialization among the performance groups. In 1402, the Confrérie de la Passion announced a monopoly on the mystery and miracle plays in order to prevent further contamination by the new secular Humanism. A lay group, the Union de la Basoche, founded to divert minds from the disastrous wars, concentrated on moralities and short political satires and on spoof sermons in the style of the Feast of Fools. They were the first to enact *Maître Pathelin* (pr. 1485), one of the earliest situation comedies based on contemporary life. The term "farce" itself comes from the word for stuffing; just as a fowl is stuffed with forcemeat, so a mystery was larded with a comic interlude. The independence of the farce from the mystery enabled it to exploit such true-to-life situations as marital strife, legal chicanery, or business shenanigans; it served as a springboard for modern comedies of character and of manners.

Another early-fifteenth century group, Les Enfants sans Souci, confined themselves to *sotties* (the word means "foolishness"): short, comical allegories made to serve both Church and State. For example, Pierre Gringore, in his *Jeu du Prince des Sots et de mère Sotte* (pr. 1511; the prince of fools and mother fool), supported Louis XII in his dispute with Pope Julius II. In nature, *sotties* were closer to satiric revues than to social comedies. The audiences for *sotties* and moralities were never as homogeneous or as large as those for miracles and mysteries, but an elite patronage allowed authors to experiment with subject matter and treatment in a manner that would have been inadmissible in a more public situation.

In England, where the comic element had been strong in the mysteries, the Vice character of the morality won enduring popularity. Originally a henchman of the Devil, the Vice, with his crude jokes, phallic sword of lath, and inept evildoing, became a popular favorite and assumed the truth-telling aspects of the court fool. This tolerated malefactor can be seen in so simple a creation as the sheep stealer Mak in the fifteenth century *The Second Shepherds' Play* (pb. 1958), as well as in the richly complex figure of Shakespeare's Falstaff.

The earliest English moralities were devoid of religious dogma, merely presenting the allegorical strife over the soul of an Everyman. After the rupture with Rome that occurred during the reign of Henry VIII, however, the morality play began to be used for propaganda. Under Elizabeth I, theological controversy was waged in *New Custome* (pb. 1573) and Nathaniel Woode's *The Conflict of Conscience* (pb. 1581), and intellectual progress was treated in John Rastell's *The Nature of the Four Elements* (pr. c. 1517) and John Redford's *Wit and Science* (pr. c. 1530-1547), which contains a hilarious spelling lesson carried on by Ignorance and Idleness. By this means, the new learning was vulgarized and disseminated. John Bale's *King Johan* (pb. 1538) made an antipapist, patriotic appeal, and by combining the allegorical abstractions of the morality with characters from England's history, he invented an embryonic chronicle play. The moral element can still be glimpsed in the figure of Rumour in Shakespeare's *Henry IV, Part II* (pr. 1598).

Others, such as Sir David Lyndsay of the Mount in his *Satyre of the Thrie Estaitis* (pr. 1540), mingled contemporary types with allegorical figures to produce an early version of the comedy of humors. This movement was also carried forward by John Heywood, whose interludes were usually based on French farces, with a dosage of British anticlericism added. An interlude, as its etymology implies (*inter* plus *ludi*, "between the plays") was originally a light, humorous presentation interpolated between the episodes of a protracted mystery. The Victorian Shakespearean scholar John Payne Collier claimed that John Heywood's interludes were the earliest form of modern drama, and he was right, insofar as Heywood's plays eschew any allegorical characters and draw their people and language from the life around them. The actions and personalities were as familiar to their original audiences as were their next-door neighbors.

Medieval drama was most technically adept and variegated in France and England. Religious spectacles of various kinds existed throughout Europe but seldom matured into more complex forms. The German Corpus Christi plays, or *Frohnleichnamsspiele*, were written in the vernacular, with an emphasis on the Last Judgment and plentiful dollops of moralizing, but audiences were too naïve to warrant the step up to the morality play. The only secular plays in Germany were the *Fastnachtsspiele*, or Shrove Tuesday shows, comic interludes played by professional strollers. In Italy, the religious drama had been subsumed by the ostentatious processionals, or *Trionfi*, the artificiality and pomp of which militated against dramatic development. The secular equivalent, the *festaiuoli*, in which opulent ornamented dishes were brought into courtly banquets to the accompaniment of dance and music, gave rise to ballet and masque. (This latter form was introduced into England as a private entertainment or masquerade around 1512-1513 and, as noted below, had an illustrious future.) The English version of the *Trionfi* were "pageants," patriotic equestrian processions of mythological heroes and allegorical abstractions, with men and horses gorgeously caparisoned. The pageant lingers on in an etiolated form in the Lord Mayor's Show, the Macy's and Rose Bowl parades, the New Orleans Mardi Gras, and the hero's ticker-tape welcome.

Contrary to Aristotle's hypothesis that dramatic forms evolve through inner necessity, medieval drama responded to external stimuli, transmuting and adapting to ecclesiastical regulations and audience demands. Relatively untrammeled by prescriptive rules, it still needed a fresh impetus to develop beyond the limited genres of morality and farce. This impetus was provided by the rediscovery of classical literature; at the same time, however, the example of the Greeks and Romans inhibited the dramatic energies of certain cultures.

The Middle Ages had known Horace's *The Art of Poetry*. Aristotle's *Poetics*, however, although available in an unabridged Latin version, was seldom consulted. After the fall of Constantinople in 1453 and the influx of Greek pedagogues into a Europe thirsting for contact with intellectual authorities outside the Church, the *Poetics* became a guidebook for every budding scholar. Within a century, it had been fully translated into both Latin and Italian, published in its original Greek, and thoroughly annotated. In the medieval period, Aristotle, although a pagan, had been respected by the scholastics for his knowledge in the fields of natural history and logic; the Renaissance merely extended his authority to the arts and, with its tacit assumption that the classical past had been a Golden Age to be emulated but never superseded, measured contemporary literature on an impossible scale. What in Aristotle had been deductions and inferences drawn from observation became, in the Humanist tradition, rigid rules to be disregarded at peril of contempt. The critics themselves were luminaries of courts and aristocratic circles. Their edicts thus were endorsed from above and integrated into the intellectual codes of the ruling society. Drama founded on the Humanist reinterpretation of Aristotle was fare intended for a powerful but narrow *cognoscenti* and took on prestige as a guide to right thinking and proper conduct at a time when the Church's authority was waning.

These Aristotelian prescriptions were most stunting to the growth of tragedy in Italy. Throughout the Middle Ages, tragedy for the Italians had meant Seneca. The *Ecerinis* (pr. c. 1314; *The Tragedy of Ecerinis*, 1972) of Albertino Mussato, though written in Latin, had tried to convey contemporary relevance by warning the Paduans that Cane Grande della Scala had designs on them, through the example of the tyrant Ezzelino. Antonio Minturno, in his work on poetry *On the Poet* (1559), was still sufficiently medieval in his thinking to define tragedy as a fall from prominence to misery, teaching one to distrust all things mortal and to bear one's griefs bravely. He was also sufficiently fashionable to explore catharsis as an unpleasant compulsion which, through pity and fear, purges the characters of such negative qualities as the mortal sins and endows the spectators with a heightened respect for virtue. This emphasis on the didactic aim of drama was less Aristotelian than Horatian, and the note would be struck ever louder by every theorist of the period.

The immensely influential Julius Caesar Scaliger pronounced that tragedy has its roots in real life and is distinguished from comedy by its unhappy ending and by the exalted rank of its characters, since only royalty and nobility have tragic potential. To suit the elevated station of the protagonists, the diction must be lofty. The dramatist's task is to teach correct behavior through pleasurable emotion and convincing imitation. Scaliger invented what came to be called the "French scene," defining a scene as "part of the act in which two or more characters speak," but he did not, despite the term by which they are known, invent the so-called *unités scaligériennes*.

These pernicious rules were, in fact, codified by Lodovico Castelvetro, who had a low opinion of the theater and its audience and was dubious about the possibility of tragedy offering moral exempla. In his view, poetry could not accommodate science and philosophy but would have to offer a surrogate world, sufficiently recognizable to be accepted by the crude commoners who beheld it. Therefore, unity of time and place are essential, though double plots are allowed in order to enhance pleasure. Misreading Aristotle's twenty-four-hour rule to mean the time of performance, Castelvetro insisted that no presentation should last long enough to frustrate the audience's "bodily necessities, such as eating, drinking, disposing of the superfluous contents of belly and bladder, sleeping and so on." Castelvetro contended that this stolid, dim-witted audience had an inelastic imagination that could not be stretched too far; it could believe only the most plausible and the most visible. The most plausible subject for a tragedy, then, is an imaginary story supported by realistic data, whose action "may admit of happening, but must never have happened." Anything that cannot be portrayed with verisimilitude, such as violence, should be deleted, and the tragedy should end happily.

Despite Castelvetro's scorn for the theater, his awareness that its entertainment value was paramount struck an especially Italian note. Tragedies that followed the ancients too closely lacked appeal, such as Cino da Pistoia's *Filostrato e Panfila* (pr. 1499), which was written in Italian and based on a story from Giovanni Boccaccio but which employed the Senecan five acts and a chorus and was even introduced by the ghost of Seneca. Giambattista Giraldi Cinthio, in a discourse of 1543, reiterated that there was no satisfaction in writing a play that met all the academic criteria and failed to please the public. He, too, recommended the *finta favola*, the invented story, both for tragedy (his *Orbecche*, pr. 1541, is a gruesome array of murder and incest on the Senecan plan) and for *tragedia mista*, "mixed tragedy," in which the characters are all of the same social class but reveal a variety of personalities. In mixed tragedy, horrific events may occur but the ending is happy, a result which is achieved through reliance on recognition scenes. Such a play, Cinthio asserted, would rouse the audience's horror and compassion (his extremist reading of fear and pity) and purge them of the obsessions that plagued the characters. His own *Gli antivalomeni* (pr. 1546; *The Changelings*, 1962) is a telling example: Tyrannies and threatened deaths are dispelled by the revelation of a cradle switch and by the marriage of two pairs of lovers, once the true identities of the exchanged infants are made known. This formula has become a staple of Western drama, sometimes used seriously (as in Shakespeare's *The Winter's Tale*), sometimes casually to tie up loose ends (as in Molière's *Les Fourberies de Scapin*), sometimes nonsensically, trading on the audience's awareness that the device is silly and stale (as in Oscar Wilde's *The Importance of Being Earnest* and W. S. Gilbert's *H.M.S. Pinafore*). The clichéd nature of this kind of anagnorisis was soon criticized even by Cinthio's contemporaries. Anton Francesco, known as Il Lasca, noted that the discovery scenes were "so irksome to the audience that, when they hear in the argument how at the taking of this city or the sack of that, children have been lost or kidnapped, they know only too well what is coming, and would fain leave the room."

Cinthio's own plays were lent interest by his originality in concocting his plots, and tragicomedy, as mixed tragedy came to be known, caught on. The genre was defined in 1599 by Giambattista Guarini as a means of freeing the audience from melancholy and disposing its soul to relaxation by portraying great characters indulging in common actions, a blend of public and private affairs, the whole expressed in dulcet, ornate language.

Whoever creates tragicomedies takes from tragedy its great charm but not its great actions, its verisimilar plot but not its historically true one, its stirred emotions, but not its furious ones, its delight but not its sadness, its danger but not its death. From comedy he takes laughter that is not immoderate, modest amusement, the fabricated complication, happy reversal and, above all, the comic order. . . .

In short, one finds the best of all dramatic worlds.

A favorite style of tragicomedy was the pastoral, originally a dramatic imitation of the bucolic idylls of Horace, Vergil, and Longus, and a neoclassical response to rustic folk comedies that also featured peasants and shepherds. The earliest Italian example is Poliziano's *Orfeo* (pr. 1480; *Orpheus*, 1879), which begins on an idyllic note and ends on a tragic one, and is performed to music—clearly an ancestor of opera. The comic element came to the fore in Agostino Beccari's *Il Sagrifizio* (pr. 1554; the sacrifice), but the masterpiece of the genre is Guarini's *Il Pastor Fido* (pb. 1590; *The Faithful Shepherd*, 1602), a tragicomedy based on a story by Pausanias. Set in Arcady, the basic plot is extremely complicated and somber in tone, involving a number of unrequited love affairs, jealous intrigues, and a threat of death looming over the protagonists. This is intermingled with a modicum of satiric comedy and ends with an anagnorisis of true relationships, love triumphant, and an oracle fulfilled. The influence of *The Faithful Shepherd* cannot be overemphasized: Guarini's play was translated, adapted, and imitated throughout Europe, confirming the age's taste for idealized swains, Platonic romances, and abstractly classical settings.

Following Aristotle's example, the Renaissance critics wasted little time in analyzing comedy. Castelvetro, Scaliger, Cinthio, and the rest all stressed the low station of the characters and the private nature of the events. Scaliger noted of the plot that it begins in confusion and ends in resolution; Castelvetro made the remarkable comment that comic characters have recourse to law, whereas tragic characters must defend their honor in other ways that lie outside the courts. He also astutely recognized that the comic characters' joy, transmitted to the audience, consisted in concealing a disgrace, saving oneself from shame, and the like. These minor victories were to remain the stuff of farcical situations. An Oedipus loses his eyes; a Monsieur Prud'homme loses his trousers. Oedipus chooses his disgrace; Monsieur Prud'homme exults in evading his.

The Italian imitation of the *palliatae* of Plautus and Terence resulted in the *commedia erudita*, or school comedy, which enlisted the conventional parasites, pedants, and so on, and tacked on snippets of morality. The slavish way in which many authors stuck to their originals was commented on by the sarcastic Lasca:

> Authors of such comedies jumble up the new and the old, antique and modern together, making a hodge-podge and confusion, without rhyme or reason, head or tail. They lay their scenes in modern cities and depict the manners of today, but foist in obsolete customs and habits of remote antiquity. Then they excuse themselves by saying: Plautus did thus, and this was Menander's way and Terence's; never perceiving that in Florence, Pisa and Lucca people do not live as they used to do in Rome and Athens. . . .

Eventually, however, dramatists managed to adapt the five-act structure and the conventions of Roman comedy to the mores of their own times.

Among others, Ludovico Ariosto in *La Cassaria* (pr. 1508; *The Coffer*, 1975), Niccolò Machiavelli in *La Mandragola* (pr. 1522; *The Mandrake*, 1911), and Pietro Aretino in *Il Marescalco* (pr. 1526-1527; *The Stable-master*, 1966) produced literate comedies in racy language about scabrous modern characters without doing damage to the classical unities. The best features of the *commedia erudita* are its well-observed types and its craftsmanlike handling of intricate imbroglios; for post-Renaissance audiences, its least effective feature is a windy verbosity, the need to tell rather than to show. It efficiently superseded such earlier forms of Italian comedy as the *contrasti*, which features disputations between pairs of allegorical characters, and the *frottola*, in which humans replace the abstractions.

The *commedia erudita* did not, however, manage to supplant forms of comedy that were firmly rooted in Italian soil. The *farsa*, an earthly medieval comedy of plebeian life, persisted, although it came to be redefined as a subcategory of tragicomedy which "accepts all subjects—grave and gay, profane and sacred, urbane and rude, sad and pleasant," and has no truck with the unities. "The scene," explained Cecchi of Florence, "may be laid in a church, or a public square, or where you will, and if one day is not long enough, two or three may be employed."

Commedia dell'arte might be translated as "plays performed by professionals," to distinguish it from the erudite drama acted by nobles and university students. Although a number of individuals, including Francesco Cherea and Angelo Beolco, have, at one time or another, been credited with inventing it, it is more likely that it originated among the wandering jugglers and entertainers who, from Egyptian times, have preserved the popular traditions of the professional theater. Many of the character-types from the Atellan farces and even the Greek *phylakes* were preserved and transmuted in it, taking on distinctive dialects and mannerisms of the Italian regions. Pappus became Pantalone, a merchant of Venice, greedy, lustful, and crabbed; the hunchback, hooknosed Maccus transformed into Pulcinello, brutal and rapacious; the pedant reappeared as Il Dottore, a grandiloquent, stuttering lawyer from Bologna; the clever slave and the dim-witted slave recur as Brighella and Arlecchino (Harlequin), the latter a peasant from Bergamo, victim of his appetites. Different troupes and regions renamed the characters at will and modified their endowments, but the basic types were conspicuous throughout Italy. Sometime in the late fifteenth century, the *capitano spavente*, a fire-eating but cowardly braggart, was added, possibly by Venturino of Pesara, partly in imitation of Plautus, and partly to mock the Spanish mercenaries who engineered the Sack of Rome.

"The Commedia dell'arte does not exist as an independent body of drama," states K. M. Lea in her classic *Italian Popular Comedy* (1934). The scripts were not finished literary products but rather scenarios (*soggetti*), offering a three-act plot line with a prologue and a sequence of incidents; within these guidelines, the players were free to improvise their dialogue, exploiting local personalities and issues, or to draw upon their stockpile of comic devices. Many set pieces, especially the love scenes, the *concetti* or aphorisms, and the elaborate physical business, known as *lazzi* (for example, two servants tied back to back trying to eat a plate of pasta lying on the ground), were known by heart and interpolated as the spirit moved. Leather masks immediately established the character and compelled the performer to use his body and voice to express what his face could not (ordinarily, the lovers were not masked). The popularity of this improvisatory genre prompted playwrights and writers in other theatrical forms to co-opt its strategies and stock characters: Lecchino, Pantalone, and their crew popped up in court entertainments; Massimo Troiano and the composer Orlando de Lasso, in 1568, regaled the Duke of Bavaria with a medley of music, *lazzi*, and *commedia* characters; and the *Ballet comique de la Reine* (pr. 1581) transported a similar divertissement to the French court. The *commedia dell'arte*'s influence on the history of comedy, dance, opera, mime, and every theatrical form in which text is subservient to performance was immense.

The transition from medieval to Renaissance genres occurred later in France. The *mystères* had been banned in 1548, at which time the Pléiade, that galaxy of poets and taste-makers, was canvassing for the classics and urging imitation of Greek and Latin models. Significantly, members of the Pléiade acted in Étienne Jodelle's *Cléopâtre captive* (pr. 1552; Cleopatra in bondage), known as the first "regular" French tragedy, and *Eugène* (pr. 1552), the first "regular" French comedy. In 1572, in a preface to *Saül le furieux* (Saul gone mad), Jean de la Taille asserted that tragedy, that "most elegant, excellent and splendid" type of poetry, essentially required unity of time and place. *Cléopâtre captive* is unregenerately Senecan, highly declamatory, with the obligatory ghost and chorus. The verse is in couplets of iambic pentameter, with occasional lapses into Alexandrines. The Alexandrine couplet was established by J. B. de La Péruse, in his *Médée* (pr. c. 1553?), as the standard verse form for French tragedy.

The most interesting experiments at this time were in adapting the biblical material of the *mystères* to the new classical format, but Scriptural stories and saints' lives were rapidly effaced by Jacques Amyot's 1559 translation of Plutarch's *Parallel Lives,* a treasure trove of incident and character. It is curious that Alexandre Hardy's dramatization of Amyot's translation of a Greek romance, entitled *Les Chastes et loyales amours de Théagène et Chariclée* (pr. 1623; the chaste and faithful loves of Theagenus and Chariclea), was divided into eight *journées,* or days, a unit of the medieval dramatic structure. It soon became clear that the public preferred five-act structures entailing one day's action, despite the occasional complaint, such as Pierre de Laudun's in 1559, that packing all the action into one day destroys illusion, while thinning the action to fit a day denudes the play.

Many of the changes were required by the physical restrictions of the playing space. The medieval *mystère,* taking place in the open, could be fluid in its movement and take advantage of numerous stage settings, such as the "mansions," emblematic indications of locale arranged to be traversed lineally. The Hôtel de Bourgogne, which very probably housed the first French professional acting troupe, had limited space, and mansions were replaced by symbolic stage properties. These proliferated to such an extent that the patrons complained that props were incapable of representing all the necessary locales; in compliance, actors and playwrights began to narrow the scope of the action and generalize the location. This they would later justify by appeal to the unities, but in reality the innovations were practical responses to public demand.

In the sixteenth century, the French theater was relatively free of control from above and could draw its subject matter from any source it chose. The first tragedy written on a contemporary subject was Gabriel Bounyn's *La Soltane* (pr. 1561; the Sultan). Under the Medicis, Italian influence made Giovanni Boccaccio and his fellow romancers the dramatist's main creditors, but Nicolas Filleul's introduction of the pastoral in his *Achille* (pr. 1563) was a failure. The biblical tragedies, infused with the Calvinist temper of the Huguenots, became more spare and took to imitating Seneca. As for comedy, it shared the subject matter of the farce, even as it strove to resemble a five-act *palliata* by Terence. It is significant that Jodelle's *Eugène* pivots on the theme of cuckoldry, which came to dominate French comedy and, later, drama for centuries. A troupe of Italian comedians settled in Paris in 1576, and suddenly French prose comedy was revitalized by a vivacious set of characters and plot devices. Basically, however, the most popular form remained tragicomedy. French tragedy and comedy would not assume their characteristic shapes until the seventeenth century.

Of the other important literatures of the European Renaissance, the Spanish and the German remained relatively untouched by the classical infection, while the English managed to survive it and render it benign. The first Spanish play of any stature was a tragicomedy, *La comedia de Calisto y Melibea* (pr. 1499), attributed to Fernando de Rojas and written more as a novel in dialogue than as a stage play. This realistic, almost cynical story of a tragic love affair, with its vivid characterization of the old bawd Celestina and her associates, proved so irresistible that later dramatists scaled down the twenty-one act version of 1499 to suit the exigencies of their own theaters. Shakespeare seems to have drawn on it for *Romeo and Juliet.* Influential though it was, *La comedia de Calisto y Melibea* was an anomaly. The first true Spanish dramas are credited to Juan del Encina, religious and pastoral eclogues that he called *representaciones* and which were imitated in Portugal by Gil Vicente.

Encina was followed by Bartolomeo de Torres Naharro, who, in 1517, published eight plays, divided into *comedias a noticia,* which dealt with actual events, and *comedias a fantasia,* which used imaginary events; each of these irregular and loosely knit pieces, uninhibited by the unities, began with an *introyto,* or argument, and was divided into three *jornadas,* equivalent to the French *journée.* Torres Naharro's influence was limited by the Inquisition, which prohibited his plays. Less ambitious and perhaps more indigenous were the *pasos,* short comedies founded on popular sayings, and the *coloquios* of Lope de Rueda, pastoral farces in the form of dialogues among shepherds and a shepherdess, which were occasionally spiced with comic interludes featuring familiar types such as the Blackamoor and the Biscayan. These *entremeses,* or interludes, were developed by Miguel de Cervantes into pungent and well-observed one-act comedies of real life; the grounding in reality was also present in his tragedies, in which he introduced a personified abstraction, as in the morality, to speak a "divine" or heightened language.

The earliest Spanish tragedies were stilted imitations of classical originals, but the genius of Lope de Vega, Pedro Calderón de la Barca, and Luis Veléz de Guevara transformed Spanish drama into a brilliantly idiosyncratic school with its own genres. The standard Spanish term for a play, *comedia,* implies a romantic drama that combines elements of comedy and tragedy. The innumerable *comedias* of Lope de Vega, for example, can be divided into several subgenres.

The *comedia de ingenio,* or *de capa y espada* (cape-and-sword dramas), derived their name from the everyday costume of the main characters, persons of noble birth. Although the plots were seldom original, the titles were ethnically Hispanic, deriving from proverbs, and the intrigue revolved around gallantry. Action was plentiful, both in the main plot and in the subplot, which concerned the *gracioso,* or rustic fop. The *comedia heroica,* or *de teatro,* dealt with royal or high-ranking figures; historical, mythological, or national themes; or current events. Its tone was more serious than that of the cape-and-sword play, concerning as it did the *pundonor,* the code of honor by which a gentleman lived, but it, too, had a comic underplot. Lope de Vega also wrote undesignated plays of the common people. All three types are notable for an alacrity of rhythm, sprightly dialogue, and a minimum of static or analytic passages.

Tragedy in the classic sense could not exist in Spain for theological reasons: God and the believer were on chivalric terms with each other. Fate could not be inexorable, since divine magnanimity left the field open to free will, and miracles could always supervene at the eleventh hour. Therefore, when all secular plays were prohibited between 1598 and 1600, Lope de Vega turned his attention to the *comedia de santos,* or *de cuerpo,* miracle plays, and the *auto sacramental*, a development from the open-air Corpus Christi pageant. These solemn proceedings in honor of the Sacrament followed a set pattern: two or more characters speaking a complimentary prologue (the *loa*), a lyric farce or two (the *entremeses*) allied in nature to the *paso*; and the *auto* itself, an allegorical depiction of the sinful soul wavering and transgressing until Divine Grace intervenes, the ultimate *deus ex machina.*

So rich and vital was the Spanish drama of this period that, well into the nineteenth century, playwrights, librettists, and novelists of other nations looted it for plots and characters. The French and English tragicomedies of the seventeenth century would have been impoverished without it, and Guiseppe Verdi would have had to look elsewhere for the stories of some of his most popular operas. The genres fixed by Calderón, Lope de Vega, and Miguel de Cervantes maintained their hold in Spain with little change until the eighteenth century endorsed French fashion. Augustín Moreto did modulate the cape-and-sword drama into the *comedia de figuron*, or comedy of character, which streamlined the plots, put the *gracioso* center stage, and claimed to cleave to nature. Similarly, the *entremes* became divorced from the religious drama and evolved into the *saynete* (as Toribio de Benavente called it around 1645), which literally means "a tasty morsel of crackling" and was a clownish little farce, usually containing a piquant moral. The flourishing of the Spanish drama can be attributed to the inability of the academic strictures to take root there; the theater always remained close to popular tastes and national sentiments.

A similar situation obtained in England, where the introduction of Seneca and Terence prompted imitation but never preempted the indigenous modes of dramatic presentation. The shapeless intermingling of these elements can be seen in the interminable tragedy *Gorboduc* (pr. 1561), by Thomas Norton and Thomas Sackville, intended for performance by lawyers for lawyers. The argument is drawn from pre-Christian Britain, pays no heed to unity of time and place, and contains allegorical dumb shows (the term itself had entered the English language only in 1561, the year before *Gorboduc* was first performed). These mimic depictions, featured between the numerous acts of *Gorboduc*, may have originated in the popular Italian *intermedii* or in the city pageants and court masques. At the same time, *Gorboduc* features a Senecan chorus and verbose messengers, for its ample violence is kept offstage. *Gorboduc* initiated act division and the use of blank-verse dialogue into English drama. Iambic pentameter established its dominion so rapidly in the English theater that when the complete translation of Seneca appeared in 1581, it failed to get a stage hearing because it was cast in fourteen-syllable lines.

Gorboduc, with its mélange of ancient and modern devices, was not thought a good model by Sir Philip Sidney. In his *Defence of Poesie* (1595), he censured native dramatic forms such as the miracles and moralities as antiquated vestiges of popery, "vaine playes or enterludes," unfit to carry out the drama's Horatian purpose "to teach and delight." Judging by Italian canons, Sidney found that *Gorboduc* was not strict enough in its observance of the rules, even though he refused to endorse the unities and allowed a messenger or chorus to span the breaks in time and place. Tragicomedy had crept into English in Richard Edwards' *Damon and Pithias* (pr. 1564), but Sidney condemned the genre as "mungrell," mixing kings and clowns with neither decency nor discretion; he maintained that even comedy must go beyond scornful laughter if it is to teach delightfully. Sidney's aristocratic strictures, however, had no bearing on the actual state of playwriting even when they were first published, and they remain an elegant if vain attempt to foster neoclassical drama in England.

Sidney extolled the poet over the historian, not only because the poet's teachings are pleasurable ("sportive" is a favorite word of Sidney) but also because tragedy exercises its own justice to punish vice and reward virtue. Ironically, even as he penned that sentiment, English playwrights were delving into their own national past for plots, to develop a native genre, the chronicle history. The clumsy but vigorous play *The Famous Victories of Henry V* (pr. c. 1588) would be improved upon by Shakespeare, who also lent a hand to the *Tragedy of Sir Thomas More* (pr. c. 1590), which added a tragic component to the chronicle by demonstrating the hamartia of the central character. This hybrid of tragedy and history was exceptionally successful in Shakespeare: *Hamlet* (pr. 1600-1601), *Macbeth* (pr. 1606), and *King Lear* (pr. c. 1605-1606) all begin with a kernel of "factual" data from Raphael Holinshed or Saxo Grammaticus but expand to treat subjects of universal import. Furthermore, the expertise of Shakespeare and his fellows in theatricalizing English history gave them a fluency and ease in handling classical history (*Julius Caesar*, pr. c. 1599-1600; Ben Jonson's *Sejanus His Fall*, pr. 1603) that is lacking in their foreign contemporaries. Their treatment of classical topics was not restrained by classical rules.

When, in *Hamlet*, Polonius reads the roster of entertainments that the players are prepared to offer, one can infer the relaxed attitude toward genres that was prevalent in Elizabethan and Jacobean drama: "tragedy, comedy, pastoral, pastoral-comical, historical-pastoral, tragical-historical, tragical-comical, historical-pastoral, scene individable, or poem unlimited." By Continental standards, Elizabethan and Jacobean tragedy, in particular, was shockingly irregular, with its blatant cruelty, rapid shifts in time and space, and the jostling of the sublime and the ridiculous. Its protagonists were extremists, exemplified by Christopher Marlowe's overreachers, the grandeur of whose ambition outweighs the failure or moral obloquy of their enterprise. Fate, viewed as contingency, rules over the passions— hence the frequent reference to astrology and omens, the strong hand of the supernatural in human affairs. Ghosts, especially, teem in the genre known as revenge tragedy, perhaps introduced by Thomas Kyd's *The Spanish Tragedy* (pr. c. 1585-1589) and the anonymous *Locrine* (1595), and honed to a fine edge by Shakespeare, John Webster, Cyril Tourneur, and Thomas Middleton. Motivated by a crime committed in the past, the lone avenger follows the thread of his vendetta through to a gory end, leaving the stage strewn with corpses.

The red-blooded (in every sense) form of Elizabethan and Jacobean tragedy was the direct result of theatrical conditions: The audience was heterogeneous, ranging from the groundlings in the pit to the exquisites in the boxes (or even onstage), and the coexistence of convoluted, image-packed poetry and exuberant action in the same play was meant to provide something for everyone. (Plays produced in the banquet halls display subtler effects and quieter moods.) In the open-air playhouse, the actors were so close to the public that soliloquies and asides could be intimately addressed to it; the two permanent doors at the back of the stage, which permitted one set of characters to enter as another departed, made for maximum overlap and speed of scene changes. (It should be remembered that the formal act and scene breakdowns of these plays were often supplied by the publishers and therefore do not reflect the actual unbroken continuity of stage action.) The doors also made for much "Look where he comes" and "But see who comes here" in the dialogue. As in the French theater of the time, limited space put greater emphasis on properties, so that crowns and mirrors, handkerchiefs and rings took on symbolic qualities. Dialogue served the function of scene painting ("This is Illyria, lady"; "This castle hath a pleasant seat") and stage directions ("See how it stalks away"; the cues for Malvolio's yellow stockings and cross garters). Duels, battles, murders, elaborate pageants, and shows were included to beguile the eye of the audience and make it attentive to the more subdued moments. With the proliferation of theaters and the need for new plays, speedy composition, often in collaboration, kept to a minimum a nice observation of literary regulations.

When Polonius jibs at a lengthy heroic speech, Hamlet derides him: "He's for a jig or a tale of bawdy, or he sleeps." The "jig," a lively interlude or afterpiece, usually in rhyme and occasionally improvised, is barely distinguishable from the "droll," a one-man farce full of topical references and catchphrases. The clowns who were the favored performers of jigs and drolls—such as Richard Tarlton, who became the first nationally known "star" in England—did not abandon their flair for improvisation even when participating in written comedies and so kept that form from congealing. Elizabethan comedy was a farrago of folkloric characters, romantic Italian plots, and mythological additives from the pastoral. The attempts to naturalize this latter genre by Ben Jonson, John Fletcher, and

Samuel Daniel were not successful, any more than were Jonson's stern edicts that classical models were the best guide to playwriting.

The irrelevance of classic genre divisions for the English drama becomes clear after a glance at the way Shakespeare's first editors, John Heminge and Henry Condell, subdivided his plays into "Comedies, Histories and Tragedies." The comedies include Plautine imitations such as *The Comedy of Errors* (pr. c. 1592-1594), an Italianate farce such as *The Taming of the Shrew* (pr. c. 1593-1594), and pastoral adventures such as *As You Like It* (pr. c. 1599-1600) in the same company with *Measure for Measure* (pr. 1604), referred to by modern critics as a "problem comedy," and *The Winter's Tale* and *The Tempest* (pr. 1611), baptized "romances" by Samuel Taylor Coleridge and heavily alloyed with masque elements. The history category is more straightforward, limited exclusively to chronicle plays of the English past. With tragedies, the sense of an *omnium gatherum* is again felt: Dramas from Roman history rub elbows with a story of private calamity such as *Romeo and Juliet* (pr. c. 1595-1596). A romantic treatment of early Britain such as *Cymbeline* (pr. c. 1609-1610) is grouped with a bleak vision of early Britain such as *King Lear*. The domestic disaster of *Othello* (pr. 1604) is neighbored by the universal span of *Antony and Cleopatra* (pr. c. 1606-1607). Admittedly, Shakespeare was more various and ingenious than his colleagues, but it is clear that form fit function in the drama of the period. A play took on the shape it needed without attention to labels.

Although they were given their modern titles only by later writers, the genres of romance and domestic tragedy assumed characteristic profiles at this time. The romance was so called because its story came from a tale or novella (any source was fair game) and often employed supernatural machinery and magic to attain its happy end; love was a leading motif. The domestic tragedy was a diminution of the chronicle play. Usually founded on a current news item of conjugal murder, it applies the structure and occasionally the tone and language of high tragedy to household events. Works such as *Arden of Feversham* (pb. 1592), Thomas Heywood's *A Woman Killed with Kindness* (pr. 1603), and *A Yorkshire Tragedy* (pb. 1608; once attributed to Shakespeare, who seems never to have dabbled in the genre) were consciously chosen as forerunners by such founders of latter-day bourgeois tragedies as George Lillo, Denis Diderot, and Gotthold Ephraim Lessing.

The masque, as noted above, was an Italian import, a blend of music and spoken dialogue, dancing and dumb show, with sumptuous decorative trappings and usually performed by amateurs. It was allegorical: a dolled-up morality without the moral, one might say. The earliest masques were mute, with the performers miming and dancing to the music, but by the mid-sixteenth century, words—both spoken and sung—had become a leading feature. Masques were generally private affairs, performed at weddings, banquets, and similar special occasions, by and for the nobility and the upper-middle class, indoors. The earliest masque may be Thomas Nabbes's *Microcosmus* (pr. 1637), whose kinship with the morality play is abundantly evident. By the early seventeenth century, the masque was the favorite entertainment at the court of King James I, who subsidized first-rate dramatists such as Jonson to lend their talents to it. The antimasque, a grotesque interlude that contrasted violently with the beauty and harmony of the masque, was created by Jonson in 1613. Despite his successes, the testy playwright gave up writing masques because, he complained with some justice, poetry was sacrificed to the splendor of scenic design; certainly Inigo Jones's settings and costumes are among the glories of decorative art. John Milton's *Comus* (pr. 1634) is the last masque to qualify as great literature before the form was submerged in the nascent opera.

Jonson was also the chief promulgator and exponent of a new style of comedy, the comedy of humors. Fundamentally related to the medieval psycho-physiological scheme that the human body was composed of four elements, or "humors" (blood, phlegm, black bile, and yellow bile), which, in disproportion, incline the personality to one excess or another, the comedy of humors exhibited characters who were not so much social types as pathological freaks. In Jonson's earliest specimens, *Every Man in His Humour* (pr. 1598) and *Every Man out of His Humour* (pr. 1599), the characters are living demonstrations of their names, and although the former play is set in Italy, Jonson had no difficulty in transferring its action to London, since the types bear few national characteristics. Having proved popular, this style evolved into a comedy of manners that reflected contemporary life as no other dramatic form had yet done. Jonson himself, however, was somewhat restricted by his allegiance to the classical authorities: He intended to scourge vice with satire in the manner of Horace and Juvenal while keeping to the unities. In a comedy such as *The Alchemist* (pr. 1610), he restricts the action to one day and one house, even as he brags of the play's topicality in his prologue:

> Our scene is London, 'cause we would make known,
> No country's mirth is better than our own;
> No clime breeds better for your whore,
> Bawd, squire, imposter, many persons more,
> Whose manners, now call'd humours, feed the stage.

Following the rules when all about him were ignoring them, Jonson was forced continually to engage in contentious prologues and inductions in which he justified his clinging to or falling from ancient precepts. His fellow comic writers, insouciant of endorsement from the ancients, were able to develop a citizen comedy that was realistic in ambience and novel in its plotting and characterization, because it was based on observation. Such plays as Thomas Middleton's *A Trick to Catch the Old One* (pr. c. 1605) and *A Chaste Maid in Cheapside* (pr. 1611) are virtual panoramas of London life.

The drama of the English Renaissance failed to have any influence on the Continent, except in Germany and points east. Hans Sachs' remodeling of the *Fastnachtsspiel* had merely smartened dialogue and brought the tone in closer touch with the rising burgher class. The *Englische Komödianten*, London players who toured Northern Europe beginning in 1585 with simplified versions of Christopher Marlowe, Shakespeare, and other staples of the Elizabethan repertory, had an immense impact on the inexperienced spectators. In garbled versions, the works of the Elizabethans permeated German Baroque drama for more than a century, and traces of English mummeries and *Hamlet* can even be found in Russian folk-plays. The residual impression was one of bloodletting and buffoonery, and the preeminence of the clown, under such names as Pickelherring, Hans Supp, and Jean Potage, was a lasting legacy.

In the seventeenth century, the scepter of artistic sway passed to France. Italy made no new experiments in dramatic form except to add music to tragedy, which was eventually swamped by the increasing popularity of opera. *Opera in musica*, Italian for "a musical work," was soon abbreviated elsewhere, while at various times it was known in Italy as *dramma per musica* (drama in music), *favola* (fable), and *melodrama* (song drama). As a form of drama wholly set to music, it may have begun as an amateur attempt to re-create Greek tragedy: According to one story, the form originated when Galileo's father, Vincenzo Galilei, a dilettante dabbling in monody in Florence in the early sixteenth century, sang the tale of Ugolino's starvation to the lute, much as Greek rhapsodists recited Homer. This fusion of drama and music was at first approved more by literary coteries than by professional musicians. Jacopo Peri's *Eurodice* (pr. 1600) was the first public performance in this mode, although Orazio Vecchi's *L'Amfiparnaso* (pr. 1594) cobbled a sort of musical comedy out of polyphonic madrigals, using characters from the *commedia dell'arte*. The step taken from these inchoate experiments to Claudio Monteverdi's operas was gigantic, though accomplished in a few years' time, and the richness of orchestration, emotional eloquence, and immediacy which were to characterize the genre are already present in Monteverdi's *Orfeo* (pr. 1607) and *Il combattimento di Tancredi e Clorinda* (pr. 1624; the battle of Tancred and Clorinda), employing a classical myth and a Renaissance romance, respectively. Recitative—that is, free musical declamation—was thought the only worthy medium of expression. Gradually, however, as opera became more popular, moving out of the court and into the theaters, tunes and melodies were introduced, and by Alessandro Scarlatti's time, in the early seventeenth century, tunes had blossomed into arias.

"From this time, until the death of Handel," wrote Donald Tovey, "the history of opera is simply the history of the aria; except in so far as in France, under Lully, it is also the history of ballet-making, the other main theatrical occasion for the art of tune-making." The *opera seria* (serious opera) of the period was a formal affair, set in classical antiquity or in an exotic clime and reliant on lavish spectacle and the exhibitionistic vocalism of castrati and female sopranos. Henry Purcell, in such works as *Dido and Aeneas* (pr. 1689) and *King Arthur* (pr. 1691), infused operatic music with emotional chromatics, and the Neapolitan composers of burlesque operas also escaped the rigidity of the French school. Not until Christoph Gluck, however, did opera change significantly, by means of the sonata, then developing into the symphony; as orchestral coloration deepened, so, too, did the possibility for musical drama. With Wolfgang Amadeus Mozart, opera achieved full theatrical citizenship. In his operas, every note of music, rather than being wholly an excuse for vocal display or instrumental virtuosity, makes a dramatic point, assists the characterizations, and contributes to the total effect. The arias and ensembles drive the action rather than impede it, and the subtlety of orchestration adds a richer texture to the script. Mozart was fortunate in having the witty Lorenzo Da Ponte as his librettist on *Le nozze di Figaro* (pr. 1786; *The Marriage of Figaro*, 1894), *Il dissoluto punito* (pr. 1787; *Don Giovanni*, 1817), and *Così fan tutte* (pr. 1790; *The Retaliation*, 1894), but even the messy text of Emmanuel Schikaneder's *Singspiel die Zauberflöte* (pr. 1791; *The Magic Flute*, 1829) is transfigured and given sublimity by the music.

After Mozart, the tight web of music and drama began to unravel, and, with the possible exception of Gioacchino Rossini, most composers neglected mood and plot in favor of display; the *bel canto* school of Vincenzo Bellini and Gaetano Donizetti was more interested in vocal pyrotechnics than in dramatic cogency, and however much one thrills to the beauty of their mad scenes and ensembles, one cannot take seriously the characters or their predicaments. Like the Romantic dramatists, these composers were inspired by Shakespeare and Sir Walter Scott, whose works they pillaged for librettos; every so often, real passion breaks through, as in Rossini's *Otello* (pr. 1816), or genuine fantasy takes over, as in Carl Maria von Weber's *Der Freischütz* (pr. 1821; the enchanted marksman). The last major school of opera as a dramatic genre, before Richard Wagner and the later Giuseppe Verdi changed the rules of the game, was that of Giacomo Meyerbeer, whose grand operas were massive machines, overloaded with flamboyant set pieces, lavish scenery, all-star ensembles, and glamorous locales; the lushness of the music and the savoir faire of the showmanship cannot disguise its quintessential, albeit enjoyable, vulgarity.

To return to the seventeenth century, the French preeminence in the arts had a political cause. While England was wracked by civil strife and Germany by the Thirty Years' War, and while Italy and Spain underwent disunion and economic distress, France was being stabilized and consolidated. The adventurous individualism of the Renaissance was giving way to the sedate orderliness of national consciousness, and unbridled fancy yielded to rationality. From 1622 on, Cardinal Richelieu, who had been centralizing the power of the French monarchy, applied the same principles to the arts. The foundation of the Académie Française marked a move to legislate for literature a code that would prevent deleterious pluralism; similarly, the theater was to be elevated and the dramatic poet patronized and honored. The unities and other conventional devices that had previously been adopted out of expediency or mutual consent would become doctrinaire.

In 1631, in a preface to his pastoral tragicomedy *Silvanire* (pr. 1630), itself founded on a prose romance, Jean Mairet endorsed the unities of action, time, and place. His endorsement was in some ways a reply to François Ogier, the last French defender of dramatic license for the next two centuries. Ogier, in support of Jean de Schelandre's *Tyr et Sidon* (pr. 1608), an earlier drama that defied the unities, insisted that plausibility is offended by the packing of many events into one day and that messengers and expository narratives are boring. Athens and Rome were not modern France, and even if they were, the ancients themselves violated the rules. Ogier, however, was fighting a losing battle. In the 1634-1635 season, three tragedies written according to the rules were presented and acclaimed by the public. Pierre Corneille's *Médée* (pr. 1635), Georges de Scudéry's *La Mort de César* (pb. 1636), and, most significantly, Mairet's own *Sophonisbe* (pr. 1634; *Sophonisba*, pb. 1956), which the Académie had qualified as absolutely "correct."

During the next decades, theorists such as Jean Chapelain, René Rapin, Charles de Saint-Denis, Sieur de Saint-Évremond, and Nicolas Boileau would write the prescriptions for drama, eventuating in the Abbé d'Aubignac's handbook for dramatists, *Pratique de théâtre* (1657). This is not the place to examine the arguments for and against the rules and the various interpretations given to Aristotle, except insofar as they affected written and performed drama. It must be borne in mind that much of the theory was composed to justify a preexisting theatrical situation, and two elements were critical in this regard.

First, the stage itself continued to be cramped, which restricted physical action; with the possibility of spectacle or strenuous movement eliminated, the focus had to be on psychological action. Consequently, French comedy (see below) specialized in comedy of character, and French tragedy in the intensive anatomy of motives and passions. Second, the audience, a mixture of aristocracy and bourgeoisie, had its taste dictated from above, by court circles and salons. This public prided itself on a nice discrimination and a fastidious judgment; it preferred to exercise its rational faculties rather than its imagination in the theater (and since many of the cognoscenti were sitting on the stage, any elaborate stage illusion would be difficult to sustain). Hence the recurrence of the term *vraisemblance* (verisimilitude) as a critical tenet expressing the need for plausibility in drama. Essentially, all the calls for unity of time, place, and action, the integrity of the genre, and the decorum of presentation aided plausibility, making a jaded and demanding audience accept what it sees—or rather, hears, since the audience had been trained in games in salon conversation—"Discourse for five minutes on the difference between self-love and selfless love"—and was alert to the subtleties of a moral disquisition. Whether it be Phaedra parsing the nuances of her guilt or Tartuffe caustically equating his lust with divine adoration, the characters of French neoclassical drama always reveal themselves in well-structured speeches, or tirades (that is, something spun out in one long filament).

The case of Pierre Corneille is revealing of the manner in which French dramatists tailored their plays to the demands of the critics. His immensely popular *The Cid* (pr. 1637) was attacked, partly for its very popularity, and submitted to the Académie for an opinion. This verdict (drawn up by the neoclassical propagandist Chapelain and redrafted at Richelieu's behest) upheld Corneille's choice in tampering with history but condemned him for breaching credibility by overloading his twenty-four hours with too much action and by outraging decorum by allowing the character of Chimene to favor passion over duty. The rest of Corneille's long career was devoted to answering this criticism and avoiding a recurrence of these so-called faults. As Saintsbury said, there is something bizarre in the picture of "a genius curbing himself to the tendencies of the times and the dictates of the wits." Can one picture Shakespeare bowing to Jonson's strictures or Milton revising *Paradise Lost* to suit John Dryden?

Corneille did, in fact, generate two new types of tragedy: The *tragédie héroique,* in fashion between 1640 and 1650, drew upon Roman history and exhibited the will overcoming obstacles set by circumstance or personal penchants, with serious consequences to the State, religion, or the family. Its set of values centers on humanistic self-respect (*gloire*), which regards each blow of implacable fate as a challenging ordeal, not as a disaster. *Polyeucte* (pr. 1641; *Polyeuctes*, 1655) is perhaps the most interesting of these in linking Christian mysticism to Roman heroism. With *Don Sanche d'Aragon* (pr. 1650; *The Conflict*, 1798), Corneille created the *tragédie romanesque*, in which "love" may be substituted for "will"; familial or civic duties, differences in rank, and merely mistaken identities are overcome by a lofty and gallant passion. Indebted to both the Spanish cape-and-sword dramas and the rambling romances of Georges de Scudéry and Gautier de Costes de la Calprenède, the romantic tragedy enjoyed theatrical popularity but was overshadowed by the heroic form. Corneille himself considered love to be too trivial to carry a tragedy, and he posited "heroic comedy" as a potential genre.

On a number of scores, Corneille refuted or modified Aristotle in order to expand the possibilities of tragedy. While accepting tragedy's moral intent, imposed by the critics, he insisted on both a just distribution of punishments and rewards to please the audience and a purgation of passion through pity and fear. The Renaissance had interpreted catharsis as the moderation of injurious emotions; Corneille denied that this occurs. In accord with a growing taste for sentiment, he suggested that one pities the protagonists and fears to fall into their dilemmas, and thus one purges the excesses that led the protagonists to their plights. He asserted that both saints and criminals could be proper heroes of a tragedy, a doctrine that he illuminated by the devout Polyeucte, and the vicious Cléopâtre in *Rodogune* (pr. 1644-1645); the touchstone for heroism was the character's *grandeur*, a magnitude of soul. This is an early glimpse at a more modern notion of tragic sublimity. He also introduced a new unity, the unity of peril, which the hero must either triumph over or fall beneath.

Many of Corneille's innovations were reactions to actual work in the theater; neoclassical doctrine had not congealed when he began playwriting, and he tried to modify critical dogma with hands-on experience—hence his subtle explanation of the locale of the action (*le lieu théâtral*) as a vague and nondescript space, like an antechamber, which would allow the actors to infringe on unity of place and move from city to city by taking a few steps. His *liaison des scènes,* the relating of each incident within a tight sequential pattern, corresponded to his audience's finicky insistence on plausibility and linear thinking. He recommended music to cover the noise of scene changes, cliff-hanging conclusions for the acts to hold the public's attention, stage directions to aid the actors in their portrayals, and an elimination of sung intermezzi.

Corneille's desire to excite commiseration by exhibiting the misfortunes of ordinary mortals was refined and heightened by Jean Racine in his *tragédies passionnées*, a genre that can be defined as any play he wrote after 1667. Physical and external action is reduced to a minimum and the audience is confronted with the spectacle of hearts rent asunder by irrepressible passion, driven to commit crimes despite any outside influences or nobler impulses. Adapting, even thriving on, the stiff etiquette of court ritual, willingly embracing unity of action, time, and place, Racinian tragedy distills its catastrophe into an urgent quintessence. The plays always begin in the middle of a crisis, with the preliminaries omitted or reduced to rapid exposition (as if *Hamlet* were to commence with its fifth act); the tense atmosphere warns that conflicting passions are about to collide in a crescendo of disaster. The cast is boiled down to a few interrelated individuals, held in uneasy balance like a colloidal suspension: Upsetting the balance results in tragedy. In his preface to *Bajazet* (pr. 1672), Racine insisted that "tragic characters ought to be regarded with another eye than that we use to observe the usual characters we have beheld close up. It might be said that the respect we have for a hero increases in proportion to his distance from us." Consequently, Racine's heroes are usually royalty, the only persons in the world of Louis XIV who could be supposed to enjoy independence of action and moral choice and who are sufficiently free of external pressures to make their own uninfluenced decisions. They are presented against an abstract and undefined background, within doors of nondescript palaces, the better to divorce them from a distracting context. The *vraisemblance* derives from portraying passion with as much shading and "truth to nature" as possible. Death becomes the only issue for the possessed characters.

Racine was less interested in Aristotle's catharsis, which in his definition meant a moderation of pity and fear, than in hamartia. Like Oedipus, Racine's characters are highly intelligent and self-analytical; their misjudgments arise when their intellects are clouded by passion. Thus, their situations are all the more ghastly, since they perceive their errors even as they make them. For the sake of verisimilitude, Racine eschewed soliloquies and replaced them with confidants of both sexes who act as listening posts and choral commentators. In his late plays drawn from the Bible, *Esther* (pr. 1689) and *Athalie* (pr. 1691; *Athaliah*, 1722), Racine introduced a chorus as lyric element, but those productions were in the nature of private experiments performed by amateurs. With Racine, French tragedy lost entirely the medieval vestiges apparent in Hardy and the Spanish influence manifest in Corneille, and became something rarefied, elitist, and basically unexportable.

Comedy, as usual, escaped from the critical straitjacket, not least because the theorists had little to say on the subject. (They stressed its intrigue, for example, so Corneille recommended that it be governed by a so-called unity of intrigue.) In any case, popular tradition was too strong to be entirely overridden. Before 1624, the favorite theaters of Paris had been the trestle stages of the Pont-Neuf, where racy dialogues known as *tabarinades* (after the famous clown Tabarin) were performed. High society's preciosity and fascination with affairs of the heart meant that the love interest of Menander and Terence would be given full value in French literary comedy. A writer such as Molière was free to draw on contemporary romances, popular street farce, the Spanish comedy of intrigue, the Italian *commedia dell'arte* with its stock types, and the French comedy of character. Corneille had tried combining intrigue and character in *Le Menteur* (pr. 1643; *The Mistaken Beauty: Or, The Liar*, 1671), which met with a storm of abuse. Molière's popularity was founded on his recensions of farces, but he brought the stereotypes up to date by commenting on the manners of his own time. *Les Précieuses ridicules* (pr. 1659; *The Affected Young Ladies*, 1732) won the laughter of the public, even as it earned the hatred of the coteries it satirized. Satire was a major element in Molière's comedies, which fluctuate between barbed attacks on fashionable follies and mirth-making slapstick. Molière was, first and foremost, a man of the theater, who had little time for rules when they conflicted with the immediacy of pleasing an audience. His famous statement, " 'Tis no easy matter to make decent people laugh," is the rationale of his method, the exaltation of nature above decorum, and common sense above theory.

Comedy, which had previously been considered a minor genre, rose in stature with Molière, not least because his royal allowance suddenly gave comic poets social prestige. Molière, who was a poor actor in tragedy but a superb comedian, had a vested interest in inflating comedy's stock. He mocked tragedy for being too easy to concoct, whereas comedy, he boasted, is based on observation and requires a genuine artist who is able to bring reality into conflict with the ideal so that their incompatibility will evoke laughter. Perhaps the play that confirmed comedy's growing importance was *L'École des femmes* (pr. 1662; *The School for Wives*, 1714), whose leading character, Arnolphe, deepens from the cliché of a wealthy old crank in love with a young girl into a three-dimensional, sympathetic portrait of a vulnerable if incorrigible human being. Moreover, Arnolphe is not a generalized eccentric but rather a recognizable Parisian bourgeois. In his *Critique de l'École des femmes* (pr. 1663; *The Critique of The School for Wives*, 1714), Molière replied to criticism that Arnolphe's amorous frenzy was overdrawn by having his character Dorante remark, "as if respectable folk, even the gravest among 'em, didn't do things in like situations—in short, if we were to take a good look at ourselves when we are really enamoured—." In other words, comedy is no longer punishment meted out to a few extraordinary social deviants; it is, as Ramón Fernandez says in his biography of Molière, "an outlook upon all mankind, a technique for arresting ourselves and others at any stage of intimacy or deep involvement. It is a mode of expression as viable as tragedy for every human reality that is to be expressed." Comedy was thus rendered capable of treating every aspect of the human experience; one could talk of a comic vision.

Molière also perfected the *comédie ballet,* a union of farcical high jinks and musical spectacle that was especially to the king's taste. *Le Bourgeois Gentilhomme* (pr. 1670; *The Would-Be Gentleman*, 1675), with its concluding Turkish extravaganza, and *Le Malade imaginaire* (pr. 1673; *The Imaginary Invalid*, 1732), with its pageant of doctors and clysters, relegated the music to interludes and finales. In the composite *tragédie ballet* introduced by Quinault and exemplified by Molière's *Psyche* (pr. 1671), music prevailed. The increasing concentration of theatrical power in the hands of the composer Jean-Baptiste Lully put new constraints on comedy, and Molière found himself the junior partner in these collaborations, which were a step on the road to *opéra comique*.

In England, the Puritan interregnum interrupted the rich theatrical tradition, forcing the actors out of London and back to the impromptu, miscellaneous fare that had preceded the founding of the playhouses. When Charles II was restored to the throne in 1660, he brought with him French manners, tastes, and techniques. Suddenly, tragedy and comedy were more sharply differentiated than they had been before. The afterpiece, a short farce to follow a serious play, which had been adopted in France by 1650, became standard practice in England, where, in 1676, Thomas Otway presented his adaptation of Racine's *Bérénice* (pr. 1670), followed in 1677 by his translation of Molière's *Les Fourberies de Scapin*. Fortunately, the example of Shakespeare still loomed large (even though he was drastically remodeled to suit Restoration fashion), and English playwrights found themselves trying to mediate between European critical positions and native dramatic instincts.

The first plays staged under the new licences were "dramatic operas," such as Sir William Davenant's earlier *The Siege of Rhodes, Part I* (pr. 1656), compounds of John Fletcher's romances and Corneille's tragedies, lightened by masque and pastoral, aglow with flames of tender love and vaunts of civic rectitude, and pompous with the blare of trumpets and the panoply of stage machines, all of it in tune with the grandiose political ambitions of the period. The heroic play, or heroic tragedy, typified by *The Black Prince* (pr. 1669), by Roger Boyle, Lord Orrery, was heavily indebted to Corneillean models. The themes came from French romances and tragedies, and the rhyme scheme of the heroic couplet was an adaptation of the Alexandrine to English numbers. Unfortunately, to the English ear it is too reminiscent of nursery rhymes and ballad meter to conduce to the highflown atmosphere its practitioners hoped to achieve. Also in accord with French emphases, the heroic play centered on a love-and-honor conflict, with the hero eventually sighing for his cake and eating it too, for endings were happy and the love portrayed exceedingly idealized and platonic. It was meant to appeal to the sentiments rather than the emotions, particularly since, as in France, audiences were skeptical and distrustful of high seriousness. The resulting form was bombastic, grandiloquent, and artificial to a fault, and it produced no masterpieces.

The critical utterances of John Dryden, who worked changes on the heroic play, reveal a tension between his awareness of imported canons of taste and his fondness for the English tradition. He began his career by championing the heroic drama and ended by abandoning it. He tried to reconcile the employment of rhymed verse with verisimilitude, but he eventually reverted to blank verse (*All for Love*, pr. 1677) despite the misgiving that Shakespeare, Jonson, and John Fletcher had exhausted it. Dryden shared his age's desire for harmony and decorum in art, pruning all the extravagancies from Shakespeare in his adaptations and adding fresh extravagancies of symmetry and operatic spectacle in their stead, along with a unified plot. Dryden favored poetic justice (a term invented by Thomas Rymer in his 1674 translation of Rapin), since the audience's sympathies lay with a basically virtuous hero. Catharsis thus was interpreted as an amelioration of aggressive emotions by the cultivation of tender emotions of fear and pity. This sentimental strain dominated the next century. For Dryden and his contemporaries, sentimentalism meant the presentation of a tragic hero as a "wondrous kind" and ordinary mortal, whose feelings could readily be understood by the spectator. Regrettably, the average protagonist of heroic tragedy was the sort later parodied by George Villiers, the second Duke of Buckingham, in *The Rehearsal* (pr. 1671), and Henry Fielding in *Tom Thumb: A Tragedy* (pr. 1730): an overblown and mouthing helmet topped with plumes surmounting a powdered periwig.

Comedy similarly narrowed its focus. Since opera and heroic drama had taken over romance, comic writers adapted the intricate Spanish and French intrigues to English situations. The result was less derivative and more brilliant than might be expected. In France, courtly conversation had been the paradigm for the verse tirade; in England, it became the model for prose dialogue. Wit was the *sine qua non* of a well-bred gentleman, and dramatic speeches in comedy were made to coruscate with finely aimed volleys of repartee and badinage. This emphasis on wit for its own sake conflicted with the demands of plausible characterization, since even the boobies and clodpolls were given clever things to say. If one reads the lesser comedies of the Restoration and not simply the much-anthologized masterpieces, the mind reels at the wearying sameness of tone and subject matter.

Urbanity is at a premium in Restoration comedy: The admirable characters are the rakes and men-about-town who conduct their affairs with finesse. The laughingstocks are the elderly, the provincial, the married, the business-minded, the foppish, or the obsessed, who are debarred from playing the game of seduction and fortune hunting. Sex, next to money, is the prime mover, a preoccupation with most of the characters, who are evaluated by their sexual viability. The prototype of the Restoration comedy of manners is taken to be Sir George Etherege's *The Man of Mode* (pr. 1676), whose hero, Dorimant, a thoroughly amoral profligate, is permitted to wed the rich and beautiful heiress at the play's end.

Restoration comedy partakes of an odd realism not to be found in the heroic plays. The comedy's locales were the haunts of the beau monde: Saint James's Park, Pall Mall, a young man's dressing room or a lady's boudoir, taverns, law courts, and china closets. Its terms of reference and allusion were more bounded than the Manhattan-minded brand-name jokes in a Neil Simon play. The plays' style and content were meant for immediate

reception by an exclusive and limited audience, with no thought of posterity or foreign royalties. Comedy's only aim, Dryden opined, was to beget
malicious pleasure, which could be gauged by the public's laughter: "The
faults and vices are but the sallies of youth, and the frailties of human
nature, and not premeditated crime."

One who did not agree and said so vociferously was the Reverend
Jeremy Collier, whose vastly popular, often reprinted, and widely read *A
Short View of the Profaneness and Immorality of the English Stage* (1698)
heralded a change of attitude of the theatergoing public. Collier's circumstantial diatribe against the comedies of his time is one of the earliest
English examples of criticism altering literature in a significant way. Attacking the lewdness, profanity, irreligion, and irregularity of the stage, he put
playwrights on the defensive. William Congreve offered a response that
failed to make a dent in Collier's spiky armor. For Collier, "the business of
plays is to recommend virtue and discountenance vice . . . to make folly and
falsehood contemptible, and to bring everything that is ill under infamy and
neglect."

The acceptance of Collier's premise (which even Congreve did not question) marks a major turning point. Throughout the eighteenth century, the
Aristotelian genres and their previous modifications would be shunted aside
by a number of new hybrid genres that catered to the tastes and under-
standings of a middle-class audience, more moralistic, less classically educated, and less sophisticated than the aristocratic circles whose tastes had
dictated to the seventeenth century. "The drama's laws the drama's patrons
give," Samuel Johnson was to write later in the century, and the new forms
proved it.

Comedy was an early mouthpiece for middle-class morality. Mrs.
Susannah Centlivre reclaimed her loose-living characters in the fourth act;
George Farquhar reiterated that comedy must not leave vice unpunished or
virtue unrewarded if it is to be "utile"; and Colley Cibber not only reformed his characters in *Love's Last Shift* (pr. 1696) but also put a moral
sentiment, pathetically handled, right at the center of a comedy in his *The
Careless Husband* (pr. 1704). In some small measure, this was a return to
the Horatian principles enunciated by Renaissance critics, that audiences
must be moved into the self-awareness that leads to moral improvement.
The difficulty was to sustain the interest of a public no longer interested in
seduction and satire. In tragedy, the new decorum spelled frigidity. Although Voltaire called Joseph Addison's *Cato* (pr. 1713) "the first reasonable English tragedy," and Addison himself despised tragicomedy as a
"monstrous invention, a motley of mirth and sorrow," regular blank-verse
tragedy dealing with Roman heroes grew increasingly literary and static,
whereas tragicomedy held the stage in numerous guises.

George Lillo's *The London Merchant* (pr. 1731) is honored as the first true bourgeois tragedy; it professed connections with Elizabethan domestic tragedy, which Lillo knew well, but was also akin to the evolving form of the novel, the "romance of everyday life." Lillo was a Low Church goldsmith, in no way different from much of his audience, and could identify with their concerns. The first audience came to the play intending to mock it and left with their handkerchiefs to their eyes; it became a traditional Christmas and holiday pastime for masters to send their 'prentices to see. This gratified Lillo's intention of enlarging "the province of the graver kind of poetry" by plays "founded on moral tales in private life" with the force "to engage all the faculties and powers of the soul in the cause of virtue, by stifling vice in its first principles." The concern with emotion and sympathy was timely; the ethical nature of tragedy had been proclaimed by thinkers more profound than Lillo to be a valuable form of responsory exercise. As one's passions are affected mournfully, one's nature softens and one becomes more charitable and altruistic, more prone to commiseration, caring, and benevolence. Since pity, without fear, marked the sentimental catharsis, the traditional protagonist of high degree was less effectual than Lillo's mercantile clerk George Barnwell and his low-born posterity.

Lillo also created the tragedy of fate, in which the moral lesson is subservient to the ironic pathos. In his *Fatal Curiosity* (pr. 1736), an elderly couple murder a traveler for his money, not knowing that he is their son. The misguided parents are not vicious criminals but rather decent folk driven to extremities by poverty. Lillo is no social critic, and he attacks neither the economic wellsprings of destitution nor the crime itself; rather, he is intent on provoking a sentimental frisson through pity for both the perpetrators and their victim. Very popular in Germany, this plucking of heartstrings would eventuate in the tragedy of "innocent misfortune," the tearjerkers of August von Kotzebue, in which virtuous characters suffer needlessly to allow the audience an object for its sympathies. By that time, the form had degenerated into sentimentalism. Nevertheless, Lillo's influence extended even into the twentieth century: Albert Camus was so taken with the ethical dilemma of *Fatal Curiosity* that he refashioned it as *The Misunderstanding* (1944).

What Lillo did for English tragedy, Sir Richard Steele had earlier done for comedy in *The Conscious Lovers* (pr. 1722), and despite attacks from conservatives such as John Dennis, the example took hold. Steele defined meliorative modes of tragedy and comedy: Tragedy was to represent domestic virtues, such as modesty and chastity, and high conceptions of virtue and merriment; comedy was to present a virtuous, honorable, gallant man whose happiness and success were proper subjects. Such a niminy-piminy prescription perfectly sums up sentimental comedy, designed to warm the cockles, not to split the sides. Steele seemed to forecast Lillo's counter-jumper hero when he protested that a tragic hero is marked by greatness of sentiment, not his external position in life. The dividing line between bourgeois tragedy and sentimental comedy was barely perceptible and was dependent chiefly on the characters' fates: If, after five acts of misunderstanding, quarrels, and heart-rending, they married, it was comedy; if they died, it was tragedy. By 1772, Oliver Goldsmith could complain that such comedies were bastard tragedies that had driven true comedy—the sort that raises laughter by "ridiculously exhibiting the follies of the lower part of mankind"—from the stage. "If [the characters in sentimental comedy] happen to have faults or foibles, the spectator is taught, not only to pardon, but to applaud them, in consideration of the goodness of their hearts."

In contrast to these pastel genres, colorful minor forms sprang up. Opera, which had almost been naturalized in England by Purcell, was too much associated with courtly entertainments and allegorical pieces to attract a popular audience; the name came to mean Italian opera, which further alienated the general public. Sterile heroic tragedies of love and honor, squawled in Italian by geldings and fat women (so the opera's enemies portrayed it), had only snob appeal as an aristocratic diversion, despite the attractions of George Frederick Handel's music. Opera was ripe for parody, which it received at the hands of the poet John Gay. Part of the incentive to write a "Newgate pastoral" (as Jonathan Swift called it) may have come from Allan Ramsay's transposition of the lovers Florizel and Perdita to the Pentland Hills in his *The Gentle Shepherd* (pb. 1725). Yet Gay's *The Beggar's Opera* (pr. 1728) was so novel that its success came as a total surprise: It wound up as the most enduringly popular play of the century. Gay's mode was basically mock-heroic: He displayed highwaymen, fences, and whores in the predicaments and uttering the sentiments of tragedy and opera. The key to the work's success was the music; Gay wrote new, sardonic lyrics to popular tunes and catches. "The audience," someone once remarked, "went in whistling the music." The ballad opera, as the form came to be known, enjoyed considerable success, presenting humble figures from British life—dustmen, sailors, farmers—in simple and tuneful tales of love versus duty, the ultimate *reductio* of the heroic tragedy. In the next century, the form would be swallowed by the more elaborate comic opera or supplanted by the vaudeville. If it had equivalents on the Continent, they were the *opéra comique* (see below) and the *Singspiel*.

English pantomime had its start between 1702 and 1716, when actors from the French fairs arrived and initiated "night scenes" in which *commedia dell'arte* characters conducted their shenanigans. By 1716, the character Harlequin (the Arlecchino of *commedia dell'arte*) received British citizenship at Lincoln's Inn Fields Theatre, and soon pantomime was the rage. At this period, a pantomime usually began with a mythological mime ballet featuring *commedia* masks; the first such piece explicitly to be called a "pantomime" was John Weaver's *The Loves of Mars and Venus* (pr. 1717).

Soon the serious and the grotesque components were separated: The first part would be spoken or sung around a trite love story; the second part would feature comic mime, often performed with complicated machinery and transformations. To accommodate the latter, improvisation had to be kept to a minimum and the byplay of the clowns carefully rehearsed. For many years, pantomime drew better houses than any other genre in London and, by the Regency period, it had taken on a distinctly national character.

Burlesque also thrived in the care of Gay, Henry Carey, and Fielding; Fielding defined it in his preface to *The History of the Adventures of Joseph Andrews and His Friend Mr. Abraham Adams* (1742) as "what is monstrous and unnatural, and where our delight, if we examine it, arises from the surprising absurdity, as in appropriating the manners of the highest to the lowest, or *e converso.*" This kind of travesty had its antecedents in the amateur productions staged at the end of Shakespeare's *Love's Labour's Lost* (pr. c. 1594-1595) and *A Midsummer Night's Dream* (pr. c. 1595-1596), and in Francis Beaumont's *The Knight of the Burning Pestle* (pr. 1607). The eighteenth century coupled facetiousness with criticism in parodies of artistic fads, social divagations, and political abuses. This type of shaft, aimed too often and too accurately at Prime Minister Robert Walpole, brought about the Licensing Act of 1737 and the formation of the Lord Chamberlain's office; these instruments of dramatic censorship effectively reduced the political (and, later, the religious and sexual) content of English drama to blandness.

Deprived of its sting, burlesque's exuberance was channeled into farce, while comedy proper coalesced with domestic tragedy. Comedy continued to preach homespun morality, and farce was free to kick up its heels and poke fun at innocuous social misfits and the vagaries of fashion. David Garrick and Samuel Foote managed to turn farce into a genuinely witty, even acerbic commentary on their times, but it remained a one-act form until W. S. Gilbert's *Engaged* (pr. 1877) expanded it to two.

In France, the old traditions died hard. Voltaire tried to breathe new life into Racinian tragedy, especially when he returned from England in 1729: After Voltaire had seen Shakespeare performed, the French stage, which allowed no more than three speaking characters at any one time, struck him as inhibiting. Nevertheless, while he introduced crowd scenes, exotic settings, and even a ghost (in *Sémiramis*, pr. 1748) to French tragedy, he loyally maintained the unities, the Alexandrine, and the trumpeting of civic virtue that he had inherited. Drawing upon Chinese, Egyptian, Syrian, and medieval history for his subject matter, he never succeeded in creating tragic characters or red-blooded diction.

Voltaire had nothing but contempt for what he called *comédie pleurnichon* (sniveling comedy), but he could not prevent the well-named *comédie larmoyante* (sentimental, or tearful, comedy) from usurping Racine's prerogatives. He himself dabbled in it with his Richardsonian *Nanine* (1749). The comedy of Molière had already been refined of its farcical elements by Marivaux, who portrayed sophisticated servants and carefully balanced wit and sentiment. The tipping of the balance into the sentimental was achieved by Nivelle de La Chaussée, who had begun by writing smutty clown shows for private theaters but whose comedies are sanctifications of marriage in the manner of Samuel Richardson's tear-stained novels. (Marivaux and Carlo Goldoni were also imitators of Richardson, whose stories of virtue in danger chimed with the call for "naïve and touching love" in comedies.) Voltaire's patron Frederick the Great sneered at La Chaussée for turning the stage into a "central depot for mawkishness," and La Chaussée apologized for the genre in a critique attached to *La Fausse Antipathie* (pr. 1733; mistaken antipathy), but soon he was insisting that improbable intrigues, caricatured portraits, and overdrawn portrayals of society be banished from the comic stage. Elié Fréron went even further and proposed "purely touching" plays without any admixture of comedy—or, in other words, bourgeois tragedy.

The answering echo came from Denis Diderot, the main propagandist for *tragédie bourgeoise* in France. Diderot divided drama into four genres: merry comedy, whose object is to ridicule vice; serious comedy, whose object is virtue and human responsibility; bourgeois tragedy, whose object is domestic misfortunes; and tragedy proper, whose object is public catastrophes and the mishaps of the great. It was the third category, the *genre sérieux,* that he promulgated as an agency of social reform and a propagator of the doctrine of philanthropy. Its author must "take the tone we have in serious matters" and advance the action "by perplexity and difficulties"; the subject must be important, a "simple, domestic" intrigue close to real life. Heroes must not confide in their valets, and, indeed, the servants' roles must be much reduced; monologues are allowable, but not episodic characters. Character must be unfolded not by personality traits so much as by a man's condition with "its duties, its advantages, its difficulties," including a portrayal of profession, status, and family situation. Consequently, the best device for such a portrayal is the tableau, in which, as in a genre painting, the *dramatis personae* are viewed in natural relationship to one another. *Coups de théâtre* (twists in the plot) are also permissible, because such accidental and coincidental surprises occur in life, and the theater must be true to nature.

Diderot was more an aesthetician than a man of the theater, and his plays failed to have the impact of those of Lillo and Edward Moore. *Le Fils: Ou, Les Épreuves de la vertu* (pb. 1757; *Dorval: Or, The Test of Virtue,* 1767) was simply the old love-and-duty tussle from heroic tragedy redecorated with middle-class furnishings. His most original suggestions came in throwaway comments about performance, with a strong emphasis on the importance of the actor's contribution, beyond the script. In the final analysis, Diderot remains a traditionalist in his view that comedy must foster morality, but he notes that genres can no longer be classified by their subject matter:

> It is less the subject which makes a play comic, serious or tragic, than the tone, the passions, the character or the central theme. The effects of love, jealousy, gambling, licentiousness, ambition, hatred, envy, may incite laughter, thoughtfulness or fear.

No spectator should be allowed to mistake the intended effect, for the theater must teach proper conduct and social concern, and reform humankind through the exhibition of what Madame de Staël was to call "the affectation of nature." This far exceeded Lillo, who simply wanted his audience to feel instructive pity; Diderot meant to disturb and provoke his audience, forcing it into a new way of thinking.

Pierre Caron de Beaumarchais embraced the cause of the *genre sérieux* by pointing out that tragedy had the wrong effect on eighteenth century persons. A Greek tragedy is so far removed from nature, so overwhelming, that the only possible response is terror, yet drama must engage the heart and remind the spectator of the rewards of practicing virtue. Therefore, said Beaumarchais in his preface to *Eugénie* (pr. 1767), "the closer the suffering man is to my station in life, the more I take his misfortune to heart." Like Diderot, Beaumarchais insisted that a serious drama—and he uses the term *drame*, first introduced by Alain-René Lesage in 1707, to describe his own *Les Deux Amis* (pr. 1770; *The Two Friends*, 1800)—be of a more urgent interest and a more direct moral than tragedy, and be written only in prose. Also like Diderot, Beaumarchais' own efforts in the field were mediocre, but his comic masterpiece *La Folle Journée: Ou, Le Mariage de Figaro* (pr. 1784; *The Marriage of Figaro*, 1784) achieved an equivalent result by putting a common man, a servant with his own rather than his master's interests at heart, at stage center.

An even more vigorous propagandist for the *genre sérieux* was Louis Sébastien Mercier, who condemned traditional tragic and comic forms because of their irrelevance to modern society. "The Drama," as Mercier names his salvational genre, will reach the greatest number and bind people through "compassion and pity" to lead them to virtue:

> Fall, fall, walls, that separate the genres! May the poet cast an unfettered sight into a vast countryside, and not feel his genius enclosed in those partitions which circumscribe and attenuate art.

The inflammatory rhetoric is striking, coming as it does ten years before the taking of the Bastille, and it heralds Victor Hugo's Romantic manifesto of fifty years later. The Drama alone, according to Mercier, can present average characters with mixed natures, the sort who make up the bulk of the audience, and can thus reveal the "manners, character, genius of our nation and our age, the details of our private life," to "form a republic wherein the torch of morality will enlighten the virtues we are still allowed to practice." As for catharsis, Mercier contended that it works best when it provokes indignation at vice and pity at adversity.

Mercier's fervor as a polemicist is less evident in his plays. *Jenneval* (pb. 1767), a reworking of *The London Merchant,* shies away from the portrayal of murder and execution and transmutes its hero into a sensitive but impressionable lad who never actually sheds blood, who marries the heroine, and who is reclaimed by society. There is something Rousseauian about Jenneval as a naturally good man who can be brought back to the fold. *La Brouette de vinaigrier* (pr. 1771) was an ancestor of the proletarian drama in its portrait of a workingman's family in difficulties. Mercier had a considerable influence on young German playwrights in his time, but the French theater was more impervious to change. The suggested reforms were attacked in a pamphlet that circulated at court, *La Dramaturgie: Ou, La Manie des drames sombres* (1776), and even the character Arlequin was teased for being "sensitive" in Jean-Pierre Claris de Florian's *Le Bon Ménage* (pr. 1782; the good household). It is ironic that during the French Revolution and the Napoleonic era, the most popular plays were neoclassical tragedies, selling the integrity and self-sacrifice of Roman heroes as exempla for the citizens who filled the seats.

The theaters of the fairs generated a number of dynamic minor forms, variations on the Italian comedy. When pantomime was infiltrated by popular airs, it began to develop into the vaudeville, cultivated by François Ponsard and Marmontel. The etymology of the word is obscure, the most likely derivation being a corruption of *vaux-de-vire*; the genre would gain importance in the nineteenth century. *Opérettes*, lesser or chamber operas, were composed by Jean-François Marmontel and Jean-Jacques Rousseau, whose *Devin du village* (pr. 1752; *The Cunning-man*, 1766) was parodied by Mozart in *Bastien und Bastienne* (pr. 1768) as a bastard pastoral. A more enduring form was the *opéra comique*, created by Michel-Jean Sedaine; a throwback to *Le Jeu de Robin et de Marion*, as it emerged from the fairground booths, it adapted musical farce to modern life.

Charles-Simon Favart popularized these light comedies, built around gallant love affairs and rural sweethearts, home-grown versions of "noble savages." In the nineteenth century, Daniel-François Auber, François-Adrien Boïeldieu, and Jacques Offenbach expanded the range of the genre, but the French long upheld the distinction that in opera proper, everything was sung, whereas in *opéra comique* there were spoken passages of dialogue. Comedy had nothing to do with the matter, and even *Carmen* (pr. 1875) first qualified as an *opéra comique*.

The sentimental bourgeois drama sent down deep roots in Germany, where the opposing traditions of literature and entertainment had long distrusted each other. They hobnobbed without marrying in the *Haupt- und Staatsaktionen* (literally, "lofty deeds of state"), whose plots came from everywhere—the *Englische Komödianten*, the Jesuit school drama, recent political history—and which paraded Hanswurst, the salty Tyrolian Harlequin, cheek-by-jowl with melancholy princes and distressed damsels. All of this was couched in a fustian and improbable diction and enlivened by the periodic deployment of stage machinery. A measure of discipline was instilled by Professor Johann Christoph Gottsched, who set out to purify German taste by administering French remedies. Gottsched's "literary cookbook," as Kuno Francke called it, taught that any event providing a moral lesson was acceptable to literature; what genre it became depended on "the names which you give to the persons who are to appear in it." In comedy, the persons are citizens, while in tragedy, they are princes and heroes; that, and the fact that the former evokes laughter, the latter wonder, terror, and pity, are the only real distinctions between the genres. Gottsched himself wrote tragedies and his wife, Luise Kulmus, comedies for Carolina Neuber's acting troupe, to serve as examples. He also banished Hanswurst from the stage to prevent him from polluting the newly cleansed genres and to keep the actors from improvising. Tame, declamatory, and backward-looking, these works laid no foundation for a German repertory, although his *Agis, König von Sparta* (pr. 1750; King Agis of Sparta) was the first treatment of a social problem in German drama. Similarly, Magister J. Veltheim copied Molière's comedies for the court of Saxony and, like Gottsched, hoped to impose French habiliments on awkward Teutonic bodies.

These attempts to set up the French as arbiters of dramatic taste were thwarted by Gotthold Ephraim Lessing, who dedicated his career to combating everything for which Gottsched stood, with the laudably patriotic goal of creating a national theater independent of foreign domination. For Lessing, the unities and similar rules were literary tyranny, repressing the natural forms that tragic poetry would take, given the chance. Tragedy should represent human character and fate and prompt a purifying, violent discharge of emotion. Dramatic poetry was the highest form of literature, according to Lessing, because it translated arbitrary signs (figures of speech, meter, and so on) into natural signs through its mimetic directness. Lessing was by no means as hostile to French drama as he has been painted, and he let the *comédie larmoyante* have a place in the German repertory, although he noted that what the French called tragedy was nothing of the sort.

According to Lessing, the only true practitioners of tragedy had been the ancients and Shakespeare, who were known to the Germans chiefly through the mangled renderings of the *Englische Komödianten*. Lessing pursued the line the Romantics were to take, seeing Shakespeare as a child of nature, the best possible antidote for an overdose of French rigor. Lessing's own plays followed different paths: *Miss Sara Sampson* (pr. 1755) imitated English domestic tragedy and was what Gottsched had named *bürgerliches Trauerspiel*; *Minna von Barnhelm* (pr. 1767) owed much to Farquhar and could be termed a *weinerliches Lustspiel*, the German *comédie larmoyante*. Lessing embraced middle-class heroes in accordance with his own dictum that small actions and personal relationships reveal character much more efficiently than do the formal postures of the *Staatsaktionen*. The only true unity was unity of moral. As to mixing the genres, "if a genius for higher purposes amalgamates several of them in one and the same work, let us forget our primer and only examine whether he has attained these higher purposes."

In fact, Lessing was shocked by the deluge of pseudo-Shakespearean plays that spewed forth in the wake of his encouragement. The *Sturm und Drang* (Storm and Stress) drama—so called from a play of that title, *Sturm und Drang* (pb. 1776), by Friedrich Klinger, so overheated in its passions as to remind Donald Clive Stewart of August Strindberg—allegedly followed Shakespeare in its numerous scene changes, national subject matter, and tempestuous emotions. The first success in the mode was Johann Wolfgang von Goethe's *Götz von Berlichingen mit der eisernen Hand* (pb. 1773; *Gortz of Berlichingen with the Iron Hand*, 1799), a drama of the German Reformation, which boasted fifty-four separate locales, some scenes being as brief as six lines. Goethe forgot that Shakespeare's stage allowed continuous action, whereas his own required scene-shifting that chopped up the play and disrupted the mood; he overlooked Shakespeare's architectonics, the poetic and theatrical devices that unify his plays.

Indeed, the assumption that Shakespeare licensed total freedom was widespread among German dramatists of the period and can be seen in Friedrich Schiller's *Die Räuber* (pb. 1781; *The Robbers*, 1792), of epic length and prolixity: The handling of crowds was exceptionally effective, but Schiller, too, missed Shakespeare's economy and balance. For a time, *Ritterstücke,* or plays of chivalry, founded on Romantic tales but tailored to a more classical form, were in vogue, but they and the traditional tragedy (or *Trauerspiel*, play of grief) never shared the popularity of the *Sturm und Drang* school. Its emotional extravagance was seconded on the bourgeois plane by the vast corpus of plays by Kotzebue, with their maudlin moralizing and extenuated virtue.

The central theme of a typical *Sturm und Drang* drama was the conflict between an unbridled genius and the corrupt and inhibiting society around him. As Goethe and Schiller grew personally more conservative, however, they turned back to a more classical ideal. Germany had rediscovered and reclaimed ancient Greece through the writings of Johann Joachim Winckelmann, who interpreted Greek art as the reflex of an inner vision that transcends nature to create ideal forms of pure beauty, which raise the mind to ecstasy. Goethe, under the influence of Roman architecture, and Schiller, under the influence of Immanuel Kant's philosophy, both espoused neoclassicism. Goethe's *Torquato Tasso* (pb. 1790) forced a man of genius to choose between social responsibility and madness, and his *Iphigenie auf Tauris* (pr. 1787; *Iphigenia in Tauris*, 1793) scaled down the drama almost to Racinian contours. Schiller turned to *Oedipus the King* as a model, hoping to find suitable tragic material in European history; for him, Sophocles' play was a tragic analysis of past events, the unfolding of the irremediable, and consequently more terrifying than a play in which the viewer's apprehension that something might befall is at work. His tribute to Sophocles was *Die Braut von Messina* (pr. 1803; *The Bride of Messina*, 1837), which revived the Greek chorus.

The German reversion to the ancients was allied with the growing Romantic interest in self-revelation, exemplified in the thought of Georg W. F. Hegel, who reduced the hamartia of tragedy to an ethical choice. The hero chooses a partial good, which he wrongly believes to be an absolute good. The tension between the partial goods espoused by the characters produces the tragedy. A synthesis or reconciliation between the opposing forces occurs not onstage, but in the minds of the audience. Hegel praised *Antigone* as the paragon of tragedies because it best exemplifies this pattern, and he dismissed those plays that did not fit his scheme. This emphasis on ethical conflict became the keynote of later, related attempts to create a modern tragedy, such as those of Henrik Ibsen and Arthur Miller; as Hegel explained, "modern tragedy is contained in a more subjective sphere, modern tragic characters contain *within themselves* both sides of their ethical conflicts." Fate or external motivation are at a discount; instead of Creon and Antigone debating their stands, a Karl von Moor or a Faust experiences a dynamic tension within his own nature.

The most important new genre at the beginning of the nineteenth century was not sponsored by philosophers or scholars. This was melodrama, which, in its various avatars, would infiltrate and finally dominate all of its rivals. Scorned by critics, it thrived in the theater because it consolidated many of the trends effected by social change: the middle-class milieu, the desire for poetic justice, the sentimental ethos, the visually illustrative, and the tolerance of mixed forms. Like so many other popular genres, it originated in the French fairground booths as a gallimaufry of pantomime and music: the *mélo-drame*, or music drama (the word first appears in 1772). It gained respectability from *Pygmalion* (pr. 1771), a *scène lyrique* by Jean-Jacques Rousseau, who found something inherently ridiculous about opera. In his playlet, he alternated words and music, each speech preceded by a mood-setting musical phrase. James L. Smith, in *Melodrama* (1973), has pointed out that the operatic melodrama survives in the grave-digging scene of Ludwig van Beethoven's *Fidelio* (pr. 1805) and in Francis Poulenc's *La Voix humaine* (pr. 1959; the human voice).

By 1800, the term had been reapplied by Guilbert de Pixérécourt to a certain type of music drama performed by the theaters of the Boulevard du Temple. His *Coelina: Ou, L'Enfant du mystère* (pr. 1800; *Coelina: Or, The Child of Mystery*, 1802), is usually cited as the first dramatic melodrama, although everything about it is derivative: Its morality and didacticism come from the *drame bourgeois*, its sensational scenic effects from the opera and ballet-spectacle, its characters from the *comédie larmoyante*, its singing peasants from the *opéra comique*, its eloquent pantomime sequences from the *ballet d'action*, and its tableaux of action and movement from the François-Thomas de Boulevard pantomimes. Even its Gothic elements can be glimpsed as early as 1764 in Baculard d'Arnaud's tragedy *Le Comte de Comminges* (pr. 1764). *Coelina* was in three acts and in prose, which became standard. Its immense popularity throughout Europe can be attributed to Pixérécourt's skill in blending his dramatic cocktail, but also to his timing.

The French Revolution churned up a new audience, semiliterate and artistically unsophisticated, impatient of the classical tirade and hairsplitting psychological analysis of tragedy. They came to the theater for amusement and excitement, less to hear than to see. Melodrama, by reducing dialogue to the essential minimum and substituting telling gesture, mood music, and detailed mime, by eliminating complex moral issues and substituting a clear-cut identification of good and evil, and by decking out the previously chaste stage with all the allurements of the circus and opera created a play easily accessible to the masses. It drew upon fashions and trends, such as the Rousseauian "noble savage," for its self-sacrificing Indians and monkeys, and upon Gothicism for its horrors. The stock characters of hapless hero and heroine, unrelenting villain and helpful comedian formed a nucleus that could be endlessly recostumed yet retain the comfort of familiarity. The audience knew from experience that the outcome would be happy, so the thrills and chills provided along the way were relatively harmless and unproductive of any genuine catharsis. As Smith has remarked, "In melodrama we win or lose; in tragedy we lose in the winning like Oedipus Rex or Macbeth, or win in the losing like Hamlet or Antony or Cleopatra." These tragic ambivalences had no appeal for melodrama's audiences, whose freedom to fear safely was abetted by an optimistic and humanitarian outlook, with poetic justice eternally operative.

Because melodrama became the common currency of the nineteenth century stage, the term "melodramatic" soon was given a pejorative connotation by those who resented the supplanting of tragedy and high comedy; even today, "melodramatic" suggests cheap theatrics, inadmissible plot manipulation, maudlin sentimentality, crass moralizing, spine-tingling horrifics—all that is coarse, crude, and arbitrary. Nevertheless, the principles and techniques of melodrama have permeated modern drama at every level, from Henrik Ibsen's *Ghosts* to the American musical comedy, and to belittle the genre's influence would be pointless. Its importance has been restated by the structuralist critics, who see in its conventional patterns a splendid array of theatrical semiotics.

The lessons taught by melodrama were not lost on Romantic playwrights, who adapted its most striking features and bent them to the service of a new style of tragedy. Much of the color, violence, and broad characterization of this Romantic tragedy was purely melodramatic, including a sumptuous change of scene for each act. Shakespeare was enlisted as a precursor, especially after the publication of Stendhal's *Racine et Shakespeare* (1823) and the Parisian appearance of Harriet Smithson and Charles Kean in *Hamlet* and *Romeo and Juliet* in 1827. A large amount of Romantic drama was, however, of native French manufacture. The Romantics also returned verse declamation to its place, varying impassioned arias with intentionally jarring colloquialisms. The opening line of Victor Hugo's *Hernani* (pr. 1830), with its enjambment—"*Serait-ce déjà lui? C'est bien à l'escalier/ Dérobé*" ("Might he be here already? 'Tis at the hidden/ Staircase")—shocked and startled an audience unprepared to hear an Alexandrine violated in its own home, the Comédie-Française.

The opening night of *Hernani* is the date given for the initial success of Romanticism in French drama, but, in fact, it merely confirmed an already entrenched development. As early as 1809, when Nepomucène Lemercier's *Christophe Colomb* flopped resoundingly, an effort had been made to advance the cause of historical tragedy. The effort was aided by François Guizot's *Vie de Shakespeare* (pr. 1821), which showed that the Bard's multiplicity of characters and incidents, the duration and diversity which seem to separate them, are actually bonded by a unity of "impression" or interest. Far from deploring Shakespeare's diffuseness as an unfortunate token of his "barbaric" times, as Goethe had done, Guizot provided the Romantics with an ideal theatrical technique to replace the neoclassical theory of genres. The German Romantics had already rediscovered the notion of drama as an organic entity, not a mechanical construct, in which, to use Samuel Taylor Coleridge's description of Shakespeare, "all is growth, evolution, genesis—each line, each word almost, begets the following— and the will of the writer is an interfusion, a continuous agency, no series of separate acts." Characters are organs or limbs of the whole, even when they have lives of their own. Furthermore, August Wilhelm Schlegel asserted, if tragedy was a sculptural group, Romantic drama (like Diderot's tableaux) is a painting in which the diverse elements of life are not rigorously categorized: "While the poet seems to be offering us only an accidental reunion, he satisfies the unnoticed desires of the imagination, and plunges us into a contemplative disposition by the feeling of that marvellous harmony which results ... and lends a soul, so to speak, to the different aspects of nature."

Victor Hugo absorbed and reshaped these provocative ideas in his contagiously enthusiastic preface to *Cromwell* (pr. 1827, the same year the English actors made a hit), a manifesto that is not new in its concepts, but is strikingly forceful in its expression. Hugo believed that the drama should have philosophic scope to encompass vast human problems—historical, social, and moral—with the numerous characters personifying and illuminating various aspects of the central idea through their own diversity: "True poetry, complete poetry is in the harmony of contrasts," a mystical alliance of soul and body, of the sublime and the grotesque. Later, in his preface to the prose *Lucrèce Borgia* (pr. 1833), he promoted the eighteenth century view that "the theatre is a tribune, a pulpit" with a social mission, and the poet has a cure of souls.

These stimulating proposals for a Romantic drama, along with those of Alfred de Vigny and Benjamin Constant, were not programmatically followed by dramatists but were realized sporadically. *Henri III et sa cour* (pr. 1829; *Henri III and His Court*, 1931), by Alexandre Dumas, *père,* set the tone with its historical local color, action-packed scenes, and brisk dialogue, and the impassioned fervor of Vigny's *Othello* (pr. 1829) astounded playgoers accustomed to the anemic mouthings of neoclassical tragedy. Hugo's *Hernani* was consciously Shakespearean with a considerable alloy of melodrama, though more important as a *succès de scandale* than for any original qualities of its own. More fertile was Dumas' *Antony* (pr. 1831), a prototypical problem play, which transported the gloomy and alienated Romantic hero from the past to contemporary society and, through a tale of illegitimacy and thwarted love, cast a gauntlet at the establishment. The terminal date for true Romantic drama is often given as 1843, the year that Hugo's *Les Burgraves* met with failure. In truth, it never left the popular theaters of the boulevard du Crime, where its flamboyant heroism, protestations of honor, and tear-stained miracles were the stuff of plebeian rejoicing; at the turn of the century, it enjoyed a resurgence in the poetic dramas of Edmond Rostand and Catulle Mendès. A new lease on life came for Romantic drama in the swashbucklers of the cinema, for the Zorros and Robin Hoods of Douglas Fairbanks, Jr., and Errol Flynn were merely Hernani and Ruy Blas stripped of their poetry. Romantic drama has also been preserved, like a fly in amber, in the librettos of operas by Donizetti, Bellini, and Verdi.

The classicists by no means perished before the onslaught of the Romantics; instead, their love of order and regularity was requited by the emergent form of the *pièce bien faite,* or well-made play, perfected and embodied by the more than four hundred plays of Eugène Scribe. Like the melodrama, the well-made play gets short shrift from critics who characterize it as an efficient machine and, like a machine, without heart, soul, or brain. This fails to explain away the abiding influence of the genre, whose precepts continue to inform not only most works for the commercial theater but also the structure of film and television drama. Its rules, declared Francisque Sarcey, "are the rules of the theatre because they are the rules of logic."

Scribe has been criticized because, unlike the Romantics and, later, the naturalists, he had no interest in "real life" or "nature" in the theater. The theater, in his view, is an art of fiction which contradicts truth and can dispense with reality. In life, nothing is ever completed or rounded off, or has a clear beginning, middle, and end; to imitate the incoherence and mystery of life in a play is to baffle and frustrate the audience. The drama's function is to take complex, obscure, inconsequential life and reshape it through simplicity, clarity, logic, and coherence—confessing, in the process, that the theater is a conventional art form. The first law of the theater is to arrest and hold the audience's attention; all other laws follow from that.

What are the structural features of the well-made play? Reduced to a formula by Stephen S. Stanton in his introduction to *Camille and Other Plays* (1957), they are:

> 1) a plot based on a secret known to the audience but withheld from certain characters (who have long been engaged in a battle of wits) until its revelation (or the direct consequence thereof) in the climactic scene serves to unmask a fraudulent character and restore to good fortune the suffering hero, with whom the audience has been made to sympathize; 2) a pattern of increasingly intense action and suspense, prepared by exposition (this pattern assisted by contrived entrances and exits, letters, and other devices); 3) a series of ups and downs in the hero's fortunes, caused by his conflict with an adversary; 4) the counterpunch of peripeteia and *scène à faire* [that is, the reversal of fortunes and the climactic confrontation to which everything has built up] marking, respectively, the lowest and highest point in the hero's adventures, and brought about by the disclosure of secrets to the opposing side; 5) a central misunderstanding or *quiproquo* [that is, misconstruing a word or situation] made obvious to the spectator but withheld from the participants; 6) a logical and credible denouement; and 7) the reproduction of the overall action pattern in the individual acts.

In other words, to make a play well is to streamline the intrigues of the situation comedy and the Romantic drama; plot, often extremely convoluted, was the be-all and end-all. Characters, themes, and ideas, mood setting and language—all had to be sacrificed to the carefully prepared action. Reductive as this formula sounds, it was based on the demands of the audience rather than on critical theories, and it gave supportive shape to otherwise minor genres, such as vaudeville and the *comédie d'intrigue*. In France, vaudeville became a highly polished morsel of social comedy, enlivened by simple songs; in Russia, it developed into a pungently realistic farce, rife with topical commentary.

Scribe's own dramaturgy cannot by any stretch of the imagination be called drama of ideas, although it is allied to his own *idée-maîtresse,* that great events are dependent on piddling causes, the "if Cleopatra's nose had been shorter" theory of history. Although, as a thinker, Scribe had little to offer, his successors welded the *pièce bien faite* to intellectual trends. Alexandre Dumas, *fils*, and Émile Augier remade high comedy along Scribean lines to create the *pièce à thèse*, better known in English as the "problem play." Following Dumas' motto of "moral and social action through dramatic literature," the problem play featured a particular case study, drawn from life, in order to deduce a general conclusion about an important social or moral issue. Typical themes, pregnant with significance for the Victorian and Second Empire world, were the double standard, women's position in society, marriage for money, divorce, and the status of prostitutes. A natural amalgamation of the sentimental comedy and the comedy of manners, it proceeded in proper Scribean fashion: The first act would wittily introduce the characters, the second and third would burgeon with colorful incidents, the fourth would bring the action to a climax by the final curtain, and the fifth and final act would furnish an optimistic denouement (or unraveling, another technical term of the genre), to quote Auguste Filon, "just before midnight, the time appointed by the police for the closing of the playhouse."

The problem with the problem play was that the strict architectonics of the well-made play did not permit open-ended conclusions or the admission of unresolvable complexities; a serious matter would be trivialized or neatly tied up by the play's end in a manner that did not reflect the complexities of real life. To relate the social issue to the otherwise independent intrigue, dramatists had recourse to the *raisonneur,* a mouthpiece who expounded the correct views, guided the other characters to the right road, and kept the audience alert to what everything meant. Usually a doctor or lawyer, the repository of other persons' secrets yet on the periphery of their lives, the *raisonneur* was described by the Russian journalist Vasili Sleptsov as a bottle brought onstage at regular intervals to pour out a bit of message and then recorked and stored away until needed again.

This disparity between form and content and its outcome are well illustrated by the career of Henrik Ibsen. When he began to write plays of contemporary life in the 1870's, he fell back upon the Scribean model, which he knew intimately from his experience as a dramaturge at the Bergen theater. The influence of this model can clearly be traced in *Pillars of Society* (pb. 1877), *A Doll's House* (pr. 1879), and even *Ghosts* (pb. 1881), but Ibsen broke loose of its restrictions and retained only its most useful elements in such works as *The Wild Duck* (pb. 1884) and *Hedda Gabler* (pb. 1890). By the last phase of his writing, in *John Gabriel Borkman* (pb.

1896) and *When We Dead Awaken* (pb. 1899), he had abandoned it totally, along with the pretense of dealing with "social problems." A similar evolution took place with George Bernard Shaw, who gained a hearing for his plays of ideas by imitating such popular Scribean offshoots as the costume melodrama, the problem play, and the drawing-room comedy. Once he was established as a playwright whose works were regularly performed, he was emboldened to invent whatever forms he needed, such as the "metabiological pentateuch" that *Back to Methuselah* (pb. 1921) purports to be.

When, in 1884, Francisque Sarcey listed the "most significant evolutions and revolutions in dramatic art," the three plays he cited (all French) were *Le Chapeau de paille d'Italie* (pr. 1851; *The Leghorn Hat*, 1917) by Eugène Labiche and Marc-Michel, *La Dame aux camélias* (pr. 1852; *The Lady of the Camellias*, 1930) by Alexandre Dumas, *fils*, and *Orphée aux enfers* (pr. 1858; *Orpheus in the Underworld*, 1865), a libretto by Henri Meilhac and Ludovic Halévy with music by Jacques Offenbach. It is a strange but telling selection. *The Leghorn Hat* is a typical piece of vaudeville, with Parisian and provincial types caught up in a comic whirlwind, yet it is fashioned with a Scribean rigor and precision that keep the action moving with diabolic *entrain*. There are astute touches of character and satire, but the convolutions of the plot are paramount. It was the forerunner of the "bedroom farce" perfected by Georges Feydeau, Armand de Caillavet, and Robert de Flers at the century's end, a fast-paced and intricate intrigue, scored for slamming doors and revolving four-posters.

The Lady of the Camellias is a crossbreeding of the *drame bourgeois* and Romantic social protest: The truehearted but misunderstood outcast and the blighted love affair were relocated amid drawing-room conversation and well-meaning editorializing on the evils of prostitution. Offenbach's *opéra bouffe Orpheus in the Underworld* is a sparkling travesty of classical themes, both tragic and operatic, with a *raisonneur*, Public Opinion, who relates the stage buffoonery to the audience's expectations. None of these plays conformed to any established genre, and none could even tenuously be considered traditional comedy or tragedy.

As a matter of fact, by the mid-nineteenth century, questions of genre were no longer an overriding concern with drama critics. Scribe's technique served as a handy manual, which virtually all drama critics—for example, William Archer—took as a given. Interpretation of Aristotle was left to classical scholars and seemed to have no relevance to stage practice, despite Scribe's redefinitions of peripeteia and anagnorisis. By the twentieth century, classification was made not along generic lines, but according to schools of art (naturalism, Expressionism) or principles of stagecraft (theatricality, total theater). In the meantime, nineteenth century drama split and subdivided into innumerable minor and ephemeral genres, often mere labels with no ideological rationale.

This efflorescence of demotic genres was particularly rich in England, where the licensing laws had, until 1843, restricted the performance of "legitimate" tragedy and comedy to two patent theaters; all other playhouses were constrained to put on musical farragos, farces, and burlettas. This last, a diminutive of the Italian *burla,* or joke, was a three-act piece featuring at least six songs. By setting Shakespeare to music, managers could circumvent the law. Nights were long and varied in the nineteenth century theater. The evening would open with a curtain raiser, usually a farce or two-act comedy; proceed to the main piece, a melodrama, burletta, or comic opera; and conclude with an afterpiece, usually a burlesque or vaudeville, to send the audience home merry, if groggy. By the Regency period, English pantomime had been relegated to the Christmas season, and a characteristic format had evolved. The opening was in rhyme and told a story from fairy-tale or nursery lore of separated lovers, ridiculous wooers, and evil geniuses. At the critical moment, a good genius would appear and metamorphose the characters into the English versions of *commedia dell'arte* types: Columbine, Harlequin, Pantaloon, and, most indigenous of all, Clown. There would ensue a harlequinade, a relatively mute series of slapstick scenes and magical transformations, at the end of which the apotheosis, a gorgeous scene change, would occur and the characters would return to their original shapes; love would triumph and wickedness be mildly rebuked.

In France, the harlequinades mutated into specialized types: the *pantomime mélodrame,* a throwback to Pixérécourt; the *pantomime réaliste,* set in everyday life; the *pantomime villageoise,* or rustic panto, a seedy descendant of the pastoral; and the *pantomime féerie,* or fairy-tale panto. This last became increasingly spectacular and opulent in presentation, with protracted dance interludes, operettic singing, and expensive scenery and costumes. A more homely version of this had been known in Austria as the *Zauberposse,* or magic farce; an outgrowth of folk comedy, it combined supernatural effects with plots of bourgeois life. A good example is Ferdinand Raimond's *Der Alpenkönig und der Menschenfeind* (pr. 1828; the mountain king and the misanthrope), in which a surly paterfamilias of the Biedermeier period is reformed through the agencies of an Alpine goblin. All of these magical genres may relate back to Count Carlo Gozzi's fantastic *fiabe,* or fables, of the 1760's, which tried to revive interest in the *commedia dell'arte* by putting its characters into exotic and nightmarish stories.

In England, the *féerie* fused with the pantomime proper and the burlesque travesty to become the "extravaganza," defined by V. C. Clinton-Baddeley in *The Burlesque Tradition* (1952) as "burlesque weakened into farce . . . a whimsical entertainment conducted in rhymed couplets or blank-verse, garnished with puns, and normally concerned with classical heroes, gods and goddesses, kings and queens." The form was perfected by the ingenious James Robinson Planché in charming revisions of fairy tales, and eventually it superseded the Regency pantomime; by the late nineteenth century, the pantomime opening had become fussily elaborate and the harlequinade had been reduced to a few perfunctory scenes of tomfoolery. The English stage also knew the subspecies of aquatic, equestrian, and dog drama, so defined by their principal attractions. In each case a melodrama, the type took its name from its external claptrap: If the action transpired around and in a great tank of water, it was aquatic; if the leading actors performed on horseback, it was equestrian; and if the denouement was effected by a canine savior, it was dog. (Aquatic drama had nothing to do with nautical drama, a sentimental melodrama about the life of a seaman that was enacted on an ordinary planked stage.)

A similar point can be made about the "cup-and-saucer dramas" introduced to the English stage by Thomas William Robertson, James Albery, and Henry James Byron in the 1860's. In essence, they were sentimental comedies that purported to give a faithful portrait of everyday life. The reality was mostly confined to the staging: Practicable doors and windows, three-dimensional furniture with operative props such as a tea service; comparatively unstilted dialogue, at least in the comic scenes; and a variegated stage picture—all providing a patina of realism, while the characters and plots remained stagy. As the audience oohed and aahed at real toast prepared onstage, the same inadmissible coincidences and the last-minute *deus ex machina* put in their appearance.

A more genuine lease on life was given to domestic tragedy in Germany, where Friedrich Hebbel, in revolt against Schiller, realized that drama must conform to the spirit of its own time. In the modern age, Hebbel reasoned, the central problems of humankind lie in social and political institutions; therefore, modern tragedy must question institutions, but not in the superficial way the problem play did. The family and caste remain important factors, but instead of being seen as a hearth of virtue, the middle class is condemned for its narrow-mindedness. Sharing the Romantic contempt for the social establishment, especially when in conflict with the individual, Hebbel went one step further by turning society into the modern equivalent of fate that destroys the hero utterly. The bourgeois protagonist of Hebbel's tragedy never achieves transcendence, never gains supernal illumination, never benefits from poetic justice; the culmination is a proof of the emptiness of existence and the vindication of the all-prevailing law. This bleak picture, which is presented in Hebbel's *Maria Magdalene* (pb. 1844), had been foreshadowed by Georg Büchner's fragmentary tragedy of an inarticulate prole, *Woyzeck* (written before 1837 but not published until 1879, and first produced in 1913).

Hebbel's unrelentingly Prussian outlook was popularized not by his own plays, which tended to feature mythological or historical milieus, but through Hermann Hettner's influential book *Das Moderne Drama* (1852):

> In the struggle of our inner character-development, in the secrets of family life, shaken down to its innermost foundations, in the volcanically undermined soil of our social conditions there lies at this moment the deepest deeps of the moral spirit. But where there are deep moral struggles there is also fate, great and gigantic, and where there is a great, that is, an inwardly necessary, fate, there also is pure tragedy.

This statement of the possibility of a distinctively modern tragedy was instrumental in directing Ibsen away from historical drama and toward plays of contemporary life, which, despite their cup-and-saucer trappings, revealed the destinies of the characters. "A Titan in a restaurant, the ancient Greeks never dreamt of such a thing!" the Russian poet Andrey Bely exclaimed about Ibsen's *When We Dead Awaken*.

Hebbel had noted that, "for the poet, nature must be a starting point and not a landing stage," and he would have been annoyed by the naturalist takeover of the bourgeois drama engineered by Émile Zola. Presupposing a materialistic and mechanistic moral world, the naturalists aligned themselves with scientists and claimed for their literary work objectivity of observation and experimentation, all in the service of social improvement. Since, in their system, human character was determined by environment and heredity, the social milieu must be reproduced in detail, and a class or stratum might be better matter for dramatic treatment than an individual. Few choices are open to the naturalistic hero, who offers the audience the spectacle of his inevitably following the beaten track of antecedent causes.

This philosophy blew to bits the tidy mechanism of the well-made play. The plays of Henri Becque, a forerunner of the naturalists, for example, kept plot to a minimum and simply displayed segments of life, the interplay of characters in a given situation; the *raisonneur* was jettisoned, forcing the audience to make its own moral judgments after seeing the evidence. In *Les Corbeaux* (pr. 1882; birds of prey), money and the lack of it become a surrogate for destiny, and the merely passive will is subjugated by desires and appetites. The direction pointed out by Becque was taken by the Théâtre Libre, founded by André Antoine to promote naturalism in drama.

The whole superstructure of French drama—the *intrigue parallèle* or subplot, the coincidences, the neat denouement, the speeches to the house, the mechanical virtuosity—were discarded, along with the specious solution of social problems. The spectator was to be presented with a slice of life, closely observed and served up without authorial interference or forced conclusions.

The Théâtre Libre gave new significance to the one-act play; previously, such short plays were comic or musical, meant to introduce or conclude an evening in the theater, not to steal focus from the main attraction. At Antoine's theater, an evening's bill might be made up of three or four one-act plays of serious import, elucidated by a lecturer. Thus, the *raisonneur* became an external adjunct to the drama. As Strindberg pointed out in his famous preface to *Miss Julie* (pb. 1888), his play runs about an hour and a half to say what it has to say; it refuses to conform to the old rule of an act lasting as long as the candles burn in the hall. Strindberg's view of naturalism was not cut-and-dried, and in an essay on modern drama, he drew a distinction between

> the misunderstood naturalism which holds that art merely consists of drawing a piece of nature in a natural way, . . . [and] the great naturalism which seeks out the points where the great battles are fought, which loves to see what you do not see every day, which delights in the struggle between natural forces, whether these forces are called love and hate, rebellious or social instincts, which finds the beautiful or ugly unimportant if only it is great.

Strindberg claimed that the Théâtre Libre was fostering this kind of epic naturalism, but he was guilty of wishful thinking. The theater was content to present *comédies rosses* and *comédies cruelles,* gloating snapshots of the seamy side of life. A *comédie rosse* was a brief episode, not unlike a thirty-minute television drama of the 1950's, that presented an incident of crime, squalor, or passion from the lives of the underprivileged. A sort of climax was reached in Auguste Liner's *Conte de Noël* (pr. 1890; Christmas story), in which an illegitimate newborn is thrown to the pigs to the sound of Christmas carols. The sardonic tone was pervasive as well in the *comédies cruelles*, popularized by Georges Courteline, which featured sick jokes or nasty anecdotes and whose despicable characters were butts for laughter.

These plays influenced two later developments. The Grand Guignol Theatre, founded by one of Antoine's disciples, alternated hilarious short comedies with grisly melodramas of fear and pain, thus sending the audience on an emotional roller coaster. "Grand Guignol" came to mean any play in which horror was the desired end, and the means, skillfully naturalistic reproductions of operations, eye-gougings, amputations, acid burnings, and the like. Its apogee came, perhaps, in the "splatter" movies of the 1970's and 1980's, wherein everything is directed toward obligatory moments of visceral panic. The influence of Grand Guignol was also felt in the opera, in the school of *verismo*, led by Giacomo Puccini, Pietro Mascagni, and Ruggiero Leoncavallo, who fluctuated between musical treatments of well-made historical dramas and the short, sharp shocks of the one-act *comédie rosse*. The ever-popular *Cavalleria rusticana* (pr. 1890; rustic chivalry) and *I pagliacci* (pr. 1892; the strolling players) also spring to mind; Puccini's less familiar *Il tabarro* (pr. 1918; the cloak), a drama of adultery and murder that is set aboard a barge in the river Seine, is an even more authentic example. Here, too, the tendency was toward ludicrous sensationalism: In Franco Leoni's play *L'Oracolo* (pr. 1905; the oracle), a San Francisco Chinese is strangled with his own pigtail.

If the objectivist drama intended by the naturalists thus dwindled into a neo-Jacobeanism of blood-and-guts, another nineteenth century approach was more successful. Richard Wagner hoped to unite opera and drama into a synthesis that he called at one time *Musikdrama*, and at another time *Gesamtkunstwerk* (composite work of art), the product of one creative mind, where music would ultimately subordinate poetry. Rather than reject Scribe, Wagner planned to employ his technical prowess while he restored the tragic denouement, moved the action away from modern life toward myth and legend, and played out the drama in the music itself. "A perfect art form," he declared, "must start from the point at which these laws" (that is, the laws of expansion and movement, of tone and light) "coincide"—in the world of dreams. As Eric Bentley has shown in *The Playwright as Thinker* (1946), Wagner's concept of music drama united three important ideas: the national idea, to identify Germanism by drawing on Teutonic folklore; the symphonic idea, with the music as endless and overwhelming, usurping the drama from the dialogue; and the theatrical idea, with the dialogue as a slow and continuous counterpoint to the raging symphonic background.

These ideals were not perfectly realized in Wagner's own music dramas, since he was a greater musician than a poet, and his pretentious librettos, often turgid and repetitious, defeated his dramatic purpose. Modern conductors and directors have tried to scrape off the accretions of tradition to reveal a hidden symbolism concerning nineteenth century industrialism, but this reinterpretation is not entirely convincing. It was what might be called Wagner's "auteur theory" that left its imprint most deeply on modern drama: his involvement in every aspect of production from stage design and casting to choral drill and audience regulation (no applause during an act, no latecomers, no encores), his relegation of the orchestra to invisibility so that the music seems to come from a "mystic gulf." All of this conduced to make the theater a separate world of superhuman proportions and atmosphere, with the playwright/composer as the unique mind pervading it. The cooperation of music, drama, and staging, with quasi-religious overtones, was a move to bring the drama back to its Greek origins, to sever its connection with the mundane, commercial, and purely literary. Denuded of metaphysical mumbo jumbo, its synthesis of rhythm, color, and design would come to underlie much Broadway and Hollywood practice, while the Symbolists and the Expressionists also tried to create dramatic atmosphere from consistency of scenic elements.

The bridge between Wagner's *Gesamtkunstwerk* and the ancient Greeks was built by Friedrich Nietzsche in *The Birth of Tragedy* (1872). The first to return to the Dionysian origins of tragedy, Nietzsche rejected the eighteenth century notion of Greek art as placid or harmonized—a child of

Apollo. Apollo was merely the mediating force that allowed the savage Dionysiac impulses to be channeled from ritual to drama. True tragedy could only be "a manifestation and illustration of Dionysian states, as the visible symbolization of music, as a dream-world of Dionysian ecstasy." In Nietzsche's conception, tragedy results from the tension between the Apollonian energies of painting, sculpture, and epic, and the Dionysian energies of acting, dancing, music, and lyric poetry: Ecstasy and incantation grapple with poise and contemplation to produce a tragic dynamism. The modern world, with its materialistic reliance on science, cannot engender tragedy, except if it be rooted in myth.

Despite the book's shortcomings—its faulty scholarship, its assumption that Wagnerian opera was a revival of Greek tragedy (a belief Nietzsche later abandoned), and its assertion that Euripides killed off tragedy—it was highly important as a catalyst. Nietzsche was the first to state that the Greeks exploited irrational forces in their art, rather than repressing them, that the tragic hero's certain annihilation clinched his heroism, and that catharsis was not a purge of emotions but a confrontation with the terrible truths of existence and the validation of human worth. Much twentieth century tragedy, with its exploration of myth, the dark side of the mind, and the braving of unknown forces, springs directly from these Nietzschean theses.

Both Wagnerian atmosphere and the awareness of irrational annihilation are present in Symbolist drama, without the possibility of heroism or the Dionysian exhilaration. The Symbolists saw human beings as trapped between the involuntary poles of birth and death: They cannot understand the meaning, if any, of the universe or their place in it, and they spend their span clocking the moments. Their very mortality nullifies any possibility of accomplishment, will, or purpose in life. For Maurice Maeterlinck, drama took place in the mind or soul of a character and could not be expressed by outward action; the "tragedy of everyday life," as he defined it, means that a higher life cannot exist in our humble reality. For Symbolist Stéphane Mallarmé, drama is a sacred and mysterious rite, which can evoke the arcane spiritual meaning of existence through dreams.

The Symbolists, therefore, eschewed all the traditional apparatus of playmaking: no strong, detailed characterizations or acting roles, no true crisis or conflict, no message or catharsis. An archetypical Symbolist play such as Maeterlinck's *L'Intruse* (pb. 1890; *The Intruder*, 1948) is brief, uses nameless characters with generic identities (the Grandfather, the Daughter, and so on) and incantatory dialogue, keeps its protagonist, Death, unseen, and creates a semblance of action through hints, allusions, suggestions, the symbolic use of doors and windows opening onto a higher reality, sound effects (the wind, a scythe mowing grass, the crunch of gravel), and narrowly focused lighting. The most intuitive characters are those, such as the old and blind, farthest removed from common life. Symbolist drama also exploited absences and pauses as major components and established waiting as a fundamental metaphor for life. Without Maeterlinck, much of the work of Anton Chekhov, Samuel Beckett, Harold Pinter, and even the *nouvelle vague* (New Wave) filmmakers would be unthinkable.

Mallarmé went beyond Maeterlinck in his rejection of spectacle; he demanded a one-man performance and an initiate audience of about twenty-four—essentially a closet drama. He was echoed in Ireland by William Butler Yeats, who looked to the Japanese Nō drama as an example of what ritualized poetic drama, performed in a drawing room for a select coterie, might be, and in Russia by Fedor Sologub, who argued for a "theater of a single will," with the dramatist reading his own works as the actors, puppetlike, illustrated his words. Such a performance actually occurred at the Théâtre de l'Œuvre in Paris in 1894, when *La Gardienne* (the wardress), by Henri de Regnier, was recited in the orchestra pit, with actors miming scenes behind green gauze, in front of a dream landscape by Jean-Édouard Vuillard. The dream itself as a dramatic structure was first employed by Strindberg in *Ett drömspel* (pb. 1902; *A Dream Play*, 1912); he stressed the subjectivity of the individual dream, the detail and grotesquerie of its images, and its lack of intelligibility to the uninitiate. The coalescence of private vision and public statement was to be influential on German Expressionism.

Symbolism was also partly responsible for the drama of mood, in which the evocation of an ambience is more important than action, and for the monodrama. Drama of mood is not so much a distinct genre as a description used in association with such figures as Chekhov and Christopher Fry, who adopted it for his plays *The Lady's Not for Burning* (pr. 1948) and *Venus Observed* (pr. 1950). It was first coined by the Moscow Art Theatre around 1899 to label their efforts in creating a psychological atmosphere onstage to convey to the spectator, through subtle transitional nuances and lengthy pauses, the characters' inner feelings. It became especially popular in the English-speaking theater in the 1940's and 1950's, when "Method" acting encouraged inwardness onstage, and it left fingerprints all over Eugene O'Neill, Tennessee Williams, Terence Rattigan, and Paddy Chayefsky.

The word "monodrama" first appears in the late eighteenth century to describe the one-man comic lecture popularized by Samuel Foote and George Alexander Stevens. It was resuscitated in 1910 by the Russian director Nikolay Evreinov, who reinterpreted it as a play in which the spectator is meant to "co-experience" exclusively what the active protagonist is undergoing. To achieve this, everything onstage must transmutate according to the emotions of the leading character: The color of the lighting, the size and shape of set pieces, even the three-dimensionality of the other characters alter in accordance with his reactions and mood changes. The monodramatic experiment was carried out only in certain one-act plays for the Crook Mirror Theatre in Saint Petersburg, such as Evreinov's *V kulisakh dushi* (pr. 1912; backstage at the soul), and B. F. Geier's cabaret sketches.

Significantly, Evreinov's proposal appeared the same year that the first Expressionist drama, Oskar Kokoschka's *Mörder, Hoffnung der Frauen* (pr. 1908; *Murderer, Hope of Women*, 1963), was staged. Expressionist drama shares monodrama's basic premise that the world is to be seen from a unique, usually skewed or abnormal, viewpoint, but it also boasts a social purpose: to reveal humankind struggling to escape the technocratic, soulless modern world. Protest can be as strident as a political cartoon, as in Georg Kaiser's *Von Morgens bis Mitternachts* (pb. 1916; *From Morn to Midnight*, 1962), while O'Neill's *The Emperor Jones* (pr. 1920) is, to all intents and purposes, an apolitical monodrama.

By World War I, dramatic genres had lost their specificity, and new terms were devised to cover the latest innovations in stagecraft and literary fashion. Playwrights felt free to give personal inflections to the once pristine generic terminology. Chekhov subtitled his *The Seagull* (pr. 1896), in which a leading character commits suicide, a "comedy," and simply denominated *Uncle Vanya* (pr. 1897) "scenes from country life." When twentieth century playwrights and critics came to redefine the dramatic genres, they either dusted off existing formulas, or they devised terms that were supererogatory. In the former case, Arthur Miller's attempt to explicate "a tragedy of the common man" is merely a rehashing of Diderot and Mercier without the profundity of a Hebbel. In the latter case, Lionel Abel's suggestion of a new genre, "metatheater," to define certain poetic plays of metaphysical import, is arbitrary and debatable in its coverage.

The dissolution of the traditional genres reflected the situation in the arts in general, as time-honored assumptions crumbled before scientific, technological, and philosophical onslaughts. A deep chasm formed between the commercial theater, controlled by entrepreneurs, landlords, and speculators intent on enlarging their audiences in competition with the newer cinema and mass media, and the experimental theater, which cared more for communicating its ideas than for entertaining in any traditional sense. While the commercial theater continued to purvey traditional genres in diversified ways (the well-made play splintered into the drawing-room comedy, the murder mystery, and the situation comedy), the experimental drama refused to be pigeonholed, and new forms proliferated.

One new form that did emerge in the commercial theater was the musical comedy. Although it bore traces of ballad opera, *opéra comique*, and burlesque, it rapidly took on a distinctive profile of its own. In the United States, where the form would reach its fullest flowering, many claimants have been put forth as the first. Traditionally, *The Black Crook* (pr. 1866), a melodramatic Faust story, ornamented with leggy dancers in glittering dance numbers, is cited as the original, but it bears closer resemblance to the Victorian burlesque, a mock-heroic treatment of a mythological or literary story, performed primarily by women in tights and broken up by song-and-dance interludes. The early musical comedy was an olio of variety acts and choral numbers loosely strung on an inconspicuous plot, and its setting could range from ancient Egypt (*The Wizard of the Nile*, by Victor Herbert, pr. 1895) to fairyland (*The Wizard of Oz*, by L. Frank Baum, pr. 1903) to modern New York (*Forty-five Minutes from Broadway*, by George M. Cohan, pr. 1906). The English tried to erect a wall between comic opera and musical comedy, based on how ambitious the music was and how tight the plotting. The score and structure of a Gilbert and Sullivan opera allow no digressions or interpolations, while musical comedies can be opened out to fit the specialties of a music-hall comedian or a novelty dance number.

France remained loyal to *opéra bouffe*, the German world to operetta, and the Spanish-speaking theater to its folkloric *zarzuela*, but musical comedy triumphed in England. Until the 1940's, it retained its baggy structure, allowing it to be dominated by clowns such as Ed Wynn and Bert Lahr. With Richard Rodgers and Oscar Hammerstein's *Oklahoma!* (pr. 1943), a serious plot began to subjugate the other elements—including the increasingly vestigial comedy and the increasingly aggressive ballet sequences—to the story line. By the 1970's, this had evolved into what might be called "the problem musical" ("comedy" had dropped out of the nomenclature), which pretended to treat social issues and personal interactions in an adult manner (as in Stephen Sondheim's *Company*, pr. 1970, and *Follies*, pr. 1971). A reaction came in a revival of the revue form.

The revue originated in France as a New Year's recapitulation of the past year's events and celebrities, presented in a lightly satiric vein. It was imitated by Planché in England and John Brougham in the United States, without much success; its format required a certain amount of up-to-date information to be shared by the popular audience. By the time the word "revue" had entered the English language, around 1913, a more sophisticated and urbane public was ready to welcome a collection of musical and dramatic scenes, often lightly satiric and roughly centered on a theme. German revues tended to be political in complexion, American revues to be more spectacular, but essentially, the form satisfied the perennial taste for variety and brevity in entertainment, with a veneer of smartness and contemporaneity.

The revue lent itself well to political propaganda, and groups such as the Blue Blouses in the Soviet Union and the Living Newspaper in the United States made revues into organs of public information and left-wing polemic. Sergey Tretyakov's "factographic" approach to drama, an insistence that one begin with raw field data and select the elements that best convey the desired message, resulted in documentary drama, or docudrama. Erwin Piscator pioneered the multimedia presentation, combining film clips, allegorical tableaux, and other heterogeneous elements, with dialogue scenes. Agitprop (from agitation-propaganda) drama was usually crude, since the medium was not allowed to get in the way of the message, and it seldom survived the circumstances that called it into being. After World War II, documentary drama became a German specialty, best exemplified by Heinar Kipphardt's *In der Sache J. Robert Oppenheimer* (pr. 1964; *In the Matter of J. Robert Oppenheimer*, 1967) and Peter Weiss's *Die Ermittlung* (pr. 1964; *The Investigation*, 1966), bald presentations of trial testimony with a minimum of authorial editing or manipulation, but chosen with an eye to the general conclusions to be drawn. The revue pattern persisted, however, in the United States, as in Martin Duberman's *In White America* (pr. 1963) and Jonathan Katz's *Coming Out* (pr. 1972), efforts to promote civil rights for blacks and homosexuals, respectively.

The discoveries made by the cinema were gradually absorbed into the drama, and experimental techniques that at first baffled and irritated theater audiences became standard operating procedure. Flashbacks, the fading in and out of momentary scenes, blackouts, rapid shifts from the public to the intimate (once known as Shakespearean contrasts)—all were intercut and spliced as needed. The popularization of Freudianism rejuvenated the well-made play by allowing the subconscious a role in the denouement: Dramas seemingly as different as Maxwell Anderson's *Bad Seed* (pr. 1954), about a homicidal child, and Peter Shaffer's *Equus* (pr. 1973), about a disturbed adolescent, are both gradual exfoliations of the truth about a mental state. Anderson's melodrama uses the basic drawing-room format with a Freudian criminologist as *raisonneur* and a neatly ironic ending; Shaffer employed a less confident exponent of R. D. Laing as his spokesman and had the benefit of a trendy theatricalist production. Both plays, however, are informed by the Scribean ambition to provide a causal "explanation" for a complex action.

The invention of photography is said to have freed painters from having to reproduce reality in an objective manner, allowing them to put their inner visions on canvas. The same holds true of the relationship of cinema to drama, although the serious drama had already moved in the direction of subjectivity by the time the first motion pictures were shown. Whereas naturalism and the commercial theater were coopted and consummated by the film, nonrealistic drama has never taken hold on the screen and continues to be called "experimental." As motion pictures replaced theater as the most popular entertainment medium in Western society, so drama should have been freed from its need to purvey standard fare in conventional ways to the lowest common denominator. Unfortunately, it has not yet become fully aware of its freedom.

Early evidence of the liberty to shock expectation and provide drama that was disconcerting and unpredictable was Alfred Jarry's anarchic puppet play *Ubu Roi* (pr. 1896), which Yeats deplored as the advent of the "Savage God," an announcement that the world was rapidly falling into chaos. Jarry was taken as patron saint by the post-World War I Dadaists and Surrealists, whose plays are acts of provocation and disorientation rather than works of theatrical merit. In his 1919 manifesto, Dada's founder Tristan Tzara advertised spontaneity and disgust with accepted values. His influence was later felt in the upsurge of improvisation that swept Western theater in the 1960's and 1970's, the "happenings," and the rejection of consecutively meaningful dialogue.

Even more influential, because better organized, was Dada's successor and rival, Surrealism. The term *drame surréaliste* had been coined by the poet Guillaume Apollinaire in 1917 to describe his play *Les Mamelles de Tirésias* (pr. 1917; *The Breasts of Tiresias*, 1964), which offered a fresh alternative to mimesis: "it was time to relate to nature, but without imitating it in a photographic manner. When man wanted to imitate walking action he invented the wheel, which bears no resemblance to a leg. Thus, he did something unwittingly surrealistic." Apollinaire's play, an exuberant lampoon of the French government's call for fecundity, was close to Jarry in its facetiousness and childish savagery.

Surrealism received more intellectual validation from Freud: André Breton, called the Pope of Surrealism, determined that the hidden reservoirs of imagination could be tapped through the subconscious. Although he retained the name "Surrealist" in homage to Apollinaire, his movement was less deliberately comic, more earnestly psychoanalytic than his predecessor's pranks. The goal of Surrealism was to disorder the mind by practicing automatic writing and studying dreams; in that way, the other aspect of the real, what was called "magical reality," is restored to its true place, and Cartesian logic is replaced by a more flexible approach to life. (Clearly, Surrealism was a reaction to the French school system as much as to anything else.) Human beings will recover their totality once they are released from loyalties to an imaginary god or rational imperatives, and will rediscover "an inner fairyland."

Originally intended as a weapon in a struggle for the revolutionary transformation of the consciousness, Surrealist drama has been more influential in its theoretical manifestos than in performance. Only in Poland, where life itself offered an irrational model, was Surrealist drama able to draw on certain preexisting popular traditions, as in the plays of Stanislaw Witkiewicz and Tadeusz Rosewicz. Many of Surrealism's devices—the abrupt juxtaposition of unrelated objects or moods, the reproduction of the dream state, the revelation of the marvelous within the mundane—were rapidly absorbed into more accessible works and have become mainstays of contemporary theater. Federico García Lorca's *Bodas de sangre* (pr. 1933; *Blood Wedding*, 1939) effects a surrealistic shift when it moves from the world of marriage contracts to the figure of Death in the forest; Jean Cocteau's *Orphée* (pr. 1926) updates the Greek myth with theatrical trickery and the effacement of stage convention. Tom Stoppard has been particularly successful in harnessing surrealistic effects, such as the acrobatic team in a logic professor's bedroom in *Jumpers* (pr. 1972), to intellectual comedy. Finally, much that is labeled Theater of the Absurd (see below) is Surrealist displacement put in aid of an Existentialist outlook, as with the growing corpse in Eugène Ionesco's *Amédée* (pr. 1954).

The most provocative offshoot of Surrealism was Antonin Artaud. Taken in his lifetime to be a talented madman, a freak on the fringes of the art world, he became, through the good offices of Jean-Paul Sartre and, later, Charles Marowitz, Peter Brook, and Jerzy Grotowski, a totemic figure. Artaud's plays, such as *Le Jet de sang* (pb. 1925; *Spurt of Blood*, 1968), are mere scenarios for spectacles; it was his pronunciamentos and manifestos that were ransacked for theatrical incentives during the 1960's and 1970's. Artaud, like most modern would-be reformers of the theater, looked around him and saw that playgoing was a hollow social function and that plays were stale restatements of conventional truisms, incapable of changing the world. In response, he predicated a Theater of Cruelty, a phrase much misinterpreted by those who see it only as a Grand Guignolesque recreation of atrocity onstage. To put Artaud's thesis bluntly, the theater was to become an arena of shock therapy; in the process, the actors would undergo such intense physical and psychic extremity that the audience would be unable to estrange itself; its preconceptions, hostilities, anxieties, and inner aggression would all be jarred loose, and it would leave the theater cleansed. This new catharsis could not be effected by texts, for Artaud discounted all but the incantatory value of words. Noises, startling sounds, violent gestures, ceremonial costumes, and unnerving lighting would all contribute, in an unfamiliar environment, to the curative result.

Although much contemporary theater practice embodies Artaud's desiderata, a corresponding drama has not been forthcoming. At most, he stimulated the notion of playwrights creating in collaboration with acting companies, to re-create their rehearsal discoveries as scenarios. Jean-Claude Van Itallie's work with the Open Theatre wrought improvisations and *études* into episodic scripts of a ritual cast. The Living Theatre's more intentionally Artaudian creations, *Frankenstein* (pr. 1965) and *Paradise Now* (pr. 1968), were joint efforts that barely existed on the page but required an abundance of live bodies and stage electricity to make an impact on an audience. The plays of Jean Genet and Fernando Arrabal are Artaudian in their exploitation of ritual and sadism, both mental and physical, but both are too rational, too political, and too fond of lapidary language to fulfill Artaud's prescriptions.

Bertold Brecht began with Artaud's premise that the modern drama, what Artaud called "culinary theater," was a *digestif* for the bloated bourgeoisie, but his solution was diametrically the reverse of Artaud's. While Artaud repudiated the brain and its reasoning faculties and extolled the purely visceral response, Brecht distrusted emotion and desired the spectator to keep his mind clear and keen throughout a performance. Brecht was a Marxist, though hardly an orthodox one, who intended to reveal through the staged scenes problems in capitalist society that could not be cured in the theater. The audience had to depart pondering the situations, challenged to find the remedy in life. Schiller had declared that the best tragedy was one drawn from history, for an audience would be more harrowed by prior awareness that the disaster had not been averted. Brecht, on the contrary, insisted on the audience's awareness that any disaster might be averted, depending on the choices made; that history was not fixed, but fluid and therefore capable of alteration. In a scene of a wedding proposal, the audience was to be informed at the start that the young girl would turn it down; in this way, the audience would not be caught up in emotive suspense over the outcome and would be free to observe how and why the outcome was reached. Similarly, characters must be seen in flux, their various facets revealed in given circumstances and, particularly, within the socioeconomic context: not the deterministic environment of the naturalists that reduced human beings to a passive residuum, but a context that permitted choice and adaptation. The idea of the "characterless character" forming and melting in response to outside stimuli had earlier been voiced by Strindberg, but in a psychological and Darwinian sense.

Where Brecht differed most from the run-of-the-mill Marxist writers was in his emphasis on "epic theater" to promote the proper estrangement (or alienation) of the audience from the drama. Most Socialist drama was ploddingly realistic if not melodramatic, anxious to get the message across at all costs. Epic theater was a synthesis of elements from the avant-garde—Frank Wedekind, Igor Stravinsky, Luigi Pirandello, Paul Claudel—and Oriental theater, forged by Brecht into a systematic and flexible tool of dialectic. As to dramatic construction, the "knots must be noticeable"; each scene exists in and of itself, to present an object lesson, a testing ground for the characters. This eliminates the sense of inevitability that comes in the course of a well-made act with its exposition, climax, and denouement. The core of the scene, as well as of each actor's characterization, is the *Gestus*, a strikingly theatrical action or expression that takes on emblematic significance. For example, in *Herr Puntila und sein Knecht Matti* (pr. 1948; *Mr. Puntila and His Man Matti*, 1977), the *Gestus* for the scene "Climbing Mt. Hatelma" is a masterful construction of a mountain from tables and chairs which the drunken landowner and his valet scale to a falsely poetic height.

As a young man, Brecht was more doctrinaire about the spareness of his means. To keep the audience at arm's length, uninvolved with the protagonist and prepared to debate issues, he created the *Lehrstück*, or didactic play, a bare, flat enactment of a moral dilemma. Later, he followed his own inclination for popular amusements and insisted on the importance of pleasure as a factor contributing to the audience's receptivity. "To entertain the children of the scientific age in a palpable manner and cheerfully," he required his actors to have the agility and improvisatory skill of a Charlie Chaplin or a Karl Valentin. The playing out of a situation should have the same gripping interest as a boxing match or a trapeze act, but without sentimental empathy.

For that reason, Brecht's own plays were never intended to be unalterably finished, and most of them exist in several versions: The meaning of a play can be defined only in performance, he believed, and it is legitimate to modify the play to suit the public's understanding. When Giorgio Strehler, directing the first Italian production of *Der Dreigroschenoper* (pr. 1928; *The Threepenny Opera*, 1964) after World War II, asked Brecht if he could change the locale from Victorian England to Chicago in the 1920's, the author gladly gave him permission. In this respect, he was the opposite of Shaw, who regarded every one of his words as sacrosanct and seldom left his plays open-ended—which is why so many of them have aged so badly.

A great deal of Brecht's theatrical technique has been absorbed by the modern theater, even when his dialectic is left outside. The linkage of disconnected scenes, the interpolation of song (not as in opera to heighten the emotion, but rather to generalize the situation, retard progress, and cool off emotion), the naked lighting, conspicuous musicians, set changes in full view, direct address to the audience, distressed costumes and realistic props in a nonrealistic setting, even the signboards to title senes, are the common tools of the modern dramatist. They have been popularized in historical dramas such as Robert Bolt's *A Man for All Seasons* (pr. 1960) and even in musical comedy. It may be suggested that in its influence, ethics, and adaptable form, Brecht's play is the modern equivalent of classical tragedies, however different their styles and philosophies are. In both cases, the format has often been adopted and altered to accommodate ways of thinking foreign to that which made the genre necessary in the first place.

One further genre must be touched on, the Theater of the Absurd, a term, if not invented, then given currency by the critic Martin Esslin, in a much-read book of that title. In it, Esslin discusses the work of Samuel Beckett, Eugène Ionesco, Jean Genet, Harold Pinter, and a few others, although Esslin warns against the dangers of generalizing. The term "Absurd" has since come into wide use to describe a play with an unrealistic or alogical complexion. "Absurd" originated as an Existentialist term to express the bitterly ludicrous meaninglessness of life, its anomie and lack of causal relation. When used that way, it can apply to aspects of Beckett and Ionesco, which are also absurd in the traditional sense of grotesquely comic. True Absurdism is hard to find in drama, because it takes great skill to dramatize breakdowns in communication and vacuousness without becoming incoherent and boring. Beckett has many affinities to the Symbolists as well as to the Absurdists, with his characters held in suspension and his eloquent pauses, while Ionesco is related to the Surrealists and their own ancestors, the *fin de siècle* farceurs whose whirligig comedies gave fantastic guises to middle-class banality. More idiosyncratic forms of ambiguity are currently practiced by the Austrian Peter Handke, whose plays test the nature of reality from a solipsist's point of view.

Another term used similarly to Absurdism is J. L. Styan's "dark comedy," propounded in his book *The Dark Comedy* (1962, revised 1968) as a fresh definition of tragicomedy. Styan recognized that the modern counterpoint of tragedy and farce was not wholly a twentieth century phenomenon but had its origins in Euripides, the mystery plays, Molière, and Shakespeare. Dark comedy, he wrote, is

> drama which impels the spectator forward by stimulus to mind or heart, then distracts him, muddles him, so that time and time again he must review his own activity in watching the play. In these submissive, humiliating spasms, the drama redoubles its energy, the play's images take on other facets, the mind other aspects, and the spectator "collects the force which again carries him onward." But now progression is more cautious, and he is on guard. He is charged with a tension as a result of which he is a more alert and therefore responsive participant. This tension is one of dramatic irony.

Dark comedy (as distinct from black comedy, which strives to derive humor from the morbid or taboo) is broad enough to encompass most of the innovative works of the contemporary repertory. It reflects the Existentialist belief in a disjunctive world where there is no possibility for heroism or tragedy. It is also realistic in its assumption that modern audiences are heterogeneous and cannot be expected to share common assumptions. It proposes a catharsis that occurs from moment to moment but that is not necessarily effective outside the playhouse—perhaps a token of the drama's relative irrelevance to the modern world. At any rate, the definition of drama by its effect on the spectator returns us to the Aristotelian ethos.

In 1817, William Hazlitt had casually predicted that "the progress of manners and knowledge has an influence on the stage, and will in time perhaps destroy both tragedy and comedy." This seems to have come to pass. In the mouth of a newscaster, tragedy means a streetcar accident or an avalanche. Comedy (and the ugly neologism "comedic") has come to mean anything that gets a laugh. Generic terms are taken so lightly that they are used as titles themselves, rather than as explanatory subtitles: Alan Ayckbourn's comedy of marriage called *Bedroom Farce* (pr. 1975),

Erich Segal's best-selling romance *Love Story* (1970), and Anthony Shaffer's thriller *Whodunit* (pr. 1982) tacitly assume that these are defunct and formulaic tags, useful only for the exploitation of their conventions. Playwrights themselves, when pressed to subtitle their works, give them the neutral designations "play" or "drama" (or "comedy," still a popular label to reassure the press and public that nothing disagreeable or brain-straining is in the offing). Semioticians study plays by breaking them down to their constituent signs, and deconstructionists repudiate any frame of reference extraneous to the author's linguistic games. Still, the drama is too public and synthetic a phenomenon for its context to be ignored, and the pluralism of modern culture is such that, by determining its generic alliances, a play may be clarified and its effect understood, just as those effects may be investigated to shed light on its genre.

Laurence Senelick

STAGING AND PRODUCTION

Plays are not in the first place literature; rather, they are performances. When they are included in literature courses, there is a danger that they will be treated as though they were intended primarily for the page; on the contrary, they should be regarded as historical events created and re-created at particular places and times. To read the script of a given play is only to begin the process of recovering some sense of one of those events. Readers must also learn all that they can about the theater and audience for which the playwright was composing. They must learn about the production practices and the acting company that brought the play to life on a given occasion; they must be able to reconstruct in their minds the physical theater and its stage, the setting, properties, costumes, acting styles, and conventions. Only with this knowledge can they begin to re-create some semblance of a performance. Lacking this background, readers will distort the script by unconsciously imposing on it the conventions of nondramatic literary forms such as poetry and the novel.

Students of drama, to begin with, must place each play somewhere along the spectrum that extends from realistic plays that attempt to create a dramatic illusion to the great variety of plays that frankly present themselves as performances. They must recognize that "representational" (realistic) drama is a recent invention, and that all drama used to be, and most drama still is, its opposite, "presentational." They must be aware that Western drama has evolved cyclically along this spectrum. All Western drama was essentially nonillusory before the Renaissance. Gradually, with the invention of perspective sets behind a proscenium arch, the possibility of a dramatic illusion began to develop, but not until the late nineteenth century did plays attempt to create a true dramatic illusion. Thus, from the sixteenth to the nineteenth centuries, the theater underwent a gradual evolution toward the illusory end of the spectrum. As soon as drama approached that absolute, however, there was a vigorous outburst of nonillusory theater that has persisted along with its opposite.

Students of drama, then, must place the play on this spectrum and in relation to theater history. They must know about the architecture of the theater that the playwright was writing for because, for example, a huge amphitheater would require a broader, more conventional acting style and a small theater would lend itself to an intimate, subtle style. They must know about the location of the stage, because a projecting stage would create a large measure of contact between actor and audience, whereas a pictureframe stage, set apart behind a proscenium arch, would foster a dramatic illusion. They must know how illusory or nonillusory the set was — how realistic or abstract it was, how flat or three-dimensional, whether the performers were in front of it or were enclosed by it. They must know

how the costumes affected the illusion—whether they were historically accurate, or contemporary, or indefinite, or simply nonrealistic in some other
way. They must also know about acting traditions and conventions, again
in order to place the conventions governing the play in question on a spectrum ranging from "natural" to highly stylized. They must know about the
organization of the acting troupe in order to grasp the nature of production, and, finally, they must know about the audience because its size, its
social and economic makeup, its behavior, and its reasons for attending
affected the playwright and the performers. Knowledge of production and
staging practices enables readers to reach a fuller sense of the play by
treating the written words for what they are—a script.

Ancient Greek and Roman Theaters

The first major theater was the ancient Greek theater from c. 500 B.C. to
c. 388 B.C., a span that embraces the four major playwrights of classical
Greece: Aeschylus, Sophocles, Euripides, and Aristophanes. There is very
little direct evidence about the staging and production of these plays, and
many of the details are still debated. The broad outline, however, can be
clearly determined.

Probably the most important aspect of the ancient Greek theater is that
it formed part of a religious festival; performances, therefore, were essentially opportunities for communal worship. Of the four major annual religious festivals in ancient Athens, three of them—the Lenaea, the Lesser
(Rustic) Dionysia, and the Great (City) Dionysia—involved drama. The last
of these, which emphasized tragedy, honored the god Dionysus, a god
associated significantly with fertility, with wine, and with the ecstasy or
frenzy that occurs when inhibitions are overcome. During the festival, the
Athenian community crowded into its vast outdoor auditorium to watch
and participate while performers reenacted the great legends of their culture. This worship, which allowed for laughter and for the expression of
approval or disapproval, released the Athenians' deepest feelings toward
their deities and reasserted their bonds to their proud community.

Behind these festivals lay considerable production efforts that involved
both private and public funds. A state official, the *archon*, appointed
choregoi, wealthy private citizens who each agreed to the honor of financing a chorus for a play. Playwrights submitted their scripts to the *archon*,
who decided which were worthy to be presented. Those selected were then
assigned a chorus, sometimes chosen by lot, and rehearsals began. While
the large expense of training, equipping, and rehearsing the chorus was privately undertaken, the cost of actors and many other expenses were underwritten by the State. It is not certain whether admission was charged, and
if so, how much of the cost was offset. The quality of the festival was undoubtedly helped by competition: At the end, a carefully chosen panel of

judges voted on the best playwrights and best actors, and the winners received prizes.

The City Dionysia lasted for several days in March; it began at dawn and probably continued throughout the day. On the day before it opened, a huge religious procession took the statue of Dionysus from his temple to a sacred grove where sacrifices were offered and rites were performed. Then, by torchlight, Dionysus was carried to the theater and placed on the central altar to watch the upcoming festival.

Because of their infrequency and their importance, the festivals undoubtedly drew most of the citizens of Athens. Although women were treated as second-class citizens, they probably attended the plays, seated apart from the men. The behavior of the audience was very different from that of a modern theater audience. The Athenians felt themselves to be participants, called on to express their reactions to the performance strongly and immediately. When it appeared to them on one occasion that Aeschylus had publicly revealed the rituals of the Eleusinian mysteries—rituals that were required to be kept secret—the audience became angry, and the playwright ran to the altar of Dionysus for shelter. Similarly, Euripides' plays were several times brought to a halt by audiences who felt that his stance was immoral. On many occasions, audiences reacted vigorously, cheering or denouncing the words of the play or the performers' abilities.

The auditorium was vast, more like a modern sports arena than a modern theater. It may have been four hundred feet across, and it seated audiences from fourteen thousand to seventeen thousand at the Theater of Dionysus. This great amphitheater focused on a round, flat playing area called the orchestra, which it more than halfway surrounded. The chorus of twelve or more performers danced and sang from the orchestra, moving around the altar of Dionysus at its center. To the rear was a structure called the *skene* (from which our "scene" is derived). Originally the *skene* was merely a tent where the actors could dress and conceal themselves; eventually, it became a wooden structure, then a stone one. Beyond this, the evidence is uncertain: It probably contained a platform somewhat above the orchestra and therefore probably had wide steps across the front. It is likely that there was a painted façade behind that, that there were columns and statues of Greek gods, and that there were doors for entrances and exits. Probably there was at most a simple backdrop set consisting of painted panels, which did not change during the play, and probably stage properties were very few. Thus, the performance focused directly on the chorus and the few actors.

The chorus was a group of performers, usually numbering twelve to fifteen in tragedies, who moved in unison through simple dance steps accompanied by music as they sang or chanted odes—elaborately structured songs. The actors, on the other hand, were primarily on the platform on the *skene* behind the chorus. In Aeschylus' plays, there were no more than two actors playing all the parts, thus, there were no more than two speaking parts onstage at one time. With Sophocles, this number increased to three.

For the modern reader, the most puzzling feature of the Greek drama is probably the chorus. It is difficult to know whether these "characters" are within the fiction of the play, and it is difficult to accept the way in which the choric passages interrupt the forward movement of the plot. The problem lies in the widespread modern assumption that a play should create a dramatic illusion. In fact, the tragic chorus was both inside and outside the play, its members alternately characters within the play world and spectators outside it. With the actors taking their pose on the *skene*, the chorus in the orchestra mediated the distance between spectators and characters. It could face the audience and speak to it or face the characters and speak to them.

Often the chorus performed the role of concerned citizens who collectively provided information to the characters, offered them advice, and commiserated with them. Equally often, though, the chorus served as the author's mouthpiece or perhaps his ideal spectator, singing or chanting about the moral issues involved, articulating the meaning of the action, or guiding the spectators' feelings toward the characters. The tragic chorus was therefore in a unique position in the performance, quite distinct from the characters of the play. (This was less true in the comedies, where the chorus consistently remained within the play, representing something such as clouds, birds, or cities.)

Actors and chorus members all wore large masks that completely covered their heads. The masks had high foreheads and a high buildup of hair (the *onkos*), and they had large open mouths. Through visual convention, the mask alone told a distant spectator instantly about the age, occupation, and general condition of the character. The actors wore simple, full clothing and high-soled boots (*kothornos*), which, with the *onkos*, added to the characters' stature. The actors in the Old Comedy, by contrast, wore tight-fitting garments and conspicuously displayed red-leather phalluses, which were sewn on. The use of masks enabled the two or three actors to change roles quickly, taking on all the speaking parts, male and female.

Various other staging matters also demand mention. The *ekkyklema* was a movable platform on rollers that provided the opportunity of displaying a tableau. It might have been wheeled out to reveal the murdered bodies of Agamemnon and Cassandra with Clytemnestra standing triumphantly over them, or to reveal Medea and her two murdered children. The *mechane* was a crane with ropes and pulleys that was probably most useful for creating flying gods and goddesses. The term *deus ex machina*, "the god from the machine," refers to the god flown in at the end of a play, as sometimes occurs in Euripides, to unravel a complicated plot. The *mechane* probably also helped raise and lower actors to and from the roof of the *skene*.

All of these features of the Greek theater point toward its basic nature: It was a stylized, nonillusory theater. The modern illusionistic or realistic theater has led today's readers/spectators to certain assumptions, causing them to be skeptical of masks and of the *mechane*, of big set speeches and of choric chants. The Greek theater, though, did not aim to create a dramatic illusion in anything like the modern sense. What the Greeks saw was without elaborate sets, curtains, or lighting effects; it was also very free of onstage action. Instead, the performance depended heavily on the skill of the chorus and the two or three actors. The choric dance and song were not realistic, nor were the actors, with their stylized masks and speeches of high-flown rhetoric. Their speech, especially in the tragedies, was heavily declamatory. Although the acoustics were remarkably good, there was little opportunity for subtle voice modulation when some spectators were so distant. Along with declamatory speech and with the broad, stylized masks, the acting was surely broad and conventional, with the actors using a shorthand of gestures to transmit emotions such as anger or sadness to the distant spectator. The performance was frankly a performance. It is clear, however, from contemporary accounts, that the audience was often deeply moved by such performances, that the spectators were drawn into participating in the experience more actively and vocally than in the illusionistic theater. For the Greeks, this conventional style was effective as a means of transporting them to a distant, legendary time when gods spoke to human beings and human beings were godlike.

Besides Lucius Seneca, whose plays are almost certainly closet drama, the Roman theater produced only two playwrights of stature, Plautus and Terence. The Roman theater, like Roman culture in general, was highly imitative of Greek models; therefore, a few points will suffice to illustrate the main aspects of the staging and production of Roman drama. In the theater of Plautus and Terence, the religious context had been lost; plays were essentially commercial enterprises. The chorus was gone, and the *skene* had grown larger and more elaborate; for Plautus, it had three doors and usually represented the houses along a city street. The actors, probably masked, performed from this larger stage, occasionally stepping outside their roles to address the audience directly. In place of the music of the Greek chorus, a large portion of Plautine comedy was either sung or delivered in a varied and musical style.

Medieval Drama

For medieval European drama, the evidence of production and staging practices is nearly as fragmentary and incomplete as for ancient drama. Nevertheless, a general picture can be drawn fairly confidently. The important genre of the mystery or miracle play developed in the fourteenth century in conjunction with the newly established feast of Corpus Christi. These plays, which were ultimately celebrations of the Eucharist, were usually, though not always, performed at the time of that holiday. On the Continent, religious guilds often produced them, but in England, workers' guilds more often took responsibility. Because the plays were presented in cycles—a series of many short plays—each guild could have independent and complete responsibility for a single play.

The assignments of the plays were appropriate in both a symbolic and a practical sense. The goldsmiths often produced the *Magi*, presumably because of their symbolic connection to the subject as well as because of the fact that they would be able to craft impressive properties. The Wakefield dyers produced the Pharaoh play: They could create a spectacular Red Sea of cloth. The bakers dramatized the Last Supper, and either the shipwrights, watermen, or fishermen produced the plays about Noah. Such decorum could verge on the grotesque: The nailmakers dramatized the Crucifixion, and the York ropers helped produce a play on the scourging of Christ.

The mystery plays were essentially amateur productions. In spite of a certain amount of doubling of parts, large numbers of actors, who had little opportunity for experience, were needed. Still, a few actors gained prominence and were well paid. Though most actors were men, women appeared in some French and English productions.

Typically, each play was mounted on a large pageant wagon, a portable stage that would be moved to a series of stations throughout the town. At each station, that guild's play would be performed, and the wagon would then move on to the next station. Through this processional staging, spectators formed small outdoor audiences watching a long panorama of short biblical episodes. Sometimes seating was provided, and sometimes a raised platform was available for dignitaries. In some cases, the windows and balconies of the houses of prominent citizens became the auditorium. A given cycle usually lasted several days, although sometimes only one day. Many productions did not use pageant wagons but instead mounted the whole performance on some sort of large fixed stage.

Many scholars have thought that the pageant wagons were very large structures with a main playing area and a secondary playing area on top where God or angels might appear. Glynne Wickham, in *Early English Stages, 1300-1600* (1959-1972), however, recognizing how awkward and crowded that would be, has theorized that two wagons were drawn up parallel to each other. The front wagon, called the scaffold cart, provided the *platea*, or playing area. The wagon behind it was the pageant cart containing the mansions and other structures of the sets and having a loft with a winch for flying angels and other special effects. Along the side of the pageant wagon farthest from the audience was a curtained-off area that served as a tiring-house (that is, a dressing room for the actors).

Typically, medieval religious plays used simultaneous staging: The stage contained mansions or structures representing various locales all present and visible at the same time. In a French mystery play set on a very large fixed stage in the courtyard of the Franciscan Convent in the town of Romans, nine structures simultaneously shown represented nine different locations—Heaven, Hell, prison, Africa, Asia, Europe, Rome, Lyons, and Vienna. For a fifteenth century Chester play, *The Slaying of the Innocents*, the stage, probably a pageant wagon, featured structures simultaneously representing three places—Bethlehem, Egypt, and Herod's throne; thus, the flight to Egypt, accomplished by the actors walking from one side of the stage to the other, was typically emblematic. In one of the fifteenth century Passion plays of the *Ludus Coventriae*, the stage presented on one side the Council of Jews, which offered Judas the thirty pieces of silver, and on the other side the Last Supper. Thus Judas is seen graphically moving back and forth between them. Frequently, stages were set with a magnificent mansion representing Heaven on one side and a Hell-mouth, or a huge grotesque mouth through which devils carried their victims, on the other. Earth, and human beings' lifelong struggle between the angelic and the demoniac, was at center stage. This method of staging corresponded well with the medieval worldview, according to which the drama of a single human life reflected a greater drama played out on a cosmic scale.

The mansions representing Heaven were splendidly built and lavishly decorated, while Hell and the Hell-mouth were frightening and grotesque. Often, Heaven was elevated above Hell, and angels flew above the stage while devils descended through trapdoors. Other mansions must have been fairly simple; often they required signs to identify what they represented.

Costumes and properties also were often emblematic (the archangel Michael with his flaming sword, for example). Characters were often "translated" into a medieval context. God's costume was essentially that of a pope or emperor, for example; similarly, angels wore church vestments with wings attached. Roman soldiers wore medieval armor. Except for the most expensive and important costumes, actors supplied the costumes that they wore.

Spectacular stage devices were employed in some medieval religious plays, in large part as a result of the development of mechanical winches, which were in frequent use by the sixteenth century. They enabled angels, devils, monsters, and disembodied souls to "fly"; trapdoors enabled characters to appear and disappear suddenly, trees to wither and bloom, and the miracle of the loaves and fishes to be staged by replenishing the baskets from beneath the stage. To carry out scenes of torture and execution, effigies were substituted for actors. Many animals were represented. While some were live, many were impersonated by actors. Finally, music was used extensively in medieval plays.

As with the ancient Greek theater, medieval drama had for its audience the entire community, and performances verged on ritual. Given its intimate playing conditions, the medieval theater must have been very much a participatory theater, one in which the spectators were intensely involved in the drama. At the same time, though, the spectators would have been able to separate actor from role, to remain aware of the local, amateur actor behind his pose. For this reason and because of the scripts and especially the stage settings, these medieval performances must have been, like those of the Greek theater, particularly nonillusory.

The Italian Renaissance Stage

Although the theater of the Italian Renaissance did not create a corpus of great plays, its architectural experimentation and its fascination with perspective exercised an enormous influence on staging and scene design throughout Europe. Under the influence of Vitruvius' writings on Roman architecture, Sebastiano Serlio developed theater designs using "wings" (flat scenes made of canvas stretched over a wood frame) and a "raked" (sloping) stage to create elaborate perspective. The front of the stage was level, but the rear sloped sharply up to help with the illusion that it receded into the distance. Four sets of wings, and a backdrop, along with the raked stage, together created a perspective scene converging on a vanishing point in the center. As designers built theaters according to Serlio's plans, they also developed in the 1630's sets that, unlike Serlio's, could be changed. There were two methods of doing this: Either the flat wings were mounted in grooves and were slid back to reveal other wings behind them, or—with the more sophisticated chariot-and-pole system—a single winch turned a pole beneath the stage attached to which were ropes connected to the flats. As the machinery moved, it drew the flats along "chariots" mounted on tracks beneath the stage. Besides the changing wings, Italian designers also revived a modification of a Greek and Roman stage device, the *periaktos*. A three-sided prism with only one side visible to the audience at a time, the *periaktos* could be mechanically rotated to present a new tableau, often with new performers. Pairs of these *periaktoi* were placed opposite each other, and each pair farther upstage (away from the audience) was closer together. In this way they functioned like wings and contributed to the perspective. It is important for the modern spectator to remember that all of these scene changes were performed in full view of the audience, thus emphasizing the theater's own capacity for sleight of hand, for illusion. There was a front curtain, but it concealed the stage only before the beginning of the play, not during scene changes.

The auditorium for these theaters consisted of a large horseshoe or semicircle of seats, left open in the middle. Everything in the scenery drew the spectator to the center of that semicircle (where a king or a duke often sat) because from there the illusion of perspective was most complete. In sharp contrast to the medieval theater, which had open sets where space was indefinite, the Italian Renaissance theater closed that space and defined it precisely. As it moved the audience toward one ideal point, it took the final step of enclosing its space by framing the stage with a proscenium arch. Probably first used in the Teatro Farnese in Parma, which opened in 1618, the arch defined the outer limit of the visual illusion, and along with the wall that it interrupted, it concealed the backstage machinery and personnel that created the illusion. Along with the front curtain, which was drawn aside at the beginning of performances, the proscenium arch increased the sense of separateness between performers and spectators. Still, some of the performance took place within the horseshoe or semicircle in front of the arch.

In their capacity for elaborate, sophisticated spectacle, the Italian theater and Italian opera also reached new heights, which, like their sets, influenced the staging of drama throughout Europe. Ships carrying many characters "sailed" onto the stage while waves rolled by and storms came and went. In other scenes, whole castle walls were rigged to collapse. Fire, smoke, flying figures, moving clouds, all sorts of magic or supernatural visions and transformations were regularly staged, suggesting a theater where the carpenter, painter, and machinist might begin to overshadow the actor.

Indeed, the ultimate impact of these developments was to reduce the role of the dramatist as well as the role of the actor, as Wickham observes in *Early English Stages, 1300-1600*:

> The stage which the Renaissance architect of the mid sixteenth century was contemplating was . . . one on which play and actor existed as vehicles for a display of the architect's own mastery of geometrical and optical sciences, the manipulation of pigment and of his own ingenuity in the technical skills of mechanical engineering.

The illusory nature of the new stage restricted dramatists from simultaneously setting their stage with Bethlehem and Egypt, for example, or with Heaven and Hell. The emphasis on illusion also restricted the movement of actors, because the illusion would be destroyed if they were to move far upstage. Such "advances" were brought about in a theater that produced hardly any lasting drama, yet they determined the course of staging and set design throughout Europe for several centuries.

The *Commedia dell 'arte*

While the Italian courts were establishing the basis for the illusionistic, proscenium-arch theater, the Italian popular theater was producing *commedia dell 'arte*. While court spectacle was overshadowing the actor, the *commedia*, perhaps more than any other theater, focused almost exclusively on the actor. *Commedia* troupes traveled constantly; therefore, they kept their physical baggage to a minimum and learned to adapt to whatever playing area was available. Because most *commedia* troupes operated on the sharing plan, whereby the performers were part owners of the enterprise, the actors were significantly involved in the whole production rather than dividing its phases up among specialists. In addition, because *commedia* relied on improvisation, the actors assumed much of the role of the playwright. These actors were highly skilled professionals who often played the same stock role in the *commedia* all of their lives. For each performance there was, not exactly a script, but a detailed description of the plot broken down scene by scene. Each actor knew dozens of *lazzi*, memorized routines or segments of action that could be inserted into the production. As the performance progressed, the actors inserted *lazzi* in accord with the spectators' reactions. In this way, each performance was slightly different from the others, tailored to the tastes of individual audiences.

English Renaissance Drama

The great age of English Renaissance drama began to flourish only as Queen Elizabeth I created economic, political, and religious stability and as she extended the Crown's protection directly to actors. Town councils had usually treated actors as vagabonds, but gradually the court managed to protect actors from these charges. Eventually, acting companies gained more security by being attached to the households of powerful noblemen whose names lent them status and shielded them from the civic authorities. In 1574, the Crown authorized the Master of Revels, an appointee of the queen, to grant or refuse the license of all acting companies.

Given these incentives, the acting company known as the Earl of Leicester's Men was formed in 1574, and in 1576 its leader, James Burbage, constructed the first building in London—perhaps the first in Europe—that was expressly designed as a commercial theater: It was called simply "The Theatre." In the 1590's, there were two major acting companies in London: the Lord Admiral's Men, under the actor Edward Alleyn and the financier Philip Henslowe, and the Lord Chamberlain's Men, which evolved out of the Earl of Leicester's Men and which was William Shakespeare's company. By 1600, there were at least five permanent theaters operating in London.

Like the *commedia* troupes, Elizabethan acting companies were organized by "sharing": The leading actors and playwrights were part owners of the company and earned a share of its profits. Less important personnel might own a half-share or a quarter-share or they might simply be employees. The more successful companies leased or owned their own theaters. Thus, the plays of the period were produced by self-governing, democratic bodies in which each member had ample incentive to succeed. The best actors, such as James's son Richard Burbage and Edward Alleyn, not to mention actor-playwright William Shakespeare, became men of considerable eminence and achieved financial success.

Companies varied in size from ten to twenty-five members. There was much doubling of roles, and certain actors were regularly confined to certain types of roles, particularly the "clowns." There were no women in the companies; boy actors played the women's roles. Under these conditions, Elizabethan playwrights usually wrote their plays with the capabilities of particular actors in mind. A famous example of this is the change in Shakespeare's lead clown character after William Kemp died and Robert Armin became the leading clown player: Kemp was a slapstick comedian, while Armin's forte was witty, sophisticated humor, and the major clown characters that Shakespeare created after Armin replaced Kemp are accordingly wittier and more urbane.

When Elizabethan companies were performing regularly for the public, they had to change their offerings frequently. Thus, there was a great demand for new plays. During the 1590's, for example, Henslowe's company offered a new play about every two and a half weeks, and each play was performed an average of ten times altogether.

The companies performed at the "public" theaters (large outdoor theaters that the lower classes could afford), at the "private" theaters (smaller, more exclusive, indoor theaters), and at court. The more important public theaters, in addition to The Theater, were the Rose Theatre, the Swan Theatre, the Globe Theatre, and the Fortune Theatre. Because the companies sometimes traveled, especially when the plague hit, they had to be quite adaptable. Often, then, they had to be prepared to perform in a great hall, in a town hall, in a courtyard—places that were not at all intended as theaters. Thus, adaptability and flexibility were important qualities in Elizabethan stagecraft.

The majority of the best plays of the period, however, were written for public theaters. The basic elements of these theaters have been summarized by J. L. Styan in *Shakespeare's Stagecraft* (1967): a tight, enclosing auditorium; a projecting platform almost as deep as it was wide; two upstage entrances onto the platform; and at least one balcony. As well as can be determined, these were the salient characteristics of the standard Elizabethan public theater. They must be examined thoroughly.

The enclosing auditorium was the circular or polygonal building that surrounded a large courtyard open to the sky. Seating ran in three tiers at least three-fourths of the way around the auditorium. The stage, raised probably five or six feet above the ground, jutted out into the courtyard. For a low admission fee, spectators known as "groundlings" were able to stand in the courtyard on three sides of this raised stage. Thus, spectators were below, above, and all around the performers; the audience was, in Styan's words, "on the point of swarming over the stage." The whole building was about eighty feet across and, with the three tiers of seats close on top of one another, the theater could accommodate twenty-five hundred to three thousand spectators, about as many as could be accommodated in the largest Victorian theater. Yet the farthest spectator in the back of the top balcony was within sixty feet of an actor at the center of the stage. Besides being economical, such a "tight, enclosing auditorium" created intimacy between actor and spectator: Actors would not have had to shout to be heard or make broad gestures to communicate visually. The Elizabethan playwright wrote for a theater with a very large capacity, but with very intimate playing conditions.

The platform stage was remarkably large: At the Fortune (probably very similar to the Globe), it was forty-three feet across and, more important, twenty-seven and one-half feet deep. Since it jutted out into the courtyard, there was no dead space—unlike a proscenium-arch theater of these dimensions. With this depth and this acting area, there was room for large processions, for exciting battles, and for large crowd scenes. Also, a stage of a thousand square feet was well suited to hold several characters or groups carrying on conversations independent of one another (the Capulet ball in *Romeo and Juliet*, pr. c. 1595-1596, for example) and allowed the author to create a counterpoint among them. A large stage lent itself to eavesdropping and to disguise: The eavesdropper or the disguised character could more effectively stand apart from the others and even address the audience privately through "asides." Finally, the large, deep stage provided the opportunity for especially effective entrances: An actor on his opening lines could quickly generate electricity in the auditorium by striding directly from the upstage door to downstage center. In contrast to later theaters, the Elizabethan theater was virtually free of sets upstage, and so upstage doors could be used for entrances and exits.

The final of the four elements of this theater was the balcony, an additional playing area that provided an important stage separate from the main platform. It enabled Juliet in her bedroom to be apparently out of reach of Romeo, Cleopatra in her tomb to be out of reach of Caesar's soldiers. It enabled other characters (such as Prospero) to stand in a position superior to those onstage, perhaps to eavesdrop on the others. More generally, it effectively provided for simultaneous staging, especially in crowd scenes. Possibly a second, higher balcony was also used for rare effects.

Above much of the main stage was a roofed structure known as the heavens, and in the stage floor was a trapdoor that provided access to what could represent Hell. The heavens usually contained a winch for flying characters. The trap could be used for the devils to drag Faustus into Hell, as a place from which King Hamlet's ghost could ascend, or for the grave scene in *Hamlet* (pr. c. 1600-1601). Thus, the Globe stage represented the world in the same way that the mansion labeled "Earth" on the medieval stage sometimes stood between the Hell-mouth and the mansion representing Heaven.

Finally, there is the vigorously debated question of the discovery space. Frequently, characters in Elizabethan plays draw aside a curtain to reveal a tableau—a scholar at his desk, someone in bed, a murdered body. This may have been a curtain covering an inner stage just behind the upstage wall and between the two doors. It might have been a curtain around a mansion or booth that had been temporarily set on the main stage. It might simply have been a curtain hanging from the projecting balcony. In any case, there is not convincing evidence of an inner stage; the other methods would have quite well suited Elizabethan staging techniques.

Just as there were no scenes in the modern sense, so there was little or no stage furniture. Probably any given scene would have no more than a single item which would "set" it—a throne, a tree, or an altar. Undoubtedly many of these devices were more emblematic than realistic: A simple structure onstage (the medieval mansion) could be identified by a character's words or by a decorative symbol as either a palace or a hut, a cave or a temple. Furthermore, there apparently was little hesitation about bringing these devices on and off in full view of the audience. This was nonillusory theater; there was not a dramatic illusion that could be shattered by such procedures.

Such a stage was neutral: Unless it was clearly "set" by the presence of, say, a throne or by a character's words, it was anywhere and nowhere; it was simply the stage. Often, when it was unimportant where characters were, neither they nor the empty stage told the audience. The same held for time: Since there was no control over the lighting in the public theaters and very little control in the indoor private theaters, the convention was that it was whatever time the playwright said it was—if he even chose to tell his audience.

Though the stage was mostly empty, there was considerable spectacle, and much of it must have been provided by costumes. The players bought and were given cast-off clothing from their royal and noble patrons. Thus, the plays, particularly those staging kings and their courts in the finery of peacetime and the armor of war, were filled with pageantry and splendor. Costumes were virtually all contemporary: Cleopatra was dressed as a fine English lady, and Hamlet wore doublet and hose like an English gentleman. Accompanying the visual spectacle was a considerable amount of music of all sorts. Drums and trumpets were frequent in battle scenes and in medieval court scenes; plays often included songs and dances accompanied by a variety of instruments. The instrumentalists were sometimes "within" the play, but probably as often they were separate from it, perhaps on the second balcony, where they could play background music.

Finally comes a feature that is difficult to assess: the nature of acting in this period. The Elizabethans were impressed by what they regarded as the lifelike manner of their best actors, but it is likely that this was a reaction to the excellence of a new kind of actor, the professional. In fact, Elizabethan acting was heavily influenced by the art of oratory and, it can be inferred, was by modern standards highly artificial. Given the heavy use of verse, the fact that boy actors played women's roles, the use of direct audience address, and the generally unrealistic nature of the staging, Elizabethan acting must have been fundamentally nonillusory.

Private theaters, the more exclusive indoor theaters such as the Blackfriars Theatre and the Whitefriars Theatre, were also important in the Elizabethan era. Shakespeare's company, which had changed its name from the Chamberlain's Men to the King's Men, leased the Blackfriars in 1608 and performed there during the colder months. Although smaller than the Globe, the Blackfriars was more profitable because the cost of admission could be set much higher. Along with being smaller and more exclusive, the private theaters managed more spectacular staging. Also, since lighting was a problem, they were especially adaptable for lurid, macabre scenes. Otherwise, their basic staging principles were the same as those employed in the public theaters.

The audience for Elizabethan theater was a microcosm of London society. In the boxes at the Globe Theatre sat the wealthiest merchants and many of the distinguished noblemen of the nation, and directly in front of them, down in the pit, stood the groundlings—craftsmen, apprentices, laborers, servants, and a few prostitutes and cutpurses. On the whole, they were by modern standards a rowdy group, but they were also quite responsive and helped to make this a participatory theater. Plays performed at public theaters were often performed at private theaters as well; frequently, a play performed at court might the next day be performed in a public theater, or vice versa. Probably not many women, and very few Puritans, attended plays, but otherwise the range of London society that the players addressed was remarkable.

In short, the Elizabethan theater was intimate, neutral, and flexible. It was also, in contrast to the picture-frame theater, distinctly anti-illusory and emblematic. As such, it stood in sharp contrast to the Italian approach to staging. Indeed, Wickham argues that in the Renaissance there was "a head-on collision of two fundamentally opposed attitudes to art: the typically medieval contentment with emblematic comment on the significance of the visual world versus a new, scientific questing for the photographic image."

This conflict can be graphically seen in the evolution of the English court masque, an art form which flourished under James I and Charles I. Much of the masque consisted of elaborate dances in which the courtiers as well as the professional performers had roles. In the earliest court masques, the

elegant mansions, which set the stage for various portions of the performance, were dispersed throughout the great hall, and the dancers moved
between and around them. In 1605, in Jonson's *The Masque of Blackness*
(pr. 1605), however, the designer, Inigo Jones, located all of the scenery on
a stage at one end of the hall. Suddenly, the English medieval conception
of simultaneous staging was replaced by the Italian pattern. Jones, who
had recently returned from Italy, also employed a perspective setting and
angled wings, all of which appeared when a closed curtain was dropped at
the beginning of the performance.

The collaboration of Jones with playwright Ben Jonson, who eventually
became furiously opposed to the encroachment of the scene designer on
the actor's and the playwright's art, reveals the steady triumph of the Italian ideal. In successive masques, Jones created a kind of *periaktos* that revolved to reveal eight dancers and created devices such as a cloud machine
that moved with many performers on it. Eventually, his masques were
framed by a proscenium arch; they also featured a series of back shutters
in grooves, which slid apart to reveal successive scenes in the performance,
and several pairs of wings that moved to set new scenes. In addition, Jones
created extraordinary effects with lighting, making the visual spectacle
more awesome by the dramatic use of light and shade. Jones began as the
scenic designer for Jonson's masques; by the 1630's, however, Jonson had
lost favor and Jones was essentially in charge of the masques, with a poet
of his choosing contributing the songs and verses where they were needed.
Here most vividly had the scene craftsman triumphed over the word craftsman, the spectacular over the emblematic.

English Restoration Drama

When, in 1642, the Puritans closed the theaters in England, tore down
the major theater buildings, and virtually eliminated English drama for
eighteen years, their actions created an unusually thorough break with the
past. As a result, when King Charles II returned to England in 1660, he
and a new generation of performers were inclined to make large changes in
the nature of dramatic production. Charles granted a monopoly on dramatic performances to two men, Sir William Davenant, founder of the
Duke of York's Men, and Thomas Killigrew, founder of the King's Men.
Both companies adapted and then built small indoor theaters that drew
audiences from the wealthiest, most exclusive circles in the court and London society. Partly because of their connections with Inigo Jones's court
masques, both companies worked with a movable set behind a proscenium
arch. A curtain rose at the opening of the play to reveal a flat scene all
across the back of the stage. This large, painted canvas was actually two
flats that met in the middle. When the scene was to be changed, either the
two flats would slide back, in full view of the audience, to reveal another

flat scene, and perhaps other characters, behind it, or another pair of flats would slide across in grooves in front of it, concealing the previous flats and perhaps also closing on the characters of the previous scenes. At the same time that the audience saw these effects, they also saw the series of wings, usually five on a side, replaced by other wings that contributed to the new scene. Some scenes would thus be set by flats in the farthest row of grooves, and therefore open up the whole stage; others would be set by flats near the proscenium arch and would thus concentrate the action of that scene downstage. The set itself could help to alter aesthetic distance.

The sets were painted with a variety of panoramas, usually generalized and never intended to be realistic. For example, they might have crowds or whole battles "frozen" on them. The theaters had machinery capable of spectacular special effects, and these were important in operas, tragedies, and heroic plays. For comedies, the simplest sets were used. Footlights were in use, and there were also lights behind the proscenium arch and behind each wing to illuminate the scenes and the actors. The auditorium, however, was also well lit during the play.

A distinctive feature of the Restoration playhouse was the forestage, or apron stage, a playing area that extended an average of twelve to fourteen feet, or seventeen feet in Sir Christopher Wren's Drury Lane Theatre of 1674, in front of the proscenium arch. Here, almost all of the play was performed, and actors entered and exited usually by doors in front of the arch. Thus, the arch framed the set, but the whole frame, rather than enclosing the action, was instead a backdrop against which the players walked, gestured, and spoke. Like the projecting Elizabethan stage, the forestage was still essentially neutral: Actors would often remain on it while the scene visibly changed behind them.

The apron extended out into a small auditorium. In the beginning, both companies worked in converted tennis courts that had inside dimensions of only about ninety-six feet by thirty-two feet. A little later, the theaters that were built were only slightly larger: Dorset Garden Theatre in 1671 was 140 by fifty-seven feet, and Drury Lane in 1674 was 112 by fifty-eight feet. The spectators sat in the pit, directly in front of the stage, in the grand boxes that were on three walls on the main floor, or in one of the two galleries above. A few boxes were actually beside the forestage and right next to it, and at some performances spectators were seated on the stage itself. Such a theater could seat probably not many more than five hundred spectators.

Following the Continental model, the Restoration theater replaced boy actors with actresses. The effect of this innovation can be best seen in relation to the mores of the Restoration audience. Some historians have found the Restoration theater extremely immoral, but John Harold Wilson, in *A Preface to Restoration Drama* (1965), sees it differently: "Reacting against Puritan hypocrisy and encouraged by the scandalous example of King

Charles and his Court, it was simply more open, more brazen, in its immorality." The king, who was often in the audience, was notorious for his many mistresses, some of whom were actresses. In fact, actors as well as actresses were often involved in amours with the most prominent lords and ladies. The theaters often drew well-dressed prostitutes who advertised themselves by wearing vizards (masks) and made assignations during the performance. Soon, ladies of quality, not willing to be left out, adopted the fashion of wearing vizards for much the same reason.

As the plays of the period constantly point out, usually satirically, people came to the theater for more than the stage performances. There were always dandies who sat conspicuously to display their fine clothes or who interrupted the play to display their wit. There were barons and earls in pursuit of a woman in a vizard, an actress, or an orange wench. Quarrels started and occasionally led to violence. Above all, with the most prominent lords and ladies present, the theater was a place to see and to be seen. Actresses were of immense importance, both onstage and off, in creating such an atmosphere. In fact, between 1660 and 1700 the majority of the plays had "breeches" parts, roles in which female characters disguised themselves as men, giving them an excuse to display their legs.

During this period, elite theater audiences were drawn from the highest and narrowest stratum of society. In *Drama, Stage and Audience* (1975), Styan describes the unusual conditions of performance: "At no time in the history of drama had so fraternal a coterie entertainment existed as that of the Restoration."

In an environment where such a small, intimate circle of acquaintances was regularly present and where the personalities and reputations of so many were widely known, performances were rich with in-jokes, with connotations that related to the actor's or actress's behavior or to the behavior of some prominent lord or lady. On one occasion, the whole audience roared with laughter when Elizabeth Barry, an actress with notoriously loose morals, recited a line claiming that she was armed in her "virgin innocence." In fact, playwrights writing for this audience filled their plays with lines that provided opportunities for ironic overtones, for knowing asides—for glances, gestures, intonations with a double meaning, often sexually suggestive. Restoration comedies are filled with cues for the performers to improvise visual or aural asides. The whole theater experience was a magnificent party shared by the actors and actresses, who reflected the preening and posturing in the auditorium, and by the spectators, who reflected the events on the stage. Restoration theater was truly participatory theater.

Seventeenth Century Acting and the Repertory System

Discussion of acting styles of periods before the seventeenth century must rely to a great extent on conjecture. By the mid-seventeenth century, one finds that there is more substantial evidence concerning acting styles. By modern standards, the acting of the period was close to oratory. Tragic actors, speaking elevated language in formal verse, usually faced the audience from the front of the stage and declaimed their lines in a way that modern audiences would find totally unnatural. In performing the works of the French tragedian Pierre Corneille, for example, the actors stood in a row successively watching the one who was delivering the speech at the moment. Later in the century, the tragedies of Jean Racine continued this highly stylized tradition, although the acting was slightly more lifelike. There is some disagreement among drama historians concerning styles of acting in comedy; it is probable, however, that in comedies such as Molière's, the acting, like the characters, involved the exaggeration or the comic distortion of human qualities as opposed to the realistic imitation of them. In English Restoration acting, a set of rules for actors, written by the great actor Thomas Betterton, describes the conventions of the grand manner. Tragic actors had big, set speeches in which they carried on a tirade, or "rant." They cultivated the "heroic tone" whereby each emotion had specific tones or inflections that must express it. For example, love must be expressed by a "gay, soft, charming Voice" and grief by a "sad, dull and languishing Tone." Similarly, the tragedian must point to his head to indicate reason and to his heart to indicate passion. When invoking the gods, he must raise his eyes and hands upward. The limits on such conventions were quite strict: The celebrated French actor Michel Baron created a scandal when he violated the rules simply by raising his arms above his head.

Related to this acting style was the repertory system that operated in European theaters from the sixteenth to the nineteenth centuries. Under this system, a company had a stock of plays, performing a new play only once or perhaps a few times before rotating it in its repertory. Actors were expected to have a large number of roles ready on short notice; they might perform in a different play every day for a week. Furthermore, rehearsals were quite short and sketchy by modern standards, and there was no attempt at blocking.

In general, there was apparently little sense of the overall unity of the production: No one person, like the modern director, was responsible for seeing that all aspects of the production cohered aesthetically. The set designer was independent of the actors, and the actors often chose their own costumes. To a large degree, this situation reflected the pre-Romantic assumption that there were not potentially a number of viable interpretations of a given script; there were only better or worse performances of the generally accepted interpretation. Under these circumstances, performances on the whole were probably not as finished or as smooth as modern ones.

(Prompters were on hand in the earliest theaters.) Therefore, a series of conventionalized gestures and speech tones helped to guide the actors. Since they were deprived of the modern actors' luxury of exploring the psychological motives of their character and thinking through each nuance of every word and movement, they could rely on the conventions to help them deliver the words effectively.

The Eighteenth Century Theater

Eighteenth century drama in both France and England, suffering from a falling off in quality of playwriting, was distinguished by spectacular scenic effects and great acting. During this century, English theater auditoriums, retaining the Italian box, pit, and gallery structure, steadily became larger. Drury Lane, which was rebuilt in the 1790's, had a capacity of thirty-six hundred. English stages were also becoming larger to accommodate more lavish sets. In France, the auditorium became ovoid in shape, and the stages became larger. Both countries had adopted Italian scenic practices, which were firmly established throughout Europe by 1700.

The many scene designers of the remarkable Bibliena family created sets for opera and for plays in most of the major European cities. Their designs stimulated the new Baroque style that replaced the classicism of the Renaissance. While the classical was symmetrical, rectangular, and restrained, the Baroque was asymmetrical, included curvilinear shapes, and, above all, was dynamic and much less restrained. In the course of the century, the importance of the scene increased, and scene painters became permanently attached to the major theaters. Traditionally, theaters had used stock sets, meaning that they owned altogether perhaps ten different generalized sets, which could be reused in a number of different plays. Scene designers, particularly the French designer Philippe James de Loutherbourg, were introducing a greater variety of locales and more detailed, slightly more realistic sets. There was a growing interest in historical accuracy in scene design and in costuming, although this ambition was not fully realized until the nineteenth century. Moreover, de Loutherbourg was effective and influential in ensuring that all the sets for a production were aesthetically consistent and coherent.

In England, the forestage was diminishing—presumably to make room for more paying spectators—while the size of the stage behind the proscenium arch was growing. Instead of performing on the forestage, actors after mid-century had, for the most part, retreated behind the arch, where they were more integrated with the set but more isolated from the audience. Improvements in lighting during the century contributed to this retreat because the actors could be clearly seen upstage beyond the footlights. In 1759, Voltaire eliminated the irritating practice of allowing spectators to sit on the stage, and three years later David Garrick made the same change at Drury Lane. Significantly, this practice was eliminated more because it blocked the view of the set than because it restricted the freedom of the actors.

The eighteenth century is sometimes described as the century of great actors. In France, the Comédie-Française, an elite, state-sponsored troupe governed by actors, was responsible for nurturing most of the finest actors. Both France and England experimented with acting schools, but usually actors learned their craft from being understudies to established performers. Actors normally specialized in one "line of business" or type of role. In France, such "lines" were particularly specialized: Tragic "lines" included types as distinct as kings, tyrants, princesses, or mothers. Particularly in England, actors jealously guarded roles once they had played them; thus, the roles of Romeo and of Juliet were occasionally performed by elderly actors. Interpretations of roles were established by tradition, and these interpretations were slow to change. Consequently, Charles Macklin was quite the exception when he radically challenged tradition by presenting a sympathetic Shylock.

Actors still performed primarily by standing downstage and addressing the audience as often as they addressed the other characters. They never turned their backs on the audience. They delivered their lines with considerable rhetorical flourish, and as they reached certain climactic "points" in the course of a scene, the audience interrupted with applause. In short, the performance mode of eighteenth century acting was essentially more like opera than like modern acting.

In 1700, the Comédie-Française was the only company in Paris besides the Opéra. After 1723, the Comédie-Italienne was also legitimized, but the Comédie-Française retained its monopoly on producing comedy and tragedy. The most important English company was at Drury Lane, associated successively with Colley Cibber, Charles Macklin, David Garrick, Richard Brinsley Sheridan, and John Philip Kemble. Lincoln's Inn Fields Theatre, the King's Theatre, Covent Garden, and the Haymarket Theatre were also important theaters. Both English and French companies became substantially larger during this century. A typical English Restoration troupe consisted of thirty-five to forty actors, whereas a troupe in 1800 had eighty. In addition, by 1800 there were about 120 other persons employed in the production. In the 1770's, the Comédie-Française consisted of about fifty actors, the Comédie-Italienne of about seventy.

English productions in the eighteenth century were planned and rehearsed by an "actor-manager," a prototype of the modern director. One of the most famous and influential managers of the period was David Garrick, who dominated the English stage from the 1740's until 1776. Garrick did much to further the receptiveness of audiences to Shakespeare, both in England and on the Continent. He strove to keep the scene subordinate to

the character and to eliminate ranting and bombast from acting. His interpretations were highly respected for expressing natural and convincing
emotions in a wide variety of tragic and comic roles.

The German Theater of Goethe and Schiller

The eighteenth century also marked a period when the theaters of northern Europe began to develop. Many rulers of the small German states
competed with one another in cultivating theaters. German theater reached
a high point in the last years of the century when Johann Wolfgang von
Goethe and Friedrich Schiller collaborated at the Weimar court Theater.
Their production mode, using stylized techniques to present plays in verse,
was not in the mainstream of development toward realism. Instead, Weimar classicism, as it was called, aimed at creating an image of the ideal.

Goethe's most significant contribution in the history of staging and production lies in his autocratic control of his productions. He has often been
described as the first director. Working with a second-rate acting troupe,
Goethe trained his actors by means of many rigid, conventionalized rules of
acting. He drilled them on enunciation, on the control of tone and tempo,
on all aspects of movement, posture, and gesture, and on blocking. He also
worked carefully with the scene painters to integrate that element of the
production. His primary aim was to create a continuously harmonious and
graceful image and sound. The result was an extraordinarily finished
"ensemble" production. By contrast, F. L. Schröder and the so-called
Hamburg school had established a more realistic, individualized style of
acting and production. For generations afterward, the German theater was
torn between these opposing aesthetics.

The Nineteenth Century Theater: Toward Realism

As the Romantic revolution transformed literature in the early 1800's, it
also affected the theater, bringing about a more passionate acting style and
even more spectacular scenic effects. Often the new Romantic plays called
for greater passion in their characters and more extraordinary locations and
action on the stage. Nevertheless, the Romantic era was essentially a step
along the way toward a realistic theater that reached its culmination late in
the nineteenth century.

First, a technological development in lighting contributed markedly to
the change in theater form. Around 1817, gas began to replace candles and
oil lamps, and this allowed for greater flexibility in lighting. In 1823 at
Covent Garden, limelight became the first crude spotlight used on the
stage. Electricity, in the form of the carbon arc lamp, was first used on the
stage in Paris in 1847, and in the 1880's, with the invention of the incandescent lamp, it superseded gas for stage lighting: Electricity was not only
safer but also brighter than gas and above all could be controlled more

effectively. By the 1860's, some productions were lowering the lights in the auditorium, but it was the opera composer Richard Wagner who fully established the practice of this "plunge into darkness."

The eighteenth century's interest in historical accuracy meanwhile became an obsession in the nineteenth century. In 1823, Charles Kemble, manager of Covent Garden, was persuaded to stage Shakespeare's *King John* (pr. c. 1596-1597) in authentic medieval dress and armor, and from then on, historically accurate costumes were the fashion. Charles Kean's productions in the 1850's, for example, were accompanied by extensive explanatory notes and scholarly references, which the producers used to justify the correctness of their costumes.

The trend toward the realistic set also progressed steadily during the nineteenth century. Doors and windows were inserted between flats, and in 1832, in Paris, Madame Vestris staged an interior with three continuous walls. In the 1860's, the English playwright Thomas William Robertson carried on a vigorous campaign for doors with real hinges and real knobs. At the same time, there was a slow but steady increase in the use of practical pieces within the set—three-dimensional objects instead of painted ones.

While these changes were occurring in staging practices, substantial new production practices were emerging. Barnard Hewitt, in *History of the Theatre from 1800 to the Present* (1970), observes that in 1800, "the acting company was still more important than the individual actor." Under the impetus of Romanticism, however, this soon changed. Reverence for the most magnetic actors verged on worship. In the 1820's, Edmund Kean ceased being a member of a company and instead was hired for specific engagements for the very high wage of fifty pounds a performance. This "star system" developed rapidly in the century. It became the star, more than the company or the playwright, who drew the audience.

Particularly in England, the star was also the manager of the company. Actor-managers such as William Charles Macready, Charles Kean, and Sir Henry Irving were among the most famous who filled this dual function. Many of these virtuosos did much to raise the quality of the theater. Above all, though, the star system led to productions that overemphasized the single central character (or two characters) at the expense of the ensemble. Shakespearean tragedy, for example, was adapted to remove or reduce many of the scenes that the hero did not dominate.

As the star system developed, the practice of the long-run production also grew, to the detriment of the repertory system. Instead of being employed by a company, actors increasingly were employed for a specific production that would simply run as long as it was successful. This practice made possible more carefully rehearsed and elaborately staged productions; nevertheless, because these actors were unaccustomed to playing together, they required a longer time to develop a sense of the kind of ensemble playing inherent in a repertory company. More important, the repertory company could gamble on a new play, knowing that if the play failed, it could easily be dropped from the repertoire. With the advent of the long-run production, however, there was less willingness to gamble on a play because so much was invested in that one production. In short, the nineteenth century theater came to value the actor more than the play, and the quality of the plays that were written declined.

The dominant English drama of the age was melodrama, a crude, but exciting, popular drama produced in huge auditoriums. Performed before large, vociferous, lower-class audiences, melodramas presented oversimplified situations where the downtrodden but virtuous miraculously triumph over the privileged and powerful. A whole lexicon of gestures developed to communicate basic emotions in these vast theaters: To show grief, for example, the actor conventionally beat his forehead, tore his hair, or caught his breath as though he were choking. Although clichés, these conventions did help to create a vibrant, participatory theater. The audience regularly applauded the young hero when he paused after stating a moral sentiment, and they loved to hiss the snarling villain as he shook his cane at the auditorium. The aside was still used, though it would soon disappear.

At the same time that the quality of playwriting was diminishing, the technical resources for creating a dramatic illusion were developing. Improved lighting, along with the period's eagerness for the authentic, caused the actor to move back into the set and caused the set to become more realistic. Acting and staging were treated more as three-dimensional elements, as aspects of an art that must move well in space: This was the picture-frame theater. As this potent new instrument evolved—this truly three-dimensional stage with such expressive power possible in its set and above all in its lighting—a great need arose for someone outside it to control it, and the potential arose for innovative artists to compose for the stage. As is well-known, in the latter part of the century there was an explosion of great dramatists composing for this revived medium. More to the purpose here, though, was the extraordinary development of the director, an artist who could manage the combined resources of this flexible but complex new instrument. What most radically and thoroughly brought about the modern theater was the inevitable assumption of power by one person outside the performance who worked to bring all aspects of the production into harmony with one another. This was partially brought about by the system of powerful actor-managers, but it was at the same time a reaction against these stars, because it meant a subordination of the actor to the aesthetic whole. No longer would actors choose their own costumes; no longer would sets be created independently of the prevailing interpretation; no longer would plays be shaped to highlight the star. Under the overseeing control of the director—or, in France, the *régisseur*—all of these elements were shaped by a single vision.

The most important and influential of the early directors was George II, Duke of Saxe-Meiningen, whose company performed throughout Europe from 1874 to 1890 and radically altered European stagecraft and production. Saxe-Meiningen or a director, whom he appointed and closely supervised, controlled every aspect of the production, seeing to it that the sets were suited to the play at hand, that every detail of the costuming contributed, and that the actors made use of the space on the stage and subordinated personal glory to the virtues of ensemble playing. Saxe-Meiningen required that all actors take part in each production; thus, actors playing the lead in one play might find themselves performing as "supers," or extras, in a crowd scene in the next. A leading actress who balked at this requirement was immediately fired.

The Meiningen Players, as they were called, became known for their crowd scenes: In accord with the concept of ensemble playing, the director devoted great attention in long rehearsals to each member of the crowd. Saxe-Meiningen also treated the stage space as much more plastic, creating different levels for the first time and moving characters around in new ways. Instead of focusing all the spectators' attention on the star, the Meiningen Players disseminated the effect so that the stage was communicating from several points at once. The duke said that he liked to find excuses for his actors to touch solid objects on the stage in order to affirm their own solidity. As the Meiningen Players traveled through Europe performing in the major cities, they established new standards for ensemble acting and for vivid productions in which every detail contributes.

If the goal of Saxe-Meiningen was unity, the goal of the revolutionary French director André Antoine was Naturalism. In 1887, when Antoine opened his Théâtre Libre in Paris, he saw the Meiningen Players and was awed by the effect of their polished production style. As a Naturalist, influenced by the work of Émile Zola, Antoine aimed to stage a "slice of life," a play whose characters were greatly influenced by their environment. Specifically, that meant the plays of Henrik Ibsen, August Strindberg, and Gerhart Hauptmann.

The meaningful stage environment of the characters in the Saxe-Meiningen productions was a tool ripe for the Naturalist theater. For his sets, Antoine designed an enclosed room that was as real as possible: It had authentic dimensions instead of dimensions designed for good sightlines. Instead of painted objects, he always used real ones, such as an actual side of meat when the setting was a butchershop. His lighting suited the place and time of day and appeared to come from plausible light sources. Not until he had designed the complete room did he decide which wall would be open for the audience to look through. Antoine thus established what is called "fourth-wall realism."

Although Antoine is best known for his realistic sets, he was more deeply committed to leading his actors to move through the stage space realistically. His actors cultivated a natural style, including the awkwardness, the pauses, even the silences of everyday speech. They completely avoided the downstage speech to the audience—in fact, any form of aside or audience address. (In addition, Antoine had the footlights lowered.) The actors addressed one another and gestured and moved in a way that gave the illusion of spontaneity, even turning their backs on the audience occasionally.

Because Antoine was continually struggling toward the best balance of all the elements that make theater, he described his work as "experimental," a word he borrowed from Zola. As a result, the notion of experimental theater has been adopted by countless small companies in the twentieth century. Antoine's "laboratory" was a low-budget operation in a tiny, makeshift theater. Soon, "free theaters" were begun in several other places. In 1889, in Berlin, Otto Brahm organized the Freie Bühne, an offshoot of the Théâtre Libre. Brahm's abilities at directing realistic ensemble productions soon made him a major power in European theater. Likewise, J. T. Grein, a Dutchman, founded the Independent Theatre in London in 1891, and the following year, it had the distinction of initiating George Bernard Shaw's career with a production of *Widowers' Houses*.

The next important phase of the realistic theater came in 1898 when Konstantin Stanislavsky, an actor and director, joined with Vladimir Nemirovich-Danchenko to form the Moscow Art Theatre. The setting for the opening scene of their first production was part of a large terrace that appeared to extend well beyond the stage. Many actors were continually moving to and from the wings, giving the impression of a large, overflowing crowd of which the audience saw only a small part. This sort of realism was typical of the Moscow Art Theatre, but in fact Stanislavsky, who soon became the dominant figure, was most heavily indebted to Saxe-Meiningen. After seeing the Meiningen Players in 1888, Stanislavsky determined that strong directing was essential to achieve his artistic ideals. Stanislavsky did not think of realism or Naturalism as such to be the goals of his company, as they were for Antoine. Instead, he aimed for artistic unity, for the ensemble effect. He was eclectic in his choice of plays, being particularly drawn to the Symbolist plays of Maurice Maeterlinck and Leonid Nicolaevich Andreyev. Nevertheless, the company became known for its realistic productions—of Ibsen and above all of Anton Chekhov. In fact, the pairing of Chekhov with the Moscow Art Theatre led to Chekhov's writing his last three great plays. Ironically, though, Chekhov continued to feel that Stanislavsky badly misunderstood the plays, and he was angry with the director for continually inserting extra touches of realism—croaking frogs, ticking clocks, crying babies.

Along with unity of production, Stanislavsky throughout his career was preoccupied with the problems of the actor. In several extremely influential books, he set forth his notions about actor training, famous as the Method. This training covers all aspects of acting from the beginning to full performance, from actors' study of their characters to their study and training of themselves. Actors, says Stanislavsky, are not asked to become the characters but rather to work within what he calls "the magic if": Actors must continually ask the question, if these are the facts of character and situation to this point, what behavior might follow? Thus, actors are always looking for motivation, for the inner cause of their characters' actions and statements. Together with the ensemble, they analyze the play and work toward discerning the "subtext" or underlying behavior patterns implied by the text. In addition, actors search for situations or experiences in their own lives that produce emotions and, through training, learn to call on these during performance. Often they might try improvising during rehearsal as a means of discovering the most expressive behavior of the characters they play. Thus, actors are not so much imitators of other personalities as they are creators who have found a method of expressing their own. Since actors do not simply copy emotions but instead recall personal events that trigger their own emotions, they are freer to create a more fresh and honest portrayal at each performance.

The Reaction Against Realism

While the Moscow Art Theatre was flourishing, many other realistic theaters were founded. A famous example was the Abbey Theatre, which was founded in Dublin, in 1904, and which, like the Théâtre Libre and the Moscow Art Theatre, evolved out of an essentially amateur group. In such theaters, the dramatic illusion was most completely created—the illusion that the action on the stage was real. At the same time, however, that such theaters were springing forth, an equally strong anti-illusory current began to develop, often under the name of Symbolism. The vigorous reaction declared that the theater must not disguise its own nature, that the real world can best be seen through forms that do not slavishly copy it but instead more indirectly resemble it.

Three years after Antoine began his "experiment," Paul Fort opened the Théâtre d'Art in Paris, whose aim was to glorify the spoken word and whose productions were markedly Symbolist. He was succeeded by Aurélien Lugné-Poë, also a Symbolist, who at first staged realistic Ibsen plays with excessive symbolic emphasis. Eventually, though, with the premiere of Alfred Jarry's *Ubu Roi* in 1896, Lugné-Poë produced an antirealistic play that was also theatrically effective and led him away from the vagueness and murkiness that often plagues Symbolist theater.

By this time, two extremely important men of the theater, Adolphe

Appia, a Swiss, and Gordon Craig, an Englishman, were at work developing theories of staging and production that would have an enormous impact on modern drama. Whereas Antoine was in one sense a revolutionary, he was, from the broadest perspective, simply bringing to a culmination the theater of illusion, the representational theater. By contrast, Appia and Craig were advocating a radical departure, a return to an elemental, ritualistic, extremely anti-illusory theater, a presentational theater.

Appia's theories stemmed from his absorption in Wagnerian opera. On the one hand, Appia, admired Wagner's notion of total theater, the notion that music, setting, costume, and acting must all cohere to create the art work. He felt, however, that Wagner's realistic, representational settings did not in fact cohere with his idealistic music, and that painted realistic settings were incongruous next to three-dimensional actors. In the 1890's, in two books that were illustrated with his own stage designs, Appia proposed radical changes in the staging of Wagner's operas. He urged greatly simplified, generalized sets with massive, solid structures and a number of different acting levels, typically connected by ramps or steps. Very important to this new stagecraft was the use of light, which in Appia's terminology became "living light": He proposed replacing the relatively even, uniform lighting of Wagner's theater with lighting that played off surfaces from different directions and with differing intensity. This, he believed, would harmonize with the rhythmic quality of music and above all would stress the solidity of the set and of the actor. The result of his books, felt at first in the staging of Wagner but eventually throughout the European and American theater, was to bring about the final giant step in the evolution from flat, painted sets to plastic, sculptural ones.

Like Appia, Craig was essentially a designer and theorizer; unlike Appia, Craig voiced his revolutionary ideas loudly and managed to have some of them staged. In his writing, Craig developed his theories about the ideal nature of art and about the central role of the director in imposing a style on all aspects of a production. Following Appia, he designed sculptural, abstract stage sets that encouraged actor movement and that could be lighted in varied ways to stress their solidity. Craig never wanted to become permanently attached to a professional theater, but he designed sets for Brahm in Germany, for an Ibsen play at the Danish Royal Theater, and for Stanislavsky in Moscow. He was cavalier about the practical aspects of his designs. For a production of *Hamlet*, in Moscow, he wanted a series of extremely tall, convex screens made of metal, stone, or wood that would move apparently all by themselves, presenting continually shifting aspects to the audience throughout an uninterrupted performance. (Such screens typify his general preference, in contrast to Appia's designs, for very tall vertical structures.) The theater building, however, could not support such heavy screens, so wood frames with unpainted canvas stretched over them were used. Even so, moments before the opening, the screen structure fell over like a house of cards and the screens were badly torn. The production went on but with motionless screens.

For Craig, a major point of contention with the current theater was the star system. As a radical theorist, Craig held that actors should become "super-marionettes." By this he meant that they should be disciplined to carry out every nuance of voice and movement called for by the director: The director, not the actor, should be the creative artist in the theater. By the term "super-marionette," he also implied his emphasis on the actor's physical presence and movement. With Appia he argued for a theater where actors moved around, beside, and on top of inanimate three-dimensional forms and thereby displayed their own solidity, liveliness, and freedom.

A quick glance at the designs of Craig and Appia, set against an array of the realistic sets of the period, gives a partial indication of how radical were their reforms. Easily seen is their simple and abstract use of line, form, and color, and something of the grandeur of the effect; and almost as easily seen is the greater three-dimensionality of their plans. Less easily grasped are the extraordinary implications of their notions of replacing the uniform footlights and border lights with lively, shifting, incandescent spotlights. As Appia in particular recognized, the argument for cultivating the three-dimensional nature of the stage comes not because theater should be realistic but because theater is inherently three-dimensional. Just as Antoine's realistic theater was created to reflect more honestly the three-dimensional world, so, too, the nonrealistic, anti-illusory theater ushered in by Appia and Craig came from a desire to reflect more fundamentally the three-dimensional world by replacing the interior decorator with the scenic artist. Behind both theaters was a desire to make the theater a flexible instrument in the hands of a creative, overseeing director.

As the revolutionary views of Craig and Appia gained advocates, the theater seemed to explode in many directions. There were Symbolism, Expressionism, and theatricalism, as well as realism. As the twentieth century progressed, there were epic theater, the Theater of Cruelty, and the Theater of the Absurd, and many other experimental theaters. Yet through this diversity were some basic trends. Theaters have generally pursued the trails mapped by Appia and Craig and have incorporated the performers and the spectators within the same space. At the same time, this space has become a flexible instrument and so the steady march toward realism has reversed itself; very quickly, the realistic picture-frame stage seemed out-of-date. Finally, with the notion of a flexible instrument that could be shaped to achieve artistic unity during production, the authority of the director was firmly established.

Indeed, in the twentieth century, the director began to compete with the playwright as the maker of plays. Seen in another light, there was actually often a blurring of the roles of director and playwright. The belief that the classics could be interpreted in radically different ways, and therefore that the director is the artist to reinterpret them, has grown enormously in the twentieth century. Adherents of this approach argue that Shakespeare's plays, for example, reveal their greatness when they can sustain a variety of conflicting interpretations. This can lead to a production that is as much the creation of the director as it is of the playwright. Conversely, playwrights have often taken over much of the director's role by writing elaborate, detailed stage directions, specifying everything from the set to the tone of voice the actors use. Shaw's instructions provide an early, extreme example of this tendency.

Spurred by Appia and Craig, a major step in the development of the three-dimensional stage came with the projecting stage. In 1907, Georg Fuchs designed the Munich Art Theater in which an open stage extended into an enclosing auditorium. Aiming to increase contact between audience and actor, Fuchs eliminated the dividing line of the proscenium arch altogether. In his structure, the basic theater plan returned to the plan of the primitive theater before scene painting and perspective drawing. As such, it influenced the construction of many similar stages, called "open" stages, in the modern theater.

Jacques Copeau in France and Max Reinhardt in Germany were influential directors who represented vastly different reactions to the new stagecraft of Appia and Craig. Copeau believed that as director he should aim to capture the intention of the playwright, that actors were of central importance and the setting subordinate to them. He produced his plays in a simplified theater, similar to the Elizabethan theater, where the performing area and the auditorium shared one continuous space without a dividing line between them. Both with new plays and with revivals, Copeau worked for aesthetic beauty and simplicity.

Reinhardt was very much the kind of authoritarian director that Craig had described: He took control of all aspects of production, which were planned in detailed promptbooks. He was willing to try any form that produced exciting theater. Although he produced chamber plays for intimate theaters, he is best known for his various extravaganzas—huge spectacles for huge audiences. In 1911, for a production of *The Miracle* (pr. 1911), he transformed a great hall in London into a medieval cathedral complete with stained glass windows and dramatic lighting. In 1911 also came a production of *Everyman* in front of the cathedral in Salzburg. Reinhardt created many other large-scale productions in the United States and Europe, but his most controversial was his production of *Dantons Tod* (pb. 1850), a play about the French Revolution, in which Reinhardt attempted to involve the audience actively in the drama. As the Revolutionary Tribunal debated, each of one hundred actors seated throughout the audience leaped to their feet to shout out support or opposition to the issues, creating a "total theater" aimed at further reducing the distance separating the audience and the performance.

Meanwhile, the Russian theater was trying bold experiments under the impetus of the 1917 Revolution. Vsevolod Meyerhold, the major innovator of this theater, directed plays in a style sometimes known as "constructivism," because of the use of machines and mechanical structures in the performance, and sometimes more broadly described as "theatricalism," because of his anti-illusionist insistence that the performance is only theater. Meyerhold set his stage with mechanical devices of all kinds and had his actors climb ropes or scaffolding, perform acrobatics on playground swings or slides, and display their physical agility in an admittedly non-illusory setting. Every movement was precisely planned by this overseeing director, so much so that Meyerhold had difficulty retaining actors in his company. All was designed to demonstrate human beings' integration in industrial society, to celebrate the Revolution, and to inculcate Communist values. The work of Meyerhold and other Russian directors before World War II, notably Alexander Tairov and Yevgeny Vakhtangov, is distinguished by a willingness to experiment with an incredible array of theatrical tricks. Many were adapted from such varied sources as the ballet, the circus, the music hall, farce, *commedia dell'arte*, and pantomime. The soliloquy was revived, and in a number of productions asides frequently appeared, some of them spoken by actors mingling with spectators, some of them completely improvised by actors.

In the 1920's and 1930's, both American and European theater were significantly influenced by agitational-propagandistic (or agitprop) productions. The "living newspaper" was one form of agitprop: Amateur actors performed social-protest skits developed around a reading of the newspaper. A fundamental assumption of such works was the oneness of performers and audience: All shared a common goal of class struggle against oppression. In such an atmosphere, Nikolai Okhlopkov in Moscow eliminated the stage entirely and placed his performers on ramps or platforms around the hall or had them walk among the spectators. Audience members would be asked to participate in the play—by holding a loaf of bread or helping to set a table. In one production, the audience was held back in the foyer and then allowed into the auditorium which they found filled with actors shouting, quarreling, singing, cooking, cleaning guns, and hanging out wash. Eventually, when the spectators had found seats, these various activities led into the main action. Another Okhlopkov production developed a plot in which a band of revolutionary fighters becomes separated from the main column during the Russian Civil War. Finally, the main body is sighted. The actors look excitedly out through the auditorium and then rush out to greet and embrace the spectator-participants—for they, the audience, are the lost comrades. At the end of an Okhlopkov play when the spectators applauded the performers, the performers responded by applauding the roles played by the spectators.

Another theater that continued the trend away from illusionism was the Epic Theater of Erwin Piscator and Bertolt Brecht. In Germany in the 1920's, these two men of the theater collaborated on a mode of composition and production that was designed to prevent spectators from losing themselves in the performance. Both men aimed to make theater serve the goals of Marxism by prodding the audience to reflect on the fundamental causes of war and injustice and on the Marxist solutions to these problems. Their plays were termed epic or narrative because they consisted of a series of brief, loosely connected episodes that were punctuated, especially in Brecht's case, by short songs, speeches addressed to the audience, or other theatrical intrusions designed to discourage the spectator from developing any sustained identification or sympathy. Both artists deliberately shattered the dramatic illusion in order to provoke thoughtful analysis of the social problems dramatized. Brecht used placards to indicate time and place and the events of an ensuing scene, employed film projectors extensively to provide an added dimension to the stage performance, and limited his stage setting to a few essential properties. He made certain that the audience could see the lamps that provided stage illumination, that a set which represented a town looked like a set rather than attempting to delude the spectator with a visual illusion. In stark contrast to Stanislavsky, Brecht trained his actors to feel distant from their roles, to feel that the roles were personae that they were putting on like clothing. In rehearsal, the actors were directed to talk about their roles in the third person and in the past tense. Brecht was not only a playwright but also, like Piscator, a director who assumed authority for all aspects of production. He developed a highly influential mode of production that was far from realistic or representational theater. He differed, however, from many of his contemporaries in his celebrated "alienation" technique—his attempt to reduce the spectator's emotional involvement and empathy with the characters.

From Artaud to the Present

Although Brecht's influence on the theater since the 1950's has been considerable, Antonin Artaud's has been even greater. Artaud was a practicing man of the theater, but it was his theoretical stance, expressed in *The Theater and Its Double* (originally published in French in 1938 and translated into English in 1958), that most affected the direction of theater experiments in the 1950's and after. Artaud wished to avoid both realistic drama and the dogmatic drama that predominated in Germany and Russia. He saw the whole Western theater as bland, decadent, and superficial, and he believed intensely that it needed a radical new beginning to bring it alive. To this end, he turned to Greek myths and to primitive beliefs and rituals—to the violence of savage rites of fertility and sacrifice.

Artaud believed that Western theater was actually only a "double," a weak imitation, of true theater because it was based on logical discourse and traditional thinking accumulated through centuries of civilization. To Artaud, the Eastern theater, based on myths and symbols, was closer to his ideal of the true theater. Artaud believed that theater should be intuitive instead of rational, magical instead of paraphrasable, that it should reach out powerfully to jar the spectators out of their complacency and awaken in them a spiritual renewal. To achieve the experience of primitive ritual, Artaud called for a theater that virtually replaced conventional language with a new language of symbols, signs, gestures, sounds. He named this the "Theater of Cruelty" referring more to the psychological trauma of life than to the physical violence. He experimented, however, with production devices that were physically shocking: He used loud, shrill, sudden sound effects and abruptly changing, disconcerting lighting effects. He staged his plays in places such as barns and factories, again to help destroy conventional audience response. He would place his spectators in swivel chairs in a large, unornamented hall with the performance occurring in the center, at the four corners, and on galleries running around the room. Instead of settings there would be plain, whitewashed walls to reflect light. In *The Theater and Its Double*, Artaud describes the flow and texture of a production in this environment, a theater of

> Cries, groans, apparitions, surprises, theatricalities . . . magic beauty of costumes . . . resplendent lighting, incantational beauty of voices, the charms of harmony, rare notes of music, colors of objects, rhythms of physical movement . . . new and surprising objects, masks, effigies yards high, sudden changes of light. . . .

Artaud's theories were a major stimulus to a generation of playwrights after World War II, playwrights such as Jean Genet, Eugène Ionesco, Samuel Beckett, and Harold Pinter. In general, they ventured far from realism and created drama that does not mirror reality but rather serves as a grand metaphorical equivalent of the world around them. They reflected the fundamental spirit of the Theater of Cruelty but varied in their response to Artaud's production suggestions. Beckett tended to simplify setting: merely a mound of sand in *Happy Days* (pr. 1961), a plain with a single tree in *Waiting for Godot* (pb. 1952), and in *Endgame* (pr. 1957), a bare room with two windows that is furnished only with a ladder, a wheelchair, and ash cans in which two old people live like animals. In contrast, Ionesco often created situations in which characters are engulfed by physical objects—by a mysteriously expanding corpse or by furniture arriving endlessly.

In the 1960's and 1970's, radical notions of staging and production were carried to their apparent extremes. Notions about the total theater environment, notions that recall the practices of Reinhardt, Meyerhold, and Okhlopkov and the writings of Artaud, have influenced, for example, Peter Brook's work, The Living Theatre under Julian Beck and Judith Malina, Jerzy Grotowski's Polish Laboratory Theatre, and Peter Schumann's Bread and Puppet Theatre. Brook produced *Oedipus* (pr. 1968) with the actors placed all around the auditorium. The Living Theatre, a group whose intention was to produce revolutionary political action, attempted to break down the barrier between performer and spectator by threatening or assaulting their audiences. Schumann took his acting company out onto the streets of New York City, adapting his performances to whatever space was available. He did not charge admission of his audience; on the contrary, the performers handed out bread to anyone who came. Many of the performers acted from behind gigantic masks, staging plays that were mythic doubles for contemporary problems.

Probably the most important and most influential of these experimenters in environmental theater is Jerzy Grotowski. Heavily influenced by Artaud, Grotowski aims to dissolve the remaining barriers between actor and spectator. His goal in a performance is nothing short of a kind of psychoanalysis: It should assist the spectator-participant to exorcise his aggressive, destructive impulses. To achieve this exorcism, he conceives of a "poor theatre," a theater almost totally devoid of settings and properties, of effects or spectacle. Instead, it focuses on, in Grotowski's words, the "holy actor," who, through tremendous self-discipline and rigorous physical training, has come to bare his psyche. Audiences are assigned various roles: They are the Dead, or the descendants of Cain, or inmates of a mental home. The plays involve renewing traditional myths and then blaspheming them, confronting them in ways that deeply disturb actor and spectator alike. This is theater for a very special audience, an elite.

These recent experimental trends are a small, though important, part of a large number of theater types, and of a huge array of production and staging patterns. Similar to the Russian and German theaters earlier in the century, many theaters in the past two decades have had explicit goals of social protest or consciousness raising. During the 1960's, a number of American theaters, such as The Living Theatre, focused on the Vietnam War and on the social evils that they saw as the source of it. At the same time, a vigorous black theater developed, especially in New York City, and provided opportunities for blacks to reflect their own experience. The women's liberation movement led to feminist theater companies with the express purpose of raising consciousness about feminist issues.

During the twentieth century, film and television have had a great impact on theater attendance and therefore on theater form. In the first half of the century, the mass audience of the theater of 1900 was greatly reduced throughout Europe and the United States. After World War II, however, government subsidies and private grants began to stem the decline of live theater. At first these subsidies aided only companies in major cities, but eventually they began to help with the establishment of regional companies. Indeed, in both the United States and Europe, the growth of these regional companies has been a promising phenomenon. In 1965, the establishment of the National Endowment for the Arts gave a firmer basis to American theater. In 1966, for the first time in the United States, there were more actors employed outside than inside New York. Still, New York remained the center of American theater. Broadway may have passed the peak of its success, but Off-Broadway and Off-Off-Broadway continued to flourish. On the whole, live theater continued its attempt to recover the large mass audience that it once had.

The 1980's and 1990's, appearing to be the tail end of the theater revolution (or revolutions) that so dominated the 1960's and 1970's, became a time for both extending and reexamining the many forms that theater has taken. Increasingly, as this essay has implied, theater has become attuned to international influences: The main theater centers have offered plays of many cultures, Eastern as well as Western. Likewise, the revival of plays of earlier theaters (for example, of ancient Greece and Elizabethan England) has influenced modern production methods. Also, the influence of reformers such as Artaud and Grotowski continued to be pervasive: Much of the most interesting work today reflects their radical approach. Partly in response to the impact of television and film, the best of the new work often features a return to the actor alone, using dance and song and mime—the actor alone being the sole focus of the drama. This is most evident with actors who are not conventionally associated with theater—street performers, who flourish wherever crowds gather. It is also true in those numerous fringe theaters that surround theatrical festivals and theatrical centers (for example, Off-Off-Broadway in New York and the Fringe Theater of London). Here, performers learn to break through the passivity encouraged by television and the politeness engendered by mainstream theater and to provoke their audience to interact with them.

Looked at in perspective, the history of staging and production has, in its most fundamental aspects, come full circle in the twentieth century. The realistic theater of the nineteenth century, creating its dramatic illusion behind the proscenium arch, was the culmination of a trend that began in the Italian Renaissance. In contrast to this "representational" theater is the "presentational" theater of ancient Greece, of the Elizabethans, and of most modern productions, a theater which frankly accepts its theater environment instead of trying to transport its audience elsewhere. In this presentational theater, the decor tends to be symbolic and the actors and spectators tend to share the same space. While actors' role in representational theater is impersonation, their role in the modern presentational theater has returned nearer to that of interpreters and spokespersons.

Although there are still many theaters that have proscenium arches and there is still much staging that is broadly realistic, the major trend of the twentieth century has been to move away from the representational toward the presentational. For much of the century, theaters such as those of the Greeks and the Elizabethans have been widely admired as models. Playing areas with seats sloping up on all sides ("arena" staging) have come into wide use, as have those with seating on three sides (often called "open" or thrust staging). A particularly characteristic phenomenon of the modern age of diversity has been "adaptable theaters," theaters whose components can be easily moved to create any number of staging arrangements from the picture frame to the arena. Particularly in such theaters, the vast array of staging arrangements throughout the past have been revived and modified as the theater develops its stages for the future.

Elliott A. Denniston

MEDIEVAL DRAMA

Liturgical Drama

In England, as on the Continent, theater in the classical sense virtually disappeared after the sixth century. With the decline of the study of Greek, classical tragedy lost its cultural currency and was almost entirely forgotten; fortunately for later ages, some copies of Greek tragedies were preserved, notably in Irish monasteries. Roman comedy seems to have had at least a minimal existence, surviving in the *histriones* and *ioculatores* of medieval entertainment. The single example of classical comedy in the Middle Ages is found in the adaptations of Terence by the tenth century Benedictine nun Hroswitha of Gandersheim. Her plays on the saints, however, seem to have been confined to her native Saxony and therefore did not affect the development of English drama.

It was through religious ceremonies that drama was reborn in Europe in the tenth century. The simplest form of such liturgical drama was the trope, an amplification of a passage in the Mass or Divine Office. The best-known writer of tropes was Tutilo, of the Abbey of Saint Gall. Tropes were known in England, for a Winchester troper (a medieval book containing tropes) dates from the late tenth century. Tropes were often expanded into lengthy poems, sometimes in dialogue form, known as "sequences" or "prose," which became universal in the Christian liturgy. Some of them, such as Saint Thomas Aquinas' *Lauda Sion* (1265), are still in use today.

The first notable development of tropes into drama occurred in the famous *Quem quaeritis*, a dialogue between two sides of the choir, one side representing the women at the empty tomb of Christ on Easter Day, the other side representing the angel who tells them that Christ is risen. It was to become the most famous of all medieval liturgical plays, eventually developing into more elaborate Resurrection plays. These dialogues were at first exclusively in Latin and were performed within the Mass and, later, during the Divine Office, predominantly by clerics. The prototype of the *Quem quaeritis*, again from the Abbey of Saint Gall, dates from about 950.

The *Quem quaeritis* was undoubtedly very popular in England. It is described in great detail in the manuscript *Regularis Concordia*, dating from about 965. The document was drawn up by bishops, abbots, and abbesses of England upon the suggestion of King Edgar. It is now ascribed with relative certainty to Aethelwold, Bishop of Winchester, as part of a book of customs relating to the Benedictine observances. It gives detailed directions for the dramatization of the *Quem quaeritis* and insists on the instructive aspect of the representation. The same manuscript also contains directions for a *Depositio Crucis* on Holy Thursday.

The development of liturgical drama in medieval Europe knew no national boundaries. The universal use of Latin and the numbers of *clerici vagantes*, or wandering clerics, made borrowings an ordinary occurrence. Thus, the growth of the *Quem quaeritis* play into a more elaborate *Visitatio sepulchri*, with more characters, many nonbiblical, followed a pattern that was evident throughout Europe. The incorporation of Peter and John, along with congregational participation, began in the twelfth century and continued well into the fourteenth. The only English manuscript of this type comes from the Church of Saint John the Evangelist in Dublin, a fifteenth century manuscript of a fourteenth century text.

Nativity plays, which were never quite as popular as the Easter cycle, began around the eleventh century and followed the same pattern of development as that of the Resurrection plays. Later Nativity plays centered on the shepherds (*pastores*) who were nearby at Jesus' birth and the three kings (*reges*), or wisemen, who came from the East to pay tribute to Him. Simple stage props and costumes were used in such productions.

That Christmas and Easter liturgical texts in Latin existed in England is evident primarily from secondary sources, since many manuscripts were destroyed during the Reformation in the sixteenth century. With the exception of the *Regularis Concordia*, the Winchester Troper, the Dublin *Quem quaeritis* of the fourteenth century, and a manuscript from the Nunnery of Barking, there are no extant texts of Latin Easter plays. The last-named manuscript probably dates from about 1363-1376 and is ascribed to Katherine of Sutton, who may have been the adapter. The text contains several standard liturgical dramas: *Quem quaeritis*, a *Visitatio Sepulchri Depositio Crucis*, and an *Elevatio Crucis*.

There is no extant text of a Latin Christmas play, but such a *representatio* is referred to in a Salisbury inventory of 1222, and similar references occur in the York statutes of 1255. Both Christmas and Easter plays are mentioned in the thirteenth or fourteenth century statutes at Lichfield Cathedral, which provide for representations of *Pastores*, a *Resurrectio*, and a *Peregrini* (depicting the disciples on their way to Emmaus, traditionally performed on Easter Monday). There are references to Latin liturgical plays at Lincoln in 1317, and a fifteenth century Cornish manuscript, with a text dating from about 1300-1325, contains an *Origo Mundi*, a *Passio Domini Nostri Jesu Christi*, and a *Resurrectio*. Numerous manuscripts indicate that such Latin liturgical plays continued to be performed until well into the sixteenth century.

Vernacular Religious Drama

By the thirteenth century, drama began to move gradually into the vernacular, and plays were performed outside the church. At the beginning, both Latin and the vernacular were used side by side. The earliest English documents are the twelfth century Anglo-Norman *Ordo representacionis Adae*, with the prophecies in Latin and in Norman French, which were probably played to French audiences, and the so-called Shrewsbury Fragments, a fifteenth century manuscript with a text dating from the late thirteenth to the early fifteenth century, with the role of one shepherd and the third Mary in English.

Although clerical objections are frequently given as an important reason for the development of the vernacular drama, critics such as Karl Young, E. K. Chambers, and A. P. Rossiter see such prohibitions as directed more toward secular drama. The most famous of these clerical prohibitions was made by Robert Grosseteste, chancellor of the University of Oxford and Bishop of Lincoln, who in 1244 called on clerics to end participation in miracle plays and mystery plays. (Mystery plays, or mysteries, dramatized biblical stories and apocryphal narratives featuring biblical figures; miracle plays, or miracles, as the name implies, centered on miraculous incidents, frequently presented as episodes in the lives of well-known saints or martyrs.) Grosseteste's main thrust, however, seems to have been against May games and other forms of popular entertainment. A book entitled *Manuel des Pechiez* (c. 1300), by William of Wadington, translated into English verse by Robert Mannyng and entitled *Handlyng Synne* (1303), approved reverent religious drama and verse but condemned outdoor mysteries and miracles.

By the thirteenth century, few of the faithful understood Latin, so that the transition to the vernacular was natural and appropriate. The elaborate ceremonies made an outdoor presentation more appropriate than an indoor one, and some roles were more suited to secular actors than clerical. The development of a truly vernacular English theater was hampered in its early stages by the fact that many educated people spoke French, whereas English dialects were the language of ordinary people; by the late fourteenth or early fifteenth century, however, a vernacular tradition had been firmly established.

The first English mystery play extant is a thirteenth century dialogue called *The Harrowing of Hell*; inferior to similar contemporary French manuscripts, it is written in a rather primitive thirteenth century East Midland dialect. The play portrays a wily, bargaining Satan and ends with the overthrow of his power—a very popular theme in the liturgical drama of the Middle Ages. There are few records of English vernacular plays on the great Christmas and Easter cycles, but from the existing manuscripts one can infer that their development was similar to that of vernacular drama on the Continent. Records tell of an Easter play performed about 1220 outside a Beverley minster, in a churchyard, and even include details of a "miracle" strikingly similar to that described in Acts, chapter 20: A child who fell from a window while watching the play, it is alleged, was miraculously unhurt.

In the South of England, the Passion play was very popular in the fourteenth and fifteenth centuries, as it was in France. At Christmas in 1378, the minor clergy of Saint Paul's presented *The History of the Old Testament*; in 1384, a mystery play at Skinner's Well, lasting five days, told how "God created Heaven and Earth out of nothing, and how he created Adam and so on to the Day of Judgement." It is not known whether these plays were associated with the Corpus Christi and with the performances of the trade guilds. Records indicate that London had its Corpus Christi procession and that the guilds marched in order of preference.

The institution of the Corpus Christi procession in the second quarter of the fourteenth century had a great impact on the mystery plays. Another important factor was the so-called *Northern Passion*, a simple poem in Northern English, translated from French, that told the story of Christ's public life, Passion, death, and burial. It seems to have been very popular, particularly influencing the York-Towneley Cycle of plays. A poetic translation of the apocryphal *Gospel of Nicodemus* into Northern English was also very popular and influenced the various mystery plays. One of the best-known episodes is the Harrowing of Hell, present in almost every cycle and generally providing the occasion for the most dramatic creativity. In fact, such vernacular sources seem to have had greater influence on the English plays than did Latin documents.

The great English mystery plays were popular for about 250 years, from the beginning of the fourteenth until slightly after the middle of the sixteenth century. At first, the mysteries were little more than translations or paraphrases of the Latin liturgical dramas, written in simple meters or stanzas. Among the most popular verse forms were octosyllabic couplets and quatrains, not always regular in rhyme or in the number of metric feet to the line. Some plays, such as those in the Chester Cycle, use the eight-line ballad stanza. As the mystery plays developed, they increasingly deviated from the Latin originals, adding apocryphal, legendary, and folk characters, much like the plays on the Continent, as well as humorous and popular elements.

The most famous English mystery plays center on the celebration of the feast of Corpus Christi. The Corpus Christi cycle may have been established in Chester as early as 1327-1328, although according to Chambers and others, this date is questionable, because no further mention of the celebration occurs until about a century later. The pageants consisted of cycles of plays performed by the various guilds in competition with one another; each guild was assigned a play related to the craft or trade of its members, so that bakers performed the Last Supper at Beverley, Chester, and York; cooks performed the Harrowing of Hell (Beverley and Chester), supposedly because of their tolerance for fire; watermen reenacted the flood; and so on. Since this was an event which included the entire town, the plays were given outdoors, with the players and their scenes transported on wagons to a given station, in the street or the public square, where the audience assembled to view them.

Although the origin of such plays at the festival of Corpus Christi has provoked much controversy among scholars, it is generally acknowledged that they fit logically into this feast. As a celebration of the Eucharist, Corpus Christi points to the origin of liturgical drama in the ceremony of the Mass. Aside from symbolic considerations, late springtime was the logical season for such performances in England's damp, cold climate; indeed, the Corpus Christi cycles seem to have been a phenomenon of Northern Europe, while in Southern Europe such pageants were more likely to take place during Holy Week, culminating in Christ's Passion.

Although records of the Corpus Christi plays are plentiful, mainly from the documents and account books of the guilds, few cycles have been preserved completely. There are only four complete extant cycles: the Chester Cycle; the York Cycle, first mentioned in 1387, and which may be the oldest if the Chester date of 1327-1328 is not accurate; the Wakefield Cycle, of about 1425-1450; and the N-town Cycle (also known as the *Ludus Coventriae*), the origin of which has not been established. There are also fragments of cycles from Norwich, Newcastle upon Tyne, and Coventry. Independent plays, which have not been proved to be parts of the Corpus Christi cycle, include *Abraham and Isaac*, the Digby plays, a mid-fifteenth century *Burial and Resurrection* (preserved in Bodleian manuscript), and the fifteenth century Croxton *Play of the Sacrament*. From these plays, one can infer something of the scope and nature of religious drama in medieval England.

The city of Chester was independent and prosperous from the fourteenth to the sixteenth centuries. Its guilds showed pride in their successful business skills, yet they remained unspoiled by modernity. Accordingly, their plays remain among the simplest and the most religious of the period. The plays in the Chester Cycle were enacted in heavy vehicles which traveled from one station to another. There were twenty-four pageants in the series, and two sets of banns, or public announcements, of which only five are extant.

Among the surviving cycles, the Chester Cycle bears the greatest resemblance to the French mystery plays. *Abraham and Melchisedek*, though popular in the French plays, is found in England only in the Chester Cycle. *Octavian and the Sybil* also resembles the French plays. Other plays unique to the Chester Cycle are *The Woman Taken in Adultery*, *The Healing of the Blind Man at Siloam*, and *Christ in the House of Simon the Leper*. Although most of the plays show great fidelity to Scripture, the treatment of Lucifer in the first play of the cycle, like many other contemporary accounts, goes well beyond the biblical text. The fourth play of the cycle, *Abraham and Isaac*, is noteworthy for its dramatic development, while the seventh play, an Adoration of the Shepherds entitled *The Shepherds' Offering*, has a degree of complexity evident nowhere else in the cycles. The latter features a clownish figure, the shepherd Gartius, who, though introducing humor, does not interrupt the reverent atmosphere of the cycle. The plays on the ministry and the Passion of Christ are very different from the others in their simplicity and lack of adornment. The Chester plays persisted until after 1570 and are best preserved in a late sixteenth century manuscript.

The York and Wakefield Cycles are linked in various ways that suggest a special relationship not found between other cycles. They are both preserved in incomplete manuscripts, in the dialect of fifteenth century Yorkshire.

The manuscript of the York Cycle is clearer and gives a fuller picture of its place or origin. York was the center of the earliest British Christianity and the birthplace of Alcuin, who brought scholarship to Charlemagne's empire through his palace school. By 1415, the period of the city's greatest growth and expansion, York was large and rich, with numerous trading companies. The York manuscript contains forty-eight plays, all of them quite short, although there seem to have been fifty-one in the complete cycle, according to a list prepared and signed in 1415 by Roger Burton, city clerk of York; a later list includes fifty-seven plays. Documents from 1399 and 1417 refer to twelve playing places, although later there were sixteen; there are many records of the plays among the regulations of the municipality. The York Cycle enjoyed a long and celebrated history: As early as 1397, King Richard I visited York to witness the plays, and they had their last performance as late as 1584.

The York Cycle has led scholars to conjecture a precyclic state of the Old Testament plays, probably without the influence of a previous Passion play. Thirteen of the York plays—the group from the Conspiracy to the Burial—are written in alliterative verse. These are excellent works, probably composed by one author of great talent. As at Chester, there were significant revisions among the various plays during their long performance history; some of the York plays were borrowed directly by Wakefield.

The Wakefield plays are known through a single manuscript that fell into the possession of John Towneley by the early nineteenth century; hence, they are also called the Towneley plays. The manuscript contains thirty-two plays which were performed by craft guilds at Wakefield, although no Wakefield records tell of such pageants. Critics hypothesize that the York plays were taken over by Wakefield at a given stage of development, after which the two cycles evolved independently of each other, since six of the plays which the cycles have in common are almost identical while thirteen of the plays which they have in common were revised at York but not at Wakefield. The York sponsors probably supplied the wagons to Wakefield after the merger of the plays. Four Wakefield plays—Isaac, Jacob, *Prophetae*, and Octavian—do not appear in the York Cycle. Several plays from the Wakefield Cycle, including those depicting Paradise, the events immediately following the Resurrection, Pentecost, and *The Assumption and Coronation of the Virgin*, have not survived.

The most significant aspect of the cycle is the work of the so-called Wakefield Master (c. 1420-c. 1450), unique in Middle English, with his clever, complicated style and wit. He uses many local allusions and colloquial idioms and adapts secular material for comic purposes. Along with the well-known *The Second Shepherds' Play*, this anonymous dramatist was the author of *The Killing of Abel*, *Noah*, *Herod the Great*, and *The Buffeting*. The Wakefield Cycle is unique in its presentation of two shepherds' plays, the second of which, as noted above, is one of the most popular of all medieval plays. *The Second Shepherds' Play* combines the liturgical *Officium Pastorum* with a folktale of a pseudo-Nativity. Mak steals a sheep from three shepherds and hides it in the cradle prepared for the child that he and his wife are expecting. When the suspicious shepherds come to find their stolen sheep, Mak and his wife claim that their newborn child is in the cradle and refuse to allow the shepherds to enter. The play shifts from witty farce to serious drama as the angels announce the birth of Christ and the shepherds go to adore him. It is not known what guild performed this play, but Wakefield was the center of a prosperous wool industry in the fifteenth century, which probably accounts for the popularity of the shepherd theme.

The last complete cycle is preserved in what is known as the Hegge manuscript, Cotton Vespasian D. VIII. Since the town to which it refers has not been identified (it had been erroneously ascribed to Coventry), the cycle is often referred to as N-town, taken from the banns (that is, the official proclamation listing the plays and their subjects) that accompany it. Many scholars believe that this cycle was performed by touring players, since there is nothing to associate it with the guilds. The banns indicate thirty-nine plays, constituting a complete Corpus Christi cycle. The N-town Cycle is notable for its strong Marian orientation; for this reason, as well as because of its dialect, Hardin Craig, Chambers, and several other critics assign the cycle to Lincoln. Lincoln was a cathedral city—at the time, one of the largest in England—with a collegiate establishment and a center of ecclesiastical study. It was a center of Marian devotion, with special honor paid to Saint Anne, the mother of the Virgin Mary, as early as 1383. (Indeed, Craig associates the N-town plays with Saint Anne's Day, July 26, rather than Corpus Christi.) Lincoln also seems to have been a center of ecclesiastical drama for many years; Robert Grosseteste was Bishop of Lincoln when he denounced abuses in Church plays.

Since the banns do not agree with the existing plays, it is supposed that considerable revision occurred. At the heart of the cycle are quatrains of four feet, although some plays use the ballad-type stanza, characteristic of the Chester plays. The plays with a Marian orientation include *The Barrenness of Anna*, *The Presentation of Mary in the Temple*, *The Betrothal of Mary*, *The Salutation and Conception*, and *Mary's Visit to Elizabeth*. There is also a complete Passion cycle in two parts—introduced, as in the Marian cycle, by a special prologue called *Contemplacio*. The most conspicuous play of the N-town Cycle is a very elaborate one on the Assumption, full of great learning and theology and based in part on the popular *Legenda Aurea* (Golden Legend). On the whole, the plays of this cycle differ from those of the York and Chester Cycles in their unity, in their learned quality, and in their greater use of liturgical Latin.

Other towns had elaborate Corpus Christi plays, which were known mainly from records rather than the plays, for with the exception of the four cycles discussed above, only fragments remain. The most important are the Coventry plays; they were so popular that the term "Coventry play" became synonymous with a Corpus Christi play. The number of participating guilds at Coventry seems to have been smaller than elsewhere. There is no evidence of Old Testament subjects, although Craig insists that they must have existed. There are only two surviving plays: the Shearmen and Taylors' play and the Weavers' play. The first shows the tendency of the Coventry plays to combine many topics into one play, for it comprises a prologue by Isaiah, an Annunciation, a Doubt of Joseph, a Journey to Bethlehem, a Nativity, a Visit of the Shepherds, a Herod and the Magi, a Visit of the Magi, and a Slaughter of the Innocents. Craig connects this play with the shearers because their guild seal shows Jesus in the arms of Mary receiving the gifts of the Magi. The Weavers' Pageant is the scene of Christ's Disputation with the Doctors and contains elements linking it to plays in the other cycles. In general, the Coventry plays are very simple, close to the Latin originals, and free from comedy. They maintain the reverent tone of the liturgical dramas, yet they constitute the least learned of the cycles. They exhibit little clerical influence, revealing the simplicity and naïve religious faith of the people.

A very important fragment comes from the Digby manuscripts, which are of uncertain origin and authorship. This fragment contains four plays: *The Conversion of Saint Paul*, a Mary Magdalen play, a Slaughter of the Innocents and Purification, and a morality play known as *Mind, Will, and Understanding*. They seem never to have been parts of a Corpus Christi Cycle, but rather of smaller cycles, belonging perhaps to the East Midlands. *The Conversion of Saint Paul*, probably destined for an outdoor performance in a small town, is rather verbose and pompous. The Mary Magdalen play is the most ambitious of all surviving English mystery plays; it was probably enacted on a circular stationary stage, with spectators viewing it from all sides. It also has a sensational and widely extended course of action, which calls for a great many scenes and seems to suggest a very extravagant performance. The play borrows allegorical figures from the morality and *Paternoster* plays—namely, the Seven Deadly Sins—and thus may have been a transitional work.

While the importance of mystery plays in medieval English drama is well documented, the place of miracle plays is less certain. Some scholars argue that miracle plays in England were related to folk plays centering on Saint George, which belong more properly to the comic theater. There are more records of miracle plays in Scotland than in England, particularly on obscure saints and topics. Because so few plays have survived, there is no conclusive study of miracle plays in English, and critical theories concerning the genre must rely on conjecture.

One of the earliest recorded miracle plays is a life of Saint Catherine. It was written by 1119, by a Frenchman, Geoffrey de Gorham, who, before becoming Abbot of Saint Albans, settled at Dunstable, where he composed the play. Unfortunately, the manuscript was lost in a fire. English scholars include the dramas of Hilarius, an Englishman, in their history of the miracle play, since he wrote the semiliturgical plays *Suscitatio Lazari* (the raising of Lazarus), *Daniel*, and *Saint Nicholas* (c. 1120-1130). These works are in Latin and French and were probably performed for French audiences. From the life of Saint Thomas à Beckett, it is clear that miracles based on the lives of confessors (that is, believers who gave heroic evidence of their faith but were not obliged to suffer martyrdom) were performed in London in the twelfth century. References to lost mid-fifteenth century miracles include a Saint Laurence and a Saint Susannah, both of Lincoln; a Saint Dionysius from York; a Saint Clara at Lincoln; and a Saint George at Kent. In the early sixteenth century, plays of Saint Swithin, Saint Andrew, and Saint Eustace were acted in Braintree, Essex; nothing, however, is known concerning the content of these works.

The only surviving example in English of a full-fledged miracle play is the Croxton *Play of the Sacrament*, found in Trinity College, Dublin, in the latter half of the fifteenth century, although it seems to have originated in Suffolk. The play resembles a French miracle, *La Sainte Hostie*; indeed, its anti-Semitic treatment of the central character, a Jewish merchant, had its counterparts in medieval drama throughout Western Europe. *Dux Moraud* (c. 1300-1325) is a fragment which contains the part of one actor only; it tells the story of an incestuous daughter who kills her mother and her child, born of her union with her father, and then tries to kill the father, who miraculously repents on his deathbed. On the whole it is similar to the French miracles of the Virgin, although she is not mentioned here.

One of the most important forms of medieval English drama was the morality play (or morality), a kind of dramatic allegory in which personified vices (such as Sloth and Envy) contend with personified virtues (such as Perseverance and Mercy) for man's soul. In addition to the vices and virtues, other personified abstractions (most notably, Death) enter the fray. The recurring theme of the English morality plays is the certainty of death and the desire of human beings to justify themselves before God. Moralities have a serious tone and were often performed in church, in the manner of liturgical plays, with appropriate costumes. The character representing Death was robed as a skeleton, and there was usually a dramatic spectacle in which the Dance of Death was played. There was a door or sepulcher into which the victims of Death disappeared, and a pulpit from which the priest admonished the congregation.

The Castle of Perseverance (c. 1440) is one of the earliest extant moralities, as well as one of the most extensive and learned. It follows Mankind (Humanum Genus) from infancy to old age. The World, the Flesh, and the Devil proclaim their intention to destroy him, and in his youth they tempt him, along with the Seven Deadly Sins. At the age of forty, he takes refuge in the Castle of Perseverance, but, after a raging battle, he is overcome by Covetousness. His old age is given to ill-humor and hoarding, and by the time Death claims him, Mankind has been deserted by all of his friends. In Heaven, Justice and Truth debate his fate with Peace and Mercy. God awards the judgment to the latter, and Mankind is admitted to Heaven.

The two most inspiring moralities on the theme of death are *Everyman* and *The Pride of Life*. The latter was found in a Dublin manuscript copied in the fifteenth century but thought to be much earlier in origin. It is the story of the King of Life, who defies Death and calls in both Health and Strength to aid him in the combat. Death wins, but the intervention of the Virgin saves the King of Life from eternal destruction. The play ends with a debate between the Body and the Soul. Although the play contains some references to the idea of personal sin, it recalls the motif of the Dance of Death in its portrayal of Death as the impersonal victor over all.

The best known of all medieval moralities is *Everyman*. Although it is dated from the early sixteenth century, it may have appeared much earlier. It closely resembles the Flemish *Elckerlijk*, first printed in 1495, and it is debatable which is the earlier; one may be a translation of the other. The play is remarkable for its classical simplicity and the concreteness of its allegorical characters. It begins with God, weary of human offenses, summoning Death to bring him the soul of Everyman. Everyman is surprised by Death's arrival and asks for time to find a companion for the journey. He first addresses Fellowship, who is interested in the adventure but turns back when he discovers the nature of the trip; Kindred does the same. Good Deeds wants to come along but cannot stand, weighed down by the heaviness of Everyman's sins. Knowledge then leads Everyman to Confession and Repentance, after which Good Deeds is able to accompany him.

Beauty, Strength, Discretion, and Five Wits accompany him to the grave, where they all bid him farewell, and he commends his soul to God as Good Deeds promises to speak for him.

After 1500, very few new moralities appeared. The best known of these are *Mundus et Infans*, or *The World and the Child* (c. 1508-1522), a compressed life-cycle play dealing with the Seven Ages of Man; *Hickscorner*, or *Hick Scorner* (c. 1513), important because it was the first morality to use a comic figure for its principal character; and *Youth* (c. 1513), resembling *Hickscorner* but limited to the problems of youth. After this, most moralities passed into the genre known as the interlude (discussed below).

Although most English plays seem to have had their origin on the Continent, especially in France, it appears that the English morality was unique in introducing the theme of death. Moralities developed into many other dramatic forms, such as the *sottie* in France, and in England exerted great influence on the Tudor drama.

Closely related to moralities are the *Paternoster* plays. The earliest reference to this genre dates from the third quarter of the fourteenth century: John Wycliffe speaks of *Paternoster* plays at York and elsewhere. In 1399, the *Paternoster* Guild of York performed a *Ludum Accidie*, or play on Sloth. From the records at Beverley, it is evident that all seven sins were presented in eight pageants, which were given at stations in the city. The *Paternoster* plays at York spanned two centuries, from the late fourteenth century to 1572, while there are records of eight performances at Lincoln during the period from 1397-1398 to 1521-1522. Unfortunately, all of these texts are lost, and conjecture concerning the genre must rely on contemporary descriptions of the plays and on the extant Mary Magdalen play (mentioned above), dating from the last half of the fifteenth century, in which there are elements of the *Paternoster* plays. Related to the *Paternoster* plays is the Creed play, which was performed at York every ten years around August 1, from about 1446, and perhaps persisting into the sixteenth century. The text of this play, unfortunately, is also lost.

Comedy

While the development of liturgical drama can be traced in some detail, the origin of comedy in medieval Europe is much more difficult to document with any certainty. Comedy was popular in the ancient world, and although there is no record of dramatic performances in the early Middle Ages, the institutions of minstrels, *ioculatores*, and *histriones* kept the comic spirit alive. That the comic tradition survived is evident from the many clerical pronouncements against it. As early as A.D. 679, the English clergy was admonished by the Council of Rome that the practice of maintaining musicians and of countenancing *iocos vel ludos* should be discontinued. In the ninth century, King Edgar chided the monks for taking part in mimes and dancing in the streets.

Among the folk customs associated with comedy is the Feast of Fools, which was celebrated around January 1. This feast was especially popular in France toward the end of the twelfth century, where a *Missel des Fous*, in Sens, dates from the thirteenth century and contains the well-known parody *Prose of the Ass*. The Feast of Fools provoked clerical interdictions throughout the Continent; in England, where this feast was least prevalent, it seems to have been strongest in Lincoln and Beverley. It was condemned by Robert Grosseteste in 1236 and, much later, by William of Courtney, Archbishop of Canterbury, who found the custom still alive in Lincoln in 1390. The custom of naming an *archiepiscopus puerorum*, or Boy Bishop, observed around the feast of the Holy Innocents, December 28, was extremely popular in England. The first mention of the custom is in an inventory of a church in Salisbury, in 1222, which calls for a ring for the Boy Bishop. Surviving accounts indicate that the ceremony was quite elaborate: The arrival of the Boy Bishop at court was accompanied by carols, New Year's gifts, jousts, tournaments, and, in the fourteenth century, by *ludi* or *larvae*, for which the common name was mummings.

Mummings were first mentioned in 1377, in a Stowe manuscript. Mummings, which were played at Christmas time and involved much gaity and pageantry, were originally dumb shows in which players, disguised as emperor, pope, knight, and so on, arrived on horseback, invited notables to a game of dice, and, at the end of the game (which the notables always won), accepted refreshments and performed dances. The first known author to employ dramatic effects in mummings was John Lydgate, a monk of the cultural center of Bury St. Edmunds: His *Mumming at Hertford* (1427-1430) involved the king himself in the action and included dialogue.

Other folk festivals which may have given rise to comedy include May Day, associated with Robin Hood plays, and Plough Monday, the Monday after Twelfth Night, which gave rise to the Saint George plays. Robin Hood is mentioned in William Langland's *The Vision of William, Concerning Piers the Plowman* (1362, c. 1377, c. 1395); the first extant ballad on this theme, *A Lytell Geste of Robyn Hoode*, dates from 1500, while the earliest Robin Hood play dates from 1475. Entitled *Robin Hood and the Sheriff of Nottingham*, it may be the play referred to in Sir John Paston's letter of 1473, in which he speaks of an unruly servant whom he kept with him to play Robin Hood and Saint George.

The Saint George plays were performed throughout England, Wales, Ireland, and Scotland, sometimes with another saint or hero but always with the same basic story. The first act is a prologue; the second act features a fight, in which George (Saint or Prince) is killed; and in the third and final act, the slain hero is revived by a doctor. The play's central action is the fight and resurrection, and the doctor is a comic figure. Ridings (or processions) were also added to the celebration. The fullest account of these plays comes from the Norwich riding, established by 1408. In 1537, the character of Saint Margaret was added to the story. The Saint George Guild survived the Reformation, and dumb shows, ridings, and pageants on the Saint George theme continued to be performed long afterward.

The earliest piece of English comedy is known as the Cambridge prologue, dated not later than 1300. A fragment, it consists of twenty-two lines of French followed by twenty-two lines of English, presenting a request for silence made by the herald of a pagan emperor who swears by "Mahum" (Mahomet). The Rickinghall fragment, from the late thirteenth or early fourteenth century, tells of a boastful king who summons his nobles into his presence; it consists of two stanzas of French followed by nine lines of English. A farcial dialogue of the *fabliau* type, *Interludium de Clerico et Puella*, dating from the end of the thirteenth century features a procuress named Eloise, suggesting an Anglo-Norman origin. *Dame Sirith*, also of the thirteenth century, is the only surviving Middle English *fabliau* outside of Geoffrey Chaucer's work. It tells how a reluctant girl, Margeri, is persuaded to accept the advances of the clerk Wilicken through a coarse folk motif known as the "weeping bitch." The use of English so early suggests a popular audience.

The farce as such is not a form indigenous to English comedy; like many other forms in English literature, the farce developed from French models. *Maître Pathelin* (pr. 1485) was well-known in England by 1535, and French actors had visited England in 1494 and 1495. Six "Minstrels of France" came to England in 1509, and it is supposed that they produced some of their farces in England.

The first English playwright who made extensive use of the element of farce was John Heywood, who believed that drama was intended to entertain and not to teach. He did not have a highly developed dramatic technique, but he excelled at farce; his *The Play of the Weather* (pb. 1533), though cast in the style of a morality in the character of Merry Report, a humorous vice, is actually a pleasing comedy. Jupiter sends Merry Report to several people to learn their preferences about the weather. They all differ, so he decides that things shall remain as they are, and all will have their turns. Heywood's most important comedy is *Johan Johan* (pb. 1533), which has no connection with any religious play. The French original for this farce, *Farce nouvelle et fort joyeuse du pasté*, was discovered only in 1949. The story concerns a jealous husband, Johan, who intends to beat his wife, Tyb, because she is visiting Sir John too long and too often. Tyb dupes her husband into inviting the priest, and when Sir John arrives, Tyb sends her husband to fetch water in a pail with a hole in it. When he finally returns, he interrupts their lovemaking, only to be sent away to mend the pail. At the end of his patience, he finally pursues the fleeing priest and Tyb. Other plays by Heywood include *The Pardoner and the Friar* (pb. 1533), *The Four P.P.* (pb. 1541-1547), and *Witty and Witless* (pb. 1846, abridged; pb. 1909).

The study of the Latin classics during the Renaissance introduced Plautus and Terence into the curriculum beginning about 1510. Original Latin and French plays were often performed in schools and universities, beginning with *Miles Gloriosus* in 1522. Schoolmasters frequently wrote imitations and adaptations for their students. One of the best of these was done by Nicholas Udall, when he was headmaster at Eaton. Udall's *Ralph Roister Doister* (pr. c. 1522), the first of the Roman-type comedies, tells with considerable wit the classic story of the braggart and the parasite. *Gammer Gurton's Needle* (pr. 1562?), by "W. S." (William Stevenson?), is also among the best of the plays written for the schools and universities; it is distinguished by a perfect accommodation of the academic to the popular.

Like the serious theater, comedy was indebted to Italian sources. George Gascoigne's *Supposes*, a well-shaped comedy of intrigue, is the best example of this type. Primarily a translation from Ludovico Ariosto's *I Suppositi*, it was first performed at Gray's Inn in 1566. Romantic comedy was popular in the decade from 1570 to 1580. The subjects were taken mostly from chivalry and Arthurian romances. Unfortunately, few of these plays have survived, though their loss is to be regretted more by the literary historians than by theatergoers. It seems that the children's companies preferred to enact plays from classical history and legend, whereas the romantic comedies were usually played by adult troupes.

Comic elements are present in many serious dramas of the sixteenth century, and the distinction between genres is frequently blurred. The influence of the morality continued to dominate, and even Heywood's farces, except *Johan Johan* and *The Pardoner and the Friar*, end with a lesson. It is therefore difficult to isolate a comic genre at this time. Even in the Middle Ages, religious drama had its comic elements, as in *The Second Shepherds' Play* by the Wakefield Master. By the end of the sixteenth century, elements of the medieval farce, though not absent, were subordinated to classical characteristics, if not themes, and the stage was set for the Elizabethan drama.

Interludes and the Tudor Drama

As the thirteenth century witnessed the development of the vernacular theater from the liturgical Latin plays, so the sixteenth witnessed a similar change. Plays moved outdoors in the thirteenth century to accommodate broader spectacle and secular actors. At the end of the fifteenth century, and particularly during the sixteenth, English plays moved back indoors— to the Court, to the Great Hall of Palaces, to the Inns of Court, and to schools and universities. Acting became a specialized profession, with companies of men, usually four in number, and boys, generally from ten to twelve in a troupe, performing plays expressly written for their company. Since the companies were relatively small, parts were often doubled. The most famous early company of adult actors was the Court Interluders, which existed from 1493 to 1559. Among the prominent boys' groups were Paul's Boys, from the choir school of St. Paul's Cathedral, and the Children of Windsor. The division between professional and amateur was not absolute, nor was the distinction between men's and boys' companies, since a given troupe sometimes included both.

Plays performed in this context—indoors, to cultivated audiences, often by professional actors—were known as interludes. These plays, generally short and featuring only a few characters, may have begun as short pieces between the acts of religious dramas, but by the sixteenth century they had developed into an independent genre with its own distinctive conventions. Thus, the interludes provided a transition between the religious drama of the Middle Ages and the full flowering of secular drama in the Elizabethan theater.

The development of interludes was influenced by mummings and similar genres and by the elaborate pageants for the Tudor court. The first mention of a proto-interlude comes from Thomas de Cabham, who died in 1313. Other early forms of the interlude include John Lydgate's *Mumming at Hertford* (1427-1430), performed as part of the Christmas entertainment for the king, and Benedict Burgh's *A Christmas Game* (late fifteenth century), a solemn work comprising twelve stanzas addressed by a presenter to the Apostles.

The first important writer of interludes was Henry Medwall, whose *Nature* dates from about 1500. Medwall was chaplain to John Morton, Cardinal Archbishop of Canterbury, and was of the household of Sir Thomas More. Medwall's sister, Elizabeth, married John Rastell (1475?-1536), a lawyer, printer, and playwright. Their daughter, Medwall's niece, Elizabeth Rastell, married John Heywood, whose plays were printed by William Rastell, Elizabeth's brother. Finally, Heywood's daughter married the poet John Donne. This illustrious family was to play a leading role in English dramatic history in the sixteenth century. Medwall's *Nature* (pr. c. 1500), despite its lofty morality theme of sensuality as unreason, contains much comedy, seasoned with tavern talk and allusions to contemporary London. It is for *Fulgens and Lucrece* (pr. c. 1497), that Medwall is best known. This interlude had the distinction of being the first purely secular drama in English; in the style of a *débat*, it deals with the question of nobility of lineage versus nobility of soul.

Medwall's brother-in-law, John Rastell, is also noted for a nature interlude, *The Nature of the Four Elements* (pr. c. 1517), the only play ascribed with certainty to him. Not unlike Medwall's play, this one depicts humanity as struggling between Studious Desire and Sensual Appetite. Rastell also has his hero listening to lectures on astronomy and geography; these lectures are given by Experience, a great traveler who speaks of newfound lands. *The Nature of the Four Elements* was the first English work to name America and the earliest printed attempt to teach astronomy in the vernacular. *Calisto and Meliboea* (pr. c. 1527) is often ascribed to Rastell, and certainly was printed by him. Called "a new comedy in English in the manner of an interlude," it was the first English work to call itself a comedy. *Calisto and Meliboea* is based on the Spanish novel *La Celestina* (c. 1502) and concludes a seduction story with the heroine's repentance, including the lustful details preceding it.

As noted above, John Heywood's interludes, especially *Johan Johan*, belong more properly to farce and the comic theater. John Redford's interlude *Wit and Science* (pr. c. 1530-1547), written for the acting company Paul's Boys, is an allegory of the undergraduate life. Wyt woos Miss Science, the daughter of Dr. Reason and his wife, Experience, yet falls into many errors before he finally achieves his goal. This play, one of the purest allegories among the interludes, is also among the wittiest; it has very good speakable parts and is still performed today. The same theme is repeated in the anonymous *The Marriage of Wit and Science* (pr. c. 1568), although with less brilliance.

One of the most notable interludes of this period is John Skelton's *Magnificence* (pr. 1516), a morality with the familiar Renaissance theme of moderation. Potter sees the originality of this play in the way that Skelton uses linguistic devices, such as alliteration, repetition, and long lists of names, to illustrate lack of measure. The play is said to have addressed the lack of measure in contemporary events, especially the growing power of Cardinal Wolsey and the extravagance of King Henry VIII.

One of the most important factors in the changing character of sixteenth century drama was the Reformation. Writers began to use the theater as a tool for propaganda purposes, to which the morality and the interlude were well suited. At the same time, the government worked to eliminate religious drama—especially the miracle plays, because of their association with the Roman Catholic Church. Moralities survived better than mysteries. The first steps in this direction were taken under Henry VIII in 1543, although some of the mystery cycles had ceased to be performed even before this time. In 1547, Edward VI repealed Henry's statute and allowed moralities to be performed, but Corpus Christi was suppressed as a feast of the English Church in 1548, thus dealing a death blow to the famous mystery cycles. Elizabeth made no effort to root out the plays, but local authorities did. Although there are records of mysteries in extreme northwestern counties as late as 1612, by the end of the third quarter of the sixteenth century, the Corpus Christi play was no longer the center of theatrical activities.

Moral interludes at first took up the Protestant cause. The most zealous Reformation writer was John Bale. In the 1530's he wrote a cycle of plays based on the life of Christ, anti-Catholic moralities, and anti-Catholic history plays. Only five of his twenty-odd plays have survived. *Three Laws* is the first Protestant morality, as well as the first play divided into five acts. The plays on the life of Christ are devoid of all imagination in an attempt to follow Scripture exactly, and thus they lack the charm that made the mystery plays so attractive. Bale's best play is the historical drama *King Johan*. Johan (John) becomes an idealized Christian hero, the noble champion of an England widowed of her husband, God, by false religions. *King Johan* is original in the choice of a historical theme for political morality.

Among other Protestant moralities and interludes, less vehement than Bale's, one of the most notable is David Lindsay's *A Pleasant Satire of the Three Estates* (pr. 1540), an excellent example of Scottish drama. The character of John o' the Commonweal approaches the memorable creations of Elizabethan and Jacobean comedy. Richard Wever's *Lusty Juventus* (wr. 1550) treats the popular prodigal son theme, which is also found in Thomas Ingelund's *The Disobedient Child* (wr. 1560) and Gascoigne's *The Glasse of Governement* (pb. 1575). This theme probably came from German sources; in the Protestant moralities, indoctrination rather than education of youth becomes uppermost. The only extant Catholic morality is the anonymous *Respublica* (wr. 1553). Since the counterattack is less vehement than the anti-Catholicism that prompted it, *Respublica* is superior to most plays in the genre, with widely differentiated characters in contemporary society and witty comic elements.

While the discovery of Plautus and Terence marked the interlude with a comic thrust, the Renaissance interest in Seneca turned serious drama away from the religious themes to secular and even tragic ones. In 1559, 1560, and 1561, Seneca's tragedies appeared in Jasper Heywood's translations, and the first notable product of the Senecan influence was also the only example of strict classical tragedy in Tudor England: Thomas Norton and Thomas Sackville's *Gorboduc* (pr. 1561; also as *The Tragedy of Ferrex and Porrex*). The play is divided into five acts and into scenes within the acts. There is absolutely no comedy, and all the principal protagonists are killed. Following the morality tradition, the play becomes an apology for the divine right of kings. This type of drama, however, did not prevail in England; more influential was a mixture of tragedy and comedy.

The first play in the tragicomic vein was Richard Edwards' *Damon and Pithias* (pr. 1564), performed at Elizabeth's court by the boys of the Chapel Royal. Edwards' prologue is the first statement of dramatic principles in English. The play has classical sources both in comedy and in tragedy; at the same time, it includes references to its contemporary audience. Not totally emancipated from the morality tradition, court tragicomedies maintained a Vice character; they also regularly featured king and counselor scenes and episodes of conflict and violence. Another typical play of this type is John Pickering's *A New Interlude of Vice, Containing the History of Horestes* (pb. 1567), wherein the Vice character is Revenge disguised as Courage.

The court tragicomedy was generally characterized by lengthy scenes and melodrama. Thomas Preston's *Cambises*, played at court during the Christmas season of 1560-1561, is a typical example. Based on Herodotus, with many accretions along the way, it features a Vice character, Ambidexter, who is both a double-dealer and a slapstick clown. "R. B." (probably Richard Bower), the author of *Apius and Virginia* (pr. 1567), presented an idealized melodrama of a seduction scene and a father who kills his daughter to save her honor. The Italian influence, along with the classical, was strong in such plays, as in Robert Wilmot's *Gismond of Salerne* (pr. 1565), based on Giovanni Boccaccio's *Decameron*, a fine play that is stageable even in modern times.

Although none of these plays is great, they represent certain important tendencies. One is the allegorical legacy of the moralities, which profoundly influenced William Shakespeare. Another is the fusion of genres, tragedy and comedy, which was to characterize mature English drama, in contrast to the strict separation of comedy and tragedy in the French theater. Finally, these plays point to the almost complete secularization of drama, which made possible a fully developed national theater.

Irma M. Kashuba

ELIZABETHAN AND JACOBEAN DRAMA

The rich intellectual life in England during the late sixteenth and early seventeenth centuries is reflected in literary works of the period. The Renaissance, with its accompanying movements, the new Humanism and the Reformation, brought with it a consciousness of artistic beauty and a love of learning little known since the days of classical Greece and Rome. From the days of Geoffrey Chaucer (c. 1343-1400), poetry bloomed in this favorable climate—a poetry different in mood and subject from that of the earlier medieval poets. Prose fiction, too, took tentative steps toward the novel as the stories people had to tell began to expand beyond the boundaries of rhyme and meter, but it was drama which overshadowed all other literary forms from the beginning to the end of the Renaissance.

The rebirth of arts and learning which came to England during the Renaissance brought with it the great drama of classical Greece and Rome. The guidance of Aristotle and the models of Sophocles, Aristophanes, Seneca, Plautus, Terence, and others brought to the Renaissance Englishman a view of humankind, of the world, and of human beings' relationship with the world in many respects different from the medieval view. Long before the introduction of classical drama into England, the citizens of cities and villages were acquainted with drama associated with the Church. The transition from native English mystery, morality, and folk plays to what is generally called "regular" English drama came about slowly from approximately the middle of the sixteenth century. The happy marriage of classical and native English drama gave birth to a hybrid type of literature.

Classical influence was strong during the Renaissance. In the early sixteenth century, Seneca's tragedies were translated into English and served as a model for regular English tragedy. The five-act structure; the observance of the unities of time, place, and action; the emphasis upon character; and the use of the ghost were Senecan devices employed by English Renaissance writers of tragedy. For comedy, the works of the Roman dramatists Plautus and Terence, with their clear plot development, wit, use of proverbs, and natural dialogue, served as models. Elizabethan dramatists adopted the five-act structure almost completely, but they did not slavishly follow classical models in observing the dramatic unities. Native English settings and humor remained dominant in drama, but they were regularized and modified somewhat by the classical models.

The Period of Transition

The period from about 1550 to 1580 may be thought of as a period of transition from mystery, morality, folk plays, and interludes to regular English drama. Classical influence was strong during this period, because those scholars who were writing and producing the plays were the same scholars who had introduced the literary works of classical Greece and Rome into England. Nicholas Udall, for example, who wrote the first regular English comedy, *Ralph Roister Doister* (pr. c. 1552), was an Oxford scholar and headmaster at Eton who studied and translated Terence. Seneca's tragedies had been translated into English by 1580 and served as an example for English tragedy.

One can see in *Jack Juggler* (pr. c. 1553-1558), perhaps by Udall, an excellent example of how Plautus was used in an English setting. The English dramatist takes the opening scene of Plautus' *Amphitruo* (186 B.C.) and transforms it into London farce. *Jack Juggler*, however, is not a full comedy, only an interlude. Not until *Ralph Roister Doister* does one see a full English comedy composed according to the classical rules. It is divided into acts and scenes and has a consistent plot with a beginning, middle, and end. The characters Ralph Roister Doister and Matthew Merrygreek are patterned after the Roman *miles gloriosus* and parasite respectively. While the pattern is classical, the setting is English. The play depicts middle-class life in London, with Dame Christian Custance and her English servants replacing the Roman courtesan and her entourage.

Another English comedy of this period is *Gammer Gurton's Needle* (pr. 1562?), probably by the Cambridge scholar William Stevenson. Like *Ralph Roister Doister*, *Gammer Gurton's Needle* is divided into acts and scenes and has a well-conceived, complex plot in the classical manner, but while the pattern is classical, the substance of the play is native English. Even Diccon, the most Roman of the characters, reminiscent of the intriguing slave of Roman comedy, is transformed into a distinctively English character. Whereas the setting of *Ralph Roister Doister* is urban, *Gammer Gurton's Needle* is set in a village. The dialogue, full of dialect and earthy language, helps to make the play more realistically English than any other early regular English drama. Its author was clearly a scholar of Roman comedy, but he was writing about and for English people.

One of the better Italian adaptations of Plautus and Terence, Ludovico Ariosto's *I Suppositi* (1509), was translated into English as *Supposes* and presented at Gray's Inn by George Gascoigne in 1566. Best known as a source for William Shakespeare's Lucentio-Bianca plot in *The Taming of the Shrew* (pr. c. 1593-1594), Gascoigne's translation is also important for having made available in English a comedy which, while modeled upon the major Roman comedy writers, eliminated the classical characters of the slave, courtesan, and pander and built the plot around a love story, as though the inspiration for the play were more from Giovanni Boccaccio or Chaucer than from Plautus or Terence.

The influence of classical tragedy can also be seen in early sixteenth century England. *Gorboduc* (pr. 1561; also as *The Tragedy of Ferrex and Porrex*, pb. 1570), by Thomas Norton (1532-1584) and Thomas Sackville

(1536-1608), the first regular English tragedy, is directly modeled on Senecan tragedy. It has five acts, observes the unities, avoids comic situations, and employs a chorus. Violence, and indeed almost all the action, takes place offstage, as in classical models, but even here the theme is English, not Greek or Roman. The play's didactic purpose is to warn Queen Elizabeth of the dangers of leaving the kingdom without an heir to rule. Taking as its plot the story from legendary British history of old King Gorboduc, who, like the legendary King Lear, divided the kingdom between his two offspring, the play would presumably offer the potential for exciting stage action involving murder, intrigue, revenge, revolution, and love. In fact, little occurs onstage except long reports of offstage action, inexplicable dumb shows, and almost endless, dull speeches. Although the play may strike the modern reader as tedious, its historical importance cannot be overstated. Not only does *Gorboduc* set the form for later Renaissance tragedy, but also, and more important, the play is written in blank verse, a meter introduced into English some few years earlier by Henry Howard, Earl of Surrey. The meter was used with good results by Thomas Kyd, refined by Christopher Marlowe into the "mighty line," and immortalized by Shakespeare.

Other adaptations of classical tragedy in English include *Jocasta* (pr. 1566) and *The Misfortunes of Arthur* (1593). *Jocasta* is a tragedy in blank verse in the Senecan style, adapted by George Gascoigne and Francis Kinwelmershe from Lodovico Dolce's *Giocasta* (1549), an Italian version of a Euripidean tragedy; *Jocasta* offered nothing new to English tragedy. The same can be said of *The Misfortunes of Arthur* (pr. 1588), by Thomas Hughes, also written in blank verse and exhibiting a marked Senecan influence. Hughes based his plot on ancient British legends from Geoffrey of Monmouth and Sir Thomas Mallory.

Another type of play introduced during the period of transition is the chronicle history play. The plays in this category drew their subject matter, as did much of the prose and both folk and street ballads of the period, from the English chronicles. John Bale's *King Johan* (wr. 1531?) showed future dramatists the way to move from morality plays to more modern ideological history plays. The play features such allegorical characters as Sedition, Dissimulation, Private Wealth, and Usurped Power, conspirators against the righteous monarch, Johan. The allegorical character Imperial Majesty (representing the Protestant monarch Henry VIII) finally sets things right. *Richardus Tertius* (pr. 1579), by Thomas Legge, although a Latin play, is noteworthy as a transitional play because it uses recent English history. *The Famous Victories of Henry V* (pr. c. 1588) also uses recent national history as its subject. It neglects classical models almost completely, patterning its form more on the medieval miracle play. It is the earliest example of a play based upon a popular rather than a scholarly view of history. In introducing Sir John Oldcastle (the prototype of Shakespeare's Sir John Falstaff) and many episodes involving Prince Hal in his madcap days, the anonymous playwright provided in rough form the material Shakespeare was later to use in creating his famous political plays involving Henry IV and Henry V.

Other chronicle history plays which may be called transitional in the sense that they showed the way for later, better representatives of the type are *The Troublesome Raigne of John King of England* (pr. c. 1591), *King Leir and His Three Daughters* (pr. c. 1594), *The Lamentable Tragedy of Locrine* (pb. 1595), and *The First Part of the Tragical Raigne of Selimus* (pr. 1594). *The Troublesome Raigne of John King of England*, perhaps written by George Peele or Christopher Marlowe, is a rather loosely constructed play written at the height of anti-Catholic sentiment. It served as the primary source for Shakespeare's *King John* (pr. c. 1596-1597). *King Leir and His Three Daughters* is more nearly a dramatic presentation of the story taken from Raphael Holinshed's *Chronicles of England, Scotland and Ireland* (1577) than it is a Senecan tragedy. Shakespeare's later treatment of the Lear legend has overshadowed the considerable value of its predecessor, but while the anonymous playwright provides neither the panorama nor many of the specific, sensual elements of Shakespeare's greater work, *King Leir and His Three Daughters* is a well-written and moving old chronicle play. *The Lamentable Tragedy of Locrine* (by "W. S.") combines both Senecan machinery and rather crude English humor in a history play. *The First Part of the Tragical Raigne of Selimus* echoes many lines from *The Lamentable Tragedy of Locrine* and uses many of the same sensational devices introduced by Seneca, but similarities end there: *The First Part of the Tragical Raigne of Selimus* takes its plot from Turkish, not British, history and features extravagant passions presumably calculated to appeal to unsophisticated theatergoers.

The Rise of Elizabethan Drama

During the latter part of the sixteenth century, the popularity of dramatic productions increased among all segments of the English population, from the rustics, who, as Hamlet tells the players, "for the most part are capable of nothing but inexplicable dumb shows and noise," to the educated middle class to the nobility. Plays on almost every conceivable subject were written to appeal to some segment of the population, and a few were able to include something for everyone. What had begun in the Church and developed in the schools had now become so popular that both the writing and the acting of drama became a business enterprise. Tropes (passages or sequences for farsing the Mass) had expanded into medieval mystery and morality plays, and those, in turn, given the stimulus of classical thought and forms, had evolved into school drama. So successful had drama been in delighting audiences while teaching them Christian morality and Humanistic concepts that the next logical step in development was into the public realm.

In religious drama, the choir as stage had given way to the nave, the porch, and the churchyard; the churchyard, in turn, had given way to the open field; and the field, to the flatbed wagons on which players performed at different locations. In secular drama there was a centuries-long period of evolution, similarly, culminating in the construction of public theaters expressly designed for the production of plays. In 1576, James Burbage (father of the renowned Elizabethan actor Richard Burbage) built The Theatre just outside the city boundaries of London. While some evidence, in the form of municipal records, exists to indicate that an earlier public theater had been built and used, Burbage's theater is generally considered to be the first major effort to establish a place where professional actors could practice their trade. The location of the public theater in Shoreditch, a name which adequately describes the area, allowed the acting companies to escape the jurisdiction of the unfriendly London authorities. When its lease ran out in 1596, The Theatre closed. The Curtain, built in the same general area, opened around 1577. From about 1592, when the Rose was refurbished there (it had been built in 1587), the Bankside, an area south of the Thames, just opposite the City but in the county of Surrey, became the "theater district" for London: The Swan was erected there around 1596, the Globe in 1599, and the Fortune in 1600.

These public theaters were built primarily for the production of plays, but they were all nevertheless built on the plan of the innyard. The roofless auditorium offered only standing room for the mob, the "groundlings," and seats in the roofed galleries for those who could pay more. These theaters were three stories high and either round or octagonal. The front of the stage extended out into the pit. Above the stage, beginning about half way back, was a balcony supported by two columns. Above this, set back somewhat, was a second balcony. Under the first balcony and in line with the second balcony was an upper stage, and behind that was a curtained-off inner stage.

Theaters built inside London had to claim that they were "private" playhouses catering to a special clientele, usually a wealthy and influential one. The first attempt to open a theater in London, in the Blackfriars district, was made in 1596 by the same man who had built the original Theatre, James Burbage, but after much time and expense, the city authorities refused Burbage permission to open the Blackfriars. The second attempt to open the Blackfriars, in 1600, was successful, but not without great difficulty. Private theaters in Stuart times, however, proliferated because of the comfortable seating, artificial lighting, and elaborate stage machinery.

The actors in early religious plays had been amateurs, controlled first by the Church and later by the trade guilds, and even after troupes of professional actors began touring England presenting interludes in the houses and castles of great families, much drama was being performed by child actors, both in school drama and in the homes of nobility. That child actors were serious rivals to the adult acting companies is illustrated by Hamlet's referring to them as "an aery of children, little eyases, that cry out on the top of question, and are most tyrannically clapped for 't." In 1574, a royal permit was given to Lord Leicester's Men, allowing them to act throughout the realm, but not until 1576, when Burbage built the first public theater, did professional companies have a place especially established for them to present their plays. Given the generally medieval view of morality of the time, the acting companies were composed entirely of men and boys, with women's roles being taken by the boys.

There were two prominent adult professional acting companies during the latter part of the sixteenth century and the early seventeenth century: Lord Leicester's Men and the Admiral's Men. The latter group was headed by the notable Elizabethan financier Philip Henslowe, whose diary is an invaluable aid to scholars as a window to the daily operations of early theater management. Henslowe's son-in-law, the great actor Edward Alleyn, was co-owner. The company, which gained its name and reputation from its patron, the Lord High Admiral, owned two theaters, the Fortune and the Hope. The company was later known as the Earl of Worcester's Men, then as the Queen's Men, and then as the Prince's Men.

The second company was considerably more famous, having as one of its members William Shakespeare. Lord Leicester's Men, managed by Richard Burbage, took its name from the patron Robert Dudley, Earl of Leicester. Its theaters were The Theatre, the Globe, and Blackfriars. At the death of Dudley, the company came under the patronage of Lord Strange, becoming Lord Strange's Men and later, when he became Lord Derby, Derby's Men. The company went on to have more patrons and therefore different names: Lord Hunsdon's Men, the Lord Chamberlain's Men, and then, in 1603, the King's Men.

Elizabethan drama evolved quite naturally from the intellectual climate of the times and was accompanied by the growth of acting as a profession. The increasing popularity of drama led to acting companies, special theaters, and the need for new material to enact. The new playwrights were not the Church scholars of medieval times or the schoolmasters of the middle sixteenth century. Rather, a new occupation developed, that of the professional playwright. Educated young men from Oxford and Cambridge, passionate young minds excited by the Humanistic spirit who had no inheritance or patrons to support their literary efforts, found in drama a way to mold language and ideas into a form which would support them. This group of educated young men, known as the University Wits, included

John Lyly, Robert Greene, George Peele, Thomas Lodge, Thomas Kyd, Thomas Nashe, and Christopher Marlowe. Because these men not only were familiar with classical models but also were trendsetters in developing a distinctively English literature, they lent to the evolving drama both a form and dignity borrowed from the Aristotelian mold and an immediacy in language and idea sparked by an awareness of the political, social, moral, and economic problems of sixteenth century England.

Others in the new profession of acting learned from the University Wits and, in some notable cases, improved upon them. Often the acting companies, both adult and children's companies, contracted with a professional dramatist to have a play written, but so hungry for material were the companies that their members, individually or in cooperation with others, would revise old plays to suit present needs or would fashion plots from old plays, poems, or tales into new dramas. These practical dramatists could often create works that combined the best of Humanistic ideas with the most practical dramatic techniques.

The predecessors of William Shakespeare, therefore, built a tradition of excellence that would have given the Elizabethan age a luster had Shakespeare himself never written a word. John Lyly (1554?-1606), although he wrote not for professional adult companies but for children's companies, nevertheless had considerable influence upon later playwrights. He carried the extravagant language of his *Euphues, the Anatomy of Wit* (1578) over into his drama with an effect thoroughly new in English drama. Many modern audiences find Lyly's style tedious and almost unreadable, marked as it is by heavy use of alliteration, antithesis, and elaborate similes and catalogs of fictitious authority to support insignificant arguments. Lyly's work is nevertheless a landmark in the history of English literature, setting a standard that showed the age that the English language was capable of art and grace. Shakespeare mocked the excesses of the euphuistic style in such works as *Love's Labour's Lost*, *Henry IV, Part I*, and *King Lear*, but his plays reveal the devotion to style, the confidence in the resources of the language, that informed Lyly's works. Excessive as Lyly's rhetoric was, he illustrated the richness of English.

Through his witty dialogue, Lyly emphasized the intellectual comedy of wit rather than farcical comedy of situation. Lyly's best play is *Endymion, the Man in the Moon* (pr. 1588), an allegory praising Queen Elizabeth and the Earl of Leicester. Elizabeth is portrayed as Cynthia, the chaste huntress, and Leicester is the faithful lover Endymion. Other plays by Lyly are *Campaspe* (pr. 1584), a prose comedy based on the classical story of Alexander, the beautiful Campaspe, and her artist-lover Apelles. In *Sapho and Phao* (pr. 1584) and *Midas* (pr. c. 1589), Lyly uses the old allegorical devices, while in *Galathea* (pr. c. 1585) and *Love's Metamorphosis* (pr. c. 1589), he employs pastoral elements. *Mother Bombie* (pr. c. 1589) is fashioned on the style of Plautus, with mistaken identity serving as its complication; *The Woman in the Moon* (pr. c. 1593), written in blank verse, satirizes women. All are pretty plays but slender in plot and significant ideas. As pieces of highly ornamental lace, Lyly's plays did not stand up well on the vigorous Elizabethan stage, but they served as models for the greatest drama the world has known.

If Lyly's plays are overly refined, those of Thomas Kyd (1558-1594) are frank, often bombastic, full of blood and thunder. Although Kyd's sensationalism often overpowers the more truly tragic elements of his plays, his realism in language and action nevertheless gave a vigor to drama theretofore unknown on such a large scale. Lyly may have showed Marlowe and Shakespeare the way to delicate artistry, but Kyd showed them how to use raw power to grab the attention of the audience. Strongly influenced by Seneca, Kyd introduced revenge tragedy to English drama. Most scholars believe that Kyd wrote an early version of *Hamlet*, called the *Ur-Hamlet* (from the German *Ur*, "origin" or "source"). His reputation, however, rests upon *The Spanish Tragedy* (pr. c. 1585-1589), the quintessential revenge tragedy. Here, Kyd introduces a ghost, insanity, and a play-within-the-play— all elements employed by Shakespeare in *Hamlet*—and, unlike the authors of *Gorboduc*, he presents violent action on the stage.

Robert Greene (1558?-1592) is perhaps as well-known for his prose as for his drama; like most of the professional writers of the age, Greene tried his hand at almost every type of writing which might bring him income. Educated at Cambridge, Greene expected to acquire fame as well as fortune, but both eluded him during his lifetime, and posterity has been only slightly kinder. Since he was not an actor himself, he merely wrote for others, a task which he did not entirely enjoy: In *Greene's Groatsworth of Wit Bought with a Million of Repentance* (1592), he calls actors "apes," "peasants," "painted monsters," and puppets "that speak from our mouths." Shakespeare is "an upstart crow, beautified with our feathers." He advises his fellow University Wits—probably Christopher Marlowe, Thomas Nashe, and George Peele—to stop writing for actors, "for it is a pity men of such rare wits should be subject to the pleasure of such rude grooms."

Nevertheless, Greene wrote drama. *A Looking Glass for London and England* (pr. c. 1588-1589), written in collaboration with Thomas Lodge, resembles earlier religious drama rather than the secular drama of its own time. *Orlando Furioso* (pr. c. 1588), based on Ariosto's work of the same title, is a play of lighter tone, but not completely successful. *James IV* (pr. c. 1591), not a history play but a serious comedy taken from a story by the Italian writer Cinthio, is perhaps most important for introducing Oberon, king of the fairies, to the English stage. Greene's best play is *Friar Bacon and Friar Bungay* (pr. c. 1589), a romantic comedy. The play draws on the legends that had grown around the thirteenth century philosopher and scientist Roger Bacon, whose thinking was so far in advance of his time that he was credited with magical powers. Greene shows that the magic of love is as inexplicable as the "magic" of Friar Bacon.

Friar Bacon and Friar Bungay was the first full romantic comedy on a pattern which Shakespeare was soon to immortalize—a pattern that was to be followed by all later writers of romantic comedy. The character of Margaret sets the ideal of the Renaissance woman: Greene's Margaret is a bright, vivacious, virtuous, and charming woman who can hold her own in dealing with any man. Whether Greene intended to help show the way to "apes" and "puppets," he did so anyway.

Another of the University Wits, George Peele (1556?-1596?), wrote poetry and drama in a vain attempt to earn a living by his literary skills. While some scholars have suggested that Peele spent some time as an actor, little evidence exists to support this contention; indeed, Peele's plays show scant knowledge of how to combine plot and character with ideas in a manner attractive to an audience. Those plays usually attributed to Peele are *The Arraignment of Paris* (pr. c. 1584), *The Battle of Alcazar* (pr. c. 1589), *David and Bethsabe* (pr. c. 1593-1594), *Edward I* (pb. 1593), and *The Old Wives' Tale* (pr. c. 1591-1594). His contribution to the development of English drama is to be found in the verse employed in his plays: He softens without destroying the mighty line of Marlowe's blank verse and makes it fit for romantic drama.

The contribution of Thomas Lodge (1558?-1625) to drama is much less than to prose romance. Along with his poems and pamphlets, Lodge wrote the pleasant prose romance *Rosalynde: Or, Euphues Golden Legacy* (1590), used by Shakespeare as a source for *As You Like It* (pr. c. 1599-1600). Like the other University Wits, Lodge extended his literary experiments into drama. He collaborated with Robert Greene in *A Looking Glass for London and England* and wrote at least one play independently, *The Wounds of Civill War* (pr. c. 1586), dealing with the civil strife between the Romans Marius and Sulla. While the play is interesting as an early treatment of Roman history on the English stage, it suffers from ponderous speeches and a confused plot.

Thomas Nashe (1567-1601) is best known for a series of pamphlets written during the famous Martin Marprelate controversy and for his anti-romantic prose narrative *The Unfortunate Traveller: Or, The Life of Jack Wilton* (1594), a precursor of the English novel. In *The Isle of Dogs* (pr. 1597; now lost), Nashe collaborated with Ben Jonson on a comedy which so pointedly portrayed the abuses of the state that Jonson was sent to jail. Nashe's only complete extant play is *Summer's Last Will and Testament* (pr. 1592), a play of courtly compliment which includes some of Nashe's characteristic satiric thrusts. The play has very little plot or action, but it has some vigorous moments and some surprisingly good poetry.

Christopher Marlowe (1564-1593), Shakespeare's famous contemporary, is remembered not only for his poetry and drama but also for his colorful, often violent life and his mysterious death in a tavern brawl; in contrast to his fellow University Wits, he seemed less interested in establishing his reputation as a writer or in earning a living than in pushing life and ideas to the limits in order to determine where the limits were. In particular, the philosophical and political ideas of Niccolò Machiavelli fascinated Marlowe, and in his plays he takes those ideas to their logical conclusion.

Marlowe's skepticism concerning the reigning medieval conception of human beings' place in the cosmos is implicit in his obsessive preoccupation with the nature of power. Some critics believe that Marlowe's skepticism is ultimately resolved on the testing ground of the plays; in their view, Marlowe should be read as a Christian Humanist. Other critics argue that Marlowe (who was accused of atheism by fellow playwright Thomas Kyd, with whom he had been living) clearly rejected the Christian worldview; according to their reading of the plays, Marlowe identifies with his proud, defiant, overreaching protagonists.

Marlowe's *Tamburlaine the Great* (*Part I*, pr. c. 1587; *Part II*, pr. 1587), based on the story of the Tartar king Timur Lenk (1336-1405), examines the nature of power as exhibited in the title character, Tamburlaine, who, as a young shepherd enamored of the riches and trappings of power, sets out to rule the world. This intoxication with power leads him to overcome all earthly adversaries, and he becomes an absolute monarch. The young Tamburlaine ignores the medieval concepts of divine intervention into worldly affairs and sets out to be his own god by becoming king; as his follower Theridamas says, "A god is not so glorious as a king." When the ruler's captive, the Turkish emperor Bajazeth, whom Tamburlaine wants to control absolutely, takes his own life, the man who would be god discovers that a power greater than his exists. Although he can take or spare life, he cannot, after all, control life and death. In the second part of the play, after defying the gods, Mahomet, and the Koran, the great Tamburlaine dies.

In *Doctor Faustus* (pr. c. 1588), Marlowe analyzes yet another search for power, perhaps the most universal of human desires. Like Marlowe himself, Faustus is an educated man, a master of philosophy, medicine, law, and theology, but he is "still Faustus, and a man," still unresolved of the ambiguities of life. Finding no absolute answers in traditional studies, Faustus decides to try his brains "to gain a deity." He turns to magic, some scholars say to science, as man's way to know all things; as Faustus says, "A sound magician is a mighty god." Faustus finds, as did Tamburlaine earlier and as does Macbeth later, that no activity of man is infinite. Although he learns a number of fascinating tricks, Faustus is still merely a man.

The Jew of Malta (pr. c. 1589) provides another Machiavellian character, at least as the Elizabethans generally understood Machiavelli. Barabas the Jew seeks power and wealth with no regard for values which might be dictated by a morally ordered universe. Because Barabas is so outrageous in his ideas and actions, so much so that Machiavelli himself would doubtless have detested him, his characterization often descends to bathos. In *Edward II* (pr. c. 1592), however, the protagonist is a more convincing figure. Marlowe's Edward, unlike the typical Marlovian protagonist, is a weak and vacillating man. As Edward's power decreases, the audience's sympathy for him increases, and as young Mortimer's power increases, the audience's sympathy for him decreases, much as in Shakespeare's treatment of the weak Richard II and the strong Bolingbroke in *Richard II* (pr. c. 1595-1596). In *Edward II*, Marlowe created a complex, well-crafted tragedy based upon an application of Aristotelian principles to English history rather than upon the Senecan model. Shakespeare was to use and build upon Marlowe's model in the plays of his second tetralogy.

While the themes and forms of Marlowe's drama were widely influential, it was the poetry of his plays that had the greatest impact. The "mighty line" which Ben Jonson and all succeeding critics saw in the blank verse of *Tamburlaine the Great* set the standard poetic form for the majestic speeches characteristic of Renaissance drama. To speculate on what Marlowe might have achieved had he lived past his twenties is irresistible but finally futile. This much, however, is certain: No dramatist other than William Shakespeare has shown more promise in his early works.

The High Period of Renaissance Drama

With Marlowe, the foundations of great Elizabethan drama had been laid—or rather, with Marlowe and the early works of Shakespeare, for in his early works Shakespeare was learning the trade of playwright. By 1595, the marriage of classical ideas and forms with native English literature and culture was consummated and secure.

William Shakespeare (1564-1616), from the village of Stratford-upon-Avon, learned his craft not from studies at Oxford or Cambridge but from his own reading of classical literature, from earlier English dramatists and poets, from his connection with the professional theater as an actor, and from his extraordinary perception of human nature. Rarely in history does an individual of genius happen along at precisely the right time for his native ability to flourish. Wolfgang Amadeus Mozart and Ludwig van Beethoven were such men in music, Albert Einstein in theoretical physics, and Shakespeare is the clear example of such a man in drama.

Shakespeare has been justly praised for his perception of human motivations and for the genius that allowed him to mirror these amazing perceptions in dramatic works of unparalleled power and linguistic virtuosity. Still, Shakespeare was not a dramatist who descended fully developed from

Mount Olympus. He was a working dramatist of the professional theater as it was taking shape in Elizabethan England. He was, without question, the greatest dramatic poet of his time, but he was also the heir of a tradition of great poetry.

It is likely that Shakespeare saw himself primarily as a working dramatist who wrote drama because his company needed plays to act, for he made no great effort to protect his plays for posterity. Sixteen texts of his plays appeared in quarto form during his lifetime, but Shakespeare himself appears not to have been involved in their publication. The result is that such quartos are of uneven quality. Some are from the author's foul papers (the texts actors used for actual performance of the plays), considered "good" quartos even though they have the kinds of errors we might expect to find in a copy when the author does not read and correct galley proofs. Other quarto publications were pirated in one way or another and show the kind of corruption of text one might expect from such "bad" quartos. Many of Shakespeare's plays remained unpublished until seven years after his death, when two of his fellow actors, John Heminge and Henry Condell, collected his dramatic works (with the exception of *Pericles*) in 1623 and published them in folio form. Of the thirty-six plays in this 1623 First Folio, eighteen had never been printed before. Even in the case of Shakespeare's 154 sonnets, although the poet had promised his patron in Sonnet 18, "So long as men can breathe or eyes can see,/ So long lives this, and this gives life to thee," the poems were not published until 1609, and some question exists about whether Shakespeare authorized the publication.

Since 1623, scholars have busied themselves with finding internal and external evidence to use in dating Shakespeare's plays. Once a chronology was established (insofar as any scholarly question concerning Shakespeare is ever "established"), certain patterns of the development of Shakespeare as a dramatist began to emerge. His plays may be categorized into four periods for the purpose of highlighting certain elements of his artistic development. Shakespeare did not so categorize his plays, nor did Heminge and Condell, and scholars can find fault with any attempt at categorization. The problems of the literary historian are compounded by the fact that Shakespeare did not limit himself to any single dramatic genre during any period of his career; he wrote comedies, histories, tragedies, and combinations and variations throughout his literary life. With these caveats posted, one may reasonably discuss Shakespeare's dramatic works in four periods of development.

The first period covers about five years, from 1590 to 1594, when, in order to supply his company with material to perform, Shakespeare began to adapt the plots and devices of earlier dramatists. He borrowed from Plautus, Terence, Lodge, Peele, Greene, Marlowe, and others; his purpose seems to have been to provide his fellows with a well-structured script that dealt with a subject already approved by audiences. During this time, Shakespeare was learning his craft, experimenting with presenting plot exposition in dialogue, with problems of characterization, with language, and with all that his predecessors had taught him. While this first period was a time of experimentation and imitation, the plays nevertheless reveal glimpses of Shakespeare's poetic genius and his clear perception of human behavior and motivation.

To this first period also belong the poems *Venus and Adonis* (1593), which the author called "the first heir of my invention," and the more mature *The Rape of Lucrece* (1594). Some of the sonnets were at this time being circulated in manuscript form, but it is not certain which ones or when they were written. The plays of the first period represent all the popular types—comedy, history, and tragedy—and they are imitative and flawed.

Which play is Shakespeare's first has been the subject of much conjecture, but evidence is inadequate to lead to any secure conclusion. *Titus Andronicus* may have been written as early as 1590 or as late as 1593, but it was certainly one of Shakespeare's first plays. Although "tragedy" appears in the full original title, *The Tragedy of Titus Andronicus*, the play is clearly a melodrama. It is a bloody play, closer to Senecan tragedy than is Kyd's *The Spanish Tragedy*; the motif of eating human flesh, for example, derives from act 4 of Seneca's *Thyestes*. Because the play includes such horrors as rape, mutilation, murder, and cannibalism, some critics want to deny that Shakespeare wrote it, but in fact *Titus Andronicus* shows a great talent for effective presentation of plot so as to achieve suspense and an acceptable conclusion. Shakespeare's purpose in this early attempt at tragedy was almost certainly to provide for his company a play which would capitalize upon the public's taste for sensational material presented with some degree of realism on the stage, and the play accomplishes that limited purpose, but in delivering a popular play to his company, Shakespeare also improved upon his source.

The comedies in this first period are reflections of what Shakespeare had seen and read in the academic theater influenced by Plautus and Terence, the courtly drama of Lyly, and the popular comedy of Greene and Peele. *The Comedy of Errors* (pr. c. 1592-1594), which was an adaptation of Plautus' *Menaechmi* (of the late third or early second century B.C.), is a farce involving two sets of identical twins separated at an early age and brought together by chance as adults. Shakespeare's play, though a farce, has a structure more complicated than and superior to that of Plautus, and while dialogue irrelevant to the plot and emotive speeches unprepared for in characterization detract from the play's artistic unity and coherence, this early comedy presents in the marital conflict between Antipholus of Ephesus and Adriana, his wife, a good analysis of the intricacies of human relationships. In *Love's Labour's Lost* (pr. c. 1594-1595), the influence of

Lyly is more clearly seen than in any other play of the period. The source of the comedy is not known, but the play at once uses and satirizes the romantic subjects and euphuistic style of Lyly. Beneath the witty dialogue and jests, however, is the serious contrast of nature·with the artificiality of society. *The Two Gentlemen of Verona* (pr. c. 1594-1595) presents a love story that is less contrived than that of *Love's Labour's Lost*, and the characters are less caricatured, but Shakespeare's attempt to make his characters more individualized and more believable causes some problems, because the plot itself is not realistic but romantic.

The history plays of this early period were doubtless written to capitalize upon the great spirit of nationalism that flourished after the English defeat of the powerful Spanish Armada in 1588. Only three authentic chronicle history plays had been written prior to 1590, but soon history, especially English history, was to become an important subject for all types of literature. Shakespeare's early efforts at historical drama presented the story much as he found it in his sources, with characterization being subordinate to plot, but, under the influence of Marlowe and prompted by his own interest in individual psychology, Shakespeare soon learned to use the stories and characters he found in history to write plays analyzing politics, love, hate, revenge, and other elements of the human condition.

The three parts of *Henry VI* (pr. c. 1590-1592) are uneven, lacking unity and coherence, but with the last play in the tetralogy, *Richard III* (pr. c. 1592-1593), Shakespeare had learned to escape the dramatic problems of episodic chronicle history by concentrating upon a single character and a single theme, complex though they both might be. Here, the clash between the ideas of divine and Machiavellian power that so fascinated Marlowe is taken up and analyzed minutely and realistically; as in *Tamburlaine the Great*, the Machiavellian Richard runs afoul of the natural order and is defeated. In *King John* (pr. c. 1596-1597), Shakespeare continues his movement away from mere episodic history to concentration upon theme—here, the theme of patriotism. Some scholars see this play as a rewrite, commissioned by his acting company, of an earlier play perhaps by Marlowe or Peele, *The Troublesome Raigne of John King of England*, but Shakespeare's treatment of the story is more than a mere rewrite. Here, he personalizes history, analyzing contemporary political concepts, an exercise he was to develop more fully in his history plays of the second period.

In his second period, from about 1595 to 1600, Shakespeare was no longer an apprentice dramatist imitating the work of others to produce plays for his company; rather, he had become a journeyman, able to plan his own work and create artistic works based upon his understanding of his material, his audience, and his perceptions of human behavior. The plays of his second tetralogy derive from Raphael Holinshed's *Chronicles of England, Scotland and Ireland* (1577) and from an earlier drama, *The Famous*

Victories of Henry V (pr. c. 1588), but these sources serve merely as a vehicle for exploring the major question of political theory: whether power derives from divine right or from military power. To serve his purpose, Shakespeare felt free to change the historical age of Richard II's queen from that of a child to that of a mature woman, of Prince Hal from a boy of fifteen to a young warrior, of Hotspur from a man of about forty-five to one about the same age as Hal. The playwright moves armies about to suit his dramatic purposes and introduces pumps, gunpowder, and cannons into early fifteenth century England, where these devices were not yet in use.

In *Richard II* (pr. c. 1595-1596), Shakespeare continues his inquiry into the nature of kingship, showing the political folly of one who depends wholly on divine power to protect his authority: "Not all the water in the rough rude sea," Richard shouts, "can wash the balm off from an anointed king," yet he discovers that vaporous angels are no match for Bolingbroke's army. The play ends with Richard's descent from monarchical power and high-flown illusions (exquisitely mirrored in the play's language and imagery) as Bolingbroke, now Henry IV, takes his place and the cycle of rise and fall begins anew.

The two parts of *Henry IV* (pr. c. 1597-1598) center on the political troubles of King Henry IV, who depends upon military strength to attain and keep the crown, and the political development of Prince Hal (the future Henry V), whose grasp of the Machiavellian principle of situational ethics eventually surpasses that of his father. Indeed, the two plays focus less upon their title character than they do upon Hal and his personal and political maturation. This development culminates in *Henry V* (pr. c. 1598-1599), which concerns the reign of England's most successful king up to the time of Elizabeth. Having learned much about human nature and the requirements of kingship through the negative examples of the profligate rogue Falstaff and the hotheaded young nobleman Hotspur (in the plays about Henry IV), Hal uses Hotspur and Falstaff as Marlowe's Tamburlaine used Bajazeth—as steps to the throne—and then rids himself of them when they are of no more political use. Unlike Tamburlaine, however, Hal acts on the basis of a mature comprehension of his place as the representative, rather than the embodiment, of divine will. His understanding of his central role as monarch in the Elizabethan hierarchy of being—responsible both to the people of his nation and to God—makes him in many ways Shakespeare's ideal ruler.

The second period of Shakespeare's dramatic development contains more festive comedies than any other type of play. *The Taming of the Shrew* (pr. c. 1593-1594) derives from George Gascoigne's *Supposes* (the previously mentioned translation of Ariosto's satiric farce), from an old tale in a medieval English jestbook, and perhaps from a comedy of about the same time as Shakespeare's, with an almost identical title, *The Taming of a Shrew*.

Shakespeare builds upon his analysis of male-female relationships begun in *The Comedy of Errors* by contrasting the love affair of the romantic young lovers Lucentio and Bianca with that of the more mature Petruchio and Katherina. Here Shakespeare turns the farcical elements he found in his sources into a carefully drawn comedy in which Kate (as she is called in the play) learns what love is. *A Midsummer Night's Dream* (pr. c. 1595-1596), written for private presentation rather than for the public theater, continues the theme of love. The five plots taken from various sources are carefully woven into a unified masterpiece showing that "the course of true love never did run smooth"—primarily because, as Puck remarks, "Lord, what fools these mortals be."

In *The Merchant of Venice* (pr. c. 1596-1597), *Much Ado About Nothing* (pr. c. 1598-1599), *As You Like It* (pr. c. 1599-1600), and *Twelfth Night: Or, What You Will* (pr. c. 1600-1602), Shakespeare's technical talents, clear perception of human relationships, and humor are developed to the point of mastery. All of these plays treat love as the noblest of human attributes and reveal an optimistic view of humankind's ability to work through conflicts to the natural harmony that love brings to human beings.

In *The Merchant of Venice*, Shakespeare contrasts the honorable friendships between Antonio and Bassanio, Bassiano and Portia, and several other pairs of lovers with the unnatural hatred of the Jewish moneylender Shylock—a figure suggested by Marlowe's Barabas. Shakespeare's villain, however, is no unmotivated monster; rather, he is a man poorly treated by the Christian characters in the play, a man who does not understand the natural model of mercy or love. The play is dominated by the clever Portia, who does understand the model and who has the intelligence and force of personality to establish it in the midst of conflict.

Much Ado About Nothing continues the optimistic spirit of romantic comedy and again features a witty woman who helps to bring natural order to chaotic situations. The relationship between Benedick and the witty Beatrice is contrasted to that between Claudio and Hero. When the two major characters learn that they love each other, they combine to make right the evil engineered by the hateful Don John. Beatrice, aware of the benefits of love and justice, leads the successful efforts to reestablish harmony among members of society; all, one is given to understand, live happily ever after.

In *As You Like It*, a wise young woman again leads the way through conflict to order. Shakespeare borrowed the plot from Thomas Lodge's prose romance *Rosalynde: Or, Euphues Golden Legacy* (1590), but the play uses only Lodge's names and settings, not his characterization. Once again, the villains, whose greed brings suffering and hardship, are pitted against a discerning young woman who orchestrates the return to order. Shakespeare's Rosalind understands that the courtly love tradition is mere nonsense and that secure love comes not from glandular secretion but from trust won by understanding.

In *Twelfth Night*, it is young Viola, shipwrecked on the shores of the fictive kingdom of Illyria, who teaches the lovesick Orsino and the morbid Olivia what love is and what it can do. There are no villains here, except for the puritanical Malvolio, who is more churl than villain, but there are clowns aplenty, as in the other comedies. Sir Toby Belch and Sir Andrew Aguecheek are buffoons in the tradition of Bottom, Launcelot Gobbo, Dogberry, and Touchstone—the play's true clowns—whereas the ostensible clown, Feste, who "wears not motley in his brain," anticipates the wise fool of *King Lear* in his position as truthteller by means of parody.

While common themes and similar devices run through all of these comedies, each play has its own flavor and emphasis. They are all examples of "high comedy," plays in which the situations, wit, humor, and developments are generated from the characters rather than the other way around. Taking traditional devices from others and adding his own understanding of human nature and of the theater, Shakespeare created romantic comedy of unsurpassed quality.

Another play of this period, *The Merry Wives of Windsor* (pr. 1597), is different in many respects from the other comedies written at about the same time, as are the characters it borrows from the second-period history plays. Legend has it that Shakespeare wrote this comedy at the request of Queen Elizabeth, who wanted to see a dramatic presentation of Falstaff in love, but because Falstaff was created specifically to fulfill a thematic purpose in the last three plays of the second tetralogy, he is in most respects a different character. The result is a low comedy, producing much fun but little of the serious thought of the other comedies of the period.

The only tragedy of the second period is different from both earlier and later tragedies. In his *Romeo and Juliet* (pr. c. 1595-1596), Shakespeare presents the story of two young people who discover the glory of honest, natural love. The English interest in romance can be deduced from the popularity of the many prose romances and from the hundreds of love poems of the period, including the source of Shakespeare's play, the poem *The Tragicall Historye of Romeus and Iuliet* (1562), by Arthur Brooke. Here, Shakespeare shuns the vagueness of sentimental courtly love to dramatize the discovery of true love that he was to use as the theme in his great romantic comedies of the second period, as well as in the sonnets and many of the tragedies and comedies of later periods. The love of Romeo and Juliet is contrasted throughout the play to other concepts of love and marriage: the youthful infatuation that Romeo had for the aloof Rosaline; the effeminate emotion that Mercutio scorns; the proper alliance between families that old Capulet seeks to arrange; the essence of decorum that Paris desires; and the sexual satisfaction that the earthy nurse believes love to be. When Friar Lawrence chides Romeo for loving Rosaline one day and Juliet the next, Romeo explains to him the difference: Juliet loves him back, honestly and without reservation. Their love is celebrated in magnificent poetry; the sonnet, epithalamium, and aubade express the couple's love in the clearest possible terms. The young lovers are impetuous and overhasty in their relationship, and they are sometimes unthinking; their immaturity is displayed not in their love for each other but in their reactions to events not of their making. The play does not indict their relationship; on the contrary, their love, because it is so natural and honest, is perhaps too pure to survive in a flawed world, and thus they must die. Nevertheless, the deaths of the "star-cross'd lovers" result in a sense of pathos rather than the sense of fear and awe that the later tragedies evoke.

The third period of Shakespeare's development, from 1600 to about 1608, is commonly referred to as his "great period," his "tragic period," or his "bitter period." The great tragedies and dark comedies written during this period analyze the most difficult problems concerning humankind, the cosmos, and human beings' relationship with the cosmos; they show the greatness of people in constant conflict with their darker nature.

The comedies of this period begin with *All's Well That Ends Well* (pr. c. 1602-1603), a play that ends with Bertram promising to love and cherish his wife, Helena, but this comic ending has been reached by a tortuous path. Bertram, forced by the King of France to marry Helena, promptly leaves his bride with this contemptuous message: "When thou canst get the ring upon my finger which never shall come off, and show me a child begotten of thy body that I am father to, than call me husband. . . ." Instead of appealing to the kind of love Benedick has for Beatrice or Orlando has for Rosalind, Helena must rely upon trickery to fulfill the requirements of her husband. Taking the place of Bertram's new mistress, Diana, in her husband's bed, she gets the ring and gets a child. The order of marriage is preserved by the so-called bed trick rather than by the dignity of human love. There is no purifying Forest of Arden here, no musical Illyria.

Neither is the world of *Measure for Measure* (pr. 1604) a happy place. The unyielding justice sought by Shylock in *The Merchant of Venice* becomes here the driving force of the play. The rule of Vienna is left by Duke Vincentio to his deputy, Angelo, who seeks by puritanical law to force morality upon immoral man. He orders Claudio, a young gentleman, to be executed for seducing his betrothed, Juliet, yet when Claudio's sister, Isabella, appeals to the deputy to be merciful to her brother, Angelo agrees to do so only if Isabella will yield her body to him. Isabella, as extreme in her prudishness as Angelo is in his hypocrisy, refuses to give up her maidenhead to save the life of her brother, much to Claudio's distress. The play is saved as a comedy only when the rampant immorality of the citizens of Vienna is controlled by Vincentio, who has been observing the situation disguised as a friar.

The third comedy of the period, *Troilus and Cressida* (pr. c. 1601-1602), is perhaps the most bitter of all, so much so that scholars have for years been undecided whether to call it a comedy or a tragedy. In the 1623 folio, Heminge and Condell gave it the title *The Tragedy of Troilus and Cressida*, but in most surviving copies of that collection the play is placed without pagination between *Henry VIII* (pr. 1613), the last of the histories, and *Coriolanus* (pr. c. 1607-1608), the first in the section of tragedies. There is a love story here, that of Troilus and Cressida, but Troilus is a lovesick young fool in the Petrarchan tradition, and Cressida is little better than a whore. The story of the Trojan War offers material to present man's nobility, but Shakespeare's treatment is anything but ennobling. Homer's great story is set in the mire, amid the petty squabbling of the Greeks and the irrationality and immorality of the Trojans. Hector is the most likely candidate to represent noble man, but after delivering a clear and rational argument to his brothers Paris and Troilus on why they should seek the high moral ground by returning Helen to the Greeks and thus end the bloodshed, he abruptly tosses godlike reason aside and agrees to continue the war. The deformed and scurrilous Thersites best expresses the theme of the play in his several remarks on what motivates man: "Lechery, lechery! still wars and lechery! Nothing else holds fashion."

Shakespeare's analysis of human beings' darker nature finds its greatest expression in the tragedies of the period. Political power, a subject which he had analyzed from a historical point of view in the second tetralogy, is presented darkly in the tragedies of this period. *Julius Caesar* (pr. c. 1599-1600), based upon Sir Thomas North's translation of Plutarch's *Parallel Lives* (105-115), continues to use chronicle history as a source, as do many of Shakespeare's later tragedies, but here the emphasis is upon individual human tragedy rather than history or politics, as is the case with *Richard III*, *Richard II*, and the other history plays with tragic overtones.

What A. C. Bradley calls "the four principal tragedies of Shakespeare" belong to this third period: *Hamlet, Prince of Denmark* (pr. c. 1600-1601), *Othello, the Moor of Venice* (pr. 1604), *King Lear* (pr. c. 1605-1606), and *Macbeth* (pr. 1606). In each of these plays, Shakespeare shows how the private virtues of great characters are, in the political and social contexts of the action, flaws leading to great suffering.

Hamlet, like the biblical character Job, finds that his expectation of a morally ordered universe causes him to hesitate to act when faced with the horror of insensitivity and injustice surrounding him in Denmark. Only late in the play does he decide that "there's a divinity that shapes our ends" regardless of the chaos existing in society, at which time he acts as a minister of Heaven to restore order, but such action in the midst of evil destroys this good man as well.

The life and death of the great general Othello follows a similar pattern. Because he is a man "who thinks men honest that but seem to be so," he is easy prey to the brilliant villain Iago, who seems to be honest but is not so. The innocence of both Othello and Desdemona in an evil plot concocted by Iago causes their virtues to work against them. Desdemona's desire to help her husband and their friend Cassio contributes circumstantial evidence to aid in persuading Othello that she is indeed the whore that Iago suggests that she is. Othello's idealistic desire to protect the order of the cosmos then leads him paradoxically to contribute to the chaos of evil manufactured by Iago: He kills his beloved Desdemona. When, at the end of the play, Othello learns of the duplicity that led him to murder the one he held most dear, he also gains insight into the aspects of his personality that made him vulnerable to such duplicity. He is, as he recognizes before taking his own life, "one who loved not wisely, but too well."

King Lear, too, is an essentially good man who learns that he lives in a world where love and virtue can be aped by mere words used by Machiavellian characters to further their own selfish ends. Two of Lear's three daughters, Goneril and Regan, "love" him only when he has power; when he gives up his power (by parceling out a third of his kingdom to each), they turn him out into the storm. He and, to a lesser extent, the Earl of Gloucester learn that power in society comes not from virtue but from soldiers. Lear is, indeed, a man "more sinn'd against than sinning," but "sin" has no real meaning for those who do not recognize a moral order. Nevertheless, Shakespeare in this play offers a tribute to the power and supremacy of love in the person of Cordelia, Lear's third daughter, who, at the play's beginning, had refused to substitute the "letter" of her love and respect for her father with the "spirit," as expressed in her refusal to flatter her father with appropriate but empty words (as had her sisters) in order to gain her third share of his kingdom. Enraged by her unwillingness to bow to his authority and astounded by the truths she expresses instead, Lear disowns the only one of his offspring who truly loves him. At the play's end, a much battered, maddened, yet wiser Lear acknowledges his wrong, and father and daughter are reconciled in one of the most touching and humanly true scenes of Shakespeare's entire canon.

The consequences of flouting the moral order are further examined in *Macbeth*, but the pattern is somewhat different, for here good and evil co-exist in the same characters. Macbeth fully understands the implications of disorder in the lives of men, as he demonstrates when he tells King Duncan that "the service and loyalty I owe,/ In doing it pays itself" and again when he tells Lady Macbeth, "I dare do all that may become a man./ Who dares do more is none," but his and his lady's lust for power eclipses his understanding, and they murder Duncan in order to gain the throne. Like Marlowe's Tamburlaine and Doctor Faustus, Macbeth becomes less than a man by trying to be more than a man; like Hamlet, Othello, and Lear, Macbeth and Lady Macbeth are tragically aware of the consequences of their actions. Lady Macbeth's conscience catches up with her, and Macbeth knows that in an ordered existence he should have "honor, love, obedience, troops of friends," whereas through his unnatural deed he has gained only "curses" and "mouth honor" in their stead. Macduff, in killing Macbeth, executes the inexorable fate due to those who deny the universal order.

The fabric of these great tragedies is so rich and varied that no literary historian can do more than select a few generalities of many to indicate the importance of these works in our culture. They show one of the greatest minds of all time analyzing philosophical problems that all thinking people consider at some time during their intellectual development, and they present these ideas in the finest dramatic poetry the world has to offer. Shakespeare's view of humanity is not always pleasant, but it is accurate, and dark though the tones and settings of the plays may be, in every case the worth and dignity of humankind is affirmed at the conclusion of the play.

The other three tragedies belonging to this period have never been accepted by scholars as of the same intellectual and artistic quality as the four principal tragedies described above. Perhaps they show the beginnings of Shakespeare's period of experimentation, but they are close enough to the great tragedies to warrant considering them alongside the others. *Antony and Cleopatra* (pr. c. 1606-1607) contains neither the horror of the proportions presented in earlier tragedies nor any hero of the stature of Hamlet, Othello, Lear, or Macbeth. Some scholars have a difficult time seeing Antony and Cleopatra as heroes at all, for, as Antony's soldiers believe, Antony is here in his "dotage" and Cleopatra is revealed as merely a capricious woman. Nevertheless, they are noble characters in conflict with others who are less noble. Antony is no Hamlet, nor was he meant to be, but neither is he merely an attendant lord. The play's only villain—and that is too strong a word—is Octavius Caesar, whose villainy consists in his wanting to be landlord of the world, a desire shared by much of the world's population. Antony and Cleopatra have discovered that "the nobleness of life" lies not in building an empire but in love, and in their struggle to live in a world that does not understand such a nonmaterialistic goal, they die.

In *Coriolanus* (pr. c. 1607-1608), a similar idea is presented. Coriolanus is an idealistic man of great talents, a nonpolitical man lured into the political world described by Machiavelli. Because he shuns the situational ethics required by anyone who operates in such an arena, he is destroyed. Similarly, Timon in *Timon of Athens* (pr. c. 1607-1608) is a generous man forced to flee society because of the greed and ingratitude of his fellowman. Timon dies hating all humankind, but Alcibiades, who was also banished by the ungrateful leaders of Athens, returns to conquer Athens and restore order to society. Shakespeare's "bitter period," thus, appears from this perspective to reflect a realistic view of human beings' actions coupled with an optimistic belief in human beings' potential.

The plays of the fourth period, from about 1608 to 1613, appear to be experimental works. Shakespeare had left London for Stratford sometime in 1611, but even before that time he seems to have left the harshness of reality for the more pleasant realm of romance. Indeed, four plays of his final period are romances. These late plays still contain evil, guilt, and suffering, but mythology and magic are ever present to set things right in a way that does not occur in reality. Some scholars have suggested that the late romances indicate that Shakespeare had found a new faith in the goodness of man, but in fact the darkness in man presented in these plays is not neutralized by rational action, as it is in the plays of the third period, but by magic or improbable chance. In *Pericles, Prince of Tyre* (pr. c. 1607-1608), *Cymbeline* (pr. c. 1609-1610), *The Winter's Tale* (pr. c. 1610-1611), and *The Tempest* (pr. 1611), evil is transcended rather than confronted.

In *The Tempest*, the best of the late plays, the Machiavellian concept of life is represented by Antonio, the usurping Duke of Milan, and Sebastian, his brother, who will murder their own kin to further their ambitions. No moral values guide their actions; as Antonio says, "I feel not/ This deity in my bosom." On another level of the action, there is a counterpoint between the bestial Caliban and the airy spirit Ariel. The action is controlled by Prospero, the rightful Duke of Milan, exiled by his usurping brother, Antonio. Prospero, who can call up spirits to do his bidding, is generally regarded as a figure for the artist; his genial magic suggests the prevailing tone of the late plays.

In the last years of his life, Shakespeare wrote no plays by himself, but on two occasions he did lend his talents to plays by his friend John Fletcher. Shakespeare's contribution to *The Two Noble Kinsmen* (pr. c. 1612-1613) appears to have been limited to a few scenes, which Fletcher reworked and placed into the play in appropriate places. In *Henry VIII* (pr. 1613), Shakespeare's part is largely a matter of conjecture, but the largest part has been attributed to Fletcher. Scholars believe, on the other hand, that the character of Queen Katherine, who is the best developed character in the play, is Shakespeare's.

The place of Shakespeare's plays in the history of Elizabethan drama is, therefore, at the peak. He was clearly influenced by his predecessors, who gave him the tools to practice his craft, but he sharpened the tools and created from the material of life works of art which have never been surpassed. As Shakespeare's famous contemporary Ben Jonson said of him, "He was not of an age, but for all time."

Ben Jonson (1573-1637) is second only to Shakespeare as a giant of the period. The two were in many ways very different kinds of dramatists. In his *Essay of Dramatic Poesy* (1668), John Dryden said of Jonson, "If I would compare him with Shakespeare, I must acknowledge him the more correct poet, but Shakespeare the greater wit. . . . I admire him, but I love Shakespeare," a view not uncommon among later scholars.

Jonson's best plays are his comedies, created, in the tradition of Plautus and Terence, to ridicule human foibles. If Shakespeare presented the mystery and complexity of human life, Jonson concentrated on human folly. His *Every Man in His Humour* (pr. 1598), with its well-constructed plot, stands as the first important comedy of humors on the English stage. In this genre, of which Jonson was the major exponent, human foibles are examined as a product of excessive personality traits (which, in medieval times, had been thought to result from an imbalance in the four bodily humors), concentrated in individual characters. A companion play, *Every Man out of His Humour* (pr. 1599), has a more complex plot and suggests that humors are cured by their own excesses. Other early Jonson comedies are allegorical and satiric. *The Case Is Altered* (pr. 1597), based upon a plot by Plautus, is a rather romantic comedy set in modern Italy, but the two other early comedies contain much more satire: *Cynthia's Revels: Or, The Fountain of Self-Love* (pr. c. 1600-1601) is a complex allegory praising Queen Elizabeth and satirizing some of Jonson's contemporaries, while *Poetaster: Or, His Arraignment* (pr. 1601) has a Roman setting and contains scathing attacks upon the dramatist's adversaries.

The comedies written between about 1605 and 1614 are generally considered to be Jonson's best, most mature comedies. *Volpone: Or, The Fox* (pr. 1605), perhaps the greatest satiric comedy in English, shows the effects of greed upon individual characters and society in general. *Epicœne: Or, The Silent Woman* (pr. 1609), thought by Samuel Taylor Coleridge to be the most entertaining of Jonson's comedies, is not so biting in its satire of humanity generally as *Volpone*; the gulling of the old recluse Morose is all in a kind of fun in which no one gets hurt. Greed and other human foibles are again satirized in *The Alchemist* (pr. 1610), a play relying upon the medieval belief in alchemy to show how the human desire to solve complex problems with quick, simple answers makes people susceptible to quackery. *Bartholomew Fair* (pr. 1614) utilizes a rather simple, though well-ordered, plot to present a realistic pageant of colorful London characters—a veritable circus of pickpockets, mountebanks, confidence men, religious hypocrites, balladmongers, puppetmasters, and many others. The good fun ends with all characters being forgiven their transgressions.

The late comedies return to the allegorical and satiric form of some of Jonson's earlier plays, with limited success. To this group belong *The Devil Is an Ass* (pr. 1616), *The Staple of News* (pr. 1626), *The New Inn: Or, The Light Heart* (pr. 1629), *The Magnetic Lady: Or, Humours Reconciled* (pr.

1632), and *A Tale of a Tub* (pr. 1633). The plots continue to be developed along the lines of classical comedy and are imaginatively drawn, but the characters remain mere emblems.

Jonson's two tragedies, both on Roman themes, are different in several respects from those of Shakespeare. Jonson, perhaps to display his superior knowledge of classical history, chose as his subjects minor incidents from Roman history; he also took as his sources the original Latin works rather than English translations or dramatic adaptations. *Sejanus His Fall* (pr. 1603), which derives from Tacitus, stretches the unity of time; the play depicts the destruction of the powerful Sejanus by the Emperor Tiberius. The psychological analysis of the tyrant's mind is well done both dramatically and intellectually, leading to the creation of Jonson's great comic character Volpone. *Catiline His Conspiracy* (pr. 1611) uses classical sources and dramatic devices, including a ghost and chorus, to show how humankind's bestial nature shapes political history. Characterization here, however, is weaker than in *Sejanus His Fall.*

Jonson wrote two pastoral plays, one of which, *The Sad Shepherd: Or, A Tale of Robin Hood* (pb. 1640), employs exquisite poetry in a mixture of pastoral and realistic traditions. The play exists only as a fragment; Jonson's other pastoral, "The May Lord," is now lost.

Jonson's poetical ability as a dramatist can be seen in the pastoral fragment *The Sad Shepherd*, but it is developed fully in his many masques written throughout his career. The masque is a highly ornamental type of drama written to provide entertainment at courtly functions and celebrations and different from the drama written for the public theater, for the companies of child actors, and for academic purposes. Jonson was the principal writer of masques during the reign of James I, and in these elaborate productions he replaced his satiric wit with his talent for writing carefully crafted poetry. Among the many masques he wrote for production at the court of James I are *The Satyr* (pr. 1603), *The Penates* (pr. 1604), *The Masque of Blacknesse* (pr. 1605), *Hymenaei* (pr. 1606), *The Masque of Beauty* (pr. 1608), *Hue and Cry After Cupid* (pr. 1608), *The Masque of Queens* (pr. 1609), *Oberon* (pr. 1611), *The Golden Age Restored* (pr. 1616), and *Gypsies Metamorphosed* (pr. 1621). These plays contain neither great character development nor profound ideas, for the purpose of masques was to provide not social commentary but courtly entertainment. What they do show is another side to this prolific and complex writer.

Like many of his colleagues, Jonson collaborated with other dramatists in writing plays. He had gone to jail for his part in writing *The Isle of Dogs* (pr. 1597) with Thomas Nashe, a play now lost. He had better luck with *Eastward Ho!* (pr. 1605), written in collaboration with George Chapman and John Marston. Scholars have been unable to determine with certainty which parts were written by which authors, for the play contains none of the biting satire of Jonson, the psychological analysis of Chapman, or the bitterness of Marston. The plot is realistic, presenting the virtues and pettiness in the lives of common tradesmen. The moral, if it can be taken at face value, is rather mundane, but the play is a pleasant comedy which presents middle-class London life in the style of Thomas Deloney or Thomas Dekker.

Drama After Jonson to the Closing of the Theaters

Had Shakespeare and Jonson never written drama, the history of the theater during the Renaissance would appear as a continuum from the late Elizabethan period through the early Jacobean period, or almost so. The tradition developed by the University Wits was continued by George Chapman, Thomas Dekker, Thomas Middleton, John Webster, John Ford, and Francis Beaumont and John Fletcher. These men, individually or in collaboration, wrote plays superior to any written for two hundred years or more thereafter. Their relative obscurity is caused simply by their proximity to the greatest dramatists in our culture. Others, such as John Marston, Thomas Heywood, Philip Massinger, Cyril Tourneur, and James Shirley, were good dramatists whose works lie even deeper in the shadows of Shakespeare and Jonson.

George Chapman (c. 1559-1634), perhaps best known in the twentieth century as the translator of Homer who impressed the English Romantic poet John Keats, was a leading literary figure in his day. He contributed both comedies and tragedies in response to the growing demand in London for new plays. His plots are generally more episodic than dramatic and are often exaggerated; his characters are distinctive and sometimes powerful, but seldom are their motives carefully analyzed. His comedies include *The Blind Beggar of Alexandria* (pr. 1596), *An Humourous Day's Mirth* (pr. 1597), *The Gentleman Usher* (pr. c. 1602), *All Fools* (pr. 1604), *Monsieur d'Olive* (pr. 1604), *The Widow's Tears* (pr. c. 1605), and *May Day* (pr. c. 1609). Three others were written in collaboration: *Eastward Ho!* (pr. 1605), with Jonson and Marston, and *The Ball* (pr. 1632) and *Chabot, Admiral of France* (pr. 1635), with James Shirley. The comedies develop interesting characters in usually improbable plots. The vulgarity of some of the subplots in *May Day* seems strange coming from the moral Chapman, but certainly the play offers a realistic treatment of its subject.

Chapman's five tragedies offer an interesting study of the Renaissance view of Stoicism. Drawing primarily on French history rather than English, Chapman created strong heroes placed in stories of political intrigue. The protagonist of *Bussy d'Ambois* (pr. 1604), the best of his tragedies, is a character much like Shakespeare's Hotspur in *Henry IV, Part I*, Othello, Kent in *King Lear*, and Coriolanus. Bussy is a tested soldier out of place in the world of courtly intrigue. His tragedy is as much a result of his surprising passion for a married woman as of political intrigue. In *The Revenge of Bussy d'Ambois* (pr. c. 1610), Bussy's brother Clermont, more of the detached stoic character than Bussy, philosophizes with himself on the subject of morality, revenges the murder of his brother, and dies by his own hand. *The Conspiracy and Tragedy of Charles, Duke of Byron* (pr. 1608) returns to the theme of *Bussy d'Ambois* to show a strong character whose passions lead to his destruction. Chapman's last two tragedies, *The Wars of Caesar and Pompey* (pr. c. 1613) and *Chabot, Admiral of France*, both present heroes who react stoically to the problems which beset them. Chapman's purpose throughout seems to be to use drama to present psychological studies of characters in the manner of Shakespeare before him and Webster after, and while his dramatic structure is often faulted by scholars, he was one of the most popular of the Jacobean dramatists.

Another important dramatist of the late Renaissance is Thomas Dekker (c. 1572-1632), a man whose love of life is reflected in his comedies. He took part in the "war of the theaters" that erupted between Jonson and Marston, writing the comedy *Satiromastix: Or, The Untrussing of the Humourous Poet* (pr. 1601)—the humorous poet being Jonson. Dekker's attack was not vitriolic, but Jonson soon realized that he was far too easy a target and withdrew from the "war." Dekker is best known for *The Shoemaker's Holiday: Or, The Gentle Craft* (pr. 1600), a pleasant comedy using a plot and characters borrowed from Thomas Deloney's prose romance *The Gentle Craft* (1597). Other comedies by Dekker are *The Whole History of Fortunatus* (pr. 1599; commonly known as *Old Fortunatus*), the two parts of *The Honest Whore* (pr. 1604 and c. 1605, respectively), *The Whore of Babylon* (pr. c. 1606-1607), *If This Be Not a Good Play, the Devil Is in It* (pr. c. 1610-1612; also as *If It Be Not Good, the Devil Is in It*), *Match Me in London* (pr. c. 1611-1612), and *The Wonder of a Kingdom* (pr. c. 1623). In addition, Dekker collaborated with other writers. His comedies are remarkable for their realistic portrayal of contemporary life and customs in essentially romantic plots. He excelled at the creation of individual scenes, although connections between the scenes are not always adequately provided.

A dramatist known to have collaborated with Dekker is Thomas Middleton (1580-1627), who probably had a hand in writing *The Honest Whore* with Dekker. Middleton's portrayal of London citizens in a decidedly unromantic manner is an interesting cross between Dekker and Jonson. His most important comedies among the many he wrote are *The Phoenix* (pr. 1604), *Michaelmas Term* (pr. c. 1606), *A Trick to Catch the Old One* (pr. c. 1605-1606), *The Old Law: Or, A New Way to Please You* (pr. c. 1618), and *A Game at Chess* (pr. 1624). Generally considered to be his best plays are *A Trick to Catch the Old One* and *A Game at Chess*. His comedies present life as he found it, in all of its coarseness, but his fine poetry and mastery of language attracted the attention of audiences during his day and of scholars since. Middleton also collaborated with Dekker on *The Roaring Girl: Or, Moll Cutpurse* (pr. c. 1610) and probably with Jonson and Fletcher on *The Widow* (pr. c. 1616). He wrote two tragedies in collaboration with William Rowley (1585?-1642?): *A Fair Quarrel* (pr. c. 1615-1617) and his best, *The Changeling* (pr. 1622), plays which contain good ideas well dramatized but which are marred by highly sensational, bloody scenes.

The plays of John Webster (c. 1580-before 1634) are second only to those of Shakespeare in their analysis of the psychology of evil. Scholars have long admired the magnificence of Webster's villains but condemned their motivations as obscure. Modern scholarship has argued that the characterizations in Webster's two best plays, *The White Devil* (pr. c. 1609-1612) and *The Duchess of Malfi* (pr. 1614), are in fact complex, virtually clinical analyses of psychological disorders. The horrors visited upon the virtuous Duchess of Malfi by her brother Ferdinand, for example, can be traced to the same source as his lycanthropy: his incestuous love for his sister and his inability to achieve his desires or even to admit them to himself.

Webster wrote only two other plays but collaborated on several others. *Appius and Virginia* (pr. 1634?) is a Roman tragedy which lacks the analysis of horror found in his other tragedies. *The Devil's Law-Case* (pr. c. 1619-1622) is a romantic comedy which illustrates Webster's grasp of comic satire. Both plays have been neglected by scholars because they do not contain the startling portrayal of horror long thought to be Webster's forte; they deserve to be reexamined in the light of modern scholarship. Webster collaborated on two plays with Rowley, *A Cure for a Cuckold* (pr. c. 1624-1625) and *The Thracian Wonder* (pr. c. 1617); he also collaborated with Dekker, notably on *Westward Ho!* (pr. 1604).

John Ford (1586-after 1639), like Webster, is known for his use of sensationalism. He explores frustrated love, as many of his colleagues did, but the problems that lead to the frustration are not the usual ones. Complex plots, as in *The Broken Heart* (pr. c. 1627-1631), lead the audience through a maze of sympathies and emphases. The play begins with a love triangle involving the unhappy heroine, Penthea; moves its focus to her brother, who is murdered by her lover; and ends by concentrating upon Princess Calantha, who stoically receives the news of the death of her two friends and of her father the king long enough to set her affairs and those of the state in order before dying of a broken heart. In his best play, *'Tis Pity She's a Whore* (pr. 1629?-1633), Ford uses the theme of incest, as Webster did in *The Duchess of Malfi*, but in Ford's play incest is much more central to the plot and more explicitly treated. Indeed, so sympathetic is Ford's treatment of the brother and sister, Giovanni and Annabella, whose incestuous love leads to their tragic deaths, that some critics have seen a conflict between the play's apparently moral conclusion (sin is punished) and its inner logic.

Among Ford's other contributions to drama are *Perkin Warbeck* (pr. c. 1622-1632), *The Lover's Melancholy* (pr. 1628), *The Fancies Chast and Noble* (pr. 1631?), *Love's Sacrifice* (pr. 1632?), and *The Lady's Trial* (pr. 1638). All the plays show clear construction and often scenes of intense passion and emotion. *Perkin Warbeck* is generally considered to be the best history play written after those of Marlowe and Shakespeare. Ford also collaborated with Dekker and Rowley on *The Witch of Edmonton* (pr. 1621) and with Webster on *The Late Murther of the Son upon the Mother* (pr. 1624). Several plays known to be by Ford are no longer extant.

The names of Francis Beaumont (c. 1584-1616) and John Fletcher (1579-1625), while they both wrote plays individually and Fletcher collaborated with several other dramatists, are almost always mentioned together because of the great success of the plays that they wrote in collaboration. The one play sometimes assigned solely to Beaumont is *The Woman Hater* (pr. c. 1606), a kind of burlesque comedy; some modern scholars believe that Beaumont was also the sole author of the mock-heroic satiric comedy *The Knight of the Burning Pestle* (pr. 1607). About twenty plays are usually assigned to Fletcher alone, including the pastoral *The Faithful Shepherdess* (pr. c. 1608-1609), a play of excellent poetry and rich imagery. Fletcher collaborated on many other plays with such dramatists as Massinger, Rowley, Middleton, and perhaps even Shakespeare.

Beaumont's and Fletcher's best work, however, is to be found among the plays jointly written by them rather than in their solo efforts. *Philaster: Or, Love Lies A-Bleeding* (pr. c. 1609), one of the finest plays of its day, is a tragicomedy which achieves genuine pathos. The play was acted often during the seventeenth century and returned to the stage well into the nineteenth century. *The Maid's Tragedy* (pr. c. 1611) suffers from sensationalism and sentimentality, but its well-constructed plot and vivid characterization made it a popular play during its day. Both Beaumont and Fletcher were men of good family and good education, giving them a familiarity with men and women of high social standing and a certain contempt for the common person. They were able to write interesting and successful plays which often achieve brilliant effects, but they seldom explored the basic questions of human psychology with the intensity of Marlowe, Shakespeare, Jonson, or Webster.

John Marston, Thomas Heywood, Philip Massinger, Cyril Tourneur, and James Shirley are usually ranked somewhat lower than the Jacobean dramatists discussed above, although some noteworthy critics would disagree with this ranking in a given case. Marston (1576-1634) began his literary career as a poet, turned playwright, and then gave it all up to become a priest. He entered the war of the theaters against Jonson with his *Histriomastix: Or, The Player Whipt* (pr. 1599) and was held up to ridicule as the character Crispinus in Jonson's *Poetaster*, but the battle ended quickly, and Marston collaborated with Jonson and Chapman in *Eastward Ho!* in 1605. He even dedicated to Jonson his most famous play, *The Malcontent* (pr. 1604), the story of a virtuoso cynic. The deposed Duke Altofronto, disguised as the jester Malevole, roams the court commenting upon immorality and injustice. In *The Malcontent*, however, as in Marston's other plays, the characters' motivations are often lost in the vigor of the action.

Thomas Heywood (c. 1573-1641) is usually listed as a major Jacobean dramatist on the strength of volume alone, for he wrote more than two hundred plays wholly or in part, many of which are no longer extant. His plays include chronicle histories, romantic comedies, realistic comedies, allegorical plays, and a number of pageants. The best of his plays are the domestic dramas, the ones in which specific elements of private life are dealt with interestingly and without undue sensationalism. Charles Lamb's description of Heywood as a "prose Shakespeare" is certainly hyperbolic; Heywood was a professional writer turning out plays for actors on proven themes. His best play is *A Woman Killed with Kindness* (pr. 1603), a kind of domestic tragedy on the order of Shakespeare's *Othello*. In Heywood's play, the woman is guilty of adultery but repentant; her husband, controlling his rage and jealousy as Othello does not, banishes his wife to a manor "seven mile off," there to live out her life. When she is near death, he goes to her side and forgives her. *The English Traveler* (pr. c. 1627) presents a similar theme of seduction, repentance, and death from shame. Most of Heywood's plays present the same kind of delicate, thoughtful reactions to sin and a kind of quiet morality. Neither the sin, if that is what it is, nor the morality, if such exists, is analyzed as in the plays of Marlowe, Shakespeare, and others.

Philip Massinger (1583-1640), who spent his dramatic apprenticeship in collaboration with John Fletcher and such other dramatists as Dekker and Rowley, wrote comedies, tragicomedies, and tragedies. His plot construction is skillful and his characterization competent, but his prejudice in favor of the nobility causes his characters to have a kind of irritating predictability. His best play is *A New Way to Pay Old Debts* (pr. 1621-1622?), with its interesting presentation of the political and financial kingmaker Sir Giles Overreach. Sir Giles is not uncommon as an overreacher—a rather usual character-type in drama of the Renaissance—but Massinger presents in Sir Giles a more subtle type of empire builder than is usually analyzed. Massinger's overreacher does not aspire to be ruler, a position dangerous because of its high profile; rather, he seeks to place others in position of power and wealth so as to secure his own position without the dangers faced by those in the forefront. So strict is the morality of Massinger's plays that Sir Giles is caught in a trap created by his own greed, and he pays for his sins. *The City Madam* (pr. 1632?), a play on a similar theme, is almost as lively and skillful, but its villain, Luke Frugal, does not quite measure up to Sir Giles in consistency and motive. Here again, the distrust that the noble audience of the private theater had of the middle class is at the heart of the plot.

Two plays are usually credited to Cyril Tourneur (c. 1575-1626), a poet and dramatist about whose life little is known. *The Revenger's Tragedy* (pr. 1606-1607), regarded by some critics as one of the masterpieces of Jacobean drama, shows the corrupting power of revenge. Vindice, the protagonist, like his predecessor Hamlet, begins the play as a moral man caught up in a plot of lust and murder; unlike Hamlet, however, Tourneur's revenger acts not as a minister of Heaven but as a man who learns to plot and murder with glee. Vindice recognizes at the end of the play that he has been corrupted when he says, "'Tis time to die when we're ourselves our foes." Tourneur's other play (if indeed he wrote either one—there is some question) is also a revenge tragedy, *The Atheist's Tragedy: Or, The Honest Man's Revenge* (pr. c. 1607). As in the earlier play, the dramatist here uses the revenge theme to express Christian virtues. A ghost is employed, as in many earlier revenge tragedies, but this time the ghost does not appear to direct revenge but to urge that revenge be left to God. The play thus offers an interesting addition to the usual revenge theme, but the idea is marred by the rather unrealistic application of reward for a moral life. Because he trusts in the moral order to set things right rather than taking the law into his own hands, Charlemont is rewarded with the same kind of material gain that has caused the villainy in the play. Interesting in the play is the presentation of the new materialism that came to late sixteenth century England.

One of the last dramatists of the period is James Shirley (1596-1666), a professional playwright of whose works more than thirty plays are extant— more than any playwright of the period except Shakespeare and Fletcher. Shirley's plays are consistently competent in structure and characterization, drawing as he did upon the models of his contemporaries over a wide range of themes and plots. Of his six tragedies, *The Cardinal* (pr. 1641) is the best. It has all the trappings of revenge tragedy sensationally displayed, as they had been presented by Kyd and the great writers of revenge tragedy who followed him. There are echoes here of Webster's *The Duchess of Malfi*, but Shirley is content to present the action without psychological probing. He wrote many more comedies than tragedies, the best being *Hyde Park* (pr. 1632) and *The Lady of Pleasure* (pr. 1635). The former is an early comedy of manners which looks forward to the drama of the Restoration. Shirley provides no hint that the pleasures of the aristocracy presented in this comedy would lead to the 1642 Civil War, only a few years away. The latter play presents a similar picture of an aristocracy for whom life is defined by their own pleasures and trivial concerns. The characters play at love in a sensual London, and the morality which is reaffirmed at the end of the play is little more than a witty refusal to sink completely into the mire.

Shirley was at the height of his career when, on September 2, 1642, the ruling Puritan administration proclaimed that "public stage-plays will cease and be foreborne," thus putting an end to the greatest period of English drama the world has known. It had its origins in the ideas and structures of Greek and Roman drama and in the realism of native English drama and life. It was able to grow to maturity because the intellectual and social climate of England was such that citizens were free politically and economically to pursue those ideas wherever they led. That persons of rare genius such as Shakespeare and Jonson happened along during the development of drama elevated the achievement to a level that has enthralled succeeding generations, but even without their contributions, the high reputation of Elizabethan and Jacobean drama would be secure. Rarely before or since has literature of any type held such a clear mirror up to nature, and never with such consistency.

Eugene P. Wright

RESTORATION DRAMA

The term "Restoration" in Restoration drama refers to the return of the monarchy to England after something more than a decade of Puritan rule. Yet the term might with equal justice be applied to the stage itself, for during the interregnum, Puritan authorities repeatedly endeavored, though with limited success, to banish public performances of plays. From September 2, 1642, when Parliament proclaimed "that while these sad causes and set times of humiliation do continue, public stage-plays shall cease, and be forborne," until August 21, 1660, when King Charles II granted patents to Thomas Killigrew and Sir William Davenant to establish theaters, drama in England led a precarious existence.

Late seventeenth century British drama enjoyed a restoration in more than a legal sense. As the political structure of the country returned to an older form, so, too, the drama, at least initially, looked back to pre-Commonwealth days to find its conventions, plots, characters, and themes. Indeed, in 1660 there was no alternative, since no new plays were available when the theaters reopened. Furthermore, both Davenant and Killigrew were products of the earlier period, having acted and written during the reign of Charles I, and most of the surviving actors—many had been killed fighting for the king in the Civil War—knew only the older dramatic conventions. During the Restoration period, about 175 pre-Commonwealth plays were revived, and among plays acted frequently over the years, about fifty percent date from before 1660.

Over the next forty years, however, English drama took on a voice peculiar to the age. The period's major contributions were the comedy of manners or wit and the heroic tragedy, both of which emerged rather quickly and endured throughout the era. Alongside these predominant forms, other types of comic and serious plays coexisted on the stage. Among the former were burlesques and farces, political satires, and comedies of intrigue; among the latter, operas and pastorals. Toward the end of the century, domestic or pathetic tragedy offered some variety to the theatergoing public.

As these plays drew from the stagecraft and literature of the Jacobean and Carolinian drama, so the plays of the eighteenth century drew from the Restoration. John Gay's *The Beggar's Opera* (pr. 1728) and Henry Fielding's *Tom Thumb: A Tragedy* (pr. 1730) differ little from George Villiers' *The Rehearsal* (pr. 1671) or Joseph Arrowsmith's *The Reformation* (pr. 1673), which satirizes the vogue for heroic tragedy. Charles Goring's *Irene* and Lewis Theobald's *The Persian Princess*, first performed in February and May, 1708, respectively, rely on the same kind of exotic settings that John Dryden was using four decades earlier for his heroic tragedies; as late as 1749, Samuel Johnson's *Irene* provided viewers with the same conflict between love and honor, as well as exotic settings and elevated diction, that Restoration audiences had found in the tragedies of Nathaniel Lee. Furthermore, late seventeenth century plays retained their popularity well into the next century. William Congreve's *The Old Bachelor* (pr. 1693) was acted six times in 1724-1725, whereas Charles Shadwell's *The Fair Quaker of Deal* (pr. 1710) was performed only three times that season. Sir Richard Steele's *The Tender Husband: Or, The Accomplished Fools* (pr. 1705) was performed no more frequently than Sir George Etherege's *The Man of Mode: Or, Sir Fopling Flutter* (pr. 1676) in that period. The persistent popularity of this last piece, which may be viewed as the epitome of the Restoration comedy of wit, so troubled Steele that in the epilogue of a revival of William Shakespeare's *Measure for Measure* (pr. 1604) he sharply criticized audiences' admiration for the play's hero:

> The perjur'd Dorimant the beaux admire;
> Gay perjur'd Dorimant the belles desire:
> With fellow-feeling, and well conscious gust,
> Each sex applauds inexorable lust.
> For shame, for shame, ye men of sense begin,
> And scorn the base captivity of sin.

Restoration drama thus does not end abruptly with the end of the seventeenth century. Nevertheless, one finds a change in both playwrights and plays. By 1700, virtually every major Restoration dramatist had died or retired from the stage. Dryden died in 1700; in the same year, Congreve, following the failure of *The Way of the World*, abandoned the theater. Thomas Shadwell had died in 1692, Sir John Vanbrugh turned to architecture, and William Wycherley, though he lived until 1715, did not write a play after 1676. The new generation of dramatists confronted an audience more bourgeois, devoted to at least the trappings of a newer, stricter morality, interested in sentiment and domesticity rather than wit and heroics. Not until the late eighteenth century, with the comedies of Richard Brinsley Sheridan and Oliver Goldsmith, did witty comedy revive, and even then the revival was only partial and sporadic. The world of the Restoration passed away, taking with it the world of its drama.

Influences on Restoration Drama

Many of the playwrights of the Restoration would fit easily into that category which Alexander Pope described as "the mob of gentlemen who wrote with ease." Among the dramatists were two dukes, four earls, a viscount, a baron, fifteen knights and baronets, and dozens of gentlemen. During Oliver Cromwell's regime, a number of these men lived in exile; as a result, they became familiar with the Continental drama of the period. Killigrew wrote *The Princess* (pr. c. 1636) in Naples, *Bellamira Her Dream* (pb. 1664) in Venice, *Claracilla* (pr. c. 1636) in Rome, *The Parson's Wedding* (pr. c. 1640) in Basle, *Cecilia and Clorinda* (pb. 1664) in Turin, and *The Pilgrim* (pb. 1664) in Paris; *The Parson's Wedding* was revived in 1664, the same year in which the other plays were published. The patentee of one of London's two theaters was obviously well versed in foreign drama. Etherege, to cite another example, lived in Paris when Molière was producing his works and drew from them for his own plays.

Molière was in fact the most influential foreign dramatist in the period; his plays served as sources for numerous Restoration comedies. *L'École des maris* (pr. 1661) was the basis of at least part of Sir Charles Sedley's *The Mulberry-Garden* (pr. 1668) and Thomas Shadwell's *The Squire of Alsatia* (pr. 1688). John Caryll's *Sir Salomon* (pr. 1669) derives from *L'École des femmes* (pr. 1662). *Le Misanthrope* (pr. 1666) gives much to William Wycherley's *The Plain-Dealer* (pr. 1676) and Shadwell's *The Sullen Lovers: Or, The Impertinents* (pr. 1668). *L'Avare* (pr. 1668) became Shadwell's *The Miser* (pr. 1672) and the fourth act of *The Squire of Alsatia*. *Les Fourberies de Scapin* (pr. 1671) was the basis of Thomas Otway's *The Cheats of Scapin* (pr. 1676).

Other French writers also influenced their English counterparts. Pierre Corneille's rhymed tragedies probably helped determine the metrical form of heroic tragedy, and the French romances provided plots for a number of these plays. Dryden borrowed from Madeleine de Scudéry's novel *Le Grand Cyrus* (1649-1653) for *Secret Love: Or, The Maiden Queen* (pr. 1667) and *The Conquest of Grenada by the Spaniards* (pr. 1670-1671). Nathaniel Lee's *The Princess of Cleve* (pr. 1680?) owes much to Gauthier de Costes de La Calprenède's novel of that title, and *Cassandre* (1644-1650) provided material for Lee's *The Rival Queens: Or, The Death of Alexander the Great* (pr. 1677) and John Banks's *The Rival Kings* (pr. 1677). From France, too, came the new convention of using women rather than boys to fill female roles; without this innovation, the comedy of wit—with its strong emphasis on sex—would have been impossible.

Other countries also contributed to the Restoration repertoire. King Charles himself asked Sir Samuel Tuke to translate Pedro Calderón de la Barca's *Los empeños de seis horas*, which became the popular *The Adventures of Five Hours* (pr. 1663), a play that started a vogue for comedies that featured Spanish settings and characters, swordplay, and also a strict code of honor. Augustín Moreto y Cabaña's *No puede ser: O, No puede ser guardar una mujer* (pb. 1661) was the basis of John Crowne's *Sir Courtly Nice: Or, It Cannot Be* (pr. 1685), also adapted at the request of the king, and Sir Thomas St. Serfe's *Tarugo's Wiles: Or, The Coffee House* (pr. 1667). Wycherley's *The Gentleman Dancing-Master* (pr. 1672) is a loose adaptation of Calderón's *El maestro de danzar* (pr. c. 1652), and George Digby, Earl of Bristol, turned Calderón's *No siempre lo peor es cierto* (pb.

1652) into his play *Elvira* (pr. 1664).

The Italian *commedia dell'arte* provided yet another source for Restoration drama, particularly the farce and burlesque. On May 29, 1673, and September 29, 1675, the diarist John Evelyn records seeing a troupe of Italian actors, led by Tiberio Fiorilli, who performed in England frequently during the next decade. Edward Ravenscroft sought to capitalize on the popularity of the *commedia dell'arte* with his *Scaramouch, a Philosopher, Harlequin, a School-Boy, Bravo, Merchant and Magician: A Comedy After the Italian Manner* (pr. 1677), and the actor William Mountfort turned Christopher Marlowe's *Doctor Faustus* (pr. c. 1588) into a farce, *The Life and Death of Doctor Faustus* (pr. 1685), introducing both Harlequin and Scaramouch into the piece. Part of the vogue for opera also came from the Italians; on October 22, 1660, Guilo Gentileschi received a patent to build a theater for Italian opera that provided a model for English extravaganzas.

Yet while foreign influences were important, they were less significant than the earlier English drama in determining the form and the content of Restoration plays. In *An Essay of Dramatic Poesy* (1668), Dryden wrote,

> We have borrowed nothing from [the French]; our plots are weaved in English looms; we endeavour therein to follow the variety and greatness of characters, which are derived to us from Shakespeare and Fletcher, the copiousness and well-knitting of the intrigues we have from Jonson, and for the verse itself we have English precedents of elder date than any of Corneille's plays.

Dryden claimed too much in denying any foreign debt at all, but he was correct in noting how much the Restoration drew from Elizabethan and Jacobean literature.

Ben Jonson was not especially popular during the Restoration: Of all of his plays, only *The Alchemist* (pr. 1610), *Epicœne: Or, The Silent Woman* (pr. 1609) and *Volpone: Or, The Fox* (pr. 1605) were performed with any regularity during the period. Yet his influence, particularly on comedy, was far from negligible. His insistence on realistic rather than romantic comedy helped steer Restoration dramatists in that direction; their comedies share Jonson's claim, in the prologue to *Every Man in His Humour* (pr. 1598), to portray "deeds and language such as men do use." Thomas Shadwell, at least in his earlier works, sought to write Jonsonian comedies of humor rather than the newer comedies of wit, claiming that the latter were immoral. His characters, like Jonson's, are obsessed with some peculiarity that causes them to act in an unusual, and therefore comical way. The *dramatis personae* of *The Sullen Lovers* describes Stanford as "a morose, melancholy man, tormented beyond measure with the impertinence of people, and resolved to leave the world to be quit of them." Emilia is "of the same humour with Stanford." Minor characters in the play include the cowardly bully Huffe; Lady Vaine, a whore who pretends to be a lady; and Sir Positive At-all, a pretender to universal knowledge. As the title to Shadwell's third play, *The Humorists* (pr. 1670), indicates, this work, too, is in the Jonsonian tradition. His characters such as Sneak, Crazy, and Briske, their names describing their particular "humor," are closely related to Zeal-of-the-Land Busy and Adam Overdo from Jonson's *Bartholomew Fair* (pr. 1614).

Wycherley, too, drew on the humors tradition. In *The Plain-Dealer*, a number of minor figures are humors characters: Novel, "an admirer of novelties"; Lord Plausible, "a ceremonious, supple, commending coxcomb"; Major Oldfox, "an old, impertinent fop." Even Manly, the main character, is described in Jonsonian terms as "of an honest, surly, nice humor." Lesser dramatists also relied on Jonson, as indicated by such titles as *The Humourous Lovers* (pr. 1667) and *The Triumphant Widow: Or, The Medley of Humours* (pr. 1674), by William Cavendish, Duke of Newcastle, and Nevil Payne's *The Morning Ramble: Or, The Town Humours* (pr. 1672).

Even after Shadwell abandoned the comedy of humors, the tradition continued in the minor characters of many comedies of wit. Sir Joseph Wittol and Captain Bluffe in Congreve's *The Old Bachelor* are like Matthew and Bobadil in Jonson's *Every Man in His Humour*, Wittol foolishly admiring his supposedly brave companion, Bluffe claiming, like Bobadil, to be the greatest hero ever but tamely submitting to a beating. The one-dimensional nature of humors characters makes them particularly suitable to farce, where they provided the bulk of the *dramatis personae*, and even in the comedies of wit the names of the chief characters—Wildair, Sparkish, Horner (that is, cuckolder), Ranger, Valentine, Sir Fopling Flutter, Lord Foppington—rely on the humors tradition.

Like Jonson, Thomas Middleton in his city comedies provided a precedent for realism. Again like Jonson, Middleton drew his characters from the lower ranks of society—they are much better acquainted with Cheapside than Hyde Park—yet they are not always content with their social status. Hoard aspires to be a country gentleman in *A Trick to Catch the Old One* (pr. c. 1605-1606), Yellowhammer stresses his Oxfordshire connections and seeks to improve his status through aristocratic marriages for his children in *A Chaste Maid in Cheapside* (pr. 1611), and Quomodo envisions his progress toward a rich country estate that he hopes to get from Easy in *Michaelmas Term* (pr. c. 1606). These characters are pretenders, the forerunners of the witwouds of Restoration comedy, who would claim a code of behavior and style of life not their own.

Richard Brome, writing shortly after Middleton, presented similar would-be aristocrats. Widgine reflects on Sir Paul Squelch in *The Northern Lass* (pr. 1629): "I have heard Sir Paul Squelch protest he was a Gentleman, and might quarter a coat by his wife's side. Yet I know he was but a Grasier when he left the country; and my lord his father whistled to a team of horses. . . . But now he is Right Worshipful." Mistress Fichow in the same play seeks to marry someone who will make her a lady. Brome also introduces a forerunner of the Restoration heroine, the sexually liberated woman. Rebecca in *The Sparagus Garden* (pr. 1635) observes, "I see what shift soever a woman makes with her husband at home, a friend does best abroad." Alicia, from *The City Wit: Or, The Woman Wears the Breeches* (pr. c. 1629) also seeks to supplement her husband with a lover. The spirit of the age was not ready, though, for their intrigues to succeed.

Brome, like Middleton and Jonson, deals with the lower and the lower-middle classes. James Shirley applied their realism to the world of leisure, contrasting those who would belong to the fashionable world with those who truly do. The silly and affected Lady Bornwell in *The Lady of Pleasure* (pr. 1635) tries to pose as a socialite; against her pretensions, Shirley juxtaposes the polished Celestina. While the play's moralizing marks it as pre-Restoration, the characterization foreshadows Etherege and Congreve.

The wife of Charles I, Queen Henrietta Maria, introduced to the court the doctrines of Platonic love. The love in Restoration comedy is anything but Platonic; the tragedies, on the other hand, borrow heavily from this tradition. The high-flown rhetoric of heroic tragedy, for example, follows the convention that refined diction is the only kind suitable for lovers. Such Platonic notions generated a strong realistic backlash, however, reflected in the poetry of the Cavaliers and in such plays as *The Country Captain* (pr. c. 1639), by William Cavendish, in which Sir Francis, a polished courtier, seduces Lady Huntlove. At the end of the play, Sir Francis reforms and urges his mistress to do likewise, but Lady Huntlove is neither condemned nor punished.

By the outbreak of the Civil War, then, English drama had developed a number of elements utilized by Restoration playwrights. Despite Puritan efforts to suppress the drama after 1642, plays were published and rather regularly produced: Under the Commonwealth, there were fourteen editions of *Mucedorus* (pb. 1598); eight of Marlowe's *Doctor Faustus* (pr. c. 1588); six editions of Francis Beaumont and John Fletcher's *Philaster: Or, Love Lies A-Bleeding* (pr. c. 1609), *A King and No King* (pr. 1611), *The Maid's Tragedy* (pr. c. 1611), and George Chapman's *The Revenge of Bussy d'Ambois* (pr. c. 1610). One bookseller advertised more than five hundred plays. A major publishing event of the period was the appearance of the Beaumont and Fletcher folio in 1647; their plays were immensely popular in the latter half of the seventeenth century, when thirty-nine were definitely performed and three others may have been performed. In 1668-1669 alone, eleven Beaumont and Fletcher plays were revived, compared to six by Shakespeare. Not only were these plays perennial favorites, but also their emphasis on genteel romance influenced comic writers, while their exotic settings and tragicomic plots were taken up by writers of serious plays.

Publication thus helped keep alive the English dramatic traditions. As Sir Aston Cokain observed in the preface to Brome's *Five New Plays* (1653), "though we may/ Not them in their full glories yet display,/ Yet we may please ourselves by reading them."

In fact, it was possible to see a number of plays in their full glory. *The Kingdom's Weekly Intelligencer* for January 18-25, 1648, noted, "It is very observable, that on Sunday January 23 there were ten Coaches to hear Doctor Usher at Lincoln's Inn, but there were above sixscore coaches on the last Thursday in Golden Lane to hear the players at the Fortune." John Evelyn attended a performance at the Cockpit on February 5, 1648, and even after the Parliament issued another ordinance against acting, it was informed in September "that stage-plays were duly acted, either at the Bull or Fortune, or the private house at Salisbury Court." On New Year's Day, 1649, soldiers broke up performances at the Cockpit and Salisbury Court. Raids occurred repeatedly at these theaters over the next several years, indicating that plays continued to be produced. Sir Daniel Fleming, on a visit to London, reported spending twopence to see a play in 1653; during the next two years, he spent a shilling and fourpence at the theater. Parliament was no more successful in suppressing plays in the provinces. The historian Anthony Wood records seeing plays at the Blue Anchor tavern, Oxford, on July 6, 1657, at the Cross Inn on July 17, 1658, and at the Roebuck on July 8, 1659. Though English actors performed "by stealth," they nevertheless performed.

Occasionally, new plays were performed, too, among them Davenant's *The Unfortunate Lovers* (pr. 1638) and *Love and Honour* (pr. 1634), the latter summarizing in its title the basic conflict of Restoration heroic tragedy. Davenant's *The Siege of Rhodes* (pr. 1656-1659) may be regarded as the progenitor of this genre. Abraham Cowley's *The Guardian* (pr. 1650) received several private performances and was revised in 1661 as *The Cutter of Coleman Street.* This work was but one of several leveled against the Puritans: Samuel Sheppard's *The Committee-Man Curried* (pr. 1647), *The Cuckow's Nest at Westminster* (pr. 1648), and *Craftie Cromwell* (pr. 1648) and John Capon's *The Disease of the House* (pr. 1649) began a tradition that continued after the Restoration with such plays as John Tatham's *The Rump* (pr. 1660), Robert Howard's *The Committee* (pr. 1662), and John Lacy's *The Old Troop* (pr. c. 1664).

Etherege's *The Comical Revenge: Or, Love in a Tub* (pr. 1664) provides a good illustration of the viability of these older dramatic traditions. The serious lovers, Beaufort and Graciana, Bruce and Amelia, speak in heroic couplets that express Platonic sentiments. The witty Sir Frederick, with his epigrams, is an early version of the Restoration truewit, but his widow-chasing recalls Fletcher. Cully is a Jonsonian coward, and his gulling is reminiscent of Easy's in *Michaelmas Term*. Cully is also a Puritan; the satire against him suggests the anti-Puritan plays of the interregnum. Dufoy, the French valet, is similar to Monsieur le Frisk in Shirley's *The Ball* (pr. 1632), to Galliard in Cavendish's *The Varietie* (pr. 1641), and to Monsieur Raggou in Lacy's *The Old Troop*.

Restoration drama thus drew from earlier literary traditions; it also re-lied on its social and political milieu. In his defense of Restoration comedy against early nineteenth century charges of immorality, Charles Lamb claimed that the plays were inoffensive because "they are a world of them-selves almost as much as fairyland." The characters "have got out of Chris-tendom into the land—what shall I call it?—of cuckoldry—the Utopia of gallantry, where pleasure is duty, and the manners perfect freedom. It is al-together a speculative scene of things, which has no reference whatever to the world that is."

Nothing could be further from the truth. John Stafford wrote in the epi-logue to Thomas Southerne's *The Disappointment* (pr. 1684):

> In Comedy your little selves you meet,
> 'Tis Covent Garden drawn in Bridges-Street.
> Smile on our author then, if he has shown
> A jolly nut-brown bastard of your own.
> Ah! Happy you, with ease and with delight,
> Who act those follies, poets toil to write.

Wycherley's prologue to *The Plain-Dealer* states that the author "displays you, as you are," and, at the end of the period, Vanbrugh's *The Provok'd Wife* (pr. 1697) makes a similar claim:

> 'Tis the Intent and Business of the Stage,
> To Copy out the Follies of the Age;
> To hold to every Man a Faithful Glass,
> And shew him of what Species he's an Ass.

The Character of a Coffee-House (pr. 1673) describes the company as composed of "a town wit, a silly fop and a worshipful justice—a worthy lawyer and an errant pickpocket, a reverend non-conformist and a canting mountebank, all blended together to compose an oglio of impertinence." That grouping could easily serve as the male cast of a Restoration comedy. So much a reflection of the times are these plays that when Etherege was serving as ambassador in Ratisbon (in Bavaria), he wrote back to England, "Pray let Will Richards send me Mr. Shadwell's [play] when it is printed, that I may learn what follies are in fashion." Etherege himself was accused by Captain Alexander Radcliffe of a lack of invention, of merely transcrib-ing what he heard at the coffeehouses: "So what he writes is but transla-tion/ From Dog and Partridge conversation." Gerard Langbaine at the end of the century declared in *An Account of the English Dramatic Poets* (1691) that Etherege's *The Man of Mode* was "as true comedy, and the characters drawn to the life as any play that has been acted since the restoration of the English stage." Sir Richard Steele, no admirer of Restoration comedy, conceded in *Tatler* #3 that, in the character of Horner, Wycherley had provided "a good representation of the age in which that comedy was written; at which time love and wenching were the business of life, and the gallant manners of pursuing women was the best recommendation at court."

Dryden's *The Kind Keeper: Or, Mr. Limberham* (pr. 1678) needed no literary precedents to satirize the practice of keeping a mistress. The vice was so ingrained that a group of powerful keepers suppressed the play after a three-day run. So fashionable was the practice that Lord Chamberlain North was advised to keep a mistress because he was ill-regarded for not doing so. By the same token, the character Foresight, through whom Congreve satirizes belief in astrology in *Love for Love* (pr. 1695), might owe something to Calderón's *El astrólogo fingido* (pb. 1633) and the humors tradition, but Dryden, the Earl of Shaftesbury, and the famous John Partridge, whom Jonathan Swift satirized, all believed in this pseudoscience. Lord Nonsuch in Dryden's *The Wild Gallant* (pr. 1663) believes that he is pregnant; this farfetched situation is based on a story that circulated about Dr. Pelling, chaplain to Charles II, who so imagined himself.

Political controversies also inspired the drama. As noted above, Puritans were frequently satirized in the years immediately following the return of the monarchy, and during the panic caused by the supposed Popish Plot, another spate of political plays appeared. Even Otway's *Venice Preserved: Or, A Plot Discovered* (pr. 1682), though much more than a representation of partisan political concerns, drew on this atmosphere of fear, and plays such as Crowne's *City Politiques* (pr. 1683) depict the period's factional strife.

Not only real situations but also real people served as models. Sir Positive At-all in Shadwell's *The Sullen Lovers* is a humors character, but he was based on Sir Robert Howard. Robert Hooke, curator of the Royal Society, was portrayed as Nicholas Gimcrack in Shadwell's *The Virtuoso* (pr. 1676). Hooke, who attended a performance, noted in his diary that the likeness was readily observed: "Damned dogs! *Vindica me Deus*. People almost pointed." Joseph Arrowsmith lampooned Dryden as Tutor in *The Reformation*, and Villiers satirized him as Bayes in *The Rehearsal*. William Chamberlayne attacked two other contemporary dramatists, Elkanah Settle and Edward Ravenscroft, as Sir Symon Credulous and Sir Joseph Simpleton in *Wits Led by the Nose* (pr. 1677). The Earl of Shaftesbury was a popular butt, especially around 1680. Sir Fopling Flutter in *The Man of Mode* was based on the notorious fop Beau Hewitt, Dorimant was modeled on John Wilmot, the Earl of Rochester, and Medley—as even his name suggests— was clearly modeled on Sir Charles Sedley. Vanbrugh's *The Relapse: Or, Virtue in Danger* (pr. 1696) portrayed Beau Fielding as Lord Foppington, even including the duel in which Fielding received a minor wound. The drama thus held up a mirror in which the age could see itself.

Comedy

This mirror was selective, though, in what it reflected. In his preface to *An Evening's Love: Or, The Mock Astrologer* (pr. 1668), Dryden wrote, "Comedy consists, though of low persons, yet of natural actions, and characters; I mean such humours, adventures, and designs, as are to be found and met with in the world," but the world of Restoration comedy is a limited one indeed. Of eighty-five successful comedies in the period, seventy are set in England, sixty-four of them in London. The characters, like the setting, reflect a restricted social environment; all but fourteen of the plays set in England treat the upper-middle class.

This limited outlook is not surprising, for, as already noted, many of the playwrights were themselves from the upper classes. Further, as Samuel Johnson noted in the next century, "The drama's laws the drama's patrons give,/ And we who live to please must please to live." The Restoration theater, especially in the first two decades of the period, attracted a much more restricted audience than did the Elizabethan or Jacobean stage. In 1642, London was able to support its seven theaters—Salisbury Court, Blackfriars, the Globe, the Fortune, the Red Bull, the Drury Lane Cockpit, and the Hope. Twenty years later, it had to struggle to support two; when one house was full, the other was likely to be empty. Thus, for example, when *Tarugo's Wiles* opened at the Duke's Theatre on October 5, 1667, Killigrew tried to counter with a revival of *Flora's Vagaries*. Samuel Pepys noted that the older play did not attract many viewers: "To see how Nell [Eleanor Gwyn] cursed, for having so few people in the pit, was pretty." Two year later, when Shadwell's *The Royal Shepherdess* (pr. 1669) was doing well, Killigrew again had difficulties. "Lord, what an empty house," Pepys wrote in his diary (February 26, 1669). In 1682, the two companies were forced to merge. Competition resumed in 1695, but with the same disastrous consequences, so that in 1707 a second merger was necessary.

In part, this situation resulted from the higher prices. Whereas an Elizabethan could see a play for a penny, a Restoration playgoer had to pay at least a shilling. The newer theaters were small, and they employed elaborate—hence expensive—scenery; prices reflected these circumstances. Also, there remained a strong bias against stage plays. Shadwell claims in the epilogue to *The Lancashire Witches, and Tegue o Divelly the Irish Priest* (pr. 1681),

> The City neither likes us nor our wit,
> They say their wives learn ogling in the pit;
> They're from the boxes taught to make advances,
> To answer stolen sighs and naughty glances.

Not only was the fare on the stage regarded by many as improper, but also the presence of prostitutes and rakes in the audience deterred many of the puritanically inclined.

The drama's patrons were therefore drawn from an educated, upper-class coterie. Literary men attended regularly: Sir Charles Sedley, Sir George Etherege, George Villiers, Thomas Shadwell, John Dryden, Thomas Killigrew, and Sir William Davenant. Among the royalty and the nobility, Charles II and the Duke and Duchess of York were frequently in the audience. So, too, were Prince Rupert, the Dukes of Ormond, Norfolk, and Albemarle, Lady Castlemagne, Lady Dorset, and Lady Elizabeth Bodvile. Pepys does occasionally record "The house was full of citizens" (January 1, 1663) or "The house full of Parliamentmen" (November 2, 1667), but the very fact that he mentions this element indicates how unusual it was to find them in the theater in any number.

While the comedies of the period reflect this upper-class London world, they are not mere reportage. The dramatists used situations and characters from real life, but they molded that material, imposing upon it a structure and outlook. What gives Restoration comedy its peculiar flavor is the ethos that informs the writing.

Chief among the beliefs expressed in Restoration comedy is the importance of being natural. Hence, the heroes of these comedies shun affectation, while the less admirable characters are pretenders, whether to wit, morality, or bravery. In Etherege's *She Would If She Could* (pr. 1668), Lady Cockwood pretends to conventional morality but tries to commit adultery. The truewit Gatty, on the other hand, hates to dissemble. Lady Fidget in Wycherley's *The Country Wife* (pr. 1675) objects to Horner's very name as well as to the word "naked" in "naked truth." Actually, it is the truth that she dislikes. She is willing enough to go to bed with Horner; she seeks only the reputation of honor, not the thing itself. In this regard, she is the antithesis of the truewit Horner, who does not care what others think of him provided he can have what he truly seeks, pleasure.

The motto of the truewit might read, "To be rather than to seem." In *The Man of Mode*, Harriet, the heroine, objects to plain women who set themselves as beauties and to dull men who try to be wits. She also criticizes the diversions at Hyde Park because she regards the supposed politeness there as mere show. When characters act in a manner that is contrary to nature—when, for example, Old Bellair in *The Man of Mode* seeks to rival his son for the hand of Emilia, when Sir Sampson Legend seeks to marry Angelica in Congreve's *Love for Love* even though he is fifty and she is less than half his age, when Lady Wishfort offers herself as a rival to her niece Millamant in *The Way of the World*—they are certain to be ridiculed and defeated. As George Savile, Marquess of Halifax, wrote in *The Lady's New Year's Gift: Or, Advice to a Daughter* (1688), "Unnatural things carry a deformity in them never to be disguised; the liveliness of youth in a riper age, looketh like a new patch upon an old gown; so that a gay matron, a cheerful old fool may be reasonably put into the list of the tamer sort of monsters." Or, as Congreve wrote in "Of Pleasing,"

> All Rules of pleasing in this one unite,
> Affect not any thing in Nature's spight. . . .
> None are, for being what they are, in fault,
> But for not being what they wou'd be thought.

Perhaps Horner in *The Country Wife* best summarizes this attitude: "A pox on 'em, and all that force nature and would be still what she forbids 'em! Affectation is her greatest monster."

Because they shun affectation, the truewit avoids excess in dress and speech. Dorimant in *The Man of Mode* objects when Handy spends too much time dressing him, exclaiming, "That a man's excellency should be in the neatly tying of a ribbon or a cravat!" Sir Fopling, as affected in his dress as in every other aspect of his behavior, notes that Dorimant's cravats never are handsome. Harriet in *The Man of Mode* also does not care for elaborate dress, again showing herself the female equivalent of Dorimant. Isabella in Aphra Behn's *Sir Patient Fancy* (pr. 1678) objects when her maid spends too much time fixing her hair; she is, of course, a truewit.

The vanity of fops is symbolized by their overattention to appearance, often expressed by their fondness for admiring their images in mirrors. Mockmode in George Farquhar's *Love and a Bottle* (pr. 1698), Sir Philip Modelove in Mrs. Susannah Centlivre's *A Bold Stroke for a Wife* (pr. 1718), Lord Foppington in *The Relapse*, Sir Courtly Nice in the play of the same name, Donna Aurelia in *An Evening's Love*, Lady Fanciful in *The Way of the World* are among the fops and fools who spend their time before a glass. Sir Courtly is so engrossed in his own reflection that he proposes to the wrong woman. Martha rejects Dapperwit in Wycherley's *Love in a Wood: Or, St. James's Park* (pr. 1671) because he is already wedded to himself.

Truewits, as the name indicates, speak well, but they do so naturally. The witwouds, on the other hand, lack this natural ability, and their various attempts to compensate for their deficiency render them ridiculous. Melantha in Dryden's *Marriage à la Mode* (pr. 1672) cannot go visiting until her maid Philotis furnishes her with her daily quota of French words. Witwoud in *The Way of the World* trusts to his memory rather than his invention for clever comments and lards his conversation with an excess of similes. Puny in Abraham Cowley's *The Cutter of Coleman Street* (pr. 1661) "scorns to speak anything that's common," and Sir Mannerly Shallow in John Crowne's *The Country Wit* (pb. 1675) seeks farfetched metaphors.

As speech should not be overdone, neither should it be too unpolished. Mere railing is not wit, a fact that Novel and Manly in *The Plain-Dealer*,

Brisk in Congreve's *The Double Dealer* (pr. 1693), and Petulant in *The Way of the World* fail to understand. Scandal and Ben in *Love for Love* are honest and likable, but they both fail the test of the truewit because their speech is inappropriate: Scandal is too willing to rail, while Ben uses jargon. Language serves as a key to character. In *The Man of Mode*, Old Bellair rambles and fills his talk with such uncouth phrases as "a dad," "out a pize," and "a pize on 'em." Sir Fopling speaks aimlessly, and Mrs. Loveit exaggerates, sounding like a tragic heroine. These mannerisms instantly reveal the characters as flawed.

This concern with the natural helps explain the sexual freedom of the plays and of the age. When Mrs. Loveit urges Dorimant to be faithful to her, he replies, "Constancy at my years! 'Tis not a virtue in season. You might as well expect the fruit of autumn ripens i' the spring. . . . Youth has a long journey to go, Madam; shou'd I have set up my rest at the first inn I lodg'd at, I shou'd never have arriv'd at the happiness I now enjoy." Restoration comedy recognizes the sexual impulse. As Dorimant says when he keeps a tryst with Bellinda at the same time that he is wooing Harriet, "I am not so foppishly in love here to forget I am flesh and blood yet." Valentine in Thomas Southerne's *Sir Anthony Love: Or, The Rambling Lady* (pr. 1690) also acknowledges the frailty of the flesh: "I may be a lover, but I must be a man."

Sexual appetite is natural in the young, both men and women; what is not natural, and hence deserving of ridicule, is prudishness. In fact, about half the prudes yield to men. Olivia in *The Plain-Dealer* claims to hate the very thought of a lover, and she objects to the immorality of Wycherley's "china" scene in *The Country Wife*. Typically, she is exposed as deceitful and unchaste. It is a flaw to deny one's sexuality; yet virtually every heroine remains chaste. A woman who goes to bed with a truewit will be well provided for and perhaps even married off to someone, but not to the hero. Dorimant sleeps with Mrs. Loveit and Bellinda, but he marries Harriet, who has not yielded to him. Mirabell has slept with Mrs. Fainall; she is married to another, and Mirabell marries Millamant in *The Way of the World*. Valentine gives money to his former mistress, Margery, by whom he has had a child, but he marries Angelica in *Love for Love*.

Like the prude, the fools and fops deny their sexuality. Because they affect virtue and are hypocritical, they are fit subjects for satire. Smuggler in George Farquhar's *The Constant Couple: Or, A Trip to the Jubilee* (pr. 1699) belongs to the Society for the Reformation of Manners, yet he offers to pay Lady Lovewell to sleep with him. Alderman Gripe, "a bellows of zeal," seeks to seduce a young girl in *Love in a Wood*. In *Sir Courtly Nice*, Testimony excuses his attempted rape by observing that despite his actions he has a sense of sin. It is not religion these plays attack, it is pretense.

This concern for natural behavior does not extend to an admiration for scenic nature. Restoration drama is social in its concerns, exploring the ways that people ought to interact with one another. The countryside is rejected because in the rural world social activity is limited. Furthermore, audiences were urban, and the plays demonstrate that bias. As previously noted, the majority of successful Restoration comedies are set in London, and rustic characters in the plays are almost always presented as foolish. Harriet tests Dorimant's love by insisting at the end of *The Man of Mode* that he follow her into the country; she can imagine no greater sign of devotion. To Alithea in *The Country Wife*, being sent down into the country is the worst fate that can befall a woman; it is the equivalent of death. Horner in that play finds that being away from the city for any length of time has a deleterious effect on a person's behavior. As Horner says to Pinchwife, "I see a little time in the country makes a man turn wild and unsociable, and only fit to converse with his horses, dogs, and his herds." In *The Way of the World*, "I nauseate walking; 'tis a country diversion. I loathe the country and everything that relates to it." In Colley Cibber's *The Provok'd Husband* (pr. 1728; completion of Villiers' play)—the tradition lingered into the next century—Sir Francis, Lady Wronghead, and Squire Richard have been reared in the country and are consequently shown as foolish and imperceptive, as is the hoyden Prue in Congreve's *Love for Love*.

The "natural" man in the Restoration is urban; he is also unselfish. The truewit seeks pleasure, but he is not the slave of lust. Characters who are driven by their appetites, such as Surly in *Sir Courtly Nice*, Heartwell in *The Old Bachelor*, and Blunt in Behn's *The Rover: Or, The Banished Cavaliers* (pr. 1677-1681), are all punished for their unbridled lechery. Surly is gulled and then beaten off the stage, Heartwell falls in love with a whore, and Blunt is gulled by a prostitute. No Restoration truewit would resort to force.

Indeed the truewit scrupulously adheres to a code of honor. Horner enjoys sex, but he does not pursue Alithea, whom he regards as the province of a fellow truewit. The wives of fools are fair game, chiefly because they are willing, but not the mistress of a friend. When Horner thinks that Harcourt has lost Alithea to Sparkish, he is truly sorry; and when the arrival of friends prevents Margery Pinchwife from leaving his room, he is careful to guard her reputation. So, too, Dorimant protects Bellinda's image. As she says, "He's tender of my honor though he's cruel to my love." Bevil lies to protect his mistress in Shadwell's *Epsom-Wells* (pr. 1672), and Roebuck is careful about what he says, since "the tongue is the only member that can hurt a lady's honor" (*Love and a Bottle*). Etherege summarizes this code when he writes, "A friend that bravely ventures his life in the field to serve me deserves but equally with a mistress that kindly exposes her honor to oblige me, especially when she does it as generously too, and with as little ceremony" (*She Would If She Could*).

Restoration comic heroes marry well, an important consideration in an age when a gentleman could attain wealth only through inheritance or marriage, but their primary aim is pleasure, not wealth—they are not mercenary. Ranger in *Love in a Wood* is sorry that the lady he loves is an heiress, because her wealth may lead others to suspect him of having selfish motives in pursuing her. Valentine in *Love for Love* wants money, but only so he may woo Angelica; once he thinks that she intends to marry another, he is ready to sign over his inheritance for her. Like their male counterparts, the female truewits are generous. Pleasant in *The Parson's Wedding* will marry a man of "wit and honor though he has nothing but a sword at his side." Lucia, too, prefers wit and honor to money, rejecting a rich suitor who is foolish in *Epsom-Wells*. Christina in *Love in a Wood* is willing to marry Valentine despite his poverty.

When people do marry for money, they are destined for unhappiness. Mrs. Brittle of Thomas Betterton's *The Amorous Widow* (pr. 1670) is ready to commit adultery because she is unhappy in her mercantile marriage. Lady Brute in *The Provok'd Wife* has engineered a financially successful marriage, but she is miserable. Lady Dunce in Otway's *The Soldier's Fortune* (pr. 1680) summarizes the lot of these women:

> Curst be the memory, nay double curst,
> Of her that wedded age for interest first;
> Though worn with years, with fruitless wishes full,
> 'Tis all day troublesome and all night dull.

Restoration comedy thus seeks to demonstrate the proper way to behave, rewarding those who abide by its social code, ridiculing and punishing those who violate it. Throughout the period, the plays stress this moral purpose. The dedication to Behn's *The Lucky Chance: Or, An Alderman's Bargain* (pr. 1686) can serve as a representative of dozens of similar statements, from Cowley's *The Cutter of Coleman Street* in 1661 to Congreve's *The Way of the World* in 1700. Behn states that plays "are secret instructions to the people, in things that 'tis impossible to insinuate into them any other way.... 'Tis example alone that inspires morality, and best establishes virtue." The examples held up for admiration are the characters who are true to their own natures, sincere, generous, clever, unaffected. The vices are hypocrisy, selfishness, pretension.

Seen in this light, Restoration comedy hardly seems immoral, but as the eighteenth century approached, the audiences' and critics' attitudes toward what was natural changed. Steele provides a measure of that shift in his attack on *The Man of Mode* in *Spectator* #65, dated May 15, 1711:

> A fine gentleman should be honest in his actions, and refined in his language. Instead of this, our hero, in this piece, is a direct knave in his designs and a clown in his language.... This whole celebrated piece is a perfect contradiction to good manners,

good sense, and common honesty. . . . There is nothing in it but what is built upon the ruin of virtue and innocence. . . . I allow it to be nature, but it is nature in its utmost corruption and degeneracy.

Good manners, good sense, common honesty, and nature—these are the very terms Etherege would have used. For Etherege, though, Dorimant is the embodiment, not the antithesis, of these qualities. Jeremy Collier, whose *A Short View of the Immorality and Profaneness of the English Stage* (1698) epitomized the new taste in drama, also spoke in the same terms as the playwrights he was attacking; it is his definition of those terms that differs from theirs. Thus, in criticizing the Restoration portrayal of women, he writes,

Now to bring women under such misbehavior is violence to their native modesty, and a misrepresentation of their sex. For Modesty, as Mr. Rapin observes, is the character of women. To represent them without this quality, is to make monsters of them, and throw them out of their kind.

To Etherege, Wycherley, Dryden, and their fellow playwrights, the prude, the one who denies her sexuality, is the monster. They recognized and accepted human frailty and appreciated human pleasures. One reason that the dramatists who responded to Collier failed to persuade him or his adherents is that the two sides could not understand each other: They used the same words but meant opposite things by them. To cite but one example, Farquhar in "A Discourse upon Comedy" (1702) claims that *The Old Bachelor* is moral because, through the character of Fondlewife, Congreve shows the folly of an old man's marrying a young woman. Such a moral was not what Steele and Collier had in mind, though; they were seeking absolute virtue, not social proprieties.

This shift in the understanding of what is natural, and hence what is moral, affected the plays of the 1690's. As early as 1668, Shadwell had criticized the moral tone of the comedies of wit, but Shadwell's was a lone voice in the 1660's, and he was sufficiently aware of his singularity to conform to the ethos of the period in his later plays. By the time Collier was writing, the world of the Restoration had yielded to the more bourgeois, mercantile forces that were increasingly prominent after the Glorious Revolution.

Representative of this new mood was the Society for the Reformation of Manners, which in 1694 published a "Black Roll," listing several hundred people whom it had prosecuted for immorality, and "Proposals for a National Reformation" that urged, among other measures, "that the public play-houses may be suppressed." Members of the society were forbidden to attend the theater. One can understand why Farquhar makes the hypocritical Smuggler a member of this society. By 1734, it claimed to have prosecuted almost one hundred thousand people for such offenses as whoring, cursing, drunkenness, and Sabbath breaking. In 1699, Nahum Tate proposed bowdlerizing all plays, and John Dennis reported in 1721 that at the turn of the century there was much sentiment in favor of closing the theaters. Grand juries brought indictments against Congreve for *The Double Dealer* and Thomas D'Urfey for *The Comical History of Quixote* (pr. 1694), and a London grand jury sought the prohibition of the posting of playbills on the grounds that they encouraged vice. On March 4, 1699, Dryden wrote to Elizabeth Steward, "This day was played a revised comedy of Mr. Congreve's called *The Double Dealer*, which was never very taking; in the playbill was printed—'Written by Mr. Congreve, with several expressions omitted!': what kind of expressions these were you may easily guess, if you have seen the Monday's Gazette, wherein is the King's order for the reformation on the stage."

Even in the plays of Congreve, who had no qualms about Restoration morality, one sees a change from the comedies of the 1660's and 1670's. Valentine in *Love for Love* had a mistress before the play begins, but he has given up wenching. Mirabell in *The Way of the World* also had a mistress, but he has forsworn gallantry before the first scene; he will not even allow himself to be seduced. The play that generally marks the real break with Restoration comedy, though, is Cibber's *Love's Last Shift: Or, The Fool in Fashion* (pr. 1696), which antedates Collier's attack on the stage and so suggests that even without such criticism dramatists detected and were responding to new audience demands. Loveless, a rake, has wasted his wife's fortune and then fled abroad. Upon his return to England, Amanda seduces him and then reveals her identity to him. Loveless repents of his former sins and promises "never-ceasing tears of penitence." Cibber conceded that for most of its length the play espouses Restoration values, but when Restoration rakes marry, neither do they promise, nor do their brides expect, fidelity. Cibber had correctly gauged the mood of his audience; Tom Davies described the reaction:

> The joy of unexpected reconcilement, from Loveless's remorse and penitence, spread such an uncommon rapture of pleasure in the audience, that never were spectators more happy in easing their minds by uncommon and repeated plaudits. The honest tears shed by the audience at this interview conveyed a strong reproach to our licentious poets, and was to Cibber the highest mark of honor.

Vanbrugh satirized *Love's Last Shift* in *The Relapse*: In Vanbrugh's "sequel," Loveless returns to his rakish ways and carries off his wife's cousin to bed while she cries "Help! Help!"—but does so "very softly." Vanbrugh, however, allows no cuckolding in his plays. John Dryden, Jr., in *The Husband His Own Cuckold* (pr. 1695) presents two cuckolding attempts; both fail. In Mrs. Manley's *The Lost Lover* (pr. 1696), Olivia has been forced to marry Smyrna, a rich old merchant, though she loves Wildman. In 1676, she would have yielded to him and everyone would have been happy; now she remains faithful to her husband. Belira does yield to her lover, who subsequently mistreats her, thus offering a moralistic warning. By 1709, Mrs. Centlivre was writing a play in which the heroes are named Faithful, Lovely, and Constant instead of Ranger, Wildair, Careless, or Horner (*The Man's Bewitch'd: Or, The Devil to Do About Her*, pr. 1709).

The older tradition did not vanish at once. William Burnaby's *The Modish Husband* (pr. 1702) harks back to the heyday of witty comedy when Lord Promise persuades his friend Lionel to court Lady Promise so that he (Lord Promise) may pursue Lady Cringe. The play failed because it was too risqué for the time. Mrs. Mary Pix's *The Deceiver Deceived* (pr. 1697) allows the heroine one chance at adultery before she reforms and gives up her lover, Count Andrew, for her husband.

Farquhar's *The Beaux' Stratagem* (pr. 1707) indicates how playwrights still sympathetic to the ethos of Restoration comedy felt obliged to cope with altered audience expectations. The wits win, but they do so morally rather than cleverly. Archer cannot seduce Mrs. Sullen but must wait for her to get a divorce so that he can marry her. Aimwell seeks to deceive the rich Dorinda into marriage by impersonating his titled brother. At the last minute, though, he repents and abandons his design in a sentimental speech: "Such goodness who could injure; I find myself unequal to the task of villain; she has gain'd my soul, and made it honest like her own; I cannot, cannot hurt her." Dorinda is so impressed that she agrees to marry him anyway. Happily, Sir Charles Freeman then enters and announces that Aimwell's brother has died, making Aimwell the viscount after all. Chastity and prudence have replaced wit and daring as the key virtues, and the plays now focus on moralistic examples of how one should act rather than on satiric portraits of how one should not act.

Tragedy

It is difficult to imagine that the same dramatists who penned witty Restoration comedies often also wrote the heroic tragedies of the age, or that audiences who appreciated the realistic portrait of a Dorimant or a Horner would endure the bombast and whining of the period's tragic heroes. Indeed, there is evidence that audiences did not appreciate the tragedies, for though more tragedies than comedies were written, a higher percentage of them failed, nor did they always elicit the expected response. When Morat in John Dryden's *Aureng-Zebe* (pr. 1675) announced, "I'll do't to shew my arbitrary power," Cibber claims that the audience laughed. Dryden's Lisideus says, "I have observed that, in all our tragedies, the audience cannot forbear laughing when the actors are to die; 'tis the most comic part of the whole play,." Pepys records a fine example of the response high-flying speeches might get. On October 4, 1664, Pepys attended a performance of

Roger Boyle, Earl of Orrery's heroic play *The Generall* (pr. 1663). Sedley, according to Pepys,

> did at every line take notice of the dullness of the poet and badness of the action, that most pertinently, which I was mightily taken with; and among others where by Altemuri's command Clarimont, the general, is commanded to rescue his rival, . . . he, after a great deal of demur, broke out, "well, I'll save my rival and make her confess, that I deserve, while he do but possess." "Why, what, pox," says Sir Charles Sedley, "would he have him have more, or what is there more to be had of a woman than the possessing her?"

In many ways, the tragedies of the period seem the antithesis of the comedies. Heroes in Restoration tragedy speak of virtue and honor, the catchwords of hypocrites in Restoration comedy. In Restoration tragedy, children are supposed to obey their parents regardless of consequences; in the comedy of the period, children do as they please. Marriage is the culmination of love in the tragedies; in the comedies, it is only the beginning of a new set of problems—hence the oft-repeated proviso scene in which lovers try to avoid at least some of the pitfalls that they foresee in the wedded state.

Such opposites are Restoration comedy and tragedy that the speeches of the heroes in the one are those of the villains in the other. The following speech could be that of Dorimant or Horner:

> Marriage, thou curse of love, and snare of life,
> That first debas'd a mistress to a wife!
> Love, like a scene, at distance should appear;
> But marriage views the gross-daub'd landscape near.

In fact, it is spoken by the evil King of Grenada in the second part of Dryden's *The Conquest of Grenada by the Spaniards*. In *The Man of Mode*, Dorimant tells Mrs. Loveit, "What we swear at such a time may be a certain proof of a present passion, but to say truth, in love there is no security to be given for the future." Maximin expresses a similar sentiment in Dryden's tragedy *Tyrannic Love: Or, The Royal Martyr* (pr. 1669):

> If to new persons I my love apply,
> The stars and nature are in fault, not I. . . .
> I can no more make passion come or go,
> Than you can bid your Nilus ebb or flow.

A witty, rakish speech, this, but Maximin is a villain.

Whereas the comedies seek to present a realistic portrait of the age, Restoration tragedy attempts to present the ideal. Dryden, whose criticism and example helped set the tone of the genre, declared in his essay "Of Heroic Plays":

An heroic poet is not tied to a bare representation of what is true, or exceeding probable: but . . . he may let himself loose to visionary objects, and to the representation of such things as depending not on sense, and therefore not to be comprehended by knowledge, may give him a freer scope for imagination.

Commenting on this lack of realism, Mrs. John Evelyn wrote to Ralph de Bohun in 1671, "Love is made so pure, and valour so nice, that one would imagine it designed for an Utopia rather than our stage." While she was referring specifically to Dryden's *The Conquest of Grenada by the Spaniards*, she might have been describing virtually any heroic tragedy.

The setting of these plays suggests their focus on the unreal; they are remote in time and space from modern England. Instead, they are placed in ancient Greece or Rome, Moorish Spain, sixteenth century Latin America, medieval Turkey, or Morocco.

In language, too, these tragedies differ markedly from the comedies. Dryden compared heroic drama to the epic; this analogy with poetry prompted tragic playwrights to turn to the heroic couplet for their dialogue. Pepys found that Dryden's *The Indian Queen* (pr. 1664) was "spoiled by the rhyme, which breaks the sense," and John Milton had rejected the use of rhyme for the epic. The debate over whether rhyme was in fact appropriate to tragedy was a heated one. In his dedication to *The Rival Ladies* (pr. 1664), Dryden defended the practice. Sir Robert Howard criticized it in his preface to *Four New Plays* (1665)—although he, too, employed couplets "not to appear singular"—and Dryden replied in *An Essay of Dramatic Poesy* (1668), calling heroic couplets "the noblest kind of modern verse" and hence best suited to the elevated form of tragedy. Prose was too realistic for the genre. Not every dramatist agreed; Thomas Porter's *The Villain* (pr. 1662), modeled in part on Shakespeare's *Othello*, is in prose and also contains some comic business, a practice shunned in heroic tragedy. John Wilson's *Andronicus Commenius* (pr. 1664) utilizes the exotic setting of heroic tragedy, in this case the Constantinople of 1185, but the play is unrhymed, as is Nevil Payne's *The Siege of Constantinople* (pr. 1674). Still, the majority of the tragedies written before 1676 are rhymed, and Dryden wrote confidently in "Of Heroic Plays: An Essay" (1672) that unrhymed tragedy would fail on the stage.

Yet, by 1677, Elkanah Settle felt obliged to apologize for using rhyme in *Ibrahim* (pr. 1676). Even Dryden abandoned the practice as unnatural after *Aureng-Zebe*. Between 1660 and 1680, forty-two plays in rhymed couplets were staged; during the next two decades, only five were. The rejection of rhyming did not, however, signal a shift to prose. Instead, dramatists turned to blank verse, which frequently had end-stopped rather than run-on lines and thus resembled the rhymed couplet it superseded.

Not only is the language of Restoration tragedy unnatural in its form; its content, too, is exaggerated. Maximin in *Tyrannic Love* declares that he can love more fervently than the gods. Caesario in Lee's *Gloriana: Or, The Court of Augustus Caesar* (pr. 1676) declares, "E'en in my childhood I was more than man." The imagery in the speeches is also marred by this penchant for hyperbole. Lee's *Sophonisba: Or, Hannibal's Overthrow* (pr. 1675) likens Hannibal to a whale, and the villain in Crowne's *The Ambitious Statesman: Or, The Loyal Favorite* (pr. 1679) compares himself to the same animal. When Ascanio is poisoned in Lee's *Caesar Borgia: Son of Pope Alexander the Sixth* (pr. 1679), he rants, "I burn, I burn, I toast, I roast, and my guts fry,/ They blaze, they snap, they bound like squibs/ And crackers. I am all fire." Roxana in *The Rival Queens* declares, "My brain is burst, debate and reason quenched,/ The storm is up, and my hot bleeding heart/ Splits with the rack, while passions, like the winds,/ Rise up to heaven and put out all the stars." Not to be outdone, Alexander in the same play claims, "I'll strike my spear into the reeling globe/ To let it blood, set Babylon in a blaze,/ And drive this god of flames [Cupid] with more consuming fire."

The characters who utter such speeches are presented as larger than life. When a character in Settle's *The Conquest of China* (pr. 1675) defeats a "few millions" at the outset of the play, he regards that action as mere prologue to serious battle. Thomazo in *The Siege of Constantinople* defeats the Turks practically single-handed. Drawcansir (*The Rehearsal*) gives an accurate, though satiric, portrait of these tragic heroes:

> Others may boast a single man to kill;
> But I, the blood of thousands, daily spill.
> Let petty Kings the name of Party know:
> Where e'er I come, I slay both friend and foe.

The plots of these tragedies tend to be all of a piece. A virtuous hero falls in love with an equally virtuous heroine. She, however, is loved by another to whom the hero owes allegiance and respect—a father, a prince, and sometimes, as in *Aureng-Zebe*, both at once. The hero thus faces a conflict between love and honor. In *Sophonisba*, Massinissa must choose between his love for the heroine and his loyalty to Scipio. Antony in *All for Love* must choose between duty (Rome and Octavia) and love (Cleopatra). Titus in Lee's *Lucius Junius Brutus: Father of His Country* (pr. 1680) must choose between Teraminla (love) and Brutus (duty). Another female, a villainess, may further complicate the situation by falling in love with the hero, as Nourmahal, the lecherous stepmother of Aureng-Zebe, falls in love with him. The hero generally chooses the path of honor, but the conflict is happily resolved at the end of the play through the deaths of the evil blocking characters and the marriage of the virtuous couple; less often, it is settled by the deaths of all the principals.

As this description implies, Restoration tragedy is gory. In Settle's *Fatal*

Love (pr. 1680), every character ends up dead except for Lysandra, preserved perhaps so that someone may deliver the epilogue. The stage direction at the end of *The Conquest of China* calls for everyone to die. Payne's *The Siege of Constantinople* ends with "a great number of dead and dying men in several manners of deaths. The Chancellor, Lorenzo, and Michael empal'd." In *The Fatal Jealousy* (pr. 1672), eleven of thirteen named characters are dead at the end of the play. Even *Titus Andronicus*, the bloodiest of Shakespeare's plays, was made more violent in the Restoration version (pr. 1687), and one of Dryden's objections to *Troilus and Cressida* is that the two leading characters are left alive at the end of the piece.

Tutor in Arrowsmith's *The Reformation* (pr. 1672) provides a good summary of these features of Restoration tragedy. He explains that he begins with an exotic situation and noble characters. Then, he says,

> you must always have two ladies in love with one man, or two men in love with one woman; if you make them the father and the son, or two brothers or two friends, 'twill do the better. . . . Then, sir, you must have a hero that shall fight with all the world; yes, i' gad, and beat them too, and half the gods into the bargain if occasion serves. Last of all . . . put your story into rhyme, and kill enough at the end of the play, and *probatum est*, your business is done for a tragedy.

Heroic tragedy, so remote in many ways from the comedies, nevertheless resembles them in its concern for strict poetic justice. In the comedies, the truewit gets the girl and the estate, while the witwouds and fools are exposed and often punished. Similarly, in the tragedies the good characters almost always survive to attain thrones and spouses, while the evil characters are killed. This insistence on meting out rewards and punishment restricted the scope of tragedy, which could not present good people struggling against forces greater than themselves or otherwise noble figures fatally flawed and so effecting their own destruction. The Nahum Tate revision of *The History of King Lear* (pr. 1681) demonstrates the consequences of this outlook: Tate's King Lear remains alive, and Cordelia marries Edgar; good characters should be rewarded. By the same logic, Dryden kills off Troilus and Cressida because they are bad and so must be punished. When Dryden presents the destruction of heroic virtue in *Cleomenes, the Spartan Hero* (pr. 1692), he feels obliged to explain this unusual practice.

This strict adherence to poetic justice explains part of the attraction of heroic tragedy. Further, because the age offered little heroism in real life, it enjoyed seeing such actions on the stage even as it laughed at the unreality of the representation. Nor can one dismiss the transmuting magic of the stage. The work that seems dull or ludicrous on the page can become quite compelling in the theater. The operas of Richard Wagner and Giuseppe Verdi appear bombastic and absurd in the reading, but in performance the effect is quite different. In the theater, one suspends disbelief, and a good actor can do much with the poorest of texts. Colley Cibber, himself a talented actor who began his career during the last years of the Restoration, emphasized this point in *An Apology for the Life of Colley Cibber* (1740):

> There can be no stronger proof of the charms of harmonious elocution, than the many even unnatural scenes and flights of the false sublime it has lifted into applause. In what raptures have I seen the audience at the furious fustian and turgid rants in Nat Lee's *Alexander the Great!* When these flowing numbers came from the mouth of a Betterton, the multitude no more desired sense to them than our musical connoisseurs think it essential in the celebrated airs of an Italian opera.

Finally, there was the spectacle, intended to attract the audience. As Richard Flecknoe noted in 1664, "Our theaters now for cost and ornament are arrived to the height of magnificence." Lee in *The Rival Queens* presented the spectacle of a bird fight in midair. His *Sophonisba* called for a heaven of blood, two suns, a battle between armies of spirits, and arrows flying through the air. So elaborate and expensive were the sets that they were often reused. Dryden's *The Indian Emperor: Or, The Conquest of Mexico by the Spaniards* (pr. 1665) was a sequel to his *Indian Queen* in costuming and stage sets more than in characters, only two of whom had survived the first piece. In the prologue, Dryden apologized for recycling the scenery and outfits, but later dramatists also used them. The prison reappeared in Settle's *The Female Prelate* (pr. 1679) and *Fatal Love* (pr. 1680) and in Joseph Harris' *The Mistakes* (pr. 1690); the grotto was used again in Lee's *Sophonisba* and D'Urfey's *Commonwealth of Women* (pr. 1685).

While heroic tragedy was the age's chief contribution to serious drama, other forms did appear on the stage. Among the most popular was opera. Davenant's *The Siege of Rhodes* (pr. 1656-1659), originally performed during the Commonwealth period but revived after the Restoration, provides an early example. In 1661, Charles II paid a French opera company under Jean Channoveau three hundred pounds for a production of *The Descent of Orpheus into Hell* (pr. 1661). *The Tempest: Or, The Enchanted Island* (pr. 1667), by Davenant and Dryden, and *Macbeth* (pr. 1663), by Davenant— operatic adaptations of Shakespeare's plays—are full of stage machinery and sound effects. Like the heroic tragedies, these plays are far removed from reality; in many cases, the characters in Restoration opera do not even pretend to be human. In the preface to *Albion and Albanius* (pr. 1685), Dryden notes that "the suppos'd persons are generally supernatural, as gods and goddesses, and heroes which at least are descended from them, and are in due time to be adopted into their number." These operas attracted large audiences, but they were very expensive to stage and hence not often produced. Shadwell's *Psyche* (pr. 1675), for example, cost eight hundred pounds, and Dryden's *The State of Innocence, and Fall of Man* (pb. 1677), a dramatization of Milton's *Paradise Lost* (1667, 1674), was never acted because it would have been too expensive. *The Fairy Queen: An Opera* (pr. 1692; possibly by Settle, music by Henry Purcell), an adaptation of Shakespeare's *A Midsummer Night's Dream* (pr. c. 1595-1596), cost three thousand pounds; despite its popularity, it lost money.

The pastoral was another alternative to the heroic. Whereas the latter stressed bravery and duty, the pastoral tragedy praised rural retirement. During periods of political crisis, tragedies as well as comedies mirrored popular concerns. In the early 1680's, when the Popish Plot and the succession weighed heavily on people's minds, about half the serious plays were political.

The most enduring rival to the heroic was, however, the domestic tragedy. Otway's *The Orphan: Or, The Unhappy Marriage* (pr. 1680) revolves around the love of two brothers for the orphan of the title, Monimia. The setting—Moorish Spain—and the rivalry of the two brothers are both heroic elements, but the play is not concerned with affairs of state. *Venice Preserved*, perhaps the most popular tragedy of the period, again is largely domestic in its interests. The background is a plot to overthrow the Venetian government, so the play may be read as an anti-Whig fable. Jaffier faces a choice between love for his wife and loyalty to his fellow conspirators—the standard heroic dilemma. Where the protagonist of heroic drama chooses duty, though, Jaffier chooses love, betraying his comrades after one of the plotters tries to rape Belvidera. This emphasis on the domestic rather than the public sphere also characterizes John Banks's *The Unhappy Favorite* (pr. 1681) and *Vertue Betray'd* (pr. 1682); the latter dwells on the love of Piercy and Anna Bullen and on young Elizabeth's affection for her mother. The political, public world supplies only the setting.

As the comedy of wit yielded to a more moralistic, sentimental form, so heroic tragedy was replaced by a more middle-class variety. In his prologue to *The Fair Penitent* (pr. 1703), Nicholas Rowe observed that "we ne'er can pity what we ne'er can share" and so rejected the presentation of kings and queens for "a melancholy tale of private woe." On the stage as in real life, the aristocratic Tory forms of the Restoration yielded to the bourgeois, Whig concerns of the next century.

Joseph Rosenblum

EIGHTEENTH CENTURY DRAMA

Most histories of the drama in Britain during the eighteenth century maintain implicitly or explicitly that the course of the development of the drama during this period was determined not so much by the playwrights as by the performers and theater managers, and that the more managers and playwrights strove to please and succeeded in pleasing their audiences, the more the quality of the drama declined. Whereas during the Restoration plays were composed by, for, and about members of the aristocracy, by the beginning of the eighteenth century, the theater had widened its appeal to include the middle class, and a higher percentage of women—especially "respectable" women—attended the theater. By mid-century, middle-class morality, tastes, and interests had gradually become the dominant shaping force in the development of the drama. As the eighteenth century theater drew to a close, audiences also included members of the lower class, for whom the cost of Restoration and early eighteenth century theater had been prohibitive. The more bourgeois the orientation of the theater, however, the more that members of the aristocracy turned elsewhere for their entertainment, and the more that gifted writers abandoned the drama to express themselves in other genres. Although theatergoers of all ranks had always considered the drama more a form of entertainment than one of artistic expression, never before the end of the eighteenth century had the rift been so great between drama and literature.

Whatever its artistic shortcomings, however, during the eighteenth century the drama proved immensely attractive to writers as well as to the general public. As a result of the greatly increased size of audiences and the consequent increased demand for entertainment, for the first time since the age of William Shakespeare it was once again possible to make a living as a playwright. Generally, playwrights would sell to a theater manager the copyright to their play for an amount somewhere between one hundred and two hundred pounds. Although playwrights would receive additional revenue based on attendance, they would get nothing for revivals. Moreover, unlike the drama of the previous century, which was dominated by a dozen or so masters, almost all of whom were male, the eighteenth century abounded with playwrights of both sexes, many of whom wrote only a single play or published their plays anonymously. Playwrights had the opportunity to work in a much wider variety of theatrical genres than had been available during the seventeenth century, as a typical evening's entertainment at the theater included, in addition to the full-length play that served as the main feature, a prologue and an epilogue, *entr'actes* of music and dancing, and finally an afterpiece of brief comedy, farce, burlesque, or pantomime. Thus, on a single evening, an audience might see both humorous and serious pieces. Usually, playwrights who attempted to write more than one dramatic work did not restrict themselves to the confines of a single dramatic genre but extended their talents as widely as they could in order to cater to the eclectic tastes of the eighteenth century audience. Aaron Hill, for example, wrote pseudoclassical tragedy, heroic tragedy, domestic tragedy, opera, and farce, as well as translations and adaptations of the plays of Voltaire. Prominent literary figures who are more important to critics for their contributions to other genres—Joseph Addison, Sir Richard Steele, Henry Fielding, James Thomson, Edward Young, and Samuel Johnson—also tried their hands at drama, with various degrees of success. Indeed, of the most famous writers in eighteenth century literary history, only Jonathan Swift and Alexander Pope chose not to pursue playwriting.

As one might expect, this wide variety of talents and diffusion of interests among playwrights occasioned a corresponding variation in the quality of the drama produced during the eighteenth century. The absence of dominant figures to direct the development of the drama, as John Dryden had done in the previous century, afforded the dramatists of the age unprecedented latitude in their choice of genre and theme. One might expect these circumstances to have generated highly individualized expression and much experimentation in drama, but such was not the case. The effect of this lack of dominant figures was almost wholly negative; particularly in the latter half of the century, the tragedy lacked purpose and direction, while the comedy became formulaic and sentimental. During the Restoration, generic distinctions had been relatively clearly drawn, and writers had tried to vary and perfect forms whose conventions the masters had established; in the eighteenth century, however, playwrights composing tragedy struggled to find satisfactory new forms by combining various elements from existing tragedies. Most of the original tragedies written during this period merely synthesized elements extracted from earlier English and Continental plays. Throughout the century, playwrights borrowed plots, character-types, rhetorical modes, and themes from classical, Elizabethan, Shakespearean, Restoration, and, later, early eighteenth century drama, as well as from French and Italian drama (especially from mid-century on) and from German drama (particularly during the final years of the century). On the whole, the comedy of this age is of better quality than is its awkwardly derivative tragedy, largely because the comic playwright generally had to choose between composing "laughing" comedy or "weeping" comedy. Unquestionably, the playwright's reliance on recombination of familiar elements contributed to the stultification of the drama. Although there was some experimentation, very little that was composed was fresh or original. Only one form that originated during this period ultimately proved lasting and significant—domestic tragedy, which was refined on the Continent but only rarely attempted in England.

A cultural movement of the eighteenth century that was reflected in and shaped by the drama was sentimentalism, which became, from the second decade of the century, an increasingly pervasive influence upon both tragedy and comedy. Sentimentalism brought to the theater a new emphasis on benevolence and pity and a new goal for the playwright, the eliciting of pathos. One's heart rather than one's reason became the guide as well as the measure of one's worth. The popularity of Jean-Jacques Rousseau's social criticism fostered the development of a humanitarian concern bred by sentimentalism, which emphasized the dignity and worth of the lives of ordinary men and women. The problems of women, especially of married women, also became serious topics for tragedy (most obviously in Nicholas Rowe's she-tragedies) and comedy alike (see, for example, George Farquhar's *The Beaux' Stratagem*, pr. 1707, and Sir John Vanbrugh's *The Provok'd Wife*, pr. 1697). Although the fully emancipated woman remained an object of satiric attack, the drama afforded greater recognition of the problems of being a woman.

As the shift in the makeup of the audience was reflected in the more sympathetic presentation of women, so, too, was this change reflected in the presentation of members of the mercantile class. Traditional butts of ridicule in the Elizabethan and Restoration comedy, merchants were presented during the eighteenth century with dignity and respect. Merchants are, for example, openly praised in two of the most successful and influential comedies of the century, by the character Sealand in Steele's play *The Conscious Lovers* (pr. 1722), and by the character Stockwell in Richard Cumberland's play *The West Indian* (pr. 1771). So, too, are they presented sympathetically in tragedy, most obviously in George Lillo's *The London Merchant: Or, The History of George Barnwell* (pr. 1731), in which Thorowgood eulogizes the dignity and worthiness of the merchant's trade in order to emphasize the tragic dimension of the protagonist's fall.

In the eighteenth century, as in every period since the beginnings of public drama, the success or failure of the plays did not depend wholly on their aesthetic or ethical merits. The fate of a play might depend, for example, on the political sentiments it expressed or was perceived as expressing. A playwright's political allegiances could boost the success or ensure the failure of a play irrespective of its intrinsic merits. The enthusiastic reception afforded Rowe's *Tamerlane* (pr. 1701), for example, was augmented by the obvious analogies Rowe drew between his hero and King William III and between his villain and King Louis XIV. Addison's *Cato* (pr. 1713) was also extraordinarily successful because of the contemporary political allusions the audience recognized. Yet politics could damn a play as well as promote it. John Home's *The Fatal Discovery* (pr. 1769), for example, was successful only until the audience became aware of Home's allegiance to Lord Bute. Similarly, Hugh Kelly's *A Word to the Wise* (pr. 1770) met with so much opposition because of his politics that Kelly had his next play, *Clementina* (pr. 1771), produced anonymously. Even at the very close of the century, because of his well-known sympathies with William Blake and Thomas Paine, Thomas Holcroft also produced many of his plays anonymously. Although politics remained a vital force in English drama throughout the century, the nature of the political allusions shifted noticeably. Whereas political allusions in drama during the first half of the century were generally faction- or party-oriented, those that followed the outbreak of the French Revolution were generally nationalistic. During the final years of the century, largely in response to the French Revolution, occasional pieces such as Frederick Pilon's *The Siege of Gibralter* (pr. 1780) and *The Battle of the Nile* (pr. 1799) were composed to express English nationalistic sentiment. Despite their exuberant patriotism, plays such as these are of little literary value.

Another political factor contributing to the decline in quality of eighteenth century theater was the Licensing Act of 1737. Sir Robert Walpole advanced the act ostensibly to help maintain order in London but actually to deter satiric attacks against himself and his party, especially those leveled by Fielding. The Licensing Act decreed that all play scripts were subject to the censorship of the Lord Chamberlain and that only the Drury Lane and Covent Garden theaters would be permitted to perform plays. This act was a particularly repressive measure, since, for the first time in one hundred years, there were five playhouses simultaneously offering plays in London. In addition to decreasing the accessibility of the theater to the audience, the Licensing Act effectively crushed the artistically stimulating competition between playhouses and vastly decreased the likelihood of playwrights and managers offering new, untried, and hence more risky plays. At first, the managers of the unlicensed theaters circumvented the law by advertising musical performances and staging plays during what purported to be the intermissions. Eager to boost their profits by eliminating their competition, however, the managers of the Covent Garden and Drury Lane theaters assisted the authorities in exposing and suppressing such practices, so that by mid-century virtually no such renegade productions were offered. Subsequent licensing acts, passed in 1756 and 1788, extended licensing from London to all of England, and the act was not officially withdrawn until 1968. The hold of the monopolies over London theaters remained unshaken until 1766, when Samuel Foote assumed the management of the Little Theatre at the Haymarket, and slowly but gradually offered the main theaters competition. At first his performances were billed as "entertainments" and staged in early afternoon, primarily during the summer season. Later the theater was given official sanction and became the third patent theater.

The Licensing Act also strongly influenced the tone and the content of plays performed after 1737. At first, only selected passages were altered, but gradually the form and content of entire plays were affected. Since self-consciously moral plays were more likely to obtain the censor's approval, these were more frequently submitted for approval, were approved, and were performed more than were plays laden with controversial matter such as sex, religion, and politics. Thus, the Licensing Act reinforced in the drama the expression of middle-class tastes and the movement toward the avoidance of controversial (and thus significant and intellectually oriented) subject matter. The effects of the act were not entirely negative, however, for in the search for plays that would be inoffensive to the censor and successful with the public, the theater managers, particularly David Garrick, began performing Shakespearean drama much more frequently than they had before. Though William Shakespeare had never disappeared from the stage, a number of his plays had not been performed in many years— *Antony and Cleopatra*, *Cymbeline*, and *Coriolanus*, for example. These Garrick revived. Largely as the result of his efforts, by mid-century, Shakespeare's romantic comedies had again become popular. Garrick himself adapted *A Midsummer Night's Dream* as *The Fairies* (pr. 1755). Later, Adam Smith transformed *As You Like It* into *The Noble Foresters* (pb. 1776), and John Philip Kemble, in 1780, altered *The Comedy of Errors* and, in 1790, *The Two Gentlemen of Verona*. Garrick thus sparked the great revival of interest in Shakespeare that would be continued by Kemble and that would greatly influence the subsequent development of drama both in England and on the Continent. Garrick is also important in the history of the production of Shakespeare for his insistence upon using more reliable texts for performance than had previously been employed.

Whether in original or adapted form, the plays of Shakespeare attracted large audiences. Though by no means as docile as the audience of today, the audiences of even the early years of the century were considerably better behaved than were their Elizabethan and Restoration counterparts. Nevertheless, at the beginning of the century, players still faced an audience whose members were often drunk and rowdy and who shouted catcalls during the performances, and playwrights still felt the need to "pack" the audience with friends and hirelings to combat "first nighters" determined to ensure the play's failure. As the drama grew more decorous over the course of the century, however, the audience, too, became increasingly self-restrained—and increasingly prudish. Perhaps because they were not as well educated and as intellectually oriented as were members of the Restoration audience, the members of the eighteenth century audience wanted their drama to be emotional, sentimental, and didactic rather that intellectually stimulating. They longed to hear effusive declarations of sentiment rather than clever repartee. Loud or open laughter they believed, reflected a distinctly unattractive lack of breeding as well as insensitivity, at a time when a tender heart and a refined mien were the most desirable traits.

As the drama became increasingly dominated by the bourgeoisie, its two traditional sustainers, the aristocrats and the artists, gradually dissociated themselves from the theater. Among the aristocrats, the French fashion of holding private theatricals became popular during the last two decades of the century. In private theaters on their own estates, they performed plays for one another. Blenheim, the home of the Duke of Marlborough, was noted for such productions, as was Richmond House. In France, where the private theatrical had arisen earlier, these plays were referred to as *scènes princières* and were given by Madame de Pompadour, Marie Antoinette, and the Duc d'Orléans. During the 1770's, Charles Collé was renowned for his productions of these dramas. By diverting aristocratic and artistic interests from the public theater, however, the fashion of the private theatrical only augmented the domination of the middle class and the mediocre over both the French and British drama. In England, the decline in the quality of the drama was also encouraged by the popularity of the "little theaters." Although only Drury Lane and Covent Garden were permitted to put on full-length plays, the little theaters were allowed to present brief entertainments, such as pantomimes, burlesques, farces, spectacles, and animal acts. Such productions, which were extremely popular with audiences, diverted the attention of both audience and playwright from legitimate theater.

Substantial architectural as well as aesthetic changes also occurred in the theater during the eighteenth century. In the beginning of the century, new playhouses were built to accommodate the expansion of the audience. In 1705, the famous playwright-architect Vanbrugh designed the Queen's Theatre in the Haymarket, where the French House was also erected, and in 1732, the Theatre Royal was erected in the Covent Garden. The Little Theatre in Lincoln's Inn Fields also thrived, serving as the home for Fielding's great comedies. The early years of the century also witnessed great interest in the theater outside London. Already well established, the theater in Dublin was prospering, and new theaters sprang up in Bath, in Tunbridge Wells, and in the provinces. This growth in the construction of theaters was abruptly checked by the Licensing Act of 1737. After 1737, the widespread interest in the drama that had been generated prior to 1737 had so greatly expanded the number of theatergoers that the Drury Lane and Covent Garden theaters were insufficiently large to accommodate all who wished to attend plays. Even before the Licensing Act, so much interest had developed in the theater that the Haymarket had expanded its maximum seating capacity from nine hundred in 1705 to thirteen hundred in 1735. Drury Lane was thus remodeled in 1762, and continuing expansion of the audience necessitated additional remodeling in 1780 and complete rebuilding in 1793. Covent Garden, too, was remodeled in 1782 and eventually rebuilt in 1792. Great theaters were built on the Continent as well. In France, for example, the two main theaters were the Comédie-Française and the Comédie-Italienne, the latter the less traditional and the more innovative of the two theaters. The Opéra Comique, which was founded in 1713, joined with the Comédie-Italienne in 1762, while the Théâtre de la Foire offered popular pieces, such as farces, vaudevilles, and *comédies à ariettes*, to French audiences.

In addition to the expansion of seating capacity, there were other physical changes within the theater. As in the previous century, would-be wits and critics continued to habituate the pit, but the more fashionable members of the audience left the first gallery to the middle class. For a substantial fee, wealthy members of the audience could still obtain seats onstage during performances until 1763, when Garrick, the manager of the Drury Lane Theatre, refused to allow this disruptive practice to continue. This restriction was not innovative on Garrick's part, for onstage seating had been banned at the Comédie-Française in Paris four years earlier. During the eighteenth century, the shape of the stage also changed: The apron grew smaller, with the performing area shrinking gradually into the familiar picture-frame stage. Thus, physically as well as spiritually, the theater was receding from the flesh-and-blood world of its audience.

Although remodeling made it possible for increasing numbers of people to attend the theater, the ultimate effect of the enlargement was to accelerate the decline in the quality of the productions and to discourage the writing of plays of depth and subtlety. Given the relatively primitive state of stage lighting in the eighteenth century, the increased distance of the audience from the stage made it more difficult to see the facial expressions and gestures of the actors. Moreover, the enlarged theaters were, as a rule, acoustically poor: The Haymarket, for example, had acoustics so dreadful that it was impossible to perform plays there, and its stage had to be given over entirely to the production of opera. Actors who wished to avoid having their words garbled into incomprehensibility or swallowed up in space were compelled to speak lines in inappropriate (albeit audible) pitches and monotonous tones. Thus, it became impossible for an actor to give a performance that had much subtlety or naturalness.

Such physical problems in the theater encouraged theater managers and audiences to become visually rather than aurally oriented and thus to prefer tragedies that relied not on great verse but on spectacle and comedies that relied on farce rather than on incisive dialogue. To ensure substantial profits, theater managers included animal acts, pantomimes, and dances in addition to the full-length play. Visual elements were incorporated into virtually every production, sometimes in very curious ways. In a revival of Rowe's grim tragedy of pathos *The Tragedy of Jane Shore* (pr. 1714), for example, a rope dance was included in the fifth act. By mid-century, audiences were drawn at least as much by afterpieces and by the dramatic periphery and spectacle as they were by the full-length play itself. Thomas Morton's *Columbus: Or, A World Discovered* (pr. 1792), for example, was well attended largely because of the startling realism of its stage effects, which included swirling clouds, thunder, lightning, a volcanic eruption, and trees being uprooted by the wind. By the end of the century, effect came to be what mattered most. Thus, when Matthew Gregory ("Monk") Lewis included black servants as characters in a play set in Wales, he explained in the preface to the play that he did so in order to make possible greater variety in the costumes. These productions lacked originality as well as literary excellence, for much as television networks reduplicate the basic formulas behind one another's successful shows, Drury Lane and Covent Garden each frantically copied the successful shows of the other rather than attempting to develop something new. Thus, in 1750, for many weeks, two productions of Shakespeare's *Romeo and Juliet* were offered simultaneously, Drury Lane's featuring Garrick and George Anne Bellamy, and Covent Garden's featuring Spranger Barry and Susannah Cibber.

Responding to and accelerating the orientation of the drama to spectacle were several very important developments in stagecraft. In 1765, Garrick adapted from the French a greatly improved technique for lighting the stage. During the first half of the century, as during the Restoration, lighting had been supplied by footlights and by chandeliers suspended over the stage in plain view of the audience. Garrick replaced the latter with "direct sidelighting," candles arranged in pyramid-shaped forms set in the wings out of the sight of the audience. In addition to being far less distracting than older methods of lighting, the new form could, with the use of colored screens, be made to shed colored light, thus providing effects that would enhance the appeal of plays dependent on visual elements.

Toward the close of the century, substantial innovations were also made in scenery, replacing the painted palaces, tombs, temples, prisons, and gardens that had served as settings. In the 1770's, under the auspices of Garrick, Philipe James de Loutherbourg developed a new type of scenery for the Drury Lane Theatre. Using transparent dye, Loutherbourg painted two different scenes, one on each side of a sheet of sheer cloth. Because only the illuminated side would be visible to the audience, scenes could be changed easily and rapidly by a simple shift in lighting. Loutherbourg was also famous for his innovative "romantic" landscapes, which presented not the symmetrical, formal scenes of past years but rugged, irregular natural shapes. Another important current in the development of scenery was also initiated at Drury Lane, under the auspices of Garrick's successor, Kemble. When Kemble hired William Capon to design scenery, Capon tried to produce scenery accurate to the most minute historical detail. This new interest in historical accuracy was also reflected in the costuming of the last quarter of the century. It was considered very innovative when, in 1764, Shakespeare's *Richard III* was presented in period costume, as it was in 1773 when the famous actor Charles Macklin performed *Macbeth* in Scots dress. Perhaps because their success depended heavily on their reputations as beauties, the actresses of the period did not adopt historical costumes but continued to wear contemporary, fashionable dress until 1790, except for the occasional "breeches parts," which afforded them the opportunity to display their legs.

Unquestionably, the actors and actresses of the century exercised great influence over the development of the drama. They encouraged playwrights to compose specific parts with them in mind, and the dramatists, eager to have plays produced, would write dramas as vehicles for famous actors' and actresses' dramatic specialities—Farquhar, for example, composed *Sir Harry Wildair, Being the Sequel of a Trip to the Jubilee* (pr. 1701) especially for Robert Wilks. As a result, plays tended to rely upon the same types rather than introducing fresh and innovative characters. Another obstacle to the development of high-quality drama was the lack of discipline with which actors approached their trade. Richard Brinsley Sheridan's *The Rivals* (pr. 1775), for example, failed miserably on its opening night largely because several principal actors did not know their lines well. Often while onstage, when not delivering their own lines, actors and actresses fell out of character entirely, even engaging in conversation with members of the audience while other actors were speaking. Actors also adopted a similarly casual attitude toward rehearsals, from which many members of the cast were absent or, if present, were inattentive. The famous tragic actress Sarah Siddons once remarked that she had played Belvidera, the female lead in Thomas Otway's *Venice Preserved: Or, A Plot Discovered* (pr. 1682), without benefit of a single rehearsal. This lack of rehearsal also encouraged actors to engage in the common practice of freely ad-libbing lines rather than adhering strictly to the script penned by the playwright, a tendency very likely encouraged by the popularity of the *commedia dell'arte*, which relied extensively on improvisation. Nevertheless, the eighteenth century witnessed an abundance of excellent actors, the most famous of whom include Colley Cibber, Booth, Wilks, James Quin, Barry, Macklin, Garrick, Kemble, Ann Bracegirdle, Kitty Clive, Peg Woffington, and Siddons.

Curiously, as the drama grew less literary, its performers and performances became more self-consciously professional. The eighteenth century also saw great changes in acting style, again largely as a result of the efforts of Garrick. Actors such as Quin, who adhered to the older style, strode out onto the apron and declaimed in a highly formal manner. Garrick and his rival Macklin, however, strove for greater realism and subtlety in performance. Macklin became famous for his natural rendering of Shylock in 1741, the same year Garrick debuted in *Richard III*. Garrick insisted upon the need to display emotion to make the drama effective. Thus, he employed facial expression and gesture to enliven his performance and, rather than adhering rigidly to the versification in the plays, used stresses and pauses to heighten the effect of the dialogue. During his visit to Paris in 1763, Garrick was asked by Denis Diderot to illustrate in practice the theory of acting presented in Diderot's *Paradoxe sur le comédien* (wr. 1773, pb. 1830).

As theater manager as well as actor and playwright, Garrick exerted great influence over the drama. Unlike the theater managers of the previous century, those during the eighteenth century were not courtiers but were, like Garrick, professional theater people. Among the more famous managers of Drury Lane Theatre were Cibber, Steele, Garrick, Kemble, and Sheridan, while the most famous manager of the Little Theatre in the Haymarket was Fielding. Theater managers were often criticized for their rude and whimsical treatment of playwrights as well as for their tendency to make financial considerations rather than artistic merit their primary criterion in selecting plays to produce. Garrick, for example, was attacked by Arthur Murphy in the preface to *Alzuma* (pr. 1773), as was Kemble by George Colman the Younger in the preface to *The Iron Chest* (pr. 1796). Because of Sheridan's erratic vacillation between irresponsibility and tyranny, Kemble resigned his Drury Lane partnership and became manager of Covent Garden. The Continent, too, had its share of famous playwright-managers. Two of the most famous German theater managers were Johann Wolfgang von Goethe, who managed the ducal theater in Weimar from 1791 until he resigned in 1817, and August Wilhelm Iffland, who directed the Mannheim National Theatre and who, like Garrick, was also the foremost actor of his day.

Thus, a variety of forces contributed simultaneously to the widening of the audience and to the decline of quality in the drama: the encouragement of mediocrity and the discouragement of the controversial stemming from the Licensing Act, the artificiality of sentimentalism, the popularity and excellence of drama from the past and from the Continent, the lack of real competition between the playhouses, the temptation offered playwright and theater manager alike of easy labor and certain profit in the production of drama other than the full-length play, the "star system," and technological advances and architectural alterations within the playhouse itself. Nevertheless, the drama of the eighteenth century is worthy of study—when not for its intrinsic literary merits, for its reflection of the age and for its influence on subsequent drama.

Comedy

Although the British comedy of the eighteenth century shares the eclecticism of the tragedy of the period in its recombination and synthesis of a wide variety of earlier forms, these plays typically adhere more to one than to the other of two theoretical positions concerning comedy—to "laughing comedy," that which is designed primarily to amuse, or to "weeping" or, more commonly, "sentimental comedy," with its overt didacticism, exemplary characters, and exaltation of pathos. When considering the comedy of this period, it is perhaps most important to remember that there was no great struggle for preeminence between the comedy of manners, the predominant comic form of the previous age, and sentimentalism, which became an increasingly pervasive influence upon drama during the eighteenth century. Although sentimentality eventually dominated eighteenth century comedy, initially it merely colored scenes, character-types, or dialogue rather than manifesting itself as an independent comic genre. In fact, very few sentimental comedies, as such, appeared during the first half of the century. Most new comedies written before 1750 relied heavily on the traditions of the comedy of manners, of intrigue, and of humors, as well as on the farce, burlesque, and, after 1728, the ballad opera. Of these forms, during the first half of the century, the Restoration comedies of manners (especially those by Dryden, William Wycherley, Sir George Etherege, and William Congreve) and the transitional plays of Vanbrugh and Farquhar were the regular comedies most frequently offered. Although sentimentalism clearly dominated the stage during the latter half of the century, the comedy of manners and other species of laughing comedy continued to thrive in abbreviated form as afterpieces.

The two main comic trends of the eighteenth century are observable in its opening decade, in the laughing comedies of Vanbrugh and Farquhar and in the more obviously moralistic comedies of Cibber and Steele. Although relying heavily on the tradition of the Restoration comedy of manners, Cibber's *Love's Last Shift: Or, The Fool in Fashion* (pr. 1696) broke with this form in its sympathetic and somewhat serious consideration of a wife's concern over her spouse's adultery as well as with the last-act repentance of her rake-husband. Cibber's impetus in writing such a play was likely more pragmatic than moralistic. He seems to have been responding to the disdain of the contemporary audience for the cynicism and immorality of Restoration comedy, to perceptions reflected by Jeremy Collier's *A Short View of the Immorality and Profaneness of the English Stage* (1698). Cibber's *The Careless Husband* (pr. 1704) similarly employs the sudden reformation of its hero and the serious consideration of the problems within marriage.

The plays of Farquhar and Vanbrugh also exemplify the movement away from both the style and the spirit of the Restoration comedy of manners. Though both playwrights satirize vice, their satire is gentler and less cynical than that of their predecessors. Farquhar's masterpieces, *The Recruiting Officer* (pr. 1706) and *The Beaux' Stratagem*, are set not in London but in the country and are peopled by coarser and more realistic characters than those in the comedy of manners. Much of the humor in these plays arises from physical movement and situation rather than from witty dialogue. *The Beaux' Stratagem* also departs from the comedy-of-manners tradition in its occasionally serious attitude toward marriage and in its emphasis on virtue as well as wit as an essential characteristic of a hero. Vanbrugh offers an even more serious consideration of the problems within marriage in *The Relapse: Or, Virtue in Danger* (pr. 1696), which he wrote in response to the facile reformation at the conclusion of Cibber's *Love's Last Shift*, and in *The Provok'd Wife*. Overt moralizing, however, characteristic of sentimental comedy, is absent from these plays.

It was with the later comedies of Steele that "genteel" or "reformed" comedy (which presents the comedy of manners form in the sentimental spirit) really seized hold on the theater. In his comedies as in his essays, Steele's purpose was the advancement of good breeding and virtue. He sought to eliminate coarseness but not wit from the comedy of manners, to transform the comedy-of-manners conception of the hero as rake into the hero as moral exemplar. Like Cibber's, Steele's early comedies largely consist of a comedy-of-manners plot with a reformation in the final act. Such is the case in his first comedy, *The Funeral: Or, Grief à-la-mode* (pr. 1701), and in the unsuccessful *The Lying Lover: Or, The Ladies' Friendship* (pr. 1703), whose purpose, Steele declared, was to elicit "generous Pity" rather than laughter, and which, he felt, was "dam'd for its piety." Again, however, like Cibber's and Vanbrugh's, Steele's early comedies depart from the comedy-of-manners tradition by focusing seriously and sympathetically on domestic issues. Whereas the sentimentality of Steele's early comedies resides largely in their conclusions, his later plays are increasingly permeated by sentimentality; his *The Conscious Lovers* was the first (and, for more than forty years, the finest) English sentimental comedy.

The Conscious Lovers, like subsequent sentimental comedies, was intended to elicit an emotional more than an intellectual response from the audience, to stir up pity and admiration (emotions more traditionally associated with tragedy) for an exemplary pair of lovers in distress. In *The Conscious Lovers*, as in subsequent comedies of this subgenre, the focal characters are middle-class lovers who are unashamed of their devotion to each other. Marriage is presented as an ideal goal, the attraction between the lovers based on the virtue rather than the wit or wealth of the potential spouse. The hero, with whom the audience is intended to sympathize, is not a cynical rake but is, like his beloved, an intensely benevolent and sensitive soul who is given not to witty repartee but to prolonged, rapturous pronouncements about love and virtue. Such plays consider not the manners but the fundamental nature of humankind, which, they optimistically assume, is inherently good and perfectible. In his preface to *The Conscious Lovers*, Steele declares that he wishes his drama to "chasten wit, and moralize the stage," to inspire in the audience "a Joy too exquisite for Laughter." Whereas Restoration comedy typically satirized vice, the principal purpose of sentimental comedy was to advance the cause of virtue and morality. Dependent as it is on the moral aphorism, the dialogue of sentimental comedy is unrealistic and formulaic, as are the plots typical of this genre. Inevitably, poetic justice triumphs, and virtue is unexpectedly and improbably rewarded, usually in tangible as well as in intangible terms. Although these plays are concerned with moral questions in social contexts, rarely do their playwrights espouse revolutionary political or social positions; the morality they advocate is wholly conventional and middle-class. Sentimental comedy is free from indelicacy and vice—and, often, from humor, for the moralistic emphasis and the rigid conception of decorum rendered many of these plays tedious and somewhat grim fare.

The sentimental comedy established by Cibber and Steele was widely imitated both at home and on the Continent. During the first half of the century, for example, sentimental comedy was written in England by the Reverend James Miller, Thomas Baker, William Burnaby, Charles Johnson, and Robert Dodsley. One of the better sentimental comedies of this period is *The Foundling* (pr. 1748), by Edward Moore, who is more commonly remembered for his tragedy *The Gamester* (pr. 1753). James Dance's *Pamela* (pb. 1741), a dramatization of Samuel Richardson's sentimental novel *Pamela: Or, Virtue Rewarded* (1740-1741), is also worthy of note in that it inaugurates the eighteenth century fashion of rendering popular novels into dramatic form.

During the decade of the 1750's, no new comedies were offered, but sentimental comedies continued to appear in subsequent decades. The foremost writers of sentimental comedy after 1750 were Kelly and Cumberland. Kelly is remembered most for his *False Delicacy* (pr. 1768), with which Garrick hoped to undermine the success of Oliver Goldsmith's *The Good-Natured Man* (pr. 1768). The conflict in *False Delicacy* arises from the characters' extreme consideration for one another's feelings, but the conclusion of the play ultimately applauds rather than criticizes the characters for their excessive sensibilities. Cumberland's play *The Brothers* (pr. 1769) is more typical of sentimental comedy than is Kelly's *False Delicacy*, but it is for his second play, *The West Indian*, that Cumberland is best remembered. In writing *The West Indian*, Cumberland was determined to present in an extremely positive light characters drawn from groups who were the victims of prejudice, traditional butts of ridicule. Such are the Irishman O'Flaherty and the West Indian Belcourt, the latter a typical hero of sentimental comedy. Belcourt is also significant as a reflection of the influence of Jean-Jacques Rousseau's conception of the "child of Nature." So successful was Cumberland in elevating the stature of the Irishman through this play that Sheridan's use of a comic Irishman in the original version of *The Rivals* elicited hostility rather than laughter from the play's audience. Cumberland again defended the oppressed in *The Fashionable Lover* (pr. 1772), in which he served as an advocate for the Scots, and in *The Jew* (pr.

1794). In concert with Garrick and George Colman the Elder, he also wrote another very successful comedy, *The Clandestine Marriage* (pr. 1766). Other sentimental comedies of the latter half of the century include William Whitehead's *School for Lovers* (pr. 1762), Frances Sheridan's *The Discovery* (pr. 1763) and *The Dupe* (pr. 1763), Isaac Bickerstaffe's *The Maid of the Mill* (a 1765 comic opera based on *Pamela*), George Colman the Elder's *The English Merchant* (pr. 1767), Hannah Cowley's *Which Is the Man?* (pr. 1782), Lieutenant-General John Burgoyne's *The Heiress* (pr. 1786), and Macklin's *The Man of the World* (pr. 1781).

At the close of the century, the most prominent writers of sentimental comedy were Elizabeth Inchbald and Holcroft, who were also participants in the humanitarian movement in literature. Inchbald's attitudes toward drama—views that are representative of her age—are reflected in her prefaces to the plays in *The British Theater* (1806), the collection that she edited. Inchbald believed that artistic success depended upon "scrupulous purity of character and refinement of sensation" and that laughter should be confined to the lower forms of comedy, such as farce and burlesque, since, in her view, the primary purpose of high comedy was to educate and edify. Her own plays offer much social criticism—*Such Things Are* (pr. 1787), for example, is based on the experiences of the prison reformer John Howard. This play is also of interest in its reflection of Rousseau's conception of the noble savage in the characterization of Zedan. Whereas Inchbald's views were expressed quite openly in her dramas, Holcroft's highly controversial political opinions were not. Holcroft's comedies are much like those of Cumberland, except that Holcroft relies more heavily on sensational and tragic elements. *The Road to Ruin* (pr. 1792), a sentimental comedy about the problems of gambling, is his most famous play.

Thus, in England, sentimental comedy gradually increased its emphasis on pathos and at the same time degenerated into a simplistic conception of the relationship between virtue and reward. Over the course of the century, English sentimental comedy neither enlarged the scope of emotions to which it appealed nor explored fresher, larger issues. The form constituted a lengthy dramatic experiment that was sustained by a belief in (and a desire to augment) the fundamental benevolence of humankind. Sentimental comedy was, however, an experiment that succeeded more in commercial than in aesthetic terms.

The sentimental comedies of Cibber and Steele were also imitated successfully in France, where playwrights came to place even greater emphasis on the pathetic and on philosophical and ethical declamation. Because of its pronounced emphasis on pathos, the sentimental comedy of France is designated *comédie larmoyante* ("weeping comedy"). Like English sentimental comedies, plays in the tradition of the *comédie larmoyante* employ bourgeois characters and are highly moralistic and overtly didactic. In

France, at the opening of the century, the most popular comic playwrights were those following in the tradition of Molière, among them Florent Carton Dancourt, from whom Vanbrugh and Foote both borrowed extensively, and Alain-René Lesage, who was extraordinarily prolific as a playwright, although he is best remembered for his four-volume novel *Gil Blas* (1715-1735). Jean-François Regnard's *Le Légataire universel* (1708), a comedy of intrigue satirizing vice in Molièrian manner, also anticipates the *comédie larmoyante* in its theme and style. Other important approximations of the form are *Le Philosophe marié* (1727), by Philippe Néricault Destouches, which John Kelly translated into English in 1732 as *The Married Philosopher* and which Inchbald later adapted as *The Married Man* (pr. 1789), and Destouches' *Le Glorieux* (pr. 1732). Although Pierre-Claude Nivelle de La Chaussée is typically credited with producing the first actual *comédie larmoyante* with his *La Fausse Antipathie* (pr. 1733), the most famous dramatist of this movement was Pierre Carlet de Chamblain de Marivaux. In an amusing rather than a satiric manner, Marivaux's plays offer a minute exploration of the sentiments of lovers, especially women. The polished dialogue he employs in scenes offering such psychological exploration and revelation led to the coinage of the literary term *marivaudage*. Two of his plays that exerted the greatest influence on French comedy are *L'Amour et la vérité* (pr. 1720) and *Le Jeu de l'amour et du hasard* (pr. 1730).

The French *comédie larmoyante* was introduced in Germany by Christian Fürchtegott Gellert's *Das Los in der Lotterie* (1747). Although many literary historians identify Gotthold Ephraim Lessing's *Minna von Barnhelm* (pb. 1767) as the finest German sentimental comedy, significantly more popular both in Germany and in England were the artistically inferior plays of August von Kotzebue. Kotzebue adapted Friedrich Schiller's type of drama, which appealed primarily to the elite, to suit popular taste. Audiences were drawn to his plays not merely because of their sentimental and humanitarian emphasis, however, but also because of their sensationalistic plots. Thirty-six of Kotzebue's plays were translated into English, and twenty of these were performed on the English stage between 1796 and 1801. In 1799, for example, translations and adaptations of *Die Spanier in Peru* (pr. 1794) were done by Anne Plumptre, Matthew Gregory Lewis, Sheridan, Thomas Dutton, Robert Heron, and Matthew West, and another version was produced by Benjamin Thompson the following year. In England, the most popular adaptations of Kotzebue's plays were A. Schink and George Papendick's rendering of *Menschenhass und Reue* (pr. 1789) as *The Stranger* (pb. 1798) and Sheridan's *Pizarro: A Tragedy in Five Acts* (pr. 1799). *Menschenhass und Reue* was again reworked in 1799 as *The Noble Lie* by Maria Geisweiler. Kotzebue's plays did not meet with unanimous praise, however, as is evident in Jane Austen's novel *Mansfield Park* (1814), in which the characters debate the degree of immorality and offensiveness to be found in Kotzebue's dramas.

In Italy during the eighteenth century, comedy developed along a substantially different course as a result of the pervasiveness and persistence of the influence of the *commedia dell'arte*. A species of improvisational comedy based on the stock characters Harlequin, Columbine, and Scaramouche, the *commedia dell'arte* ("comedy of the profession") originated during the mid-sixteenth century with the rise of the first regular Italian theatrical companies. Despite the efforts of a number of dramatists, the influence of the *commedia dell'arte* remained apparent in Italian comedy throughout the century. One of the first to attempt to break from this tradition and develop a higher form of Italian comedy was Carlo Goldoni. Of Goldoni's approximately three hundred plays, almost half are prose comedies, many of which are derived from the comedy of manners and sentimental comedy and which thus place greater emphasis on character development and dialogue than did traditional Italian comedy. Although he exposes man's folly, Goldoni's tone is typically one of warm humor rather than of harsh satire. His comedies are highly moralistic, and the morality they espouse is distinctly middle-class. His masterpieces, which were produced between 1757 and 1762, are *I rusteghi* (pr. 1760) and *Le baruffe chizzotte* (pr. 1762). Opposing the changes instituted by Goldoni was Carlo Gozzi, whose most famous play is *L'amore delle tre melarance* (pr. 1761). An advocate of the tradition of the *commedia dell'arte*, Gozzi was especially successful with the production of his nine *fiabe* ("fantastic plays"), which appeared between 1761 and 1765. Based on Oriental tales or on fairy tales, the *fiabe* were translated into German in 1777 and 1778 and exerted a strong influence upon Goethe, Schiller, Lessing, and Schlegel.

· As the result of the efforts of Diderot in France, yet another dramatic form developed at the same time as the *comédie larmoyante*—the *drame*. A *drame* is a serious but not tragic play that focuses on the concerns of middle-class characters. Although this form has comic potential in its concentration on middle-class characters and tragic potential in the seriousness with which it addresses their concerns, the tone of the *drame* does not alternate between comic and tragic but remains consistently serious. As in the sentimental comedy, the eliciting of emotion for and identification with the characters are prime considerations of the playwright. Deliberately trying to shape the development of the *drame*, Diderot published his critical theory of the drama along with his plays. Thus, the unsuccessful play *Le Fils naturel* was published with the theoretical work *Entretiens sur Le Fils naturel* in 1757, and the successful play *Le Père de famille* was published with *De la poésie tragique* in 1758. Among Diderot's many followers and imitators in the *drame* were Louis-Sébastien Mercier's *La Brouette de vinaigre* (1775) and Michel-Jean Sedaine's *Le Philosophe sans le savoir* (1765), the latter perhaps the finest *drame* produced during the century.

Sedaine did not confine his playwriting to this sober genre but also wrote plays belonging to another genre of French drama, the vaudeville, variety shows employing music, dance, and spectacle. Still another famous follower of Diderot was Pierre-Augustin Caron de Beaumarchais, whose *Essai sur le genre dramatique sérieux* (1767) both echoes and modifies the ideas of Diderot. Beaumarchais is best remembered for the trilogy that comprises *La Folle Journée: Ou, Le Mariage de Figaro* (pr. 1784), in which he attempted to revive laughing comedy; *Le Barbier de Séville* (pr. 1775), which blends the comedy of humors and of intrigue with social and political satire; and *L'Autre Tartuffe: Ou, La Mère coupable* (pr. 1792).

Despite its overwhelming popularity both in England and on the Continent, the sentimental comedy never met with universal approbation; from the time of its inception, many critics found fault with it. In "A Defense of Sir Fopling Flutter" (1723), for example, the famous critic John Dennis argues that Steele, with his "Joy too exquisite for Laughter," "knows nothing of the rules of comedy, the purpose of which is not to set up patterns of perfection but to picture existing follies which we are to despise." Indeed, so pervasive was the obsession with morality in the comedy that Garrick jokingly suggested that a steeple should be placed atop the playhouse. Perhaps the most famous criticism of the sentimental comedy is that offered by Goldsmith in his *Essay on the Theatre: Or, A Comparison Between Sentimental and Laughing Comedy* (1773), in which Goldsmith condemned the genre as "bastard tragedy," an infelicitous mingling of genres that produced unnatural, pompous plays. Goldsmith's own plays, *The Good-Natured Man* and *She Stoops to Conquer: Or, The Mistakes of a Night* (pr. 1773), aptly illustrate his views. His comedies are replete with warm humor, and though they employ low comedy, they are never coarse or obscene. He shares the sentimentalists' benevolent view of human beings but not their overt didacticism. Though Goldsmith eschewed weeping comedy, he neither advocated nor attempted a return to the comedy of manners of Congreve. Goldsmith's own dramas are *sui generis*; they set no fashion, and he had no direct imitators.

The tradition of the laughing comedy, with its roots largely in the Restoration comedy of manners, continued throughout the century, generally incorporating some sentimental elements. Early examples of such comedies include Burnaby's *The Reform'd Wife* (pr. 1700) and *The Ladies' Visiting Day* (pr. 1701), unusual for its Restoration-style cynical wit; Charles Johnson's *The Masquerade* (pr. 1719); Mrs. Susannah Centlivre's *A Bold Stroke for a Wife* (pr. 1718); Arthur Murphy's *The Way to Keep Him* (pr. 1760) and *Know Your Own Mind* (pr. 1777); and Colman the Elder's *The Jealous Wife* (pr. 1761) and *The Clandestine Marriage* (pr. 1766), the latter written in collaboration with Garrick and Cumberland. The finest eighteenth century comedy of manners after Congreve is unquestionably that produced by

Sheridan—indeed, until Sheridan, no writer after Congreve had success-fully attempted a full-length comedy of manners. Voicing his dramatic the-ory in the *Prologue* [to *The Rivals*] *Spoken on the Tenth Night* (pr. 1775), Sheridan condemned the didacticism of sentimental comedy as well as its fusion of comic with tragic elements. Sheridan's plays are primarily com-edies of manners with some reliance on "humours" characters. As in the plays of Cumberland and Goldsmith, the hero is a good-hearted prodigal. Sheridan shares the benevolence but not the pathos of sentimentalism, and the wit but not the profundity of Congreve. The object of his satire in his most famous plays, *The Rivals* and *The School for Scandal* (pr. 1777), is sentimentality, "The Goddess of the woeful countenance—/ The sentimen-tal Muse," as Sheridan describes her. Sheridan does not disagree with the basic morals and assumptions of his society, only with their corruption and distortion. Another writer in this tradition was Mrs. Hannah Cowley, who is more often remembered for her comedies of intrigue derived from Aphra Behn and Mrs. Centlivre. Like Sheridan, Cowley blended the com-edy of manners tradition with sentimental elements in *The Belle's Stratagem* (pr. 1780), *Which Is the Man?*, and *A Bold Stroke for a Husband* (pr. 1783), as did Inchbald in *I'll Tell You What* (pr. 1785) and *Every One Has His Fault* (pr. 1793).

Contemporary laughing comedy did not serve as the sole alternative to the sentimental comedy, however, for the comedy of previous ages still appeared on the stage. Philip Massinger's *A New Way to Pay Old Debts* (pr. 1621-1622?) was revived in 1748, as was Ben Johnson, George Chap-man, and John Marston's *Eastward Ho!* (pr. 1605) in 1752, and the coffin scene in Steele's *The Funeral* is indebted to Francis Beaumont's *The Knight of the Burning Pestle* (pr. 1607). Garrick adapted Jonson's *Every Man in His Humour* (pr. 1598) in 1751 as well as *The Alchemist* (pr. 1610) in 1774, and versions of his *Epicœne: Or, The Silent Woman* (pr. 1609) were pro-duced by both Francis Gentleman (in 1771) and Colman the Elder (in 1776). Of the Elizabethan comedies, however, as with the tragedies, those by Shakespeare were unquestionably the most frequently performed and the most influential. Indeed, one might attribute some of the impetus behind the development of sentimental comedy to the revival and popu-larization of Shakespeare's romantic comedies, adaptations of which were written by George Granville, Burnaby, and Charles Johnson, among oth-ers, beginning in the 1730's. In 1756, Garrick furthered the trend toward the presentation of distressed virtue and more imaginative drama by bring-ing Shakespeare's *The Tempest* (pr. 1611) and *The Winter's Tale* (pr. c. 1610-1611) back to the stage.

Despite their ostensibly distasteful immorality, the comedies of the Res-toration also retained their popularity. Though performed in an essentially unaltered form during the first half of the century, in later years these comedies appeared only in bowdlerized and moralized adaptations or in condensed versions, as afterpieces. Congreve and Dryden were frequently revived, Etherege occasionally, and Wycherley only rarely until Garrick produced his emasculated adaptation of *The Country Wife* (pr. 1675) as *The Country Girl* in 1776, the same year Bickerstaffe's adaptation of *The Plain-Dealer* (pr. 1676) appeared. Perhaps the profusion of excellent comedies already available diminished the desire of the audience for new comedies or discouraged playwrights from attempting forms that appeared already to have been perfected.

Both the comedy of intrigue and the comedy of humors, which had been very popular during the Restoration, disappeared as independent forms during the eighteenth century. A number of new comedies of intrigue did, however, appear at the opening of the century, including Francis Manning's *All for the Better: Or, The Infallible Cure* (pr. c. 1702), Cibber's *She Wou'd and She Wou'd Not: Or, The Kind Imposter* (pr. 1702), Taverner's *The Maid the Mistress* (pr. 1708) and *The Artful Husband* (pr. 1717), Christopher Bullock's *Woman Is a Riddle* (pr. 1716), and Richard Savage's *Love in a Veil* (pr. 1718). Unquestionably, the best comedies of intrigue were those produced by Mrs. Centlivre, who adroitly blended intrigue with sentimentalism in *The Gamester* (pr. 1705) and *The Busie Body* (pr. 1709). The format of these comedies of intrigue had remained essentially the same as that employed during the Restoration, except, perhaps, that the newer plays relied more heavily on farce. By 1730, however, the comedy of intrigue as a genre unto itself virtually ceased, perhaps because its atmosphere of trickery and deceit seemed antithetical to sentimentality. Traces of the comedy of intrigue persisted, however, in many plays, such as Bickerstaffe's *'Tis Well It's No Worse* (a 1770 rendering of a work by Pedro Calderón de la Barca), Joseph Atkinson's *The Mutual Deception* (pr. 1785), and Cowley's *A School for Greybeards: Or, The Mourning Bride* (pr. 1786). Similarly, though few attempted the comedy of humors as a form in itself, numerous sentimental and laughing comedies include humors characters. One of the few who did attempt to sustain the form was Charles Shadwell, the son of the famous Restoration humors playwright, Thomas Shadwell; the younger Shadwell met with little success in his attempt to follow in his father's generic footsteps. Typical of his works is *The Fair Quaker of Deal: Or, The Humors of the Navy* (pr. 1710). Another comedy of humors is Thomas Baker's *Tunbridge Walks: Or, The Yeoman of Kent* (pr. 1703). Around 1730, the form seems to have experienced something of a brief revival with the appearance in that year of both Miller's *The Humours of Oxford* and Fielding's *Rape upon Rape: Or, The Justice Caught in His Own Trap*.

Rather than devote their talents to high comedy, playwrights attempting original laughing comedies usually turned to the composition of the afterpiece, the drama that usually followed the main entertainment. Typically, the afterpiece was a farce, ballad opera, burlesque, or pantomime. Not only were such forms easier to compose than a full-length play, but also these afterpieces were often much more popular with the audience and were offered for many more performances. Although on the whole the literary merit of afterpieces is inferior to that of the longer plays, many have genuine comic appeal, and the form demands consideration in any history of eighteenth century drama as a reflection of the taste of the age.

An extremely popular form for the afterpiece was farce, which draws its humor from situation rather than from character or dialogue. Having no uniform set of characteristics, farce allowed the artist much greater latitude than did the longer play. Some of the most prominent dramatists of the century composed farces, and this form reached its pinnacle of popularity and quality during the eighteenth century. Vanbrugh, Cibber, and Rowe, for example, wrote farces during the first decade of the eighteenth century, and Mrs. Centlivre, Bickerstaffe, Bullock, and Charles Johnson did so during the second. A number of popular farces were written by Garrick also, whose best received farce was *The Lying Valet* (pr. 1741). Garrick's talent lay not in creating new characters and scenes but in heightening the humor of the old by condensing and accelerating the action. During the second half of the century, Colman the Elder, Murphy, and Sheridan also dabbled in this form. Colman's *Polly Honeycombe* (pr. 1760), which satirizes romantic novels, is a farce, as is his *The Deuce Is in Him* (pr. 1763), in which he again attacks sentimentality. Murphy's *The Citizen* (pr. 1761) and *Three Weeks After Marriage: Or, What We Must All Come To* (pr. 1776) were both very successful, as was Macklin's *Love à la Mode* (pr. 1759) and Inchbald's *Appearance Is Against Them* (pr. 1785). Less successful was Sheridan's *St. Patrick's Day: Or, The Scheming Lieutenant* (pr. 1775). The form did not change much over the course of the century, except that in later years it incorporated material from the pantomime. A unique species of farce was that offered by Foote between 1747 and 1777. Foote's farces depended on the mimicry of contemporary public figures, both public and private, including their physical defects. In *The Minor* (pr. 1760), for example, he caricatured the Methodist George Whitefield. Devoid of literary or aesthetic value, performances of Foote's plays were nevertheless enormously popular. His best piece, *Taste* (pr. 1752), satirizes virtuosi (that is, pretentious connoisseurs). Another extremely popular—and controversial—farce was Townley's *High Life Below Stairs* (pr. 1759), which satirized the pretentiousness and dishonesty of servants. So strongly did footmen object to the depiction of servants in the play that they almost rioted during the second performance.

Without question, however, it was Henry Fielding who composed the finest farces of the eighteenth century. Fielding's farces employ political, social, and dramatic satire, though his best satires of contemporary drama are more appropriately designated burlesques. Among his finest farces are *The Letter-Writers: Or, A New Way to Keep A Wife at Home* (pr. 1731), *The Author's Farce* (pr. 1730), *Pasquin: Or, A Dramatic Satire on the Times* (pr. 1736), and *The Historical Register for the Year 1736* (pr. 1737). Though "farce" is the term most appropriate to designate these works, they include elements drawn from the comedy of manners, of intrigue, of humors, and burlesque, and most also include songs. Using farce as a vehicle for satire, Fielding expanded the scope of the form to include themes such as a country election and a state lottery.

Another form of afterpiece at which Fielding excelled is the burlesque; in this genre, only John Gay is his equal. Probably the most famous burlesque of the eighteenth century is Fielding's *Tom Thumb: A Tragedy* (pr. 1730); more farcical than Gay's burlesque, the targets of Fielding's satire are not merely heroic dramas but also, as the mock annotations suggest, pompous critics, editors, and readers. Many eighteenth century burlesques are the "rehearsal plays" that follow the example of George Villiers, Duke of Buckingham's *The Rehearsal* (pr. 1671). Such are Clive's *The Rehearsal: Or, Bays in Petticoats* (pr. 1750), which satirizes female dramatists; Garrick's *A Peep Behind the Curtain: Or, The New Rehearsal* (pr. 1767); and Sheridan's *The Critic: Or, A Tragedy Rehearsed* (pr. 1779). Henry Carey's *The Tragedy of Chrononhotonthologos* (pr. 1734) satirizes tragedy, while his *The Dragon of Wantley* (pr. 1737) satirizes opera. Gay's main contribution to this genre is *The Mohocks* (pb. 1712), burlesquing Dennis' tragedy *Appius and Virginia* (pr. 1709).

A form of burlesque perfected by Gay is the ballad opera, of which his *The Beggar's Opera* (pr. 1728) is the most influential example. *The Beggar's Opera* simultaneously satirizes both Italian opera and sentimentality, parodies Shakespeare, Dryden, and Otway, and elicits genuine concern for its characters as well as laughter. For contemporary audiences, much of the play's humor derived from Gay's parodies of well-known songs. The great success of *The Beggar's Opera* stimulated a barrage of imitations, including Charles Johnson's *The Village Opera* (pr. 1729), Charles Coffey's *The Beggar's Wedding* (pr. 1729), Essex Hawker's *The Wedding* (pr. 1729), and George Lillo's *Silvia: Or, The Country Burial* (pr. 1730). Satiric, sentimental, realistic, and pastoral imitations of *The Beggar's Opera* were all produced, but none approached Gay's success. The heyday of the ballad opera was from 1728 to 1738, but the genre was revived later in the century by Bickerstaffe's *Love in a Village* (pr. 1762) and *The Maid of the Mill*. Other writers who attempted the form in the later years of the century were John O'Keeffe, Charles Dibdin, and Sheridan, whose highly successful *The Duenna: Or, The Double Elopement* (pr. 1775) was based on Wycherley's *The Country Wife*.

Perhaps the most profitable and popular form of afterpiece from mid-century on was the pantomime, a form believed to have been developed for the English stage during the 1720's by John Weaver, a dancing master at Drury Lane. So popular was the pantomime that admission prices for it were frequently twice the amount of those for other kinds of entertainment. In developing this form, Weaver drew on a variety of traditions, primarily on English farce and satire, on classical mythology, and on the stock characters found in the Italian *commedia dell'arte*. The story line of the pantomime focuses on the adventures of Harlequin, which were presented through dance, acrobatics, and gesture rather than through dialogue. The titles of these pieces reflect their curious mixture of sources and subjects: *The Loves of Mars and Venus* (Weaver, pr. 1717), *Harlequin Turned Judge* (Weaver, pr. 1717), *The Jealous Doctors* (John Rich, or "Lun," pr. 1717), *Harlequin Doctor Faustus* and *Harlequin Shepherd* (both by Thurmond, pr. 1723 and pr. 1724, respectively). Pantomime remained popular throughout the latter half of the century, as playwrights expanded the subject matter to include historical spectacle, current events, Oriental tales, and popular literature. Later pantomimes include Henry Woodward's *Harlequin Ranger* (pr. 1751), *The Genii* (pr. 1752), and *Queen Mab* (pr. 1750); Dance's *The Witches: Or, Harlequin Cherokee* (pr. 1762) and *The Rites of Hecate: Or, Harlequin from the Moon* (pr. 1763); Colman the Elder's *The Genius of Nonsense* (pr. 1780); John O'Keeffe's *Harlequin Teague: Or, The Giant's Causeway* (pr. 1782); and Garrick's self-parodic *Harlequin Invasion* (pr. 1759). The form was satirized by Fielding in *The Author's Farce*, as well as by Kelly in *The Plot* (pr. 1735) and in the anonymous *The British Stage* (pr. 1724), *The English Stage Italianized* (pr. 1727), *Harlequin Horace* (pr. 1731), and *Harlequin Student* (pr. 1741).

Tragedy

In Britain during the eighteenth century, tragedy was by no means as popular as was comedy, constituting but a small percentage of the number of plays performed. Although several dramatists made significant contributions to this genre—most notably, Addison, Rowe, Lillo, and Home—their influence was not nearly as pervasive or powerful upon either their contemporaries or their successors as was that of Dryden and Otway upon other tragic playwrights of the previous century. Generally, those playwrights who wrote tragedies did not attempt to specialize in the form but exercised their talents—or limitations—in other genres as well.

If one calculates a play's popularity according to the number of performances given, the most popular tragedies of the century were, by far, those by Shakespeare. His works were edited during the eighteenth century by Rowe (1709), Pope (1723-1725), Lewis Theobald (1733), Thomas Hanmer (1743-1744), William Warburton (1747), Samuel Johnson (1765), Edward Capell (1767-1768), George Steevens (1773), Edmond Malone (1790), and

Isaac Reed (1785), and Shakespeare was universally praised as a natural genius; nevertheless, his tragedies were often revised substantially to render them more compatible with contemporary sensibilities. Even the great Samuel Johnson, whose preface to his edition of Shakespeare is a landmark in the history of literary criticism, preferred Nahum Tate's 1681 adaptation of *King Lear* to the original. Garrick also adapted *King Lear* (in 1756), as did Colman the Elder (in 1768) and Kemble (in 1788). Lest one is tempted to dismiss automatically such adaptations as worthless, one should note that the film script for the famous production of *Richard III*, in which Sir Laurence Olivier plays the title role, is based on Tate's version of the play.

Other Elizabethan and Jacobean tragedies were also revived and adapted during the eighteenth century. Rowe's *The Fair Penitent* (pr. 1703) is based upon Philip Massinger's *The Fatal Dowry* (pr. c. 1616-1619); Lillo reworked *Arden of Feversham* (pr. 1759), and Colman the Elder adapted Fletcher's *Philaster: Or, Love Lies A-Bleeding* (pr. c. 1609) in 1763. Jonson's *Sejanus His Fall* (pr. 1603) was adapted by Francis Gentleman (in 1752) and anonymously as *The Favourite* (in 1770). More popular than the Elizabethan tragedies, however, were the heroic dramas of the Restoration, those by Dryden, Elkanah Settle, and Nathaniel Lee in particular, and the pathetic tragedies of the late seventeenth century, especially those written by Otway, Thomas Southerne, and John Banks. Thus William Addington developed Dryden's play *Aureng-Zebe* (pr. 1675) into *The Prince of Agra* (pr. 1774), while Bickerstaffe transformed *Don Sebastian, King of Portugal* (pr. 1689) into *The Captive* (pr. 1769). Southerne's *The Fatal Marriage* (pr. 1694) became Garrick's *Isabella* (pr. 1757), while *Oroonoko: Or, The Royal Slave* (pr. 1695), Southerne's adaptation of Behn's novel, underwent various transformations in the hands of John Hawkesworth (in 1759), Francis Gentleman (in 1760), and John Ferrar (in 1788).

It is not surprising that such earlier tragedy surpassed the popularity of contemporary eighteenth century tragedy, for many contemporary plays suffered from serious weaknesses in dialogue, character development, plot structure, and form. The dialogue, for example, is often bombastic or woodenly formal in plays derived from heroic drama or, as the century progresses, is laden with sentimental sententiae or pre-Romantic hyperbole. The atmosphere of many of these tragedies lacks the tragic aura of malign and inexorable fate. Many plots rely excessively upon anagnorisis (recognition or discovery) to create dramatic tension, as is done successfully in John Home's *Douglas* (pr. 1756) and, less felicitously, in William Whitehead's *Creusa, Queen of Athens* (pr. 1754), Arthur Murphy's *The Orphan of China* (pr. 1759), and Cumberland's *The Carmelite* (pr. 1784).

Perhaps the most damning flaw of these tragedies, however, is their uncertainty of generic identity: The bulk of the original tragedies written in

Britain during the eighteenth century consist of a patchwork of elements drawn from other tragedies, from tragedies old and new, domestic and foreign. The plots of these plays are generally drawn from three sources— from classical themes (such as Addison's *Cato* and Whitehead's *The Roman Father*, pr. 1750) or from Oriental tales (such as Young's *Busiris, King of Egypt*, pr. 1719; John Hughes's *The Siege of Damascus*, pr. 1720; and Hill's *The Tragedy of Zara*, pr. 1736, and *Merope*, pr. 1749, both derived from Voltaire) or from English history, especially of the medieval period (such as Hill's *Elfrid: Or, The Fair Inconstant*, pr. 1710, and Ambrose Philips' *The Briton*, pr. 1722, and *Humfrey, Duke of Gloucester*, pr. 1723). Over the course of the century, though the structure of most tragedies remained essentially classical, the subject matter became increasingly Romantic, but never did a single coherent form predominate, developed and perfected by masters and imitated by those striving to be such. Within the confines of a single scene, pathos derived from Otway, Southerne, or later from Rowe, diction derived from Dryden (if elevated) or from Shakespeare (if "natural"), and characters derived from classical drama may cohabit uneasily.

Because of their lack of fixed form, the more polymorphous tragedies of the eighteenth century are usually referred to simply as "Augustan tragedies." Those that do offer a coherent sense of form may usually be classified as belonging to the subgenres of pseudoclassical tragedy, she-tragedy, domestic tragedy, or Romantic tragedy. These categories, however, are overlapping and artificial, and do not reflect the entirety of each play, only its prevailing mode; even those tragedies that may reasonably be assigned to specific genres incorporate diverse elements from diverse sources.

Pseudoclassical tragedy is a subgenre of particular interest to the literary historian in that it reflects one of the strongest critical currents of the age, the belief, maintained by the "ancients," in the necessity of adhering to classical rules in order to produce the finest tragedy. Based upon a misreading of Aristotle, the Rules had dominated the French drama written in the seventeenth century and had exerted a profound influence upon that of Germany, Italy, and Britain. During the early decades of the eighteenth century, critics both in England and on the Continent persisted in admonishing playwrights for violating the Rules, especially those concerning the unities of time, place, and action. Thomas Rymer, Dennis, and Charles Gildon were the most influential British advocates of the Rules, and it is to their encouragement that historians owe the persistence of attempts to popularize pseudoclassical tragedy in England. Pseudoclassical plays rely heavily on classical drama for their plots, characters, structure, and themes; Dennis himself, for example, employed classical subjects as the bases for his unsuccessful tragedies *Iphigenia* (pr. 1699) and *Appius and Virginia*. Perhaps the most important force in the development of pseudoclassical tragedy was the seventeenth century French playwright Racine, who during the eighteenth century remained a force to be imitated or resisted. Charles Johnson's pseudoclassical tragedy *The Victim* (pr. 1714), for example, is based on Racine's *Iphigénie* (pr. 1674). Similarly, Philips' aesthetically and financially successful tragedy *The Distrest Mother* (pr. 1712), for which Steele wrote the prologue and Addison the epilogue, owes much to Racine's *Andromaque* (pr. 1667). Philips' tragedy is important in literary history as an example of an artistically and financially successful pseudoclassical tragedy and as an early example and progenitor of the she-tragedy. Most important, however, it was the positive reception afforded this pseudoclassical tragedy that convinced Addison to complete one of his own after a ten-year delay and to offer on the stage what would prove to be the foremost English pseudoclassical tragedy, *Cato*. Greeted with virtually universal critical approbation, *Cato* generated a legion of pamphlets and was translated into French, German, Italian, and Polish. More than any other tragedy during the first half of this century, *Cato* elevated the esteem in which English drama was held by the literati of the Continent.

Although Addison's *Cato* is unquestionably an example of a successful pseudoclassical tragedy, the play also illustrates the limitations of the genre. Strive though he does to adhere to the Rules, Addison nevertheless violates them with his inclusion of a subplot and his somewhat broad interpretation of the unities. A more serious and symptomatic defect in *Cato* is that, despite the sincerity of the sentiments this tragedy expresses, the play lacks emotional force and psychological depth. The pseudoclassical emphasis on decorum renders this tragedy, like other pseudoclassical tragedies, overly restrained and passionless; its characters are admirable but distant and unapproachable. Indeed, the best scenes of plays of this type are those that are least "classical" and that rely most on the heroic or the pathetic. Although contemporary critics praised pseudoclassical tragedy, the public, on the whole, shunned it; indeed, most historians of the theater agree that the success of *Cato* derived at least as much from its allusions to contemporary politics as from its exemplification of critical theory or its intrinsic merit as a drama. So artfully written was Addison's tragedy that the opposing political factions in the audience all claimed that Addison was a spokesman for their position.

Although the production of pseudoclassical tragedy declined in the 1720's, other playwrights continued to equal Addison's success during the century. Among these playwrights are James Thomson (who is more renowned for his poem *The Seasons*), in his *The Tragedy of Sophonisba* (pr. 1730); Samuel Johnson, in *Irene* (pr. 1749); Whitehead, in *The Roman Father* and *Crëusa, Queen of Athens*; Murphy, in *Alzuma*, based on Sophocles' play *Electra*; and John Delan, in *The Royal Suppliants* (pr. 1781), which blends Euripides' *Heraclidae* with Aeschylus' *The Suppliants*.

Pseudoclassical tragedy was popular on the Continent as well as in

Britain. In Italy, the foremost composer of pseudoclassical tragedy was Francesco Scipione de Maffei, whose *Merope* (pr. 1713) was one of very few Italian tragedies to be performed on the English stage during the eighteenth century. *Merope* was lauded by Goldsmith, both praised and condemned by Voltaire (who produced his own version in 1743), and carefully examined by Goethe and Lessing. In Germany, the most important force in the pseudoclassical movement in drama was Johann Christoph Gottsched, who tried to model German pseudoclassical tragedy on the French as part of his effort to reunite the German drama with literature. Gottsched's most famous play is the very successful *Der sterbende Cato* (pr. 1732), which is essentially a translation of François Michel Crétien Deschamps' *Caton d'Utique* (pr. 1715), with Addison's conclusion substituted for Deschamps'. Gottsched was also influential in the history of German theatrical production as well as the composition of plays, being one of the first to demand that actors adhere strictly to the script and to pursue historical accuracy in costuming, and he produced a bibliography of German drama that scholars still find useful today, entitled *Nötiger Vorratzur Geschichte der deutschen dramatischen Dichtkunst* (1757-1765).

Subsequent leaders in the German pseudoclassical movement rejected French classicism, believing that the French had misinterpreted Aristotle, and insisted on returning to the Greek texts themselves for their models. The most famous of the German dramatists advocating this Greek-oriented pseudoclassicism were Lessing, Goethe, and Schiller—the latter two more famous for their contribution to the *Sturm und Drang* movement. Lessing believed that the Rules were not "rules" per se but merely suggestions. In *Kritische Briefe, die neueste deutsche Literatur betreffend* (1759-1760) and *Hamburgische Dramaturgie* (1767-1769), Lessing enunciates his critical position, condemning the tragedies of Gottsched, Pierre Corneille, Racine, and Voltaire for their lack of action and praising Shakespeare as the greatest modern dramatist. Lessing even asserts that Shakespeare adhered to Aristotle's actual principles more closely than did Corneille. The ideal tragedy, Lessing believed, would blend Shakespearean characterization and incident with Sophoclean restraint of form, principles that Lessing incorporated in the composition of his extremely influential tragedy *Emilia Galotti* (pr. 1772).

In France, the predominant force in the shaping of tragedy was Voltaire. Like the German tragedians, Voltaire found the old models no longer satisfactory, but he offered an alternative solution. Voltaire enunciated his theories partly in response to his chief rival, Prosper Jolyot de Crébillon, whose innovation in the drama consisted of the exploitation of the horrific, as is evident in his *Atrée et Thyeste* (pr. 1707) and Voltaire's *Œdipe* (pr. 1718). Though an admirer of Racine and fundamentally a classicist who believed in clear generic distinction, decorum, and the unities, Voltaire was inspired by Shakespeare to initiate a number of significant innovations in the drama. Rather than turn back to the Greeks, Voltaire modernized and renewed classicism by placing a new emphasis on the emotions, especially on pathos, and by extending the range of characters and settings used in tragedy to include the Oriental and the exotic (as in *Mahomet,* pr. 1741, and *Alzire, l'Orphelin de la Chine,* pr. 1755). Voltaire also wrote philosophical tragedies focusing on subjects other than love. *Alzire* and *Mahomet* for example, center on religious conflict. Voltaire violated the Rules by presenting violence onstage, and he also expanded the use of spectacle. The performance of *Adélaïde du Guesclin* (pr. 1734), for example, included a riot, thunder, and the firing of a cannon. Voltaire's dramas and ideas were widely imitated and adapted: In England, Hill's *The Tragedy of Zara* was based on Voltaire's *Zaïre* (pr. 1732), which was, in turn, derived from Shakespeare's *Othello* (pr. 1604), and Murphy's *The Chinese Orphan* and *Alzuma* are also adaptations of plays by Voltaire. Voltaire's movement away from rigid classicism is sometimes regarded as a significant step toward the beginning of Romantic tragedy.

Besides pseudoclassicism, another influential force in the development of tragedy during the early part of the century was the heroic drama, with its standardized characters (great souls struggling in love), plots (bold exploits and contemptible betrayals), settings (temples, tombs, palaces, prisons, gardens), and bombastic dialogue. The plays of Racine, Dryden, and Lord Orrery were most frequently imitated by playwrights attempting to make use of this tradition. Although the eighteenth century witnessed the production of relatively few new heroic dramas, heroic elements recur in a variety of tragic genres throughout the century. This influence is evident, for example, in the popularity of Asian motifs, as in John Mottley's *The Imperial Captives* (pr. 1720), Gay's *The Captives* (pr. 1724), Marsh's *Amasis, King of Egypt* (pr. 1738), Miller's *Mahomet the Imposter* (pr. 1744), and Lillo's *Elmerick: Or, Justice Triumphant* (pr. 1740). A catalog of contemporary heroic drama would include Cibber's *Xerxes* (pr. 1699), Gildon's *Love's Victim: Or, The Royal Queen of Wales* (pr. 1701), and Charles Johnson's *The Sultaness* (pr. 1717), based on Racine's *Bajazet* (pr. 1672).

Whereas the pseudoclassical and the heroic drama both attempted to elicit admiration for their heroes, the pathetic and domestic tragedies were more designed to arouse warmer emotions, particularly sympathy. Playwrights composing pathetic and domestic tragedies during the eighteenth century turned to Shakespeare, to Otway, and to Southerne for direction, as did Rowe, one of the most famous and most influential dramatists of the eighteenth century. Although he designated Shakespeare as his guide, Rowe's concern with cultivating pathos for admirable but distressed women is more reminiscent of Otway than it is of Shakespeare. Precedents for his violation of poetic justice are, however, evident in both of his models. Although Rowe achieved success with his early political tragedy *Tamerlane*, his most influential works were his she-tragedies, especially *The Fair Penitent* (a 1703 adaptation of Massinger's *The Fatal Dowry*) and *The Tragedy of Jane Shore*. Rowe himself coined the term "she-tragedy," which refers to those tragedies whose primary purpose is to elicit pathos for the unjust suffering of a woman. Although Rowe did not initiate the form—Banks is usually credited with having done so in the previous century—it was Rowe who popularized it. Also included in this category are Rowe's unsuccessful *The Tragedy of Lady Jane Gray* (pr. 1715), Philips' *The Distrest Mother*, Thomson's *The Tragedy of Sophonisba*, Samuel Johnson's *Irene*, and Charles Johnson's *Caelia: Or, The Perjured Lover* (pr. 1732), which, with Rowe's *The Fair Penitent*, served as one of Richardson's main sources for his multivolume novelistic tragedy, *Clarissa: Or, The History of a Young Lady* (pr. 1747-1748).

Rowe's efforts in developing the she-tragedy did not please everyone: The classical critics, for example, feared that Rowe's emphasis on love would accelerate the decline of tragedy. Such fears were not without basis, for aside from Jane Shore, even Rowe's female characters elicit only pathos and lack tragic grandeur. Nevertheless, Rowe's plays are very important in the history of British drama, for in them one can observe the beginnings of the development of domestic tragedy. Although Rowe's characters are not middle-class, neither are they royalty, and though his tragedies center on historical figures who shaped the destiny of their nation, Rowe's most memorable scenes are those focusing on the characters' private, domestic concerns. Rowe's emphasis on pity and suffering and the occasional aphoristic bent of his dialogue are also interesting reflections of the growth of sentimentalism.

Fueled by an increasing emphasis upon the eliciting of emotion in the interest of advancing didactic intentions, by mid-century literary critics had turned from a preoccupation with formalistic concerns (such as the Rules) to explore the psychological sources of tragic pleasure. The focus in criticism thus shifted during the eighteenth century from the text and aesthetic concerns to the emotional response of the audience. In France during the seventeenth century, René Descartes had maintained that the stimulation of the emotion was in itself pleasurable, while his English contemporary, Thomas Hobbes, had argued that the viewer derives pleasure from tragedy as the result of remarking the contrast between others' misfortune and the viewer's own comparatively happy circumstances, a view similar to that later advanced by the pseudoclassical dramatist and critic Schlegel in *Von der Unähnlichkeit in der Nachahmung* (pb. 1764). In the eighteenth century, two rival explanations for tragic pleasure predominated. In "Of Tragedy" (1757), David Hume asserted that the pleasure obtained from tragedy is aesthetic and that this pleasure is enjoyed only so long as the beauty of the tragedy is not overbalanced by its horror. An even more influential explanation, however, was that offered disparately by Anthony Ashley Cooper, the third Earl of Shaftesbury, by Francis Hutcheson, and by Edmund Burke, each of whom maintained that the pleasure comes from exercising sympathy for the distressed characters. Thus, during the eighteenth century, audiences and critics alike reinforced dramatists' inclination to relegate aesthetic concerns to the second rank and to concentrate instead on emotional stimulation and response.

Such an emphasis on drama's mechanical rather than aesthetic essence is reflected by Lillo's *The London Merchant*, the first successful domestic tragedy in England. In his dedication to the play, Lillo asserts the importance of having a "moral" to his tragedy that will prove "useful." Its author himself a member of the merchant class, *The London Merchant* focuses on the concerns of the middle-class people, as eighteenth century comedies and the periodical essays of Addison and Steele had already done for some time. Lillo was not the first to attempt domestic tragedy in English: The anonymous Elizabethan play *The Yorkshire Tragedy* (pr. 1608) and Thomas Heywood's *A Woman Killed with Kindness* (pr. 1603) also focus on middle-class characters, as does Hill's *The Fatal Extravagance* (pr. 1721), which was based on *The Yorkshire Tragedy*. Unlike the Elizabethan domestic tragedies, however, Lillo employs the middle class for more than setting, and unlike Hill's tragedy, Lillo's was successful on the stage. Although self-indulgent in its bid for an emotional response and dogged in its didacticism, *The London Merchant* offered its audience a recognizable and convincing sense of tragic fate. Lillo was also innovative in his use of prose for his tragedy as well as in his employment of a British rather than a classical or exotic Eastern setting. Curiously, however, despite the play's overwhelming and century-long success onstage, few English tragedies were modeled upon it. Neither was Lillo's other domestic tragedy, the blank-verse *Guilt Its Own Punishment: Or, Fatal Curiosity* (pr. 1736), widely imitated, though it did spawn two adaptations, one by Colman the Elder, in 1782, and another by the novelist Henry Mackenzie, in 1784. Indeed, the only other eighteenth century English domestic tragedies of note are Charles Johnson's unsuccessful *Caelia*, Moore's *The Gamester* (which Diderot translated into French), Home's *Douglas,* and Cumberland's *The Mysterious Husband* (pr. 1783). Though comparatively well written, *Caelia* failed because of what was considered the indelicate realism of Johnson's depiction of a brothel. From the failure of *Caelia*, one may deduce a partial explanation for the paucity of fine tragedy in this period: Overly concerned with propriety and insistent in their demand for facile moralizing, the eighteenth century audience would not accept the indecorousness of realistic suffering onstage.

Lillo's domestic tragedies were, however, received enthusiastically and imitated widely on the Continent, particularly in Germany. The first German *bürgerliches Trauerspiel*, or "bourgeois tragedy," was Lessing's *Miss Sara Sampson* (pr. 1755), which owes much not only to Lillo but also to Johnson's *Caelia* and to Richardson's tragic sentimental novel *Clarissa*. Lessing's later tragedy, *Emilia Galotti*, also a *bürgerliches Trauerspiel*, is important because it anticipates the type of drama produced by those involved in the *Sturm und Drang* movement. Goethe's *Clavigo* (pr. 1774) and *Stella* (pr. 1776) are also domestic dramas in the tradition of *Emilia Galotti*. German bourgeois tragedies would be translated into English and would then stimulate the development of English melodrama and Romantic tragedy. Lillo's *Guilt Its Own Punishment* also inspired the rise of another form of tragedy in Germany, the *Schicksalstragödie*, or "tragedy of fate." Such tragedies focus on a family doomed by a curse that is fated to strike at a specific time and through a specific symbolic instrument. Although Moritz adapted *Guilt Its Own Punishment* for the German stage in 1781, the first *Schicksalstragödie* did not appear until *Der vierundzwanzigste Februar* (pr. 1810) by the Romantic playwright Zacharias Werner. His later, more famous play, *Die Schuld* (pr. 1813), affords another example of the *Schicksalstragödie*.

One of the most important movements in German intellectual and literary history was the *Strum und Drang* movement, led by young writers hostile to the artificiality and cynicism of French classicism. At its strongest between 1760 and 1785, the major proponents of the *Sturm und Drang* were Johann Gottfried Herder, who is generally credited with being its founder, Jakob Michael Reinhold Lenz, Friedrich Maximilian Klinger, Henrich Leopold Wagner, Schiller, and Goethe. It was from a tragedy by Klinger, *Der Wirrwarr: Oder, Sturm und Drang* (pr. 1776), that the name for the movement was derived. Inspired by the ideas of Rousseau, the unconventionality of Shakespeare (as interpreted by Herder), and the realism of Mercier and Diderot, the proponents of this pre-Romantic movement found classicism stifling and drama which adhered to classical principles lacking in nature, originality, and passion. Fired by nationalism, they exuberantly lauded and drew upon the folk literature of Germany, sharing the spirit with which the English turned to James Macpherson's Ossianic tales. Two professors from Zurich, Johann Jakob Bodmer and Johann Jakob Breitinger, together produced a collection of medieval literature, *Sammlung von Minnesingern* (1758-1759), as their contribution to the revolt against the classicism exemplified by Gottsched. The drama of the *Sturm und Drang* often presented the theme of resistance to tyranny, glorified the Middle Ages, and exalted relentless individualism in its heroes, who were frequently misfits in their society (see, for example, the protagonists in the plays of Goethe and Schiller). Character rather than social consciousness, however, was the more important concern of the *Sturm und Drang* drama.

Among the finest literary works produced by the movement are Goethe's *Götz von Berlichingen mit der eisernen Hand* (1773) and his masterpiece, *Faust*. Though not published until 1808, *Faust* was begun in the 1770's at the height of the *Sturm und Drang*, as Goethe's glorification of the ardent individualism of *Faust* suggests. Of the plays of Schiller, who succeeded Goethe as the leader of the *Sturm und Drang* movement, *Die Räube* (pr. 1781) had a great influence upon both Lewis' *The Castle Spectre* (pr. 1797) and Richard Cumberland's *Don Pedro* (pr. 1797). Schiller's *Kabale und Liebe* (pr. 1784) inspired an anonymous English adaptation entitled *Cabal and Love* (pr. 1795) as well as a rendering by Lewis as *The Minister* (pb. 1797). Other important *Sturm und Drang* dramas include Klinger's *Die Zwillinge* (pr. 1776) and Lenz's *Die Soldaten* (pb. 1776).

By the 1780's, however, the *Sturm und Drang* movement had largely spent its force, and its historical tragedies evolved (or devolved) into the formulaic, pseudomedieval *Ritterdrama* produced by Klinger, Graf von Torring, and Joseph Babo. The best of the *Ritterdramen* is one of the earliest examples of the form, Klinger's *Otto* (pb. 1775). From approximately 1780 until 1805, Goethe and Schiller turned from the *Sturm und Drang* ethos back to classicism and attempted to synthesize the best elements of Romanticism and classicism. During this period, Goethe produced his excellent tragedy *Iphigenie auf Tauris* (pb. 1787), and he also shaped the development of the drama from a different perspective as the manager of the ducal theater in Weimar (from 1791 until 1817). Schiller, too, contributed several superb tragedies to German drama—*Don Carlos, Infant von Spanien* (pr. 1787), *Wallenstein* (pr. 1799), which was translated into English the following year by Coleridge, and *Maria Stuart* (pr. 1800), his most popular play.

In Italy, Vittorio Alfieri also composed tragedies full of passion that were based on historical themes, but Alfieri adhered strictly to the unities as part of his efforts to achieve highly intense, concentrated effects with his drama. Among his finest tragedies are *Filippo* (pb. 1784), *Don Garzia* (pb. 1788)—which offers an interesting contrast with Schiller's play of the same title and approximate date of composition—*Saul* (pb. 1788), and *Mirra* (pb. 1789). The characters in Alfieri's best dramas are drawn from ancient, biblical, and European history, and, like the protagonists of *Sturm und Drang* tragedy, they are often presented as opponents of tyranny.

In both England and Germany, interest in the national past was accelerated by the "translation" and dissemination of the fraudulent *The Poems of Ossian* (1765), which purported to be translations of Gaelic poems by the legendary Ossian that were "discovered" by James Macpherson, as well as by Thomas Percy's *Reliques of Ancient English Poetry* (1765). Translated into German during the *Strum und Drang* era, the English Ossianic poems kindled in German intellectuals the desire to explore their own primitive literature. In Germany, the most outstanding figure involved in this bardic movement in the drama was Friedrich Gottlob Klopstock. Of Klopstock's six plays, three of them focus on biblical subjects (*Der Tod Adams*, pb. 1757; *Salomo*, pb. 1764; and *David*, pb. 1772), and three form a trilogy centering on the exploits of the national hero, Hermann (*Hermanns Schlacht*, pb. 1769; *Hermann und die Fürsten*, pb. 1784; and *Hermanns Tod*, pb. 1787). Stressing the inspiration behind the latter group of plays, Klopstock referred to the plays of the trilogy as *Bardiete*. Also important in the bardic movement in the German drama was Heinrich Wilhelm von Gerstenberg, whose tragedy *Ugolino* (pr. 1769) allows the reader to observe much anguish but little action.

A pre-Romantic concern with national history and folk literature similar to that in Germany was also a dominant force in the development of English Romantic tragedy. Henry Brooke's *The Earl of Essex* (pr. 1750), Richard Glover's *Boadicea* (pr. 1753), and Hannah More's *Percy* (pr. 1777), for example, all focus on figures derived from British history. Initially, tragedies continued to manifest the imprint of classicism at the same time that they exhibited pre-Romantic tendencies. Thus, despite its setting in primitive Britain, William Mason's *Elfrida* (pb. 1752) includes a chorus similar to that found in Greek tragedy, and though Home's *Douglas* adheres to the neoclassical Rules and also to the concept of decorum, the characters are placed in a wild, ancient setting that seems to reflect their psychological turmoil.

In England, the influence of Ossian was felt most profoundly in Romantic tragedy. Home's *The Fatal Discovery* (pr. 1769), for example, is based directly on one of the Ossian tales. Concentrating on arousing the emotions and exciting the imagination, Romantic tragedies are fixed in ancient, picturesque settings. The hero is typically one whose true worth is not recognized by those around him, and the whole world seems to echo his inner turmoil. As the century progressed, Romantic tragedies increasingly employed fantastic costuming, scenery, and staging to heighten their dramatic effect, concentrating increasingly upon spectacle rather than formalistic or aesthetic concerns.

During the final years of the eighteenth century, Romantic tragedy blended with sentimental comedy to produce two overlapping forms, the melodrama and the Gothic drama. Melodrama of the last decade of the eighteenth century employed the simplistic character delineation, moralistic didacticism, and facile poetic justice evident in lesser examples of sentimental comedy but placed a greater emphasis on sensationalism. On the whole, these early melodramas are weakly constructed, with much action but little or no attention given to providing the characters with psychological complexity or realistic motivation. The first play explicitly termed a "melo-drama" was Holcroft's *A Tale of Mystery* (pr. 1802), but included in the genre are earlier plays, such as Cumberland's *The Wheel of Fortune* (pr. 1795) and Thomas Morton's *Columbus*, which is based on René-Charles Guilbert de Pixérécourt's *Cælina: Ou, L'Enfant du mystère* (pr. 1800). In France, the most famous melodramatic playwright was Pixérécourt. Best remembered for his melodrama *Selico* (pr. 1793), Pixérécourt specialized in adapting popular novels with sensational plots.

Closely akin to the melodrama is the Gothic drama, which employs complex plots replete with hidden chambers, dire curses, and mysterious apparitions. Among the more successful plays in the genre are Colman the Younger's *The Iron Chest*, Lewis' *The Castle Spectre*, and Cumberland's *The Carmelite*. Curiously, one of the most influential plays in the development of Gothic drama was never offered on the stage—Horace Walpole's *The Mysterious Mother* (pb. 1768), which was circulated in manuscript form and which provided many dramatists with suggestions for characters and plot. The influence of *The Mysterious Mother* is especially apparent in Cumberland's *The Mysterious Husband*.

Neither melodrama nor Gothic drama constitutes either comedy or tragedy proper, for though both elicit pity and fear, they almost invariably conclude happily. Both forms of drama are nevertheless worthy of attention as illustrations of the divorce that occurred between theater and literature during the latter half of the eighteenth century. The composition of literary tragedy and comedy persisted at the century's end, in the form of plays designed not for presentation in the theater but for reading in the study. These "closet dramas" are typically lacking in theatrical technique as well as vitality—exits and entrances are omitted, the characters appearing and disappearing, speaking and remaining silent, without any apparent reason. Closet dramas tend to be abstract and philosophical, far removed from the realm of ordinary human passions. Joanna Baillie offered some of the better examples of this form in *A Series of Plays* (1798), which includes her tragedies *Count Basil* and *De Montfort* as well as her comedy *The Tryal*. Among the most popular closet dramas were German plays in translation, perhaps because these plays offered readers the genuine tragic spirit that their own contemporary tragedy no longer afforded. Benjamin Thompson's *The German Theater* (1800) was the most popular collection of German plays in translation, though many editions of translations of individual work were also available.

Although patterns of decline in both the tragedy and the comedy of eighteenth century drama have been identified in this study, it should be noted that historians of drama regard this period as a time of germination, a period preceding and thus necessarily less mature and attractive than an age of flowering. What was engendered in the eighteenth century in the theater was something fine and new, an unquestioning affirmation of the dignity and importance of the human spirit, whatever the birthright of the container in which that spirit resides. Rowe and Lillo paved the way for the plays of Henrik Ibsen, August Strindberg, and Arthur Miller; Steele and Sheridan ushered in the plays of Oscar Wilde and George Bernard Shaw. The sin to which the dramatists of the age freely gave themselves, that of pleasing the audience at the expense of artistic concerns, is one from which no age is free. One can only hope that the playwrights of succeeding generations will draw as much profit from the drama of the present age as the present has derived from that of the eighteenth century.

Laurie P. Morrow

NINETEENTH CENTURY BRITISH DRAMA

Heartless, mustachioed, black-caped villains; helpless, innocent, poverty-stricken heroines; clean-cut, upright, there-in-the-nick-of-time heroes; and "curses, foiled again"—such are the elements that make up the popular conception of melodrama. An almost equally popular conception is that the melodrama was virtually the only form of drama to hold the boards in the nineteenth century theater. While the melodrama was certainly popular and influential, the age also produced Romantic verse drama, high tragedy, sophisticated comedy, and plays of ideas. In addition, numerous extrava-ganzas, burlettas, farces, and comic operas satisfied audience demands for novelty and variety. Poets, such as Lord Byron and Percy Bysshe Shelley, novelists, such as Charles Dickens, and playwrights, such as W. S. Gilbert and Oscar Wilde, wrote for this stage and its players. John Philip Kemble, Edmund Kean, William Charles Macready, Samuel Phelps, Charles Mathews, and Lucia Elizabeth Bartolozzi (Madame Vestris) are but a sampling of the nineteenth century theater's stars. Those who acted toward the beginning of the period were illuminated by candlelight; those who succeeded them were illuminated by limelight, then by gaslight, and finally by electricity. This technological transition was only one among many other theatrical and dramatic developments of the period. While the importance of these developments cannot be slighted, it is equally important to consider the nineteenth century theater as more than merely the product of a transitional period.

Playhouses

Shortly after King Charles II was restored to the British throne in 1660, he reopened the theaters, which had been closed at the outbreak of the English Civil War in 1642. Charles II granted patents (licenses that could be sold or willed to heirs like other kinds of property) to two of his courtiers, Thomas Killigrew and Sir William Davenant. The theaters which they established and those of their successors enjoyed a veritable monopoly that was not abolished until the Theatre Regulation Act of 1843.

During the eighteenth century, this monopoly had been strengthened by the Licensing Act of 1737—a measure aimed at controlling the unlicensed playhouses that had been built during a period when the government's enforcement of the theatrical patents had been lax. Since these unlicensed playhouses had also been hotbeds of antigovernment satire, the Licensing Act further required that all dramatic manuscripts be submitted to the Lord Chamberlain for censorship. The practical effect of this legislation was that by the beginning of the nineteenth century, there were two classes of theaters: the two patent houses, Drury Lane and Covent Garden (Samuel Foote's Haymarket Theatre, which eventually was granted a patent, operated principally during the summer), and the more numerous minor (that is, nonpatent) theaters, such as the Olympic and the Adelphi. The acting of "legitimate" drama (five-act tragedies and comedies) was restricted to the patent houses, while "illegitimate" drama (melodramas, extravaganzas, burlettas, hippodramas, pantomimes, and spectacles) was the province of the "minors." This division of theatrical labor persisted until it was abolished by the aforementioned Theatre Regulation Act of 1843. The Lord Chamberlain's censorship powers, however, remained in force until 1968.

The rather intimate eighteenth century theater auditorium had been divided into pit, box, and gallery. The pit, at ground level, consisted of rows of backless benches; the rowdier elements of the audience tended to congregate there. One level up, around the sides of the theater, were the boxes—the location preferred by the fashionable. At the upper level were one or more galleries: The first gallery attracted the middle classes, while the second was often frequented by servants and apprentices.

By the beginning of the nineteenth century, the population of London had grown substantially, increasing the number of potential theatergoers, especially among the working classes. In 1792 and 1793, Covent Garden's seating capacity was increased to three thousand, while in 1794 Drury Lane's was increased to thirty-six hundred. In 1828, the King's Theatre converted some of the pit benches into seats with backs. The Haymarket followed suit in 1843, replacing these primitive "stalls" with upholstered seats in 1863. At first, only a few rows of pit benches were removed, but by the 1880's the pit had vanished entirely in favor of the stalls. With the stalls came also the practice of reserved seating.

The boxes were retained except for those at the pit level, which were removed to allow expansion of the pit and subsequently of the stalls. The number of galleries was increased from one or two to as many as four or five. New methods of theater design eventually removed the pillars dividing various sections of the galleries, thus turning them into modern balconies.

After 1860, there was a tendency to reduce theater size. The Criterion Theatre, for example, built in 1874, seated 660, and few theaters remained with a seating capacity above fifteen hundred. Smaller theaters meant fewer galleries, or balconies, so the boxes were also converted to balconies and renamed the Dress Circle. What had been the first gallery was renamed the Upper Circle, while the second gallery simply remained the Gallery. The customary horseshoe-shaped auditorium was gradually replaced by a fan-shaped one that afforded better sightlines for the new staging techniques that were being developed.

The nineteenth century theater had inherited from its eighteenth century predecessor a shallow stage framed by a large proscenium arch. Jutting out from this arch was a large apron, upon which most of the acting was done, the shallow backstage being reserved for scenery, which was changed by the pushing and pulling of painted flats and wings along wooden grooves. On either side of the proscenium arch were the proscenium doors, used for entrances and exits. (Performers normally did not enter or exit through the wings or through any other part of the scenery.)

Throughout most of the eighteenth century, scenery, though sometimes spectacular, was used primarily to suggest a general atmosphere. Under the influence of the Romantics, the nineteenth century theater began to use scenery to suggest particular places—often in minute detail. For example, when Drury Lane was enlarged in 1794, the dimensions of its stage measured eighty-five feet wide by ninety-two feet deep—sufficient to allow use of a remarkably detailed Gothic-cathedral set. Indeed, the theater's concern with architectural accuracy even went so far as the consulting of an archeologist, Sir Lawrence Alma-Tadema, whom Sir Henry Irving hired to design scenery for his productions of William Shakespeare's *Cymbeline* in 1896 and *Coriolanus* in 1901.

The larger auditoriums and stages also allowed theater managers to satisfy a growing demand by the audience for spectacle. Indeed, the large auditoriums encouraged this taste, since they made subtle, intimate scenes and actions difficult both to see and to hear. Sadler's Wells Theatre, for example, featured a water tank that enabled it to stage sea battles. Astley's Ampitheatre boasted a circus ring in front of its stage, which was used for the presentation of equestrian dramas.

Various staging devices also contributed to specular effects. Among the best known were the "vampire trap," which allowed an actor seemingly to walk through a wall, and the more complicated "ghost glide," which made an actor seem to rise mysteriously from the earth.

Alongside the grand-scale Romantic dramas, with their often spectacular sets, were smaller-scale dramas of everyday life. The box set, popularized by Madame Vestris during her management of the Olympic Theatre, was first used there in 1832. This set completely enclosed the acting area and gave the illusion of watching the action inside one or more rooms with their fourth walls removed. Thus, all the acting took place behind the proscenium arch instead of spilling over onto the stage apron. Indeed, this apron shrank considerably throughout the nineteenth century as actors began more and more to move through the scenery instead of merely using it as a backdrop while they declaimed their lines from the apron.

As the illusion of reality came to be more important, managers began to emphasize productions that integrated acting, scenery, and costuming. In 1823, James Robinson Planché persuaded Charles Kemble, manager of Covent Garden, to stage Shakespeare's *King John* with historically accurate costuming, thus beginning a vogue of theatrical antiquarianism. Planché himself extensively researched ancient modes of dress. In 1834, he published his *History of British Costume*; it remained the definitive work on theatrical costuming throughout most of the nineteenth century. Planché also encouraged Madame Vestris to devote equal care to the costuming of the "minor" drama. Thus, at the Olympic Theatre, the exaggerated costumes that had characterized comedy and burlesque gave way to clothes more like those worn in everyday life.

The illusion of reality was further enhanced by the development of new stage-lighting techniques. The eighteenth century theater had used candles and oil lamps. Varying the lighting levels, either onstage or in the auditorium, was nearly impossible. Limelight, invented by Thomas Drummond in 1816, used a mixture of hydrogen and oxygen, which heated a column of lime until it glowed. Covered with a lens, this light acted much like a spotlight and was also used for special effects. Gas lighting became popular in the 1840's, making it possible to control lighting intensity better than ever before. In 1881, the Savoy Theatre was totally illuminated by a new power source, electricity, and by 1900 almost all the London theaters had followed suit. With both gas and electricity, the lighting levels in the auditorium could also be controlled, so that the lights could be dimmed during performances, if the manager desired.

The use of the curtain also changed during the nineteenth century. It had been customary to raise the curtain at the beginning of a play and not to lower it until the end. Scene changes were accomplished in full view of the audience. Thus, the curtain usually was not used to mask scene changes or indicate the end of an act. As the penchant for the illusion of reality grew stronger, theater managers believed that such scene changes detracted from the effect they desired and so began to use the curtain to hide the process and to preserve the illusion.

This illusion was further enhanced by the use of three- rather than two-dimensional scenery. The old grooves eventually disappeared as newer methods of setting up and removing scenery were developed. Actors thus could make the most integrated use of scenery possible.

People

Although nineteenth century actors used a wide variety of techniques, three important styles can be readily identified. The first is the classic style, popularized by John Philip Kemble and Sarah Kemble Siddons. This style demanded that an actor catch the essence of a character and express it with dignity, grace, declamation, and stately poses. Naturalness resided in the catching, rather than in the expressing, of this essence. The art of the actor was not to be concealed but rather to be revealed and admired.

The second style, the Romantic, sought naturalness through emphasizing a character's passions—a stark contrast to the reasonableness of the classic style's interpretation. Actors achieved their effects chiefly through exaggeration of, and sometimes through rapid changes among, the various emotions they sought to portray. Edmund Kean helped to establish this style, though his critics judged both his acting and his personality to be somewhat erratic.

The realistic style was encouraged by Charles Fechter. Fechter, an actor, managed successively the Princess's Theatre and the Lyceum Theatre, both in London. His emphasis on the box set and his interest in creating an illusion of reality led him to demand that his actors move and speak more like persons in everyday life. Fechter's enthusiasm for this style was not limited to contemporary drama but was extended to the classics as well.

Actor-managers such as Fechter were not uncommon. For example, in 1788, John Philip Kemble succeeded Richard Brinsley Sheridan as manager of Drury Lane before moving to Covent Garden in 1803. One of the best-known managers was William Charles Macready. An actor who combined the best of the classic and Romantic styles (with a touch of realism thrown in), Macready was dissatisfied with current theatrical practices and saw managing as a way to effect reforms. He managed Covent Garden from 1837 to 1839 and Drury Lane from 1841 to 1843. Macready emphasized the importance of rehearsals, which had previously been perfunctory—the star often not bothering about them in order to conserve strength for the actual performance. Furthermore, he insisted on dictating where his actors were to stand instead of allowing them to choose the positions that were personally most advantageous. All in all, Macready strove for a unified effect that also extended to his sets and costumes, which were designed with great concern for their historical accuracy.

Among Macready's acting company was Samuel Phelps, who, as eventual manager of the run-down Sadler's Wells Theatre, attracted large audiences by offering a bill consisting almost exclusively of poetic drama. Phelps acted in his own productions and, like Macready, took great pains to achieve historical accuracy. In 1862, he left Sadler's Wells to tour, but later in the decade his productions of Shakespeare's plays revived the sagging fortunes of Drury Lane.

Madame Vestris' work at the Olympic has already been mentioned, especially her use of the box set and her insistence on more realistic costuming for the "minor" drama. She herself was famous for her roles in light comedy. Her second husband, Charles Mathews, was well-known for the same types of roles. (Her first husband, Armand Vestris, had been a dancer.) Vestris and Mathews combined their managerial talents, first at Covent Garden, from 1839 to 1842, and then at the Lyceum, from 1847 to 1856.

One of the most influential actor-managers was Charles Kean, son of the more famous Edmund Kean. Never the actor his father was, Charles gave up acting in favor of managing the Princess's Theatre in 1850. He was assisted by his wife and leading lady, Ellen Tree. He was also Master of the Revels—an appointment granted him by Queen Victoria. Kean managed to attract a fashionable audience by setting his curtain time and arranging his theatrical bill to cater to upper-class tastes. He presented chiefly Shakespeare and melodramas, using long runs to offset the cost of his productions, which had escalated in response to Kean's demands for historical accuracy.

John Baldwin Buckstone was a comedian-turned-manager of the Haymarket from 1853 to 1876. He was also the author of numerous plays, including the successful melodrama *Luke the Laborer: Or, The Lost Son* (pr. 1826). Planché twice satirized both Buckstone and his entertainments, in *Mr. Buckstone's Ascent of Mount Parnassus* (pr. 1853) and in *Mr. Buckstone's Voyage Round the Globe in Leicester Square* (pr. 1854). Buckstone's melodramas, however, found their home at the Adelphi, managed by Benjamin Webster—a former actor from Madame Vestris' company. He was also Buckstone's predecessor at the Haymarket Theatre, which he managed from 1837 to 1853, the year Buckstone took over.

Marie Wilton Bancroft, an actress in the "minor" theaters, and her husband, Squire Bancroft, a provincial actor, acquired a run-down theater, which they remodeled and reopened as the Prince of Wales's Theatre in 1865. The Bancrofts were especially successful at staging the contemporary dramas of Thomas William Robertson—plays that demanded realistic settings, though not always totally realistic acting. Among the Bancrofts' most important contributions to the theater were their reduction of the theater bill to a single play, their adoption of regular matinee performances, their refinement of the box set, and their extension of the proscenium arch across the floor of the stage, which confined all the acting behind the imaginary "fourth wall," enhancing the pictorial effect.

Sir Henry Irving gained his acting fame in melodramas. His leading lady was the equally famous Ellen Terry, who excelled in Shakespearean roles as well. Irving managed the Lyceum Theatre from 1878 to 1898. He was a proponent of pictorial realism. It was Irving who, in 1881, removed the grooves that had been used to shift scenery, thus opening the way for increased use of three-dimensional sets. He also extended historical accuracy of costume to include those of the minor characters, who had previously been neglected in favor of the major characters. Stage lighting received the same care, and Irving experimented with color as well as with intensity of lighting. It was for his acting, however, that Irving was knighted in 1895. He was the first English actor to be so honored. Two years later, Squire Bancroft followed in his footsteps.

Herbert Beerbohm Tree managed the Haymarket Theatre from 1887 until he built Her Majesty's Theatre in 1897. Although he often acted in his own productions, his fame rests chiefly on his establishment of an annual Shakespeare festival and also on his acting school, which eventually became the Royal Academy of Dramatic Art.

Another important manager was the nonacting Richard D'Oyly Carte, who brought into partnership the playwright W. S. Gilbert and the composer Sir Arthur Sullivan. In 1881, D'Oyly Carte built the Savoy Theatre especially for the production of Gilbert and Sullivan's comic operas. There, his managerial skills were needed not only to get the operas staged but also to get them written, since the stormy partnership between Gilbert and Sullivan often threatened the success of his enterprise; Gilbert insisted on supervising every detail of rehearsals, while Sullivan sulked and complained that his music had been reduced to a mere accompaniment for Gilbert's lyrics. Were it not for D'Oyly Carte's diplomatic persuasiveness, far fewer of the Savoy operas would exist to delight today's audiences.

If Gilbert and Sullivan were to some extent prima donnas, so also were some of the nineteenth century's greatest actors. The nineteenth century theater produced the star system. In the eighteenth century, actors had been engaged by a manager for an entire season, and they were hired for a particular "line of business," which meant for a particular type of part, such as tragic hero, romantic hero, or low comedian. Playwrights customarily fashioned their works to match the talents of a particular company, which offered plays on a short-run, repertory basis. In the nineteenth century, the staggering costs of mounting new productions (because of more elaborate sets and costumes) and the great popularity of leading actors and actresses (which could be used to fill the large theaters and help managers recoup their production costs) led to the hiring of a leading actor or actress only for the run of a specific play, not for the entire season. Moreover, the repertory system was generally abandoned in favor of the long run. Furthermore, ensemble acting was subordinated to the showcasing of the star, the rest of the cast sometimes being used for little more than feeding lines or enhancing atmosphere. Stars also commanded enormous salaries that often forced theatrical managers into near or actual bankruptcy. The Romantic drama, with its emphasis on the hero, encouraged the star system. The more realistic drama, such as that of Robertson, favored a return to ensemble playing, though not necessarily to the repertory system itself.

The repertory system had enabled the eighteenth century theater to sustain itself with the support of fewer audience members, since it relied on attracting the same people over and over again. As the population of London grew, so did the potential audience, enabling a theater to sustain a long run by attracting different people each night. As the eighteenth century aristocratic influence began to wane, that of the nineteenth century working classes began to assert itself both in the pit, where rowdyism was frequent, and on the stage, where the escapism of spectacle and the familiarity of realism were both indulged. The melodrama, with its simple, clear-cut morality, its appeal to emotion, and its ability, depending on whether it was a Gothic thriller or a domestic drama, to provide both escapism and realism, was the staple of this kind of audience and the salvation of theater managers. The coarse behavior of the working-class audiences also had the effect, however, of keeping a large part of the sober middle classes away from the theater. Charles Kean's reforms at the Princess's Theatre helped to change that pattern. By timing his curtain to coincide with more fashionable dining habits and by banishing some of the more objectionable incidental entertainments to the music halls, he was able to attract Queen Victoria herself to his theater. Her presence and patronage began to confer respectability on theatergoing. Replacing the pit with the stalls also helped to change the makeup of the audience to that of a more middle- and upper-class mixture. Such works as the Savoy operas of Gilbert and Sullivan were especially designed to attract and not offend this more desirable type of theatergoer.

The playwrights who wrote for the nineteenth century theater faced substantial challenges. They had to gain the attention of audiences, sometimes more intent on being seen than on seeing the entertainment: While plays were being performed, theater patrons chatted socially, arranged an assignation or two, commented on the performance, often with hisses and catcalls, and purchased refreshments from vendors. Occasionally there were riots. Furthermore, the managerial practice of allowing people to enter the theater after the performance was half over for half price created further disturbances. The gradual removal of the pit and the attracting of a bettereducated, more restrained audience produced a group of theatergoers who by the end of the century watched in relative silence the stage action going on behind the fourth wall.

During the first years of the century, playwrights did not grow especially rich from their works. They might receive the benefits from the third, sixth, and ninth night's performances. Additionally, they might sell their copyright for several hundred pounds. After that, they received nothing, no matter how popular their plays might prove. Planché's popular historical drama *Charles XII: Or, The Siege of Stralsund* (pr. 1828) is a case in point. After an unauthorized performance of this work in 1828 netted Planché nothing, he sought legal remedy. Five years later, in 1833, Planché's friend Edward Bulwer-Lytton was instrumental in getting Parliament to pass the Dramatic Authors Act, which vested copyright with the author for his lifetime plus twenty-five years and provided fines for unauthorized performances.

Shortly after mid-century, the prolific playwright Dion Boucicault successfully exploited the royalty system to earn more than sixty-five hundred pounds from his play *The Colleen Bawn* (pr. 1860). Before the Dramatic Authors Act, the same play would have netted its author only about one one-hundredth of that amount. A similar reform, which was again prompted by Planché, resulted in royalties being paid to the writers of lyrics for operettas. Previously, they had received only a very small payment, royalties being reserved for the composers of the music. All in all, the more lucrative royalty system served to attract more talented writers to the theater, so that by the end of the century, high-caliber plays were more than occasional phenomena.

This copyright protection was not extended to foreign plays until 1852, when copyright was granted to these works for five years. This copyright applied only to translations, not to adaptations, so managers seeking to evade payment for foreign dramas made minor changes in the foreign works and produced them. French plays were their favorite source, and playwrights such as Planché and Boucicault supplied the theaters with numerous adaptations. These plays coincided well with the tastes of working-class audiences. Shortly before his death, however, Planché proposed the establishment of an English art theater, in which commercialism would be subordinated to aesthetic considerations.

Better-known writers than Planché also discussed the state of English drama, often with a keen interest in its past. For example, Samuel Taylor Coleridge, writing "On the Characteristics of Shakespeare's Plays" (1836), maintained that Shakespeare's judgment was equal to his genius. William Hazlitt, in "On Wit and Humour" (1819), extended the eighteenth century discussion of this topic. Charles Lamb, in "On the Artificial Comedy of the Last Century" (1822), tried to reassess Restoration comedy using other than moral criteria. Thomas Babington Macaulay, in "Comic Dramatists of the Restoration" (1841), argued that Restoration comedy does present a moral standard—a very bad one. George Meredith, in *An Essay on Comedy* (1877, 1897), asserted that comedy requires a cultivated society since its aim is intellectual as well as emotional. Finally, Oscar Wilde, in "The Decay of Lying" (1889), emphasized the beauty of the drama's artifices (its lies) and claimed that life copies art more often than art copies life.

Plays

In the first half of the nineteenth century, theaters presented a varied bill that usually lasted five or six hours and might include two full-length plays and several other entertainments. These productions began between six and six-thirty in the evening and ended between one and two in the morning. Madame Vestris at the Olympic Theatre reduced the number of pieces offered, so that her theater let out by eleven o'clock. Charles Kean provided only a short curtain raiser and main play. By the end of the century, most managers had eliminated even the curtain raiser, presenting only the main play.

Variety was certainly not lacking among the types of nineteenth century plays. There were the Romantic verse drama, the melodrama, the comedy of manners, the problem play, the comic opera, and numerous farces, burlettas, and extravaganzas. Revivals of Shakespeare's plays were popular, especially if they starred Edmund Kean or if they featured historically accurate sets and costumes. In addition, adaptations of French plays could always be counted on to fill out a theatrical bill of fare. Many plays were adapted from novels, especially those of Sir Walter Scott and Charles Dickens. Mary Shelley's *Frankenstein* (1818) was also very popular.

The Romantic dramatists emphasized the primacy of passion over reason. Joanna Baillie, for example, was noted for writing plays in which a single passion predominated. Her *Plays of the Passions*, published between 1798 and 1812, filled three volumes. Percy Bysshe Shelley, in his preface to *The Cenci* (pb. 1819), even went so far as to assert that "the highest moral purpose . . . of the drama, is the teaching of the human heart." Shelley's play, however, had a little too much passion. Count Cenci's thoroughgoing dedication to evil and his incest with his daughter Beatrice kept the play off the boards until it was finally produced by the Shelley Society in 1886.

Both heroes and villains fascinated Romantic writers. Shelley's Count Cenci pursues his own will at all costs, even that of his own life. He both repels and fascinates the viewer, who recoils from his evil but envies his freedom and power. His villainy is straight out of Jacobean drama, but his liberty, however perverted, marks him as a creature of the nineteenth century, which admired rebels of whatever stripe. Shelley's Prometheus, the hero of *Prometheus Unbound* (pb. 1820), is a rebel, but with a noble cause. In stealing fire from the gods, he reaps great benefits for humankind and great suffering for himself. The Romantic heroes and villains eventually found their way into the melodrama, though with their stature much diminished.

Horror and the supernatural also intrigued the Romantic dramatists, whose Gothic dramas inspired terror by evoking evil, supernatural forces at work in an eerie setting, such as a ruined church or a medieval castle. This genre had become established by the end of the eighteenth century, as exemplified by Matthew Gregory ("Monk") Lewis' *The Castle Spectre* (pr. 1797). Perhaps the nineteenth century's most famous example of the Gothic drama is Charles Robert Maturin's *Bertram: Or, The Castle of St. Aldobrand* (pr. 1816). Its settings include a castle and a monastery; its special effects call for ferocious storms and midnight processions; and its villain displays a passion close to frenzy, a role tailor-made for Edmund Kean, who produced and starred in the play. Coleridge's *Remorse* (pr. 1813) also belongs in this category.

Shakespeare's history plays were much admired by Romantic dramatists, who attempted to imitate their predecessor in plays whose heroes and villains could make passionate speeches, often about liberty and tyranny. James Sheridan Knowles's *Virginius* (pr. 1820) popularized this type of play, but it was epitomized in Bulwer-Lytton's *Richelieu* (pr. 1839). Bulwer-

Lytton played fast and loose with historical data in order to create a magnificent, but unhappy, Richelieu who is ennobled by a grand passion for France. Robert Browning's *Strafford* (pr. 1837) and Alfred, Lord Tennyson's *Queen Mary* (pb. 1875) and *Becket* (pb. 1884) were also written in imitation of Shakespeare.

Such lofty subjects, however, also coexisted with the less exalted ones of domestic drama, frequently centered on conflict between social caste and a romantic love that leaps the barrier of rank; the claims of filial duty often complicate matters. Bulwer-Lytton's *The Lady of Lyons* (pr. 1838) and John Westland Marston's *The Patrician's Daughter* (pr. 1842) illustrate the type, to which may be added Browning's *A Blot in the 'Scutcheon* (pr. 1843).

Some of the most famous Romantic poets, such as William Wordsworth and John Keats, were not successful in writing stageable plays. In part, their failure resulted from their overemphasis on text at the expense of staging and from their skeptical, if not contemptuous, attitude toward the ability of the theater's mass audiences to appreciate the refined poetry of their plays. Their solution was to write "closet drama"—poems in dramatic form that were not intended to be staged. Shelley's *Prometheus Unbound*, Browning's *Pippa Passes* (pb. 1841), and Algernon Charles Swinburne's *Atalanta in Calydon* (pb. 1865) might be called "closet dramas," since they were intended to be read but not acted. Only Byron wrote at all successfully for the stage, giving it the "Byronic hero"—a combination of hero and villain, often a rebel, motivated by deep passions and given to introspection. Byron's tenure on the governing committee of Drury Lane certainly gave him the practical theatrical knowledge that his Romantic counterparts lacked. Although only *Marino Faliero, Doge of Venice* (pb. 1821) was acted in Byron's lifetime, most of his remaining plays were eventually performed, including *Manfred*, published in 1817 and finally staged at Covent Garden in 1834.

The melodrama shared many elements with the Romantic verse drama, chiefly its emphasis on emotion, its archvillains, its heroes, and its sensationalism. The *mélodrame* originated in France. Originally, the term simply meant a three-act play accompanied by music. Such an arrangement was perfectly suited to nineteenth century British theatrical conditions. Since the minor theaters were not allowed to produce five-act plays, and since their productions had to contain a specified number of songs, the melodramatic form was ideal. In fact, desirable five-act plays were often simply redivided and the requisite music added. Even *Othello* was not immune from this treatment. As the century progressed, however, the amount of music diminished until it was sometimes little more than the occasional striking of a chord in observance of the letter, if not the spirit, of the law.

The melodrama, like the medieval morality play, depicted the conflict between virtue and vice, with virtue almost always triumphant after either the defeat or the conversion of the villain. Most often, an innocent heroine (frequently an orphan) is the victim of the moral tug-of-war, but she is eventually rescued from disaster either by the hero or by an unexpected turn of events. The setting for a melodrama might be Gothic, domestic, or more specialized—nautical, for example: Douglas William Jerrold's *Black-eyed Susan* (pr. 1829) is liberally laced with the language of the sea. Indeed, stock characters from the nautical melodrama, particularly the "jolly jack tar" and the chorus of sailors, eventually reappeared in Gilbert and Sullivan's nautical operetta, *H.M.S. Pinafore* (pr. 1878).

Thomas Holcroft's *A Tale of Mystery* (pr. 1802) is commonly considered to be the first British melodrama, even though it was merely an adaptation of a French play by Guilbert de Pixérécourt, *Cœlina: Ou, L'Enfant du mystère* (pr. 1800). Holcroft's stage directions reveal his use of music to enhance mood. They also reveal his use of highly stylized acting, especially the striking of poses or attitudes.

Buckstone's *Luke the Labourer* was a domestic melodrama, notable for its use of two heroes and two villains and for its social protest against the injustice of debtors' prisons. Jerrold's *The Rent Day* (pr. 1832) protested the injurious system of farm rents that had to be paid no matter how ruinous payment might be to the farmer. Boucicault's *After Dark: A Tale of London Life* (pr. 1868) was set in the London underworld and included a thrilling rescue in the depths of London's newly opened subway system. More sentimental was *East Lynne* (pr. 1874), adapted by T. A. Palmer from Mrs. Henry Wood's 1861 novel of the same title. The heroine abandons her husband and children to live with her villainous seducer; her sufferings end only after a tearful deathbed scene. Leopold David Lewis' *The Bells* (pr. 1871) was one of the most popular melodramas of the period. The role of Matthias, a murderer who has concealed his crime for years, was one of Sir Henry Irving's favorite parts. A less spectacular play, but one often called the finest of the melodramas, is Henry Arthur Jones's *The Silver King* (pr. 1882). Its hero mistakenly thinks he has killed a man and flees to the western United States, where he makes a fortune in silver mining. He returns to England just in time to keep his poverty-stricken wife and sick child from being evicted. Detective-like, the hero finally manages to clear his name and send the real murderer to jail.

Refinements of the melodrama eventually resulted in the social problem play. As the term suggests, a social problem was presented, with varying degrees of realism. The playwright might suggest a resolution or leave the question open. Thomas William Robertson wrote a series of such plays, produced by the Bancrofts and each sporting one-word titles and dealing with a particular social problem: *Society* (pr. 1865), *Play* (pr. 1868), *Home* (pr. 1869), *School* (pr. 1869), *War* (pr. 1871), and *Caste* (pr. 1867). The latter is perhaps his best-known work; it deals with the complications of marrying above or beneath one's station. Limited movement between classes is finally condoned, while the retention of class distinctions is supported. The aristocratic George D'Alroy marries Esther Eccles, a former dancer with a theatrical company. The entire Eccles family, including the drunken father, is depicted with compassionate good humor. The play's elaborate stage directions, which called for practicable scenery—that is, real chairs, tables, teacups and saucers, and bread and butter—gave rise to the term "cup-and-saucer drama." Robertson carefully constructed his dialogue for ensemble acting—the lines and actions would not otherwise make sense. The play's most obvious elements of melodrama are its sentimentalism, Mr. Eccles' attempted villainy, and the use of tableaux (picturesque poses struck and maintained by the cast).

Arthur Wing Pinero and Henry Arthur Jones further developed the social problem play, taking advantage of the conventions of the well-made play in the process. The well-made play was originally a French product— the *pièce bien faite*. It gained prominence through the numerous plays of Eugène Scribe, Victorien Sardou, Eugène Labiche, and Georges Feydeau. Its basic formula is a well-told story, full of complications and coincidences and designed to hold the audience's attention from moment to moment. All in all, this type of play was blatantly theatrical, its artifices often barely concealed or sometimes not concealed at all.

In their use of the conventions of the well-made play, Pinero and Jones attempted to achieve greater verisimilitude than had their French counterparts, even though the former's works often seem artificial to modern theatergoers. Among contemporary reviewers, George Bernard Shaw criticized the clumsiness of the exposition in Pinero's *The Second Mrs. Tanqueray* (pr. 1893). The production of Henrik Ibsen's *Ghosts* (pb. 1881) in London in 1891 caused a sensation because, among other things, the play featured a woman with a past. Pinero did likewise: Aubrey Tanqueray's marriage to a woman with a past leads inevitably to his own social isolation and to her suicide. Pinero's play helped to popularize Ibsenism in England; indeed, by the end of the decade, the critic William Archer had translated most of Ibsen's plays.

A woman with a past also causes catastrophe in Jones's *Michael and His Lost Angel* (pr. 1896). She seduces a man of the cloth to their mutual destruction. A woman with a present, however, the notorious Mrs. Ebbsmith, is the main character in Pinero's 1895 play of the same title. Agnes Ebbsmith is an example of the new woman, but she enjoys liberation from conventions only to be defeated by those conventions at the end of the play. Despite her unconventional relationship with Lucas Cleeve and her throwing of a Bible into the fire, she discovers that she is not the leader she thought she was. While Shaw's plays are beyond the scope of this essay, many of them also dealt with social problems, often suggesting unconventional solutions.

The eighteenth century comedy of manners continued into the nineteenth century, which elevated the comedy's moral tone by banishing much of the witty sexual innuendo that had long characterized the genre. The setting is usually the drawing room, in which the social games being played are exposed for the audience's amusement as well as for its admiration, the latter being reserved for characters who can best play the game. Boucicault's *London Assurance* (pr. 1841) illustrates the type. Sir Harcourt Courtly is the ridiculous superannuated beau; his son Charles, the rakish but reformable man-about-town; and Grace Harkaway, the witty, sprightly young woman whom Charles contrives to win. The drawing room of Squire Harkaway's house provides ample space for plots and counterplots, with the best gamesters eventually winning. The most striking character in the play, however, is Lady Gay Spanker, who spends most of her life riding to hounds and dominating her husband Adolphus (Dolly). She, too, takes part in the romantic games and almost loses her husband, whom as she discovers in the process, she truly loves. Witwouds, witlings, and truewits can all be found, but even the latter seem to be at the mercy of fortune's vicissitudes in a world whose workings they do not ultimately understand. Only barefaced "London assurance" carries them through.

A year earlier, Bulwer-Lytton's comedy *Money* (pr. 1840) had depicted a different kind of game playing. In order to discover how his friends and relatives truly feel about him, the rich Sir John Vesey pretends to have lost all of his money. Sir John gets the knowledge he seeks, repudiates all the sycophants, and marries Clara, who has loved him faithfully, even without his fortune.

Toward the end of the century, Oscar Wilde's plays continued in the comedy-of-manners tradition. More than *Lady Windermere's Fan* (pr. 1892) or *A Woman of No Importance* (pr. 1893) or *An Ideal Husband* (pr. 1895), *The Importance of Being Earnest* (pr. 1895) developed the form to its utmost by subordinating considerations of theme and character to those of style. In the play's several drawing rooms, Algernon, Jack, Gwendolyn, and Cecily play the social games that will allow them to be properly paired before the final curtain. To achieve his effects, Wilde used mistaken identities, preposterous situations, witty remarks, and the pun on Ernest/earnest. In the process, however, Wilde's witty epigrams and artifices seem to hint at a reality not successfully approached by the more serious melodrama, whose conventions this play burlesques.

The Importance of Being Earnest was indebted to Gilbert's *Engaged* (pr. 1877). In this play, Gilbert turned upside down and inside out the conventions of the melodrama. His aim was to expose the mercantile morality that underlay much of Victorian sentimentality. Gilbert was to use this technique again in the Savoy operas. In *The Pirates of Penzance* (pr. 1879), for example, Gilbert uses a chorus of orphans—pirates, that is—whose king forces himself to get through much "dirty work" in the name of business. In *H.M.S. Pinafore*, the notion of caste is turned upside down as seaman Ralph Rackstraw exchanges rank with Captain Corcoran, while Sir Joseph Porter, who is engaged to the captain's daughter Josephine, resigns her hand, observing that love does indeed level ranks, but not that much. In *The Mikado* (pr. 1885), however, almost all ranks are leveled in the person of the aristocratic, bureaucratic Pooh-Bah, who among his other roles is Chancellor of the Exchequer, Archbishop of Titipu, and Lord-High-Everything-Else.

The Savoy operas were among the most popular entertainments of their era. The burletta was equally popular. It, too, was a form of comic opera, only it consisted of a play of no more than three acts with at least five songs interspersed with the dialogue. This form was especially suited to the needs of the minor theaters and offered them a chance to adapt regular plays to fit the requirements of the Licensing Act. The burlesque, on the other hand, was a play that treated a serious subject humorously. (It did not feature strippers and off-color humor, as the term's later usage, particularly in the United States, came to suggest.) The extravaganza relied on spectacle and whimsy to tell a story—often an adaptation of a fairy tale. Planché wrote a number of these fairy tales, many of them adapted from the French. The hippodrama used horses, either onstage or, more often, in a special ring constructed in front of the stage on the floor of the pit. Pantomimes, especially Christmas ones, were also popular. Finally, vaudeville and the music halls offered a mixture of songs, dances, dramatic sketches, acrobatic stunts, and other kinds of entertainment. Nineteenth century audiences were certainly not without a wide choice of theatrical diversions.

Perspective

Nineteenth century audiences were not so very different from either their predecessors or their successors. They sought to escape from their everyday lives by going to the theater, while at the same time they enjoyed seeing themselves portrayed onstage. Despite the growing pressure toward realism, these audiences were keenly aware of theatrical artifice—so much so, in fact, that writers who considered the text of their plays to be more important than their staging had a difficult time succeeding in the theater. Although these audiences were often sentimental and sententious, they were surprisingly responsive to experimentation, even at the expense of the shocking of their sensibilities.

To see nineteenth century theater only as a transition between that of two other centuries is to look at it with a far too limited vision. Indeed, the theaters of all periods are transitional to some extent. The nineteenth century theater was exactly that: the *nineteenth century* theater, a product, as well as a reflection, of its era—an era of both artificiality and realism, whose creative tensions produced some bad theater but overall much more that was good.

Valerie C. Rudolph

TWENTIETH CENTURY BRITISH DRAMA

While George Bernard Shaw is frequently lauded as the dramatic heir of the great Norwegian realist Henrik Ibsen and, consequently, as the father of modern British drama, any attempt to survey the modern movement also reveals a variety of short-lived movements and individual experiments. From the chronicle dramas of John Drinkwater to the Absurdist plays of Harold Pinter, the essence of modernism seems to inhere in experimentation, in change itself. To be sure, criticism of societal values is hardly reserved for the twentieth century playwright alone, yet the nagging suspicion that all values are relative, that existence is merely a series of personal compromises, is characteristic of the new wave.

As a result, twentieth century plays, taken in the aggregate, suggest a worldview far different from that of the nineteenth century. Pinter's dark comedies may seem unrelated to the lighthearted, whimsical operettas of W. S. Gilbert and Sir Arthur Sullivan, just as John Osborne's bitter "Angry Young Men" dramas differ radically from the farces and sentimental social comedies of Arthur Wing Pinero or Henry Arthur Jones. Both literary and historical facts—the impact of the realist Ibsen, on the one hand, and World War I, on the other—hedge the revival of British drama, as does a complicated interplay among the demise of old forms of entertainment and their administration, increasing urbanization and leisure time, technological advancement, and a new, independent dramatic spirit.

Forces of Change

Historians of the theater stress the confusion that opened the twentieth century, when the actor-manager system changed, repertories grew, and music halls and motion pictures influenced the legitimate stage. While powerful figures such as Sir Herbert Beerbohm Tree, Forbes Robertson, and Charles Frohman did provide commercial viability for the theater, they were criticized for arranging showcases primarily for their own talents. Ironically, criticism of the actor-managers was transferred almost verbatim to the music-hall managers, who offered huge salaries for cameo appearances of serious actors and who also lured promising authors by incessant demands for dramatic sketches, often presented in a triple or quadruple bill. In addition, the threat of music-hall mergers sparked the trade union movement, the effect of which was felt in 1906 when the Variety Artists' Federation called the first theatrical strike.

An important part of the revival was the transformation of dramatic form, staging, and definition—a transformation caused, in part, by increasing internationalism. Not only did the growth of the publishing industry bring an increasing number of foreign plays into the public's hands, but also a large number of foreign companies on tour presented works in their

original languages. Evidence of such ferment may be seen in William Butler Yeats's experimentation with Japanese Nō plays, as well as in the presence of actresses Etelka Gerster and Helena Modjeska; the latter had begun
her career by introducing William Shakespeare to her native Poland.

In addition, both Ibsen's use of fewer acts in his well-made problem plays
and the ever-present demand for one-act sketches for the music halls
affected dramatic structure. An entire generation of new playwrights, lured
by good remuneration, became skilled in the short play—prologue, central
action, epilogue—rather than in the classical five-act structure. Added to
the unrest was the growing popularity of the motion picture, which, silent
until the early 1920's and initially welcomed as a force to counteract the
attraction of music and variety halls, seemed to pose little threat to the
legitimate theater. Like the music-hall playlet, however, the motion picture,
with its episodic structure, found itself mimicked onstage; wordless vi-
gnettes and brief scenes became acceptable dramatic techniques.

Staging also changed as nineteenth century display gave way to twentieth
century reductionism. The heavy sets with wings and backdrops favored by
the provincial playhouses, as well as the intricate stage machinery (sometimes complete with panoramic effects) that were used in the spectacles,
were replaced by more movable sets. Gordon Craig, who used lighting as if
it were paint, revolutionized stage design, as did his contemporaries, the
Swiss Adolphe Appia and the Austrian Max Reinhardt. The efforts of
other, more modest experimenters are evident today: William Poel, for
example, founder of the Elizabethan Stage Society (1894), moved against
then current practice by employing a "modern" open stage with little scenery for his Shakespearean productions.

Undeniably, the commercial inroads made by the music halls on the
legitimate theater are in part to blame for the virtual disappearance of
tragedy during the first three decades of the twentieth century: Plays,
farces, comedies, and sketches abounded, but the audience presented with
a drama was almost certain to see melodrama, not tragedy. The overcom-
mercialization of the stage also may be seen, however, as a positive force,
encouraging by indirection the development of numerous private theatrical
societies and regional theaters for the production of literary or social plays
unlikely to make a profit in London's West End.

The first years of the twentieth century are memorable, then, not only
for such changes but also for the advent of several giants of the age as well
as important regional movements. Shaw changed the course of drama with
his "plays of ideas," which mixed serious social commentary with comedy,
while the whimsy of Sir James Barrie is still revived today in *Peter Pan* (pr.
1904). Literary dramatists appeared as well, including the poet laureate
John Masefield, the novelist Thomas Hardy, and such writers as Fiona
MacLeod (pseudonym of William Sharp), whose works were performed at

the Glastonbury Festival. Of all the regional movements, the Celtic revival in Ireland had the most profound effect. The establishment of the Abbey Theatre provided a showcase for authors such as Yeats, John Millington Synge, and Sean O'Casey, whose use of folk legends and speech patterns and whose experiments with verse and form influenced later dramatists. In addition, among the provincial repertory theaters, the Manchester deserves special credit for encouraging the production of serious social plays that appealed to the working classes.

The course of modern British drama was also shaped by the two world wars, which not only changed the physical face of London and the expectations of the audience but also decimated almost an entire generation of young men. In the city itself, no new theaters were built between 1914 and 1959, when the Mermaid Theatre opened. World War I, during which audiences escaped to farces, comic revues, and thrillers, exacerbated the split between the commercial and the literary theater. To be sure, the British Drama League began in 1919 to offer classes and other resources, and the Stage Society continued until 1930 to offer plays by Shaw and other influential writers such as Maxim Gorky, Luigi Pirandello, and Jean Cocteau. Theatrical clubs such as Ashley Dukes' Mercury Theatre appeared, and left-wing organizations such as the Unity Theatre Club offered political plays. Personalities recognized today as leading proponents of the classical style—Dame Sybil Thorndike, Sir Laurence Olivier, Sir John Gielgud, Sir Alec Guinness, and Charles Laughton among them—dominated the acting scene, while Tyrone Guthrie directed the Old Vic Theatre not only in 1933 and 1936 but also during World War II, when it was bombed and the company moved to the New Theatre.

In the aftermath of World War II, the distance between the commercial and literary theater became greater: American musicals were popular, and impresarios such as Prince Littler controlled both London and provincial stages. Interest in serious drama was widespread, however, as the actor-manager system was revived, with Gielgud at the Haymarket Theatre from 1944 to 1945, and with Olivier at the St. James Theatre from 1950 to 1951. Aided by subsidies from the Arts Council of Great Britain, provincial repertories revived, and Shakespearean seasons were presented at the Old Vic and at Stratford-upon-Avon. Traditionalists and experimentalists alike found interest in the revival of poetic drama and the conservative plays of T. S. Eliot, on the one hand, and, on the other, in the performances of Paul Scofield at theaters such as the Unity Theatre and the Arts Theatre, or the productions of the new "plays of ideas" by Terence Rattigan and John Whiting. The increasingly experimental nature of plays that looked to Dadaism and the language of gesture helped to force the end of censorship by the Lord Chamberlain in 1968. Perhaps not surprisingly, tragedy, a disappearing genre at the turn of the century, did not resurface, while playwrights moved to highlight social and political commentary with Absurdist techniques.

Melodrama in the First Two Decades

The popular conception of melodrama that features a weeping heroine in peril of "a fate worse than death," a double-dyed villain in a sweeping cloak, and a handsome, energetic hero who arrives in the nick of time is probably derived more from nineteenth century provincial performances than from fashionable West End productions. In fact, by the turn of the century, melodrama no longer incorporated music and song with sensational incident but rather focused on the sensation itself: The evocation of powerful emotions that culminated in a happy ending was the formula. Another change was evident: Melodrama became a democratic medium, not confined to well-known, sometimes "literary" authors, but open to thousands of unremembered playwrights whose works are not likely to be revived. One example is that of the owner-managers of the Standard Theatre at the turn of the century, Walter and Frederick Melville, who wrote the plays they themselves produced. While the works of their Victorian predecessors were often published, the plays of these and such authors as Charles Darrell, Emma Litchfield, and Royce Carleton exist only in manuscript, if at all. Further confusing the record is the fact that even commercial successes were likely to have premiered in the provinces under a variety of titles.

While in many cases the works of these forgotten playwrights are marred by stilted diction and superficial plots, they were above all sincere, and to that may be attributed their success. Writing with an equal belief in his endeavor was Sir Hall Caine, whose popular novels, among them *The Manxman* (1894) and *The Christian* (1897), delighted Victorian readers. Caine collaborated on a stage version of the former with the melodramatic actor Wilson Barrett; an adaptation of the latter opened to wide critical acclaim at the Lyceum Theatre in 1907. Caine himself stressed the depth of his own agreement with the "social propaganda" that he propounded in this latter play. Similarly, his revision and intensification of melodramatic patterns in *The Manxman* resulted in *Pete*, produced at the Lyceum Theatre the next year. Caine mingled melodrama with domestic, social, and religious themes, but his other triumphs resulted from his grandness of conception and his choice of exotic settings: Iceland in *The Prodigal Son* (pr. 1904), an adaptation of his 1904 novel, and the Isle of Man in *The Bondman* (pr. 1906), which was an adaptation of his 1890 novel of the same title.

Caine was not the only well-known novelist to venture into melodrama. W. Somerset Maugham produced a number of melodramas—from *The Tenth Man*, produced in 1910, to *The Sacred Flame*, produced in 1928—

that were considerably less successful than his society plays, such as *The Circle* (pr. 1921), about romantic love, and *The Constant Wife* (pr. 1926), about adultery. More surprisingly, William Archer, the pioneering translator of Ibsen and proponent of realism, achieved instant popularity with his play *The Green Goddess* (pr. 1921). Indeed, until the 1920's, audiences enjoyed revivals as well as new versions of such romantic melodramas as Charles Hannan's *A Cigarette-Maker's Romance* (pr. 1901), and Montagu Barstow and Baroness Orczy's *The Scarlet Pimpernel* (pr. 1903), as well as the historical romance *Henry of Navarre* (pr. 1908), by William Devereux. As the decades passed, however, the realistic spirit affected melodrama in such a way that chronicle plays began to replace those that had subsisted primarily on the strength of their beautiful period costumes.

Another popular movement produced the crime drama, or thriller. Perhaps the first of this genre was William Gillette and Sir Arthur Conan Doyle's *Sherlock Holmes* (pr. 1901), a remarkably well-bred exercise in detection when compared with the increasingly sensational productions that followed. As the genre developed, the hero-detective gave way to the hero-crook; the crook to the murderer; and, finally, to balance the score, the murderer to the lawyer. George Pleydell's *The Ware Case* (pr. 1915) is typical of the trial plays; *Sexton Blake, Detective* (pr. 1908), of the theme plays, this one both written and produced by John M. East and Brian Daly, who formed The Melodramatic Productions Syndicate to market their series. Arnold Ridley's long-running cult play *The Ghost Train* (pr. 1925) was more substantial than the host of plays to employ a series of tricks and thrills as a replacement for plot. Ghost plays enjoyed a vogue; *A Murder Has Been Arranged* (pr. 1930), by the Welshman Emlyn Williams, is representative of this genre. Also notable in the development of the crime drama or thriller is Williams' *Night Must Fall* (pr. 1935), a compelling and perennially revived dramatic portrait of a psychotic killer. While Williams' play typifies the psychological thriller, another kind of thriller developed in the line of the 1921 and 1922 "Grand Guignol" theater seasons, featuring plays whose emphasis on realistically depicted physical torment and hair-raising suspense, treated with a certain artificiality, gave "Grand Guignolism" its notoriety.

Noncommercial Theater in the First Two Decades

While managers of music halls and theaters were engaged in a struggle for economic survival, noncommercial, or "minority," drama proliferated. Plays of propaganda, religion, and fantasy as well as village and children's theater became popular. Regional drama and repertory companies such as the Abbey Theatre in Dublin and the Gaiety Theatre in Manchester were important parts of the dramatic revival. Political diatribe in dramatic form and "problem plays" were a novelty during the first decades of the new century; on the opposite end of the intellectual spectrum from the popular comedies in the commercial theater, they were frequently privately performed and dealt with topics such as women's suffrage, socialism, and evolution. A typical, and initially popular, example is Guy du Maurier's *An Englishman's Home* (pr. 1909), treating the astonishment of a British homeowner at a (presumed) Russian invasion.

Another movement that stressed simplicity of approach and sincerity of performance in contrast to commercial spectacle was the village drama movement, whose proponents, harking back to the Romantic belief in primitivism and the noble savage, suggested the hope that local actors, untutored by all but nature, would express their homespun philosophy about the worth of life in an influential way.

The power shift among the variety and music halls, the cinema, and the legitimate theater was complemented by the rise not only of dramatic festivals and private acting societies but also of repertory theaters throughout Britain. Some, like the St. Pancras People's Theatre, were innovative in acquiring civic funding; others, such as the Gate Theatre Studio, were private clubs formed to evade the censorship of the Lord Chamberlain, who licensed publicly performed plays. Major pageants and festivals involved well-known playwrights: The August, 1929, Malvern Festival, for example, by Barry Jackson, was dedicated to Shaw, who wrote *The Apple Cart* (pr. 1929)—political discussion masquerading as moral drama—for the occasion; Bishop George Bell inaugurated the Canterbury Festival with Masefield's *The Coming of Christ* (pb. 1928).

A number of lesser-known societies provided the foundation for the more successful repertories. Because typical nineteenth century scenery was both heavy and expensive, producers were unwilling to invest in the untried playwright; hence, such organizations as Poel's Elizabethan Stage Society and the Pilgrim Players (begun in 1904) in Birmingham came into existence. Of these, the best known is the Independent Theatre, which was set up by J. T. Grein in 1891: This association, which produced noncommercial plays by such figures as George Meredith and Thomas Hardy, is noted for introducing both Ibsen and Shaw to its members.

While Grein's theatrical association did not develop into a national theater, the movement was under way. In London, John Eugene Vedrenne and Harley Granville-Barker collaborated at the Royal Court Theatre to initiate a series of three "seasons" beginning on October 24, 1904, in which matinees were given in repertory. As some theater historians point out, these were primarily "social" events and hardly the way to introduce plays that appealed to the intellect, although John Galsworthy, famous for *The Forsyte Saga* (pb. 1922), entered the theater with his *The Silver Box* (pr. 1906). Indeed, because more than two-thirds of the 788 performances were devoted to plays by Shaw, the Court seasons are sometimes seen more as a vehicle for Shavian ambition than as a disinterested effort to introduce the repertory. Granville-Barker himself was more successful as an actor and producer than as a playwright, although he wrote in a variety of genres, from the fantastic in *Prunella* (pr. 1904) to the political in *His Majesty* (pb. 1928).

While other managers held seasons at such theaters as the Savoy, Haymarket, Bijou, St. Martin's, and Fortune, none seemed appropriate for a national theater except the Old Vic, whose history, beginning in 1818, identifies it as a house of melodrama, a music hall, a temperance coffeehouse, a cinema palace, an opera stage, and finally, in 1914, a Shakespearean theater. In 1963, the National Theatre opened its first season at the Old Vic with a production of *Hamlet*. In addition, the Stratford Memorial Theatre held annual festivals from 1879. Today, the Arts Council of Great Britain subsidizes the Royal Shakespeare Company, the National Theatre, and the English Stage Company.

Irish Renaissance

Outside London, nationalism provided the catalyst for new theatrical interest. While Welsh efforts proved unsubstantial, the Scottish National Theatre Society arose in 1922, after a number of similarly named patriotic efforts, and in 1927, Sir James Barrie and others began the touring Masque Theatre. Indeed, these efforts mimicked the success of the Abbey Theatre, rooted initially in the revolutionist Maud Gonne's political/theatrical group "the Daughters of Ireland" and brought to life by the efforts of Yeats, Lady Augusta Gregory, and Edward Martyn to create an independent theater to preserve Gaelic literary heritage.

The Abbey Theatre, housed in the Mechanics' Institute and funded by Annie Horniman, opened in 1904 with Yeats's *On Baile's Strand* and Lady Gregory's *Spreading the News*. In 1910, however, Miss Horniman withdrew from the project. In 1924, the Abbey became state-subsidized; in 1951, the company moved to the Queen's Theatre and, fifteen years later, to its own house. With B. Iden Payne and Lewis Casson, Horniman in 1908 acquired the Gaiety Theatre for the Manchester Playgoers' Association, which encouraged new playwrights such as Allan Monkhouse, Stanley Houghton, and Elizabeth Baker to explore themes of interest to the working class; interestingly enough, such plays were less concerned with jobs and living conditions than with family problems, as in Houghton's *Hindle Wakes* (pr. 1912), a sympathetic treatment of the new woman's sexual rights, or in Harold Brighouse's *Hobson's Choice* (pr. 1915).

The Abbey Theatre, however, became known worldwide as the heart of the Celtic revival with productions such as Lady Gregory's *The Travelling Man* (pb. 1909), which invokes the mystical figure of the unconventional tramp; Rutherford Mayne's *The Turn of the Road* (pr. 1910), Padraic Colum's *Thomas Muskerry* (pr. 1910), and St. John Ervine's *Mixed Marriage* (pr. 1911) deal with the despair of the young under the domination of the old. Other plays critical of the Celtic mythos, such as those by Synge or O'Casey, evoked patriotic riots or indifference.

Distinctively Celtic elements have defined the modern sense of drama, including plays by Yeats, remembered for his lyricism and symbolism; by Synge, for his Celtic linguistic patterns and ethos; and by O'Casey, for his prodigious experimentation. The Abbey also enriched the one-act play form, which in Ireland became the vehicle for expressing elemental human aspirations in such plays as Synge's *Riders to the Sea* (pb. 1903). Also to the Abbey's credit, or, rather, primarily to Yeats's, is the successful production of the verse play.

Yeats's development from the idea, in *The Countess Cathleen* (pb. 1892) and *Cathleen ni Houlihan* (pr. 1902), that reform comes through changing social institutions to the idea that the artist's concern must be with symbols representing spiritual understanding derives from his interest in the intensely ritualistic Nō drama, incorporating stylized gestures and language. Indeed, he eventually couples violence with formalism in a Sophoclean manner: To participate in violence vicariously is, in the long run, less destructive than looting and burning.

Yeats's success influenced Synge to produce *Riders to the Sea*, in which the combination of Maeterlinckian symbolism and lyric dialogue produces almost pure tragic action. Synge's best-known play, *The Playboy of the Western World* (pr. 1907), examines the Irish propensity for belief in myths of their own making. While Synge's achievements in *Riders to the Sea* and *The Playboy of the Western World* are universally acknowledged, his last play, *Deirdre of the Sorrows* (pr. 1910), has not received the recognition it deserves. Produced posthumously by Yeats, this unfinished masterpiece incorporates Irish legend and Celtic lyricism. More influential than Synge, O'Casey, self-educated hod-carrier-turned-playwright, can be seen as a symbol of modern man, able to cross class lines and to rewrite history, treating the 1916 Easter Rising in *The Plough and the Stars* (pr. 1926), the 1920 resistance in *The Shadow of a Gunman* (pr. 1923), and the new Irish Republic in *Juno and the Paycock* (pr. 1924). His experimentation is well shown in the morality play *Within the Gates* (pb. 1933), in *Red Roses for Me* (pb. 1942), a support for the transport workers' strike, and in *Purple Dust* (pb. 1940), a burlesque of the British. His later *Cock-a-Doodle Dandy* (pr. 1949), with its magnificently crested magical rooster, representing the vitalism underlying puritanical repression, is far removed from his early slice-of-life works.

Modern Religious and Verse Drama

Like the plays of the Irish Literary Revival, religious drama eventually bridged the gap between private and commercial theater. The successful dramas of T. S. Eliot and Christopher Fry, however, were preceded by many private productions. Censored on the stage and not allowed within the Church, even centuries-old morality plays such as the fifteenth century *Everyman* had difficulty finding a performance venue. In 1904, however, a modern morality play for Christmas, *Eager Heart*, by Alice Buckton, was a wildly popular nonprofit production that eventually gave rise to the Incorporated Company of Eager Heart to honor the impoverished child who gave shelter to the Holy Family. Other groups, such as the Morality Play Society, founded in 1911 by Mabel Dearmer, were established to give performances, frequently without pay, of plays with religious themes. Such productions were far removed from both commercially successful spectacles such as Wilson Barrett's *Sign of the Cross* (pr. 1896) and revisionist versions such as D. H. Lawrence's *David* (pb. 1926), yet they did contribute to the popular and critical climate that allowed Eliot's series of modern moralities, including *The Cocktail Party* (pr. 1949) and *The Elder Statesman* (pr. 1958), to be performed.

Similarly, the climate of interest generated by such private performances provided welcoming as well to quasi-religious and fantasy plays. Barrie's *Peter Pan*, for example, in its own way paved the way to A. A. Milne's *Mr. Pym Passes By* (pr. 1919) and the adaptation of Kenneth Grahame's children's book *The Wind in the Willows* (1908) as the play *Toad of Toad Hall* (pr. 1929). Jerome K. Jerome's *The Passing of the Third Floor Back* (pr. 1908), a work that makes use of an impoverished boarder as a catalyst for good, and Vane Sutton-Vane's *Outward Bound* (pr. 1923), in which a cruise ship provides, in fact, passage to Heaven or Hell, are further examples, as is Laurence Housman's *Little Plays of St. Francis* (pr. 1922), a collection of short plays reminiscent of *Eager Heart* in their simplicity.

The flourishing of religious drama in private, noncommercial theatrical clubs and associations and the production of religious spectacle plays constitute, however, only two-thirds of the story: Serious religious drama composed in twentieth century idiom and attractive to commercial ventures is perhaps a peculiarly modern manifestation. To be sure, the success of the *Eager Heart* nonprofit venture was phenomenal, but by that time managers had already learned the value of mounting lavish productions of such spectacles as Barrett's *Quo Vadis* (pr. 1900), based on the novel of the same title by Henryk Sienkiewicz, and Caine's *The Christian*. Even the medieval morality play *Everyman* was modernized and presented at the Drury Lane by the American Walter Brown as *Everywoman* (pr. 1911).

Eliot's own brand of liturgical drama is different, however, in that it partakes less of the spectacle and more of the comedy of manners, with the exception of *Murder in the Cathedral* (pr. 1935), composed for the 1935 Canterbury Festival. Even that play, however, written for an audience predisposed not only to understanding but also to participating in the tale of the martyrdom of Thomas à Beckett, is closer to the classical Greek definition of spectacle, with its choral movements and sonorous poetry, than to the profitable ventures of Drury Lane. Indeed, Eliot seems to have possessed the very divided consciousness that is depicted as the bane of modern humanity in such poems as "The Love Song of J. Alfred Prufrock" and *The Waste Land* (1922). Although he was drawn to create a new poetic idiom within the superficial comedy of manners that appeals to modern audiences, he was also deeply convinced that modern materialism and worldliness are spiritual dead ends. Somewhat like the seventeenth century French playwright Molière, who prefaced his play *Tartuffe* (pr. 1664) with the statement that moral lessons in a comic drama were more effective than sermons, Eliot employed the comedy of manners as an overlay to his more serious message.

To a modernist, Eliot appears as a reactionary. In contrast to the expansive optimism of Shaw's drama, Eliot's plays purvey a narrow asceticism far removed from the realist's call to social action. In fact, Eliot's stated intention to "redeem society" has a distinctly liturgical flavor, emphasizing individual rather than social salvation. In his plays, only the saints, such as Beckett, or Cecilia in *The Cocktail Party*, seem to be fully human; the others, even the "guardians" who have come to some sort of rapprochement with a moral system, suffer from shallowness. His light society dialogue, which at times is more polished than that of Noël Coward, the modern master of the comedy of manners, has affinities not only with Yeats's formal lyric verse but also with Synge's and O'Casey's use of dialect. Like them, as well, Eliot drew on legend or myth, reaching to Anglican traditions as well as to Greek formalism and to Aristophanes' black humor. In addition, he made extensive use of popular rhythms: Vaudeville airs, children's rhymes, and journalistic phrases are all evident, even in his first dramatic experiment, *Sweeney Agonistes* (pb. 1932).

Whether Eliot was indeed rebel or reactionary is, however, a matter of some critical debate. In his experimentation with language and in his radical attempt to align religion and life, he seems the former; in his opposition to the Liberal cause, his evident assumption that social action is placebo, not cure, and his insistence that redemption inheres in reaching the still point of the cosmic design, he seems the latter. His characters are clearly not part of a social structure larger than, perhaps, that of the family or a social circle, unlike those in O'Casey's plays; in fact, when Eliot's characters come to some measure of understanding their guilt, they become further isolated. Lord Harry Monchensey in *The Family Reunion* (pr. 1939), for example, after understanding that his sense of guilt, his harassment by the Furies, is a transference of his father's murderous wishes, gives up the family estate as well as the comfort of remarriage. Likewise,

Colby in *The Confidential Clerk* (pr. 1953) retreats from a newfound family to be a church organist, and Lord Claverton, guilty of financial chicanery and murder in *The Elder Statesman*, withdraws to die after confessing his misdeeds to his daughter.

In comparison with the more exuberantly poetic Fry, Eliot seems to have taken the *via dolorosa*, or the negative way, of the mystic Saint John of the Cross; nevertheless, his deliberate attempt to impose poetic language on a naturalistic setting and to suggest thereby another level of meaning is important to the development of religious drama. Fry's language alone poses a contrast to Eliot's work; in fact, the same criticism is made of him that was made of O'Casey, that he is carried away by the sheer poetic freight of words. Like O'Casey, too, his plays are broader in scope than Eliot's, tending to give the effect of panorama rather than of drawing-room comedy. Critics have compared Fry's dramatic structure to that of such eighteenth century writers as Richard Brinsley Sheridan, Fry's witty persiflage to that of Oscar Wilde, and his eye for absurdity to that of Pirandello and Jean Anouilh.

What Fry provides that Eliot does not is a worldly, albeit Christianity-based, optimism that finds its focus in the compassion and humanity of his characters. His theme, like Eliot's, is conversion, yet Eliot's conversions are either otherworldly or isolating, whereas Fry's are centered on life, a focus that seems to show his indebtedness to Shakespeare. In *The Lady's Not for Burning* (pr. 1948), for example, the plot is about witchcraft and the absurdity of a legal system, yet the theme is the conflict between life and death. The hero, Thomas Mendip, with logic reminiscent of Wilde's, argues for the validity of death in a society full of shortcomings, in a world that shows in its deceptiveness no evidence of God. The supposed witch, Jennet Jourdemain, argues for life, like a heroine from one of Shaw's plays. Each to some extent convinces the other. In Fry's plays, female characters typically stand at the center of perception, their higher love allowing them to help their male counterparts transfuse earthiness into sublimity.

The list of those devoted to increasing the popularity of poetic drama is long, and it includes a series of loose associations. Certainly Yeats and his associates were influential, although some critics consider their influence to have been negative: While Yeats was master of the form he developed from the Nō play, such minor lights as Gordon Bottomley and Lascelles Abercrombie were led in the direction of increasing idiosyncrasy. In *Stonefolds* (pr. 1907) and other plays dealing with the life of the worker, Wilfred Gibson combined the "Manchester School" approach with poetry.

While Yeats, Eliot, and Fry may therefore be seen as the twentieth century high points in a long tradition of verse drama, a subsidiary pool of less important dramatists did contribute to public expectations of the form. Many are scarcely remembered, such as Stephen Phillips, whose *Herod* (pr.

1900) and *Paolo and Francesca* (pr. 1902) caused him to be compared by contemporary critics to John Milton and Dante. Others were noted in other genres: The scholar John Middleton Murry, for example, ventured into satire with the play *Cinnamon and Angelica* (pb. 1920). Even those hailed, with some reason, as the precursors of a new poetic drama, such as James Elroy Flecker, whose *Hassan* (pr. 1923) ran for nearly three hundred performances, have fallen into disregard. Others are better remembered. Sir Gilbert Murray, known for his classical translations, is one: His *Oedipus Rex* (pr. 1912) was directed by Reinhardt, and his *Alcestis* was produced at Covent Garden in 1924. Masefield, named poet laureate in 1930, is another. Influenced like Eliot by Christian themes, like Yeats by Nō drama, and like Murray by classical tragedy, he wrote such plays as *The Tragedy of Pompey the Great* (pr. 1910) and *The Trial of Jesus* (pb. 1925), as well as ringing denunciations of injustice and its effects on the innocent, as in *The Tragedy of Nan* (pr. 1908).

Between the two world wars, verse drama and political drama converged in the works of Stephen Spender, W. H. Auden, and Christopher Isherwood. Spender, for example, openly castigates Nazi Fascism in his verse play *Trial of a Judge* (pr. 1938), while the others experimented with a variety of other themes. Auden and Isherwood collaborated on such plays as the symbolic *The Ascent of F6* (pr. 1936), written in both verse and prose. Auden is especially noted for his experimentation with popular verse forms and his Brechtian Expressionism. His Group Theatre, in which, along with Rupert Doone and Robert Medley, he produced innovative, noncommercial drama, sponsored Spender's play as well as others, including Eliot's *Sweeney Agonistes*. A similar convergence of verse drama and religious drama affords speculation for the critic, for much of the verse drama that is revived today achieved its popularity by attaching itself to universal themes, from Yeats's Celtic quasi-mysticism to Eliot's Anglicanism. Much must be attributed to the quality of the verse as well; while many of the unremembered playwrights of the past produced their turgid dramas with little understanding of dramatic structure and less of verse music, both Eliot and Yeats began as poets, as did Dylan Thomas, whose autobiographical *Under Milk Wood* (pr. 1953) was both a radio and a stage success.

Shapers of the Age

To consider as a pair the two playwrights who together shaped the twentieth century idea of comedy—George Bernard Shaw and Noël Coward—is to look at different facets of the genre in which the British, despite the havoc of two world wars and concomitant economic woes, have gained ascendency. Shaw was a philosophical realist whose ready wit was based on his faith in the creative evolution to which he refers in his prefaces and afterwords, as in "The Revolutionist's Handbook," appended to *Man and*

Superman (pb. 1903). Coward, on the other hand, was a comedic realist of a different stamp; his comedies of manners reproduce glittering cocktail conversation in a way that proves him the heir of the epigrammatic Wilde. As playwrights, Shaw and Coward have this in common: They are witty and take a humorist's joy in frustrating expectations, Shaw by relentlessly following the logic in the problem he poses and Coward by providing neat twists in his plots. There the similarity ends.

Unlike Coward, Shaw brought to his work as a playwright experience as a novelist, political polemicist, and critic. While to some he seemed a philosophical butterfly, sampling major theories as they became current, in fact his constant experimentation from 1885 to 1950 was firmly grounded in a belief in human perfectibility. To begin with, his interest in Karl Marx and his role in founding the Fabian Society, where he was friendly with Beatrice and Sidney Webb, dated from the early 1880's and was a reaction against the antihumanitarian society that supraindividualism seemed to encourage. Again, his attachment both to "evolutionary socialism" and "revolutionary socialism" superseded his brief attachment to Carlylian hero-worship, which paled in the light of twentieth century totalitarianism. Finally, although he postulated the existence of a "Life Force" that moves even bumbling human efforts in the direction of "creative evolution," his belief in perfectibility, dependent as it was on the operation of human will informed by moral passion, was unallied with fatalism.

In his early years, Shaw not only espoused but also revolutionized the "play of ideas" movement with his serious comedies collected as *Plays Unpleasant* (pb. 1898). These deal with poverty, war, prostitution, women's rights, and other ethical questions, rather than with what he labeled "romantic follies," which he satirizes in *Plays Pleasant* (pb. 1898). *Candida* (pr. 1897), for example, is Ibsen's *A Doll's House* turned upside down; rather than choosing to leave an apparently fruitless marriage, Candida chooses the less obviously "weaker" of her two admirers—her clergyman husband, rather than the poet Marchbanks.

Similarly, Shaw attacks the melodramatic mode in his *Three Plays for Puritans* (pb. 1901), so named because of G. K. Chesterton's attack on the playwright's sermonizing. Typically, Shaw not only subverts a popular form into comedy but also takes a generally accepted formula—in *The Devil's Disciple* (pr. 1897), for example, the exhortation that one should love one's neighbor as oneself—and applies it with inexorable logic. Hence, Dick, the black sheep of the Dudgeon family, offers his life for the minister. The minister discovers that his vocation is war, not peace, but his wife cannot understand that Dick is dying for principle, not for love of her.

Illuminated by wit and a pursuance of logic to unexpected ends, Shaw's more mature plays go beyond Ibsen. *Major Barbara* (pr. 1905) illustrates Shaw's method well: Taking as his text that "the root of evil is poverty," he gives us Undershaft, whose munitions factory has enabled him to set up a thriving socialist community, much to the horror of his daughter, who is a major in the Salvation Army. For Shaw, religion is a mere bandage that obscures the truth that only those aware of hard economic fact can indeed do good. Again, in *Saint Joan* (pr. 1923), which, next to *Man and Superman*, critics agree to be one of his greatest plays, Shaw attacks conventional religiosity as he depicts the visionary whose unconventional perceptions cause her destruction by those who in more ordinary terms are "good." In *Man and Superman*, Shaw explores the nature of good. Based on the Don Juan legend, the play illustrates the idea that the Life Force is all conquering: Although the central plot is superficially romantic, centered on the pursuit of Jack Tanner by Anne Whitfield, the dream sequence that features an argument between the Devil and Tanner on the nature of Heaven and Hell is the philosophical heart of the play. That Heaven is a state of action is underscored by the characterization of "Ricky-Ticky-Tavy," a poetic hero whom Anne rejects because his incapacity to deal realistically with life would make him an inadequate husband and father. Tanner expresses Shaw's own distaste for aestheticism as well as for the false romantic fervor that passes for moral passion.

One of Shaw's later plays, *Back to Methuselah* (pb. 1921)—a long account of human history—reaffirms his belief, somewhat sobered by World War I, that only through the eventual evolution of the Superman can the human race be salvaged. He foresees a Utopia in which those who achieve lengthy life spans evolve into pure thought. While Shaw's growing pessimism about the achievement of a present-day Utopia through socialistic means is evident, the play does demonstrate his continuing optimism about the creative evolution of humanity.

An examination of Sir James Barrie and Noël Coward is helpful in ascertaining the special genius of Shaw, whose plays, because of their undergirding in social and intellectual movements, have proved perdurable. In Barrie, intellect such as Shaw's is expressed as wisdom about human nature; in Coward, it is expressed as worldliness, savvy about human beings as social animals. Shaw's brilliance of wit is whimsy in Barrie, glittering dialogue in Coward. If Shaw is master of the mind and Barrie of the heart, Coward is neither; he is, rather, a master of repartee. Shaw's relentless logic leads to a moral imperative; Barrie and Coward, on the other hand, deal with everyday complexities, the former in terms of feelings, the latter in terms of social complications.

Coward is best known for shaping the form of the comedy of manners to twentieth century demands and expectations. He finds wit, which has sometimes been called "brittle," in diverse and intricate relations between the sexes. Typical is his first successful comedy, *Hay Fever* (pr. 1925), which, supposedly based on a biographical incident, features sprightly quarrels and a round-robin exchange of partners during a weekend visit. His *Tonight at 8:30* (pr. 1935-1936) is a collection of short plays written with himself and Gertrude Lawrence in mind as stars. His most commercially fruitful alliance with Lawrence was, however, *Blithe Spirit* (pr. 1941), in which Spiritualism is both burlesqued and made the *raison d'être* of the plot: During a séance, Elvira, Charles Condomine's first wife, mistakenly kills Ruth, his second wife, and, exorcism failing, Charles leaves on vacation while the two spirits destructively take possession of his living room. To be sure, Coward also wrote more serious drama. His *Still Life* (pr. 1936), about a love affair, became the film *Brief Encounter* (1946).

To move from the sophisticated comedies of Coward to Barrie's whimsical plays may seem to be to travel from the adult's to the child's world, especially since Barrie is most famous for *Peter Pan: Or, The Boy Who Would Not Grow Up*. Like the introductions and stage directions written by Shaw, those by Barrie go beyond the matter at hand, exploring the motives of the characters as well as the orientation of the playwright; to this degree, the plays are really readers' plays. Barrie's comedy reached its height in *The Admirable Crichton* (pr. 1902), in which he posits an impossible, albeit delightful, situation—the marooning of a well-to-do family on a desert island to demonstrate the butler Crichton's insistence that human nature makes true equality an impossible goal. Even in an unstructured situation, someone, in this case the resourceful Crichton, is a leader.

More prolific than Barrie, yet touched with the same type of fantastical humor, was James Bridie, a Scottish playwright whose reputation has suffered because of the unevenness of his work. Concentrating primarily on biblical themes, Bridie, both early and late, as in *Tobias and the Angel* (pr. 1930) and *The Baikie Charivari: Or, The Seven Prophets* (pr. 1952), provides a Shavian twist to his plots. In the first play, the blind Tobias thwarts the Devil with the help of the angel Raphael in disguise; in the second, a group of villagers are both ordinary folk and characters in a Punch-and-Judy scenario which is manned by the Devil himself. The framework gives rise to discussions about the search for truth through theoretical and practical means.

Postwar Modernism

While certain major playwrights, such as Eliot, Shaw, and Coward, seem to define much of the twentieth century, perspective is more difficult to gain on contemporary writers, not only because of their proximity in time but also because audiences still feel the implicit effects of, for example, World War II and the economic recessions that shaped a new theatrical style. Postwar playwrights faced a world in which even ultimate values seemed meaningless. Not only did faith in God seem groundless, but faith in human nature was likewise questioned, especially in the light of the concentration camps, with their suggestion of international complicity in human suffering. As some critics note, even the Nuremburg war-crimes trials affected the question of universal values, for there the question of the conflict between a nation's laws and its moral imperatives was as much on trial as were those who engaged in wartime atrocities.

The role of the mass media in publicizing details about the war and its aftermath cannot be ignored: In effect, television, with its graphic pictures and instant analysis, contributed to a general decline of the sort of optimism that Shaw espoused. Other influences were important as well, most notably the works of Jean-Paul Sartre and Albert Camus, who introduced British playwrights and playgoers to Existentialism.

Both Sartre, whose *Being and Nothingness* (1943) defined the new stance, and Camus, the father of the Absurdists, viewed the human condition as illogical. Unlike their followers, however, they insisted on the ability of the individual human being to choose to act in an ultimately meaningless world: Free of all codified moral imperatives, one might initially feel anguish or despair, but one can choose to create for oneself the standards by which one will live. Camus finds absurdity in the search for clarity in a chaotic world, in the search for answers in an ungrounded universe. His early characters in, for example, *Caligula* (pb. 1944), can overcome absurdity only by refusing to recognize it; in a later play, *The Just Assassins* (1949), however, they substitute action for denial and demonstrate the working of responsibility.

While Camus and Sartre were particularly important philosophically, Bertolt Brecht was an important influence theatrically. With his state-supported Berliner Ensemble, which incorporated not only a corps of actors but also all the other artistic and managerial personnel necessary for production, he profoundly influenced the antirealistic trend of contemporary theater.

In England, changing political and philosophical winds resulted in much theatrical experimentation. Indeed, the fragmentation of the theater at this point in the century seems to reflect the common person's schizophrenia in a war-torn society, especially since those who followed both Camus and Sartre pushed Absurdity to its extreme in denying even the possibility of creative action. Samuel Beckett is important in this regard. Born in Ireland but eventually residing in France, where his friendship with James Joyce developed, Beckett, like Yeats, experimented with static drama but developed it into an existential statement about the essential futility of action. His *Waiting for Godot* (pb. 1952), for example, presents two tramps, Vladimir and Estragon, who wait endlessly and inexplicably for Godot. "It's awful," they agree; nothing happens, except that Pozzo trails by with his slave Lucky, whose talents include a stream-of-consciousness monologue. At the end of the play, Pozzo and Lucky have gone blind and dumb, respectively, and Godot has not arrived. In another depiction of futility, *End-*

game (pr. 1957) presents characters waiting, but this time each is as visibly deformed as the ruined world outside his room. While Clov cannot rest, the blind Hamm cannot move; Hamm's legless and senescent parents are stowed in dustbins. All await death, paralyzed in an irrational world. The silence, the isolation, the endless boredom that underscore the futility of action are nevertheless balanced by the persistent survival of even the most internally ravaged of Beckett's characters.

Absurdists such as Beckett transformed the sort of stage familiar to the playgoer at the turn of the century in a number of ways. Heavy plotting went the way of heavy scenery; in addition, as the focus on existence itself intensified, plays were stripped of realistic props as well as of a linear time frame and realistic characterization and setting. Language, often grotesquely simplified, was no longer an aesthetic medium to be enjoyed for its diction or wordplay but rather an emblem of the futility of communicating, even in the most basic terms. In short, playwrights such as Beckett attempted to eliminate all that distracts from contemplation of the human condition, at times, perhaps, achieving a modern parable, the characters of which are not unrelated to the archetypes of, for example, John Bunyan, but the plots of which reflect the illogic of the postwar era.

The Absurdist worldview influenced several groups of playwrights whose interest lay primarily in social issues and whose names are associated with two important theaters. Both the English Stage Company, from 1956 to 1965 under the leadership of George Devine and his assistant Tony Richardson, and the Theatre Workshop, headed by Joan Littlewood, had profound effects, not only in encouraging new playwrights but also in providing a voice for new audiences.

Perhaps the best-known products of the English Stage Company are John Osborne and John Arden, although others contributed to the Absurdist movement. Norman Simpson, for example, whose *A Resounding Tinkle* (pr. 1956) was a Royal Court Theatre prizewinner, is distinguished by his attempt to forge Absurdism to fantasy. The English Stage Company, in residence at the Royal Court Theatre, featured John Osborne's *Look Back in Anger* (pr. 1956) as its third new production. Influenced by the Absurdist interpretation of the human condition—that one is at the mercy of an irrational, chaotic world and, by extension, of one's own unexamined impulses—Osborne nevertheless suggests that one can alleviate existential despair by attempting to change the political and social system. His characters are therefore considerably more vital and active than Beckett's Hamm or Lucky, for example, in attempting to counter such forces, if only through resounding diatribes against what cannot be helped. Jimmy Porter in *Look Back in Anger* is the original "angry young man": Disillusioned, frustrated, lashing out against the hypocrisy of social conventions, he expresses his anger against the universe by verbally lacerating his wife, who retorts through nonresponse. Among the plays that followed, both *The En-tertainer* (pr. 1957) and *Inadmissible Evidence* (pr. 1964) take declining pub-lic figures—the first, a vaudeville entertainer; the second, a lawyer, himself on trial—as their spokesmen and analyze the "evidence" behind the fa-çade. In *The Entertainer*, Osborne takes as his symbol of despair an aging music-hall entrepreneur who, through a series of monologues, verbalizes his progressive decay. Episodic in structure, the play shows the influence of Brecht: The entertainer has an abortive affair, fails to stage a financial trick, and finally is unable to arrange any star performances. More than a British version of Arthur Miller's *Death of a Salesman* (pr. 1949), *The Entertainer* is also a parable about the successive decay of Britain from strength to indifference.

Another successful Royal Court playwright who also reinterpreted the Absurdist philosophy is John Arden, whose objective pose between the elements of chaos and order and conventionality and revolt forces the audi-ence to participate by examining their own worldviews. While *Live Like Pigs* (pr. 1958) was generally considered inconclusive, *Serjeant Musgrave's Dance* (pr. 1959) seemed to espouse a pacifistic stance, suggesting that war is only one form of violence, the imposition of ideas another. Similarly, in his other plays—*The Happy Haven* (pr. 1960), written in collaboration with Margaretta D'Arcy, for example, or *Armstrong's Last Goodnight* (pr. 1964)—Arden seems interested primarily in the balance between opposites rather than in their resolution. In this sense, he seems to follow, but only conceptually, the Strindbergian notion that life is strife, and unresolvable strife at that.

Like the Royal Court Theatre, the Theatre Workshop attempted to win the allegiance of the working class to the theater by adopting some of the methods of popular entertainment. Littlewood's group, which toured from 1945 to 1953, when it settled in East London, relied on Brechtian methods and improvisation; in a departure from traditional practices, it generated plays through the cooperative efforts of actor and playwright, including, for example, Frank Norman and Lionel Bart's *Fings Ain't Wot They Used t'Be* (pr. 1959). After 1961, when Littlewood retired, the group lost much of its direct influence but remained a force in theater education. Many modern playwrights owe their subject matter and style to Littlewood's group. Henry Livings, for example, trained there as an actor, but his realistic and bitter works, such as *Big Soft Nellie* (pr. 1961) and *Nil Carborundum* (pr. 1962), display Littlewood's emphasis on the deleterious effects of work on humanity; similarly, Bernard Kops, although much different from Livings in his emotional freight, exhibits in such works as *Change for the Angel* (pr. 1960) the experimentation with language that Littlewood encouraged.

Both Shelagh Delaney and Brendan Behan were showcased by Little-wood. Delaney's one major success, *A Taste of Honey* (pr. 1958), treats illegitimacy, abuse, and homosexuality with close observation and empathy. Behan, on the other hand, produced two plays that were hailed as the Theatre Workshop's answer to Osborne's *Look Back in Anger*. Like O'Casey, Behan examines the human cost of revolution, in *The Quare Fellow* (pr. 1954) and in *The Hostage* (pr. 1958); also like O'Casey, he experiments with a variety of approaches. Perhaps Littlewood's best-known playwright was the self-taught Arnold Wesker, whose early plays demonstrate his political interests and his suggestion that the working class is oppressed because it is incapable of vision. His trilogy comprising *Chicken Soup with Barley* (pr. 1958), *Roots* (pr. 1959), and *I'm Talking About Jerusalem* (pr. 1960) traces the fortunes of the Kahn family from the strongly socialistic mother to the disillusioned children, who eventually discover that neither escapism nor self-reliance is the answer. Like Osborne, Wesker suggests that the political and social system is awry; further, he looks to collaborative efforts to solve the problem. Another play, *The Kitchen* (pr. 1959), suggests that implicit and explicit brutality stems from the adverse effects of environment on workers. *Chips with Everything* (pr. 1962) treats a similar theme within the context of the military, in which the enlisted men are equivalent to the workers in their deprivations. To encourage an active interest in theater among the working classes, Wesker founded Centre 42—which, however, eventually became a haven for the avant-garde rather than performing its intended function.

Among the host of playwrights influenced by Absurdism and the new theater movements, Harold Pinter emerges as the most important. Others, to be sure, made their marks with one or two significant contributions. John Whiting and Robert Bolt, for example, were seen as serious rivals to Pinter. From Whiting's early *Saint's Day* (pr. 1951) to his later *The Devils* (pr. 1961), his vision was uncompromising and generally bleak; his career was cut short by his premature death. While Whiting's *The Devils*, a play in which demoniac possession is explored as sexual neuroticism, achieved success in its Royal Shakespeare Company production, Bolt's plays have appealed more consistently to the West End audience. His well-known study of Sir Thomas More, *A Man for All Seasons* (pr. 1960), has more of a connection with Drinkwater's early epics than with the social commentary of the mainstream Absurdists. Again, such writers as Ann Jellicoe, who wrote *The Sport of My Mad Mother* (pr. 1958) and *The Knack* (pr. 1961), as well as Nigel Dennis, author of *The Making of Moo* (pr. 1957), have won recognition, as has David Storey, whose *In Celebration* (pr. 1969) and *The Contractor* (pr. 1969) illustrate his idea that the class system has isolated workers from their spiritual legacy.

Pinter's consistent output defines the human condition in the 1950's and 1960's. Influenced by Beckett in his Absurdist plots and simplistic language, Pinter evokes in his early plays a nameless sense of menace, as with the inexplicable darkness in *The Room* (pr. 1957). Later, the menace, existentially grounded in the human condition, is seen to emanate from the characters themselves. In *The Birthday Party* (pr. 1958), Stanley is abducted by two strangers whose motive appears to be to harangue him with meaningless questions. Similarly, in *The Dumb Waiter* (pr. 1960), the gunman Ben shoots his companion Gus on orders from an unseen "boss." Finally, in *The Homecoming* (pr. 1965), the characters' self-brutalization is evident as Teddy's wife, Ruth, panders to the various needs of the all-male family she has joined, becoming mother and sister, whore and homemaker, at the same time.

Osborne and Pinter may be seen as the prototypes of two complementary branches of postwar drama. On the one hand, the mood was Absurdist: Characters faced with a relativistic world found inaction or escape their only means of survival. On the other hand, it was political: Angry Young Men such as Osborne waged verbal war against the political and social abuses they believed could be rectified. As some critics suggest, the mood of the 1960's was a combination of these two elements. Playwrights seemed to see absurdity in the past and hope in the future, the end to be achieved through an angry response to what was dehumanizing. From this mood arose several important theaters as well as playwrights such as Peter Shaffer and Tom Stoppard.

In the 1960's, government subsidies became especially important to support the theatrical troupes responsible for the postwar dramatic renaissance. The National Theatre, for example, whose first director was Sir Laurence Olivier, began in 1963 to present a wide range of productions under the aegis of visiting directors and a permanent company. Considerably less conservative than the National Theatre, the Royal Shakespeare Company, chartered in 1961, broadened its scope not only to include Absurdist plays but also to sponsor avant-garde experiments. In 1963, for example, the troupe presented such playwrights as Antonin Artaud and Jean Genet in a Theater of Cruelty from which emanated Peter Brook's memorable production of *Marat/Sade* the next year. Although beset by subsidy problems, the Royal Shakespeare Company is best known for the modern interpretations given to Shakespeare's works by Brook, who intended less to present the original texts than to focus on, for example, elements stressed by the Theater of Cruelty or on psychological motifs. Other groups were important as well, not only in encouraging new playwrights but also in forcing the repeal of censorship. The English Stage Company continued its policy by opening the Theatre Upstairs; other subsidized groups ranged from the Mermaid, which has presented Elizabethan and eighteenth century drama, to the National Youth Theatre, established in 1956 under Michael Croft, which has presented such works as Peter Terson's *Zigger Zagger* (pr. 1967) and *Fuzz* (pr. 1969).

Outside London, provincial repertories doubled in number; one of the most important, the 69 Theatre Company, was housed in the Royal Exchange Theatre in Manchester. The company, which was fathered by the 59 Theatre Company that played at the Lyric Theatre, began its productions in 1968 at the Manchester University theater and eventually built its own theater-in-the-round, a model of innovative modern architecture. The company's best-known director, Michael Elliott, directed premieres of Ronald Harwood's plays—*The Ordeal of Gilbert Pinfold* (pr. 1977), *A Family* (pr. 1978), featuring Paul Scofield, and *The Dresser* (pr. 1980), featuring Tom Courtenay.

While government and private subsidies played an important role in the burgeoning theatrical activity, the Theatres Act of 1968 paved the way for further experimentation. For 231 years, every play produced publicly had to be licensed by the Lord Chamberlain; the 1968 act abolished the office and allowed for greater freedom not only in the commercial theater but also in such underground groups as Charles Marowitz's Open Space theater and Ed Berman's Inter-Action street theater. The drive for complete freedom of expression is evident in the works of playwrights such as Edward Bond, whose *Saved*, notorious because of a scene in which a baby is stoned to death, had to be performed privately in 1965; in 1968, his *Narrow Road to the Deep North*, which explores the way in which weakness of will leads to violence, was performed publicly.

Among the most promising of the new playwrights of the 1960's were Peter Shaffer and Tom Stoppard. Shaffer, in particular, ventured into a variety of theatrical genres, from his *Five Finger Exercise* (pr. 1958), about the domestic power brokering that a private tutor engenders, to *The Royal Hunt of the Sun* (pr. 1964), a historical drama about the communion between the powerful and the vanquished, between Pizarro and the Inca Atahuallpa. *Black Comedy* (pr. 1965) and *The Battle of Shrivings* (pr. 1970), an argument about the perfectibility of human beings, were less successful. Unlike Shaffer, Stoppard followed both Pinter and Beckett, especially in *Rosencrantz and Guildenstern Are Dead* (pr. 1966), whose Absurdist vision is incorporated in two minor characters from *Hamlet* who can make little sense of the events transpiring around them.

The Last Three Decades

British drama of the 1970's, 1980's, and 1990's features a mixture of old and new artists. Many playwrights who began their careers in the 1950's and 1960's continued to produce new dramatic works that developed their original preoccupations. For example, Beckett persisted in presenting the silence and isolation that he perceived in the modern world in plays such as *Waiting for Godot* by producing works that became briefer and briefer: *Breath* (pr. 1970) contains 120 words and lasts approximately thirty-five seconds, while *Not I* (pr. 1972) runs no more than sixteen minutes, and *That*

Time (pr. 1976), no more than half an hour. Other dramatists even returned to the same characters and situations they had presented in earlier works; in *Déjàvu* (pr. 1992), Osborne picks up the life of Jimmy Porter, his protagonist in *Look Back in Anger* (pr. 1956), thirty-six years later. Unfortunately for Jimmy, the situation in England has not significantly improved since 1956.

While some playwrights stayed on essentially the same course during this period, others took slightly different directions. In the 1970's, for example, Arden, collaborating with his wife, Irish activist and actress Margaretta D'Arcy, focused his drama more explicitly on Irish questions in plays such as *The Non-Stop Connolly Show* (pr. 1975), *The Little Gray Home in the West* (pr. 1978), and *Vandaleur's Folly: An Anglo-Irish Melodrama* (pr. 1978). Pinter also pursued a more overtly political direction. His later works often show the silencing of either an entire people, as in *Mountain Language* (pr. 1988), or an individual, as in *The New World Order* (pr. 1991), by an oppressive political power.

Two of the most promising playwrights of the 1960's—Shaffer and Stoppard—continued to mount successful productions in the 1970's and 1980's. Shaffer produced two of his most well-received plays in the 1970's—*Equus* in 1973 and *Amadeus* in 1979. He structured both works around seemingly antagonistic characters—the psychiatrist and his patient in *Equus* and Wolfgang Amadeus Mozart and Antonio Salieri in *Amadeus*—and then showed how this seeming opposition actually masked a greater number of similarities. His later work *Lettice and Lovage* (pr. 1987) also revolves around this same kind of opposition. Stoppard also enjoyed continued success during this period. Plays such as *Jumpers* (pr. 1972), *Travesties* (pr. 1974), *Night and Day* (pr. 1978), *The Real Thing* (pr. 1983), and *Hapgood* (pr. 1988) combine his characteristic wit and dazzling wordplay with an exploration of more philosophical concerns.

These earlier playwrights have been joined by a number of dramatists who emerged during the 1960's and 1970's. These writers were linked by their desire to critique contemporary British life through comedy, direct political attacks, or a mixture of both. The most successful (and prolific) playwright of domestic comedies is undoubtedly Alan Ayckbourn. He began mounting West End productions in 1967 with *Relatively Speaking*, which was modeled on Oscar Wilde's *The Importance of Being Earnest* (pr. 1895). In the early 1970's, Ayckbourn began producing one play per year at his home theater in Scarborough before moving it to London. His plays are often distinguished by their technical innovation. For example, the marital farce of *How the Other Half Loves* (pr. 1969) is intensified by having the living-dining areas of the two principal couples occupy the same physical space, while in *Taking Steps* (pr. 1979), the comic mishaps are heightened by presenting three stories of an English country house—downstairs living room, upstairs bedroom, and attic—on one level. Ayckbourn's technical innovation has also been accompanied by experiments in form and narrative structure. For example, in his trilogy *The Norman Conquests* (pr. 1973), he created a series of plays meant to be seen on three successive nights, with the onstage action in one play becoming offstage action in the other two. In *Sisterly Feelings* (pr. 1979), some of the middle scenes may vary from performance to performance depending on an actress' spur-of-the-moment decision or a coin toss. *The Revengers' Comedies* (pr. 1991) takes a classic British form—the revenge play—and puts it in a modern context; the performance itself spans two evenings. While Ayckbourn's plays have often been criticized as lightweight compared to the more overtly political concerns of his contemporaries, his later plays show the darker undertones of contemporary domestic life. *Woman in Mind* (pr. 1985) revolves around Susan, an unhappy woman, who escapes the realities of her present life by creating a more congenial dream family, while *A Small Family Business* (pr. 1987) illustrates the corruption that begins at home.

Social concerns paired with innovative staging and style also characterize the work of Caryl Churchill, one of Great Britain's most successful female dramatists. In *Cloud Nine* (pr. 1979), whose first act is set in colonial Africa during the Victorian era and whose second act is set in present-day London, Churchill comments on sexual repression and imperialism by linking them with economic repression and political imperialism. To illustrate the role conditioning present in society, Churchill utilizes unusual casting, including males playing female roles (and vice versa), white people playing black roles, and adults playing children. The Royal Court's first resident woman dramatist, Churchill deals with feminist themes in some of her works such as *Top Girls* (pr. 1982), where a number of historical female figures dine with Marlene, the owner of the Top Girls employment agency. The play illustrates the sacrifices women must make in order to succeed in a male-dominated world. Churchill, however, is not solely concerned with women's issues. In *Serious Money* (pr. 1987), she creates a "city comedy" in the tradition of Ben Jonson, John Marston, and Thomas Middleton that critiques the London financial world; she even writes the play in rhymed couplets. In *Mad Forest* (pr. 1990), she depicts the political repression in Romania and the overthrow of the Ceauşescus.

Churchill is one of many female dramatists who have been actively producing works during this period. While a number of these playwrights have presented so-called women's issues in their plays, these are not their only concern. Some of the most notable of these writers are Nell Dunn (*Steaming*, pr., pb. 1981), Pam Gems (*Dusa, Fish, Stas, and Vi*, pr. 1976, pb. 1977; *Piaf*, pr. 1978, pb. 1983; *Camille*, pr. 1985, pb. 1987; and *The Blue Angel*, pr. 1991), Sarah Daniels (*The Devil's Gateway*, pr. 1983, pb. 1986; *Masterpieces*, pr. 1983, pb. 1984; *Byrthrite*, pr. 1986, pb. 1987; and *Gut Girls*, pr.

1988, pb. 1989), and Timberlake Wertenbaker (*The Grace of Mary Traverse*, pr., pb. 1985; *The Love of the Nightingale*, pr. 1988, pb. 1989; *Our Country's Good*, pr., pb. 1988; and *Three Birds Alighting on a Field*, pr. 1991, pb. 1992).

Irish drama has also undergone a resurgence during this period, led, to some extent, by Brian Friel, who began producing plays as early as 1964 with *Philadelphia, Here I Come!*, a memory play in which Gareth O'Donnell lives through his last hours in Ireland before immigrating to the United States. Friel's plays tend to be driven by character and setting; often, characters find themselves caught in the conflict between traditional Irish life and modern-day realities. For example, in *Aristocrats* (pr. 1979), Friel shows the decline of the O'Donnell family, who must eventually leave their home, Ballybeg Hall. *Dancing at Lughnasa* (pr. 1990) returns to the form of the memory play as the narrator, Michael, recalls an important fortnight in his family's life that occurred in 1936. Friel has also greatly aided the production of new Irish drama when he cofounded, with actor Stephen Rea, Field Day Productions, a theater company dedicated to bringing professional theater to cities throughout Ireland. Its first production was Friel's own play, *Translations* (pr. 1980).

One of Great Britain's most explicitly political playwrights is David Hare, whose dramas demonstrate the failures of contemporary England. He illustrates this theme in *Plenty* (pr. 1978), depicting twenty years in the life of Susan Traherne, who never adjusts to "normal" life after her experiences as a courier for the French Resistance during World War II. Hare has also played an important role in the contemporary theater as a founder of fringe companies—including the Portable Theatre in 1968 and Joint Stock in 1974—and as a director of the work of other political dramatists, including David Edgar, Trevor Griffiths, Stephen Poliakoff, Howard Brenton, Snoo Wilson, and Howard Barker. Hare even cowrote *Pravda* (pr. 1985), a satire of Fleet Street, with Brenton. His later plays look closely at the decline of established British institutions such as the family (*The Secret Rapture*, pr. 1988), the Church of England (*Racing Demon*, pr. 1990), and the legal system (*Murmuring Judges*, pr. 1991).

Although British drama of the twentieth century has moved from Shaw's evolutionary optimism to Beckett's Absurdism, from solutions to questions, it is, on the whole, strong in a serious comic spirit. As the nineteenth century's penchant for melodrama and spectacle seems to modern eyes to suggest escapism, so the witty dialogue in the comedy of manners, the fantasy, and the exuberant Shavian donouements seem to provide relief, not resolution. The perceptive audience may suspect that the comedy is really a cover for a pressing problem, the inability of the individual human being to cope with an intractable universe. The newer playwrights exhibit a theatrical vitality that belies the bleakness of their philosophical views. Indeed, every depiction of a random, ominous universe is in itself a violation of that universe, for even an unstructured play presents some sense of form. At the end of a century in which dramatists have traveled from realism to Absurdism, from integrated dramatic structure to the episodic structure of Brechtian epic theater, from poetry to naturalistic speech and to the language of gesture, the critic thus looks for a playwright to create a new tragedy as well as a new comedy, to model a brave new world onstage as well as to reflect the old one, to show what lies beyond wordlessness and the impossibility of action.

Patricia Marks
(Updated by *Sharon L. Gravett*)

AMERICAN DRAMA

Until the post-World War I era, American drama, confronted with religious hostility and then by economic necessity and academic indifference, struggled to come into its own as a respected literary genre at home and as a force that made itself felt on foreign stages. A commonplace of American literary history is that the plays of Eugene O'Neill, in Walter J. Meserve's words, marked "America's full-scale arrival into the modern drama of western civilization."

In an article in a 1907 issue of *Atlantic Monthly*, John Corbin quoted Edmund Stedman, who proclaimed a literary declaration of independence for American drama: "Quote boldly, then, I prophesy the dawn of the American drama; and quite confidently, too, for the drama has already dawned. . . ." Decrying the exhaustion of the European-influenced melodrama, Corbin applauded dramas by William Vaughn Moody and Percy MacKaye as plays "which challenge comparison with the best work of the modern stage in any country." Moody's *The Great Divide* (pr. 1906) and MacKaye's *Jeanne d'Arc* (pr. 1906) are hardly plays for which modern historians and critics would claim such eminence, but Corbin expressed an optimism about American drama that would become a reality in the post-World War I era in the dramas of O'Neill.

Kenneth Macgowan claims, in his introduction to *Famous American Plays of the 1920's* (1959), that the book might have been entitled "The American Drama Comes of Age." When American drama finally came into its own, each decade thereafter left its unique mark on stage history. In the 1920's, Eugene O'Neill's stylistic experiments initiated a period of explosive growth and rich variety. In the 1930's, the social protest dramas of Clifford Odets and his contemporaries dramatized the personal conflicts of individuals and families at odds with themselves and with the conditions in the country. In the 1940's, Tennessee Williams and Arthur Miller emerged at the forefront of post-World War II writers concerned with psychological and moral dilemmas of individuals in a society readjusting to a peacetime economy and Cold War diplomacy. Their mood continued into the 1950's in the Beckettian plays of Edward Albee, with his bleak vision of American culture and its alienated or dismembered characters. Albee, Miller, and Williams continued into the following decades, while social-protest dramatists flourished in Off-Broadway and Off-Off-Broadway theaters such as the Open Theatre, the Living Theatre, Café La Mama, the American Place Theatre, and the Public Theatre. Although the 1970's and 1980's witnessed some gains in minority theater by gay, feminist, and black dramatists, it was Sam Shepard, with his expressionistic utilization of the cowboy myth, and David Mamet, described by Ruby Cohn as the writer with "the most concentrated American stage speech since Edward Albee," who captured critical attention as playwrights with the potential to join the ranks of O'Neill, Williams, Miller, and Albee.

A latecomer to literary history, American drama had its beginnings in the two preceding centuries, during which it slowly developed from plays modeled on foreign subjects and on the prevailing English and European styles of sentimental comedy and tragedy to those derived from native experience and characterized by a realism and literary quality that gained respectability domestically and internationally.

There was strong hostility from religious groups in colonial times, a carryover from the Puritan closing of the English theaters from 1642 to 1660. Except for the Southern states, where Episcopalians settled, the theater was considered frivolous. Puritan New England, Huguenot New York, and Quaker Philadelphia, where the American drama eventually took root, rallied against the theater. Their religious opposition was strengthened by the country's preoccupation with the Revolutionary War. The high value placed on the thrifty use of time and money further consolidated opposition to such "trivial" pursuits as the theater. Yet even in earliest times, formal functions such as commencements featured quasi-theatrical performances at the College of William and Mary, the College of Pennsylvania (now the University of Pennsylvania), and Princeton. These performances took the form of recitations of odes and, occasionally, masques. A "pastoral colloquy" at the College of William and Mary in 1702 may well have been the first college dramatic performance in America.

Over the years, still another division developed, that between "theater" and "drama," caused by purely commercial considerations. As popular entertainment, theater relied on traditional audience tastes for its survival. Theater managers and producers could not risk plays by new authors experimenting with subject matter and style. Consequently, these writers turned to the small, noncommercial theaters. Much of their success was a result of their association with groups such as the Provincetown Players and the Theatre Guild. Later, the Group Theatre and the Actors' Studio strengthened the importance of the little theater movement. The inheritors of this tradition are to be found in cities and campuses across the country and in New York in Off-Broadway and Off-Off-Broadway theaters and theater clubs such as the Manhattan Theatre Club, the Hudson Guild Theatre, the American Place Theatre, the Public Theatre, and Theatre Row, along West Forty-second Street. Some of these, such as the Public Theatre, have nurtured dramatists-in-residence. David Rabe and Lanford Wilson are but two dramatists who have had their plays steadily produced in resident theaters. Such regional theaters as the Goodman and Steppenwolf theaters in Chicago, the Actors' Theatre of Louisville, and the Long Wharf in Connecticut are among groups that continue a vital tradition that began with the Provincetown Players and the Theatre Guild in the 1920's.

On Broadway, indigenous musicals have enjoyed the financial successes denied much of the time to "serious" drama. Occasional dramatic imports such as those brought over by the Royal Shakespeare Company of London have enjoyed success with their limited runs. Serious plays by O'Neill, Williams, Miller, Albee, and others have enjoyed some financial success, but these are the exception rather than the rule.

The commercial division between theater and drama frequently has been carried over to the university level, where drama as literature is taught in English departments and plays are produced by theater departments. Until the end of the second decade of the twentieth century, the literary ambitions of the drama took a backseat to theatrical stageability and popular demand. This tardiness contrasts markedly with the national identity that native poetry and fiction enjoyed in the 1850's with the outpouring of literature by major writers such as Walt Whitman, Nathaniel Hawthorne, and Herman Melville. Not until seventy years later was American drama to experience such acceptance.

Yet in the time since, international recognition of major American plays and playwrights has come swiftly. O'Neill received the Nobel Prize in Literature in 1936, and his play *More Stately Mansions* (pb. 1964) was premiered posthumously in Stockholm in 1967. Sir Laurence Olivier played the father in *Long Day's Journey into Night* (pr. 1956) at the Old Vic in London in 1972. Miller directed—or helped direct—*Death of a Salesman* (pr. 1949) in China in 1983. Even the plays of later playwrights—Shepard's *Curse of the Starving Class* (pb. 1976) and Mamet's *Glengarry Glen Ross* (pr. 1983)—received their premieres at two of London's prestigious theaters, the Royal Court and the National, respectively.

A second major commonplace about American drama is its derivative nature. During the eighteenth and nineteenth centuries, William Shakespeare, Richard Brinsley Sheridan, and a host of lesser dramatists, both English and Continental, were popular on the American stage. As will be discussed later, the subject matter and styles of foreign dramatists influenced the American dramatists of the time. Even in the twentieth century, the influences of Aeschylus, Sophocles, Henrik Ibsen, August Strindberg, Anton Chekhov, George Bernard Shaw, Bertolt Brecht, and Samuel Beckett, among foreign dramatists, are evident in the plays of O'Neill and others. Miller's *All My Sons* (pr. 1947), for example, is an adaptation of Ibsen's *The Pillars of Society* (pr. 1877) that is placed in a contemporary American setting.

Only in musical theater has the United States contributed innovatively to the history of world drama. The musical drama is, indeed, so indigenous that its transplantation to a foreign stage sometimes seems unnatural. Its unique Whitmanesque paradoxical qualities of idealism and energetic brashness are inimitably American. Not until the 1980's have imported musicals such as the English *Cats* (pr. 1981) vied with native musicals on the New York stage.

Singular moments in American dramatic history when theater and drama coalesced to produce luminous moments on the stage must include Pauline Lord's appearance in Sidney Howard's *They Knew What They Wanted* (pr. 1924) and O'Neill's *Anna Christie* (pr. 1921), Alfred Lunt and Lynn Fontanne in Robert E. Sherwood's *Idiot's Delight* (pr. 1936), Laurette Taylor as Amanda Wingfield in Tennessee Williams' *The Glass Menagerie* (pr. 1944), Lee J. Cobb as Willy Loman in the 1949 production of Miller's *Death of a Salesman*, Jessica Tandy as Blanche DuBois in Williams' *A Streetcar Named Desire* (pr. 1947), and Colleen Dewhurst and Jason Robards (quintessentially O'Neillian actors) in the 1973 production of *A Moon for the Misbegotten* (pr. 1947).

Special events also mark stage history, such as the 1984 production of *Death of a Salesman*, with a jaunty Dustin Hoffman as Willy Loman, contrasting vividly with the defeated Willy of Cobb's portrayal. In an interesting coincidence, a new play about salesmen of another sort—this time, a real-estate salesman—appeared in tandem, as it were, with the Miller drama. *Glengarry Glen Ross* dramatizes the distinctively American confidence game that has been the subject of many dramatists since the 1920's. Hailed by critics as an updated sequel to *Death of a Salesman*, Mamet's drama is a hard-hitting, brilliant verbal choreography of a basic American myth. Rather than focusing conventionally on the causes and consequences of the conflicts created by the betrayal of ideals, Mamet transforms the disillusionment into an energetic poetry that takes on a life of its own. Like Williams before him, Mamet transforms even the harshest American realities into a celebration of the vitality and energy that are usually the domain of the musical. He brings the dynamic of Carl Sandburg's poetry to the stage. (It is an interesting coincidence that, like Sandburg, Mamet hails from Chicago.) The dapper Willy Loman of Hoffman, then, is, at least in part, akin to the spirit of Mamet's salesmen.

Early American Drama

The beginnings of American drama date back to April 30, 1598, near El Paso, Texas, when a comedy about soldiers on a march, written by a Captain Marcos Farfan de los Godos, was performed. Spanish-speaking areas, for the most part, were more congenial to theatrical entertainments than were those colonized by the English and Dutch.

Among other "firsts" on the American theater scene was a play by Virginia landowner William Darby. His *Ye Bare and Ye Cubb* (pr. 1665), "the first record of a play in English," resulted in a lawsuit against the author brought by an Edward Martin. Darby was found not guilty.

The "first play written by a native American to be performed by a professional company," reports the historian of drama Arthur Hobson Quinn, was performed "on the stage of the Southwark Theatre in Philadelphia in 1767." That play was *The Prince of Parthia*, a heroic tragedy by Thomas Godfrey. The Southwark Theatre, which replaced an earlier one built outside the limits of Philadelphia (like Shakespeare's on London's South Bank) and torn down after protests from religious groups, became the first permanent theater in America.

Written in blank verse and depicting historical events in a foreign country, *The Prince of Parthia* was influenced by many plays, including Shakespeare's *Hamlet*, *Macbeth*, *Richard III*, *Julius Caesar*, and *Romeo and Juliet*; Francis Beaumont and John Fletcher's *The Maid's Tragedy*; John Dryden's *Aureng-Zebe*; and Nicholas Rowe's *Tamerlane*, among others. The traditional tragic passions of love, jealousy, loyalty, and revenge motivate the action, involving two brothers, one of whom returns in triumph to Parthia from a military victory, and Evanthe, the maiden for whose hand the two brothers compete. Personal and political passions eventually lead to Evanthe's suicide by poison, as well as the suicide of Arsaces (the brother whom she loves). Order is restored to the kingdom by Gotarzes, a younger brother, who, like Fortinbras in *Hamlet*, is a figure outside the main action of the play. Although lacking in a native subject, the play is significant, as Quinn observes, as "the only play of American origin that was actually performed on a native stage during this period, before the Revolution. . . ." (Having died at an early age, Godfrey himself did not live to see his play performed or published.)

The history of the Southwark Theatre, at which *The Prince of Parthia* was produced, involves the beginning of the actor-manager tradition in colonial times. Plays such as Shakespeare's *Richard III*, William Congreve's *Love for Love*, Dryden's *The Spanish Friar: Or, The Double Discovery*, Joseph Addison's *Cato*, John Gay's *The Beggar's Opera*, George Lillo's *The London Merchant: Or, The History of George Barnwell*, Thomas Otway's *The Orphan: Or, The Unhappy Marriage*, and George Farquhar's *The Beaux' Stratagem*, *The Recruiting Officer*, and *The Twin-Rivals*—all were brought to America by an English actor-manager named Lewis Hallam. With his company, which included members of his family, Hallam began American theatrical history in prerevolutionary Williamsburg, New York, and Philadelphia. Contending with opposition from religious groups, he finally left for Jamaica, where he died, leaving a widow and a son to return to the United States to resume their theatrical activity. Mrs. Hallam's second husband, David Douglass, became manager of what was probably the first "American Company," the actual name of the performing group assumed. Douglass built the Southwark Theatre in Philadelphia, and his first and very long season included the production of Godfrey's *The Prince of Parthia*.

When war broke out, pursuits such as the theater, already strongly opposed on moral and economic grounds, were outlawed by an unenforceable resolution passed by the Continental Congress in 1774, which reads as follows:

> We will in our several stations encourage frugality, economy and industry, and promote agriculture, arts, and the manufactures of this country, especially that of wool; and will discountenance and discourage every species of extravagance and dissipation, especially all horse-racing and all kinds of gaming, cockfighting, exhibitions of shews, plays, and other expensive diversions and entertainments.

Douglass and his company left voluntarily for the West Indies, and the prerevolutionary period in American drama had come to a close. During the war, however, the lean beginnings of drama took on a decidedly native turn in the many satires directed against the British. Just as the prerevolutionary drama was associated with the names of Hallam, Douglass, and Godfrey, that of the war period belongs to political satirists such as Mrs. Mercey (née Otis) Warren of Massachusetts, where patriotic plays thrived. Characters, frequently military and political figures of the time, were taken from real life, and the settings were real places such as Faneuil Hall in Boston. In addition to the satiric writers, dramatists such as Hugh Henry Breckenridge portrayed generals on both sides with dignity, mostly in long speeches of blank verse.

The stern prohibitions of the Continental Congress in 1774 did not entirely prevent theatrical entertainments. Young Lewis Hallam, son of the British theatrical entrepreneur, and John Henry reestablished the American Company, and when Pennsylvania, in 1789, repealed the prohibition of theaters, moral opposition lessened and increasing emphasis was placed upon dramatic quality.

If *The Prince of Parthia* can lay claim to being the first tragedy by a native performed in the first professional American theater, *The Contrast*, produced by the American Company at the John Street Theatre in New York on April 16, 1787, was the first such comedy. Its author was Boston-born, Harvard-educated Royall Tyler, and his play met with success in New York, Baltimore, Philadelphia, Boston, Charleston, and Richmond. Like the author of *The Prince of Parthia*, Tyler had seen much British drama, and it is not surprising that *The Contrast* (advertised in Boston as "A Moral Lecture in five parts") is an American adaptation of England's memorable eighteenth century comedy of manners, Sheridan's *The School for Scandal* (pr. 1777).

In *The Contrast*, a servant, Jonathan, provides an interesting insight into contemporary attitudes toward the theater. Having purchased a ticket to an entertainment where "they play *hocus pocus* tricks," he was mistakenly directed to a "play-house," "where the devil hangs out the vanities of the world upon the tenter-hooks of temptation." In the narration of his adventure to a fellow servant, Jenny, Jonathan describes the reaction of the people sitting near him: "[they] set up such a hissing—hiss—like so many mad cats; and then they went thump, thump, thump, just like our Peleg threshing wheat and stampt away, just like the nation." When Jonathan finishes his tale, Jenny concludes that he was surely at a playhouse, whereupon Jonathan admits to having demanded a refund of his money and having been told that he had been watching not the sights he thought he had paid to see but something called the "School for Scandalization." Popular audience identification with or rejection of characters and action on the stage commonly expressed itself in strong reactions such as those described by Jonathan.

The Nineteenth Century

The second comedy by a native American to be performed on the professional stage was William Dunlap's *The Father: Or, American Shandyism* (pr. 1789), a play influenced by another English work, Laurence Sterne's novel *Tristam Shandy*. *The Father* also holds the distinction of being the first professionally produced comedy of an American author to be published.

Dunlap, born in New Jersey, was also America's first major playwright-producer. A man of many interests, he seems to have been the Samuel Johnson of the late eighteenth and early nineteenth century American stage. Among his varied publications, the first chronicle of the American stage stands out: *A History of American Theatre* (1832). Drama criticism had begun, and Dunlap records the formation of groups that gathered to support and stimulate interest in the theater by reviews in the magazines.

Especially important during the Dunlap era was his long-standing association with August von Kotzebue, a German dramatist whose domestic melodramas were very popular on the American stage. Americans during the early nineteenth century were enjoying the same kind of melodramatic fare that was popular on the English stage.

Two other major figures in nineteenth century stage history merit mention here. James Nelson Barker wrote the first surviving drama about Pocahontas, *The Indian Princess: Or, La Belle Sauvage* (pr. 1808). Taken from John Smith's *The Generall Historie of Virginia, New England, and the Summer Isles* (1624), the play used native history. Although remembered primarily for his romantic dramatizations of native subjects, Barker also wrote plays that featured exotic foreign settings. John Howard Payne, author of more than sixty plays, was known for his adaptations of foreign plays. Payne's exotic, Gothic melodramas, such as *Ali Pacha: Or, The Signet Ring* (pb. 1823), entertained American audiences, as did his domestic melodramas.

Hastily and cleverly written for performances, melodramas—domestic and exotic, drawn from sources as varied as Shakespeare, Charles Dickens, Sir Walter Scott, Kotzebue, and René-Charles Guilbert de Pixérécourt—fulfilled the expectations of early nineteenth century audiences. Major authors such as Dickens were popularized for audiences who demanded sheer spectacle, heroines saved from villains, and strong musical reinforcement of emotions.

It was in this period that the Scribean well-made play, featuring a formulaic plot fleshed out with much action and stage business, reached its peak. Victorien Sardou, Alexandre Dumas, *père*, and their countryman Eugène Scribe were the major figures grinding out such formula plays, to which the European dramatists of the latter half of the nineteenth century reacted in their realistic and psychological plays. Ibsen, Strindberg, Shaw, and Chekhov began the modern period of drama with plays in which ideas and complex characterizations replaced the melodrama that dominated the stages earlier in the century.

With beginnings, then, in Godfrey, Tyler, Dunlap, and Barker, drama had taken hold in the United States, its directions influenced by religious, economic, and historical forces.

During the Civil War period, George H. Boker, educated at the College of New Jersey, wrote tragedy in blank verse that is distinguished by its literary quality. His *Francesca da Rimini* (pr. 1855) was the first play in English to be based on the story of Dante's famous pair of lovers, Francesca and Paolo. Irish-born Dion Boucicault, who had spent some time in France before emigrating to the United States, found American culture a rich source of dramatic material. His *The Octoroon: Or, Life in Louisiana* (pr. 1859), based on Mayne Reid's novel *The Quadroon: Or, A Lover's Adventures in Louisiana* (1856), is about interracial romance. Boucicault wrote sympathetically about the poor. He was also important for his efforts (with Boker) to bring about the passage of the first copyright law in 1856. The legislation, however, came too late to give Harriet Beecher Stowe the right to have a voice in the stage adaptation of *Uncle Tom's Cabin*. Her novel was adapted with little success by Charles Western Taylor and with much success by George L. Aiken, both stage versions having been produced in 1852, the same year that the novel was published.

Other nineteenth century dramatists provide important links in the historical development of American drama. Their interest in the realism of character and events was part of a reaction (conscious or not) against the superficiality and predictability of the prevailing melodrama. In contrast to the outsized passions of melodrama, Quinn observes, James Herne's *Margaret Fleming* (pr. 1880) and *The Reverend Griffith Davenport* (pr. 1899) deal with "less obvious material and the finer subtlety of motive." William Gillette's *Secret Service* (pr. 1895) moved the drama a step further in the realism of action. Had the author not invoked an improbable ending in regard to the fate of the hero, a Civil War spy, he might have "created a tragedy of uncommon power." Even so, Quinn concludes, *Secret Service* is a "melodrama of a high order."

Clyde Fitch also produced a prodigious output of plays and earned for himself an international reputation, especially with *The Truth* (pr. 1906), a drama about a promiscuous wife, sympathetically drawn, who, in spite of her wayward nature, loves her husband devotedly. Fitch's *Beau Brummell* (pr. 1890), drawn from the novel by William Jesse and the stage adaptation of Blanchard Jerrold, features a hero-philanderer who also demonstrates heroic goodness. Fitch's sympathetic heroes and heroines constitute the melodrama's counterpart to Ben Jonson's biting studies of "humours"; Fitch's characters, Quinn notes, are "endowed with a shining virtue or possessed by one absorbing vice." Like Gillette, Fitch also wrote spy dramas, among them *Nathan Hale* (pr. 1898) and *Major André* (pr. 1903).

The 1920's

At the turn of the century, theater continued to depend on foreign influences in both style and subject matter, despite efforts to create serious native drama. The much-needed catalyst for change was provided in 1913, with the beginning of Workshop 47, the famous playwriting course at Harvard taught by George Pierce Baker. O'Neill became Baker's most distinguished student; among the many other enrollees in Baker's classes, those who were most influential in shaping the course of American drama include Robert E. Sherwood, S. N. Behrman, George Abbott, Philip Barry, and Sidney Howard. Baker's influence extended to those involved in the production aspects of the theater and to critics as well, including Heywood Broun, Brooks Atkinson, and John Mason Brown. When Baker moved to Yale, he numbered among his protégés Elia Kazan, important for his work in the Group Theatre and the Actors' Studio and for his direction of Williams' *A Streetcar Named Desire* and Miller's *Death of a Salesman* in the late 1940's. The effect of Baker's classes was eventually felt not only throughout the United States but also internationally.

At the time that Baker started Workshop 47, William Vaughn Moody, himself a Harvard graduate, had already left his Harvard teaching post to write his own poetic dramas. Others, such as Percy Mackaye, also of Harvard, had formed a band of serious writers who worked for changes in the drama. Yet even as these efforts for change were under way, financial problems continued to plague the stage, especially in New York, where the twenty theaters of 1903 had grown to eighty in 1927 and the tastes of popular audiences had to be satisfied. The demands of the "fabulous invalid," as Broadway has been labeled, created a two-tier stage system.

The earliest impetus to modern American drama came from the Provincetown Players, housed in the Wharf Theatre in Provincetown, Massachusetts. There, O'Neill's *Bound East for Cardiff* (pr. 1916) and *Thirst* (pr. 1916) were staged, and O'Neill himself played the part of the black man in the latter. In 1916, the group moved to New York's Macdougal Street, and by 1925, Quinn records, the Players had put on "ninety-three new plays by forty-seven playwrights, practically all American." It was, indeed, a playwright's theater in the sense that financial considerations were not paramount. The company was fueled by a zeal to provide opportunity to writers who would otherwise lack a forum for new ideas in the theater. As noted above, beginning with these innovations of the post-World War I years, each decade has had its own little theater movement.

The distinction between the dramatists of the 1920's and their predecessors was twofold. First, the dramatists of the 1920's achieved a genuine breakthrough in their freedom to treat every aspect of human reality. Second, they introduced a range of styles and forms that gave the American theater an unprecedented vitality.

Earlier dramatists such as James Herne and William Vaughn Moody, who had attempted to bring change to the worn-out comedies, farces, and melodramas of their time, had succeeded only partially. Herne's *Margaret Fleming* and Moody's *The Great Divide*, although inching closer to genuine realism in dialogue and plot, were still characterized by emotional excess and by the artificially theatrical big speech. Then, in one decade, the long gestation period of American drama came to an end, its birth characterized by honesty and naturalness in language and plot.

Nowhere is the phenomenon more strikingly illustrated than in three plays that were staged in the fall of 1924: Maxwell Anderson and Laurence Stallings' *What Price Glory?*, Sidney Howard's *They Knew What They Wanted*, and O'Neill's *Desire Under the Elms*. *What Price Glory?* is a realistic comedy about the futility of war. Stallings had lost a leg in World War I, and Anderson, at the time, was a committed pacifist. Like many writers of the 1920's, they shunned any romanticism about love and war in their characterizations of the two main characters, Captain Flagg and Sergeant Quirt. Whether fighting each other (over women) or the enemy in trenches, the men experience disillusionment in a fast-moving, hilarious series of events.

In Howard's Pulitzer Prize-winning *They Knew What They Wanted*, a folk drama later adapted to the musical stage as *The Most Happy Fella* (pr. 1956), Tony, an Italian immigrant grape grower, employs deception to win a girl much younger than he, sending her a photograph of his handsome young hired hand instead of one of himself. The trick backfires when Tony's bride is seduced by the hired hand, by whom she has a son. In the end, Tony overcomes his murderous rage, seeing the girl's mistake as one of the head, not of the heart.

The third play of this remarkable season, O'Neill's *Desire Under the Elms*, is, like Howard's, a drama about an older man and a young wife. Here, however, the illegitimate father is the youngest son of the old man, and the setting is a rockbound New England farm. The child is murdered by the mother as a demonstration of her love for its father, and the couple, as the play ends, is imprisoned.

O'Neill transcended his contemporaries in the tragic dimensions with which he endowed his characters. The young couple, struggling in the knowledge of events that they cannot overcome, acquire a moral wisdom in what Quinn calls their "conflict with something—fate, circumstance, moral and social law—which hampers or crushes" them. As in Greek tragedy, the wisdom comes too late. In its departure from the "virtue conquers all" endings of earlier American plays, O'Neill's Oedipal-based drama marks an important development in dramatic history. A few years later, in *Mourning Becomes Electra* (pr. 1931), O'Neill expanded the sense of tragedy in an Aeschylean attempt to trace through several generations the destiny of a guilt-haunted New England family. This tragic sense permeates O'Neill's works, despite their diversity of style, unifying the early lyric sea plays; the expressionistic plays such as *The Emperor Jones* (pr. 1920), *The Great God Brown* (pr. 1926), and *Dynamo* (pr. 1929); the naturalistic *The Iceman Cometh* (pr. 1946); and the unfinished autobiographical cycle of plays, of which *Long Day's Journey into Night* (pr. 1956) is his masterpiece.

O'Neill fused theater and drama, putting compelling theatricality at the service of psychological insight. What Nathaniel Hawthorne, Herman Melville, and Walt Whitman are to American fiction and poetry, O'Neill is to its drama. In the anguished search of his characters for something to which to belong, O'Neill joins the tradition of Ralph Waldo Emerson and Henry David Thoreau. The necessity of people to claim or reclaim something of their most primitive selves is the force that drives O'Neill's characters.

O'Neill's ambitious stagecraft, his attempts—not always successful—to combine conflicting psychological, sociological, and moral forces in the personal lives of his characters, place him in the company of such major figures in world drama as Ibsen and Strindberg. Quinn's estimate of O'Neill still holds: that "he is a great dramatist because he is more than a dramatist," for "he will be finally estimated by. . . his profound imaginative interpretation of aspiring humanity, struggling upward, even through sin and shame, toward the light." On a worldwide scale, O'Neill's dramas continue to be performed in a steady stream of productions. On the national level, his major successors have carried on his traditions, although in narrower ranges. Miller in his sociomoral plays, Williams in his psychological and poetic explorations of neurotic characters, and Albee in his highly stylized concern with the moral wasteland that the American Dream has become—all have assumed in part the mantle of O'Neill.

If the emergence of three remarkable plays within a few months of one another—a ribald comedy, a realistic folk drama, and a tragedy—stand out as a phenomenon of 1924, they are only three of a large number of dramas that vitalized the stage during that decade. Sherwood and Anderson began writing at this time, even though their major dramas were written later. Thornton Wilder wrote novels and a few one-act plays and, much later, *Our Town* (pr. 1938), *The Matchmaker* (pr. 1954), and *The Skin of Our Teeth* (pr. 1942). Elmer Rice's *Street Scene* (pr. 1947) dramatized tenement life on the streets of New York, and DuBose and Dorothy Heyward's *Porgy* (pr. 1927) did the same for the blacks of Charleston, South Carolina. George S. Kaufman and Marc Connelly, one of the most successful of many playwriting teams of the decade, were responsible for a prolific output of satires on the American success story, the most famous of which is *Beggar on Horseback* (pr. 1924). Kaufman also collaborated with Edna Ferber on *The Royal Family* (pr. 1927) and with Ring Lardner on *June Moon* (pr. 1929), and staged John Steinbeck's novel *Of Mice and Men* (pr. 1937). The decade also included bright comedies about upper-class society by Philip Barry, whose urbane wit in *Holiday* (pr. 1928) saves the play from the sentimental moralizing to which it quite easily might have descended. The 1920's were indeed a brave new world for the American stage.

The 1930's

If the playwrights of the 1920's were bold in their treatment of subject matter and dramatic form, those of the 1930's were more self-confident in their social and political commitment and, in their topicality, perhaps more brave. Their leading voice was Clifford Odets, whose *Awake and Sing* (pr. 1935) continues as a stage favorite, despite its label as a period piece. Odets and his contemporaries—William Saroyan, Robert E. Sherwood, Maxwell Anderson, and Lillian Hellman—wrote their major dramas during the Great Depression. This was the era of the Federal Theatre Project (1935-1939), which made live theater available to a general public for the first time. As the first government-subsidized theater in the United States, the project provided Orson Welles with his first directorial experience, one result of which was the formation of the Mercury Theatre by Welles and John Houseman.

A second very important development of the time was the establishment of the Group Theatre, the 1930's version of the Provincetown Theatre and Theatre Guild, which had nurtured the dramatists of the 1920's. Out of the Group emerged some of the most productive theater figures of the twentieth century: Stella Adler, Luther Adler, Harold Clurman, Lee J. Cobb, Morris Carnovsky, Elia Kazan, and Franchot Tone, among others.

The protest drama and its depressed milieu enjoyed a close relationship in the 1930's, perhaps as in no other time. Many dramatists, consequently, became the targets of criticism from conservative groups. Characterized as radical, left-wing, and tinged with various shades of "pink," some continued to be criticized for the rest of their lives, as in the case of Hellman.

The protest plays were direct descendants of the plays of the 1920's. Social, political, and moral problems, although a part of the fabric of earlier dramas, became more pronounced in the very late 1920's and throughout the 1930's. Because of their narrower thematic focus, the dramatists of the 1930's fall into the shadow of O'Neill, much as Ben Jonson and Christopher Marlowe are overshadowed by Shakespeare; however, they form an important group, and they provide a connection between the two war eras. Indeed, the tradition of the social-problem drama, whether handled satirically, realistically, or tragically, has been the point of departure for the plays of Miller, Williams, Albee, and most American dramatists since the 1930's.

Three important plays produced in 1935 stand out as representative of the 1930's. Robert E. Sherwood's *The Petrified Forest* carries its weight of social criticism, but in a melodramatic style. The setting, an isolated filling station on the edge of a desert; the plot, with its roots in the crime drama or thriller; and the use of stock characters, such as an impoverished writer, an American Legionnaire, and a banker, provide the ingredients that make for an evening of conventional theater. The requisite touch of sentimentality is provided when a gangster listens to the writer's request to shoot him so that his insurance money may go to the station owner's daughter, whom he has made his beneficiary. The play, which also became a successful film, powerfully evokes the moral bankruptcy against which the socially committed dramatists of the 1930's were reaching.

Maxwell Anderson's *Winterset*, a second noteworthy play of 1935, dramatizes the tragedy of a modern Electra and Orestes: a sister and a brother through whom the truth is brought to light concerning a crime for which an innocent Italian immigrant was convicted and executed. With his blank-verse exploration of the complex issue of crime, punishment, and their accompanying guilts, Anderson—whose reputation in the 1930's was much higher than in subsequent years—was acclaimed as a major writer of tragedy. Based loosely on the famous Sacco-Vanzetti case, *Winterset* was preceded by *Gods of the Lightning* (pr. 1928), a social-protest play about the factual aspects of the same case, which Anderson had written in collaboration with Gerald Hickerson.

A third important play of 1935, Clifford Odets' *Awake and Sing*, concerns an extended Jewish family fighting against poverty. Conflicts occur between the young and the old, the liberal and the conservative, the practical mother and the aging but still passionately Marxist grandfather—and between the characters' dreams and the realities that they all must face. Odets developed his characters within a deliberately loose plot, focusing primarily on the strong characterizations of each member of the family. Like Rice in *Street Scene* and like the Heywards in *Porgy*, Odets painted his antiheroic characters with broad strokes of dignity and compassion. In spite of its period flavor, the play is frequently produced and seems to enjoy a popularity denied by contemporary audiences to the other two plays of 1935 discussed above.

Lillian Hellman, another important writer of the era of social protest, wrote steadily until her death in 1984 and is one of America's major female dramatists. From her plays of the 1930's, *The Children's Hour* (pr. 1934) and *The Little Foxes* (pr. 1939), to her World War II drama *Watch on the Rhine* (pr. 1941), an admonitory play set in the United States, Hellman assumed a clear anticapitalist and anti-Fascist stance, yet she also made individual morality a strong issue. Often criticized for her dependence on melodramatic components and on the conventions of the well-made play, Hellman was praised for her powerful characterizations. Her characters seem driven by psychological and biological forces beyond their control. Fascinated by the darker side of experience, she dramatized such subjects as malice in children and greed in adults. Villains triumph over characters who are good but weak. Throughout her career, Hellman fought against the evil that for her became symbolized in the activities of the House Committee on Un-American Activities investigations of the 1950's.

The 1940's

If the 1930's represent, at least in retrospect, some cohesion in the use of drama as a vehicle for social protest, the 1940's seem far removed from any such unity. Thus, it is fitting that Thornton Wilder's *The Skin of Our Teeth* should be regarded by many critics as the most memorable play of the first half of the decade. An expressionistic, farcical drama of epic events that span human history from the Ice Age to the present, the play proclaims that there is no order, no cause-effect relationship in events, and, consequently, no explanation of the catastrophic events that humankind has survived from earliest times. Therefore, one can learn little or nothing from history. What pleasure or even comfort human beings can hope for is to be found in the little events of life. Wilder had said much the same thing in his realistic-sentimental play of the late 1930's, *Our Town*. Later, in the 1950's, his conventionally constructed farce, *The Matchmaker*, about two apprentices and their employer and their antics on the town, dramatized the same views.

During World War II, only two decades after an earlier war that was supposed to end all wars, the theater, like the country in general, was especially in need of optimism. Escape from the problems of the time was provided in the plethora of musicals, and muted optimism appeared in William Saroyan's *The Time of Your Life* (pr. 1939). Even some musicals, however, were tinged with problems; Anderson's *Lost in the Stars* (pr. 1949), for example, was based on Alan Paton's novel about apartheid in South Africa, *Cry the Beloved Country* (1948).

With the war's end, the American theater entered a period of extraordinary achievement, equaled perhaps only by the 1920's. Three major plays, Williams' *The Glass Menagerie* and *A Streetcar Named Desire* and Miller's *Death of a Salesman*, stand out among many fine plays of the era; the last two were directed by Elia Kazan of the Actors' Studio. In the decades since these three plays first appeared, the names of Amanda, Laura, and Tom Wingfield; Stanley Kowalski and Blanche DuBois; and Willy, Biff, and Linda Loman have become household names on the world stage. The original productions of these plays provided audiences with unforgettable performances by Laurette Taylor, Jessica Tandy, Marlon Brando, Lee J. Cobb, and Mildred Dunnock.

Criticized for writing exclusively about the weak and fragile in a society that is dominated by the strong, Williams became America's major poet of the theater. Similarly, Miller, attacked by the Right for being too negative about the American capitalistic system and by the Left for not being critical enough, has shown that artistic integrity and social commitment are not mutually exclusive.

In the plays of both Williams and Miller, the influence of European dramatic traditions is evident. In particular, Williams often recalls Strindberg, while Miller has close ties to Ibsen. Like Miss Julie in Strindberg's play of the same title, Williams' heroines are trapped by social conventions. Blanche DuBois is torn between the gentility of an Old South upbringing and the harsh realities of the lower classes into which her sister has married. Laura Wingfield is the victim of a well-intentioned, practical mother of that same Southern background and of the poet-brother who needs to escape. Like Strindberg's and O'Neill's characters, those of Williams find themselves trapped between their illusions and reality. Tom Wingfield, as character and narrator in *The Glass Menagerie*, tells his audience: "Yes, I have tricks in my pocket, I have things up my sleeve. But I am the opposite of a stage magician. He gives you illusion that has the appearance of truth. I give you truth in the pleasant disguise of illusion." Like O'Neill's, Williams' characters are haunted by a sense of doom, and, indeed, they are doomed. As misfits in society, they are neurotic, their very neuroticism striking a deep chord in the American psyche and providing their author with a rich vein of poetic drama.

In his January, 1985, review of Olof Lagercrantz's biography of Strindberg, Miller writes of Strindberg's influence on English-speaking playwrights: "Strindberg struck strongly into O'Neill, is quite directly mirrored in Beckett and Pinter, in Tennessee Williams and Edward Albee." He refers to these playwrights' concern with the "world of the subconscious, where the sexual encounter especially was a fight to the death, a world where the mother did not nurture but suffocated and destroyed her offspring, a world where domination (usually female) was the key to life." In O'Neill's *Desire Under the Elms* and Albee's *The American Dream* (pr. 1961), the fight is to the death, and in Williams' *The Glass Menagerie*, the emotional suffocation is total.

Miller, on the other hand, is an artistic descendant of Ibsen. In the latter's *The Pillars of Society*, a father builds a defective ship, only to have his son embark on that ship and go down with it. In Miller's *All My Sons*, a father who is engaged in the manufacture of airplane parts is guilty of similar negligence, resulting in unnecessary deaths during World War II.

Miller also adapted Ibsen's *An Enemy of the People* (pr. 1950), a strong condemnation of civic-minded leaders who eventually turn an entire community against an idealist who exposes water pollution, an exposure that threatens the financial health of the town, since its baths provide income for the owners and workers. The pitting of moral values against financial gain constitutes the conflict in a number of Miller's plays.

It was in *Death of a Salesman*, however, that Miller redefined tragedy and began a debate among critics and scholars. The question on which the debate turns is whether the antihero of contemporary literature can achieve tragic stature. Purists hold that since Willy Loman, Miller's protagonist, never achieves the dignity that results from wisdom gained through experience, he is not a tragic hero. To the end, Willy lacks wisdom, clinging to the illusion that his insurance money will provide his son Biff with an opportunity for a new start. Thus, Willy's death, by suicide, is tainted by incompetence: It is the last act of a loser.

Charley, Willy's old friend, comments at the funeral that no one dares blame Willy: "A salesman is got to dream, boy. It comes with the territory." Linda, sobbing at the funeral, cannot understand Willy's suicide, especially since the last payment on their home was made that day. Only Biff, the more disillusioned of the two sons, has known the truth all along: "He [Willy] never knew who he was."

The American Dream of success is exposed for the illusion that it can become when challenged by certain realities of life. The pipe dreams of O'Neill's characters and the dreams that haunt Williams' heroines find a sharp focus in the Loman family. Indeed, as noted above, selling and salesmen are at the heart of the American success story and are thus of recurring significance in American drama: Willy's brothers exist in Hickey of *The Iceman Cometh* and in the real estate salesmen of Mamet's *Glengarry Glen Ross.* This trilogy of salesmen—Willy, Hickey, and Roma—embodies the rapidly deteriorating morality of the confidence game at the very heart of the American Dream success story.

The importance of Elia Kazan's productions has already been noted in connection with the emergence of Williams and Miller. Kazan was one of three important figures from the Group Theatre of the 1930's—the others were Lee Strasberg and Cheryl Crawford—who, in the 1940's, formed the Actors' Studio. They and their graduates strongly influenced the course of American drama, as Baker had done earlier in the century at Harvard and at Yale.

The 1950's

During the 1950's, the old lines between "theater" and "drama" were redrawn, sending the "serious" and new dramatists, producers, directors, and actors scurrying to the small theaters of Off-Broadway and to the even smaller ones of Off-Off-Broadway. The Antoinette Perry Awards (or Tonys, as they came to be known on Broadway) were supplemented by the Off-Broadway selections for best plays and productions (or Obies). Regional theaters and arts complexes sprang up in the major metropolitan areas, Lincoln Center in New York being the most prominent.

The times were troubled by the Washington investigations conducted by the House Committee on Un-American Activities, which called various artists in for questioning. Arthur Miller's *The Crucible* (pr. 1953), an allegorical drama about witch-hunting in colonial Salem, dramatizes the mood of the 1950's. It was the decade of blacklisting in California, as a result of which a large number of left-wing writers, directors, and actors were unable to find work.

Writers from earlier decades experimented with new styles. Lillian Hellman, for example, wrote a loosely plotted drama in the Chekhovian style, *The Autumn Garden* (pr. 1951), while Tennessee Williams, departing from the naturalistic poetry of *A Streetcar Named Desire* and *The Glass Menagerie*, wrote the expressionistic *Camino Real* (pr. 1953).

A group of writers, some of them new, wrote social-problem plays, among them Robert Anderson, Arthur Laurents, and William Inge— labeled by critic Gerald Weales as "the new [Arthur Wing] Pineros." In support of this judgment, Weales quotes Shaw, who observed that a certain class of writers conquered "the public by the exquisite flattery of giving them plays that they really liked, whilst persuading them that such appreciation was only possible from persons of great culture and intellectual acuteness."

Another important group of writers are those whom Weales calls "the video boys," who wrote for television, almost as training for the stage. Their stage writing frequently reflects film and television technique in the fluidity realized by lighting and multiple stage sets. In subject matter, these playwrights—among them Paddy Chayefsky (*Marty*, pr. 1953) and William Gibson (*The Miracle Worker*, pr. 1957)—resemble the new Pineros.

Poets and academics also left their mark on the stage of the 1950's.

Archibald MacLeish (*J. B.: A Play in Verse*, pr. 1958) and Robinson Jeffers (*The Cretan Woman*, pr. 1954, and, earlier, *Medea*, pr. 1947) took up the mantle of Maxwell Anderson, and they, in turn, were followed in the 1960's by Robert Lowell, whose *Old Glory* trilogy (pb. 1965) is an adaptation of stories by Hawthorne and Melville. Lowell's dramas, which deal with ideological conflicts in colonial times, also carry on the tradition of social protest.

Lee Strasberg sees the 1950's as a time of "numerous playwrights, yet fewer important plays." The decade "inspires the feeling of having hit bottom, yet produces the greatest play of our time—O'Neill's *Long Day's Journey into Night*." The posthumous production of this major drama—written, it should be noted, well before the 1950's—occurred during a time that saw the successful production of two other O'Neill plays that had not fared well earlier: *The Iceman Cometh* and *A Moon for the Misbegotten*. The role of Hickey in *The Iceman Cometh* gave Jason Robards prominence in a career that was distinguished by many O'Neill roles. O'Neill's *A Touch of the Poet* (pr. 1957) and *Hughie* (pr. 1958) also were given successful productions.

The 1960's
The 1950's were not to close, however, without the emergence of a major new voice on the American stage, that of Edward Albee, whose pessimism about American cultural values seemed an exorcism of the general malaise of the time. Optimism regarding the American Dream, closely scrutinized or questioned in earlier plays and still insisted on by popular audiences, collapses under its own weight in Albee's early plays. In no other American dramatist and in no other Albee play is this collapse so total as it is in *The American Dream*. A searing comedy, the play probes the psychological dismemberment of a child by its parents and by the social institutions whose ostensible purpose it is to nurture the young. The play catapulted Albee into fame as America's own Absurdist dramatist. *The American Dream* was preceded by Albee's trio of short plays, *The Zoo Story* (pr. 1959), *The Death of Bessie Smith* (pr. 1960), and *The Sandbox* (pr. 1960), the first of which remains one of his most frequently produced plays.

The Zoo Story premiered in Berlin, Germany, in 1959, produced by the Schiller Theater Werkstatt. In a historical coincidence, its first American staging took place in 1960 at the Provincetown Playhouse, a name inextricably linked with O'Neill and the coming of age of American drama. In this strikingly accomplished debut, Albee presented a life-and-death struggle in the guise of a fight over a park bench. The combatants are a successful publishing executive and a social failure who has spent the day walking up to Central Park from Greenwich Village; their struggle is actually a desperate attempt on the part of the failure, Jerry, to attempt some human communication with the executive, Peter. The themes for the brilliant Albee dramas to follow, among them *Who's Afraid of Virginia Woolf?* (pr. 1962), are established in this first play.

As an inheritor of the mantle of O'Neill and Williams, Albee explores the dark, complex psychological and sociological forces that have shaped his characters and their worlds. O'Neill's characters search for something larger than themselves, something to which they can belong; those of Williams and Miller at least maintain tenuous links with the human family; Albee's, consciously or unconsciously, find themselves alienated from one another and from their universe. *Who's Afraid of Virginia Woolf?*, a Strindbergian battle of the sexes, presents a fascinating study in which long-repressed conflicts and guilts are exorcised, leaving both major characters, a history professor and his wife, exhausted at the end. The play enjoyed a successful initial run on Broadway and has been revived frequently, attracting major talents of the time, from the clawing, naturalistic film performances of Elizabeth Taylor and Richard Burton to the more subdued later Broadway version, directed by Albee himself and featuring Colleen Dewhurst and Ben Gazzara in beautifully and classically balanced interpretations of their roles.

Following the emergence of Albee as America's fourth major dramatist, the Off-Broadway, Off-Off-Broadway, and university and regional theaters, which had begun as independent and frequently isolated efforts appealing only to small audiences, initiated a second coming-of-age of American drama. Beginning around 1960, Broadway prices began a steady and unprecedented escalation, so that by 1985, tickets for Harvey Fierstein's *La Cage aux Folles* (pr. 1983) on New Year's Eve were bringing in seventy-five dollars apiece. Although an extreme example of the financial stranglehold in which Broadway found itself, *La Cage aux Folles* illustrates a phenomenon that has affected even the straight dramas of the day.

In *New Broadways: Theatre Across America, 1950-1980* (1982), Gerald Berkowitz traces the growth of the small theaters that began springing up independently all across the country, partly in response to the prohibitive cost of Broadway productions. In 1967, the Ford Foundation began a generous program of theater subsidy. The Alley Theatre of Houston, the Arena Stage of Washington, and the Mummers Theatre of Oklahoma City were among the major recipients. Benefiting from subsidies as well were the American Place Theatre in New York, the Center Stage in Baltimore, the Hartford Stage Company, the Seattle Rep, the Stage/West of West Springfield, Massachusetts, the Actors' Studio in New York, the American Shakespeare Festival, and the Guthrie Theatre of Minneapolis. The Ford Foundation not only subsidized writers and actors but also built new theaters for the Alley and the Mummers and bought and renovated theaters for the American Conservatory Theatre and the Actors' Theatre of Louisville. Other foundations followed with their own subsidies, but Ford has remained the most active. Additional impetus to theaters across the country was provided by the National Endowment for the Arts, which began in 1966. Even Broadway became the recipient of subsidies, by means of the Theatre Development Fund, jointly established by the Twentieth Century Fund, the Rockefeller Brothers Fund, and the National Endowment for the Arts. The Fund, Berkowitz explains, "began by buying up blocks of tickets to forthcoming plays of artistic merit but uncertain commercial strength and reselling them at a discount to students and similar groups, thereby encouraging new audiences while giving the productions a financial buffer." Among the notable plays produced as a result were Lanford Wilson's *The Hot l Baltimore* (pr. 1973), Jason Miller's *That Championship Season* (pr. 1972), and Arthur Kopit's *Wings* (pr. 1978).

Finally, the greatest of all financial boosters for both Broadway and Off-Broadway theatergoers, the half-price tickets booth on Duffy Square (called TKTS), opened in 1973, a boon sponsored by the Theatre Development Fund. Discount vouchers for Off-Off-Broadway productions supplemented the half-price sales at the TKTS booth. The impact of the Theatre Development Fund was felt across the country, and the influence of the half-price idea carried as far as London's Leicester Square, where the English implemented a similar arrangement. Ironically, the prices of theater tickets in London, already low, since many of the English theaters were subsidized, were cut in half by the English borrowing of the American half-price idea.

In time, Off-Broadway became in its way a minor Broadway as it underwent its own institutionalizing. Prominent among the theater groups in this transitional period were Joseph Papp's Public Theatre, Lynn Meadow's Manhattan Theatre Club, the Hudson Guild Theatre, the American Place Theatre, and the Roundabout Theatre. Financial pressures exerted their influence here, as they had on Broadway, and smaller groups sprouted, such as Ellen Stewart's Café La Mama. Off-Off-Broadway also enjoyed a groundswell in the 1960's.

As a result of this minor but flourishing stage renaissance, many dramatists were provided with opportunities to write and to have their plays produced, opportunities that would not have existed without the subsidies. Both the established Off-Broadway theater and the Off-Off-Broadway efforts can be seen as the offspring of the theater of the 1920's, when the Provincetown Players figured so importantly in bringing about America's coming of age in drama, but without subsidies or a tradition behind them.

Among the newcomers to the stage scene in the 1960's were a number of black dramatists. When Lorraine Hansberry wrote plays in the late 1950's, blacks were still referred to as "Negroes," and her play *A Raisin in the Sun* (pr. 1959) evokes the period flavor of her time. Amiri Baraka (LeRoi

Jones) opposed the merging of blacks into the mainstream of white drama, and his *Dutchman* (pr. 1964) has earned for itself a place in the John Gassner/Bernard F. Dukore anthology, *A Treasury of the Theatre* (1970). Ed Bullins also writes outside the mainstream theater; like O'Neill before him, Bullins has attempted an ambitious cycle of plays. His first volume of plays, published in 1969, includes *Goin'a Buffalo* (pr. 1968), *A Son, Come Home* (pr. 1968), and *The Electronic Nigger* (pr. 1968), all three of which were produced at the American Place Theatre. In the 1975 season, *The Taking of Miss Janie* won the New York Drama Critics Circle Award. The strong black movement was associated with the Negro Ensemble Company, and small theaters devoted to black populations sprang up across the country, particularly in cities with large black populations.

Another group of dramatists became vocal during the 1960's, a group which still finds itself the least accepted of minority movements on the stage. Explicitly homosexual or gay drama found expression in groups such as the Ridiculous Theatrical Company. For them, the main mode of dramatizing the homosexual experience is farce or, at least, a farcical tone, even when psychological realism and poignant emotion are central to the play. Laughter seems to be the means by which uncomfortable subjects gain some measure of acceptance on the stage. Writers, producers, and actors such as Martin Duberman, Robert Patrick, Charles Ludlam, Ronald Tavel, and Kenneth Bernard are important figures in the development of gay drama in this narrow sense.

The 1960's also saw the emergence of a number of women dramatists, most of whom were writing within the traditions of the contemporary feminist movement. The consciousness-raising function of the movement tended to limit the appeal and, some maintain, the quality of the drama thus produced. Among the groups founded to encourage women dramatists are the Womanspace Theatre in New York, the Circle of the Witch in Minneapolis, the Washington Area Feminist Theatre in Washington, and Interart Theatre in New York. As a group, the feminist playwrights were more loosely organized and more diverse in both content and style than were other minority dramatists. These women appear in Honor Moore's 1977 anthology, *The New Women's Theatre: Ten Plays by Contemporary American Women*, which includes plays by Corinne Jacker, Joanna Russ, Ursule Molinaro, Tina Howe, Honor Moore, Alice Childress, Ruth Wolff, Joanna Kraus, and Myrna Lamb and a stage arrangement by Eve Merriam, Paula Wagner, and Jack Hoffsiss.

Two women dramatists whose plays were brought to the national scene in the late 1970's through the Actors' Theatre of Louisville are Marsha Norman, whose *'Night Mother* (pr. 1981), her fifth play, won for her both critical acclaim (including a Pulitzer Prize in 1983) and commercial success, and Mississippi-bred Beth Henley, whose bizarre comedies about middle-class life in the South (most notably *Crimes of the Heart*, pr. 1979, which won a Pulitzer Prize in 1981), have enjoyed performances across the country as well as in New York.

The 1970's

All three minority movements discussed above (black, gay, female) were part of a larger new wave of American dramatists from which emerged several particularly promising playwrights. In this new wave, two interesting phenomena developed: one involving a popular playwright who wrote steadily for Broadway and for film, Neil Simon, and the other involving a quartet of dramatists who started their careers in small theaters and who have continued to develop steadily: David Rabe, Lanford Wilson, David Mamet, and Sam Shepard. The last two have demonstrated a uniqueness of style that sets them apart as writers with the potential to join the ranks of O'Neill, Miller, Williams, and Albee.

Neil Simon began his career as a writer for television comedians such as Sid Caesar. On the stage, Simon became famous for his play *The Odd Couple* (pr. 1965). Having made a reputation with his jokes (particularly his one-liners) and with his technical mastery of the television-style situation comedy, he enjoys popularity among middle-class audiences. According to Berkowitz, Simon is—"in purely financial terms—the most successful playwright in the history of the world, with (among other records) more Broadway performances of his plays in the 1960's than Williams, Miller, Albee, Inge, Pinter, [John] Osborne and [Richard] Rodgers put together." Jewish and New York-born, Simon stems from the tradition of Odets and Chayefsky in his concern with the little man who has big dreams and for whom his dreams are the only escape from a dull existence. Another recurring concern is the mismatched couple, whether they be roommates, husband and wife, or lovers. Like the British playwright Alan Ayckbourn, with whom he is frequently compared, Simon is capable of a Chekhovian brand of humor that challenges his reputation as merely an exceptionally slick writer of popular plays. His autobiographical trilogy, *Brighton Beach*, *Biloxi Blues*, and *Broadway Bound*, amply illustrates his ability to sustain a seriousness that tones down his predilection for gag lines.

Lanford Wilson arrived in New York from the Midwest and West and provided the Caffé Cino, a major Off-Off-Broadway enterprise, with its first success, *The Madness of Lady Bright* (pr. 1964). He helped establish the Circle Theatre Company and became a resident playwright at a time when Off-Broadway productions were beginning to find their way uptown. Wilson's *Hot l Baltimore*, still his best-known play, and his Missouri trilogy about the Talley family, comprising *Fifth of July* (pr. 1978), *A Tale Told* (pr. 1981), and *Talley's Folly* (pr. 1979), are deeply rooted in American social consciousness. An early play, *Balm in Gilead* (pr. 1965), enjoyed unusual success when revived in 1984; the play in a run-down New York café and its assortment of characters recalls O'Neill's *The Iceman Cometh.*

Also establishing himself by means of Off-Broadway residency (the Public Theatre of Joseph Papp), David Rabe, a Vietnam veteran, has continued the tradition of *What Price Glory?* in a trilogy of plays about the Vietnam experience: *The Basic Training of Pavlo Hummel* (pr. 1971), *Sticks and Bones* (pr. 1969), and *Streamers* (pr. 1976). During a time of civil unrest and heightened protest, *Sticks and Bones*, which concerns the return of a blind veteran to an America that does not understand him, won a Tony Award. Rabe's *The Basic Training of Pavlo Hummel* has been likened to Bertolt Brecht's *Man Is Man* (pr. 1926) for its expressionistic style.

Like Wilson and Rabe, David Mamet has a career closely tied to the small theaters. His *A Life in the Theatre* (pr. 1977) and *American Buffalo* (pr. 1975) were staged at the Goodman Theatre in Chicago, and *Sexual Perversity in Chicago* (pr. 1974) premiered at the student-founded Organic Theatre Company. Mamet himself helped found a series of small theaters in the Chicago area.

Lean in language, character, and plot, Mamet's theater has affinities with the minimalism of Harold Pinter, and like Pinter, Mamet, more than any other American dramatist, employs characters and situations that are dominated by, indeed created by, language and language rhythms. *American Buffalo* is a play in which nothing much happens except that three very limited and inarticulate would-be petty thieves hatch a plan that is never implemented. The thrust and parry of the dialogue constitutes the action of the play; the rightly controlled speech rhythms and the elemental human situations—security, threat, intrusion, and dispossession—are compelling. The same elements can be found in *A Life in the Theatre*, about a pair of actors, one aging and one young, and in *Duck Variations* (pr. 1972), a conversation between two old men on a park bench. *Glengarry Glen Ross*, about real estate salesmen in Florida selling land that does not exist, spins out a similar situation in a more complexly plotted play. Both *American Buffalo* and *Glengarry Glen Ross* were successful Broadway productions, the latter appearing during the same season in which a production of *Death of a Salesman*, as noted above, featured Dustin Hoffman's perky, energetic Willy Loman. Without the social morality of Miller as a dominant idea, but with a devastating linguistic hilarity, Mamet brilliantly accomplishes by a different means what Miller achieved in his classic play. *Speed the Plow* (pr. 1988), complementing *American Buffalo* and *Glengarry Glen Ross*, extends the selling myth in an even more scathingly comic satire on the dark undergirdings of American culture.

Sam Shepard, having written more than forty plays, has built a solid reputation among critics and scholars. The reputation rests on his archetypical view of America, in which folklore (cowboy and desperado) and fantasy blend with a high threaticality of style that is inimitably his. The heroic cowboy psyche struts through his contemporary characters in the persons of the faded rock star Hoss in *The Tooth of Crime* (pr. 1972) and of Slim and Shadow in *Back Bog Beast Bait* (pr. 1971), two Jesse James-like characters who wander in search of people with enemies. *True West* (pr. 1980) pits a slick Hollywood writer against an uncouth brother; by the end of the play, the two have reversed roles. Elemental forces are released in the conflict between a man and a woman in *Fool for Love* (pr. 1983). Like the Gary Cooper figure of *High Noon* (1952), the cowboy and the hired gun search for scores to settle, knowing that one day they themselves will become victims. In Shepard's family plays, *Curse of the Starving Class* and *Buried Child* (pr. 1978), the effects of the American myth are seen in the familial lives of the characters, while *Operation Sidewinder* (pr. 1970) demonstrates the myth at work in the area of technology. *A Lie of the Mind* (pr. 1985), more encompassing than either of its predecessors (*Curse of the Starving Class* and *Buried Child*), rounds out what constitutes a trilogy of Shepard's family plays. Shepard represents graphically the split between the commercial and the small theaters. Like Wilson, Rabe, and Mamet, Shepard has his roots in the Off-Off Broadway and Off-Broadway movement, his first play, *Cowboys* (pr. 1964), having been staged at Theatre Genesis.

Shepard's plays, mythical and fantastic, require visceral performances in which Jungian levels of American consciousness in all of their violence are explored. His unique re-creation of the American myth recalls O'Neill's concern with pipe dreams, Williams' with the strain of Puritanism, Miller's with conscience, and Albee's with a moral wasteland.

Both Shepard and Mamet have been produced frequently in London. *Curse of the Starving Class* and *Glengarry Glen Ross* were given premiere productions at London's prestigious Royal Court Theatre and National Theatre, respectively. These two playwrights, with their distinctive voices, appear to be the inheritors of the tradition carried forward by O'Neill, Williams, Miller, and Albee.

The 1980's and 1990's

Since Shepard and Mamet, no dramatist has appeared with the innovative impact of either of these two writers. Instead, a number of traditional dramatists who began writing plays in the 1970's (and even earlier) have made their mark in the Off-Broadway theaters in New York. A. R. Gurney, John Guare, and Romulus Linney, with roots in the academic/literary tradition, have assumed increasing prominence. Incorporating some elements of the prevailing Beckettian or Brechtian theater, each in his unique way has reinvented themes and styles of earlier writers.

An example is Gurney's *The Cocktail Hour* (pr. 1988), which not only plays on T. S. Eliot's themes in *The Cocktail Party* but also is replete with literary allusions. A central theme in most of Gurney's dramas is the fading tradition of the middle-class, white Anglo-Saxon, Protestant ethic in the United States. A striking illustration is *The Dining Room* (pr. 1982), about a family, depicted as each generation adheres to, or departs from, the attitudes and values of the preceding generation. The title, *The Old Boy* (pr. 1991), speaks for itself. *Who Killed Richard Cory?* (pr. 1976), a reference to a character from a poem by Edwin Arlington Robinson, and *The Perfect Party* (pr. 1985) are among the nearly twenty dramas in which the rituals of the dominant WASP class are analyzed with a mixture of poignancy, humor, and criticism.

Influenced by Chekhov, Ibsen, and Shaw, John Guare, best known for *The House of Blue Leaves* (pr. 1971), *Six Degrees of Separation* (pr. 1990), and *Four Baboons Adoring the Sun* (pr. 1992), explores the American Dream myth. *Six Degrees of Separation*, a play based on an actual event reported in *The New York Times*, focuses on an ingenious youthful impostor who finds his way into the intimate lives of the affluent. Utilizing at times, as in *The House of Blue Leaves*, elements of Absurdist techniques, Guare has said that he writes about those whose dreams "of the future and outside the house were greater than their ability to enjoy what was right there in the house." In *Four Baboons Adoring the Sun*, a couple, with children from previous marriages, realize their dreams, but at the expense of the death of one of their many children. The Greek sense of tragedy slowly evolves to a climax involving the interfering jealousy of the gods in a twentieth century re-creation of the Icarus myth.

Romulus Linney, the most academic of the three playwrights, roots his dramas in political, social, and historical matters. Influenced by O'Neill, Friedrich Dürrenmatt, Albee, and Pinter, he has written about historical and literary figures, relating these to contemporary situations and attitudes: *The Sorrows of Frederick* (pr. 1917), about a father-son relationship; *The Love Suicide at Schofield Barracks* (pr. 1972), about Vietnam War issues; *Childe Byron* (pr. 1977), about a father-daughter relationship; and *Three Poets* (pr. 1989), three one-act plays, each about a female poet.

August Wilson, an African American dramatist, developed a solid reputation in one decade with *Ma Rainey's Black Bottom* (pr. 1984), *Fences* (pr. 1985), *Joe Turner's Come and Gone* (pr. 1986), and *The Piano Lessons* (pr. 1988). All were first produced at the Yale Repertory Theater and then moved to New York. His play *Two Trains Running* (pr. 1990), Wilson has said, is yet another illustration of his interest in the folkloric aspects of black culture. An important new black voice as well as an inheritor of the Langston Hughes tradition, he updates humorously and poignantly themes to be found in earlier black writers.

Along with Gurney, Guare, Linney, and Wilson, the direction toward traditionalism includes other articulate, critically applauded writers, the youngest of these being Jon Robin Baitz (*The Substance of Fire*, pr., pb. 1991) and (*The End of the Day*, pr., pb. 1992). Scott McPherson, whose *Marvin's Room* swept nearly all the Off-Broadway awards in 1992, joins, among others, Christopher Durang, Craig Lucas, Herb Gardner, and Donald Margulies in a postmodern era, a term loosely designating a time of consolidation of tradition and innovation.

Susan Rusinko

AFRICAN DRAMA

English-language countries in Sub-Sahara Africa include Nigeria, Ghana, Sierra Leone, Gambia, and Liberia in the west; Uganda, Kenya, and Tanzania in the east; Malawi, Zambia, and Zimbabwe in the center; and the Republic of South Africa, Swaziland, Botswana, and Lesotho in the south. Several of these countries have produced a considerable body of drama and can serve as representatives of the activity that is taking place in Anglophone countries throughout Africa.

In all of these countries, scripted drama in English developed even later than other written forms, perhaps because, as Cosmo Pieterse and others have suggested, traditional community life still satisfied the dramatic instinct through rituals involving music and dance and through oral narrative—both forms in which the audience was not only spectator but also participant. The potential of African drama, once established, stemmed from its ritual character and became evident soon after independence (after 1960). African plays, in capitalizing on the ritual element, usually go beyond the need for mere entertainment in the search for cultural identity and social cohesion.

African plays fall generally into two categories: those that are immediately accessible to Western audiences, since they rely primarily on dialogue and a tightly knit structure, with personal conflict, rising action, climax, and denouement; and those that show the influence of such structures but that return to forms of community ritual. The first group seems intended partially for audiences beyond Africa, with an eye on publication by foreign presses. One effect, if not motive, of such drama is to make Africa a part of the international community. The other group often disparages such concerns and focuses attention solely on an African audience, on the education, self-awareness, and cohesion of the African community. Many such plays therefore use the local idiom and unless translated are inaccessible not only to the outside world but also to other Africans. Still, a large body of drama, even in the second group, relies on English—with only scattered uses of local language for song or intimate dialogue—because dramatists need English to reach beyond their own ethnic groups. One must insist, however, that no English-language play has the integrative quality of traditional drama, religious or secular. Cut off from the ceremonial, ritual life of the people, it is not "African" in that fundamental sense.

Some permanent theater sites exist, most notably at large universities in urban areas, but traveling companies attempt to reach the people directly. One alternative has been to encourage high schools to establish acting groups. A popular form of contemporary drama is the radio play. The British Broadcasting Corporation's African Theatre Series has twice sponsored competitions, the second one in 1971-1972, to encourage the writing and production of plays by Africans. Such plays, written for radio, were necessarily short, designed as thirty-minute programs. Brevity has been characteristic of other African plays as well. They are frequently one-acts, simple in outline and action, often using between two and five characters. The plays can be subtle, even ambiguous, in their statements. A play of simple dialogue can have far-reaching symbolic overtones. What appears to be direct statement about a social or political situation contains nuances that one should perhaps expect from a culture accustomed to proverbial and ritualistic speech. The brevity of the plays may have something to do with their appeal to a broad audience, but it does not imply any absence of subtlety or sophistication in dealing with personal or social issues. Further, even in the short, well-made plays, the characters are not so much individuals as "ritual" representations. They invite the audience to be participants rather than spectators. African plays, at their best, have suggestions of communal experience.

In East Africa, Kenya and Uganda have been the most active dramatically. Mackerere University in Uganda, with its own traveling theater company, has had a tremendous impact. The plays that have come out of this region, despite considerable diversity, have common, identifiable features. For the most part, they are well made. With the exception of Ngugi wa Thiong'o (who wrote as James T. Ngugi until 1970), the dramatists rely on simple, intimate situations, choosing to reveal the larger social setting within the microcosm of a small group. Even when the setting is a traditional village, either in the past or in contemporary times, with one or two exceptions the complicating features of song, dance, and ritual are absent. In addition, a pervasive motif preoccupies dramatists, whether they are speaking of the traditional life of the people or the modern conflict between African and non-African, both European and otherwise: On the most basic level, the motif is self-aggrandizement, an imposition of the self on others. In Ugandan plays, especially, self-aggrandizement frequently leads to self-destruction as well. Nuwa Sentongo's *The Invisible Bond* (pb. 1975) is a paradigm of this theme. Kibaate murders his wife's beloved only to have the corpse return to haunt him. While he slowly becomes a slave to this dead master, his wife is killed and joins her lover, Damulira, in death. In the background of the personal conflict, somewhat a rarity in published Ugandan plays, night-walkers (cannibals), acting as a chorus of dancers, stalk the dead, first calling up Damulira, then Kibaate's wife, as food for their tables. The feeding of one upon another attains a level of ritual condemnation. Elvania Namukwaya Zirimu in *Family Spear* (pr. 1972; radio play) and Tom Omara in *The Exodus* (pr. 1965) call into question the role of tradition in sanctioning such behavior. In both plays, the ancestral spear, the symbol of authority, signifies the continuing power of tradition to prevent a sensitive response to the human needs of the present.

Several Ugandan and Kenyan dramatists are of Asian (Indian or Pakistani) ancestry. Their special situation within the African setting raises issues of race, of belonging, and of patriotism. Significantly, however, the theme of self-aggrandizement remains the key concern. Jagjit Singh's *Sweet Scum of Freedom* (pr. 1972; radio play) ennobles the "scum," or victims, of society (the heroine is a prostitute) and suggests strongly a desire for self-destruction in those who exploit them. Ganesh Bagchi shows, in *Of Malice and Men* (pb. 1968), the difficulty an Indian, Sudhin, and an Englishman, Michael Knight, have in getting outside their ideologies to establish a personal relationship with a young Indian woman, Sona. One sees them both impose their ideologies on themselves and on her. What constitutes a modern African state, what responsibilities individuals have to themselves and to their country, what race, ideology, and tradition have to do with identity within the state, and, most specifically, what happens to individuals who fail to acknowledge the rights of others within the society—these are the concerns of Ugandan drama of the 1960's and 1970's.

Kenya's dramatists, Kuldip Sondhi and Ngugi wa Thiong'o, are representative of the same situation as in Uganda. Although he was educated in Kenya, Sondhi was born in West Pakistan and thus is sensitive to the social ostracism that characterizes the modern African state. In his plays, this emerges as an imposition of one culture's or one person's values or prejudices on another. In *The Magic Pool* (pb. 1972), it is the social rejection of a hunchback; in the radio play *Sunil's Dilemma* (pr. 1970), it is the invasion of an Asian's home by Africans identified as both thieves and police. *With Strings* (pb. 1968) warns of the imposition of the past on the present. When a wealthy uncle, who, for whatever motive, uses a promise of money to influence critical decisions in the lives of the younger generation, suddenly dies of a heart attack, the hand of the past releases its grip, the young Indian man and African woman who are the play's focus can make their decision about marriage without prejudice, and, it would seem, the two races can merge, albeit with some difficulty. In *Undesignated* (pb. 1968), Sondhi explores what appears to be a personal dilemma (he is both engineer and writer). The main character, an African named Solomon, is tempted to become the head of a department in an engineering firm so that he can have wealth and influence, motives that are ultimately self-destructive. Because another is chosen for the position, however, he is forced to use his talents as an artist instead, to the benefit of both himself and his country. Sondhi's play *Encounter* (pb. 1968) not only reiterates this theme but also does so in a context that is more common to the work of Ngugi wa Thiong'o. Two encounters, one between a British lieutenant and a fellow officer, the other between the lieutenant and a rebel, General Nyati, reveal the power of ideology and cultural loyalties. Both the lieutenant and the general are idealists, but the force of the general's personality prevails because it is ultimately in the service of freedom and not of exploitation.

Ngugi wa Thiong'o, as the most prominent figure in East African literature, deserves much more extensive treatment than is possible here. He is mainly known as a novelist and a critic of Western exploitation. His plays are not as powerful as his novels, but they explore the same themes and allow him to speak his political views directly to the people. Ngugi combines in a more complex way than the other East African dramatists the three common elements in African drama: the sociopolitical context, traditional modes of performance (song, dance, and oral narrative), and personal dialogue that captures with intimacy the consequences of forces at work in contemporary Africa. *This Time Tomorrow* (pr. 1967) contrasts a narrator-journalist, whose view of the slums in Nairobi is rhetorical, insensitive, and exploitive, and a stranger, who enters the slums just before their removal in order to incite the people against the government. When the stranger is arrested, the people fail to support him. The play ends with a young woman leaving her homeless mother to marry into wealth. This pattern of the seduced woman recurs in Ngugi's work. In *I Will Marry When I Want* (pb. 1982; with Ngugi wa Mirii), first produced in the Gikuyu language in 1977, the beautiful daughter of a poor, exploited family is seduced by the son of the family's exploiter. The family sees its condition deteriorate, partly through its own lapse of will, as even the one piece of land left to it is cleverly bargained away.

The most powerful and innovative of Ngugi's plays is *The Trial of Dedan Kimathi* (pr. 1974; with Micere Githae-Mugo). Using a variety of juxtaposed scenes, it captures the trial of this famous rebel leader, the children who grow up amid the injustices of the British system, and the seduced young woman who has recovered her identity and become a part of the rebel movement. The final act is a positive, courageous gesture of the two children, motivated by the woman's persuasive presence, to attempt to save Kimathi during the sentencing. Ngugi applies the theme of exploitation to a cultural attack against the exploiter. His concern, evident in the theme and in the form, is not primarily the self-destructiveness of the victimizer but rather the effects on the victims and the need for revolutionary change in the social structure: a return to communal values and traditional attitudes toward property and personal worth.

After his exile from Kenya in 1978, Ngugi settled in London. While less active in the theater, his novels *Caitaani Mutharaba-Ini* (1980; *Devil on the Cross*, 1982) and *Matigari ma Njiruungi* (1986; *Matigari*, 1989) and his political commentary *Decolonising the Mind: The Politics of Language in African Literature* (1986) have kept him in the public eye.

The Republic of South Africa offers a variety of plays written in English. The least compelling of them seem carbon copies of plays from other countries in Africa. They are not uninteresting, but they do not seem to arise from the particular complex of issues in the South African setting. Alfred Hutchinson's *Fusane's Trial* (pb. 1968), for example, deals with a typical conflict between the old and new cultures. A young girl, Fusane, refuses to become the fourth wife of an old man. Before the actual marriage ceremony, he forces himself upon her. In defending herself against rape, she kills him. When the court finds her innocent, her family is both penitent and joyous. New concepts of love and marriage win over the old. Arthur Maimane's *The Opportunity* (pb. 1968) deals with the ironies of a domestic situation in which a former leader in the rebel cause must divorce his wife and marry an educated woman in order to be eligible for a post as Ambassador to the United Nations. The authority he wields according to custom makes it easy to take this symbolic step into the modern world.

In other plays, technical experimentation is at least as important as the conflict itself. Cosmo Pieterse, one of the most prominent figures in the African theater—an editor of numerous texts and an actor as well as a dramatist—has attempted poetic drama in his *Ballad of the Cells* (pb. 1972). In Credo V. Mutwa's intriguing *uNosilimela* (pb. 1981), the "experimentation"—if that is what it should be called—is an incorporation of traditional modes. *uNosilimela* is an epic tracing of uNosilimela's journey from mythical origins to her experiences in modern South African settings—her fall from grace, sufferings, abuse, and eventual return to the family. The final act is accompanied by the Apocalypse: the end of the white regime, the end of apartheid, and the attainment of Eden for South African blacks. The play uses allegory, myth, dream, music, dance, and ritual. It is not a well-made play, nor does it appeal primarily to an international audience. It is an indigenous play written for the people. Though the predominant language is English, some conversation and the songs and ritual portions are conducted in local languages. It may be the most "authentically" African play yet published.

The one playwright who has most clearly spoken for the creative potential of South Africa and the entire African experience is Athol Fugard, considered South Africa's premier and most contentious playwright and "the greatest active playwright in English." Fugard, who has directed and appeared in several of his own works, has built his reputation on four seminal but highly theatrical works: *The Blood Knot* (pr. 1961, pb. 1963), *Boesman and Lena* (pr., pb. 1969), *A Lesson from Aloes* (pr. 1978, pb. 1981), and *"MASTER HAROLD" . . . and the Boys* (pr., pb. 1982). His later dramatic output includes *The Road to Mecca* (pr. 1984, pb. 1985), *Place with the Pigs* (pr. 1987, pb. 1988), and *My Children! My Africa!* (pr., pb. 1990).

Plays that are most interesting to an international audience, perhaps, are those that deal directly with the apartheid system. They are inevitably critical of the system, but with varying degrees of intensity and subtlety. The approach is generally that of most African writers, with the exception of

Ngugi: a concentration on a particularized and limited situation that reflects the social setting rather than a broad social and political attack. Harold Kimmel's two-act play *The Cell* (pb. 1972) focuses on two prisoners in the same cell, a Boer extremist and a Jewish liberal. In act 1, Peter reduces Levine to the status of a black in an apartheid state; in the second act, Levine uses the leverage of truth about Peter's activities and motives to create a Socialist state. Richard Rive, in *Resurrection* (pb. 1972), attacks racism directly and, in his radio play *Make Like Slaves* (pb. 1972), suggests more subtly the difficulty of crossing the racial line. An aggressive white woman and a "coloured" man not only have some difficulty understanding each other but also find no way to enter a third world, that of the blacks. David Lytton's *Episodes of an Easter Rising* (pb. 1972) is a sensitive treatment of two older white women who take up residence in an isolated region because racial conflict takes up too much time from the act of living. They are thrown into the conflict, however, when they humanely and instinctively befriend a revolutionary leader, "the man," and protect him from the police. They eventually realize their involvement and at the end confirm their commitment by taking in the family of a black man who has died in a seditious act. Lytton thus suggests that the line between the races is not an unsurmountable barrier.

The plays of West Africa are distinctly different from those of the East and South. Since Europeans did not settle there and take away the land, racial conflict and demands for the recovery of economic and political rights are not major themes. It is not the residual colonial presence, or ideology, or patriotism that primarily motivates West African drama. Plays from this region tend to be exposés of political, social, or economic chaos, or of the corruption among the high and low officials who have replaced the white bureaucracy. Some of the plays attempt to deal with the conflict of values between the old and new cultures; they often broach such topics with detachment and even with a comic spirit. These plays of West Africa are typically busier than their counterparts elsewhere on the continent, as though their purpose were to capture the fullness of life, especially in the modern urban centers and marketplaces, through local color, dialect, and a wide variety of characterization and mood.

Sanya Dosunmu's *God's Deputy* (pb. 1972) is a Cinderella story set in Nigeria in the late nineteenth century. The divine right of a local king is enough to overcome all obstacles to permit him to marry the beautiful princess, the daughter of a village chief. The play incorporates the paraphernalia of traditional customs—children's games, a festival, the Egungun dance, symbols of various gods such as Ogun and Esu—but it is, in the final analysis, a light piece of entertainment, a musical. Kofi Awoonor's *Ancestral Power* (pb. 1972) is a dialogue between a proponent of the past and a man of the new age. The traditionalist claims to possess powers from his dead ancestors, only to be abruptly exposed as a braggart and coward. His exposure raises questions about the tradition itself and suggests the necessity of entering reasonably into the twentieth century, yet the twist at the end is more cleverness than dramatic peripeteia. Gordon Tialobi attempts Kafkaesque nightmare in his radio play *Full-Cycle* (pr. 1971). General Maga is arrested by revolutionaries, tried, sentenced, and executed. He wakes up to find that it was all a dream but then experiences the same thing again as either another nightmare or reality. The clever ambiguity and the surrealistic mode detach the audience from the psychological and political theme. Ngugi would not dissipate the force of his attack by such dramatic devices.

As noted above, a popular vein in West African drama is the largely comic treatment of bribery, corruption, and business dealings in the modern city. Imme Ikiddeh in *Blind Cyclos* (pb. 1968) applies poetic justice to Olemu, the Minister of Housing, who uses his position to demand "kola" or bribery for his special favors. A local medicine man, also seen as a prophet, turns the tables by casting a spell on him. Not only does he charge him an enormous fee for his services, but also he puts into motion a series of events that lead to Olemu's arrest and exposure. Femi Euba's *The Game* (pb. 1968) turns the old society upside down as a wealthy businessman's second wife takes a lover (polygamy reversed), and a beggar takes advantage of the situation through deceit, bribery, and the selling of information to enter the world of high finance. There is no difference between the beggar and the businessman whom he is exploiting. The Ghanaian dramatist Patience Henaku Addo, in a typical portrait of city life, *Company Pot* (pr. 1972; radio play), traces the education of a young girl in the ways of the city; she has to face seduction, con games, drugs, and prostitution, but survives a wiser woman.

This mixture of romance, comedy, and satire, however, is not the whole picture. In Derlene Clems's indictment of Ghanaian bureaucracy in *The Prisoner, the Judge, and the Jailor*, first broadcast in 1971, the ingratiating hand of friendship and fellow suffering quickly becomes the grip of the law. The artistry of the play reinforces rather than dissipates emotional effect. Jacob Hevi, in his play *Amavi* (pb. 1975), traces a Ghanaian peasant woman's life to show how, for twenty years, she has been exploited. Among the most famous of the West African dramatists is John Pepper Clark-Bekederemo. His play *Song of a Goat* (pr., pb. 1961) makes sexual impotence a tragic event. It attempts to capture and preserve a way of life that modern audiences, even in regarding that particular play, find hard to appreciate.

Wole Soyinka, who gives an especially sensitive reading of *Song of a Goat* in his book *Myth, Literature, and the African World* (1976), is the one figure of West African drama who not only represents the qualities already mentioned but also, as an accomplished and gifted writer, has realized their potential. He has attempted practically every mode of drama, from farce to Swiftian satire and tragedy, sometimes mixing modes in one play. He has received criticism for not using his talent in more patriotic ways— for being too much the artist, not enough the social critic—but a Western reader is likely to view this "fault" as a virtue. Soyinka's successful merger of psychological realism, dramatic form, and mythical substructure gives historical continuity to a specific situation and raises drama to a ritual level. Soyinka, who won the Nobel Prize in Literature in 1986, has moved away from the dramatic genre to concentrate on poetry and essays. His later plays were *A Play of Giants* (pr., pb. 1984) and *Requiem for a Futurologist* (pb. 1985).

Scripted African drama in the English language is still in its infancy, but dramatic activity is extensive. For various reasons—political, cultural, aesthetic—the commitment to the form is real.

Thomas Banks
(Revised by *Thomas J. Taylor*)

AFRICAN-AMERICAN DRAMA

Seeking to extricate the power of African-American music and dance from the stereotypes and trivializations of minstrelsy in its various forms, African-American dramatists have struggled throughout the twentieth century to locate or create an audience receptive to the full range of their thematic and theatrical concerns. The attempt to develop an autonomous style without sacrificing all access to production confronts African-American playwrights, collectively and individually, with a paradoxical situation in which they must first demonstrate their mastery of traditionally European-American themes and techniques to dispel stereotypes concerning African-American ability and character.

Faced with tensions between their African- and European-American audiences, and with class tensions within the black audience, African-American dramatists have followed three distinct paths. Some, concentrating on commercial success in the predominantly white mainstream American theater, have contributed to Broadway-style revues only tangentially concerned with challenging inherited conceptions of African-American experience. More self-consciously literary playwrights, usually working on the margins of the commercial theater, have occasionally achieved some commercial success with plays designed to increase white awareness of the variety and complexities of the African-American experience. Increasingly, however, serious African-American dramatists have sought to address directly an African-American audience, frequently but, given the cultural and economic realities of the United States, by no means exclusively in theaters located in the black communities.

Ed Bullins, a major figure in both contemporary and African-American drama, describes this historical development and contemporary direction in a statement that has exerted a substantial impact on the subsequent development of the tradition:

> With the present Black Writers turned away from addressing an anticipated white readership and appealing the plight of Blackness in America to their masochistic delight, the literature has changed from a social-protest oriented form to one of a dialectical nature among Black people—Black dialectics—and this new thrust has two main branches—the dialectic of change and the dialectic of experience. The writers are attempting to answer questions concerning Black survival and future, one group through confronting the Black/white reality of America, the other, by heightening the dreadful white reality of being a modern Black captive and victim. These two major branches in the mainstream of the new Black creativity, the dialectic of change (once called protest writing, surely, when confronting whites directly and angrily, then altered to what was called Black revolutionary writing when it shifted . . . away from a white audience to a Black) and the dialectic of experience (or being), sometimes merge, but *variety* and *power* in the overall work are the general rule.

As Bullins suggests, early African-American dramatists and performers did in fact anticipate a white audience or, in the rare case where the plays were published, a white readership. Complicating matters was that audience's familiarity with the minstrel shows, such as that of Thomas Rice, which developed in the South as early as the 1830's and enjoyed a vogue well into the twentieth century. Originally performed by whites in blackface imitating songs and dances they had witnessed in slave communities, the minstrel shows rapidly developed into travesties with no direct relationship to any actual African-American culture. By the time blacks formed their own troupes after the Civil War, the minstrel stereotypes were so firmly established that black performers were forced to add the familiar blackface makeup if they wished to attract an audience.

Despite this pressure to correspond to preconceived stage images, however, several black dramatists, and especially black performers, established serious reputations during the nineteenth century. Actors such as Ira Aldridge and Victor Séjour, who performed primarily in Europe, also wrote plays on racial themes, as did William Wells Brown, whose abolitionist play *The Escape: Or, A Leap for Freedom* (pr. 1858) is generally credited as the first work of African-American dramatic literature. Paul Laurence Dunbar, who frequently performed his own dialect poetry for white audiences grounded in the neo-minstrel stereotypes of the plantation tradition, collaborated with Will Marion Cook on *Clorindy: Or, The Origin of the Cakewalk* (pr. 1898), the first African-American play to receive a full-scale commercial production. Although Bob Cole's *A Trip to Coontown* (pr. 1898) was produced by blacks, it was not until 1916 that a serious play written, acted, and produced by blacks was performed in the United States. Sponsored by the National Association for the Advancement of Colored People, Angelina Grimke's *Rachel* (pr. 1916), while addressed primarily to a white audience, did not pander to the stereotypes of tragic mulatto, black beast, or comic darky.

The movement in African-American drama from an exclusive address to the white audience toward Bullins' "black dialectics" began during the Harlem Renaissance of the 1920's. Responding to the growth of sizable African-American communities in northern urban centers, black playwrights seriously envisioned for the first time a theater not predicated entirely on white expectations. Companies such as Cleveland's Karamu House and Gilpin Players (named after Charles Gilpin, one of the first black actors to earn a major reputation as an actor on American stages), Philadelphia's Dunbar Theatre, and New York's influential Lafayette Players, along with the Krigwa Little Theatre movement, which under the sponsorship of W. E. B. DuBois established theaters in many large cities, provided proving ground for black actors and playwrights. At about the same time, plays by European-American dramatists, especially Ridgley Torrence (*The Rider of Dreams*, pr. 1917), DuBose and Dorothy Heyward (*Porgy*, pr. 1927), Paul

Green (the Pulitzer Prize-winning *In Abraham's Bosom*, pr. 1926), Marc Connelly (*The Green Pastures: A Fable*, pb. 1929), and Eugene O'Neill (*The Emperor Jones*, pr. 1920, and *All God's Chillun Got Wings*, pr. 1924) began to treat African-American characters and themes more seriously than had their predecessors. The presence of a black-oriented, if not yet predominantly black, audience, accompanied by the partial abatement of minstrel stereotypes, encouraged a significant number of African-American playwrights to begin working during the 1920's and 1930's.

Many, including Zora Neale Hurston (*Great Day*, pr. 1937), Wallace Thurman (*Harlem*, pr. 1929), Countée Cullen and Arna Bontemps (*God Sends Sunday*, pr. 1931), Georgia Douglas Johnson (*Plumes*, pb. 1927), Jean Toomer, and Langston Hughes, had previously worked and remain best known as poets and novelists. Others, including Frank Wilson (*Walk Together, Chillun*, pr. 1936), Hall Johnson (*Run Little Chillun*, pr. 1933), and especially Willis Richardson, established their reputations primarily as dramatists. Whatever their primary literary focus, however, the playwrights of the Harlem Renaissance responded to the call sounded by James Weldon Johnson in the preface to *The Book of American Negro Poetry* (1922) for a new type of artist who would do for African Americans "what [John Millington] Synge did for the Irish; he needs to find a form that will express the racial spirit by symbols from within rather than by symbols from without."

As Sterling Brown observed in *Negro Poetry and Drama* (1937), the plays written in response to this call were of two distinct types: the problem play, which extended the "political" tradition of Grimke and William Wells Brown, and the folk-life play, which to some extent attempted to reconstruct the materials that had been trivialized in the minstrel tradition. Among the most successful playwrights to work with both approaches was Richardson, who wrote a half-dozen plays of lasting interest, including *The Broken Banjo* (pr. 1925) and *The Chip Woman's Fortune* (pr. 1923), the first play by an African American produced on Broadway. More powerful as literature, Toomer's complex philosophical character study "Kabnis," published as section 3 of *Cane* (pb. 1923), a work incorporating prose and poetry as well as drama, presented insurmountable staging problems given the generic conventions of the era.

As the excitement of the Harlem Renaissance gave way to the political determination of African-American writing of the Great Depression era, attention gradually shifted away from the optimistic aesthetics of the influential critic Alain Locke, cofounder along with Montgomery Gregory of the Howard University Players, whose anthology *Plays of Negro Life* (1927) included work by both black and white writers. Supported by programs such as the Federal Theatre Project, playwrights such as Hughes and Theodore Ward, whose *Big White Fog* (pr. 1938) is widely considered the most powerful African-American play of the decade, contributed to the proletarian theater exemplified by European-American dramatists such as Clifford Odets. Despite the shift away from mainstream political positions, much pressure remained on black playwrights to align their views with those of their radical white contemporaries. Hughes, who began writing plays in the 1920's and had the first Broadway hit by an African-American playwright in *Mulatto*, which ran from 1935 to 1937, supported leftist political causes in plays such as *Scottsboro Limited* (pr. 1932), as did novelist Richard Wright, whose *Native Son* (1940) was a commercial success in a dramatic adaptation by Wright and white playwright Paul Green. While best known as a poet, Hughes continued to work in theater throughout his career, although he abandoned the explicitly political focus in later plays such as *Simply Heavenly* (pr. 1957) and *Tambourines to Glory* (pr. 1963).

The transition from a drama addressed to an anticipated white audience to Bullins' black dialectics accelerated after World War II, proceeding in two major phases. The first phase, involving recognition of serious African-American drama from a mainstream white audience, centered on the commercial and artistic success of a sequence of plays reinforcing the premises of the nonviolent civil rights movement of the 1950's and early 1960's. The second, heralded by LeRoi Jones/Amiri Baraka's stunning *Dutchman* (pr. 1964) and culminating in the community theater movement frequently associated with black nationalist politics, redirected attention to the internal concerns of the African-American community. By no means devoid of assertive political commitment, the plays of the first phase typically endorsed an integrationist philosophy, partially in deference to the anticipated white audience and partially as a result of the early successes and promise of Martin Luther King's interracial strategies. The first major success of the period, Louis Peterson's *Take a Giant Step* (pr. 1953), was followed rapidly by William Branch's *In Splendid Error* (pr. 1954), Alice Childress' *Trouble in Mind* (pr. 1955), and Ossie Davis' *Purlie Victorious* (pr. 1961).

The most significant plays of this phase were Lorraine Hansberry's *A Raisin in the Sun* (pr. 1959) and James Baldwin's *Blues for Mister Charlie* (pr. 1964). While Baldwin's play drew substantial critical and political attention largely as a result of his position as a novelist and community spokesman, *A Raisin in the Sun* is the first unarguably major contribution rof an African-American playwright to the dramatic literature of the United States. Focusing on the tensions between the members of an African-American family seeking to realize their individual conceptions of the American Dream, the play possesses a variety and power equal to that of any play written in the dominant realistic mode of the mainstream stage of the 1950's.

Although *Blues for Mister Charlie* failed to match the 530-performance run of *A Raisin in the Sun*, which won the New York Drama Critics Circle

Award for 1958-1959, the two plays established a lasting African American presence in American drama on Broadway, Off-Broadway, and Off-Off-Broadway as well as on community and regional stages previously devoted almost entirely to European-American drama. Douglas Turner Ward's Negro Ensemble Company has maintained a continuing presence Off-Broadway with productions such as Ward's own *Day of Absence* (pr. 1965) and Charles Fuller's *A Soldier's Play* (pr. 1982), which was the second Pulitzer Prize-winning play by an African-American dramatist. The first, Charles Gordone's brilliant Absurdist work *No Place to Be Somebody* (pr. 1969), produced by leading Off-Broadway producer Joseph Papp, reflects the developing avant-garde tradition in black theater. Several plays by Baraka, Bullins, and Adrienne Kennedy (*Funnyhouse of a Negro*, pr. 1964, and *A Rat's Mass*, pr. 1966) have had substantial influence on experimental dramatists outside the African-American community. Reflecting the continuing interaction of African- and European-American avant-garde theaters, *The Gospel at Collonus* (pr. 1983), an adaptation of Sophocles' work written by prominent white experimental playwright Lee Breuer but given its emotional power by the improvisational performance style of the all-black cast, followed *Dutchman* and several of Bullins' plays as winner of the Obie Award for best Off-Broadway play. Other plays by African American dramatists which have made a notable impact on mainstream audiences during the 1960's and 1970's include Lonne Elder's *Ceremonies in Dark Old Men* (pr. 1969) and Joseph Walker's *The River Niger* (pr. 1972).

While these playwrights have made an impact in the mainstream theatrical world, the energy of African-American drama since the mid-1960's derives in large part from the community theater movement spearheaded by Baraka and Bullins. Repudiating not only the focus on the white audience but also the emphasis of many earlier playwrights on the problems of the black middle class, these dramatists oriented their work toward the entire black community. In part, this shift can be attributed to the growing influence of the separatist philosophy of Malcolm X as the Civil Rights movement confronted a new set of problems in the North.

Baraka's *Dutchman* marked the major transition point in African-American theater, emphasizing the common position of all blacks, however fully assimilated into the mainstream. The climactic murder of the articulate black protagonist by a white woman, who has manipulated his complex self-consciousness, provided a symbol that exerted a major impact on younger playwrights such as Ron Milner, Jimmy Garrett, Richard Wesley, Marvin X, Sonia Sanchez, and Ben Caldwell. Working in community theaters such as Baraka's Spirit House of Newark, Bullins' and Robert Mac-Beth's New Lafayette Theater and Woodie King Jr.'s New Federal Theatre of New York, John O'Neal's Free Southern Theatre of Mississippi and New Orleans, Val Gray Ward's Kuumba Theatre of Chicago, and the Black Arts/

West of San Francisco, these playwrights struggled to create a theater designed specifically to reach an audience unlikely to attend traditional theatrical events. Drawing heavily on traditions of African and African-American music and dance, many of their plays, including Milner's *Who's Got His Own* (pr. 1966), Garrett's *And We Own the Night* (pr. 1967), and Wesley's *The Last Street Play* (pr. 1977), redirected "protests" intended for whites when presented in mainstream theaters toward the revolutionary, usually nationalist vision that Bullins associates with the "dialectic of change." Particularly in his Obie Award-winning *The Taking of Miss Janie* (pr. 1975) and in the plays from his ongoing Twentieth-Century Cycle that have been produced to date (most notably *In New England Winter*, pb. 1969, and *In the Wine Time*, pr. 1968), Bullins had demonstrated a thematic power and technical versatility matched in American drama only by O'Neill.

Although the community theater movement underwent substantial changes as racial issues assumed a less prominent position in public debate during the late 1970's and 1980's, its impact is evident in the works of dramatists who have chosen to work closer to the American mainstream. While African-American dramatists continue to confront pressure to orient their work toward a white audience, most of the simplistic stereotypes have been called into question to the extent that new playwrights, building on the achievements of Bullins and Baraka even while working from sharply differing political premises, are able to employ the power and beauty of the African-American performance traditions without needing to compromise their vision of the complexity of African-American life.

In 1985, African-American drama began de-emphasizing the revolutionary and recolonization aspects of the political platform, searching instead for a strong dramatic voice to tell the story of African-American assimilation into mainstream American ideals. That voice has been found in the work of August Wilson, whose series of plays, each based on a decade in the history of African-American family life, has been developed in cooperation with the Yale Repertory Theatre and the O'Neill Center, officially known as the National Playwrights' Conference. The plays have moved successfully from the League of Resident Theatres (LORT) circuit onto Broadway, a new play appearing about every two years. Wilson's *Two Trains Running* (pr. 1990), *The Piano Lessons* (pr. 1988), *Fences* (pr., pb. 1985), and *Ma Rainey's Black Bottom* (pr. 1984), which won the third Pulitzer Prize by an African American, have all been produced to wide acclaim. The link between the two not-for-profit institutions is Lloyd Richards, until 1992 the artistic director of the Yale Repertory and the institutional director of the O'Neill Center. He has guided Wilson's plays through the play development process, at the O'Neill Center in staged reading format, and at the Yale Repertory in their first professional productions, many of which moved to other LORT theaters before attempting a Broadway run.

The death of James Baldwin in 1987 took away one of the most effective African-American talents from the stage. Political activists such as Amiri Baraka, less active in the theater but vocal in other cultural affairs, continued watching the film industry for signs of vitality. Director Shelton Jackson "Spike" Lee, especially with his 1992 film *Malcolm X*, became a voice for African-American ideas, one which Baraka does not support.

Another major influence in African-American drama has been the feminist movement. The plays of Alice Childress and Adrienne Kennedy have been followed by those of Ntosake Shange's, such as *for colored girls who have considered suicide/ when the rainbow is enuf* (pr., pb. 1976) and *Betsey Brown* (pr. 1991), based on her novel of the same name.

Craig Werner
(Updated by *Thomas J. Taylor*)

AUSTRALIAN DRAMA

Although the beginnings of an identifiably Australian drama can be discerned in plays written during the 1930's, it was not until about 1960 that plays of lasting or literary merit were frequently printed or performed. For convenience, Ray Lawler's *Summer of the Seventeenth Doll* (pr. 1955) is often regarded as the precursor of modern Australian drama, yet in 1956, A. D. Hope, in a *Current Affairs Bulletin* article, "Standards in Australian Literature," published by the University of Sydney, noted that "there is not much to say about Australian drama," and Cecil Hadgraft, in *Australian Literature: A Critical Account to 1955* (1960), a highly regarded conspectus, wholly omitted any consideration of plays.

The late flowering of Australian drama is not readily explained: Though the national population has always been small, it has consistently been urban and relatively literate and affluent, sustaining almost all the other forms of culture, both popular and high. Paradoxically, both at home and abroad Australians have been keen theatergoers, and until the advent of television Australians were among the world's most frequent moviegoers, yet few local writers produced film scripts, although Australian-made and -directed films came into their own in the 1970's and 1980's.

In June, 1789, only eighteen months after the arrival of the First Fleet, George Farquhar's *The Recruiting Officer* (pr. 1706) was performed in Sydney by a cast of convicts as a King's Birthday entertainment for an audience of sixty that included the colonial governor. Thereafter, musical entertainments as well as civil and religious spectacles and stage plays were commonplace; that is, theater became an integral part of the regional culture, and, taking into account the educational background of some of the convicts, one might have expected original dramatic materials making use of the novel local milieu. Convicts, soldiers, settlers, and aborigines isolated in a generally inhospitable and inaccessible environment would seem to have offered ample scope for plays on themes of expatriation, penitence, ambition, fortitude, and rivalry set in unusual, if not exotic, locales, but a deference to established, successful models, a reluctance to experiment, and minimal leisure combined to keep local drama imitative, derivative, and repetitious in structure, theme, and characters. These traits are to be found in the other genres also; it was some time before recognizably Australian characters, speech, and subjects were widely incorporated into Australian literature.

Literary reputations in Australia were traditionally based on achievement in poetry or fiction, while the dominance of comedy and musical comedy in commercial theaters (a reflection of British theater offerings) eliminated the stimulus to attempt serious plays and tragedies, which were relegated to little theaters—located in suburbs or in the insalubrious sections of the capital cities, in the main. A publishing industry that could rarely justify poetry, short stories, and novels commercially was understandably reluctant to print plays. The almost total absence of professional theater personnel militated against successful staging of plays by Australian authors.

Although most of these impediments have been removed and there are indications that the drama—for stage, broadcast, film, and literary study— has attained the artistic level of Australian poetry and prose fiction, there is still no playwright of the international stature of South African Athol Fugard; there are, however, many of commendable achievements.

The first play written in Australia was *The Bushrangers* (pr. 1829), a typical nineteenth century melodrama set in Tasmania in 1825 and dealing with contemporary subject matter and characters. Its author was a Scots settler and editor of *The South Briton: Or, Tasmanian Literary Journal*, David Burn. In all, Burn wrote eight plays, some in prose, some in verse, that attempted most of the forms—melodrama, farce, blank-verse tragedy, and historical drama. They became the first plays published in Australia (1842). Curiously, the two plays set in Australia were never staged there.

The Bushrangers was produced in Edinburgh in 1829. In its episodic structure, satire of officialdom, social criticism, and juxtaposition of government and highwayman moralities it is reminiscent of John Gay's *The Beggar's Opera* (pr. 1728). Like Gay's ballad opera, *The Bushrangers* had its imitators: two of identical title were written by Henry Melville (pr. 1834) and Charles Harpur (wr. 1835), while a plethora of others utilized contemporary social antagonisms and issues as subjects. Some, such as Edward Geoghegan's *The Currency Lass* (pr. 1849), were original; others, such as Garnet Walch and Alfred Dampier's *Robbery Under Arms* (pr. 1891) and Thomas Somers and Dampier's *His Natural Life* (pr. 1886), were adaptations of successful Australian novels.

Throughout the nineteenth century, however, local playwrights tended to imitate the current London stage fare with melodramas, farces, and pantomimes or tableaux that made only minimal concessions to the location. When American plays were introduced, they, too, were imitated. J. C. Williamson and Maggie Williamson's *Struck Oil* (pr. 1874) had its replications in Francis R. C. Hopkins' *All for Gold* (pr. 1877), Dampier's *The Miner's Right* (pr. 1891), and his and Kenneth MacKay's *To the West* (pr. 1896). Some imaginative dramatists attempted to fuse British, American, and Australian elements, so that Euston Leigh and Cyril Clare's *The Duchess of Coolgardie* (pr. 1896), set in the Western Australian goldfields, could have an aborigine's lines written in an approximation of South Carolinian Gullah dialect and an implausible cast and improbable plot. Yet the play was successful: It was performed in Drury Lane Theatre, printed in London, and imitated by George Darrell's *The King of Coolgardie* (pr. 1897).

The increasing nationalism at the close of the century became a feature of all forms of Australian culture. With federation in 1901, chauvinism became less strident yet no less apparent: Australia's participation in the Boer War, World War I, and the Versailles Peace Treaty sustained the sense of national identity. In the drama, William Moore (who organized a writers' theater) and Louis Esson (who had met William Butler Yeats and been advised by him to write "Australian plays") accepted responsibility for the encouragement of an Australian drama.

Esson's *Three Short Plays* (pb. 1911), which included *The Woman Tamer*, *Dead Timber*, and *The Sacred Place*, helped establish the one-act play as a national norm and influenced the choice of theme and characters. (The one-act play became the dramatic equivalent of the short story in Australian fiction; Esson's role was thus similar to that of Henry Lawson.) Esson redirected the play from the melodrama of his forerunners to social realism, represented both city and country issues, and included the attitudes, problems, and antipathies of the several social classes. Accordingly, some critics have noted the influence of Henrik Ibsen and George Bernard Shaw rather than of Yeats and John Millington Synge or Lady Augusta Gregory. In *The Woman Tamer*, Esson explores interrelationships in a slum household; in *Dead Timber*, he reveals the monotonous struggle for existence and for love in the Outback; *The Sacred Place* suggests that slum life has its own morality and that this is justified. Impressive as these plays are, they have not been as popular as *The Drovers* (pr. 1923), in which an injured drover is of necessity abandoned by his mates and cared for by an aborigine whose eerie wails accompany the drover's death and enhance the pathos. In this play, the influence of Synge's *Riders to the Sea* (pb. 1903) seems obvious. Later plays, such as *Mother and Son* (pr. 1923), which reexamines the loneliness of bush life and the disconcerting effects of an inhospitable environment, and *The Bride of Gospel Place* (pr. 1926), a study of city violence, demonstrated that Esson was adept in the full-length dramatic form. His place in Australian drama is secure, though his plays are infrequently staged; his satiric, sardonic, yet sympathetic approach is largely representative of the national ethos, and his themes and subjects are at once historical and regional, continuing and universal.

Compared with Esson's plays, those of two of his contemporaries are inferior, yet they have earned a niche in Australian dramatic literature. Vance Palmer's *Hail Tomorrow* (pb. 1947), about the 1891 shearers' strike, uses characters and issues dear to the Australian heart, yet the play suffers from an inadequate comprehension of dramatic conventions. Like John Steinbeck, Palmer was a fine fiction writer but was unable to work with ease and conviction in drama. Sydney Tomholt's *Bleak Dawn* (pb. 1936) is a praiseworthy study of the divorced working-class woman living in a male-oriented society.

The role of women in Australia, which has increasingly become the focus of sociological studies, has been explored with understanding and feeling by several competent dramatists, among them Katharine Susannah Prichard, Betty Roland, and Dymphna Cusack. Prichard, author of twenty-four published novels, also wrote seventeen plays, eleven of which were produced in Australian little theaters. Only one, *Brumby Innes*, which won a drama contest run by *The Triad* magazine in 1927, was published (1940); it remained unproduced until 1972, possibly because it had been expanded into the very successful novel *Coonardoo* (1929). Set in the Outback, *Brumby Innes* is a mature investigation of black-white and male-female interrelationships, which, it suggests, follow a course from affection and accommodation to sensuality, dominance, and brutal imperiousness. *Brumby Innes*, in its analysis of alienation, self-doubt, domination, and denigration, perhaps reflects the influence of Eugene O'Neill.

Roland's *The Touch of Silk* (pr. 1928) has continued to hold a unique position in Australian drama: It was published by a university press and continues to enjoy readership and discussion, unlike Roland's later, more propagandist plays, the best known of which is probably *Are You Ready, Comrade?* (pr. 1938). *The Touch of Silk* is a study of the difficulties of a sensitive young French woman, Jeanne, to adapt to the cultureless and unaesthetic Outback, with its materialism, crudities, and primitive possessiveness, predicated on the unequal roles and status of men and women and resulting in the very denial of love. After Jeanne buys lingerie from a traveling salesman and goes to a dance with him, she pretends that she has had an affair: The illusion is a necessary balance for a loveless life in an unbeautiful and isolated environment.

Cusack's full-length plays *Red Sun at Morning* (pb. 1942) and *Morning Sacrifice* (pb. 1943) deserve greater recognition than they have gained. The first has as subject matter the flight of a mistress from an overbearing military officer, and so treats a continuing Australian phenomenon, the pervasive authoritarianism in society, while also examining interpersonal relationships outside marriage. The play's historical setting (1812), however, and the improbability of the means of escape militate against its success. *Morning Sacrifice* has a wider appeal. It is set in a girls' school, where the students are conditioned "to accept all, question nothing and grow into nice, well-behaved yes-girls": The indictment of the national educational-social outlook is forceful, the examination of teacher-supervisor roles is perspicacious, and individual weaknesses and ambitions are carefully scrutinized. The simulated sincerity, the frustrations, jealousies, and ambitions of the teachers become paradigmatic of society; the badinage and ripostes suggest the depth of animosity that underlies surface compatibility. The minuscule society of the school tragedy is a metaphor for life itself.

During the 1940's, other dramatists developed their art. Max Afford wrote and adapted plays for radio: His *Lady in Danger* (pr. 1944), a well-constructed, popular comedy-thriller, has retained its enthusiasts, though it is subliterary. Sumner Locke-Elliott, author of *Interval* (pr. 1942), a sophisticated piece set in London that demonstrated his mastery of dramaturgy, achieved fame with *Rusty Bugles* (pr. 1948), "a play of inaction" as one critic termed it, which has no principal characters, includes the coarse language characteristic of soldiers stationed in an isolated ordnance camp, and engages its characters in antiwar discussions. After the success of *Rusty Bugles*, the playwright moved to New York, where he regularly wrote and adapted plays for Studio One, Sunday Night Playhouse, and other broadcast series. He adapted his first novel, *Careful, He Might Hear You*, into a successful film in 1984.

The radio dramas and verse plays of New Zealand-born Douglas Stewart gave indications that he was properly to be compared with Louis MacNeice and Christopher Isherwood as a major dramatist in these forms, but the virtual eclipse of radio drama after World War II, the growth of theater-going, and the demise of verse drama have combined to deflect attention from Stewart's very remarkable plays. In an environment where even standard English was a rarity, Stewart's language (with its finely turned phrases and impeccable nuances of diction) clearly created an impression, but where the predisposition of the public was for musical comedy, operetta, and the domestic comedy, his expressed interest in the creation of national myths from legendary individuals established barriers to the realization of his goals. It is therefore noteworthy that he continued his course and gained wide popularity.

Stewart's principal dramas are *Ned Kelly* (pr. 1942), written in both stage and radio versions, a study of the legendary bushranger and archetypal antihero; *The Fire on the Snow* (pr. 1941), a moving radio play treating the unsuccessful polar expedition of Robert Falcon Scott in 1912; and *Shipwreck* (pr. 1947), another historical play, which treats the 1629 massacre of a majority of the passengers of the *Batavia* while the captain, Pelsart, was in search of help. In each of these plays, Stewart reexamines the popular concept of the dreamer, the visionary, the leader, with his illusions of invincibility, showing also the relationship between national legends and cultural archetypes.

Considerable attention has been given in histories of Australian literature to Lawler's *Summer of the Seventeenth Doll*, which was staged in London and New York to critical acclaim. There is a consensus that this overseas recognition resulted in a resurgence of playwriting in Australia. Certainly it provided a helpful fillip, but it should be remembered that the themes of alienation, physical isolation, mateship, and country-city and man-woman interrelationships had long been the very substance of the national drama. Yet *Summer of the Seventeenth Doll* did add dimensions to established materials: It explored with understanding the inevitable disillusionments of middle life, the disintegration of friendships, and the decreasing importance of hollow ritual and token remembrances. Lawler's subsequent play, *The Piccadilly Bushman* (pr. 1959), examined the reactions to and of a returning expatriate (a common Australian experience, treated most memorably by Henry Handel Richardson in *The Fortunes of Richard Mahony*, one of the classic Australian novels, in 1917).

Richard Beynon's *The Shifting Heart* (pr. 1957) is yet another treatment of the perennial Australian confrontation with nonnatives, whether they be aborigines or Europeans. Better than most of its genre, it shows the depth and suggests the causes of this xenophobia, exclusiveness, and even small-mindedness that is finally disappearing. Alan Seymour's *The One Day of the Year* (pr. 1961) used the artificial camaraderie of Anzac Day (the national veterans' holiday) to deflate myths, to explore the concept of mateship, and to show the irrelevance of some myths when seen across the generation gap. This play was a timely reassessment of subjects of national importance.

After 1960, Australian dramatists attempted most of the modern techniques of the theater and wrote in other than realist terms. The influences of Absurdism, Expressionism, and Symbolism could be noted. Bertolt Brecht and Friedrich Dürrenmatt became as influential as Shaw and Ibsen, Arthur Miller and Tennessee Williams, Eugène Ionesco and Samuel Beckett. As a consequence, a narrowly nationalistic and dominantly realist drama became cosmopolitan in the widest sense. The transformation was aided by the establishment of drama schools and professional theaters, extended university education, overseas travel, and the surcease of blind adherence to outdated and overused dramatic modes. Among the important new playwrights to develop were David Williamson, Alexander Buzo, Jack Hibberd, Ric Throssell, Dorothy Hewett, and Patrick White.

With four plays produced between 1961 and 1964, White—best known as a novelist—established himself as a dramatist of some stature. *The Ham Funeral* (pr. 1961), which is informed by Ibsen's theory that illusion is essential for equanimity, shows that there is poetry in even circumscribed, dreary lives. *The Season at Sarsaparilla* (pr. 1962), a patently Expressionist play subtitled *A Charade of Suburbia*, is a devastating comedy of conformism. The main characters lead lives not quite of quiet desperation but lives where "there's practically no end to the variations of monotony." *A Cheery Soul* (pr. 1963)—based on one of White's own short stories—explores the artificiality of a voluble, self-satisfied suburban do-gooder, while *Night on Bald Mountain* (pr. 1963), a darker play, subsumes all the themes and essential character-types of the author's earlier work to stress the sterility of the proud, the detached, and the intellectual. Toward the end of the play, Professor Sword says, "You and I are here on the edge of the world, and might so easily slip over, into this merciless morning light ... along with the illusions of importance and grandeur that we had." The theme of the play is summed up in Sword's later aphorism, "Failure is sometimes the beginnings of success."

David Williamson's *Don's Party* (pr. 1971) and *The Removalists* (pr. 1971), Jack Hibberd's *A Stretch of the Imagination* (pr. 1972) and *A Toast to Melba* (pr. 1976), and the several plays of the prolific Alexander Buzo are among the more inventive, substantial, and likely to survive as both literature and theater. Buzo's *Norm and Ahmed* (pr. 1968) is one of the most affecting treatments of xenophobia; *The Front Room Boys* (pr. 1969) lays bare the sterile life of the office worker confined to the routines of the large corporation. In both, there is the sure touch of the playwright who has an ear for the speech and interests of the common person and the analytic methodology of the sociologist.

By the mid-1970's, professional theaters could present local texts without suffering at the box office; an annual National Playwrights' Conference, first held in Canberra in 1971, established a link between the development of solicited works and commercial production; and the fledgling film industry achieved international success with films such as *Gallipoli* (1980), *Breaker Morant* (1980), *My Brilliant Career* (1979), and *Picnic at Hanging Rock* (1981).

The demand for published plays, stimulated by their inclusion in academic drama courses, was met by a new company, Currency Press, which was amalgamated with the established publisher Methuen in 1982. The women's movement, the development of aboriginal scripts, and the emergence of a new and vigorous community spirit—giving voice to the workplace and specific geographical areas—have challenged the beliefs and practices of established theaters. Chief among the new playwrights are Alma De Groen, whose *Rivers of China* (pb. 1988, pr. 1990) challenged the way people at the margins attempt to speak at the center; Michael Gow, who in *Away* (pr. 1987, pb. 1988) examines the coming-of-age of his teenage protagonists and deals with a 1960's society on the verge of political and social self-realization; and Stephen Sewell, who explores the domestic turmoil of a Fascist politician new to the Australian order in *Hate* (pr., pb. 1988).

An interesting aspect of contemporary Australian theater is a maturity of vision that gives recognition to the work of aboriginal dramatists, in particular Jack Davis (*No Sugar*, pr. 1985, pb. 1986; *Honey Spot*, pr. 1985, pb. 1987), and Robert Merritt (*The Cakeman*, pr. 1988; *Women of the Sun*, pr. 1989, a television series). They have pioneered a drama free of colonial and imperialist thought.

Alan L. McLeod

CANADIAN DRAMA

Until the late twentieth century, almost all Canadian literature appeared to be self-restricted to a severely circumscribed range of subjects and themes, forms, and language. The daring and inventiveness of such fiction writers as Alice Munro, Margaret Laurence, Mordecai Richler, and Morley Callaghan, however, have helped to reduce the conventionalism of Canadian literature, including the drama.

During the 1970's, the dominant metaphor in the study of Canadian literature was Northrop Frye's "garrison mentality," which he described as an unthinking herd mind that resulted in the suppression of individualism and the maintenance of the cultural status quo. Canadian drama has been particularly vulnerable to this criticism: Its themes have never ranged far from the struggle of the settler with an intimidating and almost overwhelming natural environment (including the Indians) and the struggle of the individualist against the formidable powers of conformity or cultural imperialism. Furthermore, Canadian dramatists have generally observed the methods of established, mainline American and European playwrights, rather than those of the avant-garde. The explanation for this situation might be found in a pervasive sense of cultural colonialism, the feeling that the theater—whether in text or in performance—is fundamentally an art form that has been developed elsewhere (New York, Paris, London) and is only to be imitated in Canada. Oddly, Canadians are keen patrons of modernist plays abroad, and Americans have enthusiastically supported Canadian theater festivals and actors; it would appear that even one first-rate play could effect a remarkable burgeoning of both drama and theater in Canada. So far, however, there seems to be no Canadian equivalent of Wole Soyinka, Athol Fugard, Ray Lawler, or Arthur Miller.

It is generally believed that the earliest stage piece produced in Canada (then New France) was *The Theatre of Neptune* (pr. 1606; originally *Le Théâtre de Neptune dans la Nouvelle France*), which was written by Marc Lescarbot to celebrate the return to Port Royal, Nova Scotia, of Sieur de Poutrincourt from a journey of exploration. Unfortunately, this pioneering work seems not to have created any demand for theater, because thirty years passed before there was mention of another play—Pierre Corneille's *Le Cid* (pr. 1637). In 1694, an episcopal decree suspended performances of Molière's *Tartuffe* in Quebec, and both the drama and theater in French Canada thereafter languished.

By contrast, the British authorities encouraged the theater, both literary (Elizabethan and contemporary eighteenth century authors) and popular (farces, topical sketches, and pantomimes). Moreover, long before English-language plays were written in Canada, the country was the subject of *Liberty Asserted* (pr. 1704), a tragedy by the British literary critic John

Dennis. In his play, Dennis treats of the French-Iroquois wars, the benefi-
cence of the English, and the consequences of conquest, miscegenation,
and cultural pluralism. Notwithstanding his identification of several issues
of lasting concern in Canada, Dennis' work appears to have had no dis-
cernible effect in the stimulation of playwriting in the country. In fact, for
more than 150 years, no play or dramatist of note appeared.

In the nineteenth century, in contrast, plays seemed to be as common as
volumes of poems. Despite their number, however, few Canadian plays of
the nineteenth century had any lasting interest or true merit. Many were
closet dramas; some were intended for theater production but were neither
staged nor published; a few enjoyed brief runs. In the tradition of the era,
many plays incorporated songs for diversion; most contained political subject matter or allusions—often local or regional—that restricted their
interest. Such is *The Female Consistory of Brockville* (pb. 1856), by the
pseudonymous Caroli Candidus; the play centers on the efforts of the
female members of a Presbyterian congregation to bring about the dis-
missal of their pastor. Another is Nicholas Flood Davin's *The Fair Grit* (pr.
1876), built around the dilemma of lovers thwarted by the political affili-
ations of their parents. Somewhat more imaginative is Thomas Bush's
Santiago (pr. 1866), which explores the evil that pervades a South American country and in the process utilizes songs, Elizabethan and biblical language, grand melodrama, divine intervention, and exotic scenes and characters. Clearly, it is more a potpourri than a play.

Of a somewhat different character is W. H. Fuller's *H.M.S. Parliament*,
popular immediately upon its performance in 1880 and for many years
later. While it parodied Gilbert and Sullivan's *H.M.S. Pinafore* (pr. 1878),
it added topical satire and local characters and allusions and thus suggested
a line of development that was not resumed until the plays of Robertson
Davies.

Charles Heavysege (1816-1876), who migrated from England to Montreal
in 1853, made a definite though not very lasting contribution to Canadian
literature through his journalism, poetry, and drama. Indebted to the Bible
and to John Milton in particular, Heavysege gave expression to a pessimistic worldview according to which God is a rather capricious and even vin-
dictive force Who dispenses injustice. This outlook can be discerned in
Saul (pb. 1857), a closet drama of 135 scenes, and in *Count Filippo: Or,
The Unequal Marriage* (pb. 1860), a five-act tragedy of love and intrigue.
Coventry Patmore declared *Saul* to be the greatest poem in English published outside Britain, and Henry Wadsworth Longfellow—for reasons no
more comprehensible—judged Heavysege the greatest dramatist since William Shakespeare. Today he is unread except by literary historians; Professor Desmond Pacey has aided in reassessing Heavysege's work by suggesting that his once popular *The Advocate* (1864) is the worst of the many bad

novels written in Canada.

Charles Mair (1838-1927), who was associated with the "Canada First" movement, made tentative steps toward a national authenticity but stopped short of positive achievement. His *Tecumseh: A Drama* (pb. 1886), yet another blank-verse closet drama, remains a curiosity despite its potential: It retains the fustian and bombast of late Restoration tragedy and has its Indians orate in stylized, rhetorical diction. It thus remains a dramatic curiosity.

A bibliography of Canadian drama in English compiled by Geraldine Anthony and Tina Usmiani lists more than two hundred women dramatists. Most were active during the nineteenth century; not many had their plays published; fewer saw them on the stage; and almost all remain footnotes in Canadian literary and theatrical history. Nevertheless, their range can be inferred from a listing of representative examples: *Esther: A Sacred Drama* (pb. 1840) and *The Intercepted Letter* (pb. 1845), by Eliza L. Cushing; *The Secret* (pb. 1865) and *The Talisman* (pb. 1863), by Mary Anne Sadleir; and *Laura Secord, the Heroine of 1812: A Drama* (pb. 1887), by Sarah Anne Curzon.

The founding of the Hart House Theatre in 1919 brought attention to the plays of Merrill Denison and gave a boost to Canadian playwriting, for a little theater in Toronto and another in Montreal (the Community Players) seemed to offer vastly improved chances of production in major urban centers. These theaters, however, and with them the Drama League Theatre in Ottawa, could not make a general commitment to Canadian drama and remain solvent. Besides, the plays that were written in the 1920's and 1930's were mainly one-act pieces, light and "popular" in the pejorative sense; some, such as Marjorie Pickthall's *The Woodcarver's Wife* (pb. 1922), reverted to an earlier mode of verse drama, dealt with tragic love feuds, and used overblown diction.

In some ways an iconoclast, Merrill Denison nevertheless made a niche for himself with short, ironic plays that explored the accepted mythology of the heroic Northland, national patriotism and sovereignty, and Puritan industry and frugality. His most popular plays were collected as *The Unheroic North* (1923). One of them, *Marsh Hay*, has been compared in its intensity of mood with Eugene O'Neill's *Desire Under the Elms* (pr. 1924). It depicts the moral decadence of Canada's isolated communities and questions the premise that the urban environment is the least congenial to nobility, neighborliness, and morality. Within a decade, Denison left Canada for the United States, however, and the stimulus that he helped provide was soon lost, though plays continued to be written, staged, and published.

Among other plays of the 1920's, Mazo de la Roche's four slight comedies, published as *Low Life and Other Plays* (1924), reveal a proclivity for farce; Duncan Campbell Scott's *Pierre* (pr. 1923), a domestic tragedy set in

Quebec, deals with a prodigal's return and departure with the family savings, even as he is being extolled by his mother; and L. A. Mackey's *The Freedom of Jean Guichet* (pr. 1925) offers a melodramatic mélange of characters and themes. In the following decade, Alice Chadwicke gained momentary fame with her 1937 adaptation of L. M. Montgomery's *Anne of Green Gables*. All now seem dated and culturally irrelevant.

Another generation bemoaned the state of the Canadian drama and stage; promising actors departed; the little theaters persevered. Yet the groundwork for subsequent dramatic and theatrical development was laid by the Canadian Broadcasting Corporation's radio drama series, directed by Andrew Allan.

Of the multitude of plays written between the world wars, probably fewer then half were ever staged, and of these, perhaps no more than half were ever published in any format. According to Professor Terence Goldie, who has made an analysis of this great mass of theatrical material, the primary thematic interests are the terrain, politics, history, and religious concerns of Canada. Melodramas and comedies prevail, and they are superficially about contemporary society—particularly about the difficulties of romantic affection—but the playwrights devote most of their energies to the manipulation of dramatic devices rather than to the exploration and elucidation of their subjects and themes. Those who seem to have the greatest potential and proficiency concentrate on characteristically Canadian materials: The plays that deal with the terrain are superior to those that deal with politics, and these, in turn, seem superior to the remainder. Since more than four hundred plays were written during these two decades, there is adequate proof of writers' interest in dramatic composition and theatrical presentation.

During the 1940's, such playwrights as Gwen Pharis Ringwood, John Coulter, and Robertson Davies began to attain stature as dramatists and to influence the development of an identifiably Canadian drama. Naturally, they were not alone: Dorothy Livesay, in *Call My People Home* (pb. 1948), wrote a documentary verse drama for radio about the expulsion of ethnic Japanese from the West Coast after 1941; Patricia Joudrey, in *Teach Me How to Cry* (pb. 1955), wrote a play that (in her own words), "tells the story of a troubled teenage girl who is steered away from a hazardous life of escapism by the love of a boy who has himself learned to face reality." *Teach Me How to Cry* is therefore in the tradition of Henrik Ibsen and Tennessee Williams in its juxtaposition of reality and illusion in contemporary life, but it lacks deftness in dialogue, dramatic intensity, and individualization of characters. Notwithstanding, it achieved some acclaim when staged in both New York and London.

The best of Gwen Pharis Ringwood's several plays, the one-act *Still Stands the House* (pr. 1938) and *Dark Harvest* (pb. 1945), are somewhat melodramatic studies of family relationships in farming communities during the Great Depression, but the attachment to farmhouse, family, and the infertile land is explored with great sensitivity, so that one senses the depth of the drama when a choice has to be made. Local color, despair, and the contrasted feelings for sibling and spouse are handled with unusual skill. Among Ringwood's other plays, only *The Courting of Marie Jenvrin* (pr. 1942), set in the Northwest Territories, deals with life outside Alberta. Clearly, Ringwood has the same attachment to place, and the same insights into the human condition of life on the land, that distinguished the Nebraskan stories of Willa Cather.

It has often been observed that John Coulter's plays place him in the tradition of the Irish Literary Revival. Coulter migrated from Ireland, and many of his plays, such as *The House in the Quiet Glen* (pr. 1937) and *The Family Portrait* (pr. 1937), are set there; they suggest, in many ways, the depth of his indebtedness to William Butler Yeats and Lady Augusta Gregory as well as to John Millington Synge. (Coulter wrote the libretto for an opera based on Synge's *Deirdre of the Sorrows*.) In 1962, however, Coulter produced a clearly Canadian drama, *Riel*, which deals with the Northwest Rebellions of 1869-1885, led by Louis Riel, a Manitoban of French and mulatto heritage, in the Red River settlements. The drama presents the protagonist as an enigmatic, charismatic, yet ruthless fanatic whose defense of Indian land rights resulted in his being tried and hanged for treason. The play is doubtless an advance on Mair's *Tecumseh* and helps to create a new Canadian mythology through its revisionist interpretation of the consequences of the dissolution of the hegemony of the Hudson's Bay Company and the advent of Confederation.

Robertson Davies is perhaps the best-known Canadian man of letters; his principal achievements have been in prose fiction of a light, sometimes satiric, and not always notably substantial nature. He has a droll sense of humor, a ready wit, and a good ear for dialogue, yet his plays have not often risen above the level of deft, short theater pieces of amusing and inconsequential substance; *Eros at Breakfast* (pr. 1948) is representative of his early, flippant work. Davies' later work has added to his reputation; even an early work such as *My Fortune, My Foe* (pr. 1948), the author's first full-length play, considers a serious theme: the dilemma of the intellectual in Canada, the choice between emigration for growth and fame, or residence with stultification and denigration. Today, Davies is considered his country's leading dramatist.

Davies has long been preoccupied with middle-class pretensions, and he takes delight in scrutinizing Canadians' follies and pretensions. Like most satirists, he clearly recognizes the veracity of his vision and sees the necessity and the possibility of reform and progress. Still, he is not always able to balance the romantic and the idealistic, his concern for self-knowledge becomes much too overt, and he is at times too clearly the advocate of a neo-Jungian psychology. One critic, W. M. Steinberg, notes that "it is unfortunate that in no case in his plays does he explore characters in depth—for the most part they are used as a means to present or develop ideas." This Shavian propensity is admittedly a shortcoming, yet Davies' several experiments in dramatic form, as in *A Jig for the Gypsy* (pr. 1954) and *A Masque of Mr. Punch* (pb. 1963), attest his versatility.

In the late twentieth century, a new generation of Canadian playwrights has succeeded that of Davies, and it includes a number of talented dramatists. George Ryga has drawn attention to the plight of the Indian; Norman Williams has demonstrated his skill in the one-act play form with *Worlds Apart* (pb. 1956), an anthology of six of his plays; John Reeves, in *A Beach of Strangers: An Excursion* (pb. 1961), has adapted the techniques of radio drama to the stage in a play that owes much to Dylan Thomas' *Under Milk Wood* (pr. 1953) yet has a somewhat more vast and allegorical scope; and James Reaney has worked in myriad forms, with varying success, as in *The Killdeer* (pr. 1960), an ambitious play that grapples with issues such as innocence and experience, fertility and death, and the role that the family takes in the development of personality and community.

The story of late twentieth century Canadian drama is in many respects the story of the success of a diverse and exciting theater community. The Canadian Stage Company, founded in 1988 in Toronto, continued to offer a wide range of stages, operating with an annual budget of more than six million dollars. Its members "serve the broadest possible audience with bold, relevant plays . . . in productions of superlative standards." The company's primary focus is the development and production of Canadian work; it also encourages new Canadian playwrights as they emerge.

The prestigious and highly successful Stratford Festival, whose artistic director John Neville stepped down in 1988 and was replaced by David William, continued to lead Canada's reputation for the highest-quality theater productions, encouraging new playwrights while preserving and rejuvenating the classics.

Non-Aristotelian dramas and theater pieces, often inspired by Canada's encouragement of contemporary theater from outside its borders, have been the best fare to come from the various festivals. The Montreal Theatre Festival of the Americas, Toronto's de Maurier World Stage Showcase, and Quebec City's Quinzaine Internationale du Théâtre are examples. Edmonton's Fringe Festival and, in Toronto, Factory Theatre's "Brave New Works," Nightwood Theatre's festival of women writers, and the gay theater work from Buddies in Bad Times have all given their energy to the new dramatic output. Carbone 14, a French-speaking experimental dance group, did a "textless" version of D. M. Thomas' Freudian novel *The White Hotel* (1981). Other alternative theater events of note are *The Bible as*

Told to Karen Ann Quinlan (1978) and *She Devils of Niagara* (1985), a "brilliant satire on sexuality," by the Clichettes, a leading feminist group.

The women's theater movement has been strong in every province. For example, Judith Thompson's *The Crackwalker* (pr. 1980, pb. 1981) begins a series of strong plays of "emotionally dynamic young people operating under economic, social, and mental handicaps." *White Biting Dog* (pr. 1984, pb. 1986) and *I Am Yours* (pr. 1987, pb. 1989) display her adroit handling of metaphor inside a powerful stage voice. Her later play *Lion in the Streets*, published in 1992, further demonstrates this artist's talent. Other Canadian dramatists of note are Tomson Highway, whose *The Rez Sisters* (pr. 1987, pb. 1988) won the Dora Award (1986-1987) and was presented at the Edinburgh (Scotland) Fringe Festival in 1988, and a promising newcomer, George F. Walker, born and reared in Toronto's working-class East End, who has written *The Prince of Naples* (pr. 1971), *Beyond Mozambique* (pr. 1974), *Criminals in Love* (pr. 1984), *Better Living* (pr. 1986), and an adaptation of Ivan Turgenev's *Ottsy i deti* (1862; *Fathers and Sons*, 1867) entitled *Nothing Sacred* (pr. 1988). Walker served the 1981 season as playwright-in-residence with Joseph Papp's Public Theatre in New York.

Of the well-established Canadian writers from previous generations, Robertson Davies has been long associated with the Shakespeare Festival in Toronto. The major book on Davies' dramatic output remained Susan Stone-Blackburn's *Robertson Davies, Playwright*, published in 1985. James Reaney has continued to write after several decades of excellent work and has become active in video and film. A "doll opera" based on the novel *Crazy to Kill* by Anne Cardwell was premiered at the Guelph Spring Festival in 1989. An opera, *Serinette*, in collaboration with musician Harry Somers, was commissioned and performed in 1989.

Dispassionate observers, including Canadian critics themselves, are generally of the opinion that Canada has yet to produce a dramatist of the first rank, though there are many now writing who give great promise. In the future, some of the large number of West Indians now resident in Canada will surely add their contribution, and it is likely that the range of subject matter and themes will be expanded: The resulting cosmopolitanism should itself add a measure of sophistication and interest to Canada's dramatic output.

Alan L. McLeod
(Updated by *Thomas J. Taylor*)

IRISH DRAMA

"Let us learn construction from the masters and language from ourselves," William Butler Yeats (1865-1939), one of the founders of the Abbey Theatre, advised aspiring playwrights. Indeed, an aptitude for language and humor was a distinctive feature of drama written by Irish authors, but not until the establishment of the Abbey Theatre at the beginning of the twentieth century was it possible for Irish playwrights to draw on indigenous precedents, distinct from those supplied by England's literary tradition. Since the seventeenth century, as Irish dramatists looked toward London for their audiences, Irish drama had taken British theatrical conventions for its own. As the central arena of the cultural-political movement known as the Irish Literary Revival, the Abbey Theatre placed the island's resources of myth, social custom, folklore, and language at the service of a generation of dramatists whose work is recognizably Irish. The success of this national theater continued, with some qualifications, through the years, but by the 1920's, a reaction to the preoccupations with national history and identity, rural mores, and religion led to the internationalization of theater in Ireland. As a result of these developments, dramatic writing in Ireland began to produce works of various characters: either provincially British, discretely national, or Continental. Similarly, a historical account of Irish drama falls into three main phases: Anglo-Irish, Irish national, and contemporary European.

Through most of the nineteenth century, Ireland retained some regional vestiges of mumming, a traditional folk drama which ritually reenacted significant events in the memory of the community, but it was not until the early seventeenth century that literary drama set its first roots in Irish soil with the founding of a small theater on Werburgh Street in Dublin in 1637, followed later in the century by the Smock Alley Theatre. Thereafter, the city had a continuous theatrical presence, and many provincial centers had seasonal houses. From its beginnings to almost the end of the nineteenth century, however, Irish drama was primarily of colonial character, only in minor ways distinct from what could be seen on the stages of London or provincial England. With the collapse of the Gaelic social and political order at the beginning of the seventeenth century, the cultural traditions of Ireland were abandoned, and no Irish institutions remained to graft that inheritance to the life of the cities and the new institution of the stage. Until the end of the nineteenth century, the only contacts with the ancient civilization available to the serious artist were relatively inaccessible relics in the folklore of the countryside and in the manuscript rooms of the museums and academies. These repositories held a rich lode of heroic, romantic, and folk legends which bore witness to a sophisticated, indigenous Celtic civilization.

It is not surprising, therefore, that although many of the most distinguished dramatists writing in English between 1700 and 1900 were born in
Ireland, their works were written according to the idiom and conventions
of the English stage. Neither the spirit of the times nor the conditions in
Ireland were conducive to reflections on what were considered accidents of
birth. Scions of the Anglo-Irish Protestant ascendancy, these writers typically attended an Irish grammar school and Trinity College, Dublin, before
emigrating to London to pursue professional or theatrical careers. Many of
them were Grub Street hacks, writing sentimental commercial comedy,
melodrama, or farce, as the commercial market demanded, but the most
distinguished of them were the pioneers of new developments in English
drama. Two of the earliest Irish-born dramatists were Nahum Tate (1652-
1715) and Thomas Southerne (1660-1746), best known, respectively, for
their popular adaptations of William Shakespeare's plays and Aphra Behn's
novels. William Congreve (1670-1729), whose *Love for Love* (pr. 1695) is
the masterpiece of the comedy of manners, and George Farquhar (1678-
1707), author of the genial and entertaining comedies *The Recruiting Officer* (pr. 1706) and *The Beaux' Stratagem* (pr. 1707), perhaps derived from
their Irish birth some of the detachment and humor which enabled them to
develop a satiric style. The sentimental comedy of the eighteenth century
had its chief exponents in two Irishmen, Sir Richard Steele (1672-1729) and
Hugh Kelly (1739-1777), before the arrival of Oliver Goldsmith (1730-
1774). In his 1773 "An Essay on Theatre" and his classic "laughing" comedy *She Stoops to Conquer* (pr. 1773), Goldsmith put an end to sentimental
comedy's effete mélange of tragedy and comedy by purifying once again
the springs of humor. This refreshing departure in English comic style was
continued by Richard Brinsley Sheridan (1751-1816) in *The Rivals* (pr.
1775) and his classic *The School for Scandal* (pr. 1777).

During all of this period and until the nineteenth century, the most visible Irish feature of the drama was the convention of the "Stage Irishman":
a humorous character, either gentleman or peasant, whose distinctive features were his outrageous dialect, proclivity to "Irish bulls" (blunders in
speech or logic), and pugnacious disposition. This endearing caricature has
many variants (soldier, priest, gentleman, fortune hunter, servant) and can
be found in the English theater from Tudor times—notably in Farquhar's
Roebuck (*Love and a Bottle*, pr. 1698) and Sheridan's Sir Lucius O'Trigger
(*The Rivals*), evolving in the nineteenth century into the Conn (*The
Shaughraun*, pr. 1874) of Dion Boucicault (1820?-1890). Boucicault was
the most prolific and successful Irish dramatist of the nineteenth century,
especially with *London Assurance* (pr. 1841), a comedy of manners, and
several Irish melodramas, including *The Shaughraun*. By the 1890's, two
other Anglo-Dubliners had begun to establish themselves in the tradition of
stage comedy established by their forebears: George Bernard Shaw (1856-

1950) and Oscar Wilde (1854-1900). Shaw soon became the leading social satirist and comedian of ideas in the modern British theater, and Wilde, by virtue of his brilliantly witty comedies, especially *The Importance of Being Earnest* (pr. 1895), was the most celebrated—and infamous—of the Decadents. The Irish origins of these dramatists enabled them, like so many Anglo-Irish writers before them, to view with some dispassion the English class system, English social customs, and habits of feeling and speech, and their own socially indeterminate position (as outsiders in Ireland as well as England) gave them a sense of independence and contributed to the skepticism with which they treated their English materials. On the other hand, with the exception of Shaw's *John Bull's Other Island* (pr. 1904), neither made explicit use of distinctively Irish themes.

By that time, however, the Irish Literary Revival had introduced to the stage the resources of Ireland's long-neglected cultural tradition. The father of this movement was the poet William Butler Yeats. Under the influence of John O'Leary, an aging revolutionary and *littérateur*, the young Yeats turned from a career begun in the spirit of late Victorian English letters to the folklore of the west of Ireland and the heroic legends of Celtic literature that were, by the end of the nineteenth century, becoming available in contemporary English translation. In the company of Lady Augusta Gregory (1852-1932), a folklorist and folk dramatist, and Edward Martyn (1859-1923), a landed gentleman with strong affinities for Henrik Ibsen's social, symbolic drama, Yeats founded the Irish Literary Theatre in 1899, which within several seasons became the showpiece of the national literary movement: Dublin's Abbey Theatre.

The founders of this theater took their cue from the presence of several European precursors: Ole Bull's in Norway (established in 1850), André Antoine's Théâtre Libre in Paris (1887), Germany's Freie Bühne Theater (1889), J. T. Grein's Independent Theatre in London (1891), and the Moscow Arts Theatre (1897). In contrast with these antecedents, however, Yeats, Lady Gregory, and Martyn were beginning as pioneers. Although this group had a diversity of talents, sensibilities, and inclinations, they agreed on the necessity to replace the caricature of Irish life on the stage with serious and authentic drama, drama that would be at once popular yet not ruled by political orthodoxies, and they committed themselves to experimentation with an imaginative and poetic drama that would harness heroic legend to the demands of the modern stage. Yeats developed his dramas from indigenous folk and mythic materials, the French Symbolists, Ibsen's poetic dramas, and, later, Japanese Nō drama; Martyn modeled his work on the more social and realistic of Ibsen's works; and Lady Gregory drew on folklore, local history, and heroic sources which she herself collected or translated, shaping these materials with the techniques of French comedy.

The Irish Literary Theatre opened in May, 1899, with Yeats's poetic play *The Countess Cathleen* (pr. 1899) and Martyn's problem play *The Heather Field* (pr. 1899). This initial double bill was to foreshadow the character of the Irish theater's repertoire during the ensuing decades. The low-key naturalistic acting style of the company, led by William and Frank Fay, and the financial patronage of Annie Horniman soon won for the Irish Literary Theatre a solid reputation. By 1904, it had found a permanent home on Abbey Street (thus the name Abbey Theatre), and the dramatic movement was attracting many talents in the rising generation, including John Millington Synge (1871-1909), George Fitzmaurice (1878-1963), and Padraic Colum (1881-1972). Meanwhile, under Bulmer Hobson, the Ulster Literary Theatre was providing in Belfast what the Abbey Theatre had begun in Dublin.

Yeats himself experimented with several dramatic styles, including peasant realism, farce, and modern naturalism, but his genius found its true métier in a highly sophisticated drama that combined poetry, dance, mask, and symbolic action to represent a world of ideals and pure passion. These plays borrowed from the Japanese Nō for their form, from Celtic heroic tales for their subjects, and expressed Yeats's view of the primacy of imaginative or spiritual realities of which historical change and the differentiation of humanity are emanations. In all of his work, but most comprehensively in his plays for masks, Yeats's enmity against modern realism can be seen. An attitude of detachment and impersonality shapes his works into intensely ritualized expressions, having affinities with both ancient religious drama and modern Absurdism.

In Cuchulain, the central figure of the Ulster Cycle of Celtic tales, Yeats found a symbolic conjunction of the virtues of heroic individualism, eloquence, aristocracy, and pagan self-realization—values that he sought to insinuate into the character of modern Ireland. In his *Four Plays for Dancers* (pb. 1921), and especially in *The Only Jealousy of Emer* (pb. 1919), the convergence of Japanese technique and Celtic subject is most evident. Beyond the plays themselves, with their masterful fusion of private passion and public vision, Yeats's legacy to Irish drama consists of haughty artistic independence and a heightened awareness of the possibilities for verse drama in a hostile age. Following his example, verse drama has had a small but persistent tradition in Ireland, notably in the works of the poet Austin Clarke (1896-1974) and Donagh MacDonagh (1912-1968) and in the productions of the Lyric Players Theatre, Belfast.

Before long, however, the Abbey Theatre had developed its own distinctive blend of naturalism, romanticism, and poetry, as exemplified principally by the plays of John Millington Synge during the first decade of the twentieth century and of Sean O'Casey (1880-1964) during the 1920's. Synge was the first Irish dramatist to combine successfully the influences of

Molière's design and humor, Jean Racine's musicality, Irish myth and folklore, and the extravagant dialect of English to be found in the remote regions of Ireland. Synge was the first major success of the Abbey Theatre, in terms of both the realization of its theoretical objectives and its becoming the focus of consciousness for the emerging nation. Synge's reputation rests on the output of the last seven years of his brief life: six plays, two of which, *Riders to the Sea* (pb. 1903) and *The Playboy of the Western World* (pr. 1907), are masterpieces. These plays in particular exhibit the characteristic qualities of intense, lyric speech drawn from the native language and dialects of Ireland, romantic characterization in primitive settings, and dramatic construction after the classics of European drama. Three central themes dominate Synge's work: the enmity between romantic dreams and life's hard necessities, the relationship between human beings and the natural world, and the mutability of all things. The production of some of his plays, notably *The Playboy of the Western World*, aroused public controversy, provoking riots and a bitter public debate over the play and over freedom of expression on the stage. In retrospect, *The Playboy of the Western World* is universally acclaimed as one of the classics of dramatic comedy and marks the zenith of the Abbey Theatre's early years. Synge had considerable influence in shaping the style and theme of subsequent Irish drama, as exemplified by the works of Fitzmaurice, Michael J. Molloy (born 1917), and John B. Keane (born 1918), and some influence outside Ireland, most notably in the work of Federico García Lorca and Eugene O'Neill.

While Synge's work was the most accomplished transmutation of Irish rural life into lyric realism, other dramatists in the literary movement made worthy contributions to the style that was to become the hallmark of the Abbey Theatre: Lady Gregory's many comedies based on folklife rendered in humorous and colorful "Kiltartan" dialect, Colum's realistic tragedies of peasant life set in the midlands, Fitzmaurice's fantasies and realistic tragedies set in his native Kerry. These writers had many inferior imitators, and the Abbey Theatre went into a decline. That decline was arrested, however, by the arrival of O'Casey in 1923.

In many ways Synge's city equivalent, O'Casey brought the language, the humor, and the sufferings of the Dublin poor to the stage, especially in his three "Dublin plays": *The Shadow of a Gunman* (pr. 1923), *Juno and the Paycock* (pr. 1924), and *The Plough and the Stars* (pr. 1926). In these works—set against the political struggles of the previous decade—he showed himself a master of tragicomedy and a trenchant critic of personal and national self-deception. When he submitted his play *The Silver Tassie* (pb. 1928) to the Abbey Theatre, codirectors Yeats and Lady Gregory rejected it for what they considered an ill-conceived expressionist second act; an acrimonious public exchange followed, and O'Casey severed his relationship with the Abbey Theatre. His later plays are marked by a more strident Marxism and by less certainty in the handling of the Irish materials that he continued to employ throughout his long remove to the south of England.

During the 1920's, the talented "second generation" of Abbey playwrights emerged: T. C. Murray (1873-1959), Lennox Robinson (1886-1958), and Brinsley MacNamara (1890-1963). These dramatists helped establish domestic realism as the hallmark of the Abbey Theatre, a preference relayed in Belfast by the Ulster Group Theatre in the 1940's. Murray's work is stark tragedy, Robinson's ranges from farce to historical treatments of the decline of the Anglo-Irish class, and MacNamara wrote many popular comedies of small-town life. As the official state theater, the Abbey benefited from a modest subvention but suffered from some restrictions. A fire in 1951 caused a temporary move, remedied in 1966 with the building of the new Abbey Theatre on the same site and realizing Yeats and Lady Gregory's plans for a large, commercial auditorium along with a pocket theater, The Peacock, for poetic and experimental works.

It was not entirely a coincidence that in the same year as O'Casey's falling out with the Abbey directorate, Dublin got its second serious theater: the Gate Theatre. Founded by Hilton Edwards and Micheál MacLiammóir, the Gate Theatre set out to bring European and international classic theater to Ireland, in contrast to the perceived introversion of the Abbey Theatre. Almost immediately, with Denis Johnston's sensational expressionist play about Irish nationalism, *The Old Lady Says No!* (pr. 1929), the Gate Theatre began its signal service to Irish audiences in importing contemporary European and American drama as well as encouraging much of the best experimental work by Irish playwrights.

During the 1950's, three dramatists emerged who represented quite different traditions and social sectors: Brendan Behan (1923-1964), a political dramatist from Dublin's working class; John B. Keane, author of many popularly successful folk melodramas; and Dubliner Samuel Beckett (1906-1989), whose inimitable theatrical genius blends some Anglo-Irish coloration into his dramas of persistence in the face of dissolution and death (most notably in *All That Fall*, pr. 1957). Behan, whose two plays *The Quare Fellow* (pr. 1954) and *The Hostage* (pr. 1958) were produced by Joan Littlewood at the Theatre Royal, London, gained an international reputation of spirited tragicomedy.

Drama in late twentieth century Ireland is in a healthier state than in any other period since the 1920's, despite commercial demands and the counterattractions of other media. The annual Dublin Theatre Festival, state subventions to the Gate Theatre and individual dramatists, and the nationwide amateur dramatic societies encourage potential writers for the stage; although there have been complaints about the trend toward producing adaptations from novels and biographies on the Abbey Theatre's main stage, both The Peacock and the national television network (RTE) offer incentives to new dramatists.

Contemporary Irish theater, while socially diverse, continued to be dominated by the political voices of such committed writers as Brian Friel, Margaretta D'Arcy, and Frank McGuinness. Friel, whose play *Translations* (pr. 1980, pb. 1981) stands as the ultimate metaphor for the inability of Irish nationals to talk with their Protestant counterparts in a mutually respectful language, has dedicated his creative life to the continued discourse between the disparate sides. With *The Communication Cord* (pr. 1982, pb. 1983), the metaphor is continued. More important, Friel has founded the Field Day Theatre to develop new plays and playwrights and to accomplish on a larger scale what his plays try to do individually. Besides the encouragement to new playwrights, however, the most important contribution of the Field Day Theatre has not been a theater piece but a series of pamphlets, somewhat in the manner of fellow-Irishman Jonathan Swift in the eighteenth century. These pamphlets deal in particular with the development of theater in Ireland and with Irish problems in general. They are grouped as published, under separate titles: The first six pamphlets are collected as *Ireland's Field Day* (1985); the next three as *The Protestant Idea of Liberty* (1985); and the next three as *The Apparatus of Repression: Emergency Legislation* (1986). Friel has also begun work on a dictionary of Irish English.

McGuinness' play *Observe the Sons of Ulster Marching Towards the Somme* (pb. 1985) can be compared to the work of Friel in stage technique and in McGuiness' obsession with cleansing Irish history through recapitulations of its past. His *Baglady/Ladybag* (pb. 1988) opened in 1985; *Carthaginians* opened in 1988 and is concerned with the Northern Catholic psyche faced with death in the streets of Derry on Bloody Sunday. It was developed in a Derry theater workshop in 1987.

D'Arcy, best known for her collaborations with John Arden, is another Dublin-born playwright active in examining and dramatizing the political questions of the country. Long productions (sometimes as long as twenty-six hours) revolving loosely around the life and activities of James Connolly (the six-part *The Non-Stop Connolly Show* was produced through the 1970's but was published in full in 1986) have set her work apart even from the more radical Irish theater. Her plays have been described by Michael Etherton as emphasizing "the central and unresolved conflict between revolution and reform: the relationship of socialism to republicanism in the context of north and south, and the issue of land in Ireland which continues to underscore the struggle today; their particular depiction of women; the emblematic theatre which they have recreated and its antecedents in carnival and the Corpus Christi cycle of the medieval theatre."

Hugh Leonard, whose work is well known in other parts of the world, is an Irish playwright and television writer less involved with political questions and more concerned with the family and small social groups of typical urban Irish life. His touching play *Da* (pr., pb. 1973) received considerable attention and was made into a film starring Jack Lemmon. Leonard's memoirs, the last installment of which, *Out After Dark*, was published in 1989, are rather more typical of his laconic humor and sometimes distancing technique found in such commercial work as *Pizzazz* (pr. 1984, pb. 1987).

Other playwrights of note, all of whom are benefiting from Friel's and play development techniques, are Thomas Kilroy (*Double Cross*, performed in 1986 at the Field Day Theatre), Anne Devlin (whose *Ourselves Alone*, *The Long March*, and *A Woman Calling* were produced and published together in 1986), Bernard Farrell (*All the Way Back*, pr. 1985, pb. 1988), and Tom MacIntyre (*Dance for Your Daddy*, pr. 1987).

Cóilín D. Owens
(Updated by *Thomas J. Taylor*)

WEST INDIAN DRAMA

Since Christopher Columbus' voyage, the people of the West Indies have been sharply divided between the privileged and the dispossessed, the elite and the common, the rich and the poor. (Until 1838, there was as well the division between the free and the enslaved.) The development of drama in the West Indies closely follows the region's historical and cultural development, from its colonial beginnings, through the periods of slavery and emancipation, to the growing national consciousness in the twentieth century that led to political independence for most of the English-speaking islands. From the first theater in the region, in Jamaica in 1682, until the 1930's, drama in the West Indies largely followed English fashion, serving to maintain the colonizers' identity with their mother country. The goal of creating an indigenous West Indian drama—that is, one that addresses the West Indian experience and is created by and for the native West Indian— has determined the direction of theatrical endeavor since the 1930's.

The gradual blending of European and African cultural traditions over nearly five hundred years has produced the modern West Indian Creole languages and cultures. Thus, the question of what is and is not distinctively West Indian in drama is part of the larger issue of cultural heritage. African elements in the folk traditions are strongly dramatic, especially in the carnival and Calypso of Trinidad, the mummers in many smaller islands, and the pantomime and Pocomania in Jamaica. Participants in the carnival masquerade called "The Pierrot," for example, wear elaborate costumes, usually with a headpiece and a long train held by a small boy. Each man carries a whip. They set out through the city, and whenever they encounter one another, they exchange long speeches. If one falters in his elaborate oratory, he feels his rival's lash. The mummers of Nevis and Saint Kitts perform in the streets during Christmas and Easter holidays. They recite, play, dance, and mime stories, many of them derived from medieval English mumming plays, Arthurian legends, and Renaissance drama. The argument that theater is a European institution and therefore alien to the West Indies ignores the significant assimilation of English custom into the culture.

Nevertheless, it is true that for the first 250 years of its existence, the West Indian theater was the property of the elite. The colonial theater existed for the privileged, for the plantation owner, the governor, the young Englishmen who came in search of wealth and exotic experience. Actors and plays were English, performed for audiences whose cultural identity was still centered on Great Britain, rather than on the New World. Eighteenth century New York actors would proudly add to their credits a brief respite in the Jamaican theater, a theater, however, almost wholly British in character and content. The few plays from that period that included West

Indian characters or settings used them for exotic appeal or to support the antislavery movement, as in Richard Cumberland's *The West Indian* (pr. 1771) and the romantic comedy *Inkle and Yarico* (pr. 1787) by George Colman the Younger. More typical of the dramatic treatment of slave life is Thomas Southerne's *Oroonoko: Or, The Royal Slave* (pr. 1695), a Restoration tragicomedy, based on Aphra Behn's novel, about an African prince who is kidnapped by an English captain and sold into slavery in Surinam. The prince's wife becomes the object of the deputy-governor's passion and the subject of a comic underplot.

Barbados had its first dramatic society in 1729, Antigua in 1788, and Saint Lucia in 1832. By the 1820's, Port of Spain, the capital of Trinidad, supported three theaters and five performing companies. The repertoire was imported, except for a few short plays by Edward Lanza Joseph, who came to Trinidad from Scotland in 1820, and wrote plays and poetry until his death in 1840. He was dubbed "the Bard of Trinidad" because his plays, notably *Martial Law* (pr. 1832), were set locally and dealt with timely subjects.

Through the nineteenth and early twentieth centuries, plays by local playwrights were generally written in the Shakespearean manner, with West Indian characters providing comic relief. The Jesuit C. W. Barrand wrote two such five-act plays in blank verse: *St. Thomas of Canterbury* (pr. 1892) and *St. Elizabeth of Hungary* (pr. 1890). The epic *San Gloria* (pr. 1920), by Tom Redcam (the pen name of Thomas H. MacDermott), a play about Columbus, is in a similarly Elizabethan vein, but Redcam's sympathetic treatment of the Afro-West Indian presents a marked contrast to the usual treatment of blacks as lowlife characters speaking comic, pidgin English. The few black characters appearing in West Indian drama of this period were always played by white actors in blackface, but even when the situation would appear to demand black characters, they were usually omitted. The eighty percent black majority of Trinidad had no part, for example, in the first West Indian historical drama, Lewis Osborn Iniss' *Carmelita: The Belle of San Jose* (pr. 1897). Written for the centenary of England's takeover of the island from Spain, the play concerns a young English officer who falls in love with the young Spanish beauty Carmelita. Their union is a symbol of England's affectionate husbandry of its colony, yet the black population whose labor sustained the colony had no part in the historical drama.

The playwright George Bernard Shaw visited Jamaica in 1911 and in a press interview told Jamaicans that they ought to nourish their own culture by, among other projects, building a theater and keeping the American and English traveling companies out of it. He said that if the Jamaicans would write their own plays and do their own acting, the English would soon send their children to Jamaica for culture, instead of the other way around.

As he so often lamented, Shaw went unheard. For the next three decades, wealthy Jamaicans continued to travel to the United States and England to attend plays and maintain cultural connections, and in January of each year, a touring English company would stage plays at very high prices in Kingston.

Nevertheless, given the growing national consciousness of West Indians in the 1930's, Shaw's advice proved prophetic. The first play about the black experience in the New World to feature a historical figure of heroic stature was *Touissant l'Ouverture* (pr. 1936), by the Trinidadian writer C. L. R. James. The play was produced in London with Paul Robeson in the title role. A number of West Indians who had been studying or working in England at that time returned to the Caribbean with an interest in changing the theater to include working-class people who had largely been excluded from productions (except for Marcus Garvey's outdoor theater in Jamaica in the early 1930's). Una Marson returned to Jamaica in 1937 to produce her play *Pocomania* (pr. 1938), which was the first play to use the African-derived religion named in the title as dramatic material.

Later, once again in England, Marson founded the British Broadcasting Corporation program *Caribbean Voices* (1942), which, along with a number of new magazines and drama groups, gave strong impetus to a new generation of West Indian playwrights, poets, and novelists. Magazines that published local writers were founded: *The Beacon* (1931) in Trinidad, *Bim* (1942) in Barbados, *Focus* (1943) in Jamaica, and *Kyk-over-al* (1945) in Guyana. An upsurge of interest in drama created a number of groups, including the Little Theatre Movement (1941) in Jamaica, the White Hall Players (1946) in Trinidad, the Georgetown Dramatic Group (1948) in Guyana, and the St. Lucia Arts Guild (1950) in St. Lucia. Committed to developing an indigenous drama, such groups needed more work from local playwrights. Edna Manley in the 1948 edition of *Focus* published Cicely Howland's *Storm Signal* and George Campbell's *Play Without Scenery*, but lamented in the issue's foreword that the Little Theatre Movement was still in great need of Jamaican plays.

Little more than a decade later, the Trinidadian playwright Errol Hill claimed that there were twenty-seven West Indian dramatists writing at home or abroad, and twenty years later, the Georgetown Public Library published a list of more than one hundred Guyanese plays, many of which had been produced by the Theatre Guild of Guyana, founded in 1957. The University of the West Indies has published its Caribbean Plays Editions from its extramural departments in Jamaica and Trinidad since the 1950's, and has made available scores of plays.

The theater groups have done a great deal to encourage both writing and production of West Indian plays. While strongly identified with the annual pantomime, the Little Theatre Movement of Jamaica has produced work by many West Indian playwrights, notably Errol Hill, Errol John, Barry

Reckord, Trevor Rhone, and Dennis Scott. The Theatre Guild of Guyana gave the first Caribbean production of John's *Moon on a Rainbow Shawl* (pr. 1957), which won the London *Observer*'s play competition of 1957 and has been produced in Europe, North and South America, and Australia. The Guild also premiered Evan Jones's *In a Backward Country* (pr. 1959) as well as work by many Guyanese playwrights, most notably Frank Pilgrim's *Miriamy* (pr. 1962) and Sheik Sadeek's *Porkknockers* (pr. 1974).

The St. Lucia Arts Guild has the distinction of having produced the two most prolific and important playwrights in the Caribbean, the brothers Derek and Roderick Walcott. Both are legendary in the region, Derek Walcott having won the 1992 Nobel Prize in Literature. Though less well-known outside the Caribbean than his brother, Roderick Walcott is highly regarded for his dramatically powerful use of the Creole of St. Lucia, as well as his integration of folk traditions and music in dramatic situations. His best-known plays include *The Harrowing of Benjy* (pr. 1958), *A Flight of Sparrows* (pr. 1966), *Banjo Man* (pr. 1972; performed at Carifesta, Guyana), and *Chanson Marianne* (pr. 1974), which was commissioned for the Conference of Prime Ministers of the West Indies meeting in St. Lucia in 1974. The commitment of a playwright of Roderick Walcott's stature to remain in the West Indies gives reason for hope that the exodus of writers that has plagued the region since Claude McKay left Jamaica in 1912 is at least slackening.

Derek Walcott is the one West Indian playwright of truly international stature; he is also widely regarded as one of the foremost contemporary English-language poets. He has written some fifty plays, of which twenty are available in print. His accomplishments are legion. The production of his verse play *Henri Christophe: A Chronicle* (pr. 1950), about the Haitian monarch, is widely regarded as the foundation of an indigenous West Indian drama. Though the production was staged in London, the cast and crew were West Indian, and included many of the region's leading writers. The Barbadian novelist George Lamming wrote the prologue; Hill, who directed the London production, and John, the lead actor, are both prominent Trinidadian playwrights. When the newly independent Caribbean nations attempted to unite under a federal government, Derek Walcott was commissioned to write a play for the inauguration of the first Federal Parliament. The result was an epic drama, *Drums and Colours* (pr. 1958), that spans four hundred years of history in episodic scenes framed with interludes of carnival dancers. Walcott founded the Trinidad Theatre Workshop in 1959, after studying theater in New York under a Rockefeller Foundation Fellowship. In 1966, the workshop became the first company to produce a complete theatrical season with West Indian players, and in 1967 it became the first West Indian company to tour internationally. In those successive seasons, the workshop premiered two of Walcott's most ambitious plays, *The Sea at Dauphin* (pr. 1950) and *Dream on Monkey Mountain* (pr. 1967). In 1972, the Royal Shakespeare Company commissioned his musical *The Joker of Seville* (pr. 1974).

While a truly indigenous West Indian drama began only in the 1930's, the centuries-old folk traditions have readily lent themselves to the creation of unique West Indian theatrical styles. Critical debate in the theater continues, however, over which heritage, the African or the European, best expresses the West Indian experience. Critical judgments continue to be based on the use of European and African elements in the work, such as metropolitan versus Creole English in dramatic speech. Using the poetic richness of Creole is to limit appeal outside the region, but using metropolitan English in favor of a larger audience is to falsify local character.

C. L. R. James, foremost scholar of Caribbean literature, died in May of 1989 and left behind a legacy of critical understanding of not only Caribbean literature but also world literature. In many respects, with the awarding of the Nobel Prize in Literature to Derek Walcott, West Indian drama came of age in 1992, but Walcott's work has been popular for some time, and Caribbean drama history acknowledges his contribution of *Dream on Monkey Mountain* (pr. 1967, pb. 1970) as the central dramatic work of his canon. His poetry collection *The Arkansas Testament* was published in 1987. Robert D. Hamner, who wrote a definitive book on Walcott in 1981, discusses the "chiaroscuro" metaphor in Walcott's work in an article published in *International Literature in English*, edited by Robert L. Ross, and published by Garland in 1991.

West Indian drama became more popular and accessible in 1985 with the publication of *Caribbean Plays for Playing*, edited by Edith Noel, in which new West Indian playwrights were introduced to a more general public, and whose introduction gave the student of West Indian drama some valuable insights into the origins of experimental theater. The book explains the experimental basis of the folk comedies of Ed Bim Lewis in Jamaica, Freddie Kissoon in Trinidad, and Dennis Scott, Rawle Gibbons, "Sistren" (the all-female Jamaican group that does documentary theater), and the actors' theater of Ken Corsbie and Mark Mathews in Guyana. Younger writers such as Kendel Hippolyte of St. Lucia and the commercially oriented works of Trevor Rhone are also mentioned. Other playwrights represented in this important anthology are Zeno Obi Constance and Aldwyn Bully. Less well known but gaining more critical attention is Earl Lovelace, primarily a novelist but also a playwright of several plays, including *Jestina's Calypso* (pr. 1976). Reed Way Dasenbrock, in his article on Lovelace in *International Literature in English*, offers a brief overview of his work and a valuable bibliography of articles about Lovelace to 1989.

Robert Bensen
(Updated by *Thomas J. Taylor*)

ENGLISH LANGUAGE OPERA

The history of opera written to an English libretto or book (either sung throughout or with spoken dialogue interspersed between the musical numbers) is one of long, deep valleys separated by but a few noteworthy crests. Following the invention of opera as a recognizable form by the Florentine camerata (a Humanistic discussion group that met in the late 1570's and early 1580's in the Florentine palace of Giovanni Bardi, Count of Vernio) just before the start of the seventeenth century, first France and then Germany joined Italy in developing a distinctly national form both in content and sound. This was not to be the case in Great Britain and, collaterally, the United States until the early twentieth century. Pure chance and ill fortune, combined with less definable causes such as public taste, account for the absence of an ongoing tradition. Equally curious, however, is the development of a sturdy form of English opera since the 1930's and its dominance in international theater, so that without benefit of indigenous prototypes, a powerful force in the lyric theater has been produced out of the thinnest of rarefied air.

The Seventeenth and Eighteenth Centuries

At the beginning of the seventeenth century, after the accession of James I to the English throne, the masque, a court pastime combining an allegorical story, dialogue, and vocal and dance music with scenic and costume spectacle, became dominant as royal entertainment. Although none of the great Elizabethan composers contributed music, masques incorporated lyrics, accompanied recitative, and scenic and costume design that later would appear in the first acknowledged English operas. The mighty forces behind the masque were the scenarios and words of Ben Jonson and the scenery and costumes of designer-architect Inigo Jones, whose knowledge of Italian practices introduced the British to the stage picture and craft of Italian scene painters and machinists. In 1617, Nicholas Lanier composed for Jonson's masque, *Lovers Made Men* (pr. 1617), what was most likely the first English recitative, a type of vocal composition patterned on the natural rhythms of speech, in the Italian style of Claudio Monteverdi. Although the music is lost, it is doubtful that it would have exerted much influence on an English public that had come to prefer the traditional structure of the masque, with its fast-moving dialogue separating the songs known as "ayres." Even before the execution of Charles I, the Commonwealth government suppressed theater, but the ruling Puritans did not as vigorously oppose secular music. This situation led to the curious attempt by practitioners of theater to circumvent the harsh laws by presenting stage spectacles under the guise of musical concerts. It was in this context that, at Rutland House in 1656, William Davenant's *The Siege of*

Rhodes (pr. 1656-1659) was given a private performance. Davenant's work was subtitled *A Representation by the Art of Prospective in Scenes and the Story Sung in Recitative Musick in Five Acts*; the music (now lost) was contributed by a number of composers, including Matthew Locke and Henry Lawes. The changeable scenery in the Italian style was designed by John Webb, a student of then recently deceased Inigo Jones.

The first irony in the development of English opera came with the restoration of Charles II four years later, when the ban on spoken drama was lifted. The English, including Davenant, who was given one of the two monopolies to present plays in London, returned to their love of words and virtually abandoned their earlier attempts at opera. Incidental music for the theater and interpolated songs persisted, as did remnants of masques, now heavily influenced by the court of Louis XIV of France, where the new English king and much of his court had found refuge during the interregnum of the Puritan Parliament. Chief among these influences was Jean-Baptiste Lully, the Italian-born composer who had become the titan of French music.

Indeed, that a native English music survived to the end of the seventeenth century was somewhat miraculous, considering the English tendency to look to the Continent for what they thought was true genius. The slim promise of an English school of opera in the closing years of the seventeenth century rested with three composers: the previously mentioned Locke, with his setting of Thomas Shadwell's adaptation of Lully's *tragédie lyrique* entitled *Psyche* (pr. 1675); John Blow, with his one complete work for the musical stage, *Venus and Adonis* (pr. 1684?); and, most important, Henry Purcell. Purcell's one complete work for the stage, *Dido and Aeneas* (pr. 1689?) with a superb libretto by Nahum Tate, is the earliest English opera to achieve a place in the international standard repertory. Despite his short lifetime, with *Dido and Aeneas* and his incidental music for spoken drama, Purcell seemed to light the way for future generations of theater composers.

Such, however, was not to be the course followed by theatrical history. Between the time of Purcell's death and the arrival of George Frederick Handel and his *Rinaldo* in 1711, operatic as well as theatrical tastes changed radically in London. In the theater, the forty-year reign of the rather prurient comedy of manners came under successful attack and was replaced by a more sentimental comedy meant to inspire a higher moral tone. Even the continued revivals of William Shakespeare's plays were marked by adaptations to the prevailing sentimental tone found in the new comedy. Purcell's prototype of what might have been a truly national form of opera virtually disappeared, overwhelmed by the change in popular taste that saw French and French-inspired English music fall out of favor, succumbing to the wave of Italian music and musicians that flooded England.

With this wave came a type of singer known as a castrato, who had been sexually neutered prior to puberty so that his voice would not change. The unique sound which these male sopranos or altos produced made them the most celebrated singers in eighteenth century Europe.

Another sign of the triumph of the Italian style was the unchallenged preeminence of the German-born Handel, whose four-decade dominance of English opera was to obscure other English stage composers from history's notice. Despite Handel's conquest of London's opera stage, his works fall outside the scope of this essay, because all of his operas composed in England were in Italian, adhering to the international craze for that genre known as *opera seria*. Although Handel wrote forty such operas, his dramatic oratorios, sung in English, but similar in structure and style to his *opera seria*, proved his greatest legacy to English musical theater. A performance in 1732 of his greatly revised *Esther* (pr. 1718) initiated a long series of these quasi-dramatic works based on biblical subjects, such as *Samson* (pr. 1743), *Saul* (pr. 1739), *Judas Maccabaeus* (pr. 1747), and *Solomon* (pr. 1749). Originally intended to be presented during Lent, even in Handel's time these oratorios found their way out of season into more than one theater. Such was their success that the audiences of England have still not lost their taste for Handel's semioperatic works and their successors, including Sir Arthur Sullivan's *The Prodigal Son* (pr. 1869), Sir Edward Elgar's *The Dream of Gerontius* (pr. 1900), Sir William Walton's *Belshazzar's Feast* (pr. 1931), and Michael Tippett's *A Child of Our Time* (pr. 1941).

The attempt to write Italianate full-length operas continued through the 1760's. Thomas Augustine Arne, the most accomplished composer of his day, based his own English text of *Artaxerxes* (pr. 1762) on that of *opera seria*'s most prolific librettist, Pietro Metastasio. This isolated attempt to transfer Italian opera into the English language coincided with the last gasps of *opera seria* on the Continent, where comic opera had already begun to supplant and cause modification to the older form. In England, as if in response to playwright and librettist Joseph Addison's anguished pleas about not allowing Italian music to "entirely annihilate and destroy" English music, new forms of English musical stage works appeared. The most successful of these new forms was known as "ballad opera," and its first major author, John Gay, made a direct assault on the Italian norm with his satiric *The Beggar's Opera* (pr. 1728). Gay supplied the play and lyrics, and Johann Christoph Pepusch arranged sixty-nine popular tunes, including a march from Handel's *Rinaldo*. Although the play and lyrics of ballad operas were almost always original, the music was usually borrowed, in a popular vein, and often uncredited. The success of *The Beggar's Opera* inspired hundreds of other attempts in the same style. For the next sixty years, the ballad opera was a uniquely English form of theater that combined dialogue (generally superior to that of any Continental comic or serious opera), catchy tunes, and a talent for satire seldom found elsewhere. Besides satire of politics and politicians, the middle classes, and the legal profession, *The Beggar's Opera* poked fun at Italian opera and its performers, who at the time so dominated the London musical scene. One of its successors, *The Devil to Pay* (pr. 1743), by Charles Coffey, is historically important as the direct progenitor of German comic opera. It was also one of the first operas performed in the American colonies, in Charleston, South Carolina, in 1736.

A relative to the ballad opera was the *pasticcio*, which took pieces of successful works and tied them together on a very slender string. Usually the *pasticcio* was found as an afterpiece during the standard eighteenth century evening of entertainment that included a spoken drama. In the last decades of the century, both the ballad opera and the *pasticcio* were replaced in public favor by an English comic opera with spoken dialogue and original music by one or more composers. Of these, Richard Brinsley Sheridan's *The Duenna: Or, The Double Elopement* (pr. 1775), with music by Thomas Linley the elder and Thomas Linley the younger, was very popular and has remained of interest primarily because of the reputation of its playwright. Despite the bold success of ballad opera, the eighteenth century produced little of an enduring nature in terms of English opera. If this is true in the Old World, the fate of the few comic operas composed in the newly independent country of the United States was even less impressive.

The Nineteenth Century

The transition between the eighteenth and nineteenth centuries was tumultuous both politically and culturally. The shock waves of the French Revolution, followed as it was by Napoleon Bonaparte's initially republican-inspired conquests, found artistic expression in so-called rescue operas, of which Ludwig van Beethoven's *Fidelio* (pr. 1805) is a major example. In prose, poetry, and dramatic literature, revolution found its expression in the Romantics' assault on the bastilles of neoclassical drama and the worn-out *opera seria*. Although England was one of the dominant forces in the new movement with the novels of Sir Walter Scott, the poetry of William Wordsworth, and the scenic designs for antiquarian, medieval productions of the now faithfully restored plays of Shakespeare, it was left to the Italians and the French to set these works in operatic form. While the Germans were developing opera rooted in their own mythology and medieval history, what little that passed for English opera retained the form of comic opera with musical selections separated by spoken dialogue and introduced the style of semiserious opera emphasizing sentimentality over history and tragedy. During the first seventy years of the nineteenth century, England produced only a handful of successful or important musical works for the stage, and these were products of non-English composers and found little audience outside England.

The first of these works was by the influential founder of the German Romantic school of opera, Carl Maria von Weber, whose *Der Freischütz* (pr. 1821) was to set a standard for subsequent developments by Richard Wagner. In 1826, shortly before his death in London, Weber opened *Oberon: Or, The Elf-King's Oath*, an opera in English to a libretto by James Robinson Planché. Its overture remains a concert favorite, and its fairy music became the model for popular future incarnations such as those found in W. S. Gilbert and Sir Arthur Sullivan's *Iolanthe: Or, The Peer and the Peri* (pr. 1882). With the exception of Giuseppe Verdi, who was commissioned to write an opera for Jenny Lind in Italian for a London production in 1847, this was the last work by a non-British composer to be specially written for London. That England went from a perpetual importer of European music, especially French and Italian in origin, to semi-isolation in less than sixty years is difficult to explain except as a consequence of cultural chauvinism.

The two works that were to prove the most enduring in England for the rest of the century were products of Ireland. Dating back to the time of Handel and even before, Dublin had been London's only rival as a center for works in English for the lyric stage, and it was from there that Michael William Balfe's *The Bohemian Girl* (pr. 1843) and William Vincent Wallace's *Maritana* (pr. 1845) emerged. Coupled with *Lily of Killarney* (pr. 1862), by Sir Julius Benedict, a German émigré, these works made up the trio of successful romantic dialogue-operas that neither broke new ground nor established a distinctive national style or sound, since their music was based primarily on the approach of Gioacchino Rossini and Antonio Gaetano Donizetti. Only two through-composed operas of note during the nineteenth century must be mentioned: John Barnett's *The Mountain Sylph* (pr. 1834) and Sullivan's *Ivanhoe* (pr. 1891), the latter a failure but a notable attempt at English grand opera with an English subject.

Despite his failure at grand opera, Sullivan, working with established author W. S. Gilbert as librettist, was to create the most enduring works of the English musical theater. These comic operas or operettas, inspired by the *opéras bouffes* of Jacques Offenbach in Paris, became a regular feature of the London theatrical scene in 1875 when impresario Richard D'Oyly Carte brought them together to write a short afterpiece to his production of Offenbach's *La Périchole* (pr. 1868). The resulting one-act comic opera, *Trial by Jury* (pr. 1875), ushered in a string of artistic and financial hits, including *H. M. S. Pinafore: Or, The Lass That Loved a Sailor* (pr. 1878), *The Pirates of Penzance: Or, The Slave of Duty* (pr. 1879), *Patience: Or, Bunthorne's Bride* (pr. 1881), *The Mikado: Or, The Town of Titipu* (pr. 1885), and *The Gondoliers: Or, The King of Barataria* (pr. 1889). As had been the English tradition in comic operas since the days of Gay, the emphasis in these works was on the inventive, sparkling, and truly satiric words, which made Sullivan's role mostly subservient. Although Gilbert and Sullivan's works have failed to become as popular in Europe, where operetta tradition used words simply as a skeleton on which the composer draped the muscle of the music, in the English-speaking world the mercurial words and the close-fitting music continue to hold the stage as easily and delightfully as they did when they were first presented. Gilbert and Sullivan's comic operas represent the major legacy of English musical theater of the nineteenth century.

The fortunes of English opera in England are mirrored in the first hundred years of the history of the United States, although in the latter more interest was focused on native themes, as in George Frederick Bristow's *Rip Van Winkle* (pr. 1855). While imported operas in foreign languages were regularly performed in New Orleans after 1805 and in New York after 1820, it was difficult for American composers to get their works produced: Many organizations, such as the New York Philharmonic Society (1842), were under the control of foreign-born musicians. With native opera expensive to produce, especially by reluctant theaters, many American stage composers turned to writing dramatic cantatas which were similar in form to the English dramatic oratorio. These works, which collectively concentrated on natural or sea disasters (and almost every incident in American history), were produced into the twentieth century. Examples include *The Pilgrim Fathers* (pr. 1854), by George F. Root, and *The Wreck of the Hesperus* (pr. 1887), by Arthur Foote. At the end of the century, the Indianist movement inspired a number of stage works, including Charles Wakefield Cadman's *Shanewis: Or, The Robin Woman* (pr. 1918) and Victor Herbert's *Natoma* (pr. 1911)—one of his two excursions away from popular operettas and Broadway shows into through-composed opera (that is, opera for which new music is composed for each stanza).

The Twentieth Century

The first thirty years of the twentieth century saw opera in both the United States and England dominated by neo-Wagnerian principles in structure and sound, although modified by the *verismo* school of Italian operatic naturalism. Perhaps the closest of Wagner's disciples was the English composer Rutland Boughton, who conceived of a festival home modeled on Wagner's Bayreuth for his own works, based primarily on Celtic and Old English legends. Boughton completed a massive tetralogy based on the Arthurian legends and gave a performance of the second piece, *The Round Table*, in 1916 at the Glastonbury Festival, his Bayreuth. The entire work has never been produced, and Boughton's reputation rests on a much simpler work, *The Immortal Hour* (pr. 1914). Other composers influenced by Wagner, perhaps less ambitious than Boughton but equally or more successful, included the only internationally acknowledged female opera composer, Dame Ethel Smyth, whose works include *The Wreckers* (pr. 1906), which is still able to hold the stage in revivals. Frederick Delius, who lived most of his life outside England, wrote six operas, of which *A Village Romeo and Juliet* (pr. 1907) is still performed.

In America, the late German Romantic school was represented by Walter Damrosch's *The Scarlet Letter* (pr. 1896) and *The Man Without a Country* (pr. 1937), as well as Deems Taylor's *The King's Henchman* (pr. 1927) and *Peter Ibbetson* (pr. 1931), both of which premiered at the Metropolitan Opera House in New York. Howard Hanson's *Merry Mount* (pr. 1933), based on a novel by Nathaniel Hawthorne, made its debut at the Metropolitan and remains one of the grandest of grand operas using an American setting.

Two trends in opera written to an English libretto have been dominant since 1930; the first is the introduction of folk elements or reworked folk music into the story, setting, and texture of the work; the second employs naturalistic psychological studies of characters and music that embodies the emotions generated from within them. To be sure, there have been experiments in impressionism and other non-naturalistic forms, but most of these have been found in French, German, and Italian works. Exceptions include Virgil Thomson and Gertrude Stein's collaborations on *Four Saints in Three Acts* (pr. 1934) and *The Mother of Us All* (pr. 1947), with their focus on stimulation of the senses rather than content; Igor Stravinsky's *The Rake's Progress* (pr. 1951), based on drawings of William Hogarth with music consciously aping the style of Wolfgang Amadeus Mozart; and Marc Blitzstein's agitprop opera, *The Cradle Will Rock* (pr. 1937), modeled on the style of Bertolt Brecht and Kurt Weill.

In the mainstream of folk opera, England saw the work of two major composers, Gustav Holst in *At the Boar's Head* (pr. 1925) and Ralph Vaughan Williams in *Hugh the Drover* (pr. 1924) and *Sir John in Love* (pr. 1929), while in the United States a steady stream of folk or folk-related operas appeared during the 1950's and 1960's. Many American composers' contributions in this field were given active encouragement and first performances at the New York City Opera. Included in the long list of works that fall into this category are *The Tender Land* (pr. 1954) by Aaron Copland, *The Ballad of Baby Doe* (pr. 1956) and *Carrie Nation* (pr. 1966) by Douglas Moore, *Susannah* (pr. 1955) by Carlisle Floyd, and *Lizzie Borden* (pr. 1965) by Jack Beeson.

The second trend, into psychological naturalism, is highlighted in the United States by Kurt Weill's setting of Elmer Rice's play *Street Scene* (pr. 1947), the highly charged *The Medium* (pr. 1946) and *The Consul* (pr. 1950) by Gian Carlo Menotti, and the lyric *Vanessa* (pr. 1958) by Samuel Barber. In England after World War II, a titan of English opera emerged within a month after the fall of Germany. On June 7, 1945, the Sadler's Wells Opera reopened with the premiere of *Peter Grimes* by composer Benjamin Britten, and onto the international scene burst a universally acknowledged operatic genius. In his twelve operas, Britten mixes rich orchestral textures, extensive choral music, and an almost unerring sense of characterization. In addition to *Peter Grimes*, Britten's *Billy Budd* (pr. 1951)—based on the Herman Melville story—and *Death in Venice* (pr. 1973)—based on Thomas Mann's novella—have found their way into the standard repertory of the world's major opera houses and have elevated English opera to a status unknown since Purcell. Two other major English opera composers have works approaching the same international status: the established Michael Tippett, with works such as *The Midsummer Marriage* (pr. 1955) and *The Knot Garden* (pr. 1970); and the younger Peter Maxwell Davies, with *Taverner* (pr. 1972) and *The Lighthouse* (pr. 1979).

As the dividing lines among opera, operetta, and musical comedy have blurred in the United States, and to a lesser extent in England, the commercial theater has become the proving ground for new works. Beginning with George and Ira Gershwin's jazz-inspired collaboration with DuBose and Dorothy Heyward, *Porgy and Bess* (pr. 1935), which took fifty years to reach the stage of the Metropolitan Opera House, a long list of works originally produced on Broadway have taken their places in both European and American opera houses. Among these are Menotti's *The Medium* and *The Consul*, Blitzstein's *Regina* (1949), Lillian Hellman and Leonard Bernstein's *Candide* (pr. 1956), Arthur Laurents and Bernstein's *West Side Story* (pr. 1957), Frank Loesser's *The Most Happy Fella* (pr. 1956), and Stephen Sondheim's *A Little Night Music* (pr. 1973) and *Sweeney Todd, the Demon Barber of Fleet Street* (pr. 1979). With the growing acceptance of a broader definition of opera, the efforts of English and American composers have assumed a central position in the operatic centers of the world.

The dividing line between opera and musical theater has become more obscured as the two disciplines merge: musical theater demanding stronger voices with more complex melodic lines and more sung dialogue, and opera moving toward popular themes and more accessible librettos. Musicals such as *Les Misérables* (first produced in French in 1980 and in English in 1985) and *Phantom of the Opera* (pr. 1986) can be described as operas, since a large part of the dialogue is sung. Similarly, *Miss Saigon* (pr. 1987) and *Chess* (pr. 1986) can be seen as opera and are regularly reviewed in such periodicals as *Opera News*. Musical composer Ned Rorem said in *Opera News* (July, 1991) that "the sole difference between opera and musical comedy is that one uses conservatory-trained voices while the other uses show-biz voices." Stanley Silverman put it less somberly, noting that "opera is merely musical comedy an octave higher."

As examples of popular themes in English language opera, the 1980's saw Henry James's *The Aspern Papers*, John Steinbeck's *Of Mice and Men*, James M. Cain's *The Postman Always Rings Twice*, and Luigi Pirandello's *Six Characters in Search of an Author* all transformed into operas. As opera experiments with its forms, the now traditional English language operas of Gian Carlo Menotti continue to find their way into the seasons of regional companies. For example, the double bill of *Help! Help! The Gobolinks!* (pr. 1969) and *Amahl and the Night Visitors* (pb. 1952, pr. 1953) was part of the Buffalo, New York, opera season in 1990.

The best names in English language opera occur again and again. Carlisle Floyd's completely rewritten *Passion of Jonathan Wade* was performed in 1992 in Houston, Miami, San Diego, and Seattle; the tale of a Reconstruction-era clash between North and South, it was billed as a world premiere, despite its original production in 1962. Floyd became famous for his *Susanna* (pr. 1956, pb. 1957) and the less successful *Willie Stark* (pr., pb. 1981). Douglas Moore's *Ballad of Baby Doe* (pb. 1955) is also performed occasionally. Leonard Bernstein revised *Candide* (pr., pb. 1956) in 1988 and recorded the new version in 1989.

Closer to the avant-garde are the productions of Judith Weir's *A Night at the Chinese Opera* (pr. 1987, pb. 1988) and *The Vanishing Bridegroom* (pr., pb. 1990), both performed in Scotland. Philip Glass's *Hydrogen Jukebox* (pr., pb. 1990) continued this composer's assault on the definition of music; Peter Sellars' direction of John Adams' *Nixon in China* (pb. 1981) and *The Death of Klinghoffer* (pr., pb. 1991) is notable for the plays' unusual staging and subject matter. *Atlas*, by Meredith Monk, was staged at the Houston Grand Opera in 1991, after being workshopped from 1988 to 1990. William M. Hoffman and John Corigliano collaborated to bring *The Ghosts of Versailles*, after Pierre-Augustin Caron de Beaumarchais' *La Mère coupable*, to broadcast form in 1992.

Finally, no discussion of modern English language opera can be complete without the mention of Robert Wilson, a writer/designer/director whose avant-garde, multifaceted works combine operatic size and musical complexity with the visual possibilities of the stage and the meditative concentration of philosophical speculation. Wilson began his experimental career with theater pieces, "demonstrations," workshops, and other alternative theater activities. Often he tried "sound" pieces, whose function was to experience pure sound rather than the contextual tyranny of words. After his early "sound" works gained acceptance, Wilson tried an actual opera, *The Life and Times of Joseph Stalin* (pr. 1973), with music by Alan Lloyd, Igor Demjen, and others. It previewed in Copenhagen as a production of the Byrd Hoffman School of Byrds and premiered at the Brooklyn Academy of Music in December of 1973. Truncated versions of the opera were subsequently performed, along with Wilson's next opera, *A Letter for Queen Victoria* (pr. 1974). The following years continued Wilson's collaborations with his team of composers, choreographers, visual artists, and actors: *Einstein on the Beach* (pr. 1976), one of the most successful of this series of works, with music by Philip Glass, premiered in France. Among several "plays," Wilson designed and directed *Medea* (pr. 1981) and *the CIVIL warS* (pr. 1983, 1984), as well as some operas in other languages.

From these ambitious operatic constructions, usually performed at the Brooklyn Academy of Music, Wilson became more and more accepted in the world of English language opera. Wilson's imaginative and demanding productions have forced opera to expand its self-definition to include works as far removed from nineteenth century notions as his collaborators— Meredith Monk, David Byrne, Allen Ginsberg, Christopher Knowles, Laurie Anderson, Richard Foreman, and many others—are different from their classical counterparts in dance, theater, and dramaturgy.

John R. Lucas
(Updated by *Thomas J. Taylor*)

MUSICAL DRAMA

The musical drama, musical play, or simply the musical is an evening-length theater piece integrating spoken dialogue and sung music in order to tell a story. The story, or book, while it may take up serious matters, always has a significant, if not dominant, comic element, and the characters in the story are recognizable and accessible to all members of the audience. The music, usually a set of songs, is composed in a popular idiom.

The foremost criterion for evaluating a musical's artistic success is the integration of book and music. In the best musicals, songs are like compressed scenes of dialogue, revealing character and moving the plot along. A song should never impede the action of the story. Also, in the very best musicals there is a unity of style or tone to the songs; they constitute a musical suite.

Secondary criteria for judging musicals are often derived from the relation of the story and musical idiom to the audience. A story can stray too far from an audience's experience or expectations, either in the general nature of the narrative events or in the relative degree of comedy in the plot. Music similarly challenges an audience when it approaches the technical or conceptual complexity of classical forms. Such musicals, even if they come from Broadway or London's West End, are frequently denied the label "musical," sometimes by their composers. Instead, they are called operettas or even operas.

Since *Porgy and Bess* (pr. 1935), *Sweeney Todd, the Demon Barber of Fleet Street* (pr. 1979), and, by some accounts, even *My Fair Lady* (pr. 1956) and *Oklahoma!* (pr. 1943) belong to this group of musicals, the confusion of terminology ought to give pause. Definitions and criteria for the musical cannot be rigidly fixed. At the most superficial level, many a musical with a weak or poor book has become fantastically successful at the box office. From the artistic viewpoint, it would seem almost inevitable that a creative integration of story and music will challenge an audience's experiences and expectations; this is the quality of good art. During the 1984-1985 season, *Porgy and Bess* and *Sweeney Todd* were taken into the repertories of, respectively, the Metropolitan Opera and the New York City Opera. Perhaps the two works are operas—or perhaps labels such as "musical" and "operetta" and "opera" have outlived their usefulness: There is only musical theater. Indeed, perhaps no works ever written fulfill the criteria outlined as essential to musicals as successfully as do Wolfgang Amadeus Mozart's comic operas, which even include spoken dialogue. It is instructive to recall that *The Magic Flute* (pr. 1791), which is called an opera, was written for the *Singspiel*, the German language vaudeville, and that it satisfied a commercial craving for music, story, and spectacle as great as any possessed by contemporary audiences.

Evolution of the Musical

Musical theater in English goes back to the court masques of the Renaissance—private productions which, in the case of Ben Jonson's works, achieved a highly wrought integration of poetry, music, and spectacle. William Shakespeare first made a musical production number part of public theater when he inserted a full masque into the action of *The Tempest* (pr. 1611).

Strangely, the vicissitudes that beset English drama over the next century had the effect of encouraging musical theater. The Puritan Commonwealth's proscription extended to plays only; while few dared to indulge in this loophole with impunity, opera in English first dates from this period. The Restoration authorities also restrained legitimate drama, this time by awarding exclusive patents to the Covent Garden and the Drury Lane theaters; again musical theater went unrestricted. Even when musical entertainment was finally brought under governmental regulation early in the eighteenth century through the issuing of burletta licenses, the effect was to further musical theater, for the licensing rules established a minimum of five musical numbers per act as a requirement for a license; the real purpose of the burletta licenses was to provide further protection for the two legitimate theaters.

With all this opportunity, one might suppose that musical theater in England matured rapidly during the reign of the Georges, but this is not so. The artistic success of John Gay's *The Beggar's Opera* (pr. 1728), the earliest theater piece identifiable as a musical drama or musical play, was singular. No exceptional work of popular musical theater appeared again for 150 years, until the musical plays of W. S. Gilbert and Sir Arthur Sullivan, which are most frequently labeled "comic operas."

Gay's purposes in *The Beggar's Opera* were satiric, his victim the Italianate opera made fashionable by George Frederick Handel, but his approach to musical theater clearly foreshadows that of the modern musical play. For opera's knights and princesses, Gay substituted highwaymen and whores. Instead of recitative, Gay used spoken dialogue. Finally, the music for *The Beggar's Opera* was not classical; Gay's characters sang lyrics set to the popular tunes of the day.

Gay's success spawned many imitations. Indeed, burlesquing the pretentions of high art, whether opera or literature, never lost its popularity, although, after Gay, few of these works were evening-length pieces. Also popular were shows such as *Tom and Jerry: Or, Life in London* (pr. 1823), Pierce Egan's theater work that was part comic sketch, part travelogue, part musical. Shorter early musicals were performed on bills in variety or vaudeville theaters. Variety was the most popular of all the musical theater forms; in and out of favor over the decades were pantomime (only partly mute) and the "extravaganza," a form that featured dance (frequently with an element of titillation), elaborate stage machinery, and, often, burlesque or parody.

The Beggar's Opera came to America in 1751. All the early musical entertainment forms flourished in America, except perhaps pantomime, which was never as popular as in England. Early in the nineteenth century, America added its own indigenous musical theater form, the minstrel show, whose three-part structure allowed for musical sketches as the final feature of the performance. The larger import of the arrival of musical theater in the United States is that the history of musical theater in English thereafter became mostly an American story. Indeed, the popular musical drama is most often said to be an American art form.

During the second half of the nineteenth century, the distinctions among the various types of musical theater (never rigid to begin with) began to blur. *The Black Crook* (pr. 1866), by Charles M. Barras, often cited as America's first important musical theater production, was famed for its scandalous ballets but also included in its full evening's worth of entertainment a plot, dialogue, and songs. The pantomime *Humpty-Dumpty* (pr. 1868) kept all the production values, and it added much-needed comedy. Edward Harrigan and Tony Hart's short plays with original songs about a group of New York Irish called the Mulligan Guard, which appeared regularly from 1877 to 1885, are often credited with popularizing the musical play's interest in the common folk. Probably the most commercially successful musical of the nineteenth century was an elaborate 1874 burlesque of Henry Wadsworth Longfellow's *Evangeline* (1847) by J. Cheever Goodwin and Edward E. Rice. *Evangeline* incorporated nearly all the elements of all the forms of musical theater and had a full original score. *Adonis* (pr. 1884), William Gill's evening-length burlesque of the Pygmalion myth, was another proof that integration of plot and musical elements was well under way.

It is England, however, that is usually given credit for producing the first musical comedies. Ironically, George Edwardes, an English impresario, had seen a number of American theatrical imports in London and had been struck both by their integration of story and music and by their popularity. He created for his own theaters, the Gaiety and the Prince of Wales, a series of musical comedy plays whose use of musical elements to tell a story was subtle enough to seem original. His three principal productions, *In Town* (pr. 1892), *The Gaiety Girl* (pr. 1893), and *The Shop Girl* (pr. 1895), all employed the same plot: A poor girl, an actress or a shop girl, succeeds in marrying into the upper crust. By modern standards, the plot was simply an excuse for the musical numbers. Still, it was a beginning.

One of Edwardes' goals was to make the musical theater more respectable, and so more profitable. His chorus girls, the wildly popular Gaiety Girls, the ancestors of the Florodora and Follies girls, were fully and fashionably clothed. The general quest for respectability in musical theater had already banished "waiter girls" from the music hall, creating thereby both wholesome vaudeville and modern burlesque. Perhaps no other single event contributed to the moral legitimizing of popular musical theater as did the advent of the collaborative works of W. S. Gilbert and Sir Arthur Sullivan; especially influential was their first success, *H.M.S. Pinafore: Or, The Lass That Loved a Sailor* (pr. 1878). The artistic superiority of their work was also quickly recognized, but curiously enough their influence on popular musical theater, despite a few quick-penned imitations, was not significant. Musical comedy went its own evolutionary way.

In part, the explanation of this may lie in the perception of Gilbert and Sullivan's works as operas, albeit comic operas or operettas. Continental comic opera shared a similar fate. Jacques Offenbach was popular but did not directly influence the progress of musical drama in England and the United States. Johann Strauss, Jr., was never popular; *Die Fledermaus* (pr. 1874) was not even produced in England or the United States until decades into the twentieth century. Largely because of its famous waltz, Franz Lehár's *The Merry Widow* (pr. 1905) became one of the greatest stage successes in the English-speaking theater, but again, there was no sudden burst of English-language operettas. Behind musical comedy or musical drama looms opera, the foremost integration of plot and music. One cannot fail to wonder whether the popular musical establishment simply grew skittish about pursuing a course that led, in its perception, away from the expectations and desires of its audience.

Yet there was a kind of American operetta, or rather there was one composer. The English-language version of *The Merry Widow* did not appear until 1907. Victor Herbert's *Babes in Toyland* had been produced in 1903, and *The Red Mill* had appeared in 1906. *Naughty Marietta* dates from 1910, and without question Herbert stands as one of two dominant figures in popular musical theater in the period from 1900 to World War I. Herbert was an immigrant who began his American career as a cellist with the Metropolitan Opera; his wife, Therese Förster, sang in the first American *Aida* (pr. 1871) in the late 1880's. Not surprisingly, his musical plays follow European models; there are lush melodies and improbable stories mostly about Europeans. There is another element in Herbert's shows, however, perhaps most forthrightly apparent in *The Red Mill*. *The Red Mill* is the story of two Yanks in Holland. The operetta part of the show is complemented by American show biz. The Yanks were played by Fred Stone and Dave Montgomery, who made famous L. Frank Baum's 1903 musical *The Wizard of Oz*, and who, along with Joseph M. Weber and Lew Fields, were the most popular vaudeville-type comics of the age. America flirted again with operetta in the 1920's. Rudolf Friml's *Rose-Marie* (pr. 1924) and *The Vagabond King* (pr. 1925) and Sigmund Romberg's *The Student Prince* (pr. 1924) and *The Desert Song* (pr. 1926), among the most successful shows of the decade, are perhaps the closest counterparts to the Continental models of Offenbach and Lehár in American musical history.

The other major figure of the twentieth century's first musical theater decade was George M. Cohan. Cohan's roots were in vaudeville; his parents were headliners, and he and his sister grew up as part of the act. When he began to write and star in musical plays, he never lost a rousing affection for the vaudeville style of performing, and he admitted openly that he played to the balconies. In plays such as *Little Johnny Jones* (pr. 1904) and *Forty-five Minutes from Broadway* (pr. 1906), he also introduced songs such as "Yankee Doodle Dandy" and "Give My Regards to Broadway" and, along with Herbert, helped establish the dominance of the composer in popular musical theater. Cohan's productions are also notable for their flag-waving patriotism. What had been only popular entertainment now became American entertainment, and henceforth one of the recurrent criteria for the musical was its Americanness as expressed in subject and theme, American topics for an American art form, even though Cohan's overt chauvinism grew too simplistic for the sophisticated entertainments of the decades to come.

In the second decade of the twentieth century, a series of musicals were produced at the small Princess Theatre in New York. *Nobody Home* (pr. 1915), *Very Good Eddie* (pr. 1915), and *Oh, Lady! Lady!* (pr. 1918) brought to prominence their composer, Jerome Kern. Just as important for the development of the musical play, the shows' librettist, Guy Bolton, publicly expressed his belief in the importance of integrating all theatrical elements into the plot of the musical. In particular, he pointed out with pride how comedy in the Princess shows evolved from the dramatic situation; heretofore, comic material in musicals had the quality of comic acts from vaudeville. Kern and the Princess musicals were seminal to the development of the modern book musical.

The plotless musical evening, though, was far from dead. Vaudeville went on more or less triumphantly, and the revue appeared. Unlike vaudeville acts, revue numbers were prepared especially for that edition of the revue. The most famous revue was the *Ziegfeld Follies*, which began in 1907. Florenz Ziegfeld's imitators followed the same formula: stars and show girls in elaborate production numbers. The big revues died out in the late 1930's, but smaller-scaled revues such as *The Garrick Gaieties* (pr. 1925) and the *New Faces* series (various years from 1934 to 1952) were still popular. One of the most famous revues was George S. Kaufman and Howard Dietz's *The Band Wagon* (pr. 1931), with a score by Arthur Schwartz and lyrics by Dietz. Revues are important to the history of musical theater, because every major composer and performer important to the development of the musical play worked in revues.

After World War I, English-speaking audiences were briefly infatuated with shows such as *Irene* (pr. 1919), new versions of the Cinderella tale so successful in the Gaiety musicals, and with, as noted, American-made operettas. The 1920's, however, will be remembered as the time when the great popular composers—George Gershwin, Richard Rodgers, Cole Porter, Irving Berlin, Noël Coward—came to dominate the musical stage. The subjects of their musical shows were for the most part drawn from the upbeat society of the jazz age. (Lest anyone credit audiences with a complete switch to musical sophistication, the most successful 1920's-type musicals were Vincent Youman's *No, No, Nanette* of 1925 and 1927's *Good News*, the apotheosis of college football musicals, with a score by Ray Henderson.) George Gershwin's *Lady, Be Good!* (with lyrics by Ira Gershwin) opened in 1924. Rodgers and Lorenz Hart's *Dearest Enemy* followed in 1925. (Rodgers and Hart shows such as *Dearest Enemy* and the 1927 show *A Connecticut Yankee*, despite being set in the past, have modern scores.) Berlin had already been on the theatrical scene for nearly as long as Kern with revues, especially the wartime show *Yip, Yip, Yaphank* (pr. 1918); revues remained his favored form throughout the 1920's, while his success with musical comedy began with Moss Hart's *Face the Music* (pr. 1932) and the films of Fred Astaire. Porter's first successes came at the end of the 1920's, with *Paris* (pr. 1928) and *Fifty Million Frenchmen* (pr. 1929). Coward's romantic *Bitter Sweet* opened in London in 1929, before crossing the Atlantic. Songs from these 1920's shows and their 1930's cousins help form the backbone of the body of popular standards. Gershwin's "I Got Rhythm" comes from *Girl Crazy* (pr. 1930); Porter's "Night and Day" was first sung in Dwight Taylor's *The Gay Divorce* (pr. 1932)—the list can go on and on. As book musicals, however, these shows are less successful. The plots are trivial excuses for the songs; the songs are virtually interchangeable with the songs from every other show by the same composer.

As already noted, the 1930's and the Depression changed things hardly at all for the musical theater. There was a small vogue for musicals with political satire. (One of these, the mild *Of Thee I Sing*, pr. 1931, by George S. Kaufman and Morrie Ryskind with music and lyrics by the Gershwins, became the first musical to win the Pulitzer Prize in 1932.) Serious dance entered the popular theater, most memorably with George Ballanchine's ballet to Rodgers' "Slaughter on Tenth Avenue," but even this landmark work comes from a featherweight musical, Rodgers and Hart's *On Your Toes* (pr. 1936). It was the 1940's that brought major change—with two exceptions that not only prefigured what was to come but equaled it.

Kern's *Show Boat* was produced in 1927 and is most often credited with being the first modern book musical. Oscar Hammerstein II wrote the libretto (based on Edna Ferber's novel) and most of the lyrics. (The words to "Bill" are by P. G. Wodehouse, Kern's Princess Theatre collaborator.)

The theatrical setting of the story lent itself to musicalization; some of the songs, such as "Bill," are introduced during performances or rehearsals in the story, and somehow it seems natural in the play for the characters to go on singing and dancing offstage. The showboat setting also adds variety and balance to the bitter-sweet romance of the leads, and in particular the black characters, the workman Joe, who sings "Ol' Man River," and the mulatto Julie, who sings "Bill," give the musical weight and insight. The story sprawls, and the plot may turn too much on coincidence, but *Show Boat* continues to be successful musical drama; any list of the standard repertory of musical plays must begin with it.

Gershwin's *Porgy and Bess* (with lyrics by Ira Gershwin) is a tighter musical play, and DuBose and Dorothy Heyward's story of the black cripple and the fancy woman has an inherent focus which is lacking in the romantic tale in *Show Boat*. For some, Heyward's attitude toward blacks is paternalistic. Such a view, though, fails to consider how libretto and music complement each other in the work, transfiguring the characters into outsized, commanding theatrical figures. Unfortunately, even in the first production, with Anne Brown and Todd Duncan, and in the most famous of the revivals, the touring *Porgy and Bess* of 1952 with Leontyne Price as Bess, there were compromises and deletions from the score. Not until the 1974 revival by the Houston Opera (which also toured and played Broadway) was the complete score performed. While the all-black nature of the story may have affected the work's popularity, another difficulty for the play has been producers' distrust of the score's operatic character. In truth, opera seems an appropriate label for *Porgy and Bess*. There is no spoken dialogue; there is recitative. The arching vocal lines for the women or the interwoven vocal lines of the trio at the end of the work reflect a musical complexity unique among musical plays in both technique and concept until the mature works of Stephen Sondheim.

Black performers in both *Porgy and Bess* and *Show Boat* emphasize the place of blacks in the history of the musical. Harrigan used black actors in his Mulligan Guard sketches, and Bert Williams was one of Ziegfeld's headliners. Black revues were a part of the Broadway experience throughout the 1920's and 1930's. Yet even the kindest interpretation of the facts sees the presence of institutional racism. The all-black label, the label of separateness, draws attention away from serious works such as *Porgy and Bess* and Vernon Duke's *Cabin in the Sky* (pr. 1940), and despite the limited integration of a show such as *Show Boat*, black actresses never played Julie, the mulatto accused of miscegenation. Also part of black musical history are black versions of white materials such as *The Hot Mikado* (1939), a swing version of Gilbert and Sullivan's *The Mikado* (pr. 1885), and *Carmen Jones* (pr. 1943) and all-black casts in white shows such as the 1967 Pearl Bailey version of *Hello, Dolly!* (pr. 1964) or Harold Arlen and

Truman Capote's lovely *House of Flowers* (pr. 1954). The first major musical created by blacks was *The Wiz* (pr. 1975), with a soul and disco score by Charlie Smalls. A new *The Wizard of Oz*, the show was a great hit, but a serious look at black life, Melvin Van Peebles' *Ain't Supposed to Die a Natural Death* (pr. 1971), failed. Ossie Davis' *Purlie* (pr. 1970; based on his 1961 play *Purlie Victorious*) and *Raisin* (pr. 1973; based on Lorraine Hansberry's 1959 play *A Raisin in the Sun*) treated racism less angrily and were successful. Thereafter the black musical revue returned again with shows such as *Bubbling Brown Sugar* (pr. 1976), *Eubie!* (pr. 1978; based on the life of Eubie Blake), and, most popular of all, *Ain't Misbehavin'* (pr. 1978). These shows renewed interest in black composers such as Eubie Blake and Fats Waller, and the same period saw the first production of Scott Joplin's ragtime opera *Treemonisha* (pr. 1975). Michael Bennett's production of *Dreamgirls* (pr. 1981) marked a return to the book musical. All of these shows increased black theater audiences and the opportunities for black performers. Still, the sociological element remains a conspicuous part of the black musical theater experience.

The Modern Book Musical

The 1940's established the book musical as the dominant form of popular musical drama. *Pal Joey* (pr. 1940), the penultimate Rodgers and Hart musical collaboration with a libretto by John O'Hara, set the stage with its cynical romance about the scheming Joey and the older, hard-edged Vera, who dumps him at the end; the show's songs were character studies and depictions of the gritty nightclub world of the story. The most important show of the decade, however, was *Oklahoma!*, which opened in New York on March 31, 1943.

Oklahoma! was not the first book musical. The production's real innovations were the integration of Agnes de Mille's dances into the drama, particularly Laurie's dream ballet, and the striking tonal unity of the song score. Nevertheless, the show, which was Rodgers' first collaboration with his new partner Hammerstein, did establish the book musical, with its integration of story and music, as *the* form of popular musical theater. The songs from *Oklahoma!* were truly memorable, and the composer remained the principal creative force in musicals, but after *Oklahoma!* a composer was expected to put his music at the service of the drama rather than the other way around.

The heyday of the book musical coincides almost exactly with the years of the Rodgers and Hammerstein partnership, a partnership that ended only with Hammerstein's death in 1960. Their first four hits—*Oklahoma!*, *Carousel* (pr. 1945), *South Pacific* (pr. 1949), *The King and I* (pr. 1951)— raised the partners to a position of eminence and influence in the popular musical theater unknown before or since. In most people's minds, a musical play was a Rodgers and Hammerstein musical play. In addition, the partnership changed Rodgers' music. Instead of the worldly tunes that had accompanied Hart's lyrics, Rodgers wrote melodies less specific to the musical times, more in the style of Kern, and this generalized approach also influenced and continues to influence many a Broadway score.

Carousel is probably the most innovative of the Rodgers and Hammerstein plays. Whole scenes are set to music. Instead of an overture, the show opens with a musical pantomime. *Carousel*'s big musical moment is nothing less than a full-blown musical soliloquy. By comparison, *South Pacific* is best remembered for its songs and its stars, Mary Martin and Ezio Pinza. It was a great show, but as an integrated musical drama, *South Pacific* represents a falling-off from the level of its two predecessors. *The King and I* marked a successful return to a more seamless approach to musical storytelling, although its originality lies more in the choice of subject, Margaret Landon's *Anna and the King of Siam* (1944) than in the play's musical dramaturgy. The partners' last two commercial successes, *Flower Drum Song* (pr. 1958) and *The Sound of Music* (pr. 1959), do not equal the earlier landmark works. Still, Rodgers and Hammerstein's influence on the musical play's development did not lessen, and all the important musicals for twenty years show this influence.

Other great popular composers also wrote scores for the new book musical play. Berlin's *Annie Get Your Gun*, with Ethel Merman as Annie Oakley, opened in 1946. (Another Merman vehicle, *Call Me Madam*, followed in 1950.) Porter's finest work, *Kiss Me, Kate* (with book by Bella and Samuel Spewack), appeared in 1948. Some would argue that both shows are throwbacks to the musicals of the 1920's and 1930's, and, in truth, *Annie Get Your Gun* is a lot of old-fashioned American show biz mounted on a lightweight (but serviceable) plot. *Kiss Me, Kate*, however, though similarly lighthearted, is a highly crafted theater piece about a warring theater couple cast in a musical version of Shakespeare's *The Taming of the Shrew* (pr. c. 1593-1594). Porter's memorable score was his first to belong to the characters and storyline. Among musicals, *Kiss Me, Kate* must be reckoned the equivalent of Oscar Wilde's *The Importance of Being Earnest* (pr. 1895). One other composer must be mentioned with Berlin and Porter: Kurt Weill is a giant in the history of musical drama, but he stands a bit to the side of this story, since his masterwork (with Bertolt Brecht), *The Threepenny Opera* (pr. 1928), and other works such as *Rise and Fall of the City of Mahagonny* (pr. 1930), were originally written in German and are most often grouped with operas. Weill fled Nazi Germany in 1935 and began writing American musicals, but until the 1940's his greatest success was "September Song," written for *Knickerbocker Holiday* (pr. 1938), a deserved Broadway failure. In 1941, Weill collaborated with Moss Hart to create *Lady in the Dark* (pr. 1941), a successful book musical whose intriguing musical numbers were the dreams of a woman undergoing psychoanalysis. Although originally unsuccessful, the Weill-Maxwell Anderson collaboration *Lost in the Stars* (pr. 1949), based on Alan Paton's novel *Cry, the Beloved Country* (1948), earns respect today, and *Street Scene* (pr. 1947), based on Elmer Rice's 1947 play, entered the opera repertory, the frequent fate of ambitious works in the popular musical theater. In 1954, Marc Blitzstein's famous English translation of *The Threepenny Opera* began a long successful run with Weill's widow, Lotte Lenya, in the cast. This production would significantly influence the darker musicals of the following decade.

The 1950's added many works to the musical repertory. Following the lead of *Oklahoma!* and *South Pacific*, many if not the majority of the best shows were evocations of some part of Americana. The plots stressed comedy at the expense of sentiment, but perhaps audiences found a special kind of nourishment in recognizing an America in part real, in part based on popular fiction, even if that fiction embraced crooks and disreputable show business types, and even if there were, as there often was, a small amount of satire mixed in with all the celebration and fun.

Perhaps the two best-loved shows from this group, Frank Loesser's *Guys and Dolls* (pr. 1950) and Meredith Willson's *The Music Man* (pr. 1957), nearly bracket the decade. Both shows center on disreputable characters: *Guys and Dolls* sets to music Damon Runyan's New York world of showgirls and lovable crooks; the Music Man of the title is a traveling con man who preys on gullible Midwestern towns. With "Seventy-six Trombones" and "Till There Was You," *The Music Man* probably had the more memorable score. (One more often thinks of the musical busyness of the nightclub acts or the floating crap game in *Guys and Dolls* than of "Take Back Your Mink" or "Luck, Be a Lady.") Both shows, while they poke fun at their essentially American subjects, do so affectionately; these are lighthearted entertainments. Loesser's other hits were *Where's Charley?* (pr. 1948), *The Most Happy Fella* (pr. 1956), and *How to Succeed in Business Without Really Trying* (pr. 1961), the latter a satire on the business world that, once again, was only joshing. Willson is also remembered for *The Unsinkable Molly Brown* (pr. 1960).

There is a simple enjoyableness to these shows and their fellows. *The Pajama Game* (pr. 1954) is a comedy about a garment workers' strike, and *Damn Yankees* (pr. 1955) is a comic setting of the Faust legend in the baseball world. Both (with books by George Abbott and songs by Richard Adler and Jerry Ross) are loud and brassy compared to *Carousel* or *The King and I*, but perhaps this hardworking zeal to entertain, which infects every aspect of the shows, is exactly what makes these musicals so winning. In the same category are *Fiorello!* (pr. 1959), a musical biography of Mayor Fiorello La Guardia by Abbott with songs by Jerry Bock and Sheldon Harnick, and *Bye Bye Birdie* (pr. 1960), the Charles Strouse musical that looked at the Elvis Presley phenomenon. Composer Jule Styne contributed his *Gentlemen Prefer Blonds* (pr. 1949), which made Carol Channing a star, *Bells Are Ringing* (pr. 1956), which added luster to the star of Judy Holliday, and *Gypsy* (pr. 1959). Of all the Americana musicals, *Gypsy*, based on the memoirs of Gypsy Rose Lee, is the darkest. Its central character is Mama Rose, the grasping stage mother. Arthur Laurents' book was funny; Styne's score (with lyrics by Sondheim) was strong, and there was a star at the center, Merman, but in *Gypsy* Merman did more than merely perform; she acted, showing fully the abrasive, destructive side of Mama Rose, most memorably in the show's finale, "Rose's Turn." *Gypsy* showed some of the darker side of human nature and was one foreshadowing of musicals to come.

The 1940's and 1950's also produced musical orphans and distant cousins, plays nearly or completely removed from the musical theater vogue for things American. Burton Lane's *Finian's Rainbow* (pr. 1947) was an odd mix of the American South with an Irish leprechaun. After its debut on television, Mary Martin's version of *Peter Pan* (music half by Styne, half by Carolyn Leigh) moved to Broadway in 1954, costarring Cyril Ritchard as Captain Hook. Two small Off-Broadway shows, Rick Besoyan's operetta spoof *Little Mary Sunshine* (pr. 1959) and *The Fantasticks* (pr. 1960) by Tom Jones and Harvey Schmidt, asked audiences to turn to a nostalgic past with a quieter kind of sentiment than that in the big noisy Broadway musicals. In 1956, Leonard Bernstein, who had written the music for two Americana shows, *On the Town* (pr. 1944) and *Wonderful Town* (pr. 1953), wrote one of the most famous and most atypical of musical scores, *Candide* (pr. 1956). Setting the Voltaire satire to music, Bernstein mocked many of the standard set pieces of both light and serious musical drama such as the soprano's aria and the lovers' duet, and in the process made memorable additions to their numbers. It is said that the book (by Lillian Hellman) and the staging (by Tyrone Guthrie) caused the show's failure, but at least a suspicion remains that the work appeared at the wrong time. (A 1974 revival by Hal Prince, with a new book and an environmental staging, was a success.) Appearing at exactly the right time, though, was *West Side Story* (pr. 1957); the street-gang setting for a tale of a modern Romeo and Juliet both shocked and attracted audiences. Bernstein's song score (with lyrics by Sondheim) included "Tonight" and "Maria," but as important was the musical writing for director-choreographer Jerome Robbins' ballets and dances. No musical has ever made such integral dramatic use of dance as *West Side Story*, with its choreographed wars on both the dance floor and the asphalt.

Alan Jay Lerner and Frederick Loewe had also written an Americana musical, *Paint Your Wagon* (pr. 1951), and an oddfellow, *Brigadoon* (1947), a pseudo-Scottish fantasy. Neither show (nor their 1960 production of

Camelot) hints at the artistic and popular success of Lerner and Loewe's *My Fair Lady* (pr. 1956), which starred Rex Harrison and Julie Andrews as the phonetics professor and the flower girl. While few of even Rodgers and Hammerstein's song scores can boast as many hits (which include "I Could Have Danced All Night" and "On the Street Where You Live"), the backbone of *My Fair Lady* is its book, adapted from George Bernard Shaw's *Pygmalion* (pr. 1913). Lerner switched one scene from Mrs. Higgins' home to the Ascot racetrack (giving Cecil Beaton the opportunity to create the most famous setting and costumes in recent theater history), but he resolutely retained much of Shaw's text from the final authorized version. Lerner's faith in Shaw was well-placed; *My Fair Lady* probably has the strongest musical book ever written. Certainly, few other musical plays approach so ideal an integration of music and plot.

By the 1960's, conditions no longer favored the book musical in the form dominant for twenty years. Almost all the major composers of shows were silent, or nearly so, or had given up the musical. More important for the musical's future, the arrival of rock and roll and, later, of the Beatles had irrevocably split popular music in two. In *Bye Bye Birdie*, Broadway had observed the rock phenomenon from a bemused, secure distance, but once the theater realized that the musical play was nearly on the brink of obsolescence, a few rock shows came forward, the most famous being the nearly plotless *Hair* (pr. 1967), the religious *Godspell* (pr. 1971), and *Grease* (pr. 1972). All were very popular and continue to be performed, but even Galt MacDermot's fine score for *Hair* is more rock-influenced than it is rock. The musical has not historically been successful in competing with rock on rock's own terms. Perhaps this fact, as it revealed itself, was at least partly responsible for the outsized importance that directors of musicals assumed during the 1960's. If musical theater could no longer deliver the musical goods, it could still produce an evening of theatrical magic and wonder.

Still, in the 1960's and the 1970's, and even into the 1980's, old-fashioned book musicals continued to appear. (Since the importance of the book seems to have been sacrificed to outsized production concerns, most of these shows seem old-fashioned even when set beside *Oklahoma!* or *My Fair Lady*.) The total number of shows produced during these years may have been fewer than in previous decades, but the financial bonanzas for shows such as *Hello, Dolly!*, *Mame* (pr. 1966), *Annie* (pr. 1977), or *La Cage aux Folles* (pr. 1983) were enormous. It is staging that made these shows theatrical events of note. Naturally, theatrical technology had advanced, but much of the credit for what happened onstage must be credited to plain ingenuity. Suddenly the stage could do more, faster, and in cleverer ways than ever before. Gower Champion's staging of *Hello, Dolly!* was a model of the new staging. *Hello, Dolly!* had Jerry Herman's title song and Carol Channing's starring presence already working for it, but what made the show exciting was the sleek, elegant look and move of the thing, its theatrical élan. By comparison, the staging of even the original *My Fair Lady* was stodgy.

The directors who rose to stardom during this period—Gower Champion, Bob Fosse, Hal Prince, Michael Bennett—had worked in the musical theater throughout the 1950's. As they developed, they gave an individual flavor to the musicals they mounted, and in short order there appeared the "concept musical." At least the beginnings of the concept musical can be seen in *Fiddler on the Roof* (pr. 1964), Jerome Robbins' last Broadway assignment before returning to classical choreography. The show had a tuneful score by Bock and Harnick and a star, Zero Mostel. It was Robbins' staging, however, that attracted critical comment. Anatefka and its inhabitants appeared out of the shadows. Boris Aronson's settings, inspired by Marc Chagall, were simple; most often Tevye's little toy house sat alone on the dark stage. When Tevye rejects his daughter's marriage to a Gentile, he reprises the song "Tradition" and joins a hallucinatory march across the stage of all the town's inhabitants.

The musical plays that most often bear the label "concept musical" place less stress on plot than *Fiddler on the Roof* does. Prince's 1966 production of *Cabaret* (score by John Kander and Fred Ebb) is more typical. Set in Christopher Isherwood's Berlin of the 1930's, the show alternated between two failed love stories and the musical numbers at the cabaret itself; the production numbers commented on the action. Influenced by Weill's *The Threepenny Opera*, the show's real subjects were Berlin's decadence and the rise of the Nazis. As must be apparent, *Cabaret* shares some common assumptions with the more densely plotted *Fiddler on the Roof* and *Man of La Mancha*, 1965's ambitious, if sentimental, musical adaptation of Miguel de Cervantes' *Don Quixote de la Mancha* (1605-1615). All three are played more in darkness than in light; all three end unhappily. While comedy is present, all three insist on their seriousness. Occasionally the seriousness might be relaxed, as in Fosse's 1972 production of *Pippin* (although after his film *Cabaret* Fosse returned to the theater with the gritty *Chicago*, pr. 1975, notable for its anti-star turn by the great Gwen Verdon), but the aim of all of these works was to provide a gripping kind of experience that could be had nowhere else but in the theater. Interestingly, the setting for the most popular of these shows was the theater. Bennett's production of *A Chorus Line* was an instant hit in 1975. The setting was an audition for a Broadway dance line, and this idea seemed to triumph over a score by Marvin Hamlisch (by most accounts, more serviceable than memorable), over a book by James Kirkwood and Nicholas Dante that indulged unabashedly in the old-fashioned sentimentality of backstage musicals dating back to *A Gaiety Girl*, over choreography that, as the estimable Arlene Croce noted, was curiously mundane for a musical about dancing. Bennett, who was both the director and the choreographer, saw the dancer's life as one of endless repetition in class, audition, rehearsal, performance, and he etched this idea in the audience's mind nowhere more memorably than the show's finale, the gold-lamé-costumed, high-kicking chorus line that to some audiences celebrated the musical theater and to others criticized the musical show for its dehumanization of the people who did the singing and the dancing. (Bennett's next two shows, 1979's *Ballroom* and 1981's *Dreamgirls*, while almost musical opposites, shared a greater concern with a linear plot.)

The evolution of the concept musical and the emphasis on a newer, bolder theatricality also confirmed England as a small reliable source of musical plays besides those of Coward. Sandy Wilson's 1920's spoof *The Boy Friend* (pr. 1954) had delighted New York audiences during the book musical's heyday, and Anthony Newley and Leslie Bricusse's *Stop the World—I Want to Get Off* (pr. 1962) and *Oliver!* (pr. 1963), a clean-scrubbed version of Charles Dickens' *Oliver Twist* (1837-1839), were successfully imported to Broadway. The innovators were Marguerite Monnot's gentle *Irma la Douce* (pr. 1960), and Joan Littlewood's strong and lively anti-war revue *Oh, What a Lovely War* (pr. 1964), but it is the Andrew Lloyd Webber musicals in their New York productions—the "rock opera" *Jesus Christ Superstar* (pr. 1971), *Evita!* (pr. 1979), and *Cats* (pr. 1983)— that permanently enlivened the British musical show. The stagecraft of these shows has been applauded loudly, but the reception of Webber as a composer has been less universal. He is an innovator—his works contain no spoken dialogue—and his melodies have proven enormously popular, but the musical writing does not achieve the complexity and sophistication of the operatic form to which it avowedly aspires.

The one composer to achieve greatness during the decades that have been dominated by the concept musical and the director-as-star is Stephen Sondheim. Sondheim wrote the lyrics for *West Side Story* and *Gypsy*, and his first musical score was the farcical *A Funny Thing Happened on the Way to the Forum* (pr. 1962), but his breakthrough work was *Company*, the 1970 landmark concept musical. *Company* was less a play than a set of situations about a bachelor and his married friends. The married couples also doubled as the singing-dancing chorus and in solos or trios sang commentary on the ensuing action. There were songs within the scenes. In any case though, Sondheim resisted the easy melody (a frequently heard criticism of all of his important works) in favor of musical and emotional sophistication. Other concept shows followed: *Follies* (pr. 1971), which found Sondheim brilliantly imitating the styles of decades of musical theater for a reunion of old follies girls; *Pacific Overtures* (pr. 1976), a historical pageant about the modernization of Japan; and *Sunday in the Park with George* (pr. 1984), a musical about Georges Seurat's painting *Sunday Afternoon on the Island of La Grande Jatte* in which Sondheim chose classical music's minimalism as an equivalent for Seurat's pointillism. All of these shows were theatrically compelling, all but the last staged by Prince, *Cabaret*'s star director, but while Sondheim's musicals are very much of his moment, the dominating force of his music recalls the older decades when musical theater was the composer's forum. Two other Sondheim plays (both Prince collaborations), though they share the customary shadowed affinities with concept musicals, have, like *Fiddler on the Roof* before them, a vital story to tell. *A Little Night Music* (pr. 1973) is a musical setting of Ingmar Bergman's *Smiles of a Summer's Night* (1955) and includes the song "Send in the Clowns." *Sweeney Todd* was adapted from Christopher Bond's version of the Victorian bogey story about the homicidal barber. Faithful to two strong dramatic sources, the books for these musicals rival that of *My Fair Lady*. Musically, the interwoven vocal lines, the rhythmic counterpoint, and the soaring quality of the music (especially in *Sweeney Todd* where the music is almost continuous) rival Gershwin's equally ambitious vision for *Porgy and Bess*.

Sondheim's preeminence in musical theater during the 1970's and 1980's was unprecedented, yet while providing a just measure of his talent, his position also pointed out something about the health of the popular musical theater. The hoped-for show was the big new show, whether the stirring *Sweeney Todd* or the brassy *La Cage aux Folles*, but with spiraling costs, the number of musicals decreased. Sensing that audiences still loved singing and dancing, producers backed a variety of revues, and a few small musicals appeared, including Cy Coleman's *I Love My Wife* (pr. 1977) and William Finn's *March of the Falsettos* (pr. 1981). Unique was Fosse's dance revue, called simply *Dancin'* (pr. 1978). One of the most lucrative ventures in the musical theater became the revival, from *No, No, Nanette* to *My Fair Lady* and *The King and I* to *Man of La Mancha*, frequently starring leads from the original casts. Some of these revivals were sparkling; many, though, were tired. Freed from copyright restrictions, *The Pirates of Penzance* came to Broadway in a Broadway version in 1981, and some of the more forward-thinking opera companies talked about taking into their repertories not only musicals such as *Porgy and Bess* and *Sweeney Todd* but also the regular solid book musicals such as the legendary *Oklahoma!*

The later 1980's and the first years of the 1990's, however, witnessed a widening split between entertainment extravaganzas and more serious musical drama. The huge success of British imports such as *Cats* (Lloyd Webber's musical based on T. S. Eliot's 1939 poetry collection *Old Possum's Book of Practical Cats*) and *Les Misérables*, first produced in French in 1980 and in English in 1985 (by Alain Boublil, and Claude-Michel Schönberg, from Victor Hugo's famous novel), meant that the economics of

Broadway theater had turned toward investment-and-return criteria, rather than theatrical complexity of character and integrity of vision. The ambitious *Chess* (pr. 1986), by Benny Andersson, Tim Rice, and Bjorn Ulvaeus, also moved from London to the United States, with a revised score and new cast but still burdened with a massive electronic backdrop of sixty-four television sets and a revolving chessboard stage. Typical of the gaudy extravaganzas is *Phantom of the Opera* (pr. 1986), Lloyd Webber's musical version of the classic story, complete with a falling chandelier on which the phantom rides over the audience. Less successful were his *Starlight Express* (pr. 1987) and *Aspects of Love* (pr. 1989). In Lloyd Webber musicals, one strong theme song typically emerges as the signature of the musical itself: "Phantom of the Opera," a song that makes use of the famous musical line from the motion picture, and the recurring "Don't Cry for Me, Argentina," from *Evita*, are examples.

In the meantime, almost single-handedly keeping the concept musical intact, Sondheim paired with several book writers in musicals such as *Into the Woods* (pr. 1987, with James Lapine), which is based on fairy tales, and *Assassins* (pr. 1991, with John Weidman), a remarkable musical defense of the impulses of presidential assassins from John Wilkes Booth to Lee Harvey Oswald. Tributes to Sondheim included a staged concert revue of *Follies*, with an all-star cast of Sondheim's favorite vocalists, and a 1992 Carnegie Hall retrospective, featuring his greatest songs from a twenty-five-year career. Sondheim, however, is famous for the complex rhymes and high-intensity deliveries of his songs, and his difficult lyrics, which are almost always integral to the play's dramatic moment, and the harmonic sophistication of the musical score, preclude extracting Sondheim songs for popular consumption.

Broadway continued to see its share of revivals and remakes filling the ever-diminishing musical stage: the 1980's and early 1990's witnessed re-stagings of *Gypsy*, *Guys and Dolls*, and *Camelot*. Professional theaters (part of the League of Resident Theatres) in other cities cashed in on the popularity of such revivals as *Bye Bye Birdie*, *House of Flowers*, and *Damn Yankees*. Sondheim musicals such as *Follies* and *Company* continued to be revived in all parts of the United States, with varying degrees of professionalism.

Given the expense of producing on Broadway, many shows went on the road quickly, often with multiple casts, and made their profit not on Broadway but from major-city tours and film rights. The Toronto staging of *Phantom of the Opera*, within a half-day's drive of a large portion of the American population, became a mainstay vacation and group-ticket sellout, while other casts and production companies move from city to city with the play as well. *Les Misérables* broke all box-office records for touring shows, and Lucy Simon's *The Secret Garden* (pr. 1991) had a longer run on the road than on Broadway.

Finally, the history of musical drama must henceforth include *A Chorus Line*, a collaborative production of Joseph Papp's New York Shakespeare Festival Theatre, which moved to Broadway in 1975 and held the record for the longest run of any musical (6,137 performances) when it closed on April 29, 1990. The work dramatized the life of the Broadway chorus dancer, personalizing the private dramas of the dancers' struggles with an impossible career choice. Ironically, the no-star character of the dance-oriented play allowed for literally hundreds of otherwise unknown dancers, singers, and actors finally to find a place, however briefly, on the Broadway stage.

Dale Silviria
(Updated by *Thomas J. Taylor*)

EXPERIMENTAL THEATER

"Experimental theater" is an often-used term that has a variety of possible definitions. In a broad sense, every great artist is essentially an experimenter; in this sense, the plays of modern dramatists such as T. S. Eliot, Eugene O'Neill, and Tennessee Williams were demonstrably experimental. Clearly, this is not the sense of the term as it has come to be used to describe a kind of theater that has developed in the United States and in Europe from the 1960's to the present. In this specialized sense, "experimental theater" seems to suggest a willingness, within a theater environment, to militate aggressively against social and aesthetic conventions. The proximate cause for protest—the one most ardently espoused—by theater artists in the United States was a political and social one, the escalation of the war in Vietnam. Other targets of protest were racism, sexism, oppression of the disadvantaged, and bureaucratic intransigence. A popular means of expressing this protest was shock tactics, in the streets and on campuses, often involving personal insult or property destruction. On the stage, shock was effectively achieved through the use of unconventional theatrical techniques. Directors and writers often abandoned or directly attacked traditional aesthetic standards, looking for untried means of expression in staging and in writing, enabling audiences to reassess their own experience in fresh, illuminating perspectives.

While the motivating causes may have shifted since the 1960's, the essential principles of experimental theater remain relatively unchanged: Robert Wilson's production of *the CIVIL warS* in 1984 qualified as "experimental theater" at least as validly as did Megan Terry's *Viet Rock* in 1966.

Experimental Theater in the United States

The history of American experimental theater is conventionally dated from 1958, the year that Joseph Cino opened his coffeehouse, Caffé Cino. Begun mainly as a haven for artists and offering exhibits, poetry readings, and a café menu for its growing clientele, Caffé Cino soon expanded its fare to include, first, play readings and then productions of complete plays, evolving into a regularly operating theater. Perhaps its most enduring contribution to the development of experimental theater in New York was its influence: Other companies began to emerge following the Caffé Cino example (notable among them Ellen Stewart's Café La Mama).

Thus was Off-Off-Broadway born, reflecting some of the features of what had been called Off-Broadway (equity waiver, small house, low budget) theater, but containing one relatively new element: the will to experiment, to break rules—both aesthetic and, often, social. Small companies proliferated during the 1960's and 1970's, many achieving little more than the thrill of the ephemeral moment of artistic freedom (sometimes all that was desired), but a few achieving fame (desired or not). To this liberated milieu were attracted a new wave of writers whose work has left an enduring stamp on the American experimental theater: Jack Gelber, Rochelle Owens, Ed Bullins, Leonard Melfi, Adrienne Kennedy, and the brilliantly prolific Sam Shepard. The work of others, such as Arthur Kopit, Lanford Wilson, and Amiri Baraka, has also continued to nourish the growth of this theater. Still others, though perhaps less widely known, have been integrally involved in the development of experimental theater, both in the United States and abroad; it is these latter writers whose work will be discussed under the heading "Playwrights," below.

Companies and Theaters

In 1959, another watershed event occurred: the production of Jack Gelber's *The Connection* by the Living Theatre of Julian Beck and Judith Malina. The history of the Living Theatre actually begins in 1951, when Judith and Julian, recently married, began theater productions in their apartment. The Becks soon moved into the Cherry Lane Theatre but were forced out because of fire-law violations. In 1954, they relocated to a rented loft. Forced out again in 1956 because of safety violations, they eventually reopened in a building of their own at the corner of Fourteenth Street and Avenue of the Americas. One of their most significant offerings was Gelber's *The Connection*, a production that set important precedents for the emerging experimental theater movement in at least two respects. First, it dealt in a free and forthright manner with the still somewhat taboo subject of hard-drug addiction. Second, it challenged the barriers that separate actors-characters from audience in conventional theater environments. It is not that the methods that Gelber and the Becks used to accomplish this effect were new—their antecedents could be found in Antonin Artaud, Luigi Pirandello, Bertolt Brecht, and others. The particular distinction of *The Connection* was, rather, its ability to bring some of these unconventional techniques together in an especially forceful and memorable fashion, at a time that was marked by growing restlessness both within the theater community and in American society at large.

As *The Connection*'s audience entered the theater, they encountered an uncurtained stage—something relatively unknown at the time—with actors sprawled about in assorted postures (one sleeping on a bed, one slumped over a table). As the audience would soon discover, these were junkies waiting for their "connection"—the fix to be brought by their pusher, Cowboy. Others, musicians in this jazz play, were dozing in their places, also waiting for Cowboy. After the audience was seated, two men came down the aisle and jumped onto the stage: Jim, a film producer, and Jaybird, a writer. Jim explained that they were doing a documentary on narcotic addiction and that they had assembled the junkies for this purpose, with the bait of the fix. This was, then, a play-within-a-play, and the audiences were often completely taken in by the realism of the conversations of the addicts, who later would mingle with them, at intermission, looking for handouts. It was this altering of the traditional actor-audience relationship—the blurring of the distinctions between actor-character and viewer, and the effective expansion of the stage environment to include spectators as participants—that became the Living Theatre's trademark and would powerfully influence the development of experimental theater not only in the United States but also in Europe.

The Becks took their repertoire—William Carlos Williams' *Many Loves* (pr. 1959), Brecht's *In the Jungle of Cities* (pr. 1960), and *The Connection*—on a successful tour of six cities in France, Germany, and Italy that would prepare the way for their later years of expatriate work in Europe. After one more New York success, Kenneth Brown's *The Brig* (pr. 1963), the Becks' chronic financial difficulties became overwhelming. The theater was ordered closed, and the Becks were arrested and imprisoned (Julian for sixty days, Judith for thirty) for unauthorized use of the theater and for failure to pay taxes. The European odyssey followed: four years in twelve countries, the performances reflecting continually changing ideas and techniques (*Mysteries and Smaller Pieces*, pr. 1964, and *Frankenstein*, pr. 1965, both developed by the company collectively, and Bertolt Brecht's *Antigone*, pr. 1967, which focused on the actor as actor, rather than as character). These new dimensions, and the Becks' ever-present anarchist disposition, were evident in the eight-section *Paradise Now* (pr. 1968), a "rite of guerrilla theatre" ending in "permanent revolution," first produced in Avignon, then, that same year, back in the United States. More arrests followed, more financial problems, but also a successful tour of American cities and universities, another visit to Europe (in 1970), then thirteen months in Brazil (ending in arrest). Among later productions, in the United States and Europe, were *The Legacy of Cain* cycle (pr. 1975), *The Money Tower* (pr. 1975), and *Prometheus* (pr. 1978). The Living Theatre continued its zealous campaign of revolution in traditional theaters as well as in street performances, but was often on the move, with brief stays in American cities (Pittsburgh, 1974 to 1975) and longer ones in Europe. In 1984, from their base in Paris, the Becks brought four plays—*The Yellow Methuselah* (pr. 1984), *The Archaeology of Sleep* (pr. 1984), Ernst Toller's *The One and the Many* (pr. 1984), and *Frankenstein*—to New York. The critics were disappointed, noting with regret that the Becks' group—now made up mainly of European actors—had not adequately adjusted to the changing needs of changing times.

Ellen Stewart founded Café La Mama in 1960, partially influenced by her interest in the Caffé Cino operation. Like Joseph Cino, a former dancer, Stewart had no experience in theater production. With her background in retail clothing and fashion design, she opened a boutique in New York. From the boutique, Stewart ("La Mama" to some of her friends) began working with writer Paul Foster to produce plays, and Café La Mama came into existence (licensed as a café to accommodate city codes). Like the Becks, Stewart was plagued by city officials and was forced to change the location of her theater a number of times. Like the Living Theatre, Café La Mama went to Europe (under Tom O'Horgan's direction) and returned highly acclaimed. Back in New York, Café La Mama's production of Rochelle Owens' *Futz* (pr. 1965) received Obie Awards. Stewart took *Futz* and Paul Foster's *Tom Paine* (pr. 1968) on a second trip to Europe and returned with more raves. Suddenly Owens, Foster, O'Horgan, and Stewart were established in New York theater. Throughout this period of its growth, Stewart dedicated her time and energy exclusively to the enterprise, which was sometimes barely existing. She performed every task from making soup and washing floors to selecting the plays for production and introducing each performance. She was completely in charge. The company continued to grow and to change and to move. In 1969, operating from a complex of two theaters, it became La Mama ETC (Experimental Theatre Club). As one of the most consistently prolific of the experimental companies, La Mama has continued to wield an extraordinary influence. Playwrights whose plays have been produced at La Mama include—besides Owens, O'Horgan, and Foster—Tom Eyen, Megan Terry, María Irene Fornés, Leonard Melfi, Israel Horovitz, Lanford Wilson, and Sam Shepard. La Mama groups sprang up in other cities in the United States and in more than a dozen cities all over the world.

Joseph Chaikin began appearing in roles at the Living Theatre in 1959. He acted in *The Connection* during the first European tour and performed the role of Galy Gay in Brecht's *Man Is Man* (pr. 1926) on their return. In 1963, he left the Becks and founded his Open Theatre. The main focus of Chaikin's work was on the actor, not the character—what Chaikin called "presence." The performance itself concentrated on the "inside"—the interior of the person and the situation, a kind of subtext distinguished from the "outside" illusion of conventional theater. Chaikin's actors were required to work on "inside-outside" techniques, moving, for example, back and forth from nonverbal to verbal contexts. The main productions of the Open Theatre were generated through workshops featuring such techniques—collectively developed performances to which the writer contributed but did not dominate. Terry's *Viet Rock* was developed in Open Theatre workshops, though it was presented in 1966 at Café La Mama. Other major productions were Jean-Claude van Itallie's *The Serpent* (pr. 1967); *Terminal* (pr. 1969), with a text written by Susan Yankowitz; and *The Mutation Show* (pr. 1971), written by Chaikin and Roberta Sklar. The Open Theatre toured extensively both in the United States and in Europe.

Chaikin's techniques—actor-focused performance, collective workshop creation, and "transformations" (actors shifting into and out of roles)—had grown out of early influences, such as Konstantin Stanislavsky, Brecht, and Artaud, as well as contacts with Jerzy Grotowski, Peter Brook, the Living Theatre, and interaction with his own actors. The Open Theatre, in turn, profoundly influenced the development of experimental theater during its years of operation, and although it was disbanded in 1973, its influence has continued in acting workshops throughout the United States and Europe. Chaikin himself, after recovering from a serious illness, continued acting and directing in some relatively conventional productions; coauthored (with Shepard) two experimental pieces, produced as *Tongues and Savage/Love* (pr. 1979); and collaborated (with former Open Theatre members and others) on productions for the Winter Project, such as *Tourists and Refugees* (pr. 1980-1981) and *Trespassing* (pr. 1982), performed at La Mama ETC.

Richard Schechner formed his The Performance Group in 1967 at what he called the Performing Garage on Wooster Street. Schechner, a university professor, had emigrated from Louisiana, where he had been involved with a theater group and had edited the *Tulane Drama Review*, which also migrated to New York, becoming *The Drama Review*. Like Chaikin, Schechner had been influenced by Grotowski's laboratory methods. Another main Schechner interest was "environmental theater," a chief dictum of which was that "all the space is used for performance; all the space is used for audience." His *Dionysus in '69* (pr. 1968; based on Euripides' *Bacchae*) epitomized Schechner's Performance Group doctrines. Developed in rigorous workshop sessions, *Dionysus in '69* was language-transcending ritual theater in which the audience was encouraged to participate—chanting, dancing, or disrobing when the actors did. The "environment" consisted of three- to five-level scaffolding around an irregular central space. Audiences climbed the scaffolding or sat on the floor. Actors moved in and out of character, sometimes speaking and acting on their own, as themselves. *Dionysus in '69* was followed by *Makbeth* (pr. 1969), *Commune* (pr. 1970), and a variety of other works, including some by outside writers, such as Shepard's *The Tooth of Crime* (pr. 1972), Ted Hughes's adaptation of *Seneca's Oedipus* (pb. 1968), and Jean Genet's *The Balcony* (pr. 1979). After Schechner left the group in 1980, it continued, quite actively and prominently, as the Wooster Group, directed by Elizabeth LeCompte and including some of the former Performance Group actors, notably Spalding Gray.

Many other companies were noteworthy in the development of American experimental theater. The San Francisco Mime Troupe, begun in 1959, has continued to generate excitement with its abrasively original work. In 1961, Peter Schumann formed the Bread and Puppet Theatre, sharing bread with his audiences and using large sculptured bodies in his productions, which were frequently conducted outdoors, in streets or fields. The company dissolved in 1974 but continued to reunite for periodic specific projects (*A Monument for Ishi* in 1975, *Ave Maris Stella* in 1978) and an annual one, *The Demonstration Resurrection Circus* (pr. 1974), at Schumann's Vermont farm. A collective originally formed by Lee Breuer, Ruth Maleczech, and JoAnne Akalaitis in San Francisco in the 1960's toured Europe until 1969, when it settled in New York, calling itself Mabou Mines (after a Nova Scotia mining town) and pioneering a variety of mixed-genre works; Mabou Mines quickly became a major force in New York avant-garde theater.

Other early influential companies were the Judson Poets Theatre, founded at the Judson Memorial Church in New York by the Reverend Al Carmines in 1966; the Firehouse Theatre, begun in Minneapolis in 1963 and moved to San Francisco in 1969; Theatre Genesis, formed by Ralph Cook in 1964; The American Place Theatre, also formed in 1964, by Wynn Handman; the Play-House of the Ridiculous, founded by John Vaccaro in 1966; and Charles Ludlam's spinoff, the Ridiculous Theatrical Company. In 1967, the OM-Theatre Workshop was developed by a group at a Boston church. Richard Foreman began his Ontological-Hysteric Theatre in 1968, and Robert Wilson established his Byrd Hoffman Foundation in 1969. The Squat Theatre, originally formed in Budapest in 1969, arrived at New York's Twenty-third Street in 1977. Among other groups outside New York were the Iowa Theatre Lab, the Omaha Magic Theatre, the Empty Space Theatre in Seattle, and the Changing Scene in Denver.

In addition to the San Francisco Mime Troupe, a number of other important groups have developed in California. Laura Farabaugh and Christopher Hardman founded the Snake Theatre in 1972, working with "found space"; it divided into two companies in 1980: Farabaugh's Nightfire and Hardman's Antenna Theatre. A major California theater for decades has been El Teatro Campesino, begun by Luis Valdez in 1965, in connection with the United Farm Workers' movement of César Chávez. The Padua Hills Playwrights' Workshop/Festival was formed by Murray Mednick in La Verne, California, in 1978. Like the Snake Theatre, it made liberal use of "found" environments. Padua Hills moved to the California Institute of the Arts in Valencia in 1984. Other important California theaters have been the Magic Theatre in San Francisco and the Odyssey Theatre, the East-West Players, the Los Angeles Actors' Theatre, and the collective Provisional Theatre in Los Angeles.

The proliferation of small companies on both coasts and across the United States notwithstanding, the need for social protest and the new, sometimes shocking techniques with which to express that protest dwindled by the early 1990's. In their place is a consolidation of sorts that is symbolized in the move, for example, of Akalaitis from the Off-Off-Broadway Mabou Mines to the Off-Broadway Public Theater. In 1992, when Joseph Papp, founder and guide of the Public Theater for many years, died,

Akalaitis took over the leadership of the theater, but under her direction the theater lacked the energy and creativity that characterized it at the height of the Papp years. In fact, the play *The Sisters Rosensweig* (pr. 1992), by a feminist protégée of the Public Theater, Wendy Wasserstein, was performed in 1993 in the more comfortable, uptown Mitzi E. Newhouse Theater at Lincoln Center in a fairly traditional and highly successful production.

Off-Off-Broadway groups continued to produce plays, but a quick run-through of their offerings reveals more classical than new dramas in their repertoire, with companies such as the Play-House of the Ridiculous remaining static with productions similar to those of the early days. Theatre Row on Forty-second Street—more than half a dozen tiny theaters, including Playwrights Horizons—continued to accommodate inexpensive productions of risky plays by new playwrights.

The Roundabout Theater has gone one step further in its move from a downtown New York City location to the Criterion Theater in the heart of the Broadway district, its production of *Anna Christie* in 1992 giving new life to an old play that even its author, Eugene O'Neill, did not consider important. Actor Tony Randall, feeling the need for a national theater for the classics, in 1991 opened the National Theater, its declared purpose to produce the classics—American as well as European. On the West Coast, the Mark Taper Forum, the La Jolla Playhouse, and the South Coast Repertory Theater function similarly in their "Off-Broadway" capacities—as do the Goodman Theater of Chicago, the Actors' Theater of Louisville, and the Seattle Repertory.

Consolidation of the traditional and the innovative is the modus operandum of the experimenters in the 1990's, as writers take advantage of the new without sacrificing the traditional. These playwrights, such as Larry Kramer, Wasserstein, August Wilson, and Tony Kushner, are to be found mostly in Off-Broadway houses and regional theaters.

Playwrights

Jean-Claude van Itallie, Belgian-born, arrived in the United States in 1940. His first play, *War*, which had opened in 1963, was given a production in March of 1965 at the Caffé Cino. In April, *America Hurrah!* (the *Motel* sequence) was performed at Café La Mama. *War* had introduced some of the techniques that would characterize van Itallie's work: symbolic action, expressionistic mixing of visuals and dialogue, an emphasis on highly stylized antirealism. *Motel*, which would later be combined with *Interview* (pr. 1966) and *TV* (pr. 1966) to complete the *America Hurrah!* trilogy, remained, in the view of many, the play with which van Itallie would be most readily identified. With its exaggerated doll figures (designed by Robert Wilson) and its Absurd counterpointing of violent behavior within cliché situation, it soon became a symbol of the avant-garde view of the American mid-1960's. In *Motel*, while the voice of the Motel-Keeper carries on a rambling monologue of trivial patter, the Man and Woman (also doll figures) come into the room. As the Man begins his violent antics, jumping on the mattress, the Woman throws her clothes out from the bathroom, then reenters the room naked, marking her body with lipstick and blotting it on the walls. The Man and Woman eventually destroy everything in the room, drowning out the Motel-Keeper's voice, which has been droning on, oblivious to the violence. The play ends with the Man and Woman tearing off the Motel-Keeper's head and walking out via the theater aisle.

Most of van Itallie's subsequent work was done with Chaikin's Open Theatre: *I'm Really There*, *Almost Like Being*, *The Dream*, *The Hunter and the Bird*, all in 1966, and *The Serpent* in 1967-1968. In *The Serpent*, van Itallie had worked collectively with Chaikin and his group. In their workshop sessions, the actors had been considering doing episodes from Genesis. Van Itallie combined these ideas with others (sequences depicting the assassinations of President John F. Kennedy and Martin Luther King, Jr.) and developed them into a working script, with spaces to permit improvisation. Using the Adam and Eve/Cain and Abel archetypes, the performance included the audience, with the actors portraying the serpent, offering audience members bites from their apples so that the audience might share the sense of lost innocence. Van Itallie has continued his experiments in *Take a Deep Breath* (pr. 1969), *Photographs: Mary and Howard* (pr. 1969), *Eat Cake* (pr. 1971), *Mystery Play* (pr. 1973), *Nightwalk* (an Open Theatre collaboration with Terry and Shepard, pr. 1973), *The Sea Gull* (a 1973 adaptation of Anton Chekhov's play), *A Fable* (pr. 1975), and *The King of the United States* (pr. 1973), among others. *America Hurrah!* and *The Serpent* have remained his most influential works.

In May, 1966, a year after its production of the *Motel* sequence of *America Hurrah!*, Café La Mama produced another landmark work, Terry's *Viet Rock*. Although presented at Café La Mama, *Viet Rock* was developed, much like *The Serpent*, in workshop sessions at Chaikin's Open Theatre. In their characteristic manner, Chaikin's actors developed material improvisationally, which was then finished as script by Terry. Chaikin's and Terry's shared interest in "transformations" was evident throughout this work. Actors moved freely from one character to another, assuming rapidly changing moods and outlooks to fit the roles and sometimes even becoming inanimate objects. In this rock opera (contemporary with the 1968 *Hair*), the actors entered to the music of "The Viet Rock." They became, first, infants crying, then children playing war games, then mothers and their drafted, Vietnam-bound sons, the mothers becoming an airplane carrying their sons off to war. Terry and Chaikin ended the performance with a "celebration of presence," the actors moving into the audience in what was becoming a typical gesture of communal touching, dissolving the barrier separating actors from audience.

Other of Terry's plays have been equally inventive, if ultimately less influential. *Keep Tightly Closed in a Cool Dry Place* (pr. 1965), her earlier experiment with transformations, was followed by *Comings and Goings* (pr. 1966). *The Gloaming, Oh My Darling* (pr. 1966) was an experiment with Absurdism and feminist statement; *Sanibel and Captiva* (pr. 1968) was another Absurdist effort, and *Approaching Simone* (pr. 1970) another feminist one, a historical portrait of Simone Weil. *The Tommy Allen Show* (pr. 1969) was social satire and television parody; *Hothouse* (pr. 1974) was a relatively conventional melodrama; *American King's English for Queens* (pr. 1978) and *Brazil Fado* (a 1977 musical) returned to the transformational style. Both of the latter plays were performed at the Omaha Magic Theatre, which Terry had joined in 1971.

María Irene Fornés is a Cuban who moved to the United States in 1945. Two of her early works, *Promenade* and *The Successful Life of 3*, opened in the same year, 1965—*Promenade* at the Judson Poets Theatre and *The Successful Life of 3* at the Open Theatre. *Promenade*, with music by Judson's Al Carmines, is a subtle, complicated satire depicting the adventures of two escaped prisoners, 105 and 106, whose elemental innocence remains untarnished throughout their bizarre travels. The play's mood is broadly comic and whimsically absurd by turns, its style partly lyric expressionism, partly popular entertainment. *The Successful Life of 3*, an altogether different vehicle with its constant shifts of character and situation, allowed the Open Theatre actors the opportunity of making extensive use of their "transformations" techniques. *Fefu and Her Friends* (pr. 1977), a feminist (all-women) excursion, requires for performance a series of different rooms, with the audience separated into four groups moving from room to room in order to follow the action. Another multilocation play, *No Time* (pr. 1984), was performed by the California Padua Hills group in Valencia, on a roof patio at the California Institute of the Arts and in rolling fields below. The action of this play blends lyric dialogue and violence in a Latin American setting of romantic love and political intrigue. Other Fornés plays include *Tango Palace* (pr. 1964), *Aurora* (pr. 1974, anticipating the simultaneous scenes of *Fefu*), *A Vietnamese Wedding* (pr. 1967), and *Molly's Dream* (pr. 1968).

Representing another side of experimental theater were the formalists— writers such as Robert Wilson, Alan Finneran, and structuralist Michael Kirby. These were often artists of the minimalist and postmodernist schools who strove to free their subjects from all traditional, received content and styles, reducing them to their elementary forms. Of those working in theater, many came from other artistic disciplines (Wilson was originally a painter, Finneran a painter-sculptor, Kirby a sculptor).

Robert Wilson's Byrd Hoffman School of Byrds, many of whose members were physically disabled, provided a rich environment for this work. By giving his performers freedom of interpretation, he was able to explore new and unexpected perspectives. Although most of his work since founding the Byrd Hoffman School in 1969 has been done by professionals, he has retained these perspectives in productions such as *Deafman Glance* (pr. 1970), which, with its prologue, *The Life and Times of Joseph Stalin* (pr. 1973), has a playing time of twelve hours. Wilson's *Ka Mountain*, performed at the Shiraz Festival in Iran in 1972, requires seven days and nights. *A Letter for Queen Victoria* followed in 1974, and *Einstein on the Beach*, perhaps Wilson's best-known work, followed in 1976.

Philip Glass composed the music for *Einstein on the Beach*, and Andrew de Groat and Wilson's longtime associate Lucinda Childs choreographed it. This work exemplifies many of Wilson's formalist techniques—the stressed slow motion by means of which Wilson hopes to engage the audience's "interior screen," the random language patterns, the repetition of movements and sounds. It consists of nine major sections connected by short "knee plays" (connecting sequences). The work touches the life and ideas of Albert Einstein indirectly, mainly through images suggesting the relationship between time and space. Other Wilson compositions include his two-person (Wilson and Childs) *I Was Sitting on My Patio This Guy Appeared I Thought I Was Hallucinating* in 1977 and *the CIVIL warS*, planned for the Los Angeles Olympic Arts Festival but aborted for lack of funding, although it has since been finished, and segments have been produced in various parts of the world, including a 1985 performance in Boston.

Boston artist Alan Finneran founded Soon 3 in San Francisco in 1972, as a group to present his "performance landscapes," theatrical renderings of his mobile sculptures. His productions have included *Desire Circus* (pr. 1975), *Black Water Echo* (pr. 1977), *A Wall in Venice/3 Women/Wet Shadows* (pr. 1978), *Tropical Proxy* (pr. 1979), *The Man in the Nile at Night* (pr. 1980), and *Renaissance Radar* (pr. 1980). In each of these, mobile sculptures have dominated the sets, with people moving through silent "tasks" against a background of music and taped dialogue.

Michael Kirby's structuralism has grown out of his 1975 manifesto. His works focus on structure—objects, scene fragments, unrelated language passages—to enable the audience to respond as nondirectively as possible. In his plays, *Revolutionary Dance* (pr. 1976), *Eight People* (pr. 1975), *Photoanalysis* (pr. 1976), and *Double Gothic* (pr. 1978), he has attempted to accomplish the objective of structural prominence by means of repetition of language, objects, and images. The work of Kirby and other formalists suggests, but is not limited to, the surreal, with echoes of Adolphe Appia, Vsevolod Meyerhold, and the Futurists.

The beneficiaries of experimental fervor (new feminist, gay, and African-American dramatists), who in the 1960's would have had a hearing only Off-Off-Broadway, continued to have their works produced in the 1990's in more comfortable Off-Broadway and even Broadway theaters. Their subject matter is now readily accepted by regular theatergoers: For example, Wasserstein's *The Sisters Rosensweig*; Kramer's *The Destiny of Me* (pr. 1993); August Wilson's *Ma Rainey's Black Bottom* (pr. 1984), *Fences* (pr. 1985), and *The Piano Lessons* (pr. 1988); and Kushner's *Angels in America* (pr. 1993).

Experimental Theater in England

In the fall of 1955, Peter Brook was astonishing traditional Shakespeare audiences with his bold version of *Titus Andronicus*, starring Sir Laurence Olivier and Vivien Leigh, at the Shakespeare Memorial Theatre in Stratford. In the same season, Samuel Beckett's *Waiting for Godot* (pb. 1952) was being given its London premiere. A few months later, in 1956, George Devine formed the English Stage Company at the Royal Court Theatre. A revolution was under way in English theater, and John Osborne, Harold Pinter, John Arden, Arnold Wesker, Edward Bond, and Tom Stoppard (to name a few of the major writers) began their domination of the stage. Also by 1956, Joan Littlewood's Theatre Workshop, which she had established in the Theatre Royal in London's East End in 1953, had garnered wide recognition as an alternative to mainstream theater, both attracting a working-class audience and developing an art-audience engagement radically different from the existing relationships of London's commercial stage.

New theaters were being erected and new companies continued to emerge in this fresh environment, which would become known as England's "Fringe" theater. The Belgrade Theatre, built in Coventry in 1958, was the first of many postwar theater buildings that would be constructed over the next ten years. The Chichester Festival Theatre was formed in 1962, and in 1963, Jim Haynes, an American, established the Traverse Theatre Workshop Company in Edinburgh. Haynes managed the Traverse as chairman (of the Theatre Club) and artistic director for the next three years, developing it into what would become an indispensable base for the eventual expansion of Fringe theater in England.

In the autumn of 1963, another American, Charles Marowitz, joined Peter Brook in developing the "Theatre of Cruelty" group, with the object of applying some of Antonin Artaud's theories and techniques in a series of experimental exercises. The group, comprising twelve actors and sponsored by the Royal Shakespeare Company, spent twelve weeks in rehearsal at the London Academy of Music and Dramatic Arts (LAMDA) Theatre Club, then presented (in 1964) a five-week program consisting of the premiere of Artaud's three-minute *Spurt of Blood* (pb. 1925), some short "nonsense sketches" by Paul Ableman, a mimed dramatization of an Alain Robbe-Grillet short story, two collages written by Brook, three scenes from Jean Genet's *Les Paravents* (pr. 1961, Berlin) entitled *The Screens*, the premiere of John Arden's short play *Ars Longa, Vita Brevis*, and Marowitz's collage *Hamlet* (1966).

In 1965, Jeff Nuttal began The People Show and Roland Muldoon and Claire Burnley formed their agitprop group CAST (Cartoon Archetypal Slogan Theatre). Both companies were to have considerable impact on the later development of London's alternative theater environment.

One of the most popular forms of alternative theater, lunchtime theater, began in 1966 with the founding of Quipu by David Halliwell and David Calderisi at the Arts Theatre Club. This midday phenomenon would foster two essential ingredients of the Fringe movement: low-budget production and an unfettered working environment for the artist.

The year 1967 was a crucial one in the development of London's Fringe; the visit of two important American companies to London galvanized the existing experimental English groups into a major theatrical phenomenon. Chaikin's Open Theatre performed van Itallie's *America Hurrah!* in the Royal Court Theatre in Sloane Square in the summer of 1967, and soon afterward, Stewart's Café La Mama arrived at the Mercury Theatre with Owens' *Futz*. Café La Mama's Tom O'Horgan also directed a brief run of *Tom Paine* at the Vaudeville Theatre in London's West End.

World events in 1967 and 1968 provided an atmosphere in which the flames of the American-inspired counterculture theater could be fanned. The student rioting in France, the turbulence of the Democratic party's national convention in Chicago, the Soviet invasion of Czechoslovakia, and the continuing conflict in Vietnam all invited protest. The American theater companies had set exciting examples of how this protest might be articulated, and the British Fringe groups responded accordingly.

The flourishing of the Fringe theater movement was later given added impetus by the success of the unprecedented "Come Together" Festival of autumn, 1969. Like American experimental theater, the Fringe developed both through the willingness of producers and companies to present nontraditional performances or provide space for them, and through the innovative work of individual playwrights.

Companies and Theaters

Besides those already mentioned (Theatre Workshop, Belgrade Theatre, Chichester Festival Theatre, Traverse Theatre Workshop, People Show, CAST, Quipu, Royal Court, and Mercury Theatre), the main Fringe theaters by 1968 included the Arts Laboratory in Drury Lane, formed by Traverse founder Jim Haynes; Ed Berman's Inter-Action (which would spin off other influential sections such as the lunchtime Ambiance Basement, The

Other Company, and the children-oriented Dogg's Troupe); and William Gaskill's Theatre Upstairs at the Royal Court Theatre. David Hare and Tony Bicat (later joined by Howard Brenton, Snoo Wilson, and Trevor Griffiths) began Portable Theatre; Nancy Meckler, also American, founded Freehold; and the Pip Simmons Theatre Group was formed—all in Haynes's Drury Lane. John Fox started The Welfare State in Leeds; performing in a variety of outdoor settings, Fox's Welfare State quickly became one of the strongest influences on theater outside the London area.

These were the major theater groups working in the key year of 1968. Other important theaters providing spaces for these companies from 1968 on were the Roundhouse, the Institute of Contemporary Art (ICA), The Half Moon, The Oval House, The Bush, and The King's Head. Other companies would continue to emerge, such as the Young Vic, 7:84 (seven percent of the population possessed eighty-four percent of the nation's wealth), and IOU, which had separated from its parent, Welfare State, in 1976.

The most prolific of the London groups were the Portable, Freehold, and Pip Simmons. Portable, as its name implies, designed its productions to allow flexibility, both in format and in playing space. For example, in 1971, Portable was able to put on three productions concurrently at the Edinburgh Festival. Portable also experimented, as had the Traverse earlier, with collaborative productions in which one or more writers, along with other members of the company, would develop a performance script in a workshop environment, combining ideas of everyone involved, actors as well as writers; Brenton's *Hitler Dances* (pr. 1972) had been created in this way by the Traverse Workshop. From an actual incident that he had observed, Brenton suggested the idea of children playing around a bomb site to the Traverse actors. On a tour to Amsterdam's Mickery Theatre, the Traverse group then developed Brenton's concept into workable play elements that Brenton later finished as a script. The final product thus combined Brenton's ideas, such as a projected image of the children resurrecting the body of a German soldier from the bomb crater, with the actors' individual memories of their own wartime experiences in London, and other ideas mutually derived from film and news sources.

In contrast to the Traverse's writer-actors collaboration, the Portable Theatre's workshop plays were the efforts of writers only. The first and most celebrated of these was *Lay By* (pr. 1971). In 1971, during an informal get-together of writers at Gaskill's Royal Court Theatre, David Hare proposed the idea of writing a collaborative play. Trevor Griffiths found a newspaper item concerning a sensational event that had occurred on a motorway lay-by—an act of fellatio involving two women and a truck driver. In all, seven writers participated in the writing of the script, including Brenton and Stephen Poliakoff. Although unified in style, this first joint effort was thematically disjointed, superficial, and luridly sensational, providing no evident justification, aesthetically or otherwise, for its pornographic excesses. Other Portable collaborations, none more noteworthy than *Lay By*, were *England's Ireland* and *Point 101*, both produced in 1972. These early collective efforts, flaws notwithstanding, established a powerful precedent which influenced later group collaborations both in England and in America.

Meckler's Freehold, by contrast, used a script by one author only but worked it out communally in a laboratory environment. With her New York La Mama background, Meckler concentrated on expressionistic image statement, partly through the use of mime techniques. Freehold's *Antigone* (pr. 1969), adapted from Sophocles by Peter Hulton, was galvanized in the intense discipline of Meckler's workshop into a powerful modern combination of feminist statement and antiwar protest. Other productions developed similarly in the Freehold workshop were Roy Kift's *Mary Mary* and Meckler's own *Genesis*.

The Pip Simmons Theatre Group has been one of the consistently most popular of the Fringe companies. Having started in 1968 with the Absurdist material of Jean Tardieu, Simmons soon began developing his own plays and his own style of theater. His *Superman* (pr. 1969), a group creation, was representative of the Simmons style, mixing cartoonlike, fast-paced action, characters reminiscent of cardboard caricatures, flashing strobelight "framing," vaudeville situations, and rock music. *Superman* echoed American protest, satirizing American society and depicting aspects of the civil rights movement, with Superman coming to the rescue of the distressed. *Superman* was followed by *Do It!* (pr. 1971), adapted from Jerry Rubin's book of the same title; *George Jackson Black and White Minstrel Show* (pr. 1972), a powerful racial satire using a minstrel format; and *An Die Musik* (pr. 1975), exploiting—as did *George Jackson Black and White Minstrel Show*—audience voyeurism, but shifting the theme from racial bigotry to the Holocaust.

As in the United States, the focus for protest plays in Great Britain dissipated in the late 1980's, lunchtime theater having almost disappeared, other fringe theaters such as the King's Head (a pub) reviving plays by Noël Coward and the Victorian author of the "well-made" play Harley Granville-Barker, and the new little Almeida Theater in North London reviving in 1993 Harold Pinter's *No Man's Land*, with Pinter himself in one of the two leading roles. The tiny Pit Theater at London's Royal Shakespeare Theater and the Cottesloe at the Royal National have become homes for risky new plays, interestingly, by writers such as American Richard Nelson and Hare, respectively, and Brenton has become a mainstay on the big stages of the prestigious Royal National Theatre.

Playwrights

Howard Brenton's first play, *Ladder of Fools*, was performed while he was a student at Cambridge in 1965. This was a sprawling piece, which Brenton himself has described as "jokeless, joyless." From that point on, however, his work would be marked by tight, spare construction and fast-paced dialogue liberally sprinkled with humor. His next play was a farce entitled *Winter Daddikins* (pr. 1965), written after his graduation from Cambridge; *Wesley* (pr. 1970) and *Gargantua* (pr. 1969) were among the plays that followed. In 1969, Brenton wrote his first full-length play, *Revenge* (pr. 1969), exploring what would become, for him, a central situation: the criminal versus the police in a morally blurred environment. *Christie in Love* (pr. 1969), written for the Portable Theatre, epitomizes this theme and demonstrates as well Brenton's technique of mixing the surreal (in his depiction of the social-moral milieu) and the naturalistic (the character of Christie). Of the many plays he wrote during the next several years (*The Education of Skinny Spew*, pr. 1969; *Scott of the Antarctic*, pr. 1971; *A Sky-Blue Life*, pr. 1966, an adaptation of William Shakespeare's *Measure for Measure*; and the aforementioned *Hitler Dances*), *Magnificence*, commissioned by Gaskill and performed in 1973 at the Royal Court Theatre, perhaps best reflects the deepening and maturing of Brenton's attitudes. The central character, Jed, personifies what for Brenton are the essential contradictions of modern life—the "magnificence" of extreme, violent social reaction as well as its utter stupidity and futility—and the uncontrollable frustrations that result from them. The urban terrorism of *Magnificence* reappeared in *The Saliva Milkshake* (pr. 1975) and *Weapons of Happiness* (pr. 1976), while its political satire was reprised in *The Churchill Play* (pr. 1974), commissioned by the Nottingham Playhouse. With *Weapons of Happiness*, presented in the new Lyttleton auditorium of the National Theatre, the seemingly inevitable blending of Brenton into mainstream theater was completed. His bold, caustic polemics continued in *The Romans in Britain* (pr. 1980), but Brenton's work became no longer Fringe. His 1983 production, *The Genius*, is, by his earlier standards, quite conventional in both form and content.

David Hare wrote his first play, *How Brophy Made Good* (pr. 1969), to meet a crisis when a play promised by Snoo Wilson for the Portable Theatre failed to materialize. Two following efforts were both successes: *Slag* in 1970 and *The Great Exhibition* in 1972. Although not produced in the Fringe, but rather in the fashionable Hampstead Theatre Club, both plays reflected Hare's underground proclivities as director of the Portable Theatre. *Slag* offered a close look at three women, mistresses of a girls' school, each a unique study. *The Great Exhibition*, written while Hare was resident dramatist at the Royal Court Theatre, satirizes the tendencies, both in the mainstream and in the Fringe, of intellectuals and artists to court working-class audiences. In 1974, Hare helped found another Fringe group, the Joint Stock Theatre Group, for which he wrote *Fanshen* (pr. 1975, adaptation of William Hinton's novel), a play set in revolutionary China. Hare's later work, including the highly successful *Plenty* in 1978 and *A Map of the World* in 1983, has generally been in the mainstream of contemporary British theater.

Brenton and Hare collaborated on *Brassneck*, a tour de force written for the Nottingham Playhouse in 1973. It enjoyed an extensive run in Nottingham and was highly acclaimed by critics, who saw the best talents of both artists combining to produce this family saga with its biting satire on capitalism. *Brassneck* was later made available to a much wider audience through a television performance.

A third member of the Portable group, Snoo Wilson, is generally regarded as the most characteristically Fringe in his personal philosophy as well as in the unrelenting originality of his work. Whereas both Brenton and Hare have, in different ways, moved into commercial theater, Wilson has steadfastly sought alternatives.

Wilson's first professional work was an adaptation of Shakespeare's *Pericles, Prince of Tyre*, entitled *Pericles, The Mean Knight* (1970), in which he stripped the original play down to a one-hour program and darkened the tragicomic ending; this was followed by *Device of Angels* (pr. 1970), written for the Portable Theatre. The techniques which have set Wilson's stamp indelibly on alternative theater—visual intrusions, incongruous juxtaposing of episodes, slapstick comedy, eloquent patches of carefully reasoned dialogue—first appeared in *Pignight* (pr. 1971). This breakthrough play deals with its subject, a family pig-raising farm gradually taken over by criminals, on many levels, centering on the problem of haves living off of have-nots and incorporating jolting images of animal slaughtering. *Blow Job* (pr. 1971), a more conventionally conceived play, also portrays the criminal element, this time raiding safes by blowing them up. Wilson, a prolific writer whom Brenton has described as "a real voyager . . . a writer of nerve and daring," followed these plays with, among others, *The Beast* (pr. 1974), *Vampire* (pr. 1973), *The Pleasure Principle* (pr. 1973), *The Soul of the White Ant* (pr. 1975), *The Glad Hand* (pr. 1978), *A Greenish Man* (pr. 1975, 1978), and *Flaming Bodies* (pr. 1979). Each manifested the distinctive Wilsonian combination of intelligent social comment and outrageous or astonishing visuals—*Flaming Bodies*, for example, calling for a car to crash through a window.

Heathcote Williams wrote only one important play, but that one, *AC/DC* (pr. 1970), has come to be widely regarded as one of the best and most influential produced by Fringe theater. It accomplished, in ways that perhaps eclipsed even Snoo Wilson's bold techniques, a kind of Artaudian nonrepresentational statement, an organic blending of subject matter and stage device. *AC/DC* presents two schizophrenics, Maurice and Perowne, and three hyped-up characters, one of whom—Sadie—becomes dominant by the end of the play. All of the characters are ruled by electronically transmitted influences: rock music, television images, news reporting. In their electrically wired world, they become automatons, bereft of personality. Sadie finally exorcises the schizophrenics by tearing down their media icons and cutting Perowne's brain out of his skull.

The other major Fringe playwrights, Trevor Griffiths, David Edgar, John McGrath, Howard Barker, Stephen Poliakoff, Barrie Keeffe, John Grillo, Steven Berkoff, Charles Marowitz, and Peter Brook, although important in varying degrees to the growth of the movement, seem to have been less centrally influenced than were Howard Brenton, David Hare, and Snoo Wilson. Griffiths, Edgar, McGrath, and Barker were more specifically political in their objectives—McGrath, for example, in his 7:84 Company; Griffiths with plays such as *Occupations* (pr. 1970), written for 7:84, and the award-winning *Comedians* (pr. 1975); and Edgar, with his highly acclaimed *Destiny* (pr. 1976). The plays of Poliakoff and Keeffe have tended to deal with the young and disadvantaged. Much of Brook's later work, though experimental, was performed outside the Fringe, in commercial theaters or in specialized productions abroad (on the Continent, in the Middle East, in Africa). Marowitz and Berkoff worked almost exclusively through their own companies—Marowitz in the Open Space (which closed in 1983, after which Marowitz returned to the United States and joined the Los Angeles Actors' Theatre in 1983) and Berkoff in the London Theatre Group.

Like New York's Off-Off-Broadway, London's Fringe is not what it was in the heyday of the 1960's and 1970's. The experiments, however, continue, as evidenced in the work of writers as divergent as England's Snoo Wilson and María Irene Fornés. Experimental theater remains at the vanguard of performance art in both countries. The "Theatre of Cruelty" experiment that Brook and Marowitz conducted in 1964, for example, had a direct influence on Brook's 1965 triumph, *The Persecution and Assassination of Jean Paul Marat as Performed by the Inmates of the Asylum of Charenton Under the Direction of the Marquis de Sade (Marat/Sade)*, which in turn has had a continuing pronounced influence on the general development of theater in Europe and in the United States. For his part in 1985, Marowitz returned to his Shakespeare collage experiments with a reworking of *A Midsummer Night's Dream*. It is true that, because of the vanguard position of experimental theater, many of its artists and productions have, after brief moments of triumph, either moved into other, less militant roles or simply faded from view.

By 1993, Thatcherite England had replaced the political subjects of earlier experiments with the subjects of writers as stylistically different as feminist Caryl Churchill—whose *Serious Money* (pr., pb. 1987) added to her innovative *Cloud Nine* (pr., pb. 1979) and *Top Girls* (pr., pb. 1982)—and traditionalist Alan Ayckbourn (*A Small Family Business,* pr., pb. 1987 and *Man of the Moment,* pr., pb. 1990). Expanding her feminist subjects and her Brechtian techniques, Churchill in *Mad Forest* (pr., pb. 1990) takes on post-communist Eastern Europe in a gripping Brechtian-style play about life in Romania. Representative of newer playwrights from the working class is Willy Russell, with *Educating Rita* (pr. 1980, pb. 1981).

The Marowitz-Brook directorial experiments, however they have loosened the strictures of conventional techniques, have themselves become history. The lines between experimental and traditional are increasingly blurred by easy transfers of plays among the Fringe, provincial, subsidized, and even commercial theaters.

Joseph H. Stodder
(Updated by *Susan Rusinko*)

RADIO DRAMA

The first radio station in the United States, Pittsburgh's KDKA, began broadcasting in 1920. The idea of competing networks scheduling program slates to win listeners from one another was almost a decade away. By 1922, only thirty stations operated in the United States, but radio was already becoming the new-appliance phenomenon that later television, the videocassette recorder, and the personal computer would become: By 1923, 556 stations broadcast an assortment of programs. The production of receiver sets shows the same explosion of growth: From only a few receivers being produced in 1921, the Radio Corporation of America (RCA, incorporated on October 17, 1919) and others such as Atwater Kent and Westinghouse Electric Corporation manufactured one hundred thousand sets in 1922 and five hundred thousand in 1923. For the first time in 1923, both Sears, Roebuck and Company and Montgomery Ward offered radios in their catalogs.

Tom Lewis' book on the genesis of radio further points out that the end of the 1920's saw another surge in the popularity of the medium, sparked by the public's desire to follow the heroics of Charles A. Lindbergh. When William S. Paley combined two small networks into the Columbia Broadcasting System (CBS) and named himself president, he established conditions that would affect not only the development of American radio drama but also the basic nature of the medium.

Paley sought to compete with the National Broadcasting Company (NBC) and its president David Sarnoff by widening the types of programs broadcast. NBC had until then been featuring programs that often played to the highest tastes of listeners. Paley eschewed classical concerts and educational fare and instead found a receptive audience that enjoyed jazz, vaudeville comics, and soap opera. It was NBC that eventually broadcast the most popular radio series ever, *Amos 'n' Andy* (beginning in 1926 as *Sam 'n' Henry* on Chicago's WGN, the show first aired on NBC under its familiar title on August 19, 1929), and the national sensation of that comedy spurred further sales of radios.

Worthington Miner wrote about the early days of the medium and how the expenses of creating a national industry were absorbed by the broadcasters, the manufacturers, and the sponsors. The listeners, however, had to pay too: "[T]he price to the public was the stamp of a salesman's mind on the dramatic content and intent of every program put on the air. . . . [A] vigorous theater thrives on controversy, and in precisely those areas of prejudice and conviction—sex, politics, and religion—that are taboo for the salesman." Miner added that "the wonder is that anything of quality or substance ever reached the public air."

His comments identify both the main propellant and the main obstacle for first-rate radio drama in the United States: commercialization. The revenues generated by the sale of airtime made possible innovative, intelligent plays such as those produced by Orson Welles, Norman Corwin, and Arch Oboler in the 1930's and 1940's; the need, however, for large audiences to satisfy the sponsors virtually guaranteed that most radio shows followed the safe rather than the experimental. Howard Fink tabulated the extreme imbalance toward the popular in American radio drama and concluded that during the twenty-year span from the rise of radio to the rise of television at most only twelve radio series (out of some six thousand listed by the *Variety Radio Directory*) attempted serious plays written expressly for the radio or adapted from other media. That comes to less than half of 1 percent.

The natural comparison to radio in Great Britain tells a different story. The work of John Reith as the first general manager of the British Broadcasting Corporation (BBC) saved British radio and later television from the American type of commercialization by having the BBC set up as a public utility partly paid for by the small fees of listeners. The history of serious radio drama in England has never been a summary of isolated plays and programs of merit but rather the story of the development of an art form that continued even after the rise of television.

It may be unfair to blame Paley for the paradox of American radio— how commercialization alternatively abetted and retarded literary drama. The facts support different readings. Paley may have lowered the quality of the airwaves by broadcasting to a wider audience, or he may have begun to recognize that the growth of the industry was great enough to make room for smaller audiences of different tastes. Paley, along with Irving Reis, for example, became the driving force behind *The Columbia Workshop* (1936), one of the best dramatic anthologies in American radio.

A half-hour "sustaining series" (that is, free from commercial sponsorship), *The Columbia Workshop* debuted with a suspense drama written by Reis, *Meridian 7-1212*, a work that Fink described as going "behind the mechanical illusions of realistic sound to show a real understanding of the *space* of the medium, especially the necessity of creating verbal and intellectual complications to replace the visual complexities of the theatre." The following year, *The Columbia Workshop* offered the first American verse play written for radio, Archibald MacLeish's *The Fall of the City: A Verse Play for Radio* (pr., pb. 1937). MacLeish had written a polemic against Fascism, and Reis cast young Welles as the narrator who describes the subjugation of thousands of people to a conqueror who turns out to be a fearful-sounding but empty suit of armor. The narrator's description of the lifting of the visor and the hollowness inside placed a vivid image in the minds of radio listeners. The broadcast became the single most famous radio show until that time. Blending sound techniques and poetry to exploit the theater-of-the-mind capabilities of radio, Reis broadcast the show from an armory to approximate the acoustics of a town square. He recorded the sounds of two hundred extras and timed the playbacks during the performance so that, following the live cheers of the extras, the echoing crowd noise sounded overwhelming. Welles had to perform his lines in the quiet of an isolation booth, a change made out of necessity but one that created a type of verbal concerto through the balance of contrasting sounds of the crowd and the narrator.

Just as *Amos 'n' Andy* fueled the growth of popular radio, the MacLeish broadcast made serious radio drama exciting and more popular. Soon writers of note such as W. H. Auden and Stephen Vincent Benét were crafting scripts directly for the radio; later, other literary figures such as Sherwood Anderson, Maxwell Anderson, Edna St. Vincent Millay, William Saroyan, and Dorothy Parker would work in the medium. Welles's next radio assignment continued the innovations. His seven-part version of Victor Hugo's *Les Misérables* for the Mutual Network was called by Welles a "projection" rather than an adaptation or dramatization. To prepare what may have been the first broadcast miniseries, Welles chose important selections from the novel to be read by himself as narrator or by actors performing the characters. He used sound effects and music to accompany Hugo's prose and also played the part of Jean Valjean. The result, according to Welles's biographer Frank Brady, was that "Welles developed the character of Jean Valjean more fully than it had been in the novel."

With his growing experiences in radio, Welles, unlike many radio actors, by now knew the difference between reading lines in front of a microphone and sounding on the air like a real person. In such a context in which sound is the only medium for communication, to refer to the actor's voice as an instrument risks understatement. Brady wrote that Welles would position himself before a microphone as if it were a kind of sonic mirror, and "he would seemingly be able to gesture with sound and move himself in space, creating illusions of intimacy or distance by employing only certain voice changes."

In 1938, CBS offered Welles total artistic control of a new sustaining series to begin on July 11. The network hoped that the program would receive enough favorable attention to bring in advertisers as continuing sponsors for the hour-long show. *First Person Singular*, the name that was eventually chosen, would also provide another vehicle for Welles's Mercury players, a repertory company performing in theater works that Welles and John Houseman were directing and producing. The limited budget and the weekly demands of radio (and also perhaps the satisfactions of total artistic control) kept Welles from commissioning original scripts, so he settled on the popular classics to adapt himself with the help of Houseman, Howard Koch, Richard Brooks, Abraham Polonsky, and Herman J. Mankiewicz. Their first offering was *Dracula*, restructured from the letters-and-diary approach in which Bram Stoker had written it into a style more suited to radio. His other shows in his first season were adaptations of *Treasure Island* (on July 18), *A Tale of Two Cities* (July 25), *The Thirty-nine Steps* (August 5), three short stories (August 8), *Hamlet* (August 15), *The Affairs of Anatole* (August 22), *The Count of Monte-Cristo* (August 28), and Welles's favorite novel, G. K. Chesterton's *The Man Who Was Thursday* (September 5). CBS renewed the series for the fall and renamed it *The Mercury Theatre on the Air.*

The most famous Mercury performance came later in 1938 on Halloween Eve, when CBS broadcast an adaptation by Koch of H. G. Wells's novel *The War of the Worlds* (1898). Welles decided to tell the story of the Martian invasion in the format of a special-report newscast. His inspiration may have partly been the popular show *The March of Time* (1931), which dramatized actual news events in a radio studio with sound effects and a live orchestra. Such a format smudged the line between the real and the fictional and testified to the power of drama on radio. In an age before the ubiquitous camcorder gave television newscasts their immediacy, radio simply manufactured its reality, re-creating baseball games and news events as needed. *The March of Time* was the most popular news program on the air. In interviews years later, Welles said he also intended in the broadcast to lampoon the seriousness of radio and the way listeners passively accepted everything they heard over the airwaves.

For the man-from-Mars broadcast, Welles wanted to develop the novel's science-fiction premise realistically. The actor playing a field reporter, for example, listened to the recordings of on-the-air accounts of the burning of the dirigible *Hindenburg* and tried to mimic the eyewitness panic. According to Houseman, the opening of the show was intentionally boring in its protracted use of simulated dance music from a Brooklyn hotel to contrast the later urgency of the supposed news bulletins. The show would switch its listeners from the network newsroom to remote feeds from the invasion sites. Welles played Professor Pierson, an astronomer at an observatory. Although the beginning of the broadcast explained that the program was a dramatization of *The War of the Worlds* and repeated that disclaimer later, the show nevertheless created widespread panic when many listeners thought that the world was actually being invaded. Welles and the Mercury players were front-page news the next morning. Ironically, for all Welles's ambitious literary efforts in the medium, this was the broadcast that eventually won the program a sponsor. On December 9, 1938, the *Mercury Theatre on the Air* became the *Campbell Playhouse.*

Although nothing matched the invasion broadcast for sensationalism, some of Welles's other shows perhaps illustrate better his mastery of radio as a storytelling medium. On the whole, he tended to think of the scripts for broadcast as stories rather than as plays. As Richard Wilson, of the Mercury actors, describes it: "Radio is the medium for the story. The best storyteller was Orson. . . . He likened radio listeners to the audience that gathered around a storyteller in the town square, held spellbound with imaginative and fanciful tales." The show for October 29, 1939, was a radio version of Booth Tarkington's novel *The Magnificent Ambersons.* In 1942, Welles would also choose Tarkington's novel as the subject for his second film, but he knew that he could not play the part of George Amberson Minafer on screen, since the tall Welles was too heavy and mature looking to portray convincingly a spoiled adolescent. On radio, however, Welles played George and succeeded at bringing out both the proud and the whiny sides of pampered youth. The overlapping dialogue and sound montage that Welles's early films *Citizen Kane* (1941) and *The Magnificent Ambersons* (1942) employ so effectively have their roots in the techniques of radio drama. (Certainly Welles's radio talents invigorated his own films and even motion pictures in general; the use of sound montage in radio, however, is sometimes mistakenly credited to Welles when the work of True Boardman on the CBS anthology *Sunday Afternoon Theatre*, 1937—also known as *Silver Theatre*—probably deserves that distinction.)

Welles adapted Joseph Conrad's *Heart of Darkness* (1902) twice for radio. The second Conrad broadcast, from March 13, 1945, appeared on the series *This Is My Best* (1944), for which Welles had become director as well as host. Welles, playing the narrator Marlow, used the grunts of the natives lugging ivory to suggest the ominous climate of Africa. After journeying up the river to find Kurtz, his predecessor, Marlow hears Kurtz's last anguished whisper "the horror, the horror" and senses the degree to which Kurtz has viewed, and become involved in, the dark side of human behavior. When Marlow, however, returns to meet with Kurtz's fiancée and is asked to relate the dying man's last words, he lies and says that Kurtz spoke his fiancée's name. The audience hears the ghostly echo of Kurtz, however, repeating "the horror, the horror" and understands in that single aural image that the evils experienced by Kurtz have found their way into the subconscious of Marlow.

Shows such as *The Mercury Theatre on the Air* owed part of their mystique to the live nature of the broadcasts. In the days before magnetic tape, scratchy acetate discs were the only way engineers could reproduce sound, and so programs were aired live. Colorful stories exist about Welles, who was widely employed as an actor in live radio, using a blaring ambulance as his crosstown transportation between one show and another. Sometimes still in his theater makeup, he would race from the ambulance into a private elevator to be whisked up to a broadcast studio and handed a script minutes before airtime. Photographs show him as director of his own program, standing on a raised platform before a podium and a microphone with an engineering booth in front of him, actors and the sound-effects staff to his left, and Bernard Herrmann and his orchestra behind him. Everyone wore headphones, and Welles worked the creative ensemble like a conductor of sorts, reading lines and cuing others in order to obtain the right sound mix. John Houseman deserves credit for disciplining Welles's productive but often uncontrolled genius. In a rare surviving disc of a rehearsal session, Welles can be heard intoning perfectly the lines from a Shakespearean soliloquy and then bursting into a profane string of epithets because at the end of the speech he elided the *t* in "restless." Such a slip might not be noticed on stage or on film, where both the eye and the ear are occupied, but radio augmented the aural dimension to a degree that the speech had to be consonant perfect. Such dramatic heights were never far from the mercantile, since Welles frequently read the commercials too. One critic of the time lamented: "It's a shock to hear a plug for prune juice by someone who sounds like the Archbishop of Canterbury."

Just as fascinating as the way live shows were prepared are the accounts of resourcefulness of those in charge of sound effects. Before the invention of tape libraries of effects, sound engineers had to re-create live on the air the sounds needed for a particular show. For their broadcast of *A Tale of Two Cities*, Welles and Houseman, for example, experimented for hours in order to find the right vegetable to hack for the severing crunch of the guillotine (they finally selected a cabbage). The jobs of sound-effect engineers required them to cultivate a lore all their own. Trial and error taught them that a knife plunged into a potato or grapefruit close to the microphone made the sound of a stabbed torso. Shaking wheat stalks whistled like wind blowing through the brush. Squeezing a box of corn starch scrunched like footsteps in the snow. Hitting a sponge simulated the thud of a punch to the stomach.

Along with Welles, Norman Corwin and Arch Oboler also stand out for their important work in creating serious radio drama. Corwin's first series was *Words Without Music* (1938), which combined Corwin's own scripts with adaptations of classics such as the poetry of Walt Whitman and Carl Sandburg. In setting free verse for the radio, Corwin let each poem suggest the best approach, but he is particularly remembered for using choral speech effectively. Corwin's next series, *Pursuit of Happiness* (1939), introduced what Corwin called a "radio opera," a blend of music, documentary, and drama. If Welles's gifts to radio were primarily those of the consummate actor-director, Corwin's legacies were those of the writer. His sensitivity to language aided in his broadcasts of poetry and in imparting a lyrical dimension to his own scripts. Like Welles, Corwin was associated with *The Columbia Workshop*. His script coauthored with Lucille Fletcher, *My Client Curley*, about a luckless theatrical agent who happens on a boy with a dancing caterpillar, became one of the classics of radio and was later made into a film. Another series, *Columbia Presents Corwin* (1944), continued his originality and is regarded as perhaps his best work. Some of Corwin's memorable plots for this series include a story about a boy's visit to heaven in search of his lost dog and a dramatization of the return of Abraham Lincoln's body by train to Springfield, Illinois.

Oboler first gained attention in popular radio by working with performers such as Rudy Vallee, Eddie Cantor, Milton Berle, and Edgar Bergen. The incongruity of a ventriloquist performing on radio did not deter millions from enjoying Bergen (nor for that matter a radio dance show featuring Fred Astaire), and Oboler learned the techniques of radio drama in this apprenticeship. Oboler's first work as a writer-director came on the NBC suspense program *Lights Out* (1936), which made his name well known. His sustaining series *Arch Oboler's Plays* (1939) offered anthology programming and competed with both Welles and *The Columbia Workshop.* Oboler relied often on the psychological element of radio and explored the consciousness of the central character to carry forward the story. For example, Oboler's episode from *Lights Out* called "Oxychloride X" focuses on a college student hazed by fraternity men. The highlight of the show occurs when the student decides to get even and travels across campus at night to break into the science laboratory and concoct an all-powerful solvent. His wild mutterings organize the scene, reveal his insecurities, and establish an eerie tone. Like Corwin, Oboler worked during the war on propaganda plays for radio, which, more centered on messages, were less innovative in technique.

The mainstream of American radio, though utilizing the dramatic form, featured almost exclusively popular rather than serious programs. Freed from seriousness of purpose and depth of thought, these shows nevertheless reveal at times aspects of technique that showcase the medium well. The sound effects and voice characterizations of Mel Blanc, for example, greatly enhanced the comedy of Jack Benny. When Benny started up his Maxwell, Blanc's exaggerated sputters all but gave the car a personality; when Benny opened his vault, Blanc's creaks and groans made the comedian's stinginess something that could be heard. Benny moved his show to television in the 1950's, and audiences actually saw a set designer's version of the famous vault. This reality, however, probably did not measure up to the medieval picture in the minds of listeners. Fibber McGee's closet of junk, the clip-clop of horse-drawn hansom cabs in Sherlock Holmes's Victorian London, and the Wild West of the Lone Ranger illustrate the power of radio serial drama to unlock the imagination.

One of the longest-running detective programs, *The Shadow* (1931), also used the medium well. The Shadow of the pulp magazines published during the run of the radio show was a sinister figure in black who used blazing revolvers to fight crime. The character on radio, however, was never seen. Having the power "to cloud men's minds," the hero seemed to appear and penetrate the psychological defenses of the criminals with his uncanny powers. In the episode titled "The White Legion," The Shadow (performed by Welles) intimidates a secret society by exposing its members' identities. The final scene takes place in open court, where suddenly the mysterious voice of The Shadow disrupts the proceedings and names the judge himself as the ringleader of the criminals. The series' atmosphere catered to the imaginative powers of its audience.

Another gifted writer from the flowering of radio is John Dickson Carr. Carr is mainly remembered as a detective novelist whose books employ locked-room puzzles. Since he was also a master of atmosphere and mood, his talent thrived in radio. Carr wrote mystery plays on both sides of the Atlantic, and his experiences point out some of the differences between American and British radio drama. Carr submitted his first radio play, a three-part work featuring his Chestertonian hero Dr. Gideon Fell, to Val Gielgud, the head of drama programming for the BBC. In England, Carr learned, writing took precedence over time limits and genre. Gielgud did not feel obligated to adhere to the formula conventions of mysteries or even to preset lengths of programs. In addition, he wanted the writer present at rehearsals to explain his intentions and, if necessary, to make any revisions. Contrary to the American custom, Gielgud fostered a radio drama that minimized musical bridges, clichéd "knife-chords," and sound effects. In "The Black Minute," Carr's second script for the BBC, for example, a transition is accomplished by simply fading from a frightened woman's cries to the relaxed voice of the taxi driver who had brought her moments ago to a sinister house. The contrast between the sound of her anguish and the cabdriver's calm makes the heroine's plight more fretful for the audience. Carr's script also shows how sound effects, used sparingly, can assume greater force. The key scene in "The Black Minute" is a séance in which the characters join hands in a locked, darkened room. As the tense characters await the words of the medium, the only sound is the background scratch of a gramophone. As with the earlier transition, less becomes more. The methodical grinding of the gramophone makes the lengthening silence more unbearable.

With the United States' entry into World War II, Carr returned to the United States and wrote plays for the CBS series *Suspense* (1942). There, he encountered a work situation nearly the opposite of that in England. The American show was timed to the last second, and Carr's scripts were tailored to fit the predesigned pattern. With its own orchestra, *Suspense* also made generous use of background music and strident knife-chords as sonic punctuation. Censorship, too, hampered Carr, who had to choose ethnically indistinct villains to placate the network and avoid giving offense. Carr wrote "The Dead Sleep Lightly" for *Suspense* in the thirty-minute format of most American shows, but when he returned to England in 1943, he expanded the script to forty minutes, added his detective Dr. Fell as a foil, and boldly changed the ending to let the culprit, exposed by Fell, avoid arrest.

It is a mistake to imply that the worlds of American and British radio drama were irreconcilable. Though clear differences existed, Gielgud could also see the comparative merits of the other style. Carr served as a go-between when he offered Gielgud more of his scripts from *Suspense* to develop into a series on the BBC (*Appointment with Fear*, debuting on September 11, 1943, was the result). Gielgud's reaction to "all the trimmings of atmospheric bass-voiced narrator, knife-chords and other specially composed musical effects, and a regular length of half an hour timed to the split second" was that "the temptation to compete 'on the home ground' [was] irresistible." Carr's program proved to be a success.

The development of British radio plays can be traced to the broadcast of *Twelfth Night* on May 28, 1923. The first original work for British radio was Richard Hughes's *Danger* (1924), a fifteen-minute play about three characters trapped in the pitch black of a coal mine. Reginald Denny's *The White Chanteau* (1925) became the first original, full-length play on the BBC. In the 1930's, as technology improved, more attention to original programming brought forth the experimental play by Tyrone Guthrie *The Flowers Are Not for You to Pick* (1930). Guthrie's play takes place in the mind of the protagonist—a young missionary who drowns on his way to his first assignment in China—and breaks up the traditional linear plot by moving the audience via flashbacks through a number of formative moments in the hero's life. Guthrie understood that time could be manipulated more effectively by the radio dramatist than space, something that holds true even though stereo broadcasts in later years have made space a more important dimension. The emphasis on the psychological can also be seen in Louis MacNeice's verse play *Christopher Columbus* (1944), in which different actors voice different parts ("Doubt," "Faith") of the hero's mind. MacNeice's fantasy *The Dark Tower* (1947) emphasizes sound effects and music more than his previous plays and is sometimes mentioned as MacNeice's best work. *Under Milk Wood: A Play for Voices* (pr. 1953) is Dylan Thomas' highly regarded radio play about small-town life in Wales. The broadcast elements of language, sound, and silence may in part explain the interest of Harold Pinter and Samuel Beckett in radio. Explorations of the ambiguities of communication and the richness of silence lend themselves ideally to the medium. Pinter's radio plays *A Slight Ache* (pr. 1959) and *A Night Out* (pr. 1960) preceded his first stage success, and Beckett's radio plays *All That Fall* (pr. 1957), *Embers* (pr. 1959), and *Words and Music* (pr. 1962) have taken a place in importance next to his stage works. The tradition continued. Robert Bolt's play about Sir Thomas More,

A Man for All Seasons (1954), appeared first on BBC radio. John Arden, Tom Stoppard, and John Mortimer also made contributions to British radio drama.

If the term "radio drama" may be slightly altered to "sound drama," then the development of the genre can be charted through the rise of the long-playing record and audio cassettes. One of the first stage works preserved on sound recordings was Arthur Miller's 1949 play *Death of a Salesman.* Miller had written radio plays after graduating from the University of Michigan, and his expressionistic play about Willy Loman centers on Willy's mind and its slipping hold on reality, material well suited for sound drama. Columbia recorded the play with Thomas Mitchell as Willy; later, Caedmon Records issued a version with Lee J. Cobb as the salesman. Eventually, technology permitted a nostalgic renaissance for radio drama when many old-time radio shows (such as Basil Rathbone's and Nigel Bruce's work as Sherlock Holmes and Dr. Watson, respectively) were issued as record albums and audio cassettes.

Both Caedmon Records and London Records have produced unabridged disc and cassette recordings of the complete plays of William Shakespeare. This should come as no surprise. Before CBS radio had begun *The Columbia Workshop*, it had experimented in the summer of 1937 with a series of adaptations and selected scenes from Shakespeare. Welles worked on the *Hamlet* broadcast. While CBS prepared its series, NBC quickly signed John Barrymore for its own Shakespeare series to start in late June. Though the casting on CBS emphasized film stars rather than stage performers (Rosalind Russell as Beatrice, Edward G. Robinson as Petruchio, Humphrey Bogart as Hotspur), Shakespeare proved ideal for radio. With stage directions and action incorporated into much of the poetry, Shakespeare's dramaturgy minimized props and relied on the aural. The rhymed couplets signaled the close of a scene for radio listeners just as they did for their original spectators in Elizabethan England. In 1964, the Broadway cast of *Hamlet*, directed by Gielgud and starring Richard Burton, recorded the play on a four-disc set for Columbia Records. BBC radio has often released some of its best Shakespeare productions on audio cassettes as well.

Glenn Hopp

TELEVISION DRAMA

In the early days of television broadcasting, there was little reason to suspect that the medium viewed by many as a passing novelty would in time become the single most pervasive and influential aspect of popular culture. Certainly, the grainy, problem-prone early broadcasts seemed to pose no real threat to radio, television's predecessor in American living rooms, and unlike radio and films, the technology of television did not catch on quickly with the public. Indeed, the necessary technical knowledge had existed since the 1920's, but it was not until the late 1940's that the medium began to become a real presence in American life.

In its earliest incarnation, television was a local phenomenon, with broadcasts limited to the East Coast of the United States, within easy range of New York. Slow developments throughout the 1930's were largely put on hold during World War II, and it was in the postwar years that the medium began to grow with a force and speed that surprised many skeptics. Both the National Broadcasting Company (NBC) and the Columbia Broadcasting System (CBS) had received commercial broadcasting licenses in 1941, and by 1946 commercial television had become a reality. Joined by the short-lived DuMont network and later by the American Broadcasting Company (ABC), the networks began searching for programs to fill their expanding schedules. By 1948, the four networks offered almost complete prime-time broadcasts—the hours between seven and eleven o'clock in the evening—seven nights a week.

The Rise of Television Drama

In the late 1940's, television was a technology in search of content. Yet radio, its closest relative, could provide only limited inspiration because of the key difference between the two mediums. Despite early predictions, television was not simply "radio with pictures." Actual radio with pictures would have offered the sight of actors speaking lines into a microphone while technicians supplied sound effects and music to one side. What television required of its content was that it provide the visual imagery that radio left to the listener's imagination. What had taken place in the mind of the radio listener would now take place on the screen of the television viewer.

With New York City as their headquarters, it was not surprising that the networks would turn to the legitimate theater for programming ideas. The alliance between live theater and television was established early, when NBC in its experimental stages offered New York viewers a production of Rachel Crothers' play *Susan and God*, with Gertrude Lawrence. DuMont, lobbying hard to prove its worthiness for a broadcasting license, offered the first regularly scheduled live dramatic series, *Television Workshop*, to a limited audience during the early 1940's. NBC followed suit with *NBC Television Theatre* in 1945 and later with *Kraft Television Theatre* in 1947, a show that would prove to be among the most important in shaping the face of television.

Sponsored by Kraft Foods, *Kraft Television Theatre* would remain on the air for eleven years and would help set the standard by which television drama would be judged. With generous budgets and talented people working both on and off camera, the series brought high-quality productions into American homes each Wednesday night, offering viewers classical and contemporary dramas and providing them with their first glimpses of such actors as Paul Newman, Joanne Woodward, James Dean, and Grace Kelly. Rod Serling, whose acclaimed teleplay *Patterns* aired in 1955, established his reputation as a writer on the show. The series was also one of the earliest to experiment with color in the mid-1950's.

The show's influence was also felt in another, crucial area of television's development: the growing interest of commercial sponsors in the medium as a format for advertising their products. As the popularity of *Kraft Television Theatre* grew, sales of Kraft cheese skyrocketed, demonstrating conclusively that television had potential as a sales arena undreamed of by radio or print advertising. The impact of visual imagery offered a marketing tool that would be seized by every corporation that had a product to be sold and the advertising dollars needed to purchase airtime. Gradually, the influence of sponsors would become a shaping force in television's content and format. What had begun as an effort by Kraft Foods to associate its products with quality productions in viewers' minds would evolve into a relationship that would determine the face of commercial television in the decades to come.

In the early years, however, the ability to link company products to fine drama had a galvanizing effect on corporate America, and by 1948, Chevrolet, Philco Corporation, and Westinghouse Electric Corporation had all become sponsors of dramatic series. They were joined in the 1950's by Goodyear Tire and Rubber Company, Aluminum Company of America (Alcoa), Kaiser Aluminum, and U.S. Steel. All these companies believed—in tandem with the networks—that high-quality programming was the surest way to attract viewers.

Television's Golden Age

By 1948, all four networks were offering their viewers live drama, and the period often referred to as television's golden age had begun. With hours of airtime to fill and budgets underwritten by powerful sponsors, live television drama became a testing ground for talented young actors and writers and a showcase for the kind of work that had previously been available only to paying audiences in theaters. Viewers could see Maurice Evans performing the plays of William Shakespeare, a live production of Reginald Rose's *Twelve Angry Men*, or a young Sidney Poitier—one of the first African-American actors to appear on television in a leading role—in Robert Alan Aurthur's *A Man Is Ten Feet Tall.*

In an attempt to distinguish themselves from their competitors and establish their own niche in a rapidly burgeoning field, several shows specialized in particular forms of television drama. *Robert Montgomery Presents* offered adaptations of popular films and managed to lure such Hollywood stars as James Cagney and Claudette Colbert to the small screen. *Philco TV Playhouse* began in association with Actor's Equity and presented adaptations of Broadway plays before joining with Book-of-the-Month Club and featuring dramatizations of current novels. *The U.S. Steel Hour* also drew on the legitimate theater, offering a production of *Hedda Gabler* starring Tallulah Bankhead, while *Goodyear TV Playhouse* offered a wide range of original teleplays, including several by the young Paddy Chayefsky. Chayefsky's *Marty*, telecast in 1953 and regarded as one of the finest dramas in television history, would reverse the trend of borrowing from other media when its feature-film adaptation received an Oscar as Best Picture in 1955.

Perhaps the two most highly acclaimed live dramatic series were *Playhouse 90* and *Studio One.* Each in its own way represented not only that which was best in television drama but also that which was unique. For five years, *Playhouse 90* produced weekly, ninety-minute live dramas, sparing no expense on either production values or talent and setting a standard of excellence that is still singled out as an example of the best that television's golden age had to offer.

Incredibly, the series' second telecast was the landmark *Requiem for a Heavyweight*, written by Rod Serling and starring Jack Palance. With its combination of fine performances, careful staging, and well-crafted writing, the production proved to be a declaration of the course that the series would follow in the years to come.

The best teleplay writers were those who, like Serling and Chayefsky, realized that television was a medium particularly well suited to the staging of complex, intimate dramas. Unable to compete with feature films in scope, television could reach directly into its viewers' homes and present them with stories of ordinary individuals, so-called kitchen sink dramas. If Hollywood represented glamour, then good teleplay writing was characterized by its ability to turn television's lack of glamour into an effective asset.

Studio One, on the other hand, concentrated less on its material and more on the manner in which it was staged. Although the series grew out of an unsuccessful radio program, under producer Worthington C. Miner the television version set out to explore the possibilities of the new visual medium and became one of the most highly praised dramatic series of the 1950's. Miner was one of the earliest television pioneers to grasp the fact that television's power lay in its images rather than its dialogue. Radio's complete reliance on words and sounds to tell a story led many early dramatic television series to offer productions in which the staging was an accompaniment to the story. Under Miner's guidance, however, *Studio One* explored ways in which to tell a story through visual means. Although good writing also characterized the show, its main emphasis was on its imagery. It is not surprising, therefore, that the series helped to launch the careers of a number of notable feature-film directors, including George Roy Hill, Franklin Schaffner, and Sidney Lumet.

Despite their individual differences, live dramatic series had several factors in common that were unique to the medium of television. Unlike motion pictures, teleplays were performed live, offering audiences an immediacy that films were unable to match, and "live" on television involved risks and complications that neither the radio nor the stage faced. The lack of pictures allowed radio performers to work from scripts, unseen by their audience, and mistakes that occurred could often be covered. Stage productions have long rehearsal periods, out-of-town tryouts, and the luxury of rewrites if a play contains material that does not work well when tested in front of a live audience. Additionally, mistakes made on a stage are seen by a limited audience; television actors faced the daunting prospect that their gaffes would take place in front of an audience that was literally nationwide.

The newness of the technology also brought its share of complications. The history of live television drama is filled with anecdotes of "dead" bodies that crawled offscreen or, conversely, actors who unwittingly stepped out of the picture, uncertain of the limits of the camera's range. As television technology developed and performers became more familiar with the medium, the potential for on-the-air mishaps lessened, but the rawness, the sense that anything might happen, is remembered with great fondness by participants and viewers alike.

Ironically, one of the boons of live television drama would eventually also prove to be a factor in its decline. With a burgeoning market of prime-time hours to fill, dramatic series gave many young and untested writers a forum for their talents. Young actors also benefited when many better-known performers expressed little interest in appearing in the new medium. Yet these same factors gradually led the networks to the realization that live drama was both costly and a strain on available resources. The growing success of shows such as *Dragnet* and *Gunsmoke* heralded the development of what would become the core of television drama: the weekly filmed or taped dramatic series.

Although live television drama was at the heart of the medium's golden age, it was in the realm of the prerecorded dramatic series—and its comedic counterpart, the situation comedy—that television would find its most lasting voice. Episodic series, performed live, had also been a staple of radio programming, although the technological advantages of television and the longer running times of the shows allowed television drama series to develop in ways that had not been possible on the radio. That development took two distinct paths: the weekly anthology series and the weekly episodic drama.

Of the two, the anthology series is by far the road less traveled. Its earliest example was *Four Star Playhouse*, which each week offered a filmed, thirty-minute drama featuring one of its four stars, Charles Boyer, David Niven, Dick Powell, and Ida Lupino. In 1955, Alfred Hitchcock lent his considerable presence to the anthology format with *Alfred Hitchcock Presents*, which he hosted for ten years. Thirty-minute, and later hour-long, tales of suspense with surprise twists at the conclusion characterized the show, which also played with the medium of television itself in Hitchcock's droll introductions and conclusions of each episode. Often mocking his commercial sponsors, Hitchcock would also negate any possible censorship problems over an episode's content by adding a humorous coda that seemed to belie a story's message of evil triumphing over good.

The most ambitious and successful anthology series was Serling's *The Twilight Zone*, which used the genres of suspense and fantasy to tackle such subjects as intolerance, racial prejudice, and human beings' capacity for violence and greed. Introduced each week by Serling, the series combined the best elements of live television drama—solid writing, talented casts, serious subject matter—with the added advantages of filming. Often dismissed at the time of its initial run as simply a science-fiction series, the show later grew in critical stature.

Characters, Genres, and Themes

The lack of widespread success for anthology-style shows, however, demonstrated what would become a truism of programming philosophy; viewing audiences prefer series with recurring casts of familiar characters. This piece of television wisdom is the motivating factor behind both episodic dramas and situation comedies, and it has shaped the style of programming that has dominated the airwaves since the early 1960's. The episodic dramatic series has taken many forms and covers a wide range of genres, from Westerns and crime shows to medical dramas and soap operas, and has managed at its best to surpass in quality the majority of Hollywood feature films released in any given year.

In the late 1950's and early 1960's, Westerns, long a favorite of Saturday matinee film audiences, became among the most popular shows on the air. If theater had been the chief inspiration for live television productions,

Westerns, with their outdoor locations and action-based stories—not to mention livestock—had their roots directly in Hollywood. With *Gunsmoke* leading the way, such series as *Rawhide*, starring Clint Eastwood, *Have Gun Will Travel*, *Wagon Train*, and *The Virginian* were soon changing the format of television drama. The most successful Western was unquestionably *Bonanza*, which ran for a total of fourteen years and established characters so well known and loved by its audience that the show was able to shift from an action emphasis to one of personal drama. *Bonanza* would prove to be the last of a dying breed, however, and fitful efforts to revive Westerns in subsequent years would meet with little success.

The crime drama borrowed heavily from both radio and motion pictures. *The Untouchables* was a fast-paced, often violent thriller that drew on period settings and cinematic depictions of dramatic Feds-and-mobsters confrontations, while *Dragnet*, with its much-parodied deadpan style, had its roots in radio, a connection apparent in the show's static visual style and reliance on dialogue over action to tell its stories. *Perry Mason* centered its action in the courtroom in mysteries that were enhanced by visual imagery but that would have been easily rendered through dialogue alone. Unlike that of Westerns, the popularity of crime dramas has not diminished, and a look at any given period of television programming reveals a number of such shows, with the standouts including *Naked City*, *Kojak*, and *Columbo*.

As episodic drama developed, a dominant storytelling device began to emerge. On medical shows such as *Dr. Kildare*, *Ben Casey*, and *Marcus Welby, M.D.*, the recurring star or central cast of characters remained constant while each new patient provided the springboard into that week's story or issue. "Road" shows such as *Route 66*, *Run for Your Life*, and *The Fugitive* also used the device, moving their central characters from place to place each week and setting up problems for a new set of individuals whom the hero would assist before once again moving to a new place. The result was shows in which the central characters showed little emotional change or growth, functioning instead as the anchor on which each week's story was hung. Although individual episodes might feature stories in which the series' star fell in love or suffered a loss, these events did not translate into internal changes that made themselves felt in later episodes.

The better shows adopting this device used it as a means of exploring a wide range of ideas and issues. The critically praised series *The Defenders*, starring E. G. Marshall, used its legal setting to examine not only personal dramas but social problems as well, a direction also taken by the short-lived *East Side/West Side*, which starred George C. Scott as a social worker. While individual films and stage plays were forced by constraints of length to focus on one or two issues, a continuing television series could encompass a remarkable range of ideas in a single season. Television was also at an advantage in this area over radio, which had reached its zenith at a more restrictive period in broadcasting history.

The Soaps

One form of radio drama, however, did make itself felt in the realm of television soap operas. The backbone of daytime television, series such as *General Hospital* and *Days of Our Lives*, beginning in the 1950's, engaged loyal viewers with their ongoing emotional melodramas. If prime-time series concentrated on new stories each week, soap operas examined the loves and losses of their recurring casts of characters. Perhaps no form of television drama has shown the endurance of the soap opera, and although changing social mores and relaxed censorship restrictions have served to spice up their content, the shows themselves remain constant in their approach. Working under enormous time constraints, soap operas retained a degree of the rawness and immediacy of early live drama, although the quality of work involved was far lower.

In 1964, the first prime-time version of a soap opera made its appearance. Based on the best-selling book by Grace Metalious, *Peyton Place* premiered on ABC on September of 1964 and was an immediate success. Telecast two to three nights per week during most of its five-year run, the show brought daytime television's blend of scandal, intrigue, and melodrama to a nighttime audience that watched in droves. The show launched the careers of Mia Farrow and Ryan O'Neal, among others, and paved the way for the later prime-time soap operas that would dominate television in the 1980's. Their arrival was heralded by *Dallas* in 1978, a series that would go on to achieve international popularity and make its central character, Larry Hagman's unscrupulous J. R. Ewing, one of the most famous characters in television history. Adding opulent wealth to the familiar soap-opera formula, *Dallas* inspired several imitators and garnered one of the highest television ratings ever with its much-hyped "Who Shot J. R.?" second-season opener.

Focus on Character Development

It was not until the 1970's, however, that television drama other than soap operas began to use the format of the episodic series to explore in depth the lives of the shows' permanent characters. The family drama *The Waltons*, with its Depression-era stories drawn from the childhood of writer Earl Hamner, Jr., managed after near-cancellation in 1972 to find its viewers and engage them for eight years with its heartwarming tales of the series' large, close-knit country family. *The Waltons* soon opened the door to several similar family dramas, including *Little House on the Prairie* and the aptly named *Family*.

In 1978, television took a dramatic leap forward with the debut of *Hill*

Street Blues. Produced by Steven Bochco, the series drew on the best elements from television drama in the past and combined them with not only innovative visual techniques but also an original plotting structure. Set in an urban police precinct, the show interwove the personal and professional lives of its large ensemble cast of characters with stories and issues often drawn from recent headlines. Each week's episode involved both limited subplots that were concluded by the hour's end and segments of ongoing plot lines that were often strung out over several weeks. Within this format, the lives of the characters underwent gradual yet substantial development, aided by exceptionally fine performances from a talented cast. The show frequently raised unresolvable social and political issues and explored the ways in which these conflicts affected individual lives. By the time it left the air in 1987, *Hill Street Blues* had become one of the most honored and acclaimed series in television history and a powerful influence on television drama as a whole.

In its ensemble cast, interlocking plot lines, and concentration on serious drama, *Hill Street Blues* had hit upon a formula that took full advantage of the specifics of television as a medium. Its documentary-like realism and densely staged scenes place it beyond the reach of radio, while its episodic structure allows for character development and continuing story lines that are not possible in film or theater. *St. Elsewhere* adapted the show's structure to a hospital setting and eventually went on to find its own strikingly original voice in episodes that featured fantasy sequences and a strong self-reflexive sense that obliquely called the viewer's attention to the subject of television itself. *L.A. Law* would prove to be the most successful of the shows to follow the format, consistently drawing high ratings with its wealthy law-firm setting and frequently outrageous plot lines. Shows such as *thirtysomething* and the cult favorite *Twin Peaks* also owe their formats to *Hill Street Blues*, using variations on the structure to develop their particular dramatic themes.

Made-for-TV Movies

Surprisingly, with Hollywood to draw on as an example, the concept of movies made for television did not keep pace with other forms of television drama. NBC began experimenting with the idea in 1964, but it was not until 1966, with *Fame Is the Name of the Game*, that the format really began to gain popularity. Aired as part of the network's popular *Saturday Night at the Movies*, which featured broadcasts of Hollywood films, the film earned impressive ratings, as did Serling's *Doomsday Flight* later that year.

The success of these two projects sparked what would become an important part of network broadcasting fare. Although many made-for-television movies are mundane and unexceptional—or, conversely, a format for titillating or headline-grabbing subjects—they have also done much to bring a variety of social and personal issues to the small screen. *Brian's Song* drew praise for its touching story of football player Brian Piccolo's death from cancer, *My Sweet Charlie* dealt with the controversial subject of an interracial love affair, *The Autobiography of Miss Jane Pittman* traced the history of African Americans from the Civil War to the Civil Rights movement, and *That Certain Summer* presented the story of a young man dealing with his father's homosexuality.

The made-for-TV movie proved to be a boon for television actors who longed to play serious roles outside their familiar series personas. In *Sybil*, which was telecast over two nights, Sally Field offered a harrowing portrait of a young woman suffering from multiple personalities, while *The Burning Bed* featured Farrah Fawcett as a victim of domestic violence, and *Something About Amelia* cast *Cheers* star Ted Danson in a drama about incest. Abortion, acquired immune deficiency syndrome (AIDS), Alzheimer's disease, school desegregation, homelessness, and the nuclear holocaust have also found their way to the small screen via television film, making their presence felt among less notable efforts.

The Miniseries

Once the idea of the television film was established, the groundwork was laid for a dramatic format eminently well suited to the medium: the miniseries. What the miniseries could offer was the opportunity to tell a complex story in greater depth than the traditional two-hour length of a feature or television film would permit. This structure lent itself especially well to adaptations of novels, which did not need to be drastically edited when presented in the miniseries form. NBC's *The Blue Knight* in 1973 defied conventional programming wisdom by scheduling its four installments on consecutive nights, paving the way for the popular *QB VII* and *Rich Man, Poor Man*, at twelve episodes one of the longest miniseries.

In January of 1977, ABC broadcast the landmark miniseries *Roots*. Adapted from the best-selling book by Alex Haley, it would become one of the highest-rated series in television history, as audiences watched in unprecedented numbers the saga of a black family from the slave-trading days to the aftermath of the Civil War. Produced by David Lloyd Wolper, the series boasted an exceptional cast, a powerfully written script, and a subject of both sweeping historical scope and intimate emotional detail. The popularity of *Roots* stunned skeptics who doubted that television audiences would commit to better than a week's worth of viewing. *Shogun*, *Holocaust*, and *The Winds of War* would also enjoy remarkable viewer response before the format began to fade in popularity. *War and Remembrance*, the latter series' sequel, failed to match the success of its predecessor, and the longer miniseries gave way gradually to two-night series. Given the proper subject, however, the format remained capable of resurrecting its earlier success, as in the case of *Lonesome Dove.* Not only a miniseries but a Western as well in a medium that had pronounced the genre officially dead, *Lonesome Dove* garnered not only critical acclaim but also a rapt viewing audience.

British Television

No discussion of the miniseries—or indeed of television drama—would be complete without the inclusion of British television. The format of the miniseries did not originate with American television; it was borrowed after the success of such British dramas as *The Six Wives of Henry VIII* and *The Forsyte Saga. The Prisoner*, shown on CBS in 1968, also captivated viewers with its enigmatic tale of a former secret agent held against his will in a nameless village. Although British programming also featured episodic series that returned from year to year, programming philosophy evolved in a markedly different fashion from that of its American counterpart. While American networks strive to establish popular series that will continue to draw viewers from year to year, British television has never balked at the idea of a successful series that is constructed to last for only one season.

The result has been a vast array of dramatic series that have found a home on public television. Through the umbrella series of the Public Broadcasting Service (PBS), such as *Masterpiece Theatre* and *Mystery*, much of the best of British television—with an emphasis on historical drama, literary adaptations, and elaborate period pieces—has made its way to American screens. *Elizabeth R* introduced Glenda Jackson to American viewers and provided a compelling history of the monarch's reign. *Upstairs, Downstairs*, which ran for five seasons, traced the first three decades of the twentieth century through the lives of an upper-class family and their servants. The widely seen *I, Claudius, Masterpiece Theatre*'s most requested series, offered a vivid, witty, often gruesome look at the early Roman emperors, while *The Jewel in the Crown* took a scathing look at the last days of the British rule in colonial India. Perhaps the most successful export from England was the immensely popular *Brideshead Revisited*, an elegant adaptation of Evelyn Waugh's novel. Adaptations of Agatha Christie, Dorothy L. Sayers, P. D. James, and Arthur Conan Doyle's Sherlock Holmes have made *Mystery* one of public television's most-watched series.

For much of its history, television drama has been a series of experiments and evolutions that have sought to make full use of the medium's potential. From bold themes and talented contributors to programming aimed solely at the lowest common denominator, television drama has evolved in front of the eyes of a watching nation, and its ability to influence that nation has become a source of much controversy and concern. In the hands of those with the viewers' best cultural and intellectual interests at heart, television drama has produced some of the most memorable productions in any medium in the decades since its inception. In less responsible hands, it can misinform, distort, and simplify. Its future is as open-ended—and as subject to popular opinion—as the episodic drama series that fills its ranks.

Janet Lorenz

ACTING STYLES

The primary task of actors is to illuminate the text for the audience. The style in which actors accomplish this is determined in part by the nature of the literature that they are called on to perform: A fiery melodrama with stock characters requires broad gestures and declamatory speech, whereas a realistic play with complex characterization necessitates a more lifelike approach. At the same time, actors, as the principal instruments of drama, reflect, as all artists do, the values, tastes, and fashions of the society in which they perform. Since the theater audience can register its approval or disapproval at the moment that the artistic work is "created" (in the sense that all stage plays are fully created only when they are performed), the actor is one of the few artists who immediately responds to the demands of the public. As an evolving society creates new trends in dramatic literature, so do acting styles change with time. A twentieth century American audience viewing a nineteenth century melodrama would find the broad gestures and declamatory speech laughable; conversely, the nineteenth century audience would be bored and confused by the stark realism of the twentieth century American stage.

Actors are their own instrument. Whereas sculptors have their clay with which to mold their art, the actors' clay is themselves—the voice, the body, and individual characteristics. The actors' methodology—how they create a role—is at the center of a debate that has raged for centuries. One theory holds that actors should create the role through mechanical means—that they should not experience the emotion of the character but should simulate it through logical and deliberate choice of gesture and vocal inflection. In contrast, the creative or psychological approach insists that the actor should create from the inside, emphasizing motivation and emotion. The first theory, or external approach, presupposes the importance of characterization over the personality of the actor, whereas the second, or internal approach, emphasizes the importance of the actor's emotions projected through the character. It was not until the early 1900's that the two theories were fused into one system by the great Russian actor-teacher Konstantin Stanislavsky (1863-1938).

The two great actors from the English Renaissance—Richard Burbage (c. 1567-1619), the leading actor of William Shakespeare's company the Lord Chamberlain's Men, and Edward Alleyn (1566-1626), leading actor of Christopher Marlowe's company the Lord Admiral's Men—typified some of the differences in acting styles that characterized the period. (It must be added that relatively little is known about acting styles on the Elizabethan stage.) It is probable that Shakespeare's company employed a more lifelike approach than that of its rivals. The Globe Playhouse precluded the use of much scenery, thereby focusing the audience's attention on the actor.

Surrounded relatively closely by the audience on three sides, the Shake-spearean actor must have followed Hamlet's advice not to "o'erstep the modesty of nature." Moreover, the characters in Shakespeare's plays (espe-cially in the later ones) are complex compared to those of his contempora-ries. Burbage, who played Othello, Hamlet, and King Lear, must have employed a subtle style in order to capture the many nuances of those multifaceted heroes. Nowhere is the disparity in characterization more evi-dent than in Marlowe's treatment of Barabas in *The Jew of Malta* (pr. c. 1589), a role played by Alleyn, and Shakespeare's treatment of Shylock, probably played by Burbage, in *The Merchant of Venice* (pr. c. 1596-1597). Compared to the complex Shylock, Barabas is a one-dimensional arch-villain roaring his way through a melodramatic revenge tragedy. Broad characters require the actor to use broad strokes, and Alleyn, like Bur-bage, must have adapted his delivery to suit the material. Perhaps Shake-speare had Alleyn in mind when Hamlet, in his advice to the players, speaks of actors who "tear a passion to tatters, to very rags, to split the ears of the groundlings. . . ."

Acting styles on the Restoration stage borrowed heavily from the French Baroque theater. English audiences traveling to France to see plays during the Commonwealth expected similar fare when the English theaters re-opened. The actor's delivery, particularly in tragedy, was highly formalized and declamatory. Reflecting the classical tastes of high society, aristocratic norms of decorum, temperance, politeness, and simplicity governed the actor; actor-playwright Colley Cibber (1671-1757), in *An Apology for the Life of Colley Cibber* (1740), said that the theater should be "a school of manners and virtue." Discussing the actor's methods, the leading actor of the period, Thomas Betterton (c. 1635-1710), said that the actor carefully catalogs "the passions and habits of the mind [which] discover themselves in our looks, action and gestures." That the Restoration actors' approach to their role was external and technical is evident in Betterton's assertion that acting should "never transport the speaker out of himself." The actors played primarily on the wide apron, or forestage, in front of the prosce-nium arch; they rarely sat. Scenery functioned as a backdrop within the proscenium and was almost never used. In 1712, theater manager Christo-pher Rich, to increase audience capacity, removed the apron at the Theatre Royal, Drury Lane. This moved the actors farther from the audience and forced them to utilize the scenery.

Nevertheless, the grandiloquent style of acting flourished. In the early 1700's, James Quin (1693-1766) specialized in vocal effects and formalized acting which exhibited the form rather than the content of tragedy. Versa-tility was nonexistent, since actors were hired to play specific roles which then became their property. Gradually, however, some actors, such as Charles Macklin (1699?-1797), referring to the "hoity-toity tone of the tragedy of that day," adopted a more natural delivery. Macklin taught his students first to speak the lines as they would in real life and then to add force to them for the stage.

It was the great actor-manager David Garrick (1717-1779) who thoroughly revolutionized acting. Criticizing the artificiality of oratorical delivery, Garrick emphasized the use of the correct gesture suited to the spoken line, as well as a more natural delivery. A masterful technician, he observed people in real life, then meticulously cataloged gestures and movements for the stage. Garrick's natural delivery caused Quin to remark, "If this young fellow is right then we have all been wrong." A highly versatile actor, Garrick excelled at both tragedy and comedy and, while his style was considered fresh and natural, he was "not above the stops and starts and drawn-out death scenes that drew applause." Sarah Siddons (1755-1831), a protégée of Garrick, fulfilled the ideal of tragic acting espoused by François Talma (1763-1826); he described her style as "the union of grandeur without pomp and nature without triviality."

Excessive emotional display, considered undesirable by actors throughout the Restoration and eighteenth century, became the norm with the rise of English melodrama and the nineteenth century tragedians. Melodrama, which flourished in both England and the United States, afforded the actor an opportunity to "tear a passion to tatters." Since the characters were stock—villain, hero, heroine, comic man, comic woman—characterization was simple. So important did action become to the melodrama that authors wrote elaborate stage directions for the actors, including descriptions of facial expressions such as "revenge burning in his eye" or "his countenance disordered." Strict conventions governed each stock character, and each type was marked by its idiosyncrasies. The comic characters dressed ludicrously and indulged in such low comedy as face-slapping, falling down, and bumping into one another. The villain generally sported a black top hat, frock coat, and cape and boots; his delivery was marked by facial contortions and furtive asides. William Brady, writing of New York's Bowery Theatre around 1870, recalled a special technique for the villain's death: "elbows stiff, spine rigid, then fall over backward square on the back of your head." Audience participation was not discouraged. The villain was regularly hissed and booed and the hero cheered on in his efforts, and it was not uncommon for audience members to comment aloud on an actor's performance or a piece of stage business. In turn, audience involvement required the actors to become more aggressive in their style. Movement and gesture were performed as broadly as possible, and speech was marked by peculiar pronunciation and special rhythm. Each syllable was voiced with elaborate distinction and sometimes elongated for effect.

The flourishing of melodrama spawned a number of star actors in both England and the United States. These giants of the stage, most of whom got their start in melodrama, assayed the great Shakespearean tragic roles, developed their repertoires to include the parts in which they particularly excelled, and honed their talents to such a degree that their dramatic feats became legendary. The first of these great actors in England was Edmund Kean (1789-1833), whose powers were so great that he reportedly caused an actress playing a scene with him to faint; Lord Byron allegedly was so carried away by Kean's performance of Hamlet that he was seized with convulsions. Samuel Taylor Coleridge's comment that watching Kean act was like "reading Shakespeare by flashes of lightning" was doubtless meant as a compliment but also provides some insight into the histrionics of Kean's acting style.

The first great American actor of the period was Edwin Forrest (1806-1872). The feud that developed between Forrest and the English actor William Charles Macready (1793-1873) initiated a lively rivalry between English and American actors that continued into the twentieth century. Since Forrest was not as well trained as his English counterpart, his style was considered blunt, natural, and impulsive, while Forrest and other critics accused Macready of being artificial, cold, and mechanical. The feud culminated in 1849 when Macready, attempting to perform Macbeth at the Astor Place Theatre in New York City, was booed off the stage. A riot ensued, and 134 persons were killed. The interesting facet of the Forrest-Macready feud is how acting styles reflect the *Zeitgeist*. The United States was a young country living out a spirit of revolution and pioneering, and it was natural that Forrest's simplicity appealed to Americans, just as Macready's sophistication played successfully to a more complex English culture that had been developing for centuries.

Versatility was of little importance to the nineteenth century tragedians. They adapted the character to suit their personalities, and, unlike the leading actors on the twentieth century English stage, who would later play virtually every role of importance in the Shakespearean canon, these earlier stars played only a few parts and were best known for one or two portrayals. Kean was most famous for his King Lear, Macready for his Macbeth and his Hamlet, and Charles Kemble (1775-1854) was regarded as the outstanding Mercutio of his day. Later in the century, Sir Henry Irving (1838-1905) was acclaimed for his Hamlet, and in America Edwin Booth (1833-1893) was most famous as Othello. Another American, Joseph Jefferson (1829-1905), achieved star status with his portrayal of Rip Van Winkle. Audiences did not go to the theater to see *King Lear* or *Othello*—they went to see Kean as Lear or Booth as Othello. English actress Ellen Terry (1847-1928) noted that although Henry Irving "expressed himself in a multiplicity of parts, . . . he was always the same Irving."

This practice of infusing the part with the actor's personality was criticized by the French actor Benoît-Constant Coquelin (1841-1909). Writing for *Harper's Monthly* in 1887, he asserted that the English practice resulted in "revolting hideousness" and "naked realities. People do not go to the theatre for that sort of thing." This prompted a reply from Irving, who wrote that Coquelin "had lost sight of the fact that in tragedy . . . it is rather the *soul* of the artist than his form which is moulded by the theme." Dion Boucicault (1820?-1890) joined the debate, saying that while Shakespeare's great heroes suffer from different causes, they suffer alike, in the same histrionic key: "Booth, Forrest, Macready, Kean, Salvini always presented the same man in a different costume." Coquelin fired a parting salvo, saying that the French actors are great "generalizers," whereas the English concern themselves with the individual.

The French actress Sarah Bernhardt (1844-1923), when asked to list the requirements of great acting, replied "voice, voice and more voice." Her English and American contemporaries probably concurred, as there is ample evidence to suggest that vocal technique was the principal instrument of tragic acting of the late nineteenth century. Drama critic and author William Winter, commenting on the English actor James William Wallack (1795-1864), said that "his sonorous tones flowed over the action in a veritable silver torrent of musical sound." Shortly before his death in 1893, Edwin Booth recorded, on one of the earliest phonographs, some lines from Othello's senate speech. Booth employed a distinct vibrato—a slightly tremulous effect—in reading the lines. Booth's contemporaries doubtless used this vocal device, and the custom of "singing the lines" continued well into the twentieth century.

A number of factors caused the decline of melodramatic acting. With the deepening complexity of society, the trauma of World War I, and the twentieth century fascination with psychology, artists began focusing on the realistic and naturalistic aspects of life. The stately grandeur of the nineteenth century theater gave way as playwrights and actors began creating complex characters in real-life situations.

Another factor that contributed to the decline of melodramatic acting—perhaps the most significant—was the advent of the cinema. As the filmic art developed, audiences expected actors to adopt cinematic techniques for the stage, and by the time sound motion pictures were made, the broad style of melodrama was considered cheap and hammy. Ironically, the earliest films were heavily influenced by melodrama, and some of the more famous melodramas were made into motion pictures, including *Uncle Tom's Cabin* (1903), *The Count of Monte Cristo* (1913), and *Under the Gaslight* (1914). The broad gestures that actors employed in the silent cinema provide an insight into the acting styles of the nineteenth century stage.

In the early 1900's, disillusioned by the staleness of his own acting and in part inspired by the work of the Italian tragedian Tommaso Salvini (1829-1916), Konstantin Stanislavsky set about to formulate a system of acting that would allow actors to develop their character properly and sustain the portrayal through many performances. The precepts which Stanislavsky set forth in *An Actor Prepares* (1936) and *Building a Character* (1949) did more to revolutionize acting styles on the English-speaking stage than any factor prior to that time. Stanislavsky divided his "System," as it came to be known, into roughly two parts: the actors' work on themselves and their work on their roles.

In *An Actor Prepares*, Stanislavsky asserts that actors must establish the inner life of the character through the use of realistic action combined with their own creative imagination, their concentration, and their physical relaxation. Stanislavsky points out that since emotion is a result of action, it cannot be acted; a correct lifelike action will produce a correct lifelike emotion. Actors stimulate the creative imagination through the use of the "magic if," postulating an imaginary situation, as in "What would I do *if* my father died?" The notion is that actors can believe in imaginary or theatrical truth as sincerely as they can believe in real truth, just as a little girl believes in the existence of her doll. The System maintains that actors placing themselves in an imaginary situation similar to a real-life situation will experience a real emotion onstage. This concept of emotion memory later played a key role in the American adaptation of the System. To help the actor develop concentration, Stanislavsky introduces the concept of "public solitude": Even in a crowd, Stanislavsky notes, individuals have their own capsule of space, which moves with them. Tension, Stanislavsky emphasizes, is a barrier to natural action, and actors must relax their muscles.

Stanislavsky's chief teaching tool was improvisation, wherein the actors, working without a text, were given a set of lifelike circumstances and, using their creative imaginations, reacted accordingly. Improvisation became especially popular in the United States, so much so that by the 1960's some American groups used improvisation even in performance.

Building a Character addresses the external methods by which the actor creates a characterization. Here, Stanislavsky stresses the importance of such technical factors as tempo and rhythm, voice and diction, fluidity of movement and observation of nature. Stanislavsky asserts that the actor must cultivate a sense of aesthetics and likens the composition of a role to that of a musical opus.

By combining the internal or creative approach with the external or technical approach, Stanislavsky evidently thought he had defined the actor's creative process. He objected to its being called "his System," saying there is only one system—creative organic nature. Stanislavsky's teachings and derivatives of them, especially as practiced by the Group Theatre and the Actors' Studio, have been the most important influence on acting styles in twentieth century America.

Although articles describing the System had appeared in American journals as early as 1906, it was not until Richard Boleslavsky (a protégé of Stanislavsky) came to the United States from Russia that the System became known to American actors. Boleslavsky was the first proponent of the System in America, teaching at the Neighborhood Playhouse in New York City in 1923. He also published an article, "Stanislavsky: The Man and His Methods," in the April, 1923, issue of *Theatre* magazine. That same year, American Lee Strasberg journeyed to Moscow to study the System and attend performances at Stanislavsky's Moscow Art Theatre. Strasberg, an immigrant from Austro-Hungary, had grown up speaking only Yiddish and had spent his early years as an actor in the Yiddish theater. He became fascinated with the acting process and would spend his life teaching and writing on the subject.

In 1931, Strasberg, Harold Clurman, and Cheryl Crawford, united by a common interest in the System, founded the Group Theatre. Until that time, actors in American theater—following the nineteenth century practice—were cast by type. The Group Theatre founders believed that typecasting stifled the actor's artistic growth, and they set out to form an ensemble of actors who could express their creative imaginations in the tradition of Stanislavsky. The Group located a farm in Brookfield Center, Connecticut, and retreated there to live and work together. Some of the notable actors in the original Group were Franchot Tone, Elia Kazan, Sanford Meisner, Morris Carnovsky, and Stella Adler. Using improvisation as their principal rehearsal technique, the actors began preparations for the first production. Strasberg's insistence that emotion or affective memory was the most important element of an actor's creative life led to divisiveness among the Group's members and caused a controversy that lasted for many years. Nevertheless, the initial production of Paul Green's *The House of Connelly* (pr. 1931) was successful, with drama critic Stark Young pointing out that "there was not an instance of stage cheating for effect, or of hollowness."

Not all the actors, however, were happy with this approach. Stella Adler, an actress with a decided flair, felt out of place with what she called the "untheatrical" personalities of some of the others. Strasberg termed her style of acting "Jewish emotionalism," and a disenchanted Adler traveled to Russia to meet with Stanislavsky himself. In Moscow, she worked with Stanislavsky for five weeks, during which time she took careful notes. Upon her return to the Group, Adler accused Strasberg of misinterpreting Stanislavsky's writings. Some of the other actors agreed with her, and Strasberg and Crawford, angered by the revolt, promptly resigned.

The Group Theatre's influence on American acting style was enormous, in that the Group introduced to the stage a new realism which evidently appealed to audiences. Elia Kazan's performance in Clifford Odets' *Waiting for Lefty* (pr. 1935) was so believable that many in the audience thought Kazan was a real cabdriver. The acting style of the Group was not without its detractors, however, and drama critic Brooks Atkinson accused Kazan of "getting to be a self-conscious actor with purple patches," who is "studiously spontaneous." Angered by Atkinson's review, Kazan quit acting and turned to directing. Other critics accused the Group of clannishness and of cultivating a mystical reverence for Stanislavsky. Actress Laurette Taylor asked, "Why must they make acting a malady?" Hampered by continuing criticism and financial difficulties, the Group Theatre was forced to close its doors in 1941.

Believing that the actor was undervalued in the American theater, and united in a desire to pursue realism on the stage, Elia Kazan and Robert Lewis founded the Actors' Studio in 1947. At their headquarters on West Forty-eighth Street in New York City, twenty-six actors gathered to study their craft. Marlon Brando, Montgomery Clift, Julie Harris, Kim Hunter, Karl Malden, E. G. Marshall, and Maureen Stapleton were among the original ensemble. Lee Strasberg was invited to join the Studio in 1951, and he eventually assumed control. Strasberg and Kazan continued the work they had begun at the Group Theatre, stressing improvisation and emotion memory. Actors were required to perform simple exercises such as threading a needle or peeling an orange—the goal of the tasks was not to achieve a mimetic effect but to capture the sense or emotion of the moment. The emphasis on emotion and the private moment was a definite departure from Stanislavsky, and Strasberg referred to his technique as the "Method," or an "adaptation of the Stanislavsky system." Absolute verisimilitude onstage was the Method actor's goal, especially in terms of the actor's own feelings. Thus, the audience became a kind of voyeur, and this unique actor-audience relationship bred in some Method actors a contempt for the audience.

In 1947, Marlon Brando, considered by many as the prototype of the Method actor, stunned the theater world with his remarkable performance as Stanley Kowalski in Tennessee Williams' *A Streetcar Named Desire*. Probably more than any other actor, Brando deeply affected the realistic acting style in both theater and cinema. Film actors were naturally intrigued by the Actors' Studio and its Method, and in the 1970's actors such as Robert De Niro, Robert Duvall, and Jack Nicholson joined the Studio. Boleslavsky and Michael Chekhov (another of Stanislavsky's protégés) had been teaching the System in Hollywood for years, and in 1966, responding to a demand from the film community, Strasberg founded the Actors' Studio West.

The Method created an enormous debate in American theater. Critic Robert Brustein described the Method as a "subjective, autobiographical approach to acting . . . through a mistaken reading of Stanislavski." Other critics complained that the Actors' Studio's "torn T-shirt school" ignored the technical aspects of an actor's training, resulting in actors with poor diction and sloppy stage movement. The emphasis on emotional reality evidently caused some actors to hang on to an emotion at all costs, thus isolating them and preventing interaction with other players on the stage. Indeed, many non-Method actors believed that practicing the Method was neurotic, and indeed Method actor James Dean called acting "the most logical way for people's neuroses to manifest themselves." By the 1970's, the Actors' Studio catered more to film actors than to stage actors, and by the 1980's, the Method was so out of vogue in American theater that the stage actor generally used the term "Method actor" as an insult.

English actors, too, were influenced by the movement toward realism, though much less so than the Americans. The English had their acting schools, most notably the Royal Academy of Dramatic Art and the London Academy of Music and Dramatic Art, but the emphasis was more on the technical aspects of acting. Courses in fencing, stage movement, and voice and diction were a regular part of the English student actor's curriculum. While the American theater had become indigenous, its actors performing in the heavily realistic style of their native drama, the English were more eclectic in their tastes. The proliferation of the repertory system and the founding of the National Theatre of Great Britain (1963-1964) allowed the English actors to continue their classical tradition. Twentieth century English actors gained respect for their important contributions to society: Actors such as Laurence Olivier, John Gielgud, Ralph Richardson, and Michael Redgrave, who worked their ways up through the repertory system to emerge as major stars, much like their nineteenth century predecessors, were awarded knighthoods, and Olivier was the first actor to be made Lord of the Realm. Mid-twentieth century English and American actors regarded one another's styles with a mixture of admiration and scorn. While the Americans admired, and even envied, the English actors' ability to perform the classics, many believed that the English actors were cold and artificial. Conversely, the English admired the emotional exuberance of the American actors, but it was not in the English character to attempt such style. With the possible exceptions of John Barrymore and Paul Robeson, the American theater in the first half of the twentieth century produced no stars in the English classical tradition.

The dramas of Shakespeare played a key role in changing acting styles. The twentieth century witnessed a renaissance in performances of Shakespeare's plays in both England and the United States, Shakespeare being the most frequently performed playwright. Shakespeare festivals had been held regularly since 1879 at Stratford-upon-Avon, Shakespeare's birthplace, and in 1961 the Royal Shakespeare Company was formed. Interest in performing Shakespeare quickly spread to Canada and the United States, the Bard's plays becoming so popular in the latter that by the 1980's virtually every state in the United States had at least one Shakespeare festival.

By the 1960's, American actors, growing disillusioned with the Method, were searching for new techniques. The politicization of American society at that time led to the formation of agitprop theater companies such as the San Francisco Mime troupe (formed in 1959 by R. G. Davis), whose chief aim was to make a political statement. The acting style of these groups was rough, broad, and forceful, borrowing from the Italian *commedia dell'arte*. The performances were often improvised, with the actors working only from a scenario. This kind of "street theater" was not in the mainstream of American theater; further, the orientation of such groups was political, not artistic.

By the 1960's, the American actor's training had fallen primarily into the hands of the universities. Most universities had a drama department, and some institutions, such as the Yale School of Drama and the University of Washington, were associated with professional companies. There was a renewed interest in performing the classics, especially Shakespeare, and those universities with professional training programs provided the student actor with a broad base of classical training, including, like the English schools, courses in voice and diction and stage movement.

In 1962, as artistic director of the Royal Shakespeare Company, Peter Brook captured the attention of the theater world with his innovative staging of *King Lear* with Paul Scofield and Peter Weiss's *The Persecution and Assassination of Jean-Paul Marat as Performed by the Inmates of the Asylum of Charenton Under the Direction of the Marquis de Sade* (pr. 1964), commonly known as *Marat/Sade*. The acting was rough, blunt, and simple, and Brook's work with the actors at the Royal Shakespeare Company resulted in a new physicality in acting style. In the early 1970's, Brook's controversial production of Shakespeare's *A Midsummer Night's Dream* toured the United States. Brook staged the play metaphorically as a circus, requiring the actors to perform feats of tumbling, juggling, and trapeze-swinging. The idea of "physicalizing" the dramatic moment caught on, and the resultant acting style was one of physicality, simplicity, and clarity of expression. Brook's insistence that the only essentials for theater were an empty space, an actor, and someone to watch (that is, the audience) elevated the actor's role in theater to preeminence. The thrust stage became the most popular form of theater architecture, since it brought the actor closer to the audience and minimized the use of scenery. The actor's task was to find the simplest form of expression.

Brook's ideas, as outlined in his book *The Empty Space* (1968), have had the most significant influence on acting style since Stanislavsky. Brook asserts that only when the actor's work is "immediate" can it be fresh, compelling, and exciting. He argues that "Deadly Theatre," or bad theater, is made deadly in part by preconceived notions about how a particular play should be staged or how a particular role should be played, and "nowhere does the Deadly Theatre install itself so securely . . . as in the works of William Shakespeare." Brook points out that it is virtually impossible for actors to speak Hamlet's "To be or not to be"—probably the most famous line on the English-speaking stage—and make it sound fresh. Only by rephrasing the line in their own words can actors begin to make the phrase live. Thus, improvisation is an important tool in that it forces the actor to create from moment to moment—a technique the actor must possess even in performance. Brook objects to the phrase "building a character," adding that only the mediocre actor builds a character the way a mason builds a wall, brick by brick, working up to a finished product. Truly creative actors, Brook asserts, must be willing to forsake all that they have learned, to "discard the hardened shells of [their] work," so that in performance they appear "in front of an audience, naked and unprepared." Only then will the actor's performance be immediate. Brook arrives at a formula: Theater = R r a. That is, theater is repetition, representation, and assistance. Repetition is the mechanics of the actor's performance, the repeating night after night of the same gestures and lines; representation is the actor's performance; and assistance is the communication that the actor receives from the audience.

Stanislavsky no doubt would have agreed with much of Brook's thesis. Both attempted to provide the actor with techniques that would allow the actor's performance to remain fresh and exciting. Both also shared a concern that the actor continue to explore new styles and techniques. Long after Stanislavsky's death, the Moscow Art Theatre continued to stage his productions exactly as he directed them. Stanislavsky would have disapproved of these carefully preserved museum pieces, since he cautioned actors that his System was itself subject to ceaseless revision, changing every day. Brook agreed, arguing that in theater "the slate is wiped clean all the time." He stressed the importance of Stanislavsky's "magic if," pointing out that while in life "if" implies fiction and evasion, in the theater it is truth. When the actor and audience "are persuaded to believe in this truth, then the theatre and life are one."

William Frankfather

DRAMATIC TERMS AND MOVEMENTS

Academic drama. See *School plays*.

Act: One of the major divisions of a play or opera. The practice of dividing a play into acts probably began in Rome but is derived from Greek drama, which separated the episodes of a play by choral interludes. In classical theory (notably in France in the seventeenth century), a play is divided into five acts; since the eighteenth and nineteenth centuries, however, the typical number of acts has varied from four to one, while some plays have entirely eliminated structure by acts and use only scene division. (See also *Scene*.)

Action. See *Plot*.

Afterpiece: A short farce meant to follow a serious play, a practice adopted in France by 1650, which became a standard part of English drama during the Restoration.

Agitprop: This term combines the words "agitation" and "propaganda" to describe drama performed as social protest rather than for its dramatic or literary merit. A German labor group called the Prolet-Bühne first used this term in New York City in 1930. Agitprop drama was performed throughout the 1930's by the American labor movement and continues to be performed in Europe and in the United States.

Agon: Greek, meaning "contest." A segment of Greek drama in which two participants become involved in verbal conflict. The two participants may be a character and the chorus; two characters, each backed by part of the chorus; or two parts of the chorus.

Alazon: The impostor or braggart of Greek comedy. The type survives in Roman comedy, as with the *Miles Gloriosus* of Plautus. (See also *Miles gloriosus*.)

Alexandrine: In French, a verse of twelve syllables generally containing four accents (in English, the iambic hexameter is sometimes referred to as an "Alexandrine"). Established as the standard form for French tragedy in the mid-sixteenth century, the Neoclassical dramatists of the seventeenth century (Pierre Corneille and Jean Racine, for example) used the Alexandrine to create the serious, elevated tone that was theoretically considered proper for the tragic mode.

Alienation: The German dramatist Bertolt Brecht (1898-1956) developed the theory of alienation in his epic theater. Brecht sought to create an audience that was intellectually alert rather than emotionally involved in a play by using alienating techniques such as minimizing the illusion of reality onstage and interrupting the action with songs and visual aids. Brecht hoped an intellectually alert audience would relate the dramatic action to problems in the real world and seek solutions to those problems. (See also *Epic theater*.)

Allegory: By representing abstract ideas or concepts through the symbolic use of character, plot, and situation, allegories are intended to instruct the audience in moral or political values. Allegory is an important component of classical drama and medieval morality plays.

Anabasis: Greek, meaning "a going up." The rising of an action to its climax. (See also *Rising action*.)

Anagnorisis: A recognition or discovery. Aristotle uses this term in the *Poetics* to refer to the moment of recognition in which a character moves from a state of ignorance to one of knowledge. In Sophocles' *Oedipus Rex*, which Aristotle considered the ideal example of tragedy, an anagnorisis occurs when Oedipus discovers that he himself is the slayer of his father, as predicted by the seer. This recognition is accompanied by a "peripeteia" (or reversal) in which the whole action of the play is reversed.

Antagonist: The major character in opposition to the protagonist or hero.

Antimasque: A grotesque interlude within a masque which contrasts violently to the beauty and harmony of the preceding episodes. Ben Jonson created the antimasque, which typically includes grotesque dances of clowns and monsters. (See also *Masque*.)

Antistrophe: In classical Greek drama, the antistrophe is a stanzalike unit of song and dance responding to the strophe and mirroring its structure. (See also *Strophe*.)

Apollonian and Dionysian: Friedrich Nietzsche proposed in *The Birth of Tragedy* (1872) that Greek tragedy was composed of two opposing elements, which it held in tension and finally unified. One element, the Dionysian, represented the savage, frenzied, passionate nature of man. The Apollonian stood for reason, moderation, and order. Nietzsche believed that the choral songs provided the Dionysian element and the dialogue the Apollonian element. Characters were often torn between these opposing forces within their personalities, which personified larger philosophical and moral issues.

Apron stage: The apron is that part of the stage which extends beyond the proscenium arch. A stage that consists entirely or primarily of an apron and on which the action is not "framed" by a proscenium may be called an "apron stage."

Aside: A short passage generally spoken by one character in an undertone, or directed to the audience, so as not to be heard by the other characters onstage.

Auto sacramental: A Renaissance development of the medieval open-air Corpus Christi pageant in Spain. A dramatic, allegorical depiction of a sinful soul wavering and transgressing until the intervention of Divine Grace restores order. During a period of prohibition of all secular drama in Spain from 1598 to 1600, even Lope de Vega adopted this form.

Avant-garde: A term describing plays intended to expand the conventions of the theater through the experimental treatment of form and/or content.

Ballad opera: A type of burlesque opera popular in eighteenth century England and modeled upon (as well as parodying) contemporary Italian operatic conventions. The story is conveyed in both spoken dialogue and songs (the latter mirroring the arias of the more serious form) set to old folk songs or ballads. The most successful work in this genre was John Gay's *The Beggar's Opera* (pr. 1728).

Black comedy: A general term of modern origin that refers to a form of "sick humor" that is intended to produce laughter out of the morbid and the taboo. The term is sometimes inappropriately confused with "dark comedy."

Blank verse: A term for unrhymed iambic pentameter, blank verse that first appeared in drama in Thomas Norton and Thomas Sackville's *Gorboduc*, performed in 1561, and later became the standard form of Elizabethan drama.

Boulevard drama: The body of plays produced in the mid- and late nineteenth century in Paris by writers such as Ludovic Halévy and Eugène Labiche. The term properly refers to comedies of some sophistication, designed as commercial products. In the twentieth century, the plays of Noël Coward would fall into the category of boulevard drama.

Bourgeois drama: A term generally used to describe the modern realistic drama which deals with the situations and social problems of the middle class.

Burlesque: A work which, by imitating attitudes, styles, institutions, and people, aims to amuse. Burlesque is distinguished from a closely related form, satire, in that its aim is ridicule simply for the sake of amusement rather than for political or social change. An example of burlesque drama is Gilbert and Sullivan's comic opera *Patience*, which is a parody of the Aesthetic movement in late nineteenth century England.

Burletta: A short comic play with music, the burletta became popular in eighteenth and nineteenth century English theater.

Buskin (also *cothornus*): A half boot covering the foot and calf, worn by actors in Greek tragedy. The purpose of the buskin was to designate the stature of the characters; while comic actors wore low, flat foot coverings, tragic figures wore platform buskins. "To put on buskins" became a term for performing or writing tragedy. (See also *Sock*.)

Capa y espada: Spanish for "cloak and sword." A term referring to the Spanish theater of the sixteenth and seventeenth centuries dealing with love and intrigue among the aristocracy. The greatest practitioners were Lope de Vega and Pedro Calderón de la Barca. The term *comedia de ingenio* is also used.

Caroline: Of or referring to the reign of King Charles I of England, lasting from 1625 to 1649. Political strife and the violent opposition to the theater by the Puritans informed Caroline drama with a rather decadent morality and generally a quality inferior to the plays of the preceding Jacobean and Elizabethan periods, although Caroline drama did produce the noted tragedian John Ford and his counterpart in Caroline comedy, James Shirley. Caroline drama was effectively halted in 1642, when the Puritans closed all public theaters for the next eighteen years.

Catastrophe: The conclusion of a play or narrative, especially tragedy, the catastrophe is more often called the "denouement," meaning the unknotting or resolution of the situation. (See also *Freytag's pyramid*.)

Catharsis: A term from Aristotle's *Poetics* referring to the purgation of the emotions of pity and fear in the spectator aroused by the actions of the tragic hero. The meaning and the operation of this concept have been a source of great, and unresolved, critical debate.

Cavalier drama: A term given to a type of play performed at court in the 1630's during the reign of Charles I of England until the ascendancy of Oliver Cromwell in 1642 and the closing of the theaters. The plays featured elaborate plots, political conflicts, lustful villains, beautiful and virtuous ladies, and their brave, honorable lovers. Dialogue was typically florid and artificial. The most notable dramatists in this genre were Thomas Killigrew and John Suckling.

Character: A personage appearing in any literary or dramatic work.

Chorus: Originally a group of singers and dancers in religious festivals, the chorus evolved into the dramatic element that reflected the opinions of the masses or commented on the action in Greek drama. In its most developed form, the chorus consisted of fifteen members: seven reciting the strophe, seven reciting the antistrophe, and the leader interacting with the actors. The development of the role of the chorus is generally seen as one of diminishing importance: In Aeschylus, the chorus often takes part in the action; in Sophocles, it serves as a commentator; and in Euripides its function is sometimes purely lyric. The Romans adapted the Greek chorus to their own stage, and the Elizabethans occasionally imitated the Roman chorus (reducing it to a single actor), but it never became an integral part of the structure. The chorus has been used during all periods, including the modern (for example, in T. S. Eliot's *Murder in the Cathedral*), but has survived most prominently in the opera and other forms of musical theater. (See also *Parodos*.)

Chronicle play: A dramatization of historical material (or material believed to be historical), the chronicle play became popular at the end of the sixteenth century. Drawing heavily on the chronicle histories of Raphael Holinshed and Edward Hall, dramatists originally strung together loose scenes from history, but the form later developed greater unity in works such as Christopher Marlowe's *Edward II* and the *Henry IV* plays of William Shakespeare. Also termed "history plays," the chronicle plays developed into subtle studies of character and became more important as examinations of human strengths and frailties than as accounts of historical facts.

Classical drama: Classical drama originally referred to the literature and theater of ancient Greece and Rome, but later the term also included theater composed in imitation of the Greco-Roman tradition, which was often called "neoclassical." In more common usage, the term refers to art which possesses at least some of the following characteristics: balance, proportion, control, unity, and simplicity.

Climax: The moment in a drama at which the action reaches its highest intensity and is resolved. The major climax of a play may be preceded by several climaxes of lesser and varying intensity.

Cloak-and-sword play. See *Capa y espada*.

Closet drama: A play meant to be read rather than performed; two examples of closet drama are Alfred de Musset's *Fantasio* or Lord Byron's *Manfred*. Also, a play which, although meant for performance, has survived only as literature.

Comedia: Principal form of nonreligious drama during the Spanish Golden Age (*Siglio de Oro*) of the sixteenth century that mixed tragic and comic elements in a complex, suspenseful plot, used a variety of verse forms, and favored realistic language and action. The *comedias* of the early sixteenth century were written in five acts, but by the 1580's the number of acts had been reduced to three by playwrights such as Lope de Vega.

Comedia erudate: Latin term for "learned comedy." In the Renaissance, scholarly imitations of classical comedies (particularly Roman) were practiced by such writers as Pietro Aretino, Ludovico Ariosto, and Niccolò Machiavelli (the latter's *Mandragola* is frequently cited as an example of the genre).

Comédie ballet: A theatrical form mixing elements of comedy, farce, and musical-balletic spectacle popular in seventeenth century France. Molière's *Le Bourgeois Gentilhomme* and *Le Malade imaginaire* are the two best examples of the form.

Comédie larmoyante: French term meaning "tearful comedy." This sentimental comedy was popular in eighteenth century France. A development from the earlier style of comedy, *comédie larmoyante* aimed to produce not critical laughter (as in the earlier style exemplified by Molière) but pleasurable tears. The chief practitioners were Philippe Destouches and Pierre-Claude Nivelle de La Chaussée. (See also *Sentimental comedy*.)

Comedy: Generally, a lighter form of drama (as contrasted with tragedy) that aims chiefly to amuse and ends happily. Wit and humor are utilized to entertain. The comic effect typically arises from the recognition of some incongruity of speech, action, or character development. The comic range extends from coarse, physical humor (called low comedy) to a more subtle, intellectual humor (called high comedy). When comedy tends toward the judgmental or critical, it is referred to as satiric; when it is mixed with sympathy or pathos, it moves in the direction of tragedy. There are many specific comic forms and manifestations. (See also *Burlesque, Burletta, Comedia erudate, Comédie larmoyante, Comedy of humours, Comedy of manners, Commedia dell'arte, Dark comedy, Farce, High comedy, Interlude, Low comedy, New Comedy, Old Comedy, Romantic comedy, Satire, Sentimental comedy, Slapstick,* and *Tragicomedy.*)

Comedy of humors: A term referring to a type of drama, developed in the late sixteenth and early seventeenth centuries by Ben Jonson and George Chapman, which dealt with characters whose behavior is controlled by some single characteristic, or "humor." In medieval and Renaissance medicine, the humors were the four bodily fluids (blood, phlegm, yellow bile, and black bile), any excess of which created a distortion or imbalance of personality (by extension, the term came to mean "mood" or "disposition"). Jonson used this theory of character in several of his works, such as *Every Man in His Humour* and *Every Man out of His Humour.*

Comedy of manners: Sometimes known as "genteel comedy" (in reference to its lack of coarseness), a form of comedy that arose during the eighteenth century, dealing with the intrigues (particularly the amorous intrigues) of sophisticated, witty members of the upper classes. The effect and appeal of these plays are primarily intellectual, depending upon quick-witted dialogue and cleverness and facility of language. The Restoration period was particularly fond of this form, as can be seen in the plays of such dramatists as William Congreve, Sir George Etherege, and William Wycherley.

Comic relief: A humorous incident or scene in an otherwise serious or tragic drama intended to release the audience's tensions through laughter without detracting from the serious material.

Commedia dell'arte: Dramatic comedy performed by troupes of professional actors, which became popular in the mid-sixteenth century in Italy. These troupes were rather small, consisting of perhaps a dozen actors who performed stock roles in mask and improvised upon skeletal scenarios (often derived from the traditional material of ancient Roman comedy). The tradition of the *commedia*, or masked comedy, was influential into the seventeenth century and still, in fact, exerts some influence. Some of the more famous stock roles are Pulchinella, Arlecchino, Pantalone, Il Dottore, and Il Capitano.

Commedia palliata: Roman comedy produced in Greek costume and refined by Plautus during the second century B.C.

Corpus Christi plays: These religious plays depicting biblical events were performed on Corpus Christi Day in England during the fourteenth, fifteenth, and sixteenth centuries. The plays originated in the liturgy of the Church, but they came to be staged outdoors on large wagons that moved through towns (such as York and Chester) in a procession, so that each play was performed before several different audiences. (See also *Liturgical drama*, *Miracle play*, *Trope*.)

Cothornus. See *Buskin*.

Counterplot: A secondary action coincident with the major action of a play. The counterplot is generally a reflection on or variation of the main action and as such is strongly integrated into the whole of the play. A counterplot may also be referred to as a subplot, but this more general term may refer to a secondary action which is largely unrelated to the main action. (See also *Subplot*.)

Coup de théâtre: An unusual, striking, unexpected turn of events in the action of a play.

Cup-and-saucer drama: A type of play that furthers the illusion of reality onstage through the realistic portrayal of domestic situations among the upper classes and through the use of realistic sets and authentic properties. The English playwright Thomas William Robertson (1829-1871) was the chief practitioner of this type of drama.

Curtain raiser: An entertainment, sometimes a one-act play, performed at the beginning of a program. In the late nineteenth and early twentieth centuries, a curtain raiser often served to entertain an audience during the arrival of latecomers, thus avoiding disturbances when the main presentation began.

Cycle play. See *Miracle play*.

Dark comedy: A term coined by J. L. Styan in *The Dark Comedy* (1962), referring to the modern concept of the play between tragedy and farce (which evolved from the work of a wide range of predecessors, such as Euripides, medieval mystery plays, Shakespeare, and Molière). The concept reflects the existential belief in a disjunctive world where there is no possibility for conventional notions of heroism and tragedy. Such a concept imposed upon drama tends to produce a catharsis from moment to moment (not a climactic one). The term is broad enough to encompass most of the innovative works of the contemporary repertoire.

Denouement: Originally French, this word literally means "unknotting" or "untying" and is another term for the catastrophe or resolution of a dramatic action, the solution or clarification of a plot.

Deus ex machina: Latin, meaning "god out of a machine." In the Greek theater, the use of a god lowered by means of a mechanism called the *mechane* (usually a crane with rope and pulleys) onto the stage to untangle the plot or save the hero. In the *Poetics*, Aristotle condemned the use of the *deus ex machina*, arguing that ideally the resolution of a dramatic action should grow out of the action itself. The term has come to signify any artificial device for the simple or easy resolution of any dramatic difficulties.

Deuteragonist: The second actor in Greek drama, the addition of whom was an innovation of Aeschylus. The term is often synonymous with antagonist. In subsequent usage, the term has indicated a major character of secondary importance or position, such as Claudius in William Shakespeare's *Hamlet*.

Dialogue: Speech exchanged between characters or even, in a looser sense, the thoughts of a single character.

Dionysian. See *Apollonian and Dionysian*.

Dithyramb: Originally a choral hymn sung and danced during the ancient Greek rites of Dionysus, the tone of which was passionate and excited. In the *Poetics*, Aristotle postulates that the tragic form developed from the dithyramb.

Documentary drama: Also popularly referred to as "docudrama," this term refers to the dramatization of actual events in a journalistic style that explores the ethics and responsibility of issues of public concern. Documentary drama developed in West Germany in the 1960's and is represented by works such as German dramatist Rolf Hochhuth's *The Deputy* and American dramatist Eric Bentley's *Are You Now, or Have You Ever Been?*

Domestic tragedy: A serious and usually realistic play, with lower-class or middle-class characters and milieu, typically dealing with personal or domestic concerns. The term has been used to refer to works from the Elizabethan age to the present. Examples of domestic tragedy include George Lillo's *The London Merchant*, Thomas Heywood's *A Woman Killed with Kindness*, several of the plays of Henrik Ibsen, and Arthur Miller's *Death of a Salesman*.

Drama: Generally speaking, any work designed to be represented on a stage by actors (Aristotle defined drama as "the imitation of action"). More specifically, the term has come to signify a play of a serious nature and intent which may end either happily (comedy) or unhappily (tragedy).

Dramatic irony: Irony is a means of expressing a meaning or significance contrary to the stated or ostensible one. Dramatic irony often lies more in the action or structure of a play than in the words of a character. Oedipus' search for the murderer of Laius (whom he later discovers to be himself) is an example of extended dramatic irony. Dramatic irony may also occur when the spoken lines of a character are perceived by the audience to have a double meaning.

Dramatis personae: The characters in a play. Often, a printed listing defining the characters and specifying their relationships.

Dramaturgy: The composition of plays. The term is occasionally used to refer to the performance or acting of plays.

Drame: French term employed chiefly by Louis-Sébastien Mercier (1740-1814) to denote plays that mixed realistic and comic elements with a serious, often tragic, plot. Such plays featured middle-class characters and situations and a preponderance of sentimentality.

Drame héroique. See *Heroic drama.*

Dumb show: A dramatic performance communicated entirely through gestures, not words. The play-within-a-play in *Hamlet* is a famous example of the dumb show. The term "pantomime" is occasionally used to signify the same type of performance. (See also *Play-within-a-play.*)

Elizabethan: Of or referring to the reign of Queen Elizabeth I of England, lasting from 1558 to 1603, a period of important developments and achievements in the arts in England, particularly in poetry and drama. The era included such literary figures as Edmund Spenser, Christopher Marlowe, William Shakespeare, Ben Jonson, and John Donne. Sometimes referred to as the English Renaissance.

Entr'acte: A brief performance, often musical, intended to entertain an audience between the acts or scenes of a drama.

Environmental theater: A production style developed by the experimental theater groups of the 1960's, emphasizing a flexible approach to the total theater space and aimed at eliminating the traditional separation between audience and stage. Environmental theater is often performed in "found" spaces such as streets, warehouses, and fields.

Epic theater: A style of drama in which the action is presented in loosely related episodes, often interspersed with song, that are designed to distance the audience from the drama. Epic theater was developed by the German director Ervin Piscator in the late 1920's but came to be associated chiefly with the work of Bertolt Brecht. (See also *Alienation*.)

Epilogue: The closing section of a play, or a speech by an actor or chorus at the end of a play, which makes some reflection upon the preceding action or simply, as in Puck's speech at the end of *A Midsummer Night's Dream*, requests the approval and applause of the spectators. The term is sometimes used to refer to the actor who recites such a closing speech.

Episode: In Greek tragedy, the segment between two choral odes. In the larger sense, an episode is a portion of a plot or dramatic action having its own coherence and integrity.

Exodos: The final scene in a classical Greek drama.

Expressionism: A movement dominant in the decade that followed World War I, particularly referring to German painting. External reality, including the appearance of objects, is consciously distorted in order to represent reality as it is felt or "viewed emotionally." Among examples of Expressionist drama (which often used distorted scenery, props, music, and unrealistic lighting effects) are Frank Wedekind's *Pandora's Box*, Eugene O'Neill's *The Hairy Ape,* and the operas of Alban Berg (*Wozzeck* and *Lulu*). A play may contain Expressionistic devices without being specifically Expressionistic (for example, Tennessee Williams' *The Glass Menagerie* or his *A Streetcar Named Desire*).

Extravaganza: James Robinson Planché (1796-1880) developed this form in England. An elaborate musical presentation, the extravaganza was usually based on a fairy tale.

Falling action: The part of a play following the climax. (See also *Freytag's pyramid*.)

Farce: From the Latin *farcire*, meaning "to stuff." Originally an insertion into established Church liturgy in the Middle Ages, "farce" later became the term for specifically comic scenes inserted into early liturgical drama.

The term has come to refer to any play that evokes laughter by such low-comedy devices as physical humor, rough wit, and ridiculous and improbable situations and characters. A play may contain farcical elements without being, properly speaking, a farce.

Flashback: A scene in a play (or in film or literature) depicting events that occurred at an earlier time.

Foil: Any character who sets off or contrasts with another by means of different behavior, philosophy, or purpose.

Folk drama: Generally, plays on folk themes performed at popular or religious festivals by amateurs. Sometimes the term is used to indicate plays written by sophisticated, practiced dramatists on folk themes or in "folk settings" and performed by professional actors. John Millington Synge's *The Playboy of the Western World* may be considered, in some sense, a folk drama by this latter definition.

Fourth wall: Theatrical convention intended to heighten the illusion of reality onstage and employed extensively in the late nineteenth century. An invisible fourth wall is imagined to exist between the audience and a stage, enclosed on three sides by the stage set and framed on the fourth by the proscenium arch. The audience, in effect, looks in on the action "through" the fourth wall.

Freytag's pyramid: In 1863, the German critic Gustave Freytag described the theoretical structure of a typical five-act play in *Die Technik des Dramas*. He categorized the dramatic action into the following segments: introduction, rising action, climax, falling action, and catastrophe—all of which can be diagramed in a pyramidal form with the climax at the apex.

Grand Guignol: A type of theatrical presentation in which horror is the desired effect. This is typically achieved by skillfully naturalistic depictions of situations causing physical pain, such as amputations, eye gougings, and burnings. The effect is invariably grisly and is sometimes meant to produce an uncomfortable sort of laughter.

Hamartia: Greek word for "error," specifically an error in judgment. Aristotle, in the *Poetics*, states that a true tragic hero should be a character "preeminently virtuous and just, whose misfortune, however, is brought upon him not by vice and depravity but by some error." This error of judgment may proceed either from ignorance or from moral fault and is sometimes referred to as a "tragic flaw."

Harangue: A speech, usually of some length, often addressed to a crowd to influence the attitudes and actions of the addressees. Antony's ironic speech to the citizens of Rome over Caesar's body in William Shakespeare's *Julius Caesar* is a well-known example.

Harlequinade: A play or pantomime in the *commedia dell'arte* tradition featuring Harlequin, the stock buffoon who has a shaved head and particolored tights, and carries a wooden sword.

Hero/Heroine: The most important character in a drama. Popularly, the term has come to refer to a character who possesses extraordinary prowess or virtue, but as a technical dramatic term it simply indicates the central participant in a dramatic action. (See also *Protagonist*.)

Heroic drama: A type of play usually written in heroic couplets and of elevated diction and seriousness of action (although there might be a happy ending). Heroic drama was popular for a short period, predominantly during the Restoration in England, and its practitioners were John Dryden, Bronson Howard, and Thomas Otway, among others. In France, the *drame héroique* was likewise popular during the seventeenth century (here the verse form was the Alexandrine). The *drame héroique* reached a level of accomplishment and art far surpassing its English counterpart. The great French practitioners were Pierre Corneille and Jean Racine.

High comedy: A term broadly used to refer to comedy whose impulse is often satiric and whose appeal is primarily intellectual. Intellect, wit, style, and sophistication are the trademarks of this type of comedy. Plays such as William Congreve's *The Way of the World*, Molière's *Le Misanthrope*, and Oscar Wilde's *The Importance of Being Earnest* are all examples of high comedy.

History play. See *Chronicle play*.

Hubris: Greek term for "insolence" or "pride," the characteristic or emotion in tragic heroes of ancient Greek drama that causes the reversal of their fortune, leading them to transgress moral codes or ignore warnings. An example of hubris in Sophocles' *Antigone* is Creon's overweening pride, which, despite Tiresias' admonitions, brings about the deaths of Antigone as well as those of Creon's wife and son.

Hypokritēs: An expositor performing recitations in early Greek tragedy that advance the action by brief dialogues with the chorus.

Imitation: From the Greek *mimesis*, used by Aristotle in his *Poetics* to describe tragedy as "an imitation of an action" of a good man. Aristotle perceived artistic imitation not as an exact replica of life but as an artistic representation that transcends reality to convey universal truths, which produces pleasure in the observer. This term has remained central to Western literary and dramatic criticism, although it has been subject to various interpretations through the centuries.

Improvisational theater: Performance in which action and dialogue are created spontaneously by the actors, and which is often based upon a rough scenario rather than a written, rehearsed script. The *commedia dell'arte* of the Italian Renaissance featured improvisation, and many contemporary theater groups use improvisation both as a performance and as a training technique.

Interlude: A short play, often a farce, popular in fifteenth and sixteenth century England. The English interlude has Continental counterparts in such works as the anonymous French farce *Pierre Patelin* and the comedies of the German mastersinger Hans Sachs. Henry Medwall and John Heywood were practitioners of the interlude in England.

Intrigue: The incidents which make up the plot or action of a play. The term is most frequently applied to plots that are elaborate and in which the schemes of various characters are involved. A play such as William Congreve's *The Way of the World* is sometimes referred to as a "comedy of intrigue."

Irony. See *Dramatic irony*.

Jacobean: Of or pertaining to the reign of James I of England, who ruled from 1603 to 1625, the period following the death of Elizabeth I, which saw tremendous literary activity in poetry and drama. Many writers who achieved fame during the Elizabethan age were still composing (notably William Shakespeare, Ben Jonson, and John Donne). Other dramatists, such as John Webster and Cyril Tourneur, achieved success almost entirely during the reign of James I. The theater of this period is particularly noted for its interest in the violent and the fantastical.

Kabuki: A form of theater in Japan which was, traditionally, established by a former priestess of the early seventeenth century, O Kuni. O Kuni organized a troupe of actors which included men who were female impersonators. Kabuki enjoyed immediate popular success, and the number of companies (with both male and female performers) increased rapidly. As early as 1629, the presence of female performers caused a scandal and was banned, a situation which was not relaxed until well into the nineteenth century. Female impersonators kept the tradition alive and, indeed, still perform today. Kabuki actors wear no masks (unlike the performers of the aristocratic Nō theater). The Kabuki drama is typically melodramatic and violent, with complex plotting.

Laughing comedy: The English playwright Oliver Goldsmith coined this term in 1772 to describe a comedy, such as his *She Stoops to Conquer* (1773) or Richard Brinsley Sheridan's *The Rivals* (1775), that exposes human follies and vices for the amusement and edification of the audience, as opposed to the sentimental comedy, which dominated eighteenth century drama and which was intended to move audiences to pleasurable tears with sentimental stories about the middle class. The respective merits of these two types of comedy were hotly debated throughout the 1770's.

Lazzo: Term for the stage business that the actors of the *comedia dell'arte* troupes routinely improvised during their performances, selecting the appropriate *lazzi* (plural) for the scenario that they were following. Usually humorous, a *lazzo* might express fear, or anger, or surprise.

Leitmotif: From the German, meaning "leading motif." Any repetition—of a word, phrase, situation, or idea—which occurs within a single work or group of related works and which serves to unify the work or works. The term has special meaning in musical drama (a signal melody or phrase of music), and the technique was used by the nineteenth century composer and theoretician Richard Wagner not only to unify his operas (most notably the four-opera cycle *Der Ring des Nibelungen*) but also to add dramatic and psychological resonance and depth to the action.

Libretto: Italian for "little book." The text or script of an opera, operetta, or other form of musical theater.

Liturgical drama: The term refers to plays performed as part of the liturgy of the Church during the Middle Ages. The origin of these plays was in the tropes or interpolations into the Latin text of the liturgy, which was chanted by the clergy. These interpolations were expanded and eventually developed into independent performances in the vernacular. The performances eventually moved out of the church proper and were performed by members of the laity. While the plays ceased to be liturgical, they continued to deal with religious themes, particularly drawn from the Old and New Testaments. (See also *Corpus Christi plays*, *Miracle play*, *Trope*.)

Low comedy: A term broadly used to refer to the coarse elements in a play designed to arouse laughter. Such elements include physical comedy (slapstick, practical jokes) and off-color humor. Low comedy elements are to be found not only in such comic forms as farce but also in plays of high artistic repute, such as William Shakespeare's *A Midsummer Night's Dream* and *The Merry Wives of Windsor*.

Masque: A courtly entertainment popular during the first half of the seventeenth century in England. Derived from Italian court entertainments, it spanned from the latter part of the reign of Elizabeth I through that of James I and into that of Charles I. It was a particularly sumptuous form of spectacle including music (song and dance) and lavish costumes and scenery (the great Baroque architect Inigo Jones and the great Baroque composer Henry Purcell were frequently involved in the nonliterary aspects of these productions). Masques often dealt with mythological or pastoral subjects, and the dramatic action often took second place to pure spectacle. Ben Jonson was the greatest writer of masques during this period, and even the young John Milton composed a masque, *Comus* (1634), whose interest was, atypically, more literary than spectacle-oriented. (See also *Antimasque*.)

Melodrama: Originally a drama with occasional songs, or with music of any kind (*melos* is Greek for "song"). It was also one of the original Italian terms for opera. By the early nineteenth century, the term acquired a new meaning: a play in which characters are clearly either virtuous or evil and are pitted against one another in suspenseful, often sensational situations. This type of play became so common that the term took on a pejorative meaning which it still retains today: any dramatic work characterized by stereotyped characters and sensational, sometimes improbable situations.

The Method: An approach to acting developed by the Russian director Konstantin Stanislavsky (1863-1938). Commonly referred to as "the Method," this approach emphasizes a realistic acting style based on each actor's self-knowledge and on the entire cast's careful analysis of the script. An understanding of the motivation behind the character's speech and actions is essential to a believable performance, according to the rules of the Method, which was popularized in the United States by the noted acting instructor Lee Strasberg (1901-1982).

Miles gloriosus: The braggart soldier character-type found in many plays from antiquity to the modern age, particularly in Elizabethan and Jacobean drama. The term derives from Plautus' play of the same title. Nicholas Udall's Ralph Roister Doister and William Shakespeare's Sir John Falstaff are quintessential examples of the type in sixteenth century English drama. (See also *Alazon*.)

Mime: Dramatic action portrayed by means of gesture and movement without speech. An actor who performs such actions is also called a "mime."

Mimesis. See *Imitation*.

Miracle play: In English drama, this term refers to medieval religious plays dramatizing the lives of the saints and divine miracles. The term "mystery play" (derived from the French term *mystère*) is used to designate plays derived from the Scriptures as opposed to those dealing with saints' lives. These plays were originally associated with the celebration of saints' feast days and with religious processions (particularly the Corpus Christi festival) and were performed in Latin as part of the liturgical services. Later, these plays were expanded, performed in the vernacular, and moved into the streets. Trade guilds were often responsible for the performance of a particular play, so that in time a series of performances by various guilds would create a cycle of plays. Some examples of subjects derived from Scripture include Christ's Passion, the Fall of Man, and the story of Noah. This form of dramatic entertainment reached its height in the fifteenth and sixteenth centuries. (See also *Corpus Christi plays*, *Liturgical drama*, *Trope*.)

Mise-en-scène: The staging of a drama, including scenery, costumes, movable furniture (properties), and, by extension, the positions (blocking) and gestures of the actors.

Monodrama: A theatrical presentation featuring only one character. Jean Cocteau's *The Human Voice* is an example of this form.

Monologue: An extended speech by one character in a drama. If the character is alone onstage, unheard by other characters, the monologue is more specifically referred to as a soliloquy. (See also *Soliloquy*.)

Morality play: A dramatic form of the late Middle Ages and the Renaissance containing allegorical figures (most often virtues and vices) that are typically involved in the struggle over a person's soul. The anonymously written *Everyman* is one of the most famous medieval examples of this form.

Motoriae: A loosely structured play, refined by the Greek writer Epicharmus of Cos during the fifth century B.C., the violent action of which combines mythological plots with realistic stories.

Mummery: This term refers broadly to a theatrical presentation in which actors or dancers are masked or in disguise. The term is occasionally used to refer to acting in general.

Musical comedy: A theatrical form mingling song, dance, and spoken dialogue which was developed in the United States in the twentieth century and is derived from vaudeville and operetta. In its earliest stages, the music often had little to do with the libretto (the text or script), but a closer integration of these elements has occurred since the early 1940's. (See also *Musical theater*, *Opera*.)

Musical theater: A dramatic production in which music, lyrics, and sometimes dance are fundamental elements. Opera, operetta, and musical comedy are all forms of musical theater. (See also *Musical comedy*, *Opera*.)

Mystery play. See *Miracle play*.

Neoclassicism: Aesthetic movement that influenced seventeenth century French and English drama and was characterized by an admiration for and an emulation of classical Greek and Roman culture. French neoclassical drama is best represented by the tragedies of Pierre Corneille and Jean Racine, who followed the strict rules of unity and verisimilitude advocated by the Académie Française. In England, neoclassical dramatists such as John Dryden wrote heroic tragedies—highly artificial dramas, featuring exotic settings, improbable and spectacular action, and high-flown language, usually written in heroic couplets. (See also *Renaissance drama*.)

New Comedy: The Greek comedy of the third and fourth centuries B.C. that coincided with the decline of Greek political power and with the decline of the satiric comic theater of Aristophanes. The New Comedy featured stereotyped plots and characters: courtesans, young lovers, foolish miserly old men, and scheming servants. After many amorous intrigues, the plays typically ended in a happy marriage. Menander was the chief proponent of the form, and the Romans Terence and Plautus were much influenced by it, finding in it an abundant source for material.

Nō: A form of theater developed in fourteenth century Japan from ritual dance associated with Shinto worship. The plays were designed for aristocratic audiences and were highly restrained and stylized. The plays are typically mysterious and gloomy in plot and atmosphere. Performers (who are always male) wear masks and employ a distinctly unrealistic form of acting. The text is sung or chanted to musical accompaniment in low- and high-pitched voices. The influence of this Eastern form can be seen in the

West in certain twentieth century works such as William Butler Yeats's *At the Hawk's Well* and *The Only Jealousy of Emer*.

Obligatory scene: The scene that a playwright has led an audience to expect (usually an emotional confrontation between characters) and without which the audience would be disappointed (also called a *scène à faire*).

Old Comedy: The Greek comedy of the fifth century B.C. that originated in the fertility festivals in honor of Dionysus. Of the plays in this form, only those of Aristophanes survive. His work is notable for its biting personal and political satire as well as its lyric beauty. The chorus takes an important role in the action, notably delivering the parabasis, an extended speech usually expressing the views of the playwright. With the decline of Greek political power in the fourth century B.C., this form was replaced by New Comedy. The plays in this form relied heavily on stock characters and situations.

One-act play: Although there have been short, unified dramatic works that might properly be termed one-act dramas earlier on, this term has typically been employed for such works written since the late nineteenth century. The one-act play is usually quite limited in number of characters and scene changes, and the action often revolves around a single incident or event.

Opera: A form of dramatic entertainment consisting of a play set to music. Opera is the most important and most sophisticated form that combines music with theatrical representation. It is a complex combination of various art forms—music (both vocal and instrumental), drama, poetry, acting, stage design, dance, and so on. Like other art forms, it has its own conventions; these are sometimes derived more from a musical perspective than from a purely theatrical perspective or tradition. The origin of opera in the late sixteenth and early seventeenth centuries in Italy resulted from the attempts of certain Humanist literary figures and musicians to re-create classical Greek drama, with its combination of speech, music, and dance. From its inception through the present, opera has undergone a diverse history of its own (which sometimes mirrors the history of purely spoken drama). Practitioners of the form include Claudio Monteverdi, George Frederick Handel, Wolfgang Amadeus Mozart, Gioacchino Rossini, Vincenzo Bellini, Giuseppe Verdi, Richard Wagner, Richard Strauss, Giacomo Puccini, and Alban Berg. (See also *Musical comedy, Musical theater*.)

Pageant: Originally the platform or movable stage upon which medieval miracle and mystery plays were performed, the term has come to refer to any large-scale outdoor procession or performance.

Pantomime: A dramatic action communicated entirely by gesture and movement but not speech. Also, a type of theatrical entertainment developed in England in the eighteenth century. The story was usually acted out in both song and dance, and the scenery and stage effects could be quite lavish and spectacular. The form still survives in England in special Christmas entertainments designed for children.

Parabasis: A seven-part choral number occurring toward the middle of a Greek comedy that makes a direct appeal to the audience, requesting a prize or offering advice on current events.

Parodos: In classical Greek tragedy, the first scene in which the chorus appears and the first ode that the chorus sings are called *parodos*. The name derives from the entryway used by the chorus for entrances and exits. (See also *Chorus*.)

Passion play: A play that depicts the life, or incidents from the life, of a god. These plays had their origin in the pagan rites of ancient Egypt and the Near East. In Christian Europe, many medieval plays presented episodes from the life of Christ and are also referred to as Passion plays. The form still survives in various pageants in Europe and America (particularly notable is the famous Oberammergau Passion play of Germany, performed every ten years).

Pastoral drama: A form of tragicomedy particularly that was popular in the sixteenth and seventeenth centuries, originally a dramatic imitation of the bucolic idylls of Horace and Vergil. Pastoral drama represented a neoclassical vision of the rustic, Arcadian life and typically mingled such elements as unrequited love, intrigues of jealousy, and threats of death to the protagonists. These tragic elements are often happily resolved by the revelation of true relationships between characters or the triumph of love. The masterpiece of the genre (and one of the most influential theatrical works of the sixteenth century) is Giambattista Guarini's *Il Pastor fido* (*The Faithful Shepherd*). Another famous example is Torquato Tasso's sixteenth century play *Aminta*.

Pathos: The quality in a dramatic character that evokes pity or sorrow from the audience.

Peripeteia: A sudden reversal of situation in a dramatic action. Aristotle gives as an example the arrival of the messenger in *Oedipus Rex*, who believes he will relieve Oedipus' anxiety and accomplishes the reverse effect.

Pièce à thèse. See *Problem play.*

Pièce bien faite. See *Well-made play.*

Play-within-a-play: A play or dramatic fragment, performed as a scene or scenes within a larger drama, typically performed or viewed by the characters of the larger drama, such as the farcical "whodunit" in Tom Stoppard's *The Real Inspector Hound* (pr. 1968). In Elizabethan drama, the play-within-a-play was often performed as a dumb show, as in the players' scene in Hamlet. (See also *Dumb show.*)

Plot: The sequence of the occurrence of events in a dramatic action. A plot may be unified around a single action, but it may also consist of a series of disconnected incidents—it is then referred to as "episodic."

Presentationalism: An approach to playwriting and stage production that presents drama as an artificial, theatrical event rather than as a realistic representation of life. For example, classical Greek drama, with its masks, chorus, and circular stage, and Elizabethan drama, with its stark stage sets and blank verse, are presentational. (See also *Representationalism.*)

Problem play: A drama in which a social problem is illustrated and, usually, a solution is suggested. This form is also referred to as a thesis play (from the French *pièce à thèse*) and originated in the mid-nineteenth century in France. *Le Fils naturel*, by Alexandre Dumas, *fils*, is an early example. A number of Henrik Ibsen's plays can be categorized broadly as problem plays.

Prologue: The opening section of a play, which often provides introductory information concerning the central action of the play. Also, a speech by an actor or chorus at the beginning of a play of an expository nature. The term is sometimes used to refer to the actor who recites such an introductory speech.

Properties: Usually abbreviated as "props." Properties are the movable objects (other than scenery or costumes) that appear onstage during a dramatic performance.

Proscenium: The part of a stage in front of the curtain. Also, the wall that separates the stage from the auditorium of a theater and provides the arch that frames the stage.

Protagonist: Originally, in the Greek drama, the first actor, who played the leading role. In a more general sense, the term has come to signify the most important character, usually a hero, in a drama or story. It is not unusual for there to be more than one protagonist in a play. (See also *Hero/Heroine*.)

Protasis: The section of a classical drama in which the characters are introduced and the dramatic situation is explained. The term "protatic character" has come to signify a character used only to assist in the exposition of a play and appearing nowhere else in the action.

Proverbe dramatique: A term referring to a play, typically a one-act play, that illustrates an aphorism which forms the play's title. This form began in France in the eighteenth century and was developed by Carmontelle, but its most famous practitioner was the nineteenth century poet and dramatist Alfred de Musset.

Psychological realism: Sigmund Freud's analysis of the complex psychological motivations behind human behavior led dramatists in the late nineteenth century to try to reproduce this psychological complexity in their characters rather than relying on character-types. One of the earliest proponents of this psychological realism was August Strindberg (1849-1912), who argued that since human actions are caused by complex motivations in real life, they should be similarly portrayed on the stage.

Raisonneur: A character in a play, typically somewhat detached from the action, who acts as a spokesman for the author. This character observes the other characters involved more directly in the action and comments upon the action, expressing the author's views.

Recognition. See *Anagnorisis*.

Renaissance drama: European drama produced from the early sixteenth to the late seventeenth centuries and often characterized by a concern for the classical ideals of composition and structure that are set forth in Aristotle's *Poetics* and are demonstrated in the works of classical dramatists such as Seneca, whose five-act plays were considered to epitomize the classical structure. Renaissance drama was also characterized by a humanitarian interest in secular subjects such as history, politics, and social issues, and this interest constituted a quite marked departure from the exclusively religious/ allegorical concerns of medieval drama, evidenced in the miracle and morality plays. Renaissance drama first appeared in Italy during the early and mid-sixteenth century with Niccolò Machiavelli's comedy *The Mandrake*, Ludovico Ariosto's comedy *The Casket*, Giangiorgio Trissino's tragedy

Sophonisba, and the Senecan tragedies of Giambattista Giraldi Cinthio. From about 1580 to 1680, Spain experienced a renaissance in drama called the "golden century" (*Siglio de Oro*) during which the prolific playwright Lope de Vega wrote thousands of *comedias*, romantic plays, mixing comic and tragic elements, which were followed by the more intellectual, and at times pessimistic, plays of Pedro Calderón de la Barca. In France, the classical influence of Renaissance drama was strictly observed, resulting in the famous Cid controversy when the noted tragedian Pierre Corneille's *The Cid* departed from the principles of neoclassicism. Jean Racine's superb tragedies were written according to the rigid classical strictures imposed on French tragedians after the Cid controversy. Ironically, this somber atmosphere produced one of the most brilliant writers of comedy of all time, Molière. In England, the Renaissance drama flowered during the Elizabethan and Jacobean periods, bringing forth not only William Shakespeare—indisputably the finest dramatist in the English language—but also a host of other outstanding playwrights, such as Christopher Marlowe and Ben Jonson, who singly and in collaboration created one of the greatest bodies of dramatic works known to the world. (See also *Caroline*, *Comedia*, *Elizabethan*, *Jacobean*.)

Repertory: A theater troupe or company that presents several different plays in alternation during the course of a season.

Representationalism: An approach to playwriting and staging that seeks to create the illusion of reality onstage through realistic characters and situations and/or through the use of realistic stage sets, properties, and acting styles. The Naturalistic drama advocated by the French novelist Émile Zola (1840-1902) and practiced by French director André Antoine (1858-1943) at the turn of the century is an example of representationalism. The opposite approach to drama is presentationalism, which presents drama as a stylized, theatrical event. (See also *Presentationalism*.)

Restoration: The period in English history beginning with the restoration of Charles II to the throne, bringing an end to the Puritan interregnum, which had abolished the monarchy in 1649 and closed the theaters. The Restoration period has no precise end but is commonly held to have ended about 1700. As a result of the reopening of the London theaters, there was a surge of theatrical activity, and the period was known for the wealth of new drama produced by such dramatists as William Congreve, Sir George Etherege, William Wycherley, George Farquhar, and Oliver Goldsmith.

Revenge tragedy: A type of drama, particularly associated with the Elizabethan and Jacobean periods, in which revenge is the central motive. Thomas

Kyd's *The Spanish Tragedy* (pr. c. 1585-1589) is said to have established the genre in English drama. Some other examples are Christopher Marlowe's *The Jew of Malta* and John Marston's *Antonio's Revenge.* William Shakespeare's *Hamlet* is, in an enlarged and very sophisticated sense, an example of this type of drama.

Reversal. See *Peripeteia.*

Revue: A theatrical production, typically consisting of sketches, song, and dance, which often comments satirically upon personalities and events of the day. Generally there is no plot involved, although some semblance of a unifying action or theme may unite the individual sketches and musical numbers.

Rising action: The part of a play preceding the climax. (See also *Anabasis, Freytag's pyramid.*)

Romantic comedy: A play in which love is the central motive of the dramatic action. The term often refers to plays of the Elizabethan period, such as William Shakespeare's *As You Like It* and *A Midsummer Night's Dream*, but it has also been applied to any modern work that contains similar features.

Satire: Dramatic satire employs the comedic devices of wit, irony, and exaggeration to expose and condemn human folly, vice, and stupidity. Although subject to political and societal repression throughout the centuries, dramatic satire appears in the classical Greek comedies of Aristophanes, in the personification of vices in the medieval morality plays, in the Renaissance plays of William Shakespeare and Ben Jonson, in the social satires of Oscar Wilde and George Bernard Shaw in the late nineteenth and early twentieth centuries, and in the twentieth century dramas of such dissimilar playwrights as Sean O'Casey and Harold Pinter.

Satyr play: In Greek drama, a performance composed of choric dances performed exclusively by actors dressed as Satyrs. Not necessarily comic, the story was often derived from epics or legends and was associated with Dionysus.

Scenario: An outline of the dramatic action (plot) of a theatrical work, specifying the characters and the order of acts and scenes.

Scene: A division of action within an act (some plays are divided only into scenes instead of acts). Sometimes scene division indicates a change of setting or locale; sometimes it simply indicates the entrances and exits of characters; this latter case was, for example, the typical practice of the French neoclassical dramatists such as Pierre Corneille and Jean Racine. (See also *Act.*)

Scène à faire. See *Obligatory scene.*

School plays: Plays performed at secondary schools in sixteenth century England. These plays showed the influence of the classical comedy of Terence and Plautus and were composed both in Latin and in English. The earliest known example of the form in English, of about 1566, is Nicholas Udall's *Ralph Roister Doister*.

Sentimental comedy: With the rise of the middle class in the eighteenth century, a "new" audience patronized the theater, demanding drama which related to their social class and milieu and which upheld the traditionally accepted moral code that had brought them into increased position and power. The sentimental comedy was a type of play generally centered on the distresses of the middle class and intended to evoke the sympathies of the audience. Good and bad characters are often presented in a very schematic way without psychological complexity. Pleasurable tears, not laughter, were the mark of the successful sentimental drama. In England, the Restoration playwright George Farquhar (1678-1707) anticipated some of the features of the sentimental comedy, but the true practitioners of the unadulterated form were playwrights such as Sir Richard Steele, Hugh Kelly, and Richard Cumberland. The corresponding development in French eighteenth century drama was the *comédie larmoyante* (tearful comedy), of which Philippe Destouches and Pierre-Claude Nivelle de La Chaussée are the chief proponents. (See also *Comédie larmoyante.*)

Set speech: A long, uninterrupted speech made by a single character to set forth a number of points. This device is prevalent in verse drama.

Setting: The time and place in which the action of a play happens. The term also applies to the physical elements of a theatrical production, such as scenery and properties.

Slapstick: Low comedy in which physical action (such as a kick in the rear, tripping, and knocking over people or objects) evokes laughter.

Sock: The flat foot covering worn by actors in Greek comedy. In contrast, tragic actors wore high platform boots (buskins), which endowed them with increased stature, both physically and metaphorically. The sock was literally more down-to-earth. (See also *Buskin.*)

Soliloquy: Properly, an extended speech delivered by a character alone on-stage, unheard by other characters. Soliloquy is a form of monologue, and it typically reveals the intimate thoughts and emotions of the speaker. (See also *Monologue*.)

Sottie: A form of medieval French farce that presented political, religious, or social satire.

Stasimon: Term for the odes sung by the chorus in classical Greek tragedy after the chorus had taken its place on the stage.

Stichomythia: In dramatic dialogue, a term referring to single lines, spoken alternately by two characters, which are characterized by repetitive patterns and antithesis. The Elizabethans, modeling after classical drama, used this type of dialogue with some frequency.

Stock character/situation: A frequently recurring dramatic type or dramatic incident or situation.

Strophe: In the choral odes of Greek drama, the strophe is a structural unit of lyric song and dance, similar to the stanza. The chorus sang and danced a strophe, followed by an antistrophe, which corresponded in form to the strophe. (See also *Antistrophe*.)

Sturm und Drang: A dramatic and literary movement in Germany during the late eighteenth century that took its name from Friedrich Maximilian Klinger's play of that title, published in 1777. Translated in English as "Storm and Stress," the movement was a reaction against classicism and a forerunner of Romanticism, characterized by extravagantly emotional language and sensational subject matter.

Subplot: A secondary action coincident with the main action of a play. A subplot may be a reflection (by means of contrast or similarity) upon the main action, but it may also be largely unrelated. (See also *Counterplot*.)

Surrealist drama: The term *drame surréaliste* (literally, "super-realistic drama") was originally coined in 1918 by Guillaume Apollinaire to describe his play *The Breasts of Tiresias* and was later modified and expanded by André Breton to describe a form of drama that focuses upon subconscious reality. The composition of such drama was often achieved by the practice of "automatic writing" and the study of dreams. The goal of Surrealist work is to restore the neglected subconscious to its rightful place alongside conscious perception.

Symbolism: A term commonly signifying a literary movement that originated in France in the latter part of the ninetenth century. Symbols have always been used in literature and drama, but as a conscious movement and practice, Symbolism achieved its most highly developed and defined form in the poetry of Stéphane Mallarmé and Arthur Rimbaud and in the plays of Maurice Maeterlinck. Drama was conceived as taking place in the mind and soul and was not felt to be truly expressed by outward action. The Symbolists, therefore, avoided the more traditional apparatus of dramatic construction: There are no strong, detailed characterizations; no true locus of crisis or conflict, no message or catharsis is intended. Action exists almost exclusively on a symbolic level and is conveyed through symbolic language, settings, lighting, sound effects, and so on. The influence of Symbolism was widespread and appears in the work of dramatists such as Leonid Andreyev, William Butler Yeats, Sean O'Casey, Anton Chekhov, and Eugene O'Neill.

Tableau: A silent, stationary grouping of performers in a theatrical performance. Also, an elaborate stage presentation featuring lavish settings and costumes as well as music and dance.

Theater of Cruelty: A term, coined by French playwright and theorist Antonin Artaud, which signifies a vision in which theater becomes an arena for shock therapy. The characters undergo such intense physical and psychic extremities that the audience cannot ignore the cathartic effect in which its preconceptions, fears, and hostilities are brought to the surface and, ideally, purged. Startling noises, violent gestures, incantatory words or phrases, and unnerving lighting, music, and scenic effects all contribute to an atmosphere conducive to this curative goal.

Theater of the Absurd: The general name given to a group of plays that share a basic belief that life is illogical, irrational, formless, and contradictory, and that human beings are without meaning or purpose. This philosophical perspective led to the abandonment of traditional theatrical forms and coherent dialogue. Practitioners have included writers as diverse as Eugène Ionesco, Samuel Beckett, Jean Genet, Harold Pinter, Edward Albee, and Arthur Kopit.

Théâtre Libre: French for "free theater." A private theater club founded by André Antoine in Paris in 1887 for the production of new Naturalist plays. The innovations in settings, dramaturgy, direction, and acting had a great influence on the modern theater, helping liberate the stage from its early and mid-nineteenth century artificiality.

Thesis play. See *Problem play*.

Thespian: Another term for an actor; also, of or relating to the theater. The word derives from Thespis, by tradition the first actor of the Greek theater.

Three unities. See *Unities*.

Tirade: A technical term used in French drama (and particularly associated with the seventeenth century neoclassical theater) for a long set piece or uninterrupted speech delivered by a single character to other characters onstage. A tirade is not necessarily of an angry or violent nature, as signified by the English cognate. The English term "harangue" is sometimes used as the technical equivalent.

Tragedy: In its broadest sense, a form of drama that is serious in action and intent. More specifically, Aristotle defined tragedy as an imitation of an action that is serious, complete in itself, and of a certain magnitude. He also specified that this action rouses pity and fear in the audience and purges these emotions. These rather broad criteria originally had specific meanings, which have undergone tremendous evolution from their inception through the present age—a single example is the notion of the tragic hero. Where in the ancient Greek theater the tragic heroes were typically personages of high rank and position (a king, queen, or nobleman), in the modern concept (particularly since the rise of the middle class in the eighteenth century) he or she would be a member of the middle or lower class. There has been much debate on the issue of whether "true tragedy" is even possible in the modern theater, and playwrights such as Eugene O'Neill and Arthur Miller have tried to incorporate the criteria of Aristotelian concepts in evoking tragic feeling or effects.

Tragic flaw. See *Hamartia*.

Tragicomedy: A play in which the dramatic action, which ostensibly is leading to a tragic outcome, is reversed and concluded happily. This somewhat loose form mingled elements theoretically associated with tragedy (such as noble characters and an action ending in death) and those theoretically associated with comedy (such as lower-class or trivial characters and an action ending happily in celebration). The term is often associated with the early seventeenth century plays of Francis Beaumont and John Fletcher. Wolfgang Amadeus Mozart's opera *Don Giovanni* is a famous example of this form in musical theater.

Travesty: A broad, often grotesque, satiric imitation (a form of burlesque) which might take a lofty theme and treat it in trivial terms. The term also refers to the appearance onstage of characters in the roles and costumes of the opposite sex.

Trope: A brief dialogue, often accompanied by music, used in early medieval religious services to dramatize certain portions of the liturgy. As tropes became more elaborate, they were separated from the religious service and evolved into liturgical drama, which later evolved into the medieval mystery and morality plays. (See also *Corpus Christi plays*, *Liturgical drama*, *Miracle play*.)

Unities: A set of rules for proper dramatic construction formulated by Italian and French Renaissance dramatic critics (particularly Ludovico Castelvetro), purported to be derived from the *Poetics* of Aristotle. The "three unities" were concerned with the standards governing the action, time, and setting of a drama: A play should have no scenes or subplots irrelevant to the central action, should not cover a period of more than twenty-four hours, and should not occur in more than one place or locale. In reality, Aristotle insists only upon unity of action in tragedy, and simply observes that most extant examples of Greek tragedy covered a period of less than a full day (there is absolutely no indication of the concept of unity of place). This formulation held particular sway over dramaturgy in France in the seventeenth century and persisted there virtually unchallenged until the introduction of the Romantic drama in the early nineteenth century.

Vaudeville: A variety show popular in the United States and Europe from the 1890's to the 1930's, vaudeville featured songs, comic playlets, animal acts, and sketches. These theatrical entertainments were a refined version of the nineteenth century form of burlesque.

Verse drama: Written in a poetic form and intended primarily as theater rather than as literature, verse drama was the prevailing form for Western drama throughout most of its history, comprising all the drama of classical Greece and continuing to dominate the stage through the Renaissance, when it was best exemplified by the blank verse of Elizabethan drama. In the seventeenth century, however, prose comedies became popular, and in the nineteenth and twentieth centuries verse drama became the exception rather than the rule.

Weeping comedy. See *Comédie larmoyante*.

Well-made play: From the French term *pièce bien faite*, a type of play constructed according to a "formula" which originated in nineteenth century France. The most prolific practitioner of the form was Eugène Scribe (1791-1861). Scribe took dramatic devices, which had been part of comedy and tragedy since the classical theater, and wove them into a formula that he repeated with little or no variation as the underlying frame for the plot construction of his enormous theatrical canon. The plot of a *pièce bien faite* often revolves around a secret known only to some of the characters, which is revealed at the climax and leads to catastrophe for the villain and vindication or triumph for the hero. Misunderstanding, suspense, and coincidence are some of the devices used in the unraveling of the plot. The well-made play provided a form for the developing social drama of such playwrights as Émile Augier and Alexandre Dumas, *fils*, and influenced later playwrights such as Henrik Ibsen and George Bernard Shaw.

Zanni: A stock buffoon character from the *commedia dell'arte* representing the madcap comic servant. Harlequin is the best known of this type.

Theodore J. Baroody

BIBLIOGRAPHY

To locate works relating to a particular dramatist, see the bibliography appearing in the article on that dramatist.

Criticism

Altshuler, Thelma C., and Richard Paul Janero. *Responses to Drama: An Introduction to Plays and Movies.* Boston: Houghton Mifflin, 1967. Students' guide to such topics as "Popcorn and Caviar," "Page, Stage, and Film," and morality in drama.

Balmforth, Ramsden. *The Ethical and Religious Value of the Drama.* New York: Gordon Press, 1925. Opinionated, mostly outdated, but specialized essays on religious and moral themes in the drama.

Banks, Morwenna, and Amanda Swift. *The Joke's on Us: Women in Comedy from the Music Hall to the Present Day.* London: Pandora, 1987. This feminist-oriented survey provides an in-depth study of such topics as women in music halls and cabarets, male and female humor, and women in comedy. Illustrations, often provocative.

Barish, Jonas A. *The Antitheatrical Prejudice.* Berkeley: University of California Press, 1981. From Plato to Yvor Winters, the author examines critics and moralists who oppose certain freedoms of the theater.

Barnet, Sylvan, Morton Berman, and William Burto. *Aspects of the Drama.* Boston: Little, Brown, 1962. Brief but valuable handbook for students. Contains selections on critical theory from Aristotle through modern critics and playwrights.

Benson, Carl Frederick, and Taylor Littleton. *The Idea of Tragedy.* Glenview, Ill.: Scott, Foresman, 1966. Benson divides his text into two parts—"Idea," treating critical theory by significant critics, and "Tragedy," covering six representative works, with useful comments by different authors.

Bentley, Eric. *The Playwright as Thinker: A Study of Drama in Modern Times.* New York: Reynal & Hitchcock, 1946. Reprint. San Diego: Harcourt Brace Jovanovich, 1987. Seminal book that includes essays entitled "Bernard Shaw," "Varieties of Comic Experience," and "Broadway—and the Alternative."

_____. *The Theatre of Commitment, and Other Essays on Drama in Our Society.* New York: Atheneum, 1967. This book contains such essays as "The American Drama from 1944 to 1954" and "What Is Theatre?"

_____, ed. *The Theory of the Modern Stage: An Introduction to Modern Theatre and Drama.* Harmondsworth, Middlesex, England: Penguin Books, 1968. Collection of essays by notable drama commentators; chapters include "Ten Makers of Modern Theatre" and "Toward a Historical Over-View."

_____. *Thinking About the Playwright: Comments from Four Decades.* Evanston, Ill.: Northwestern University Press, 1952, 1987. Contains wide-ranging critical essays, always stimulating, such as "Did Stanislavsky Know Any Psychology?," "The Political Theatre of John Wayne," and "Offenheimer, Mon Amour," among others.

Black, Michael. *Poetic Drama as Mirror of the Will.* London: Vision Press, 1977. Sound scholarly work that is particularly good on William Shakespeare.

Blau, Herbert. *Take Up the Bodies: Theatre at the Vanishing Point.* Champaign: University of Illinois Press, 1982. Primarily "a meditation," according to the author, this complex but original study includes chapters entitled "Conspiracy Theory," "The Power Structure," "Missing Persons," and "The Future of an Illusion."

Boulton, Marjorie. *The Anatomy of Drama.* London: Routledge & Kegan Paul, 1960. A popularization of literary criticism, especially useful in its treatment of conventions.

Brockett, Oscar G., ed. *Studies in Theatre and Drama.* The Hague: Mouton, 1972. Scholarly essays written in honor of Hubert C. Heffner; most of the studies are specialized.

Brooks, Cleanth, and Robert B. Heilman. *Understanding Drama.* New York: Holt, Rinehart and Winston, 1945. This clearly written text on the theater was very influential during the late 1940's. It includes such general topics as dialogue and action, and special problems of the drama and how to solve them. Also contains representative scenes from plays.

Brown, John Russell, ed. *Drama and the Theatre, with Radio, Film, and Television: An Outline for the Student.* London: Routledge & Kegan Paul, 1971. A collection of essays, including J. F. Arnott's "Theatre History," Kenneth Muir's "Plays," John Fernald's "Acting," and George Brandt's "Radio, Film, and Television." Augmented by a few illustrations.

Brustein, Robert. *Who Needs Theatre: Dramatic Opinions.* New York: Atlantic Monthly Press, 1987. Genial, sometimes controversial opinions on Shakespeare, modernism, apartheid, and other topics.

Calderwood, James L., and Harold E. Toliver, eds. *Perspectives on Drama.* New York: Oxford University Press, 1968. Collection of critical essays ranging from Thornton Wilder to Eric Bentley; strong on aesthetics and dramatic theory.

Cameron, Kenneth M., and Theodore J. C. Hoffman. *The Theatrical Response.* New York: Macmillan, 1969. Brisk, readable account; especially effective are chapters entitled "The Critical Analysis of Drama" and "Some Theater Futures."

Carlson, Marvin A. *Theories of the Theatre: A Historical and Critical Survey from the Greeks to the Present.* Ithaca, N.Y.: Cornell University

Press, 1984. Massive, scholarly work of great range, from antiquity to twentieth century drama.

Clurman, Harold. *The Naked Image: Observations on the Modern Theater.* New York: Macmillan, 1966. Collection of reviews and essays by the noted critic.

Cohn, Ruby. *Currents in Contemporary Drama.* Bloomington: Indiana University Press, 1969. Scholarly treatment of English drama, as well as Continental and classical plays.

Cooper, Charles W. *Preface to Drama.* New York: Ronald Press, 1955. Some of the examples from this textbook for undergraduates are outdated, but Cooper's discussion is generally sound.

Dawson, S. W. *Drama and the Dramatic.* London: Methuen, 1970. Brief study of dramatic conventions, influenced in part by the method of F. R. Leavis; chapters on "Drama, Theatre, and Reality," "Action and Tension," "Character and Idea." Useful to actors as well as to students of the theater.

De los Reyes, Marie Philomene. *The Biblical Theme in Modern Drama.* Quezon City, Philippines: University of the Philippines Press, 1978. Specialized study on aspects of the religious treatment in selected plays. Effective chapters on the language of biblical themes and on dramaturgy.

Dickinson, Hugh. *Myth on the Modern Stage.* Urbana: University of Illinois Press, 1969. Chapters on Robinson Jeffers, Eugene O'Neill, T. S. Eliot, and Tennessee Williams.

Ditsky, John. *The Onstage Christ: Studies in the Persistence of a Theme.* Totowa, N.J.: Barnes & Noble Books, 1980. Insightful essays on George Bernard Shaw, John Millington Synge, T. S. Eliot, John Osborne, Tennessee Williams, Harold Pinter, and others.

Dyer, Richard. *Now You See It: Studies on Lesbian and Gay Film.* London: Routledge, 1990. Includes chapters entitled "Shades of Genet," "Underground and After," and "Lesbian/Woman: Lesbian Cultural Feminist Film." Photographs and illustrations.

Ellis-Fermor, Una. *The Frontiers of Drama.* 2d ed. London: Methuen, 1964. This brief but valuable study by the noted critic treats such topics as "The Limitations of Drama," "Shakespeare's Political Plays," and "The Universe of *Troilus and Cressida*"; scholarly but readable.

Esslin, Martin. *The Theatre of the Absurd.* 3d ed. Harmondsworth, Middlesex, England: Penguin Books, 1980. Famous critical study that includes essays on Harold Pinter, Edward Albee, Arthur Kopit; brilliant treatment of Samuel Beckett.

Fergusson, Francis. *The Human Image in Dramatic Literature.* Garden City, N.Y.: Doubleday, 1957. Brief but stimulating series of essays by the noted critic. Includes an essay on Bertolt Brecht, Thornton Wilder, and

T. S. Eliot, on the American theater between the wars, as well as essays on Shakespeare.

Filewood, Alan D. *Collective Encounters: Documentary Theatre in English Canada.* Toronto: University of Toronto Press, 1987. Studies such matters as the evolution of Canada's documentary theater, collective creation, and documentary theater and politics. Bibliography.

Freedman, Morris, ed. *Essays in the Modern Drama.* Lexington, Mass.: D. C. Heath, 1964. Collection of essays by notable commentators on a number of playwrights and a variety of themes.

Gassner, John. *Dramatic Soundings: Evaluations and Retractions Culled from Thirty Years of Dramatic Criticism.* New York: Crown, 1966. This memorial volume ranges widely, with particularly good sections on perspectives on American theater and on productions of the 1960's.

_____, ed. *Ideas in the Drama: Selected Papers from the English Institute.* New York: Columbia University Press, 1964. Excellent collection of essays by such authorities as Vivian Mercier, Edwin A. Engel, Victor Brombert, and others. "From Myth to Ideas—and Back" and "Ideas in the Plays of Eugene O'Neill" are some of the essays.

Gassner, John, and Ralph G. Allen. *Theater and Drama in the Making.* Boston: Houghton Mifflin, 1964. Excellent chapters on the medieval theater, the Renaissance theater, and the American theater; essays on theory, criticism, and stagecraft by playwrights and distinguished commentators.

Goodlad, J. S. R. *A Sociology of Popular Drama.* Totowa, N.J.: Rowman & Littlefield, 1971. Insightful and clearly written study of drama as ritual, with excellent chapters such as "Roles: Society as Unscripted Drama," "Drama as Mass Communication," and "The Drama of Reassurance."

Granville-Barker, Harley. *The Use of the Drama.* Princeton, N.J.: Princeton University Press, 1945. Brief but stimulating essays by the distinguished playwright and critic on such topics as "The Sort of Play to Study," "The Casting of a Play: Among Actors, Among Students," and "The Cooperative Task."

Grawe, Paul H. *Comedy in Space, Time, and the Imagination.* Chicago: Nelson-Hall, 1983. Genre study with such general chapters as "Theoretical," "Lucrative," "Popular," and "Sombre."

Grene, David. *Reality and the Heroic Pattern: Last Plays of Ibsen, Shakespeare, and Sophocles.* Chicago: University of Chicago Press, 1967. Brief but insightful essays; especially convincing in the studies of Shakespeare's *The Winter's Tale* (pr. c. 1610-1611) and *The Tempest* (pr. 1611).

Grossvogel, David I. *Four Playwrights and a Postscript: Brecht, Ionesco, Beckett, Genet.* Ithaca, N.Y.: Cornell University Press, 1962. The essay on Samuel Beckett is scholarly and precise; other essays are on Bertolt Brecht, Eugène Ionesco, and Jean Genet.

Guthke, Karl S. *Modern Tragicomedy*. New York: Random House, 1966. Excellent criticism, including material on "The Philosophy of the Tragicomedian."

Hobson, Harold. *Verdict at Midnight: Sixty Years of Dramatic Criticism*. New York: Longmans, Green, 1952. Particularly interesting essays, primarily from a historical rather than critical standpoint, on such playwrights as Henrik Ibsen and George Bernard Shaw.

Hogan, Robert Goode, and Sven Eric Molin. *Drama: The Major Genres: An Introductory Critical Anthology*. New York: Dodd, Mead, 1962. This collection of essays includes particularly useful sections on comedy and tragicomedy.

Hoy, Cyrus. *The Hyacinth Room: An Investigation into the Nature of Comedy, Tragedy, and Tragicomedy*. New York: Alfred A. Knopf, 1964. Directed to specialists in the history and criticism of the theater, this volume is written in a lively style that will appeal also to serious general students.

Innes, Christopher D. *Holy Theatre: Ritual and the Avant Garde*. New York: Cambridge University Press, 1981. Mostly treats European theater but includes sections on Samuel Beckett and Shakespearean adaptations.

Jones, Thora Burnley, and Bernard de Bear Nicol. *Neo-Classical Dramatic Criticism: 1560-1770*. Cambridge, England: Cambridge University Press, 1976. Scholarly treatment of Restoration and early eighteenth century drama criticism.

Kernodle, George Riley. *Invitation to the Theatre*. 3d ed. San Diego: Harcourt Brace Jovanovich, 1985. This popular students' introduction to theater contains such chapters as "The Performance Place," "Dramatic Action," "Black Liberation," and "Ethnic Theatre and the Realistic Impulse."

Kerr, Walter. *Tragedy and Comedy*. New York: Simon & Schuster, 1967. Clearly written chapters such as "The Tragic Source of Comedy," "The Tragic Ending," and "Comic Despair and Comic Solace."

Klein, Maxine. *Theatre for the Ninety-eighth Percent*. Boston: South End Press, 1978. A social-action study (often dogmatic but also insightful) of the popular theater, used to advance social and political concerns.

Kott, Jan. *Shakespeare Our Contemporary*. Translated by Boleslaw Taborski. Garden City, N.Y.: Doubleday, 1964. Of interest not only for the light that it casts on Shakespeare but also for its influence on both the production and ways of reading dramatic works.

_____. *The Theater of Essence, and Other Essays*. Evanston, Ill.: Northwestern University Press, 1984. Contains excellent discussions in chapters entitled "Shakespeare's Riddle," "Ionesco: Or, A Pregnant Death," "Noh: Or, About Signs," and "The Icon of the Absurd." Introduction by Martin Esslin.

Kuritz, Paul. *The Making of Theatre History.* Englewood Cliffs, N.J.: Prentice-Hall, 1988. A succinct discussion of a wide range of topics, including theater and Buddhism, Confucianism, Zhan Buddhism, and mythology. Illustrations.

Leech, Clifford. *The Dramatist's Experience, with Other Essays in Literary Theory.* New York: Barnes & Noble Books, 1970. Scholarly, lucid treatment of such topics as "The Shaping of Time," "On Seeing a Play," and "The Dramatist's Experience."

Littlewood, Samuel Robinson. *Dramatic Criticism.* London: Sir I. Pitman & Sons, 1939. Once-influential study, with essays such as "To Meet the Puritans," "Criticism as a Profession," and "The Future of Criticism."

McCollom, William G. *Tragedy.* New York: Macmillan, 1957. Study of the general nature of tragedy as well as of tragic drama.

Matthews, Brander. *Playwrights on Playmaking, and Other Studies of the Stage.* 1923. Reprint. Freeport, N.Y.: Books for Libraries Press, 1967. Classic study by the distinguished scholar. Insightful chapters such as those entitled "Tragedies with Happy Endings," "Mark Twain and the Theater," and "Memories of Actors."

_____. *Rip Van Winkle Goes to the Play, and Other Essays on Plays and Players.* New York: Charles Scribner's Sons, 1926. Reprint. Port Washington, N.Y.: Kennikat Press, 1967. Once-influential and still stimulating essays such as "The Question of the Soliloquy," "Second-Hand Situations," and "Memories of Actresses."

Michel, Laurence Anthony, and Richard B. Sewall, eds. *Tragedy: Modern Essays in Criticism.* 1963. Reprint. Westport, Conn.: Greenwood Press, 1978. Essays by notable commentators.

Moreno, J. L. *The Theatre of Spontaneity.* 1947. 3d ed. Ambler, Pa.: Beacon House, 1983. Translated by the author from the German, Moreno's specialized study includes such chapters as "Machine-Drama and the Spontaneity Principle" and "Psycho-catharsis."

Morley, Sheridan. *Shooting Stars: Plays and Players, 1975-1983.* New York: Quartet Books, 1983. Provides twenty years of drama criticism and reviews.

Nathan, George Jean. *The Critic and the Drama.* New York: Alfred A. Knopf, 1922. Historically interesting views on the post-World War I American theater; essays, among others, on drama as art, the place of the theater, and dramatic criticism in America.

_____. *The House of Satan.* New York: Alfred A. Knopf, 1926. Witty, sometimes strident essays by the dean of New York drama reviewers of the 1920's. Includes "Housebroken Drama," "Intelligence and Drama," and "Geniuses."

_____. *Materia Critica.* New York: Alfred A. Knopf, 1924. A collection of stimulating essays by the once-influential American drama critic. Contains opinionated chapters on "Certain Familiar Types of Entertainment" and "Certain Actors and Actresses."

Nelson, Robert J. *Play Within a Play: The Dramatist's Conception of His Art.* New Haven, Conn.: Yale University Press, 1958. The study ranges from Shakespeare to Jean Anouilh, with such chapters as "The Drama: Ritual or Play?"

O'Connor, William Van. *Climates of Tragedy.* Baton Rouge: Louisiana State University Press, 1943. Reprint. New York: Russell & Russell, 1965. Treats the general psychology and aesthetic of tragedy, as well as its dramatic uses.

Pavis, Patrice. *Languages of the Stage: Essays in the Semiology of Theatre.* New York: Performing Arts Journal Publications, 1982. Treatment of such topics as "Gesture and Body Language" and "Examples of Semiotic Analysis."

Peacock, Ronald. *The Art of Drama.* New York: Macmillan, 1957. Reprint. Westport, Conn.: Greenwood Press, 1974. Excellent treatise on aesthetics of drama, with sound chapters entitled "Images and Representation," "Imagery and the Interpretation of Experience in Art," and "Art and Experience."

Reiss, Timothy J. *Tragedy and Truth: Studies in the Development of a Renaissance and Neoclassical Discourse.* New Haven, Conn.: Yale University Press, 1980. Scholarly work that treats, among other topics, plays by Shakespeare.

Reiter, Seymour. *World Theater: The Structure and Meaning of Drama.* New York: Horizon Press, 1973. Critical resource of students of the Chinese and Japanese theater, as well as of the modern Continental drama; particularly good chapters on modern drama and play premises and audience response.

Roberts, Patrick. *The Psychology of Tragic Drama.* Boston: Routledge & Kegan Paul, 1975. Studies of Harold Pinter and Shakespeare, among other writers.

Schechner, Richard. *Public Domain: Essays on the Theatre.* Indianapolis: Bobbs-Merrill, 1969. Contains such provocative essays entitled "Pornography and the New Expression," "Happenings," and "The Politics of Ecstasy."

Sedgewick, Garnett Gladwin. *Of Irony: Especially in Drama.* 1935. Reprint. Toronto: University of Toronto Press, 1967. Great series of lectures on irony.

Seltzer, Daniel, ed. *The Modern Theatre: Readings and Documents.* Boston: Little, Brown, 1967. Handbook that comprehensively treats aspects of theory, the actor, and the creative audience. Good selection of critics and playwrights.

Smiley, Sam. *Theatre: The Human Art.* New York: Harper & Row, 1987.

Clear and copiously illustrated discussions in such chapters as "Classical and Medieval Drama," "The Rise of National Theatres," "The Modern Theatre," and "Contemporary Innovations."

Smith, Susan V. H. *Masks in Modern Drama.* Berkeley: University of California Press, 1984. Specialized scholarly study of ritual, myth, spectacle, satiric masks, and other topics.

States, Bert O. *Great Reckonings in Little Rooms: On the Phenomenology of the Theatre.* Berkeley: University of California Press, 1985. Dedicated to Kenneth Burke, this profound study of the "theatre phenomenon" treats rhetorical strategies originally articulated by Burke.

Styan, J. L. *The Dark Comedy: The Development of Modern Comic Tragedy.* 1962. 2d ed. London: Cambridge University Press, 1968. Interesting discussion of dark comedy as a fresh manifestation of tragicomedy. Traces the origins of this twentieth century genre to Euripides, the mystery plays, Molière, and Shakespeare.

_____. *The Elements of Drama.* Cambridge, England: Cambridge University Press, 1960. Among other subjects, the critic examines, with theatrical examples, "Dramatic Dialogue Is More Than Conversation," "The Behavior of the Words on the Stage," and "Tempo and Meaning."

Tennyson, G. B. *An Introduction to Drama.* New York: Holt, Rinehart and Winston, 1967. Helpful general essays entitled "The Language of Plays," "Character," and "The Reader and the Play," among others.

Thomas, Geoffrey Arden. *The Theatre Alive.* London: C. Johnson, 1948. Outdated but sometimes insightful treatment of such topics as "War," "Fools, Fairies, and Fantasies," and "Thrillers and Killers."

Thompson, Alan Reynolds. *The Anatomy of Drama.* Berkeley: University of California Press, 1942. 2d ed. Freeport, N.Y.: Books for Libraries Press, 1968. Thompson treats such topics as drama as a narrative medium, reality and illusion, and sources of dramatic effect.

_____. *The Dry Mock: A Study of Irony in Drama.* Berkeley: University of California Press, 1948. This volume on irony contains such chapters as "Emotional Discord: The Nature of Irony," "Self-Mockery: Romantic Irony," and "Painful Laughter: Comic Irony."

Whitman, Robert. *The Play-Reader's Handbook.* Indianapolis: Bobbs-Merrill, 1966. Clearly defined instruction on "Concepts of Reality in the Great Periods of Drama."

Wickham, Glynne. *Drama in a World of Science, and Three Other Lectures.* Toronto: University of Toronto Press, 1962. Especially useful discussion of the postwar revolution in British drama and university theater; the title lecture ranges widely on intellectual background.

Williams, Raymond. *Modern Tragedy.* Stanford, Calif.: Stanford University Press, 1966. Treats the theme in fiction as well as drama; good material on Eugene O'Neill, Tennessee Williams, T. S. Eliot, and Samuel Beckett.

Historical

Adams, Joseph Quincy. *Shakespearean Playhouses: A History of English Theatres from the Beginnings to the Restoration.* Boston: Houghton Mifflin, 1917. Reprint. Gloucester, Mass.: P. Smith, 1960. A classic scholarly work that is still basically reliable.

Agnew, Jean-Christophe. *Worlds Apart: The Market and the Theatre in Anglo-American Thoughts, 1550-1750.* Cambridge, England: Cambridge University Press, 1986. A specialized study of commercial aspects involved in theater production.

Albright, Victor E. *The Shakespearean Stage.* New York: Columbia University Press, 1909. Reprint. New York: AMS Press, 1965. Once-influential account of the theater. Although dated, it is still generally sound.

Bentley, Eric. *What Is Theater?* New York: Atheneum, 1968. Compilation of dramatic reviews, from 1944 to 1967, together with "The Dramatic Event"—important documents in the history of the modern theater.

Bentley, Gerald Eades. *The Jacobean and Caroline Stage.* Oxford, England: Clarendon Press, 1941-1968. 7 vols. Multivolume work that is still generally reliable.

_____, ed. *The Seventeenth-Century Stage.* Chicago: University of Chicago Press, 1968. A collection of essays such as "Shakespeare's Celibate Stage" by Michael Jamieson, "Elizabethan Actors: Men or Marionettes?" by Marvin Rosenberg, and "The Numbers of Actors in Shakespeare's Early Plays" by William A. Ringler, Jr.

Besset, Jean-Marie, et al. *Gay Plays: An International Anthology.* New York: Ubu Repertory Theater Publications, 1989. The preface, by Catherine Temerson and Francoise Kourilsky, sets the critical background for such works as Besset's *The Function*, Copi's *A Tower Near Paris*, and Hervé Dupuis' *The Return of the Young Hyppolytus.*

Booth, Michael R. *Victorian Spectacular Theatre, 1850-1910.* Boston: Routledge & Kegan Paul, 1981. Treats such topics as spectacle, melodrama, and pantomime.

Boughner, Daniel C. *The Braggart in Renaissance Comedy: A Study in Comparative Drama from Aristophanes to Shakespeare.* Minneapolis: University of Minnesota Press, 1954. Specialized scholarly criticism that illuminates certain conventions.

Bradbrook, M. C. *The Rise of the Common Player: A Study of Actor and Society in Shakespeare's England.* London: Chatto & Windus, 1962. Great work of scholarly reconstruction.

Bradby, David, Louis James, and Bernard Sharratt, eds. *Performance and Politics in Popular Drama: Aspects of Popular Entertainment in Theatre, Film, and Television, 1800-1976.* New York: Cambridge University Press, 1980. Especially useful to historians of the drama; valuable essay on spectacle, performance, and audience in nineteenth century theater, as well as essays on many specialized topics, such as water drama, by notable scholars.

Campbell, Lily Bess. *Scenes and Machines on the English Stage During the Renaissance: A Classical Revival.* Cambridge, England: Cambridge University Press, 1923. Classic study that treats English and Italian stage decoration at different times, from the sixteenth century to post-Restoration.

Chambers, E. K. *The Elizabethan Stage.* Oxford, England: Clarendon Press, 1923. Famous scholarly work that is still generally reliable.

_____. *The Medieval Stage.* 2 vols. London: Oxford University Press, 1903. A classic, comprehensive history of the drama and staging of the Middle Ages.

Clark, Barrett Harper, and George Freedley, eds. *A History of Modern Drama.* New York: D. Appleton-Century, 1947. Treats the drama of England, Ireland, and the United States, as well as Continental drama.

Conolly, L. W. *The Censorship of English Drama, 1737-1824.* San Marino, Calif.: Huntington Library, 1976. Specialized scholarly work that helps the reader understand problems in the playwright's licensing of plays.

Cook, Ann Jennalie. *The Privileged Playgoers of Shakespeare's London, 1576-1642.* Princeton, N.J.: Princeton University Press, 1981. Specialized study on aspects of the elite class who attended the theater.

Cunningham, Peter, ed. *Extracts from the Accounts of the Revels, in the Reigns of Queen Elizabeth and King James I.* London: The Shakespeare Society, 1842. Reprint. New York: Kraus Reprint, 1966. In spite of its date of publication, this classic text is still useful for its reproductions of the original "Office Books of the Masters and Yeomen."

Dent, Thomas C., Richard Schechner, and Gilbert Moses, eds. *The Free Southern Theater by the Free Southern Theater: A Documentary of the South's Radical Black Theater, with Journals, Letters, Poetry, Essays, and a Play Written by Those Who Built It.* Indianapolis: Bobbs-Merrill, 1969. As the title reflects, this volume examines black theater in the South.

Dobbs, Brian. *Drury Lane: Three Centuries of the Theatre Royal, 1663-1971.* London: Cassell, 1972. Surveys the theater from "Royal Favours" of the seventeenth century to "Shows and Stars 1939-71."

Donohue, Joseph. *Theatre in the Age of Kean.* Oxford, England: Basil Blackwell, 1975. Treats topics from "The Demise of Sheridan's Theatre" to "The Age of Kean and Its Prospects."

Dutton, Richard. *Mastering the Revels: The Regulation and Censorship of English Renaissance Drama.* Iowa City: University of Iowa Press, 1991. A scholarly study that grew out of Dutton's research on Ben Jonson.

Elsom, John. *Erotic Theatre.* New York: Taplinger, 1974. Contains an introduction by John Trevelyan. Covers a wide range of topics, from eroticism to theatrical performances.

_____. *Post-War British Theatre.* Boston: Routledge & Kegan Paul, 1976. "Language and Money," "The Search for Self," and "Breaking Out: The Angry Plays" are some of the chapters in this study.

Evans, Chad. *Frontier Theatre.* Victoria, British Columbia: Sono Nis Press, 1983. A scholarly study of such topics as "Early Amateur Theatricals," "Troupes of the Gold Era," and "The Northwest Reflection." Evans also discusses opera and the circus.

Evans, G. Blakemore, ed. *Elizabethan-Jacobean Drama: The Theatre in Its Time.* New York: New Amsterdam, 1988. Contains discussions of London theaters, repertories, and the underworld. The sober tcxt is enlivened by thirty black-and-white illustrations, some of them reproduced for the first time.

Fuchs, Elinor, ed. *Plays of the Holocaust.* New York: Theatre Communications Group, 1987. This international anthology includes an annotated bibliography of Holocaust plays.

Galloway, David, ed. *The Elizabethan Theatre, II.* Toronto: Macmillan of Canada, 1970. One of a series of volumes, edited by Galloway and other distinguished scholars, treating specialized papers.

Genest, John. *Some Account of the English Stage, from the Restoration in 1660 to 1830.* 1832. Reprint. New York: B. Franklin, 1965. Classic multivolume that should be read with some understanding of later scholarship.

Gildersleeve, Virginia. *Government Regulation of the Elizabethan Drama.* New York: Columbia University Press, 1908. Reprint. Westport, Conn.: Greenwood Press, 1975. Classic essay that treats censorship and related matters up to the "Puritan Victory."

Glasstone, Victor. *Victorian and Edwardian Theatres: An Architectural and Social Survey.* Cambridge, Mass.: Harvard University Press, 1975. Beautifully illustrated work that offers insight concerning the staging and audience reception of plays.

Gurr, Andrew. *The Shakespearean Stage, 1574-1642.* Cambridge, England: Cambridge University Press, 1970. Specialized work that brings later scholarship to supplement older sources.

Harbage, Alfred. *Shakespeare and the Rival Traditions.* New York: Macmillan, 1952. Reprint. Bloomington: Indiana University Press, 1970. Influential study that treats, among other topics, "The War of the Theatres."

Henslowe, Philip. *Henslowe's Diary.* Edited by R. A. Foakes and R. T. Rickert. Cambridge, England: Cambridge University Press, 1961. Chief sourcebook for the theatrical history of the English stage between 1590 and 1604.

Herrick, Marvin T. *Tragicomedy: Its Origin and Development in Italy, France, and England.* 1955. Reprint. Urbana: University of Illinois Press,

1962. Scholarly treatise that covers English tragicomedy from before Francis Beaumont and John Fletcher through Sir William Davenant, along with other topics.

Hillebrand, Harold Newcomb. *The Child Actors: A Chapter in Elizabethan Stage History.* New York: Russell & Russell, 1964. Major scholarly work on the subject, examining various theaters and companies.

Hotson, Leslie. *The Commonwealth and Restoration Stage.* New York: Russell & Russell, 1962. Influential work that treats such topics as "The Playhouses," "The Duke's Company, 1660-1682," and "The King's Company, 1682-1694."

Hudson, Lynton Alfred. *The English Stage, 1850-1950.* London: Harrap, 1951. Brief but useful text, with selected illustrations.

Hughes, Leo. *The Drama's Patrons: A Study of the Eighteenth-Century London Audience.* Austin: University of Texas Press, 1971. Comprises chapters such as "A Varied Response," "Changing Tastes," and "Morality and Sensibility."

Hume, Robert D., ed. *The London Theatre World, 1660-1800.* Carbondale: Southern Illinois University Press, 1980. Collection of scholarly essays by notables.

Hunt, Hugh. *The Abbey: Ireland's National Theatre, 1904-1978.* New York: Columbia University Press, 1979. A survey of such subjects as "The Troubled Years, 1914-1923," "The Years of Exile, 1951-1966," and "The Abbey in the Seventies."

Joseph, Stephen. *The Story of the Playhouse in England.* London: Barrie and Rockliff, 1963. Not about plays and playwrights but a "history of the playhouse, the place where actors perform to their audiences." Illustrations.

Kavanagh, Robert Mshengu. *Theatre and Culture Struggle in South Africa.* London: Zed Books, 1985. Includes many excerpts from plays. Among the chapters are "Culture and Social Relations in South Africa Before 1976," "The Struggle for Social Hegemony," and "The Development of Theatre in South Africa up to 1976."

Kelly, Linda. *The Kemble Era.* New York: Random House, 1980. Treats John Philip Kemble, Sarah Siddons, and the London stage.

Kemble, Fanny. *Journal of a Young Actress.* New York: Columbia University Press, 1990. "Proud, high-spirited, and, withal, not entirely unselfcritical," Kemble embarked, with her father, the celebrated actor Charles Kemble, on an American acting tour. Her journal is a delight. Contains a foreword by Elizabeth Fox-Genovese.

King, Thomas James. *Shakespearean Staging, 1599-1942.* Cambridge, Mass.: Harvard University Press, 1971. Authoritative work that supplements and corrects older works on the same general subject.

Kitchin, Laurence. *Drama in the Sixties: Form and Interpretation.* London:

Faber, 1966. Includes material on "Compressionism," "Epic," and "Malice Domestic."

Knapp, Bettina L. *Theatre and Alchemy.* Detroit: Wayne State University Press, 1980. Very specialized. A scholarly but fascinating work. Especially intriguing is the chapter entitled "Spiritus Mundi/Anima Mundi."

Lancashire, Ian. *Dramatic Texts and Records of Britain: A Chronological Topography to 1558.* Cambridge, England: Cambridge University Press, 1984. This detailed, in-depth study contains a "finding list" that is a topographical guide to British dramatic records. Includes illustrations and many reproductions of rare documents.

Landa, M. J. *The Jew in Drama.* London: P. S. King & Son, 1926. Rev. ed. Port Washington, N.Y.: Kennikat Press, 1968. Scholarly treatment of such topics as "Hebrew Origins of Drama," "The Original of Fagin," and "The Yiddish Theatre."

Lawrence, William John. *The Elizabethan Playhouse and Other Studies.* Philadelphia: J. B. Lippincott, 1912. Once-influential work that is still useful for specialists, although the general reader must be cautious.

_____. *Pre-Restoration Stage Studies.* Cambridge, Mass.: Harvard University Press, 1927. Classic study that is, despite its older material, still generally sound.

Lowe, Robert W. *A Bibliographical Account of English Theatrical Literature: From the Earliest Times to the Present Day.* London: John C. Nimmo, 1888. Reprint. Detroit: Gale Research, 1966. This standard annotated bibliography (with brief commentary) contains some entries that are unique from a historical point of view. The works include opinionated judgments, such as the one on Ralph Wewitzer calling him "[a]n actor of no great ability."

Lumley, Frederick. *New Trends in Twentieth Century Drama: A Survey Since Ibsen and Shaw.* 1956. Rev. ed. New York: Oxford University Press, 1972. Broad approach to the modern theater, with material on English, Irish, and American dramatists, as well as European writers.

McAfee, Helen. *Pepys on the Restoration Stage.* New Haven, Conn.: Yale University Press, 1916. Reprint. New York: B. Blom, 1964. Classic account of references in Samuel Pepys' diary to the Restoration theater.

McCollum, John I., ed. *The Restoration Stage.* Boston: Houghton Mifflin, 1961. Selections of historically significant critical texts by John Dryden and others.

MacKaye, Percy. *The Playhouse and the Play, and Other Addresses Concerning the Theatre and Democracy in America.* New York: Macmillan, 1909. Reprint. New York: Johnson Reprint, 1970. The addresses by the author are historically significant for the American theater prior to 1909.

Macqueen-Pope, Walter Jones. *The Curtain Rises: A Story of the Theatre.*

Edinburgh, Scotland: Thomas Nelson, 1961. A good historical survey, with illustrations, of the stagecraft of the English theater. Chapters include "Burbage—The Father of the Theatre," "Giants of the Elizabethan Theatre," and "Victorian and Edwardian Pantomime."

Mander, Raymond, and Joe Mitchenson. *A Picture History of the British Theatre.* London: Hulton Press, 1957. Remarkable, often rare illustrations, with brief commentary on such topics as the Elizabethan and Jacobean stage, the Restoration period, and the twentieth century.

Miles, Bernard. *The British Theatre.* London: Collins, 1948. A special delight is the series of eight stunning plates in color, in addition to twenty-one illustrations in black and white. Brief chapters on such topics as "The Restoration," "Macklin and Garrick," and "Strolling and Barnstorming."

Milhous, Judith. *Thomas Betterton and the Management of Lincoln's Inn Fields, 1695-1708.* Carbondale: Southern Illinois University Press, 1979. Excellent specialized material on "The Lincoln's Inn Fields Experiment" and other topics.

Mullaney, Steven. *The Place of the Stage: License, Play, and Power in Renaissance England.* Chicago: University of Chicago Press, 1988. This brief, cogent study contains such chapters as "Toward a Rhetoric of Space in Elizabethan London," "The Place of the Stage," and "Lying Like Truth: Riddle, Representation, and Treason."

Murray, John Tucker. *English Dramatic Companies, 1558-1642.* Boston: Houghton Mifflin, 1810. Reprint. New York: Russell & Russell, 1963. Multivolume work that treats "Greater Men's Companies," "Lesser Men's Companies," and "Children's Companies."

Murrie, Eleanore Boswell. *The Restoration Court Stage, 1660-1702, with a Particular Account of the Production of Calisto.* Cambridge, Mass.: Harvard University Press, 1932. Reprint. New York: Barnes & Noble Books, 1966. Based on previously unpublished material from the Accounts of His Majesty's Office of Works and other sources.

Nicoll, Allardyce. *The English Theatre: A Short History.* London: Thomas Nelson, 1936. Reprint. Westport, Conn.: Greenwood Press, 1970. A once-influential and still readable account by the great scholar of the English stage.

_____. *The Garrick Stage: Theatres and Audiences in the Eighteenth Century.* Edited by Sybil Rosenfeld. Athens: University of Georgia Press, 1980. Covered are such topics as the playhouses and old and new costumes.

_____. *Masks, Mimes, and Miracles: Studies in the Popular Theatre.* London: Harrap, 1931. Reprint. New York: Cooper Square, 1963. Classic, still useful work, with such chapters as "The Fate of the Mime in the Dark Ages" and "The Commedia Dell'Arte"—scholarly material that indirectly touches later English drama.

Roose-Evans, James. *London Theatre: From the Globe to the National.* Oxford, England: Phaidon Press, 1977. Lively work that surveys the scene from 1567 to the twentieth century.

Rosenfeld, Sybil M. *Strolling Players and Drama in the Provinces, 1660-1765.* Cambridge, England: The University Press, 1939. Reprint. New York: Octagon Books, 1970. Classic scholarly study that treats different groups of players and various theaters.

Rowell, George. *Theatre in the Age of Irving.* Totowa, N.J.: Rowman & Littlefield, 1981. Studies "Setting the Scene," "Traditional Airs," and "Accolade."

_____. *The Victorian Theatre, 1792-1914: A Survey.* 2d ed. New York: Cambridge University Press, 1978. Covers "The New Drama," "The Return to Respectability," "The Era of Society Drama," and other subjects.

Schechner, Richard. *Between Theatre and Anthropology.* Philadelphia: University of Pennsylvania Press, 1985. A psychological-anthropological study that includes such essays as "Peter Brook's Company in Africa," "Balinese Dancer Demonstrating Her Walking Technique," and "Shakers Dancing in the Nineteenth Century." Foreword by Victor Turner.

_____. *The Living Book of the Living Theatre.* Greenwich, Conn.: New York Graphic Society, 1971. As much a photographic essay as a discussion on the social and improvisational theater during the late 1960's. Offers historical insight into the political and social concerns of the time, especially of the "street theater" of confrontation.

Seilhamer, George O. *History of the American Theatre.* New York: B. Blom, 1968. Massively documented and persuasive study, but difficult for the general reader.

Seller, Maxine Schwartz, ed. *Ethnic Theater in the United States.* Westport, Conn.: Greenwood Press, 1983. Comprehensive study examining ethnic theater from Armenian American to Yiddish.

Shapiro, Michael. *Children of the Revels: The Boy Companies of Shakespeare's Time and Their Plays.* New York: Columbia University Press, 1977. A scholarly account of "The Companies," "The Occasion," "The Style," and "The Plays." Fully annotated.

Smith, Irwin. *Shakespeare's Blackfriars Playhouse: Its History and Its Design.* New York: New York University Press, 1964. Specialized scholarly work that treats the Blackfriars from the origins in 1275 to 1642.

Southern, Richard. *The Medieval Theatre in the Round.* 2d ed. London: Faber, 1975. Scholarly, comprehensive study that provides an astonishing reconstruction of the age.

_____. *The Staging of Plays Before Shakespeare.* New York: Theater Arts Books, 1973. Monumental scholarly work that treats the earliest surviving interludes (1466-1508) and shows how the ways in which they were staged affected the technique of later playwrights such as Shakespeare.

Steele, Richard. *The Theatre*. Edited by John Loftis. Oxford, England: Clarendon Press, 1962. Scholarly edition treating the distinguished eighteenth century essayist's views on the theater.

Stephens, John Russell. *The Censorship of English Drama, 1824-1901*. New York: Cambridge University Press, 1980. Specialized scholarly study.

Sturgess, Keith. *Jacobean Private Theatre*. London: Routledge & Kegan Paul, 1987. A scholarly account, with black-and-white illustrations. Devotes chapters to the audience, the Blackfriars, and the court theater.

Summers, Montague. *The Restoration Theatre*. 1934. Reprint. New York: Humanities Press, 1964. Once-influential work that must be read with some scholarly caution. Treats, among other topics, costume, realism on the stage, and the epilogue.

Taubman, Hyman Howard. *The Making of the American Theatre*. New York: McCann, 1965. Ambitious work that includes chapters on "Realism of a Sort," "Disarray in the Sixties," and "New Forces and New Hope."

Thompson, Elbert N. S. *The Controversy Between the Puritans and the Stage*. New York: H. Holt, 1903. Reprint. New York: Russell & Russell, 1966. In two parts: "The Puritan Attack" and "The Dramatists' Reply."

Thorndike, Ashley H. *Shakespeare's Theater*. New York: Macmillan, 1916. Influential study that is still generally sound.

Trewin, J. C. *The Edwardian Theatre*. Totowa, N.J.: Rowman & Littlefield, 1976. Brief but useful study on such topics as "The Drawing-Room," "The Study," and "Closing the Door."

_____. *The English Theatre*. London: P. Elek, 1948. A brief guide to plays and playwrights of the first quarter of the twentieth century. The chapter entitled "College Wit-Crackers" includes discussions of Noël Coward, Frederick Lonsdale, A. A. Milne, and others.

Troubridge, St. Vincent. *The Benefit System in the British Theatre*. London: Society for Theatre Research, 1967. A scholarly account of payments and "benefits" to British actors, from the 1680's to the 1880's, with such chapters as "Patronage and Sale of Tickets," "Making Up the Bill," "The Bespeak," and "Stars and Benefits in the Provinces."

Wellwarth, George E. *The Theater of Protest and Paradox: Developments in the Avant-Garde Drama*. 1964. Rev. ed. New York: New York University Press, 1971. This fine critical survey treats twentieth century dramatists under "The Experimentalists" and "The Traditionalists"; "New American Drama" discusses Edward Albee and others.

Welsford, Enid. *The Court Masque*. Cambridge, England: The University Press, 1927. Reprint. New York: Russell & Russell, 1962. Massive work of scholarship that is still reliable.

Wickham, Glynne. *Early English Stages, 1300 to 1660.* New York: Columbia University Press, 1959-1981. 3 vols. Multivolume work of great utility to the student of English dramatic history.

Wilson, John Harold. *A Preface to Restoration Drama.* Boston: Houghton Mifflin, 1965. Concise study on such topics as "The Restoration Theater," "The Poets," "Villain Tragedy," and "Pathetic Tragedy."

Woods, Leigh. *Garrick Claims the Stage: Acting and Social Emblem in Eighteenth-Century England.* Westport, Conn.: Greenwood Press, 1984. More than an account of the remarkable David Garrick's historical contributions to the theater, Woods's book treats such topics as refinement in acting and illusionism on the stage.

Yamazaki, Masakazu. *Mask and Sword: Two Plays for the Contemporary Japanese Theater.* Translated by J. Thomas Rimer. New York: Columbia University Press, 1980. The plays are *Zeami* and *Sanetomo.* Includes an interview with Yamazaki, who discusses modern Japanese drama.

Yates, Frances A. *Theatre of the World.* Chicago: University of Chicago Press, 1969. Discussion of such masters of stage illustration as John Dee, Robert Fludd, and Inigo Jones, relating them historically with their contributions to the theater.

Technical

Archer, William. *Play-Making: A Manual of Craftsmanship.* Boston: Small, Maynard, 1912. Reprint. New York: Dover, 1960. Historically interesting essays by the distinguished English drama critic who translated and popularized the work of Henrik Ibsen.

Baker, George P. *Dramatic Technique.* New York: Houghton Mifflin, 1919. Reprint. Westport, Conn.: Greenwood Press, 1970. A once-influential treatise by the distinguished teacher of a generation of American dramatists.

Barranger, Milly S. *Theatre: A Way of Seeing.* Reprint. Belmont, Calif.: Wadsworth, 1980. Barranger's illustrated volume (mostly photographic) examines theatrical illusions and rituals. Includes several photographic essays.

Barton, Robert. *Acting.* New York: Holt, Rinehart and Winston, 1989. Includes many practical exercises. Among the chapters are "Dueling Performances," "Stage Fright Substitutes," and "Accepting the Audience."

Beckerman, Bernard. *Dynamics of Drama: Theory and Methods of Analysis.* New York: Drama Book Specialists, 1979. Useful for both the actor and the student of theater; good chapters on foundations, variations, and response.

Benedetti, Robert. *The Actor at Work.* 5th ed. Englewood Cliffs, N.J.: Prentice-Hall, 1990. Contains technical advice for actors, including a list of exercises. Foreword by Ted Danson.

Bowman, Walter Parker. *Theatre Language*. New York: Theatre Arts Books, 1961. A dictionary of technical terms, some of them historical but most of them current, used by actors and stage directors.

Brown, Ivor John Carnegie. *What Is a Play?* London: Macdonald, 1964. Cogent essays such as "Play and Player," "The Play Screened," and "Playing with the Play."

Brown, John Russell. *Effective Theatre: A Study with Documentation*. London: Heinemann Educational, 1969. Includes useful material on actors, stage design, and production.

Burgess, Charles O. *Drama: Literature on Stage*. Philadelphia: J. B. Lippincott, 1969. Directed to students of the drama, this clearly written book has useful chapters (with examples). Among them are "Symbolism and Other Devices," "Theme: Meaning in Drama," and "Judging Plays."

Burns, Elizabeth. *Theatricality: A Study of Convention in the Theatre and in Social Life*. New York: Harper & Row, 1972. Treats such topics as acting, spectators and critics, and "Roles, Symbolic Types, and Characters."

Busfield, Roger M. *The Playwright's Art: Stage, Radio, Television, Motion Pictures*. New York: Harper, 1958. Reprint. Westport, Conn.: Greenwood Press, 1971. Includes such topics as the play and fiction, playwrights and their audience, and finding dramatic material.

Campbell, Paul Newell. *Form and the Art of Theatre*. Bowling Green, Ohio: Bowling Green State University Popular Press, 1984. Treats such topics as the theater audience, the performers and the performance, and the genres of theater.

Corrigan, Robert W., and James L. Rosenberg, eds. *The Context and Craft of Drama: Critical Essays on the Nature of Drama and Theatre*. San Francisco: Chandler, 1964. Excellent selection of theoretical and critical essays on dramaturgy, including sections on the actor, director, designer, and critic.

Culp, Ralph Borden. *The Theatre and Its Drama: Principles and Practices*. Dubuque, Iowa: Wm. C. Brown, 1971. Good material on children's theater and creative dramatics, playwrights and playwriting, playhouses and players.

Delgado, Ramon. *Acting with Both Sides of Your Brain: Perspectives on the Creative Process*. New York: Holt, Rinehart and Winston, 1986. Using modern insights from brain hemisphere research, the author provides such chapters as "Touching Both Sides of Your Brain," "The Level of Words," "The Level of Unconscious Role-Playing," and "The Level of Aesthetic Distance."

Downer, Alan S., ed. *The Art of the Play: An Anthology of Nine Plays*. New York: Henry Holt, 1955. Clear, concise introduction to nine plays, with essays on the player and action.

England, Alan William. *Scripted Drama: A Practical Guide to Teaching Techniques.* New York: Cambridge University Press, 1981. Brief but pointed chapters on acting the text, planning a production, and improvisation.

George, Kathleen. *Rhythm in Drama.* Pittsburgh: University of Pittsburgh Press, 1980. Contains such chapters as "The Panoramic Stage," "The Symbolic Gesture," and "Repetition of Verbal Strategy."

Glover, J. Garrett. *The Cubist Theatre.* Ann Arbor, Mich.: UMI Research Press, 1983. Treats such topics as "Geometricization," "An Anti-Climactic Landscape," "Condensed Signs," and "Cubist Lighting."

Goldman, Michael. *The Actor's Freedom: Toward a Theory of Drama.* New York: Viking Press, 1975. Brief but stimulating essays on actors and audience and hero and play.

Grebanier, Bernard. *Playwriting.* New York: Thomas Y. Crowell, 1961. Essays on such topics as "The Theater *vs.* Life," "Sources for Ideas for Plays," and "Plot and Character."

Greenwood, Ormerod. *The Playwright: A Study of Form, Method, and Tradition in the Theatre.* London: Pitman, 1950. Sections on the playwright's choices and kinds of theater.

Hagen, Uta. *A Challenge for the Actor.* New York: Charles Scribner's Sons, 1991. Provides sound techniques explained in simple language. Includes a list of acting exercises.

Hamilton, Clayton M. *The Theory of the Theatre and Other Principles of Dramatic Criticism.* New York: Henry Holt, 1939. Although the examples are outdated, this book provides a sound treatment of the theory of the theater and the problems of the playwright.

Hartnoll, Phyllis, ed. *The Concise Oxford Companion to the Theatre.* Oxford, England: Oxford University Press, 1972-1979. Based on *The Oxford Companion to the Theatre* (1951), this concise edition (by the same editor) updates and revises the original brief definitions.

Hayman, Ronald. *The Set-up: An Anatomy of the English Theatre Today.* London: Eyre Methuen, 1973. Among the chapters are "The Actor's Motives," "The West End," "Repertory," and "The Fringe."

Hermassi, Karen. *Polity and Theatre in Historical Perspective.* Berkeley: University of California Press, 1977. Very specialized but cogent study, with excellent essays entitled "Power Without Love," "Workable Pictures of the World," and "The Political Vocation of Theatre."

Holtan, Orley I. *Introduction to Theatre: A Mirror to Nature.* Englewood Cliffs, N.J.: Prentice-Hall, 1976. Valuable source for such subjects as the language of theater, the actor, theater space, and confrontation and communion.

Hull, S. Loraine. *Strasberg's Method as Taught by Lorrie Hull.* Woodbridge,

Conn.: Ox Bow, 1985. A lucid account with many practical examples of relaxation techniques and sensory exercises. Among the chapters are "What Is Good Acting?" and "The Trained Actor."

Kernodle, George R. *Invitation to the Theatre.* 3d ed. San Diego: Harcourt Brace Jovanovich, 1985. Useful textbook in clear language that treats kinds of plays, the play in production, and the mass media.

Kohansky, Mendel. *The Disreputable Profession: The Actor in Society.* Westport, Conn.: Greenwood Press, 1984. Contains clear and sometimes amusing discussions of the acting profession. Chapters include "The Bawdy Restoration Theatre" and "Salaries and Sex Symbols."

Kuritz, Paul. *Playing: An Introduction to Acting.* Englewood Cliffs, N.J.: Prentice-Hall, 1982. This technical volume studies such matters as the response to acting, the memory's power, and role playing.

Le Vay, John. *Margaret Anglin: A Stage Life.* Toronto: Simon & Pierre, 1989. More than a biography of this distinguished actor, the work makes clear the conventions of acting during the early decades of the twentieth century.

Mabley, Edward. *Dramatic Construction: An Outline of Basic Principles.* Philadelphia: Chilton, 1972. Analyses of the texts of classic and modern plays; material on realism and its predecessors and "The Revolt Against Realism."

McGrath, John. *A Good Night Out, Popular Theatre: Audience, Class, and Form.* London: Eyre Methuen, 1981. Includes "Toward a Working-Class Theatre," "Theatre as Political Forum," and "The Challenge of Cinema and Television."

Marx, Milton. *The Enjoyment of Drama.* New York: F. S. Crofts, 1940. 2d ed. New York: Appleton-Century-Crofts, 1961. Handbook on the theater, with clear exposition of such topics as the purpose and aim of drama and how to judge a play.

Mitchell, John D. *Actors Talk: About Styles of Acting.* Midland, Miss.: Northwood Institute Press, 1988. Contains interviews with such noted actors as Tony Randall, Jessica Tandy, and Stephen Daley, who discuss their craft. Also provides brief biographies of many actors, including European and Asian ones.

Rice, Elmer. *The Living Theatre.* New York: Harper & Row, 1959. Wide-ranging essays by the distinguished American playwright, including chapters entitled "What Does the Public Want?" and "The Noncommercial Theatre."

Selden, Samuel. *The Stage in Action.* New York: Appleton-Century-Crofts, 1941. Reprint. London: Peter Owen, 1962. Treats such matters as "Magic in Rhythm and Tone" and "The Player Singing."

Simonson, Lee. *The Stage Is Set.* New York: Theatre Art Books, 1963. Comprehensive handbook that contains such general chapters as "Scenery in the Theatre of Ideas" and "Players in the Pulpit."

Smiley, Sam. *Playwriting: The Structure of Action.* Englewood Cliffs, N.J.: Prentice-Hall, 1971. Material on spectacle, problems of production, diction, and the writer's vision.

Van Druten, John. *Playwright at Work.* 1953. Reprint. Westport, Conn.: Greenwood Press, 1971. Informal but useful essays by the distinguished dramatist.

Van Laan, Thomas F. *The Idiom of Drama.* Ithaca, N.Y.: Cornell University Press, 1970. Scholarly treatment of "The Medium," "The Immediate Action," and "The Action of Depth."

Wilson, Garff B. *A History of American Acting.* Bloomington: Indiana University Press, 1966. Treats such topics as "The School of Emotionalism," "The Comic Stage," and "Comedians in Transition."

Worsley, T. C. *The Fugitive Art: Dramatic Commentaries, 1947-1951.* London: J. Lehmann, 1952. Brilliant essays, addressed to the technically advanced student, on the production of various plays, mostly those on the London stage for the designated years.

Wright, Edward A., and Lenthiel H. Downs. *A Primer for Playgoers.* 1958. 2d ed. Englewood Cliffs, N.J.: Prentice-Hall, 1969. Nontechnical, clear discussion of such topics as the script, the audience, and the production.

Leslie B. Mittleman

INDEX

INDEX

Abbey Theatre, 481, 1046-1047, 2893-2894, 2967, 2969, 2970-2972.
ABC. *See* American Broadcasting System (ABC).
Abdelazer (Behn), 211.
Abe Lincoln in Illinois (Sherwood), 2241-2242.
Abraham Lincoln (Drinkwater), 631-633.
Absurd Person Singular (Ayckbourn), 80, 83.
Absurdism. *See* Theater of the Absurd.
Academic drama. *See* School plays.
Accentual meter, 1539.
AC/DC (Williams, H.), 3022-3023.
Achilles (Gay), 914.
Acropolis (Sherwood), 2238-2239.
Act, **3057.** *See also* Scene.
Acting styles, 2445-2747, 2748, 2845-2846; classical, 2874; realistic, 2875; romantic, 2874-2875.
Action, 2658. *See also* Plot.
Actors' Studio, 3053-3054.
Adding Machine, The (Rice), 1987-1989.
Addison, Joseph, 1-11, 2697; *Cato*, 4, 7-9, 2861; *The Drummer*, 6-7; *Rosamond*, 4-6. *See also* **Steele, Sir Richard.**
Adler, Stella, 3052.
Admirable Crichton, The (Barrie), 156-158.
Advertising, and television, 3036.
Aeschylus, 2654-2655.
After (Anderson, R.), 52.
After Dark (Boucicault), 311.
After the Fall (Miller), 1684-1686.
Afterpiece, 2695, 2855-2858, **3057.**
Agathon, 2655.
Agitprop, 2722, **3057.**
Agon, 2655, **3057.**
Air Raid (MacLeish), 1540.
Akalaitis, JoAnne, 12-19; *Dead End Kids*, 15-16; *Dressed Like an Egg*, 13-14; *Green Card*, 16-17; *Southern Exposure*, 14-15.
Alazon, 2663, **3057.** See also *Miles gloriosus*.
Albee, Edward, 20-34, 2929-3930; *A Delicate Balance*, 28-30; *The Man Who Had Three Arms*, 32; *Marriage Play*, 32;

Seascape, 30-32; *Tiny Alice*, 26-28; *Who's Afraid of Virginia Woolf?*, 24-26, 2930.
Alchemist, The (Jonson), 1289-1291, 2804.
Alcibiades (Otway), 1822-1823.
Aldridge, Ira, 2947.
Alexandrine, **3057.**
Alfieri, Vittorio, 2867.
Alfonso, King of Castile (Lewis), 1421, 1427-1428.
Alfred Hitchcock Presents, 3039.
Ali Pacha (Payne), 2918.
Alienation, **3058.** *See also* Epic theater.
Alison's House (Glaspell), 970-971.
All Fools (Chapman), 415-417.
All for Love (Dryden), 643-644.
All My Sons (Miller), 1677, 2927.
All That Fall (Beckett), 190.
Allegory, **3058.**
Alleyn, Edward, 3046-3047.
All's Well That Ends Well (Shakespeare), 2123-2124, 2799.
Alphabetical Order (Frayn), 831.
Alphonsus of Arragon (Greene, R.), 2789.
Amadeus (Shaffer, P.), 2093-2095, 2099-2101.
Ambitious Step-Mother, The (Rowe), 2040-2041.
Amen Corner, The (Baldwin), 97-99.
American, The (James, H.), 1259.
American Broadcasting System (ABC), 3035.
American Buffalo (Mamet), 1564-1565, 2934.
American Dream, The (Albee), 2929.
Amorous Prince, The (Behn), 211.
Amos 'n' Andy, 3027.
Amphitryon 38 (Behrman), 224.
Anabasis, **3058.** *See also* Rising action.
Anagnorisis, 2661, 2677, **3058.**
Ancestral Power (Awoonor), 2943-2944.
And Miss Reardon Drinks a Little (Zindel), 2649-2651.
And Things That Go Bump in the Night (McNally), 1550-1551.